Radical Poetics and Secular Jewish Culture

MODERN AND CONTEMPORARY POETICS

Radical Poetics and Secular Jewish Culture

Edited by Stephen Paul Miller and Daniel Morris

The University of Alabama Press
Tuscaloosa

Typeface: Minion and Goudy Sans

∞

The paper on which this book is printed meets the minimum requirements of American National Standard for Information Sciences-Permanence of Paper for Printed Library Materials, ANSI Z39.48-1984.

Library of Congress Cataloging-in-Publication Data

Radical poetics and secular Jewish culture / edited by Stephen Paul Miller and Daniel Morris.

p. cm. — (Modern and contemporary poetics)

ISBN 978-0-8173-1675-4 (cloth : alk. paper) — ISBN 978-0-8173-5563-0 (pbk. : alk. paper) 1. American poetry—Jewish authors—History and criticism. 2. American poetry—20th century—History and criticism. 3. American poetry—21st century—History and criticism. 4. Jews—United States—Identity. 5. Judaism and literature—United States. 6. Judaism and secularism. 7. Jewish poetry—United States—History and criticism. I. Miller, Stephen Paul. II. Morris, Daniel.

PS153.J4R33 2010
811'.54098924—dc22

2009020576

For Emma Bee Bernstein,
Joy, Isaac, Aaron, and Hannah Morris,
and Noah Miller, Rabbi Burt Seigel,
Elizabeth Wissner-Gross, Cameron McLinden,
William Kwok, and Dominick Casazza

Contents

Acknowledgments

Merle Bachman's essay "An 'Exotic' on East Broadway: Mikhl Likht and the Paradoxes of Yiddish Modernist Poetry" originally appeared in different form in her book *Recovering "Yiddishland": Threshold Moments in American Literature* (Syracuse University Press, 2007).

Marjorie Perloff's essay " 'Sound Scraps, Vision Scraps': Paul Celan's Poetic Practice" originally appeared in *Reading for Form,* edited by Susan J. Wolfson and Marshall Brown (University of Washington Press, Seattle, 2007).

The essays by Charles Bernstein, Jerome Rothenberg, Kathryn Hellerstein, and Stephen Paul Miller originated as a presentation, "Secular Jewish Culture / Radical Poetic Practice," a panel at the Center for Jewish History, 16 West Sixteenth Street, New York City, New York 10011, on September 21, 2004.

The authors wish to thank Purdue University and St. John's University for providing funds to support this publication. Debbie Self, Ruth Joynton, and Nick Mohlman did a great job with editing and proofing. Cameron Xavier McLinden did the index in a timely fashion.

Meet the Preface

Stephen Paul Miller

there's ecstasy in God being one

With God-in-one
distances between creation and judgment collapse,
and since there's nothing stopping us—
ongoing intensity, neurotic ongoing intensity
marks not only the best Jewish poetry but simply
hot poetry.[1]

If God's one, time's blue toothed to
the portable eternity in
his or her belly—

perhaps the portability
of monotheism's and
iconoclasm's
literally lighter idol load suits
nomadic shepherds, and
nonnegotiable, scorched earth,
theocratic identification with
and domination of a place is
the iconic, and thus sacrilegious, elephant in the room.[2]

If God's one, I'm an other,[3] a junk-to-junk jumping[4]
and boat-borrowing James Bond,[5]
segueing between wildly reserved
Jewish feedback mechanisms, and
powerfully unattached Judaisms.[6]

You beat it, Red Sea parts,
escape again, and Charles
Bernstein's eyes light up. The Center
for Jewish History asks I propose
poetry events. Everyone I tell
suggests they and their friends

read, period. They fear fundamentalism
getting too close to
the text.[7]

But Charles meets my preface at the boat.
Knowing no religion but wildly liberating textual scrutiny,
Charles suggests talking
"secular Jewish culture /
radical poetic practice."
Read this note first.[8]

Notes

1. Many of the essays in this collection acknowledge that however one characterizes "Jewish poetry," you need not be Jewish to write it. Hank Lazer, for instance, describes Jewish qualities in Fanny Howe's work; Benjamin Friedlander construes Saint Paul as an innovator within secular Judaism; Norman Fischer illustrates how a continuum between silence and articulation blends Jewish and Buddhist perspectives; Marjorie Perloff sees beyond simplistic historicizing to recognize Paul Celan and Wallace Stevens as poetic contemporaries; and my poem-essay points out Spalding Gray's self-portrayal as Jewish.

2. Anita Feldman, in a 2008 conversation, said, "Some Israeli settlers have turned their idea of 'the land' into an icon, a sacred image, like the golden calf that the erring Hebrews set up as an object of worship. They've identified 'the land' as a sacred object replacing the moral law and the Jewish commitment to justice. Remember the person in the audience [at the Center for Jewish History 'secular Jewish culture / radical poetic practice' panel] who faulted Jewish writers for not 'making aliyah' to Israel? I think of her as someone who has replaced the Jewish devotion to justice with reverence for 'the land' as sacred." Feldman's critique of the "sacredness" of Israel does not, I believe, negate but rather enhance the cultural value of Israel.

3. "To speak means to be forever on the road." Osip Mandelstam, "Talking about Dante" (1933), trans. Clarence Brown and Robert Hughes, *Delos* 6 (1971): 75.

4. "The quality of poetry is determined by the rapidity and decisiveness with which it instills its command, its plan of action, into the instrumentless, dictionary, purely qualitative nature of word formation. One has to run across the whole width of the river, jammed with mobile Chinese junks sailing in various directions. This is how the meaning of poetic speech is created. Its route cannot be reconstructed by interrogating the boatmen: they will not tell how and why we were leaping from junk to junk." Osip Mandelstam, "Talking about Dante" (1933), trans. Clarence Brown and Robert Hughes, *Delos* 6 (1971): 66.

5. Like the Homeric depiction of Odysseus, the cinematic James Bond is a wan-

dering "man who is never at a loss," and, since James Joyce in perhaps the proto-postmodern English language text re-characterizes Odysseus as Jewish, through a twisted metaphoric logic, Bond can also be reimagined as Jewish.

6. See Edward Mendelson, "New York Everyman" (book review essay of Richard M. Cook's *Alfred Kazin: A Biography*), *New York Review of Books,* June 12, 2008. Mendelson juxtaposes the Jew as "an outsider, with no special loyalties to any collective" with the Jew as "a member of a separate and unique group of people." He associates Alfred Kazin's literary strength with the former and "temptation" with the latter. Kazin believes some "tempters" trivialize the Holocaust for unrelated political purposes. Other "tempters" had been Kazin's childhood Brooklyn friends and CCNY classmates who became Reagan followers and "neoconservatives." Indeed, Kazin quips that he "saves his soul" by writing scathingly about them, likening them to "useful idiots."

Alfred Kazin believed the "ambiguity" of being Jewish, in Mendelson's words, "central to all aspects of modern culture." Kazin likens Jewish sensibility to American literary character itself by paradoxically planting "our alienation on native ground." Mendelson points out: "Kazin quotes Thorstein Veblen on the ability of a Jew to become an intellectual leader by escaping from his native culture and refusing to be assimilated into a Gentile one. As an outsider to both cultures, the unassimilated Jew is necessarily a skeptic, and 'the first requisite for constructive work in modern science, Veblen continued, is skepticism.' Kazin . . . thought it wholly appropriate for a lapsed Norwegian Lutheran to portray himself by describing a Jew."

7. Strictly literal interpretation seems to have been anything but a given for early Jews and Christians. For instance, discrepancies within and between favorite gospels did not seem to bother early Christians. Similarly, Chief Justice John Marshall, in his 1819 *McCulloch v. Maryland* decision, apparently was stating the obvious when he said the Constitution was "intended to endure for ages to come, and consequently, to be adapted to the various crises of human affairs." Even Thomas Jefferson, who advocated limited government, did not equate checks on government with a future generation's reluctance to reinterpret the Constitution. Jefferson compared Americans accepting laws and constitutions uncritically as dead and limited terminal language to full-grown adults wearing their childhood clothes. Both religious and "judicial fundamentalism" (a term used by Arthur M. Schlesinger Jr. and others) occur after original intent recedes so far in the past and can seem so obscure that the positing of original intent's sacredness can easily facilitate interpretive manipulation illegitimatizing rather than incorporating valid interpretations. Indeed, Schlesinger marvels at how U.S. Supreme Court justices combine judicial fundamentalism with post-eighteenth-century philosophy: "For them all [the 1935 Supreme Court's 'conservative four'], life was an evolutionary contest in which the intervention of government, by permitting the unfit to survive, could only mean catastrophe. This view had seized the Supreme Court so deeply that its devotees might well have supposed that Herbert Spencer had been in Philadelphia in 1787. It was against this view that Holmes had vainly protested thirty years before when he wrote, in a celebrated dis-

sent: 'The Fourteenth Amendment does not enact Mr. Herbert Spencer's *Social Statics.*'" Arthur M. Schlesinger Jr., *The Politics of Upheaval* (New York: Houghton Mifflin, 1960), 460.

8. Paul Mariani, in an April 6, 2009, talk at St. John's University, drew attention to the need for ways to describe religious sensibilities in poetry, particularly as concerns clearly present Catholic sensibilities. I commented that religious and cultural connections are particularly apparent when considering Judaism because for thousands of years there was so little differentiation between Jewish religion and culture. Indeed, Judaism was arguably an innovative way of achieving and disseminating culture. Even today one born into a Jewish family is often presumed, by both oneself and others, as irrevocably Jewish because what one as an adult believes or endorses about religion appears insignificant on some other personal level when compared to one's initial Jewish acculturation. One therefore often notes seemingly distinctive tonal and dialogical progressions within the products of what might be called a "Jewish" writing process. A practitioner of this kind of writing certainly need not be raised Jewish for one's writing to appear Jewish, and many Jews do not write in anything that might be called a discursively inflected "Jewish" manner. Nonetheless, assimilating various forms of Jewish culture seems to be one way of kindling this kind of Jewish writing.

Before the Napoleonic Codes and often afterward, interrelations between Jewish culture and Jewish religion were further enhanced by an often-tenuous identification between Jews and the lands they inhabited. Increased Catholic participation within nation-states may tend to deflect and diminish a similar Catholic equivalence between religion and culture. Nonetheless, I told Paul Mariani that my sense is that there is also a distinct Catholic cultural identification. Saint Paul modifies Judaism culturally, and eventually the power of the shared communion seems to contribute to the communing upon an individuated subject with a correspondingly individuated focus as an artistic and a poetic component that is detectable as characteristically Catholic (or Anglican) in works as diverse as T. S. Eliot's poetry and Alan Ball's screenplays.

This mode of focus, Mariani reminds us, is very much in keeping with Gerard Manley Hopkins's notion of inscape in which all things are unique and rippling from a divinity. The sense of perceptual transformation implicit in a concept such as inscape perhaps speaks to a distinction between a Catholic cultural tendency and ones associated with Buddhism and some other Asian belief-systems. Whereas Noh plays and Buddhist ceremonies call for objects of presentation to be presented starkly, these focal points might not tend to be reimagined into anything like Hopkins inscape.

Introduction

Daniel Morris

In 2003, the American Jewish Historical Society at the Center for Jewish History in New York asked Stephen Paul Miller to host a poetry event. Miller sought a dynamic topic in itself generating discussion, yet those he talked with simply suggested that he or she and their friends be asked to read and participate. However, when Miller posed the problem to Charles Bernstein the drive and specificity of Bernstein's plan surprised him.

Bernstein seemed to have seen a need and was responding to it. Conservative and fundamentalist coalitions were dominating the religious institutional and political terrain, and Bernstein proposed an alternative that would facilitate the public life of imaginative and interpretive, as opposed to fundamentalist, forms of religious life and support. Bernstein also stressed the "secular," which significantly underscores practical realities of religious life and culture and its relations with culture at large.

Miller happily deferred to Bernstein, and the result was "Secular Jewish Culture / Radical Poetic Practice" on September 21, 2004, at the Center for Jewish History. The event featured talks by Bernstein, Miller, Marjorie Perloff, Jerome Rothenberg, Kathryn Hellerstein, and Paul Auster. Many of these responses to Bernstein's guiding questions are reproduced in this volume, in addition to other "answers" written for this collection.

For "Secular Jewish Culture / Radical Poetic Practice," Bernstein asked: "What are the innovations and inventions of American Jewish poets over the past century? Can we say that there is a distinctly Jewish component to radical modernist and contemporary poetry? What is the relation of Jewish modernist and contemporary poets to the historical avant-garde and to contemporary innovative poetry? How do Jewish cultural life and ethnic and religious forms and traditions manifest themselves in the forms, styles, and approaches to radical American poetry? What role does a distinctly secular approach to Jewishness by poets and other Jewish artists mean for 'radical Jewish culture'?"

When we decided to edit a book based on the ideas the symposium generated, we added these foci: traces of religious Jewish texts and practices in secular Jewish radical poetic practice, including relations of poetry to prayer and other uses of sacred materials in secular poetics; assumptions that there is a "Jewish" essence, identity, or quality that a poet may express prior to the act of writing; asking how Jewish poetry can be written by non-Jews; expanding how "Jewishness" might look and sound and act in a poetic context; relating intense textual scrutiny with secular rather than, for instance, fundamentalist religious considerations; Yiddishkeit poetry and culture and Yiddish modernism; contemporary Jewish American culture and poetics on a continuum with pre-Holocaust European Jewish culture and poetics; "eclectic strategies" for "doing Jewish" (as opposed to simply "being Jewish"); Jewish cultural life and ethnic and religious forms and traditions in experimental American poetry; work that accounts for the large body of experimental poetry concerning secular Jewish culture; secular approaches to Jewishness by poets and other Jewish artists and their relations to "radical Jewish culture": the secular as a paradoxically religious and in some ways characteristic Jewish concern that is germane to radical poetic process; Jewishness as an alternative to religious and cultural forms of classification, an alternative positing identity crises as positive; Hebraic and Jewish poetic form in modernist and contemporary experimental poetry; Jewish aspects in non-overtly "Jewish" work.

This volume contrasts with *Telling and Remembering: A Century of American Jewish Poetry* (1997), in which the editor Steven J. Rubin presented the first anthology devoted to Jewish American poetry. In his introduction, Rubin writes that his "purpose throughout this collection is to present the best and the most representative work of those writers who can properly be classified as American Jewish poets" (11). He goes on to state that he has "not included those poets who, although nominally Jewish, do not deal significantly with the American Jewish experience." How did he define "best" or "representative?" What does he mean when he says that certain "nominally Jewish" poets "do not deal significantly with the American Jewish experience?" Does Rubin consider certain kinds of American Jewish experience insignificant? Would Rubin consider a text such as "The Artifice of Absorption," an eighty-plus-page "essay" in the form of lineated verse by Charles Bernstein, an insignificant expression of American Jewish experience? Although his poem does not focus overtly on Jewish themes (such as the Holocaust, immigrant experience, Diaspora, anti-Semitism, the family, the place of Yiddish in American poetry, or the Bible), Bernstein seems to express his Jewishness in many ways, especially through the poem's half-serious / half-comic scholarly tone, the concern with issues of "absorption" and "exclusion," the way he tests the borders between genres, and argues for the instability of the relationship between "content" and "style." Rubin as editor does not venture a guess about how such a poem could be understood as the work of a Jewish author. He does not include Bernstein, or Bob Perelman, two prominent Jewish experimental poets, in his anthology. Rubin's project is commendable, but his anthology fails to offer a sustained critical apparatus or theoretical perspective through which readers could evaluate how his selections were made. We mention the critical lacunae and theoretical shortfalls of Rubin's anthology because it is precisely in such gaps and silences that our collection would like to lay stress.

A discussion of the problems associated with "Jewish poetry" begins our collection with a transcript of Charles Bernstein's comments on September 21, 2004, at the Center for Jewish History. Describing "betweenness" as the (not) space of the radical Jew, Bernstein constitutes his Jewish identity by way of his distance from a secure sense of what it means to be Jewish. "I am no more Jewish than when I refuse imposed definitions of what Jewishness means," he writes. Ambiguity (such as the distinction between ethnic and religious meanings of Judaism), hybridity (such as Bernstein's fascination with the Glatt kosher Peruvian restaurants he frequents on the Upper West Side), and an absence of explicit Jewish themes, paradoxically, constitute for Bernstein the "site" of radical secular Jewish texts and identities. Following in the tradition of queer theorists such as Judith Butler, who emphasize the performative, rather than the essential, aspects of identity, Bernstein understands Jewishness as something made, not given, as a "practice of dialogue and as openness to the unfolding performance of the everyday. Call it the civic practice of Jewishness" (5). Bernstein's invocation opens Secular Jewish Culture / Radical Poetic Practice, and in the spirit of a tradition of Jewish commentary, subsequent works will address one another.

The emphasis on a lost or erased origin that maintains its spectral power over the secular Jewish culture of America, as well as the acceptance of an unstable, linguistically oriented sense of self that exists in between clearly delineated spaces is as evident in the poetics of Charles Bernstein's *Shadowtime,* which imagines the tragic life of the German Jewish theorist Walter Benjamin, as it was already in the Yiddish modernist poetry of Mikhl Likht, whom Merle Bachman refers to as an "Exotic" on East Broadway. Born in a Ukrainian village in 1893, Likht became immersed in the vibrant Café culture of New York Yiddish modernism in the 1920s, where immigrant writers and intellectuals gathered to debate the latest developments of both American modernist culture (Likht was a translator of Stevens, Pound, and Stein) as well as of international modernism. Likht describes himself as a modernist's modernist, an author so committed to an introspectivist poetics and kaleisescopic stylistics—he was the poet "who took chaos seriously," writes Bachman—that even fellow Yiddish modernist found him to be utterly incomprehensible. Occupying a "threshold position," Likht may well have been a writer who committed himself to having no legitimate readership. Doubly inaccessible, Likht positioned himself as a Yiddish writer who eschewed proletarian themes, and as an American modernist who wrote in a language—Yiddish—that none of his peers (Stevens, Mina Loy, Carl Sandberg) could have understood. No poet discussed in our collection could be said to have occupied the precarious space between interpretative communities other than Mikhl Likht, whose strangeness is recovered in Bachman's translations. Following Bachman on Likht, our volume stays with the modernist period in order to discuss several strains of radical poetics in the work of Charles Reznikoff, Louis Zukofsky, and Gertrude Stein.

Ranen Omer-Sherman reads Charles Reznikoff as a poet who translates diasporism from a deficit state into a literary opportunity in which the possibility of redemption coexists with the face of loss. Omer-Sherman speaks of the "joys of cosmopolitanism and the ingenuity of adaptability and renewed life—in the context of the humiliating connotations of exile." Far from being a Pollyanna when describing the plight of disenfranchised Jews, African Americans, and the working poor during the modernist period, Omer-Sherman notes Reznikoff's political radicalism in his "powerful commitment to neglected histories . . . particularly in his caustic responses to the forces of industrialization, poverty, and violence" (1). Imagining identity as an unstable interplay between self and other, Omer-Sherman reads Reznikoff as an exemplar of the French Jewish philosopher Emmanuel Levinas's Abrahamic emphasis on the duty of the self to the other. Describing Reznikoff's poetics as one of "acute responsibility" (5), Omer-Sherman argues that the poet performs his poetics of care without the presumption of "a loving deity or even one remotely interested in the human world" (5).

According to Joshua Schuster, Louis Zukofsky, like his contemporary Reznikoff, attempted to transform his alienation from traditional Judaism and the situation of diasporism into the grounds for a radical humanistic ethics and a poetics that celebrates the sublimity of the particular things found in everyday life. Demonstrating the influence of the non-Jewish Jew Baruch Spinoza's naturalist pantheism on Zukofsky's major long poem "A," Schuster argues that Zukofsky thus "uses Judaism to get out of Judaism" as he tries to "invent the very notion of secularism out of Judaism" (6). Arguing that the "age of Jewish exile is closing" (7), Schuster views Zukofsky's Spinoza-oriented search for a "positive relatedness" and "elective affinities" between persons and things as a harbinger to the revision of Diaspora as a state of affirmation, not deficit.

Amy Feinstein considers the startling proliferation of explicit references to Jewish motifs in Gertrude Stein's compositions of the 1910s and 1920s, which at first glance seem to be ahistorical and nonreferential writings. In a radical process of creating abstraction through decontextualization, Stein makes the word "Jew" both strange and familiar as part of a varied and often-ambiguous Jewish lexicon that includes terms of endearment to Alice Toklas (Stein's "little Hebrew") and references to the Old Testament, Disraeli, Zionism, and Palestine. Such references radically change the story of the Jew in modernism, uniting the historical with the quotidian, the cultural and the racial, and the personal with the political. A reading of these Jewish motifs also allows us to revise the sexual, racial, and political history of modernist literature.

Charles Reznikoff's diasporic poetics is carried forward in the work of several important contemporary Jewish American poets, such as Alicia Ostriker, Norman Finkelstein, Rachel Blau DuPlessis, and Michael Heller, who offer personal reflections and theoretical speculations on their work and its (at times contested) relationship to the core themes of this book. In "Remains of the Diaspora," poet and memoirist Michael Heller, following Haim Bialik, argues that for the diasporic Jew "language replaces essence" and that the space of the "between" becomes an ironic foundation for poetic utterance. For Heller, as for other contemporary radical Jewish poets such as Norman Finkelstein in *Tracks,* the late Armand Schwerner in *Tablets,* and in *The Nakedness of the Fathers* by Alicia Ostriker, the Bible and other religious texts remain important sources of inspiration, even as these texts no longer possess canonical authority or signify the poet's allegiance to Judaism as a religious practice. Law turns into lore, according to Heller, and the radical Jewish poet operates in a void, "suspended between the religious and secular worlds" (3). For Heller, as was the case for Reznikoff and Zukofsky, the emphasis is on what Gershom Scholem called the "holiness of the secular" (12). For Ostriker, the gaps, silences, and omissions in the biblical proof text paradoxically represent a literary opportunity to, metaphorically, give birth to the feminine and maternal aspects of Judaism, which, she argues, have been repressed in the patriarchal tradition, but like the grandmother swallowed by the wolf in the fairy tale, await a return. Like Reznikoff, Ostriker also emphasizes a poetics of immanent spirituality, which she links to the Shekinah, or the feminine principal of a non-transcendent God. Ostriker's project is to "encounter the physical selves of women," especially through attempts to reimagine the voice of the Jewish mother as something much more complex than the stereotypical smothering figure of Roth's Mrs. Portnoy. In yet another way Ostriker's contemporary feminist midrashic project dovetails with Reznikoff, whom she cites in her text, she imagines radicalism, and her version of cultural Jewishness, in a political context, as a call to "social change . . . designed to benefit the powerless." As was the case with Reznikoff, the contemporary Jewish poets in this collection upend exclusionary ways of thinking about "sacred" and "secular" spaces, preferring to struggle to determine what Ostriker calls the "sacredness immanent within matter."

The idea of recovering a repressed or ignored aspect of the tradition of Jewish poetics also informs Rachel Blau DuPlessis's remarks on an Objectivist forebear, Carl Rakosi (1903–2004). Where DuPlessis shows that Rakosi viewed his Jewishness as a mere coincidental aspect of the loosely connected group of poets known as Objectivist (Reznikoff, Oppen, and Zukofsky), DuPlessis, who is careful to historicize and thus de-essentialize Jewishness, nonetheless attempts to "out" Rakosi's Jewishness, especially to account for the specific characteristics of the post-Haskalah Jew that Yosef Yerushalmi called the "gottloser Jude" or "godless" or "secular" Jew. In a powerful revision of modernist culture, DuPlessis speculates that what Raymond Williams called a "structure of feeling" tended toward a Christian emphasis on epiphany that by itself excluded a Jewish way of deferring closure through "this Jewish sense of textuality involved with endless writing, multiple commentary and vectors" that suspends New Critical ideas of climax or the "unveiling of Presence" in a text. Oppen, for DuPlessis, becomes a metonym for a repressed Jewish relationship to textuality in the context of Eliotic modernism.

DuPlessis's sense of a Jewish poetics of "endless writing" certainly resonates with Norman Finkelstein's observations about identity and poetics in his reflection on *Tracks*. Self-consciously working within a (paradoxical) tradition of experimental American long poems that includes work by Oppen, Creeley, Duncan, and Spicer, as well as the midrashic tradition, Finkelstein describes *Tracks* as a "self-interrupting whole," in which the "shape of a life lived" is constituted through the "open work of self-discovery, the renewal of meaning and answerability, the overcoming of undeadness" (9). If DuPlessis was interested in reimagining modernist poetics by recovering a repressed Jewish element of Objectivism, then we could say that Finkelstein is interested in considering the "congruence between Jewish textuality and 'radical' poetic composition" in a postmodern and Derridean context.

In her essay on Muriel Rukeyser and George Oppen, Meg Schoerke underlines many of the aspects of a secular Jewish poetics that have remained so influential to contemporary authors such as Heller who came of age in the 1960s and 1970s. For Schoerke, Rukeyser and Oppen are above all else figures of hybridity, of betweenness, that defy easy categorization. Both sought contact with others through language, and yet each wondered if the individual could escape isolation. Oppen, for example, wrote that "somewhere half-way between the fact of being singular and the fact of being numerous is the fact of being Jewish" (5). Language, for them, remained a gateway and an obstacle to communication between people. Poetry mediates between the perceptions of the isolate self and appears for community, between difficulty and clarity, silence and speech, and between linguistic experimentation and direct assertion (5). Oppen and Rukeyser, who both rejected privileged yet emotionally traumatic upbringings, and the bourgeois version of Jewishness upheld by their families, rallied against capitalist exploitation, spoke out about the wrenching traumas of world wars, and about the barriers of social conditioning and self-interest, but both for long stretches refused to write poetry (Oppen joined the Communist Party in 1935 and did not write again until 1958) because they did not feel that avant-garde poetry and the radical individualism associated with it were commensurate with a communal politics. For them both, Jewishness remained a form of liberalism, an openness to all that is human, what Rukeyser called a "guarantee," "against many kinds of temptation to close the spirit" (11).

The emphasis on a lost or erased origin that maintains its spectral power over the secular Jewish culture of America, as well as the acceptance of an unstable, linguistically oriented sense of self that exists in between clearly delineated spaces is evident in the poetics of Marjorie Perloff and Charles Bernstein. Discussing his libretto for *Shadowtime,* the opera about the German Jewish theorist Walter Benjamin, Bernstein imagines his work—and the project of the radical Jewish intellectual in general—as a projection of European Jewish culture circa 1937–1945 into the context of contemporary New York culture. In his essay on the poetics of Marjorie Perloff, Daniel Morris argues that Perloff's childhood experience as an Austrian Jew who was forced to flee Vienna in 1938 affects her theories of poetry and identity as an American academic in the postmodern period. Trained from youth in the German classics, and then at graduate school in High Modernism during the heyday of the New Criticism in America in the 1950s, the memoir *Vienna Paradox* shows how Perloff in the early 1960s begins to rework her relationship to the meaning of a hyphenated identity as a highly cultured, immigrant American Jew during her early teaching career. In the memoir, she does not dwell on her Jewish background as an influence to her rise to becoming a successful American academic whose topics of study from the modernist Yeats to the postmodernist O'Hara have not tended to be Jewish, but she also does not deny the indelible fact of her Jewishness. Countering her Viennese forebears' dissociation from their Jewishness as a significant identity marker, and at least qualifying the contemporary trend in academic cultural theory to perceive all identity markers as antiessentialist, and thus to view the self as a performance in which Americans, à la Gatsby, or, more to the point, Barbra Streisand as the cross-dressing Yeshiva girl in the film version of I. B. Singer's story "Yentyl," have the freedom to compose and re-compose their character as often as they should like, Perloff responds: "Jewish identity can never be merely expunged, for the simple reason that, as the refugees from Hitler were forced to learn the hard way, one is always a Jew in the eyes of the Other" (234). She continues: "Given this state of affairs, one cannot stop being a Jew, whatever one's response to the Jewish religion and however strong one's rival affiliations, whether professional, intellectual, national, or familial. It is a reality the upper class Viennese Jewish refugees were reluctant to face: many remained staunchly in denial even after they came to America" (236). We may thus read Perloff's endeavors as critic and scholar as a conversation about identity formation that pivots between essentialist and constructivist modes.

According to Charlie Bertsch, Charles Bernstein's libretto for the 2004 opera *Shadowtime,* which uses the 1940 death of Walter Benjamin as the starting point for a rich engagement with that Jewish thinker's ideas about language, time, and spirituality, superbly demonstrates the poet's ability to balance theory and craft. Ranging widely through different techniques, the text manages to be both accessible and esoteric, channeling the populist cadence of the Beats and the avant-garde silence of OUILIPO with equal strength. As impressive as the libretto is, however, reading it in book form can be deceptive. Bernstein's words take on a much different aspect when placed within the context of composer Brian Ferneyhough's unapologetically Modernist score. Indeed, the opera casts the bulk of the libretto in shadow, making it close to impossible to pick out most of the words that comprise it from the stream of sound. And that's no accident. Ferneyhough often layers the text until it becomes a palimpsest in which it's possible to perceive the presence of language stripped of its communicative function. Even the portions of the opera that present the libretto "straight" manage to obscure meaning through the interplay of word and music. Interestingly, however, Bernstein has expressed complete approval of the violence done to his poetry in the service of art.

Bertsch's essay takes the status of language in *Shadowtime* as a starting point for a consideration of Bernstein's relation to the legacy of the Modernist avant-garde and the cutting-edge criticism, of which Benjamin's work is a prime example, that emerged alongside it. Paying close attention to Benjamin's writings on language and the work of his friend Theodor Adorno on both literature and music, Bertsch first places *Shadowtime* within a tradition of thinking about death and redemption in terms of the experience of totalitarianism. Next he submits a number of pieces in Bernstein's libretto to close readings that demonstrate his own take on those themes. After then describing how those pieces are presented in Ferneyhough's score, Bertsch uses material from interviews conducted with Bernstein in order to argue that Bernstein's willingness to subordinate the music of his words to the music of another provided him the ideal opportunity to probe the limits of language in the age of technological reason and, furthermore, to consider the implications of those limits for Jewish thought in the wake of the Holocaust. In the end, Bertsch concludes that the loss of control to which Bernstein consented in signing on to Ferneyhough's project actually gave him the opportunity to make points that his printed work, for all of its brilliance on the page, is unable to achieve.

In his reading of Bernstein as part of an omnibus essay on a group of contemporary Jewish American poets who each strive for democratic belonging, but express skepticism about its possibilities in the context of what he calls the "hyperamnesia" of a culture that is often complacent about remembering past horrors that would provoke democratic vigilance, Tom Fink emphasizes the "radical morphogenerativeness of language" in Bernstein as a way to emphasize the polysemous nature of identity that wants to avoid "dangerous and reductive forms of Jewish identity." Working in the tradition of Gertrude Stein, as well as language-oriented comics such as Groucho Marx and Lenny Bruce, Fink sees Bernstein as occupying an interstitial relationship to Jewishness that turns away from Yiddish without embracing assimilationism. Stephen Paul Miller, another contemporary poet-theorist discussed by Fink, then follows with a hybridic work, *Relentlessly*, that offers a relentless sort of ongoing discourse (which Miller associates with the Jewish secular poet Kenneth Koch) in the form of a type of lineated verse that captures the Yiddish-inflected swing cadences and at times the anapestic rhythm that Miller (and his ninety-year-old mother, Rita) associate with dovening, the oral and bodily prayer ritual that Miller reminds us stems from a term for the "divine" in Indo-European root languages. Miller de-essentializes

Jewish identity by finding what Jewish sounds like in such non-Jewish and even anti-Jewish figures as Eliot and Pound, Whitman, Duke Ellington, and Spalding Gray.

Like Fink's essay on Bernstein, Miller and several other younger Jewish American poets with a radical bent, Eric Murphy Selinger's contribution is capacious in that it covers many writers who are discussed elsewhere in the volume, including Charles Bernstein by way of Stein, Norman Finkelstein, and Alicia Ostriker, but also writers we don't discuss elsewhere such as Jackie Osherow, Jay Ladin, and a detailed reading of the political poetry of Ammiel Alcalay, as well as Howard Nemerov. As disparate as is the group of poets mentioned above, Selinger's argument is to foreground Jewish difference and Jewish differences, as well as a persistent "Jewish way," that he describes variously as obstinacy, rebelliousness, or the biblical idea of Jews as a "stiff-necked people." He speaks of the "Jewish way" of "resistance [that] trumps any more obedient Judaism as a marker of identity" (11). Quoting from several poems that foreground debates among rabbis in classical Judaism, such as the question and answer style of "Debate with the Rabbi" by Nemerov and "Rabbi Jose the Angel" by Jay Ladin, as well as the dialogic format of Ostriker's *The Volcano Sequence.* Following upon the idea that "God likes a lively opponent" (3), Selinger argues that "Debate itself as Jewish, indeed as more Jewish than either religious faith or communal affiliation" (11).

Selinger transfers the Rabbinic idea of dialectical Jewishness into a Freudian (and Derridean) context of internal dialogue and debate that he argues goes on within the psyche of the individual Jew in poems by Osherow and Finkelstein. He thus foregrounds what Harold Bloom calls the "ceaseless agon within the self" (5). Quoting Finkelstein ("the one is two"), Selinger emphasizes a Jewish poetics that acknowledges "the other within the self" as well as the ethical dimension of Judaism which honors (as in Leviticus 19:34) the stranger among us in a social context. In his moving discussion of the political poetry of Ammiel Alcalay, who writes not only on the Israel-Palestine conflict, but also on the wars in the Balkans, Selinger notes the Levinasian "ethics of responsibilities for and to the Other, indeed a willingness to see the ethnically, historically, and linguistically Other as inextricably part of the self" (23).

In a stunning verbal display of jouissance that includes linkages to Phil Spector's Wall of Sound, the beehive hairdos of the Ronettees, Walter Benjamin's observations about the detritus of history in "The Angel of History," and the relationship between arc-hives and beehives, Maria Damon playfully addresses "The Wall" and other multimedia and electronic performance pieces by Adeena Karasick, a Canadian Jewish feminist Kabbalist poet. Damon interprets "The Wall" as a visual/verbal pastiche that resembles (or re-assembles or dis-assembles) our interpretation of the meaning of the "Wailing Wall," or the Western Wall, the remaining fragment of the Second Temple in Jerusalem. Damon reads Karasick's "wall" as a hypermediated space that also resembles the polymorphous pleasure zones of the female body. In Karasick's poem the supposedly solid-state Western Wall becomes instead a figure of bricolage, a "dynamic ecosystem," and an "archive of feeling. Damon focuses on both the poem's and the Western Wall's "multitude of cracks and fissures stuffed or unstuffed with paper, [which] reads like a female body whose orifices have been dammed up" (8). An archival site that is continually producing and reproducing knowledge in the context of a missing original source (the destroyed first and second temples), Damon points to the alternate meaning of the Western Wall in Karasick to the standard narrative of exile and return to a point of origins. Instead, we have the language of the poem (and in the wall) as a terrain in which the fluctuating movements of history and culture are performed. Karasick's own comments about the relationship of her poetry to Kabbalah follows Damon's remarks.

If Damon's essay on Karasick is perhaps the most radical in the collection in terms of style, it is fair to say that in terms of stretching the idea of a Jewish poetics the most radical essay in the collection belongs to Benjamin Friedlander, who interprets secular Jewish culture as a radical sect within Judaism by claiming the precedent of Saint Paul. Friedlander shows that, like Michael Heller in his essay, and like the Reznikoff represented in Ranen Omer-Sherman's essay, Paul proclaimed an ethics without adherence to the law. A harbinger of a nonobservant Jewish culture that emphasizes love over law, Paul without Christ, for Friedlander, anticipates a wide grouping of contemporary Jewish American poets in promoting a tradition of reading the Torah radically and of offering a critique of tradition from within.

Along with the essays I have briefly described above, *Radical Poetics and Secular Jewish Culture* also includes poetry by Bob Holman and Paul Auster, commentary by Hank Lazer and Jerome Rothenberg, as well as writings by Bob Perelman and Marjorie Perloff.

Radical Jewish Culture / Secular Jewish Practice

Charles Bernstein

1. Some years ago, one of the editors of a forthcoming, prominent anthology of Jewish American literature mentioned to me that he thought Gertrude Stein (among other poets of particular importance for innovative American poetry) would not be included in the book. It struck me as deliciously odd that in a time of affirmation of the many distinct cultures that make up U.S. literature, these editors would consider leaving out of their anthology perhaps the most famous Jewish poet of the modernist period. Evidently, being Jewish was not enough to be a Jewish poet. By the same token, my children go to a Jewish camp for those who have no religious Jewish beliefs, a camp with a seventy-five-year history of secular Jewish commitment; but I wonder whether there are Muslim or Pentecostal or Catholic camps for nonbelievers? But that's because, at least in some sense, you can't really be a lapsed Jew.

Yes I know I am trading on the ambiguity of religion and ethnicity. I mean to continue to do so.

9. Here are the set of questions I posed to a 2004 panel on "Radical Jewish Poetry / Secular Jewish Practice": What are the innovations and inventions of American Jewish poets, over the past century? Can we say that there is distinctly Jewish component to radical modernist and contemporary poetry? What is the relation of Jewish modernist and contemporary poets to the historical avant-garde and to contemporary innovative poetry? How do Jewish cultural life and ethnic and religious forms and traditions manifest themselves in the forms, styles, and approaches to radical American poetry? What role does a distinctly secular approach to Jewishness by poets and other Jewish artists mean for "radical Jewish culture"?

4. Over the weeks leading up to the panel, several of the participants, but most notably me, expressed confusion about the topic—are we being asked to

put forward some positive correlation between Jewish poets, or we might say poets of Jewishness, and innovative poetic practice, or to affirm the value of Jewishness in reading or valuing such work? I feel a deep ambivalence on all these issues and I want to insist that this ambivalence itself, the questioning of Jewishness, is just as Jewish as the designer yarmulkes and Glatt kosher Peruvian restaurants of my neighborhood, the deep Upper West Side.

Remember Kafka's question: "What have I in common with Jews? I don't know what I have in common with myself." Or, in a recent translation, I wouldn't want to have an ethnicity that would automatically count me in its number . . . when the saints go marching in . . .

Am I Jewish? Is this Jewish? I am no more Jewish then when I set my Jewishness adrift from fundamentalist religious practice. I am no more Jewish than when I refuse imposed definitions of what Jewishness means. I am no more Jewish than when I attend to how such Jewishness lives itself out, plays tunes not yet played. Jewishness can, even must, in one of its multiple manifestations, be an aversion of identification—as a practice of dialogue and as an openness to the unfolding performance of the everyday. Call it the civic practice of Jewishness.

10. Amos Oz, in an essay published in 1993, writes:

> Now suppose a new Kafka is growing up right now, here in San Francisco, California: Suppose he is fourteen years old right now. Let's call him Chuck Bernstein. Let's assume that he is every bit of a genius as Kafka was in his time. His future must, as I see it, depend on an uncle in Jerusalem or an experience by the Dead Sea, or a cousin in a kibbutz or something inspired by the Israeli live drama: Otherwise, with the exception of the possibility that he is growing up among the ultra-Orthodox, he will be an American writer of Jewish origin—not a Jewish American writer. He may become a new Faulkner, but not a new Kafka.

Fortunately, we have America so as not to need a Mr. Oz to police who is Jewish or, indeed, what is Jewish. But this America, unfortunately, is still somewhere over the rainbow.

2. The obsessive focus in literary journalism on the American Jewish novel has had the effect of cutting off consideration of the formal and processural features of secular Jewish art. We have ended up with a set of representative figures for an approach in and to a culture that highly values the rejection of such graven representations.

In other words, the often frame-locked focus on Jewish content as the sine qua non of Jewish literature has distracted from recognition—not so much of Jewish forms, whatever they might be, as from formal, rhythmic, dialectical and dialogical and colloquial, dimensions of literary, musical, and visual works that do not have explicit Jewish thematic focus. In happy contrast, we do have such recent anthologies as *The Norton Anthology of Jewish American Literature* and *Jewish American Poetry: Poems, Commentary, and Reflections,* ed. Eric Selinger and Jonathan Barron, along with Jerome Rothenberg's groundbreaking *A Big Jewish Book* (and its shorter version, *Exiled in the World*).

5. & yet, increasingly, official American Jewish discourse has been dominated by concerns for Jewish demographic sustainability viewed through the frame of Jewish family life and defined by affiliation to organized religious institutions, when it is not strafed by concern over the catastrophe of Israel. This duel focus—the Scylla of ethnic preservation (as if Jewish life was already a museum show, a kind of Lower East Side Sturbridge Village) and the Charybdis of Palestine—is explicitly (and legitimately) paranoid in orientation; but the effect is counterproductive insofar as it disenfranchises sectors of current and future, and indeed historical, Jewish life, just that part of Jewish culture that can be called secular—and which had its greatest flourishing in the United States in the left Yiddishkeit culture of the 1920s and 1930s, that world of nonreligious—indeed often antireligious—Jewish artists, intellectuals, socialists, comedians, musicians and songwriters, and assorted free thinkers that thrives in New York even to this day.

7. While Jewish secular culture has sometimes—well maybe often, well sometimes or often, I really can't be sure—wanted to erase—or shall we say put under erasure?—its explicit Jewishness, especially insofar as such identity-politic might remove or ghettoize us from the larger culture of which we are an integral part—nonetheless there is no particular reason, in other words, no necessity, to take such bracketing of Jewishness as anything other than Jewish. *Read the text of this aversion. Interpret it. Talk back to it.* Within historical Jewish time there are certain icons of radical secular Jewish thought, icons that don't define a poetic practice for Americans but suggest a constellation of possibility. This is a constellation most explicitly noted by Isaac Deutscher in his *Non-Jewish Jew* and that includes Spinoza, the three Marxes (Chico, Karl, and Groucho), & the three Steins—Ein, Wittgen, & Gertrude; our own Yiddishe Trinity: Freud, Kafka, and Celan; Irving Berlin's "White Christmas" and the Gershwins's "It Ain't Necessarily So"; Emmanuel Levinas's faces,

Emma Goldman's dancing at the revolution, & Fanny Brice's Baby Snooks; Alfred Steiglitz& Chaim Gross; Allen Ginsberg's "Kaddish," Edmond Jabes's imaginary rabbis, and Jacques Derrida's midrashic commentary, Hannah Weiner's dialogic voices and Larry Eigner's linguistic fields, Ad Reinhardt's shades of black & Lenny Bruce's "Religion, Inc.," the space between Morton Feldman's notes and Arnold Schoenberg's scales; and, lest we forget, Mickey Katz's foundational "Borcht Riders in the Sky."

In this respect, I want to acknowledge the important work of John Zorn's Radical Jewish Culture series & beyond that the work of Sander Gilman and Daniel and Jonathan Boyeran and Maria Damon.

6. The weekend before the panel, several of us participated in a centennial celebration at Columbia and Barnard for Louis Zukofsky, who along with Charles Reznikoff, George Oppen, Muriel Rukeyser, and Laura Riding constitute an important constellation of Jewish second-wave modernist poets. The interest in this work should not be understated: the capacious philosophy hall lounge was filled to capacity. But of course the interest was not primarily because of Zukofsky's Jewishness.

The first conference to celebrate the Objectivist poets, and, in effect, Jewish-American modernist poetry, was not in America at all but in France, in 1989 at Royaumont. I remember after a talk I gave on Reznikoff, Carl Rakosi sternly reprimanded me for the Jewish motifs in my piece: "We were secular," he said, and Jewishness was not a legitimate lens through which to read the work. While Rakosi's remarks seemed particularly ill-suited to Reznikoff, for whom Jewishness is an explicit and central concern, it is, nonetheless, an important statement of poetic license that I do not wish—entirely—to ignore. (An even more striking rejection of Jewish identification is to be found in Laura [Riding] Jackson.) But you can't separate Jewishness, and in particular the Jewish cultural context from which, for example, Zukofksky emerges as a poet, from his work, even if this aspect of his poetry was rarely mentioned at the conference (Rothenberg's concluding address being a significant exception). Consider only that Zukofsky's first major work, "A Poem Beginning 'The'" is not only a Jewish response to Eliot's "The Waste Land" but also an extraordinary poem about the tensions of assimilation for the young poet with Yiddish in his ears into an Anglophilic literary culture. In this respect, I want to commend Stephen Fredman's recent book on Reznikoff, *A Menorah for Athena*, the title itself playing out the tensions that would underlie some of the most important formal innovations in second-wave modernist American poetry; for example, the way Reznikoff, Oppen, and Zukofsky insist on resistant particulars against airy generalization.

8. Several years ago I wrote the libretto for *Shadowtime,* an opera about Walter Benjamin. A collaboration with composer Brian Ferneyhough, *Shadowtime* was commissioned by the Munich Biennale. The opera opens with the death of Benjamin; not the suicide, by the way, because whatever else, to think Benjamin committed suicide is too easy an out for all of us. Perhaps "suicided." After this scene, the opera envisions a journey for "our" imagined Benjamin, as told, largely, through a chorus of angels, a chorus of the angels of history. The whole secular Jewish culture in Europe was completely wiped out between 1937 and 1945, along with the rest of European Jewish culture. What would have become of all these intellectuals and artists? We have to imagine our character "Benjamin" living in New York. It is interesting that two people living in America created an opera in English, commissioned and premiered in Munich, on this character. Our "Benjamin" is born in the space of contemporary American thought. The historical person leaves the face of the earth, but not our imagination. How do we "hear" him? How do we hear the flapping of the wings of history? That's also a translation: how is "Beniamin" translated into "Ben*j*amin"?

In other words, at a certain point it became apparent to me, and not just me of course, that the secular Jewish culture that was wiped out in the Second War—I realize this was not the only Jewish culture destroyed—stranded the correlative developments in America. Imagine Klezmer music played by Jews in Poland, not as museum pieces but as a living culture? Imagine European poetry and philosophy by the descendants of Benjamin and Heine. But, to a large extent, this is not to be, or anyway, insofar as it to be, it too must be the task of secular Jewish culture on this side of the Atlantic and of our radical poetry and ambiguating poetics. I think it is difficult to acknowledge this unwanted and perhaps even insufferable task, certainly it has been difficult for me. But perhaps this is what we have been chosen for.

11. Not long ago I had an extended discussion with the secular Jewish zen poet and priest Norman Fischer. Our questions wove in and out of the midrashic practice of textual dialog and interpretation: the insistence that the fixed text was nonetheless open to multiple, possibly infinite (but then again, *maybe not*) interpretations; the revelation that any text, like any word, poem, event, person, or people, requires complex interpretation in terms of its multiple levels. Call it the **PRDS** of interpretation – the truthfulness of the refusal of the literal in the pursuit of meaning: *Peshat*—literal meaning; *Ramez* (remez)—suggested meaning; *Drash* (derush)—allegorical meaning; *Sod*—hidden or mystical or esoteric meaning. You can call it Paradise but maybe it's just **P**eople **R**eally **D**igging the **S**ecular. We wondered whether

such a practice of deliberately delicious ambiguation and intoxicating complexifaction could lead to a greater ethical and aesthetic responsiveness in and resonance with the social world, such as we associate with secular Jewish politics and art. *Some dare call it reason.* Norman and I ended with more questions than we started with; this is how we knew that the conversation had value for us. But how Jewish was it? As Bartleby might put it, I'd prefer not to say.

Originally presented as part of a program I organized for the American Jewish Historical Society at the Center for Jewish History in New York on September 21, 2004. Paul Auster, Kathryn Hellerstein, Stephen Paul Miller, Marjorie Perloff, and Jerome Rothenberg joined me on the panel. The quote from Amos Oz in section 10 is from "Imagining the Other: 1" in *The Writer in the Jewish Community: An Israeli-North American Dialogue*, ed. Richard Siegel and Tamar Sofer (London: Associated University Presses, 1993), 122. I quote the same passage in the autobiographical interview in *My Way: Speeches and Poems.*

Who or What Is a Jewish American Poet, with Specific Reference to David Antin, Charles Bernstein, Rachel Blau DuPlessis, and Jerome Rothenberg

Hank Lazer

There is no need for me to Mintz my words, and thus whatever Perl-of wisdom I can come up with, I will say it.

~

I have learned, for example, that Halakah is a secret anagram, an amalgam of Hanukah and my own name, Hank Lazer, and thus the particular Halakah citations I will make, in answering that vexing question, who is a Jew?, will have the requisite Halakic authority.

~

Who is a famous Jewish American poet? I have it on the best authority. I googled. The very first source listed indicates, "This is a list of famous Jewish American poets." And the website itself is answers.com, so how much better can it be?

Charles Bernstein (I'm not making this up—he really is listed first), Joseph Brodsky, Allen Ginsberg, Louise Glück, Jorie Graham, Allen Grossman, Marilyn Hacker, Anthony Hecht, John Hollander, Richard Howard, Chester Kallman, Bob Kaufman, A. M. Klein, Kenneth Koch, Maxine Kumin, Stanley Kunitz, Emma Lazarus, Denise Levertov, Philip Levine, Howard Nemerov, Alicia Ostriker, Robert Pinsky, Carl Rakosi, Charles Reznikoff, Adrienne Rich, Jerome Rothenberg, Muriel Rukeyser, Delmore Schwartz, Karl Shapiro, Gerald Stern, Mark Strand, Boris Zubry, Louis Zukofsky, Zvi Yair.

~

As for who is a Jewish poet, there is one fundamental test: humor. If not ever funny, then not Jewish. Pound is probably not Jewish. Zukofsky maybe. Oppen may have a problem.

~

For me, it all comes down to one story. If your son—let's give him a happy name: Felix—doesn't want to have a Bar Mitzvah, makes that his decision, and you don't push him, but very near to his thirteenth birthday he decides he does want to have a Bar Mitzvah, and you contact a good friend, say, a poet you have known for a long time, perhaps a poet who is a Buddhist priest, and also a Jew, to do the ceremony, and, thank god this is in New York City, you inquire around, and, in fact, it is possible to rent a Torah, and you do so for the sake of your son's Bar Mitzvah and to assist the Jewish-Buddhist-poet-friend, then you are a Jew.

What I do not have time to take up in this essay, but hope to do so perhaps at a later date, is what is a poem and who, therefore, is a poet.

A Test of Jewish American Poetry: If Philip Levine was stopped by the side of the road and was being questioned by the police, would you pull over to help him? If Philip Levine's poetry was under attack by a prominent, non-Jewish critic, would you come to his defense? Does your response change if I say that in the *New York Review of Books* the noted Christian American literary critic Helen Vendler attacks the famous Jewish American poet Philip Levine for his sentimental poetry? Or, do you hold back and think to yourself that perhaps Oscar Wilde was right when he said that "all bad poetry is sincere"?

(Note: Bernstein, DuPlessis, and Rothenberg have all contributed to this present collection of essays on Radical Jewish Poetics edited by Stephen Paul Miller and Daniel Morris. Many of my citations originate with these talks/essays.)

Kafka's question (written in his diary of 1914)—interestingly, cited by both Bernstein and Rothenberg—"What have I in common with Jews? I have hardly anything in common with myself"—points toward a refusal, an uneasiness, a discomfort with identity itself, with the particularity of an identity-based or ethnic taxonomy. The paradox of this particular refusal of identity—the Jew who refuses the Jewish American or Jewish label—is that it has become an identifying *Jewish* trait. I wonder if there are similar traditions of refusal among Catholics, Baptists, Episcopalians, and Muslims, particularly among poets born into these groups who, nonetheless, in spite of their gestures of distancing, remain figured within such terminology. Rachel Blau DuPlessis cites Edmond Jabès asking, "How come the non-believer as much as the believer can claim, can presume on the same Judaism?" Or, as Rachel continues, "as Yosef Hayim Yerushalmi remarks: 'In the often turbulent process of social and cultural change that accompanied or succeeded the Haskalah, there emerged that modern species of "*gottloser Jude*" [Godless Jew] whom we know as the secular Jew' . . . that's pretty much a description of me" (R, 2). I think that such a discomfort with a seemingly fixed identity is not just Jewish but perhaps also Zen Buddhist. Though it also occurs to me, using Rodger Kamenetz's wonderful term, there are many JuBu's . . .

Perhaps such a refusal or discomfort with Jewish identity or with identification as a Jewish American poet may also be linked to an Orthodox Jewish interpretation of the First Commandment. No false idols means no fixed representation of the divine, no image, not even a pronounceable name. Perhaps such a deeply imbibed cultural insistence upon the *most* important things being protected by an injunction on behalf of *non*-representation comes to apply as well to ethnic identity and religious/spiritual particularity?

"One might be a writer and a Jew, but not a Jewish writer. This is a formulation from Edmond Jabès, said in conversation with Rosmarie Waldrop, and told to me by Waldrop in conversation" (R, 4).

I am intrigued by the boundaries of discomfort, acceptance, and rejection. That one might affirm and deny so clearly: "Prayer, I do not do, but the injunction to study, I have followed" (R, 8) and in affirming "a post-particularist, Emersonian kind of faith" as part of a movement that also "left behind liturgy, stained glass, and the mysticism and sensuousness of religion (except as art appreciation)" (R, 9)—yet still say about one's own writing that "I feel, increasingly, as the work goes on, *that I am being spoken through*, almost as if I were single-handedly building into existence some of the works of the lost" (R, 10; italics mine).

Makes me want to get a wrist band and wear it: What Would Robert Duncan Say?

I am after a religious phenomenology that not only scrupulously avoids the bad faith of particularity and fixed identity (and fixed dogma), but that also resists its own too-easy residence in the inability to be swept up into moments and passages of mystical experience.

I am intrigued by when it is permissible to give in: "When one enters such a gigantic task as a long poem, it is difficult not to think of *being called* and of struggling with something large, multi-dimensional and fundamentally unknowable *by which you have been touched*" (R, 11; italics mine).

Oy vay. Touched by what? Called by what or whom? Cf. Heidegger—not just what is called thinking, but what calls us into thinking?

Or, "Paul Celan says that the Beyond is inside us, immeasurable and imponderable" (R, 14).

So, which mumbo jumbo is to be sanctioned, and which is to be deemed retrograde or an impermissible mysticism, and why? Does one cite a progressive cultural history to support what exclusions and refusals are ok, and which mysticisms we inhabit (somehow ok because they are "text" or "book" but not the now completely *traif* "spirit" or "the divine" or, God forbid, "religion")?

Why is "a way of living in textuality characteristic of a Jewish heritage" (R, 17) not its own form of chauvinism or superiority or particularity? Aren't *many* cultures living in textuality? Is "our" love of the Book—cf. the problematics of being the Chosen People—both the location of a truth and an arrogant blindness (to our generic nature)?

In one tradition, the panic or compulsion is to make it cohere, as if somehow a fit conclusion could be found. In another, what we hope to do is to encourage and sustain an ongoing conversation. Is anything gained by linking this other tradition to a particular religion or ethnicity?

This talk, occurring as it does shortly after the conference in Iran denying the Holocaust, is *not* a denial of Jews or of Jewishness but of flat-footed versions of Jewishness, of an insistence on boundaries and characteristics that do not hold up when examined skeptically, of flat-footed versions of Jewish American poets and poetry.

For example, *which* Jews are we talking about in the first place. The general introduction to the *Norton Anthology of Jewish American Literature* (2001) has some interesting facts to consider: (1) there are now about 5.5 million Jews in America; (2) Conservative Judaism is now the largest of the four main branches of the religion; the others are Orthodox Judaism, Reform Judaism, and the relatively recent Reconstructionist Judaism (by the way, these branches disagree in fundamental ways over who is a Jew); (3) Jewish religious observance today is in decline; more than 50 percent of American Jews have no synagogue or religious affiliation; i.e., so, nonaffiliation, in fact, is the norm; (4) Jews have settled in the US in greater numbers than they ever have in any other land, including Israel (N, 7, 9, 3).

When I look out of my old office window from the main administrative building at The University of Alabama—the Rose Administration Building—at this time of year I see a forty-foot-tall Christmas tree fully decorated and lit. In that administrative building, the president and the provost, for whom I work, wonder why our university does not do better at recruiting Jewish students. Exams sometimes fall on Yom Kippur, as did homecoming one year. The one temple in town was just sold (to an institute for the deaf and blind).

I identify myself as Jewish-Buddhist-agnostic. I am proud to be a member of the temple; I do not attend services.

Is the question of Jewish identity simply binary? Someone is a Jew, or not? Someone is a Jewish American Poet, or not? Are there degrees? Would it make sense for us to ask, who's *more* Jewish, Poet A or Poet B?

One of my favorite essays on contemporary poetry is by Susan Schultz. The essay, "Of Time and Charles Bernstein's Lines: A Poetics of Fashion Statements," appears in her book *A Poetics of Impasse* (2005). Susan's essay, which covers more territory than my pointed summary will suggest, establishes an interesting parallel between Bernstein's modes of writing—his peculiar ability to mimic (and mock and interrogate) prior and current modes of poetic composition—and Bernstein's father's profession, which Schultz summarizes nicely: "The elder Bernstein worked as a dress manufacturer for Smartcraft Corporation, which sold imitations of designer dresses in the fifties" (183). The art of the knockoff; the selling of a substitution or simulation; the classic *shmatta* business . . . Is *this* a Jewish story? What if Neil Gaiman wrote it, and instead focused on the mythology of the cuckoo who lays eggs in another bird's nest? Would that version of the story still be Jewish? By the way, does anyone know, is Neil Gaiman Jewish? (He is.)

In a speech delivered to the National Writers Union, Jack Foley offers a concise definition: "SPIRITUALITY—God without the hard stuff."

I think that just the opposite might be the case. Can't we think of spirituality as everything else but a definiteness about the divine? In other words, everything but God?

"Adam and Eve heard the First One's voice 'in the garden walking' with them. This voice—Memra in Hebrew—was Yahweh, the Law, the Logos, and it was moving around beside them like a radio with legs. This same voice of the Logos was later heard speaking to Moses, whose face, afterwards, burned like hot gold until no one dared go near him.

"The sound of that voice comes and goes in other human and angelic forms throughout Scripture; then it recedes and disappears. The Gnostics felt it fading into eternity and becoming that eternity. The Logos spread out so far, and became so thin after the crucifixion, that contact with it from then on occurred only in much the same way as Proust's involuntary memory experience: 'It depends on chance whether we come upon it before we die or whether we never encounter it'" (FH, 73, *The Wedding Dress: Meditation on Word and Life*).

"In the Old Testament the voice in the garden, Memra, means the wisdom that flows without ceasing in the human mind. It is inaudible, not even a whisper, and is located in thought which is silent. Sometimes—out of this silence—there is a whisper, and this is when Yahweh manifests that which comes as a parade of thought words with the sound of Itself. It enters thought and speaks softly" (FH, 78) . . .

"I know that a sentence contains only as much language as it can bear, and so it can be viewed as an image of temporality" (FH, 79) . . .

"God is one word that he prays we will be liberated from, because God cannot be reduced to the word God" (FH, 80) . . .

"We may not know if there is a God or not, but we do know that there is a word" (FH, 81).

To my way of thinking, this is very Jewish writing. It is by Fanny Howe. She is a Catholic. For the term Jewish to be properly inclusive, it needs to include Catholics, such as Fanny Howe and Donald Revell. Somewhere, there is an echo of W. C. Fields's punch line about Catholics being the worst kind of Jews . . .

Charles Reznikoff, Louis Zukofsky, George Oppen, and Carl Rakosi.

(R, 2): "Once . . . I asked Robert Creeley why, in his view, the Objectivists were so under-known and so under-acknowledged. He replied, 'Anti-Semitism.' 'Anti-Semitism,' he replied."

It's tempting to say that today anti-Semitism is not a factor in the way poets are esteemed, read, recognized, and appreciated. After all, fairly recently, there have been Jewish American poet laureates. But maybe it's also worth considering whether it may be more accurate to say there's no anti-Semitism so long as you're of the secular Jewish affiliation.

With great thanks to Rachel Blau DuPlessis, who, in Madrid several summers ago, referred me to Susan Handelman's extraordinary book, *The Slayers of Moses: The Emergence of Rabbinic Interpretation in Modern Literary Theory,* let me quote a passage from that book: "Perhaps one can also understand the Biblical ban on images in this light. The Jewish idea of the invisible God culminates in the confession of faith: '*Hear* O Israel.' In the account of the revelation at Sinai, the Biblical text relates, 'And all the people saw the thunderings and the lightnings, and the voice of the horn, and the mountain smoking' (Exod. 20:15). Comments Rashi, the famous Jewish medieval commentator, 'They saw that which should be heard which is impossible to see in another place.' The revelation was to see what is *heard,* a voice, not an image. The invisible is manifested through sound and the divine word does not become 'fulfilled' or hypostatized into a present being. Revelation is not appearance" (34).

And so, by analogy, to be a Jewish American poet (in the radical tradition I am exploring) is also *not* an appearance, *not a thing*, but perhaps, at most, at best, something heard?

~

I find Edmond Jabès's writing—and Jacques Derrida's too—to be the most important religious writing of our time. Yet I find myself wondering how that comes to be: how a nonbelieving Jew, an atheist, writes a poetry (or, truly, a generically unclassifiable writing) that has such a powerful capacity to engage and to instruct. Perhaps Jabès's writing demonstrates to us—in book after book—how inadequate and crude terms such as "belief" and "nonbelief" are, and that while Jabès may be classified as being a "non-believing Jew" and an "atheist," the opposing qualities of belief are, throughout his writing, of equal intensity. Perhaps what matters, then, is the intensity (and credibility and the nuanced nature) of Jabès's relationship to these fundamental portals of "Jew" and "God," and in this regard his writing is unsurpassed. I sometimes suspect (or entertain the thought) that for Jabès (and for Derrida as well) a direct or simple profession of belief, particularly a profession that assumed a static or definitive quality, would not only be a betrayal of the fundamentals of their thinking and writing and of their profound sense of thinking as always being *in motion*, but also a violation of an orthodox interpretation of the commandment prohibiting one to have or worship any false images of the divine. For such a fixity of belief carries with it the hazard of actually standing between one and one's relationship to the divine by becoming a sign or site or formulation that one mistakenly substitutes for that engagement.

This passage is from a longer essay I wrote on Rosmarie Waldrop's *Lavish Absence.* A couple of years ago, Charles Bernstein sent me this passage with a very brief, affirmative comment. Honestly, when I read the passage, I did not know who had written it. A day or two later, I realized that I had. I have been friends with Charles for a little over twenty years. This e-mail exchange and his sending of this passage to me may be the only time we have exchanged views about spiritual matters.

~

When I suggested earlier that the Jewish American poet is not an appearance and not a thing but something heard, so that I am not misunderstood, I do not mean that the Jewish American poet ought to achieve a distinctive voice. Such an accomplishment, or such an act of lazy repetition, too readily becomes a caricature or a shtick (as in, for example, the poetry of Gerald

Stern). As Norman Fischer notes in his remarks at the 1987 conference called "The Poetics of Emptiness," "I think if meditation can show you that there is really no such thing as, nor would one want, a poetic voice, then it is already worthwhile."

"So you are not interested in 'poetic' experience nor in 'poetic' language. These seem unnecessary exaggerations. Only that you know, as a human, that you live intimately, intensely, with language, honestly with it, in it, as it, and it is necessary to keep that up, to clarify and deepen it."

"Somewhere we've developed the misconception that poetry is self-expression, and that meditation is going inward. Actually, poetry has nothing to do with self-expression, it is the way to be free, finally, of self-expression, to go much deeper than that. And meditation is not a form of thought or reflection, it is a looking at or an awareness of what is there, equally inside and outside, and then it doesn't make sense anymore to mention inside or outside." (*House of K,* Norman Fischer, 31, 30, 29–30)

I think that Norman may well be the most important Jewish Buddhist American poet writing today. Let's add him to our list, and with him, a few others that evaded answers.com:

Norman Fischer, Norman Finkelstein, Stephen Fredman, Bob Dylan, David Antin, Beth Joselow, Maria Damon, George Oppen, David Ignatow, Hannah Weiner, Bob Perelman, Larry Eigner, Tom Mandel, Ben Friedlander, and Gertrude Stein.

An axiom for Derrida's later writing might be: "Deconstruction means to be the delimitation of totalization in all its forms" (C, 126). I am tempted to say that the same axiom may apply equally well to Buddhism, to mystical Judaism, and to innovative poetry. What each strives to preserve in its resistance to totalization, its refusal of finality, its insistence upon a perpetually active and ongoing hermeneutics, its passionate engagement with thinking as ever open at one end, is the preservation of an ever-changing phenomenology of spiritual experience. Or, as Caputo concludes about "deconstruction" (where, as I think it, "deconstruction" becomes a counter or a term subject to substitution with the aforementioned off-rhyming cognates), we are "able to see how deconstruction is a certain way of putting something that is *also* religious, but over which the religions do not have exclusive rights or hegemonic power, a way of freeing something religious from the religions" (190).

Perhaps "finding one's voice" or becoming a poet with *a* distinctive voice constitutes one aspect of totalization and one aspect of a fixed identity, of a commodified identity, and of a premodern and nostalgic version of the Jewish American poet. Interestingly enough, a just-published review of Charles Bernstein's *Girly Man* in the *Jewish Daily Forward* (David Kaufmann; December 22, 2006) praises Bernstein's work for offering an alternative to poetry as finding one's voice. The *Forward* praises Bernstein for coming up "with a way of being both a very political and a distinctly Jewish writer."

And yet I wonder, really how Jewish are the features cited for praise in Bernstein's poetry? "As a rule, his poems do not aspire to recount some experience that lies tantalizingly out of the reach of language. They have nothing to do with the tasteful matching of situation and epiphany." Or, "For the point is on the one hand to undermine our lazy desire to rest not on our laurels but on the stereotypes of our language, and on the other to make some new, ungainly music from those stereotypes."

The *Forward* locates Bernstein's essential Jewishness in his humor: "It is the spirit of the punch line and the one liner and the pun—that is, of Jewish vaudeville and its stand-up heirs—that animates so much of Bernstein's work." And, "By his own account, Bernstein grew up watching television in the late 1950s and early '60s—that is, at the moment when a certain unabashed Jewish sensibility went mainstream. And Bernstein learned his lessons well. His choppy, chopped rhythms are both nervously, if not nervily, Jewish." This description begins to sound uncannily like Bernstein's own psychological profile in "Standing Target." For me, the funniest sentence in the *Forward* review is the observation that Bernstein "is, as *everyone* who has *ever* written about him has noted, a funny guy" (italics mine). My own sense is that much of the criticism, particularly by voice-finding poets and voice-praising critics, particularly in the 1980s and 1990s, was not focused on how funny Charles could be or how much fun he made the reading of poetry. Perhaps the *Forward* is more on target in linking Bernstein's work to what it calls the "genius of Jewish comedy" and "the genius of Yiddish," which "puts linguistic invention at the service of a militant deflationary zeal."

~

Susan Handelman concludes, "Jews adhere to signs because reality innately is constituted as linguistic for them. For the Jew it is precisely the cancellation of the sign or word for a thing that is idolatrous" (117).

David Antin, Charles Bernstein, Rachel Blau DuPlessis, and Jerome Rothenberg have, it seems to me, engaged in an increasingly proximate relationship to elements of Jewish culture and textuality *without* becoming a fixed target for the label "Jew" or "Jewish American Poet," and in so doing, have set in motion an ever-changing, necessarily evasive, nonessential (though critical) "being Jewish," that does not have its at-times self-contradictory particularity canceled or contained by the term "Jew" or "Jewish American Poet."

~

Charles Bernstein, in "Radical Jewish Culture / Secular Jewish Practice," notes that "at least in some sense, you can't really be a lapsed Jew" (CB, 1). It seems to me that the essential feature of Bernstein's Jewishness is an active evasion of any essential identity: "Am I Jewish? Is this Jewish? I am no more Jewish than when I set my Jewishness adrift from fundamentalist religious practice. I am no more Jewish than when I attend to how such Jewishness lives itself out, plays tunes not yet played. Jewishness can, even must, in one of its multiple manifestations, be *an aversion of identification*—as a practice of dialogue and as an openness to the unfolding performance of the everyday. Call it the civic practice of Jewishness" (CB, 1).

Such a viewpoint, oddly, intersects in intriguing ways with Harold Bloom's introduction for the recent Library of America anthology *American Religious Poems* (2006). In some sense, defining what is an American religious poem is not a whole lot easier than defining a Jewish American poet. Bloom, in his introduction to the anthology, creates a decisively Emersonian framework for his collection of American religious poetry, beginning with Emerson's remark in "Self-Reliance" that "As men's prayers are a disease of the will, so are their creeds a disease of the intellect" (HB, xxv). Bloom suggests that "religious poetry, in the United States, has little to do with devotional creeds of the Old World" (xxv). And Bloom proceeds to construct—by means of Emerson, Whitman, and Dickinson—a New World religious poetry. But he offers an observation which, while somewhat off-target, is provocative and pertinent to my own ambiguous attempts to consider a radical Jewish American poetry (which demonstrates a refusal to be precisely that). Bloom notes: "The United States, already a plutocracy, flickers these days toward theocracy. A theocratic America doubtless will distinguish between sacred and secular utterances, but Whitmanian democracy fuses them in the divinity of the self, which is our native understanding of the Resurrection as an escape from history, that is to say, from European time" (xxviii–xxix).

I think that Bloom gives us a political framework for understanding the contemporary cultural and historical value of the refusal of fixed religious identity in the poetry of Bernstein, DuPlessis, Antin, and Rothenberg—particularly during these last years of Bush II. Where I think he is utterly off-base is in identifying "the divinity of the self" as our native escape valve (from theocracy, plutocracy, and a fallen European culture). In fact, all four poets that I have mentioned *undermine* residency in a singular self, and each is eager to critique, mock, lampoon, and question a poetry that is fundamentally or principally personally expressive.

Even so, while I admire and share much with an ambiguating individual Jewishness that marks its Jewishness by its refusal to be one thing, something is missing. Perhaps one can invoke a joke and sidestep the issue: a Jew is stranded on a desert island. What's the first thing that he does? He builds two temples. One that he attends, and the other that he absolutely refuses to attend.

But what is missing is even a temporary residence in the experience of a *social* religious practice and even a sporadic but intense engagement with belief. That social force and that participation in a collective or group experience is not only a part of religious institutions (i.e., the congregation and the temple); it also lends another quality to the force and experience of worship, song, and prayer, where the social is constitutive perhaps of a qualitatively different experience. I say this not as a criticism of Charles, Rachel, David, and Jerry, but as one who also stands outside of sustained social and collective Jewish experience.

As for the issue of belief (or faith or mystical experience or moments of intensely felt spiritual awareness), I find that most discussions and poetry in that vein assume a binary nature and a steady-state quality. Either one has it, or one does not. I think that the opening that a radical Jewish poetics suggests is a phenomenology and a poetry of the inconstancy of belief. Perhaps that is why the phrase "*lend* credence" comes to mind. When Charles writes of Jewishness as involving "openness to the unfolding performance of the everyday," perhaps the inconstancy of spiritual engagement can be one such avenue of attention and performance.

What to say about David Antin? Apparently, judging by the evidence, since he is not in the Norton for Jewish American poets and he's not in Bloom's anthology of American religious poems, he may not be a *real* Jewish American poet nor a religious poet. Some, who have not acquired a taste for David's talk-poems, hear him as pontificating ad nauseam. But I hear him more as rabbificating, as conducting and performing his own midrash, a somewhat improvised creation of text-and-commentary on the spot. Or perhaps we can consider the amazing record of his approximately thirty-five years of talk-poems as a profound performance of a Jewish intellectual intensity and genius that came to fruition in New York City in the 1950s and early 1960s. His talk-poems often tell aspects, narratives, and anecdotes of that era. But it is not really the subject matter, not really the content that I have in mind; I mean that David himself, in the *manner* of his talk-poems, *is* that energy and excitement, an appealingly inventive flashy intelligence *in motion.*

Jerry Rothenberg's case bears many similarities to the positions staked out by Charles and Rachel. He describes his first deliberate attempt at writing "the Jewish poem" as a bringing together of serial techniques from Stein's poem "Dates" with "mystically loaded and sexually charged vocabulary from Isaac Bashevis Singer's novel *Satan in Goray*" (JR, 6). Among the works that Jerry himself identifies as part of his exploration of traditional Jewish linguistic practice and current modernist forms of poetic experimentation we find *Poland/1931* (1974), *A Big Jewish Book* (anthology, 1977), *Khurbn & Other Poems* (1989), *Gematria* (1993), and *14 Stations.* The story that Jerry tells of his childhood is a classically Jewish one:

> Like Louis Zukofsky and Charles Reznikoff, among other children of Jewish immigrants, my first language (to the age of three or four) was Yiddish. (I learned later from reading T. S. Eliot, who I know had *me* in mind, that this disqualified me as a poet within the English mainstream [& probably out of it as well], and I came to take that as a challenge and an opportunity.) My parents (unlike Zukofsky's) were avowedly secular, from late adolescence on, but my mother's mother, who lived with us from a month or two before my birth, was an orthodox Jew, though the relations between her and them were never less than cordial. The outside world—in street and school—was emphatically secular, extending even to the Jewish school where I would go most afternoons for Yiddish lessons. (JR, 4)

Jerry describes his relationship to Jewish textual sources as centered on his desire to "steal that language and make it my own" (JR, 5) and his allegiance, in terms borrowed from the Dada poet Richard Huelsenbeck, was for a transfer from the misbelievers to the disbelievers of religion. Jerry concludes, "I wanted to stand here firmly with the disbelievers" (JR, 5).

Like Bernstein, Rothenberg has no interest in "finding his voice" or in creating or professing or establishing some conventional sense of "identity." Jerry claims, "The intention throughout was not so much to discover or exploit identity (in the ethnic/tribal sense) but to put identity into doubt or question" (JR, 6). He seeks "a secularization of the mystical and supernatural" as he transfers "a body of work and language from religion to poetry & from poetry to the domain of Huelsenbeck's *dis*believers" (7). His desire is "to hold onto the energy and ferocity/intensity that we found there [in the realm of the mystical, supernatural, and religious] but without the 'mind-forg'd manacles' of orthodox religious thought" (7). But what makes Rothenberg's work so remarkable is the range of that investigation of the mystical, his proximity to its intensity, while at the same time his desire and ability to maintain a sense of separation (that in no way negates the validity of the mystical). It is that double bind that creates the tension, energy, and importance of Rothenberg's poetry—a double bind that applies not just to Jewish source materials, but to Jerry's investigation and residence in/with materials from many cultures. For Jerry, the fit description of this situation is "exile," of being (in Edmond Jabès's phrase) "exiled in the word" (8, 9). In its most sweeping version, Rothenberg articulates "a sense of exile both as cosmic principle (exile of God from God, etc.) & as the Jewish fate, experienced as the alienation of group & individual, so that the myth (gnostic or orthodox) is never only symbol but history, experience, as well" (8). In one sense, Rothenberg's position is a classically deconstructive one (developed independently of Derrida's writing). It is another aspect of a critique of presence—a critique that we see throughout the antiessentialist Jewish Americanness of Antin, Bernstein, and DuPlessis as well. The affirmation of an exilic state for Rothenberg includes the hope that the female side of God—Shekinah/ Shekhina—as herself in exile and evaded by orthodoxy will now return to astound us (9). Rothenberg's embrace of astonishment and wonder, his simultaneous engagement with the mystical and his exile from it, mark his work as unique among the four poets I am considering. Politically, his energetic state of exile resists as well the orderings of the present authoritarian state, in Jerry's words, "the Jews identified as mental rebels, who refuse consensus, thus become—even when bound to their own Law, or in the face of 'holocaust,' etc.—the model for the Great Refusal to the lie of Church & State" (9).

I wonder, though, if the state of exile that Jerry describes must also involve an exile from prayer. Returning to Rachel's remark (mentioned much earlier in this talk/essay)—"Prayer, I do not do, but the injunction to study, I have followed" (R, 8)—I link it to an intriguing phrase found in Bloom's Introduction to *American Religious Poems* where he praises the poetry of Frost and Stevens as being "untinged by devotional impulses" (xlv). But what if "devotion" and "prayer" were reconceived, as Norman Fischer does in "Are You Writing?" a brief essay soon to appear in *Shambhala.* Ten or fifteen years ago, Fischer took part in a symposium at Stanford on poetry and meditation, and he and fellow panelists Leslie Scalapino and Michael McClure were asked, "Who do you write for?" Each, in different ways, answered, "No one." Norman explains, "What we meant was not that we were uninterested in readership—we all publish a fair amount—but that in the *act* of writing we did not consider who the reader is or what he or she is going to make of what we are writing. We write to someone, but that person is essentially Nobody, without a name or social circumstances—we write for God. The Beyond. The Empty Nature of All Phenomena. Buddha Nature. The Mystery" (NF, 2). He goes on to remember, "Years ago I went to the Wailing Wall in Jerusalem and did what all tourists do, wrote some words on a scrap of paper that I tucked into a crevice in the wall. When I closed my eyes and touched my head to the warm stone, it came to me, 'All language is prayer.' This must be so. Who are we speaking to when we speak to anyone? To that person and also past him or her to Out There. If there is language it means there is the possibility of being heard, being met, being loved, and to reach out to be heard, met, or loved is a holy act. Language is holy" (NF, 3).

The tinge of devotion that Bloom refers to and the aversion to prayer that Rachel announces stem from notions of prayer, devotion, and writing that do not have to be the case. These gestures and activities do not need to be addressed to a specific location or person or an imagined deity, nor do they require a predetermined dogma or belief. Perhaps the gesture, the activity of engaging in a heuristic language practice, writing as a process of seeing what turns up, is itself hopeful if not prayerful, and perhaps even in some odd way devotional? Perhaps an aspect of that devotion is to an actively engaged mode of not-knowing, a perpetually inconclusive, midrashic mode of writing, which may or may not be Jewish American poetry.

If, in this essay, I have begun to establish some parameters for a peculiarly conceived Jewish American poetry, perhaps the chief quality that I have been pointing out is *a minority voice that undoes its own identity through a radical skepticism with regard both to representation and to the labels, terms, and validity of ethnic and religious identity itself.*

My concluding regret in this essay is that I have had nothing to say about Bob Dylan, Larry David, Matisyahu, and, most important of all, Red Auerbach.

The House of Jews

Experimental Modernism and Traditional Jewish Practice

Jerome Rothenberg

1

Every time I appear in a Jewish anthology—except those of my own devising—something goes wrong. Lines are omitted or placed out of sequence, prose is set as verse or verse as prose, and footnotes are used that represent an editor's imagining of what a word might mean or a place-name represent. I believe that the God of the Jews has something to do with this—a punishment for my deliberate withdrawal from Him or Her or It. Or else, to be more Jewish about it in the manner of a writer whom I like, it is as if one of Isaac Bashevis Singer's imps or demons had been there to gum up my works—not when I'm being a Jew on my own terms but when I give in to temptation and let myself be part of somebody else's order or communion.[1]

I will speak, then, *on my own terms* [my own grounds], though with continuing doubts as to whether there is any particular "*radical* poetic practice" that can be viewed as distinctively Jewish. That isn't to say that there aren't plenty of Jews (however defined) who have been active in avant-garde (or twentieth- and twenty-first-century) poetics, still less to deny that many—perhaps too many—Jewish poets have actively engaged in a Jewish version of identity writing, though I don't think that that's what "radical practice" is intended to mean in the present context. I would also say, in my own case at least, that I would be willing to construct a connection between aspects of traditional Jewish linguistic practice (much of it religious or mystical rather than secular) and current [modernist] forms of poetic (i.e., language) experimentation. I have in fact done this at some length, along with a proposition that Jewish history has been marked as well by an ongoing and more obvious resistance, by *the Great Refusal,* as I once put it, *to the lie of church and state.* (I would include here synagogue as well—at least for some of us.)

That resistance may not have been secular in the first instance, but it carried the mark of outsider or *outrider* traditions (to use Anne Waldman's word); or that was how it felt to me when I first turned to it.

It was in the sense of such an outsiderness—and placing it clearly in "this most Christian of worlds"—that Marina Tsvetayeva spoke of *all poets* as *Jews* [much like Norman Mailer's "White Negro" of the 1950s]. That was in her poem "Poem of the End," later quoted by Paul Celan in the cyrillic epigraph to his own poem "Und mit dem Buch aus Tarussa" and by me in *A Big Jewish Book,* where it became a central proposition of the stand I was then taking. My argument here wasn't for some kind of Jewish exclusiveness but toward a recognition that such resistances existed both there and elsewhere and that my address, in Tsvetayeva's sense, was to "all poets" or to all poets who share the outrider stance or to all, poets and others who resist the rule of totalizing states and constrictive religions. I saw myself—then as now—not writing in a specifically Jewish context for a Jewish audience as such, but opening the Jewish mysteries to all who wanted them. And I dramatized some of that in the dream that opens *A Big Jewish Book:*

> There was a dream that came before the book, & I might as well tell it. I was in a house identified by someone as THE HOUSE OF JEWS, where there were many friends gathered, maybe everyone I knew. Whether they were Jews or not was unimportant: I was & because I was I had to lead them through it. But we were halted at the entrance to a room, not a room really, more like a great black hole in space. I was frightened & exhilarated, both at once, but like the others I held back before that darkness. The question came to be the room's name, as if to give the room a *name* would open it. I knew that, & I strained my eyes & body to get near the room, where I could feel, as though a voice was whispering to me, creation going on inside it. And I said that it was called CREATION.
>
> I now recognize that dream as central to my life, an event & mystery that has dogged me from the start. I know that there are other mysteries—for others, or for myself at other times, more central—& that they may or may not be the same. But CREATION—*poesis* writ large—appeared to me first in that house, for I was aware then, & even more so now, that there are Jewish mysteries that one confronts in a place no less dangerous or real than that abyss of the Aztecs:
>
> *. . . a difficult, a dangerous place, a deathly place: it is dark, it is light . . .*
> & with a sense too that this space must be bridged, this door opened as well—the door made just for you, says the guardian in Kafka's story.

> Yet Kafka, like so many of us, poses the other question also: "What have I in common with Jews? I have hardly anything in common with myself."

That last, of course, is an extraordinarily Jewish statement.

2

Having gotten this far by way of introduction, I want to say something of how I came to be here, and to launch a few other comments, in no particular order but as they came to me while writing.

Like Louis Zukofsky and Charles Reznikoff, among other children of Jewish immigrants, my first language (to the age of three or four) was Yiddish. (I learned later from reading T. S. Eliot, who I know had *me* in mind, that this disqualified me as a poet within the English mainstream [& probably out of it as well], and I came to take that as a challenge and an opportunity.) My parents (unlike Zukofsky's) were avowedly secular, from late adolescence on, but my mother's mother, who lived with us from a month or two before my birth, was an orthodox Jew, though the relations between her and them were never less than cordial. The outside world—in street and school—was emphatically secular, extending even to the Jewish school where I would go most afternoons for Yiddish lessons. I had no problem with my grandmother's love of God, though as the terror of the Holocaust came back to her—two of her sons and their families having vanished by then—I heard it rather as an argument—an interrogation and rebuke—that came into her nightly prayers. For myself the experience of the war—viewed fitfully but at an easy childhood distance—brought out, with regard to that, my first poetic stirrings and what Tristan Tzara, in an earlier war, had spoken of "not [as] the beginnings of an art, but of a disgust." Such in a nutshell was the story of my early turn to poetry.

I grew up knowing a little about Jewish religion and lore but almost nothing about Jewish mysticism (the richest source for a poetics, as I later found). What came to me at some time in my teens was what I felt to be a need for poetry and for the intensities and disgust that brought the poetry I knew to life. At a still later point—I don't know just when—I was surprised to find something like that intensity in the language of religion—more likely in pagan and Christian sources than in Jewish ones. It soon seemed to me that I wanted to steal that language and to make it my own.[2] In doing so I meant to shift the field from religion to poetry, while not denying but even emphasizing the origins of what I took as poetry in areas of religious languaging and ritual. The transfer here, as the Dada poet Richard Huelsenbeck once pointed out for his own borrowings and deformations, was from the *mis*believers to the *dis*believers of religion. *I wanted to stand here firmly with the disbelievers.*

The involvement with Jewish materials as such came about when it had to, coterminous with *Technicians of the Sacred* (in 1968), and with a need I felt then "to explore ancestral sources of my own," most specifically and deliberately (I wrote) "in the world of Jewish mystics, thieves, & madmen." That project—experimental through and through—began for me with *Poland/1931*, continued with *A Big Jewish Book* (as Jewish anthology or assemblage), and returned in *Khurbn, Gematria,* and *14 Stations* (Holocaust poems using modified aleatoric procedures). (Even so, I would remind you, I was producing a still larger body of poetry and poetry gatherings that wasn't part of my Jewish experiment as such.) The intention throughout was not so much to discover or exploit identity (in the ethnic/tribal sense) but to put identity into doubt or question.

For this I applied or meant to apply the full range of modernist techniques and procedures to identity thematics, taking the resultant work, if it's right to say so, as itself a form of romantic/modernist *irony*.[3] In that sense too I saw what I was doing as the continuation of an aborted Jewish/Yiddish poetry in another language (American or English rather than Yiddish) and by every means at my disposal. Once into it I also found that I could draw from procedures and imageries imbedded in traditional Jewish sources. This was true in particular with gematria (traditional Jewish numerology), which I adapted and *secularized* as a processual form of composition, culminating in the book-length poem *Gematria* (from Sun & Moon Press) and *14 Stations* (gematria turned to memorialization of the Holocaust). But *Poland/1931*, my first experiment with a constructed Jewish poetry, is also full of fragments (verbal and visual) appropriated from traditional sources.[4]

I've been involved, then, with a secularization of the mystical and supernatural, a project which I share with others going back to at least the eighteenth century, but with twists and turns of my own and reflective also of the times in which we've lived. What this involves is the transfer of a body of work and language from religion to poetry & from poetry to the domain of Huelsenbeck's *dis*believers. My effort—but hardly mine alone—has been to open the field of poetry into areas of *poesis* (oral *and* written, sacred *and* secular) that have not had an adequate accounting. In so doing it was *our* intention to hold onto the energy and ferocity/intensity that we found there but without the "mind-forg'd manacles" of orthodox religious thought.

For me the process went beyond my engagement with Jewish sources, and before I assembled *A Big Jewish Book* I had already assembled "a big Indian book" (*Shaking the Pumpkin*) and before that "a big human book" (*Technicians of the Sacred*). [I would, still later, do the same with Christian and Buddhist imageries.] In those non-Jewish gatherings, the act of assemblage or construction was similar but my position was different in that I couldn't be thought of as writing from *within* the subject or with myself identified *as* subject. *A Big Jewish Book,* then, was an experiment along the lines of the other anthologies but with myself as a participatory subject in a shared subjectivity. With an awareness of all of that, I set out to explore what was possible at extremis and with no holds barred. I thought of myself as operating here through a secular/poetic consciousness that set the content and form of the sacred against that of the not-so-sacred, the heretical, the heterodox, the blasphemous, and certainly the secular as such.

But even in *A Big Jewish Book* or *Poland/1931*—a plunge into a constructed world based on real witnessings and documents as "data-clusters" (Ed Sanders's term in his argument for an "investigative poetry")—if I were to play it from within, I had to perform some part of it in costume, which I did in fact with the additional aid of photographs and films, something I would never had done in the Indian instance. Similarly, when I was writing, or rather performing, *That Dada Strain,* I costumed myself again—in imitation this time of Hugo Ball and Tristan Tzara (a.k.a. Sammy Rosenstock)—but that was still another kind of identity poetics that would get us too far afield if I stopped to speak about it here.

There was a time, then, when I became concerned with "the jewish poem" as such and even wondered—in light of Tsveteyava—where I might, if I continued, place its final boundaries. ("Jewish American" was of far less concern to me than "Jewish," which in itself was international in scope.) In the Pre-Face to *A Big Jewish Book,* I even made a list of Jewish "topics & conflicts/tensions," with the caveat that many of these were not unique to Jews although the history of the Jews might—up to a point—offer an exemplary instance. I presented these as characteristics that still held me to the Jewish work, as follows:

- a sense of exile both as cosmic principle (exile of God from God, etc.) & as the Jewish fate, experienced as the alientation of group & individual,

so that the myth (gnostic or orthodox) is never only symbol but history, experience, as well;
- from which there comes a distancing from nature & from God (infinite, ineffable), but countered in turn by a *poesis* older than the Jews, still based on namings, on an imaging of faces, bodies, powers, a working out of possibilities (but principally, the female side of God—Shekinah/ Shekhina—as herself in exile) evaded by orthodoxy, now returning to astound us;
- or, projected into language, a sense (in Edmond Jabès's phrase) of being "exiled in the word"—a conflict, as I read it, with a text, a web of letters, which can capture, captivate, can force the mind toward abstract pattern or, conversely, toward the framing, raising, of an endless, truly Jewish "book of questions";
- &, finally, the Jews identified as mental rebels, who refuse consensus, thus become—even when bound to their own Law, or in the face of "holocaust," etc.—the model for the Great Refusal to the lie of Church & State.

[And I concluded]: . . . it's from such a model—however obscured by intervening degradations from *poesis,* impulse to conform, etc.—that I would understand the Russian poet Marina Tsvetayeva's dictum that "all poets are Jews."

Two points to end it, and then, if I may, a poem.

There is also a curious way in which Jewish writers—contrary to Harold Bloom, say—have had an advantage, a leg up, *as poets* and as long as they maintained their sense of *otherness,* even as a counterpoint to the at-homeness they may have sought in the language that surrounds them and is nevertheless, for all of us, a place of exile. As my brother-in-arms Pierre Joris has written, in defense of a "nomad poetics": "It is only when constantly aware that the writer is not 'at home' in language (or anywhere else, for that matter) that any real and critical engagement with the enemy forces is possible." It is then too that the strongest engagements with language *qua poetry* take place.

The context for such remarks is of course diasporic/dispersed, and it's in the condition of diaspora—not exclusively but largely—that our poetics (Jewish and not so Jewish) has been constructed. That has led me, in the course of preparing this talk, to wonder about the *state* of Israel and the emergence of a Jewish *home*land—whether the connection between Jews and an exilic/nomadic/diasporic poetics isn't by now distressingly anachronistic. To say "all poets are Jews" in an Israeli-Palestinian context in which Jews are the privileged insiders, is something quite different from Tsvetayeva's 1926 context "in this most Christian of worlds" and gives me the accute sense that history has somehow overwhelmed us.

I think that I may pursue this at a later point but for now it seems to me enough simply to have said it.

To conclude, then, I'll read a poem from *Poland/1931,* that speaks both to the persistence of Jews in history and to my bewilderment at being called on as an expert in this kind of forum. (The irony is even more obvious today than when I wrote it.)
[reads]:

THE CONNOISSEUR OF JEWS
if there were locomotives to ride home on
& no jews
there would still be jews & locomotives
just as there are jews & oranges
& jews & jars
there would still be someone to write the jewish poem
others to write their mothers' names in light—
just as others, born angry
have the moon's face burnt onto their arms
& don't complain
my love, my lady, be a connoisseur of jews
the fur across your lap
was shedding
on the sheet were hairs
the first jew to come to you is mad
the train pulls into lodz
he calls you
by your polish name
then he tells the other passengers a story
there are jews & there are alphabets
he tells them
but there are also jewish alphabets
just as there are jewish locomotives
& jewish hair
& just as there are some with jewish fingers
such men are jews
just as other men are not jews
not mad

don't call you by your polish name
or ride the train to lodz
if there are men who ride the train to lodz
there are still jews
just as there are still oranges
& jars
there is still someone to write the jewish poem
others to write their mothers' names in light

Notes

1. Made-up footnotes in *Norton Anthology of Jewish-American Literature;* prose changed to verse in *Princeton University Library Chronicle* (Jewish American issue, gathered by C. K. Williams); poem truncated and missing part added to another poem, in Steven J. Rubin, *Telling and Remembering: A Century of American Jewish Poetry.*

2. Thus William Carlos Williams, when I met him as a student at City College: *Seize the language! Smash it to hell! You have a right to it!*

3. My first deliberate attempt at writing "the Jewish poem" was a mix I created by bringing together structures from Gertrude Stein's serial poem "Dates" with mystically loaded and sexually charged vocabulary from Isaac Bashevis Singer's novel *Satan in Goray.*

4. And even here, let me add, I was not alone, but entered a discourse with poets I had known or was soon to meet, like David Meltzer, Nathaniel Tarn, Jack Hirschman, Edmond Jabès, and even (from our one meeting) Paul Celan; or others, important to me at different times, like Robert Kelly and Robert Duncan. In addition the totalizing impulse of *Technicians of the Sacred* and, later, *Poems for the Millennium,* may itself have been part of a secular Jewish thrust, something, as Charles Bernstein has suggested, that may have even influenced a similar tendency in Ezra Pound and others still more obviously outside the Jewish context.

Zukofsky at 100

Zukofsky as a Body of Work

Bob Perelman

[This piece was originally a talk at the "Zukofsky at 100" at Columbia in September 2004. It echoes "*A*"-1, minimally, by mentioning a cultural venue at the beginning.]

1. The session title, "Zukofsky at One Hundred," suggests a crucially ambiguous vantage.
2. Louis Zukofsky, person, would have been 100 this year.
3. But Zukofsky, the body of work, as in "Have you read Zukofsky," is of indeterminate age.
4. Is a body of work born when the first attested or accepted work appears? If so, then we should start counting with the earliest work, "I Sent Thee Late," the 1922 poem that appears in "*A*"-18, and we should be celebrating "Zukofsky at 82."
5. Or is a body of work a body only when the work stops appearing? In that case, though it feels harshly ironic, we should make the birth year of "Zukofsky the body of work" coincide with the year that "Zukofsky the person" died.
6. So if we count from the date of the last work, *80 Flowers* and the publication of the completed "*A*" then it should be "Zukofsky at 26."
7. While 26 is poetically significant in the Anglo-American alphabet, 100 is the most august, barely reachable of the human-sized numbers. (The Hebrew alphabet has 24.)
8. For modernists seeking mastery, 100 beckoned.
9. In "An Instant Answer or A Hundred Prominent Men" [*Useful Knowledge*] Stein repeats "and one" 100 times.
9a. Of course, Stein can always be being sarcastic: it isn't A Hundred Prominent Women after all.
10. For much of the time Pound was writing them, 100 was the magic

number for *The Cantos* given that that was the number of cantos in Dante's *Comedia.*

11. In our day, there's Bruce Andrews's *I Don't Have Any Paper, So Shut Up (or, Social Romanticism)* and his *Lip Service* each with 100 sections.

12. Zukofsky was drawn to 100 as well: both "A"-22 and -23 contain 1,000 lines.

13. (1,000 is the epic version of 100.)

14. There's also the progression of his last planned projects: at the beginning of his 8th decade he begins *80 Flowers* with *Gamut: 90 Trees* planned for the decade after that. Isn't 100 the teleological goal there?

15. (At this point, it's hard to resist Ron Silliman's prediction for the next project: *101 Dalmations.*)

16. Why am I so drawn to that joke?

17. Is it because Zukofsky now stands for avant-garde mastery and completion and yet that oxymoron is particularly distorting when applied to him?

18. In resisting the equation Zukofsky = 100 I also am resisting the equation Zukofsky = 1.

19. Also the equation Zukofsky = music.

20. This in the face of the fact that it is hard to miss the ubiquitous instructions to construe his work into a unified, musical totality.

21. I.e., "Each writer writes one long work whose beat he cannot be entirely aware of."

22. I.e., the last words of "A"-24, the tiny coda written by Louis to Celia Zukofsky's *LZ Masque;* "the gift / she hears / the work / in its recurrence."

23. I.e., this from the *Autobiography:* "The form of the poem is organic—that is, involved in history and a life that has found by contrast to history something like perfection in the music of J. S. Bach."

24. Celia's basic gesture in "A"-24, composing Louis's poetry, drama, fiction, and criticism into cadenced musical voices, insists on this analogy and grants Louis's words, originally written in various genres and various historical circumstances, the retrospective perfection of music.

25. That's 'music' in the Paterian, Poundian sense: poetic 'music'.

26. My scare quotes around music makes it plain that I am an apostate from this grand synaesthesic synthesis.

27. I am acting as the tritone, the augmented fourth, C/F#, / *diabolus in musica* / as the medievals had it, and will try to make audible my perception of the value of the dissonance I hear in Zukofsky.

27a. To paraphrase what he writes in "A"-6 [26] perhaps "it has something to do with" his being Jewish.

28. While this dissonance does not accord at all with the emphatic simplicity

of his pronouncements of poetics, nevertheless it continues—in my ear at least—to resound in the deadpan slippages, extravagant layerings and uncoded leaps of much of his writing practice.

29. Zukofsky's critical practice is an instrument whose use is intended to suppress such extravagance.

29a. If you took *A Test of Poetry* as a bible of poetics, poetry like Zukofsky's would be the last thing you'd write.

30. In *A Test*, the Milton of *Samson Agonistes* gets a low mark for his "inability to leave words alone"; he is "infatuated with sound, thunder, and fury, and is 'building' a verse paragraph"; LZ puts scare quotes around building, implying that yielding to verbal infatuation results in mere imaginary work on an imaginary building. Air guitar (as opposed to the *St. Matthew Passion*).

31. But as any reader of Zukofsky knows, he himself is infatuated with sound and with building verbal contraptions that had never been imagined before:

32. O dear cool you couldn't a virile—you couldn't a parent he—
salvé! take weight bone ah Jupiter act it open,
Janus, door! when Balbo thickened—serviced his benignant
ol' him—home say days hipped seized say next tenure heat—
how come fare runt hearsways 'n how the door serve very malignantly
posthumously poor wrecked torn father's young married son—eh. [C, 67]

33. Of course, such un*Test*able extravagance does not resound everywhere in Zukofsky's body of work; a considerable portion is as verbally neat as *A Test* suggests is proper:

34. The miracle of his first job
On the lower East Side:
Six years night watchman
In a men's shop
Where by day he pressed pants
Every crease a blade
The irons weighed
At least twenty pounds
But moved both of them
Six days a week
From six in the morning
To nine, sometimes eleven at night
Or midnight;
Except Fridays
When he left, enough time before sunset
Margolis begrudged.

His own business
My father told Margolis
Is to keep Sabbath. [A, 152]

35. These passages from *"A"*-12 and *Catullus* were chosen at random.
36. Nevertheless it strikes me as an instructive coincidence that both involve fathers and that their respective styles match the degree of seriousness with which paternity is addressed.
37. The second passage is pious, taut with restraint.
38. The passage from in *Catullus* is rife with vaguely anti-paternal, comic-phallic noises: "O dear cool you couldn't a virile," "couldn't a parent," "weight bone ah Jupiter," "ol' him," "posthumously poor wrecked torn father's young married son—eh."
38a. Incidentally, Jupiter does not = Jehovah.
39. But to simply split Zukofsky along a paternal axis of obedience and rebellion isn't sufficient.
40. Zukofsky's impiety is sly, a Talmudic impishness more profound than disobedience, an ecstacy of syntactic teleporting to no world that anyone lives in yet.
41. However, Zukofsky did in fact live in the historical world, inextricably as one might say.
42. In trying to establish a place for his writing in that world he continually did two things:
43. in his critical work he would insist vigorously on an extreme decorum of style;
44. while in his poetry he would display his powers, of construction and construal,
45. displays that were neither decorous nor indecorous: the categories don't apply.
46. *A Test* is a line on the C. V. Zukofsky submitted for some imagined position of permanent authority. For an unrecognized poet aspiring to be a major modernist there was a defined set of tasks, a sequence of labors that would authenticate the laborer as a true Hercules.
47. What did proto-Hercules have to do to become Poet Hercules?
48. In Milton's time the schedule of tasks for a major-poet-in-training was Virgilian:
49. first, eclogues,
50. then georgics,
51. and finally an epic.
52. In the 1930s when Zukofsky was marshaling his own forces Pound was his model and the requirements had changed. Now it was:

53. notable editorial intervention,
54. a collection of short poems,
55. an epic,
56. and a codified statement of poetics.
57. Pound remained the model of the poet for Zukofsky.
58. *Prepositions* was on Zukofsky's desk when he died, open to his essay on Pound.
59. When *Catullus* was published, Zukofsky wrote Pound, asking what he thought: "I understand Mary de R[achewiltz]. has been receiving my Catullus translations in *Origin*—sometimes wonder what '/you/" might think of 'em if you <can> read 'em> <'Don't matter what anyone else thinks—even the praise. Still obstinate you see" [PZ, 218].
60. Thus Zukofsky's 1, his life, adds up to more than 1.
61. Zukofsky carries Pound on his back, like Aeneas carrying Anchises out of burning Troy.
62. Except there's no Roman Empire as a fated destination. The Lower East side is not a seat of empire.
63. Zukofsky also carries Bach: "The form of the poem is organic—that is, involved in history and a life that has found
by contrast to history
something like perfection
in the music of
J. S. Bach."
64. And not to forget Williams.
65. "5, Song of Degrees" begins, "William / Carlos / Williams / alive!" and ends with Billy the Kid
66.. . . torn,
shot

so quickly
it sounds
water:

purls

a
high
voice

as with
a lien

on
the sky

that becomes

low now
frankly

water—

called also—

softly—

a kill

67. The lines just before this are:

68. the
same word

that
may have,
to touch
two faces—
the heart
sees into—
of one
sound:

69. It's not just that Zukofsky's 1 always sounds with 2 faces, though it does—a not un-Yiddish sound perhaps.

70. It's that Zukofsky's celebration of the poetically perfected life—"William / Carlos / Williams / alive!"—also contains the countervailing gesture: "a kill."

71. A little symbolic mathematics: if the authorized perfected life-works—Catullus, Bach, Pound, Williams—are 100 and the individual aspiring life—Louis Zukofsky—is 1, then the result should be that the poetry produced by said 1 (e.g., Louis Zukofsky) will also be perfected, since 100 divided by or multiplied by 1 = 100.

72. But clearly that's not the case.

73. *Gai Valeri Veronensis Catulli* when divided or multiplied into English by Louis (and Celia) Zukofsky does not equal the purportedly perfect original.

74. Purportedly perfected forms, when divided or multipled by Zukofsky, produce irrational numbers.

75. As he writes in *A Test:* "*The Sonnet Form* is *not* a matter of 14 lines, set rhyme scheme, 10 syllables to a line, alternating ascending accents, as the rhetoric books have it. *Sonnet*... implies the form of the short tune, to which certain Italian poets—Dante, Cavalcanti, and others—wrote words;. . . . Dissociated from music, the *sonnet* became merely the poor versification of amateurs, without emotion or sense of the relation of the parts of a composition to the whole" [67].

76. This statement comes from a poet who had, a few years earlier, written this:

77. Clavicembalo—Nine less two, Seven
Were the diggers, seven sang, danced, the paces
Seven, Seven Saviours went to heaven—
Their tongues, hands, feet, eyes, ears and hearts, each face as
Of a Sea looking Outward (Rose the Glass
Broken), Each a reflection of the other.
Just for the fun of it. And 't came to pass

(/Open, O fierce flaming pit!/)
three said: Bother,

Brother, we want a meal, different techniques."
Two ways, my two voices . . . Offal and what
The imagination . . . And the seven came
To horses seven (of wood—who will?—kissed their stomachs)
Bent knees as these rose around them—trot—trot—
Spoke: words, words, we are words, horses, manes, words. [A, 42]

78. Now, clearly, this *sonnet* would not fit very happily to any Dantescan or Cavalcantian "short tune."

79. A crucial component of its deviation from 'musicality' is its use of the conventional sonnet form.

80. Its relation to that form is not parodic, but para-poetic. The *sonnet* armature is a perpetual occasion for verbal display.

81. This 7th sonnet that concludes "*A*"-7 insists on the traditional rhyming quatrains: Seven, paces, heaven, face as; Glass, other, pass, Bother (with the truer rhyme Brother enjambed to begin the next line).

82. But onto this armature, Zukofsky casts a remarkably diverse concatenation of verbal matter, social tone, and allusion to things inside and outside of "*A*."

83. What are some of the techniques employed by Zukofsky in this sonnet?

84. It starts with the last word of a sentence, Clavicembalo.

84a. It is an extremely odd sentence, by the way. It's far from easy to tell where it begins, but my opinion is that it starts four lines back: "A sign creaked—LAUNDRY TO-LET—(creaked—wind—)—SUN— / (Nights?) the sun's, bro', no months' rent in arrear— / Bum pump a-dum, no one's cut out, pump a- / Ricky, bro', Shimaunu-Sān, yours is the / Clavicembalo."

85. Zukofsky mixes tonal registers: the language of mathematics ("Nine less two") with the singsong of a fairy tale ("Seven were the diggers . . . the paces Seven, Seven Saviours went to heaven").

85a. False messiahs taking the next plane out. Saviour with a u can only = Christ. But here there are seven.

86. He uses typography (clearly not a 'musical' device!): capitalization to mythify and personify in a comic manner: "a Sea looking Outward (Rose the Glass / Broken)." By the way, in those last two words, the glass doesn't break until the line breaks. That linebreak is not easy to conceive within the universe of Poundian/Zukofskyan 'music'. There's the dramatic use of white space and italics, parentheses too, for the reference to "*A*"-1, "Open, O fierce flaming pit!"

87. "Pit" there encompasses the Christian Hell of the *St. Matthew Passion,* a Hell Zukofsky doesn't believe in, sung to music he does believe in; the pit where the orchestra is playing, and the pit that the miners are locked out of.

88. There's the use of extra-poetic speech: Bother, / Brother, we want a meal, different techniques. The voices of the unemployed are clear here, but Zukofsky folds his own poetic and social concerns into the quoted speech. It's hardly likely that a person who said "Brother, we want a meal" would begin with "Bother, brother." Nor is it likely that the person asking for a meal also asked for "different techniques." But Zukofsky at this time believed, along with Pound and many others, that to supply different writing techniques was at least as valuable as supplying physical necessities.

89. There's the use of phrase fragments to suggest fleeting half-formed thoughts of great intensity: "(of wood—who will—kissed their stomachs)."

90. That last phrase especially is striking. "Kissed" sounds out a completed action, but it doesn't sound out the agent or the object. Kissing a stomach can be very innocent fun (making babies chortle, etc.), but it's hardly likely that at the end of "*A*"-7 the poet had suddenly taken on childcare duties. Outside of childcare, kissing a stomach is a charged erotic act. So who kissed which stomachs here? Did Zukofsky kiss—at least in the written world of these three words—the stomachs of the poetically invoked horses, or of the barely employed diggers, or of the wooden sawhorses?

91. Whichever it is, and it might be all three, there is great power of suggestion in the phrase, which is emphatically *not* clear or exact in the way that *A Test* demands.

92. My polemic here is not against Zukofsky's use of musical structures as analogies to instigate his writing. It is against the ahistorical and really terribly vague use of music as a description of a poem. It is an impoverished sense of music. The actual practice of music, after all, has as tumultuous a history as poetry. Schoenberg had been writing 12-tone music for decades before Pound wrote *ABC;* the riots over Stravinsky's harsh polyrhythms were old news; Antheil's airplane engines had already roared.
93. Think of how we feel when "poetry" is used in such a tepid, generalizing way: the poetry of Robert Ryman's white canvases, the poetry of Alex Rodriguez's swing, the poetry of Spring.
94. But my fulmination feels a bit quixotic when common sense reminds me that music is widely used in poetics to point to a quality that is exciting and beautiful—"those wonderful sounds good poetry makes."
95. Perhaps my final negotiating stance should be this: not to proscribe music or to proscribe the use of 1 or of 100 but rather urge that the lower limit of Zukofsky's famous integral be kept in mind.
96. If a poetic integral is a process that actually integrates, then the poetics that Zukofsky affirms will indeed be music while also being speech. It will exist between 1, the life, and 100, the completed work. Throughout that range, simultaneously.
97. Why is it good to focus on only the upper, or for that matter only on the lower limit?
98. Instead, I propose a toast to the uncompletable gamut.
99. Bottoms up!
To Zukofsky at 100.

Addendum

On "The Jewish Question": Three Perspectives

Bob Perelman

Given the intractableness of the question, it's fitting that my three approaches are incommensurate. The first, based on Susan Handelman's scholarship, neatly divides Jews and Christians; the second, my own musings, agonizes about the possibility of any dividing line; the third, a nonserious application of homeopathic notions, is obviously counterintuitive but may represent my most serious thinking on the subject.

1. Susan Handelman posits an intriguing and far-reaching distinction in *The Slayers of Moses: The Emergence of Rabbinic Interpretation in Modern Literary Theory*, drawing a contrast between the Rabbinic and the ancient Greek perspectives on language. For the Rabbis, word and thing were indistinguishable, while for the Greeks they were separate. The Hebrew *davar*, she writes, means both word and thing, and for the Rabbis God was as much the producer of writing as maker of the world, and the Torah was as real as, if not more real than, the world. (Sometimes, quasi-heretically, God was more the product of the Torah than its author.) For the Greeks, in contrast, language was descriptive, belonging to the predicate, its function being to distinguish substantive from substantive. Handelman sees this contrast between Jewish and Greek conceptions continuing into the Christian era, with the Church Fathers opposing language to the Word. Handelman's analysis opposes Rabbinical thinking to Aristotle and Augustine both, undoing the opposition between pagan and Christian. For thinkers such as Augustine and Origen, language was ultimately a barrier to the presence of Christ, the one and only Word. The advent of Christ's Embodiment provided access to the spirit, superceding the letter. The desire to "escape from textuality," she writes, "permeates Christian thought" [115].

Handelman uses this large distinction to frame an account of what she calls "modern literary theory," discussing Freud, Lacan, Derrida, and Bloom (and in a later book, Benjamin, Scholem, and Lévinas). I want to borrow her model and apply it to poetry, where it will be merely an analogy, dividing poets up into "Jews" and "Christians." Still, it will turn out to make sense in some surprising ways. Coleridge is obviously Christian. In his famous distinction between imagination and fancy the validated half, imagination, would be Christian ("a representation in the finite mind of the eternal act of creation in the infinite I AM [of God]") as opposed to the denigrated part of poetic composition, fancy, which only plays with "counters" that are "fixed and dead," mere language (or, as one might say, Talmudic wordplay). Whitman would be Christian ("Who touches this book touches a man"); Pound would be Christian (pagan-Christian) with his insistence on the ideogrammic method as essential in capturing 'thing-ness' in writing (and avoiding Talmudic 'slither'—entanglement in verbiage). Zukofsky, happily living in and via letters ("z-sited paths are but us"), would be Jewish. Stein would clearly be Jewish.

Would Ginsberg, Whitmanian that he is, be Jewish? We'd have to say no, since the body and the embodied voice are so clearly the origin, locus, and telos of his work. Even what at first look like his "language-centered" moments are directed, ultimately, past language. True, the following excerpt from the end of the first part of "Howl" starts with a focus on juxtaposition, verbal collage and disjunction (which by itself could almost be a glimpse of the new sentence):

who dreamt and made incarnate gaps in Time & Space through images
   juxtaposed, and trapped the
                  archangel of the soul between 2 visual images and joined the
                     elemental verbs and set the
            noun and dash of consciousness together jumping with sensation
               of Pater Omnipotens Aeterna Deus

. . . .

who rose reincarnate in the ghostly clothes of jazz . . . and blew the suffering
   of America's naked mind for
            love into an eli eli lamma lamma sabachthani saxophone cry . . .
with the absolute heart of the poem of life butchered out of their own
   bodies good to eat a thousand
                  years.

This is suffused with Christian vocabulary: "incarnate," "archangel," "Pater Omnipotens Aeterna Deus," "who rose reincarnate"; and it quotes Christ's last words on the cross ("eli eli lamma lamma sabachthani"). And while the last line seems most directly a reference to Aztec sacrifice, isn't a heart that's good to eat for a millennium awfully close to the Eucharist?

It's really not fair to allow this concentration of Christologic vocabulary to nudge "Howl" into alignment with something like *Jesus Christ Superstar.* Nevertheless, it is a bit weird how explicitly Christian this seems, since Alicia Ostriker's reading of Ginsberg as Jeremiah always seemed suggestive and since Ginsberg the person always seemed (and sounded) vaguely Rabbinic.

Again, "Wichita Vortex Sutra" can at first seem to be linguistically focused, but the more emphatic frame is the body. While at first there is the repeated insistence on language ("The War is language"): the bad magic of congressional language and the good magic Ginsberg hopes to create; and the rhetorical and political climax of the poem is "I make mantra of American language . . . I here declare the end of War!" (407). However, that mantra is ultimately *not* primarily language. Ginsberg uses his voice as an embodied sound to act on the language and change it, which will then change the world, stop the Vietnam War, pacify and enlighten the bodies of those who listen. The action ultimately is meant to reach from the poet's body to the bodies of those receiving the poem (listeners more than readers); the poem is a conduit connecting these:

Not the empty sky that hides
the feeling from our faces
nor our skirts and trousers that conceal
the bodylove emanating in a glow of beloved skin,
white smooth abdomen down to the hair
between our legs,
It's not a God that bore us that forbid
our Being, like a sunny rose
all red with naked joy [405]

2. "You don't have to be Jewish to love Levi's" was the slogan in a series of New York subway ads for rye bread a few decades back. There was a series of posters each displaying a deliberately various demographic of non-Jewish consumer: the African American cop, the Puerto Rican broadcaster, the Chinese student, the WASP, etc., each one grinning while he or she held a corned-beef on rye with a neat bite missing. Always the same bite it seemed. Did it suggest circumcision and the unalterable singularity of Judaism? Or on the contrary was the bite evidence that the African American cop, the Puerto Rican broadcaster, the Chinese student, the WASP, etc., had swallowed and happily incorporated the missing Jewish bite, now signifying assimilation?

Is there a Jewish radical poetic practice? In one sense, of course there is: "Jewish" can simply designate the fact that writers such as Louis Zukofsky, Gertrude Stein, Laura Riding, and Charles Reznikoff were Jews. But if anything is wanted beyond this then the question quickly gets more vexing. Is there something Jewish about Zukofsky's, Stein's, Riding's, and Reznikoff's writing? If so, can the same or a similar something be found in the work of writers who weren't born Jews? If not, is it just a matter of keeping score, tallying up how many Jews there are in our pantheons? Do fractions count? By parentage, Mina Loy was half Jewish, even William Carlos Williams was one-eighth or was it one-sixteenth Jewish?

If one accepts transhistorical analogy then there are many ways in which Rabbinical writing anticipates modernism and contemporary innovative writing. The Rabbis were concerned with textuality, wordplay, letterplay, and there is a thick tradition of semantic pole-vaulting over obstacles created by the absolute givenness of the words of the Torah. Such verbal exploration across boundaries of what was previously accepted makes it possible to read the Rabbis, by analogy, as innovative poets *avant la lettre.*

Such analogizing is a kind of assimilation, but moving chronologically backward. Rather than second-generation Jews turning away from Jewish ancestry to become modern Americans, it's contemporary innovative poets discovering that their Jewish ancestors were poetic innovators. Another, more contentious example of genealogical back-formation occurs in the epigraph to *A Big Jewish Book,* where the translation makes the Talmud explicitly Poundian, not only using his famous slogan but also his emphatic capitalization:

Rabbi Elieser said
                    "prayer 'fixed'?
                    "his supplication bears no fruit
. . . .
the question then came up: what
                    is FIXED?
Rabba & Rabbi Yosef answered
                    "whatever blocks the will
                    to MAKE IT NEW

This strikes me as a pledge of allegiance to a tradition, declaring that Pound *is* one's ancestor while erasing, forgiving, reframing, putting into perspective, bracketing his vigilant and vigorous anti-Semitism. A more direct encounter between the postwar innovative tradition and Pound would be Allen

Ginsberg's forgiving embrace of the old modernist during their meeting in Venice.

Where Jerome Rothenberg's translation might simply be read as an homage to Pound's poetics rather than to the person, Ginsberg's embrace was directed to Pound himself. It seems a similar gesture to his "mantra" moment in "Wichita Vortex Sutra": by means of the enlightened clarity of embodied action, Ginsberg will effect change. "I here declare the end of the War" ≈ I here declare the end of anti-Semitism (of Pound's, at any rate). Whatever change may or may not have been effected in Pound himself, the embrace is something of an emblematic moment in poetic history. Along with a range of other (literary) actions (by Kenner, Olson, Zukofsky, etc.), it insisted on placing Pound firmly into the center of the innovative tradition. But what, if anything, did it do with respect to "the Jewish question"? Did it do much to change the fact that, in poetry at least, anti-Semitism was a major characteristic of modernism?

It may not have been the most *modern* part of modernism since it was basically a reprise of the tradition, most notably articulated by Richard Wagner, that sees Jewish art as irredeemably ersatz: Jews can't write real music, they can only ape the techniques, and the more dextrous the imitation the more insidious for the unwary listener or reader. Pound writes: "Until [T. S. Eliot] succeeds in detaching the Jewish from the European elements of his peculiar variety of Christianity he will never find the right formula. Not a jot or tittle of the hebraic alphabet can pass into the text without danger of contaminating it." That's Pound near his worst, but the aesthetic vehemence is of a piece with his saner railings; the dynamics are the same, though the referents differ. On a less specifically anti-Semitic note, Pound often defined his art, and to a lesser extent Eliot and Wyndham Lewis defined theirs, against unbounded exfoliation of verbalism. He writes in *Guide to Kulchur,* "When a code ceases to be regarded as an approximate expression of principles . . . and is exalted to the rank of something holy in itself, perversion ineluctably sets in. . . . Code-worship appertains properly to tribes arrested at nomad level" (164). And while it may seem that such identification of Jewishness with the ersatz is now old hat, unfortunately, it remains alive and well in such moments as Harold Bloom's essay that refuses the possibility of there being a "major" Jewish poet.

Anti-Semitism doesn't permeate the multiplicious fact of modernism, of course, far from it. But it is there and, insofar as it is, doesn't it insist that Jewish writing, if it's *Jewish,* can't be innovative? and that MAKE IT NEW can only lead to NEW testaments?

For decades, Pound had been hypervigilant to notice who or what felt Jewish. Was Ginsberg's embrace of him enough to render that vigilance beside the point? What is involved in rendering anti-Semitism beside the point? Perhaps it is just personal, affecting Pound so that the old guy comes off it and accepts Jews. Or, a little shockingly, did Ginsberg, symbolically at any rate, cease being Jewish after the embrace? He forgave Pound as a Buddhist: "Anti-Semitism was just your hang-up." Isn't that phrase spoken from a perspective that is itself no longer hung up on Jewish identity? Does Ginsberg become trans-Jewish at this point?

Along with Zukofsky, Charles Olson, Robert Duncan, and Robert Creeley among others, Ginsberg is one of the *filii Poundiani.*

Of course Ginsberg remains Jewish. What about *Kaddish?*

(But what about the last two times in his published work he wrote "Jew," both times using the lower-case "jew"? I will discuss this poem, "Multiple Identity Questionnaire," below.)

The insistent singularity of Jewishness is hard to avoid. After all, Judaism is not ecumenical.

Biographically, Stein *is* Jewish and Loy (nee Lowy) *is* half Jewish. In terms of poetics, though, what can be meant by the notion that Stein's and Loy's writing *is* Jewish? (Or, in Loy's case, half Jewish?)

In terms of subject matter, there are clear examples to apply to the question: Reznikoff's subject matter is often insistently Jewish; Loy's "Anglo-Mongrels and the Rose" insistently explores the rift between Anglo and Jewish identities; "Poem beginning 'The' " brilliantly mocks Western philosophic and poetic traditions, with Zukofsky, who had just attended Columbia under a narrow quota system, showing how a Jew could ace the Modernism exam set by *The Waste Land.*

But that's Jewish subject matter or subject position more than Jewish writing. How is Stein's writing Jewish? Yes, there's the pun on Yiddish, "Yet Dish," and, I think, similar instances; but such moments are rare (and isn't there, equally rare, an instance or two of anti-Semitism?). But what in Stein's poetics, style, mechanics, rhythm could be identified as Jewish? If we simply leave it that Stein's writing is Jewish because of its ever-present textual play, then isn't Joyce's writing utterly Jewish?

3. Another way of coming at Jewishness in innovative writing, what I'll call homeopathic Jewishness, will restore the commonsense fact that Ginsberg is a Jew, though in a non-commonsense way.

To present it requires a brief autobiographical excursus. Back in hippie days, alongside other branches of knowledge (macrobiotics, astrology, and the collective unconscious), I had a brush with homeopathy. There, besides the more well-known notion of curing like with like (e.g., pills against poison ivy contained minute bits of poison ivy), I learned or at least now remember learning the following amazing fact: the more you diluted a homeopathic medicine the stronger it got. (It had something to do with the 'molecular memory' of the water, if you needed an explanation that touched anywhere near physics.) So, for low strength, dissolve a drop of a homeopathic medicine in a pint of water. If the medicine needed to be made stronger dissolve the same one drop into a quart of water. Full strength would be one drop per gallon.

It was at a conference on Jewish American writing at Penn three decades after my homeopathic hours—after hearing much talk of hybridity and borders crossed, Yiddish as a porous anti-essentialist tongue incorporating other languages easily, vocabularies adopted and instantly changed, new boundaries embroidered with old and new shapes—that it struck me that there was something deeply amusing about applying my homeopathic lore to the question of being a Jewish American writer. It made a good punchline to some poetic, philosophic, or religious joke I haven't finished hearing yet.

Crudely, the homeopathic model says that the more diluted the Jewishness the more Jewish the writer.

(It can be objected that the homeopathic method is intensely circular since the original homeopathic "drop" that it starts with is the biographical fact of a given writer's Jewishness.)

Still, the question can be asked: how Jewish is the writing? Homeopathic poetics is equipped to provide an answer. It doesn't look for characteristically Jewish language or Jewish content—quite the reverse. It looks for non-Jewish 'water'. The less overt Jewishness there is in the writing—the more diluted it is—the more Jewish the writing.

Take Reznikoff, where the central framework is much more often than not clearly Jewish and where there is certainly a great deal of explicitly Jewish vocabulary and subject matter: *Jerusalem the Golden,* the shtetl narratives, not to mention the plain old religious stuff. There is quite a lot of it in R's oeuvre—more than enough for my taste:

I am Joseph, your brother, whom you sold into Egypt.
And now be not grieved, nor angry with yourselves,
for I was sent before you to save us all alive;
you meant evil against me, but it was meant for good.
Go unto our father and say to him,
your son Joseph has become head of all Egypt;
without Joseph no man, except Pharaoh on his throne, lifts hand or foot
  throughout Egypt.
you have not thought to see his face and you shall see his sons also.
Come to him and you shall dwell in the land of Goshen— (I, 81)

I find this pretty difficult going; it sounds much too much like what I remember from one of my few visits to religious school. Still, however my taste feels about it, this is nothing if not Jewish. Therefore, when read through a homeopathic lens, this flood of undiluted Jewish subject matter makes Reznikoff's Jewishness much less strong than Zukofsky's Jewishness. And Zukofsky's Jewishness becomes less strong than Ginsberg's.

There may not be a physical explanation for homeopathic intensification-by-dilution, but there is a grammatical one in the literary sphere: commonsense uses the adjective Jewish to refer to Jews; homeopathic criticism uses the adjective Jewish to refer to an undiscovered or not yet fully realized substantive. There's no noun yet, only the adjective pointing suggestively.

Here, lest my hippie heritage be seen as completely out-framing my tepidly Jewish upbringing, is the quasi-homeopathic parable that Gershom Scholem uses to conclude his book *Jewish Mysticism:*

> When the Baal Shem had a difficult task before him, he would go to a certain place in the woods, light a fire and meditate in prayer—and what he had set out to perform was done. When a generation later the "Maggid" of Meseritz was faced with the same task he would go to the same place in the woods and say: We can no longer light the fire, but we can still speak the prayers—and what he wanted done became reality. Again a generation later Rabbi Moshe Leib of Sassov had to perform this task. And he too went into the woods and said: We can no longer light a fire, nor do we know the secret meditations belonging to the prayer, but we do know the place in the woods to which it all belongs—and that must be sufficient; and sufficient it was. But when another generation had passed and Rabbi Israel of Rishin was called upon to perform the task, he sat down on his golden chair in his castle and said: We cannot light the fire, we cannot speak the prayers, we do not know the place, but we can tell the story of how it was done. And, the story-teller adds, the story which he told had the same effect as the actions of the other three. (350)

Back to "Ginsberg is more Jewish than Zukofsky." Really, isn't it simpler to reframe their difference-amid-genealogical-similarity as a difference in historical generation, both poetic and chronological?

Zukofsky grew up speaking Yiddish; two decades later, Ginsberg grew up speaking English—his father concocted poems in rhyme and meter and sent the results to *The New Yorker.*

And, extrapolating, would this make me, a generation later (and much less Jewish than Ginsberg since in my case there was no Bar Mitzvah, only the most desultory attendance at "Sunday School"—held at Temple on Sundays), would this make me even more Jewish? But my writing is not particularly Jewish at all, outside of two poems in *The Future of Memory:* "Chaim Soutine" and "Religion in the Regions of Matter." I'm a *filius avant-gardus.*

Let's do a practice problem on Ginsberg and Zukofsky.

"A"-1. What's the HJQ quotient there? (Homeopathic Jewish Quotient.) It's hard to say. *"A"*-1 is a composition with many agendas. One thing it purports to do is to enact a memory of a true act of art-worship by the embodied author. Zukofsky presents himself as the purest auditor of Bach in Carnegie Hall, imagining the original performance of the piece, which sets Kapellmeister-genius Bach amid his fellows, his auditors, and his performers in Leipzig hurrying to church to conduct what we now italicize as *The St. Matthew Passion,* observed breathlessly (as a celebrity really) by the heaving, starched "matronly flounces" of Leipzig housewives who are themselves rushing to sing alto or soprano in one of the double choruses. We compare this with the present, where the concert-subscribers in Carnegie Hall haven't a clue, can't hear a note since their ears are stuffed with money. (Never mind that Zukofsky's picture of Bach in Leipzig turns out to be as idealized as Milton's depiction of Eden. The actual people seemed to have been getting tired of "old Bach" and his fusty counterpoint, which was simply forestalling the superior excitement of the coming gallant style.) As an art maker, Zukofsky himself is in a highly diluted position: he's not Kapellmeister, not a musician (and, as the context expands in the next lines, we find out that he's not a miner, not a propagandist, not a demonstrator).

But the original "drop of medicine," at least at this moment of the poem, that is to be made stronger-by-dilution is Bach (and *The St. Matthew Passion* has more overt anti-Semitism than anywhere else in Bach). (Zukofsky had a nose for anti-Semitism.)

Zukofsky himself, at this point had no truck with homeopathic transmissibility. He does present himself as a Jew, but also as a worker (marxist if not necessarily Marxist), and a poet, collaging almost typologically. When "the great Magnus" is quoted,

Executive's not the word, use *engineer,*
Single handed, ran 'em like soldiers,
Seventy-four yesterday, and could run 'em today,
Been fishin' all Easter
Nothin' like nature for hell-fire

the analogies are meant to unify, with Magnus's hell-fire matching the same term in Bach's libretto. Such collage disturbs any easy calculation. But, conservatively, let's say that Zukofsky is a quarter Jewish here (Jewish, marxist, modernist, art lover), thus showing an HJQ of 4.

In his late "Multiple Identity Questionnaire" Ginsberg writes from many subject positions, but at least one of them is as a Jew.

I'm a jew? a nice Jewish boy?
A flaky Buddhist, certainly
Gay in fact pederast? I'm exaggerating?
Not only queer an amateur S&M fan, someone should spank me for saying
  that
Columbia Alumnus class of '48, Beat icon, students say.
White, if jews are "white race"
American by birth, passport, and residence
Slavic heritage, mama from Vitebsk, father's forebears Grading in
  Kamenetz-Podolska near Lvov.
I'm an intellectual! Anti-intellectual, anti-academic
Distinguished Professor of English Brooklyn College,
Manhattanite, Another middle class liberal,
but lower class second generation immigrant,
Upperclass, I own a condo loft, . . . (41)

Let's check the proportions, looking at the beginning of the list: jew, nice Jewish boy, flaky Buddhist, gay, pederast, queer, amateur S&M fan, Columbia Alumnus, Beat icon, White (if jews are 'white race'), American, Slavic, intellectual, Anti-intellectual, anti-Academic, Distinguished Professor, Manhattanite, middle class liberal, lower class, second generation immigrant, Upperclass . . .

The math gets fuzzy because most categories are put comic-polemically, insisting on what is not yet common. And then there's the pretty shocking anti-Semitic orthography Ginsberg insists on, writing "jew" twice although he uses caps elsewhere conventionally (Vitebsk, Kamenetz-Podolska) and comically (Another middle class liberal). But, fuzzily, let's say that Ginsberg presents us here with a quotient of roughly 3 or so Jewish or Jewish-inflected identifications in a total of 20. So, roughly, he's showing an HJQ of 7.

But don't those lower-case "jew"s go right back to one of Ginsberg's originary anti-institutional moments, his "Fuck the jews" graffito at Columbia? Even via this self-hating orthography, Ginsberg here remains a Jew. He does end his written career projecting his ashes to the cemetery with his father: "Things I'll Not Do (Nostalgias)":

Never go to Bulgaria, had a booklet & invitation
. . . .
No more sweet summers with lovers, teaching Blake at Naropa,
Mind Writing Slogans, new modern American Poetics, Williams
        Kerouac Reznikoff Rakosi Corso Creeley Orlovsky
Any visits to B'nai Israel graves of Buba, Aunt Rose, Harry Meltzer and
    Aunt Clara, Father Louis
Not myself except in an urn of ashes.

Light(silence)word

Norman Fischer

1.

Light is mysterious. Both a wave and a particle, and therefore neither, light is a universal constant; neither medium nor content, light is strangely all-pervasive. Seeing anything is not so much seeing that thing as seeing the light that falls on it; and it's not even the light that we see; we see only its afterglow. Light activates eye and consciousness only after it has disappeared, its faded radiance bouncing off objects. Uncanny in these ways, light is in almost all religious traditions associated with the divine, the supernal, with God, with Consciousness; so much so that it seems possible that light actually *is* consciousness or a form of consciousness, matter a coagulation of light, light's grosser form. In Heaven, in Nirvana, in Pure Consciousness (or whatever other ethereal realm anyone would conceive of), objects with all their stubborn messiness and grossness fade away and there is only light, sheer luminosity, in its pure state.

The word "Zohar," title of the great thirteenth-century Spanish Jewish mystical text attributed to Moses de Leon, translates as "radiance." The Judaic scholar Daniel Matt has for some years now worked on the definitive English translation of Zohar (the Pritzker edition, of which four volumes have so far been released by the Stanford University Press). Volume I of the text includes an introduction by Rabbi Arthur Green. What follows is my digest of the historical context of the text, as discussed by Green:

Kabbalah, though existent in various disorganized forms probably as early as the second century C.E., remained a secret tradition until the twelfth century in Spain, when Kabbalistic works went public in reaction to the influence of the work of Moses Maimonides, the great Aristotelian physician and rationalist, probably the most influential rabbi in history. The whole of Judaism as it exists now, East and West, bears the Rambam's (as he was called) stamp. Inspired by Greek philosophy, as mediated through Islamic culture, Maimonides thought of God as an abstruse entity, logically necessary. Like Freud (though of course, unlike Freud, not an atheist), the Rambam saw ancient Judaism as essentially childlike, and felt that with him Judaism now came to its mature form as a path of religious contemplation and ethics. The purpose of Jewish observance, according to the Rambam, was not to honor or appease God (who, it seemed obvious to him, had no need of this) but to educate, tame, and improve human beings, so that we would be capable of coming into line with the divine plan, which foresaw universal goodness and the final perfection of the world.

The Kabbalists opposed this view so bitterly they felt compelled to go public to attack it. To them, the Rambam's concept of Judaism as a gradual path of human self-improvement trivialized the tradition. In contrast, they saw Jewish daily observance as a desperately urgent mechanism for revolutionizing the cosmic order, which, in its fallen state, was perilously close to endlessly being lost, without possibility of redemption. For them God was not an impersonal philosophically necessary entity; God was intimately, even personally, wrapped up within the world and within human contemplations, actions, and language. Especially Jewish actions and language. So that Jewish religious acts were constantly crucially critical to the fate of the universe. The burden of the Kabbalistic mythology and practice is the mysterious and direct correspondence between the world below and the world above, between human action and the divine plan. Creation had gone terribly awry from the beginning; the divine sparks had broken through their vessels and plunged into the darkness of the world; it was up to Jews to raise the sparks up on behalf of the entire human race and the cosmic order. Where the Rambam and his followers were patiently and wisely hopeful, the Kabbalists were constantly urgently grasping at straws.

In discussing this historical background to the Zohar, Arthur Green writes: "to know God is a necessary condition of proper worship—on this the Kabbalists agree with the philosophers [i.e., Rambam and his followers]." Of course the two camps differed radically as to the significance of the phrase "knowing God." The philosophers understood intellectual contemplation of teaching and creation as the path to knowledge of God; for the Kabbalists knowing God meant mystical union, achieved mainly through language-based ecstatic concentration practices.

The Kabbalists were obsessed with language. They were not interested merely in analysis, contemplation, and interpretation. Study for them was not an intellectual act. Instead, every word of text masked hidden depths that revealed operations crucial to the salvation of the world on a moment-to-moment basis; and every word was related not only to every other word of text but to everything else throughout the whole of the mundane and supernal realms. Things of the world were, in their essence also "words" (in Hebrew *devar* means both word and thing), because God had after all, in the most hidden of all parts of the Bible, Bereshit ("In the beginning," the Jewish name for Genesis, and the main subject of the Zohar) created the physical universe exactly by uttering words. What was the nature of God-speech, God-word? And how did it relate to human speech, in which it lay hidden?

The Torah, it was said, was written in light. Every letter was light. And within this light all mysteries were contained. The book was the world, the world was the book. To those who then and now complain that the Torah is a primitive text, full of the violence and vindictiveness of a terrified people and a terrible God, the Kabbalists had little to say; they knew otherwise, but how could one explain, for without faith, spiritual practice, and intimate knowledge, what could be understood? They knew that certainly the Torah was not saying only what it seemed to be saying, what the black letters on white seemed to indicate, it was saying that and everything else, in multifaceted, ineffable ways. The words, the letters, were fire; the page was burning. (In an essay on Buber's vision of Chasidism, Kenneth Rexroth, who felt that the Bible was the most destructive text ever written, said that the Chasidim had managed to read the Bible in such a way that it said exactly the opposite of what it actually did say; Rexroth was seemingly both right and wrong about this.) Behind every letter of the text, every infinite pinpoint of light, lay universe upon universe.

Long before the Kabbalists the rabbis of the Talmud saw the profundity of the biblical text, which they had fashioned into a substitute for the cult of the now-destroyed temple. Judaism has for centuries been a cult of ritual action; it was now a cult of the book, into which all the mysterious efficacy of ritual action had disappeared. The Talmudists saw that the book therefore could not be merely what it seemed to be. Words could not merely be words. Each was subject to infinite interpretation, and there were infinite approaches to interpretation. Within these infinite approaches, the tradition delineated four: Peshat, the plain meaning, what the text seemed to be saying on the surface; Remes, the level of linguistic correspondence and textual operation through which completely unexpected meanings could be derived; Drash, the vast literature of legends and stories that purported to tell incidents and details (many quite anachronistic and clearly manufactured to suit situations long lost to history) that had been left out of the highly elliptical original text; and Sod, the level of mystical vision, trance, dreams, visitations, etc. (There are various interpretations and glosses on these four levels; the foregoing is my own, based on reading in various sources.) Together the four (PRDS) spell the Hebrew pardes, garden, or Paradise.

Pardes
The trees bear fruit, the book
Binds
Like water brimming in the pitcher's
Poured out steady till no drop's left
By a firm hand, an outstretched arm,
The book bears them on through the storm
Tree tops twisting, stripped debris shattered
In the violent nights
Though the fruit's sweet lingers on the tongue
Like melody—
That's the plain meaning

Beyond that and embedded in it
Like seeds in a winter earth
(Officially only a thin layer
Atop a hard dark mystery below
Exactly as deep as the plow turns)
The meaning-fingers splayed forth
Like hairy roots laterally
Entangling other letters, heterodox tales, bits and strands

(The third level now)
Of lives, songs, opinions, certainties
Wild stories, rewordings, revisions
Attempts to harmonize or humanize
Upheaval, sickness, fierce mistaken force
The worm in the infinite, how sky
Reflects the turmoil of the sea
The soul's own sequential poisoning
In its reversing desire to crawl out
Of its own skin, like the famous snake
That spoke for it in the orchard
That had no hands to touch with, to grasp

Then the inner turning
The quiet of snow falling on rock and twig
With a hush beyond speculation and thinking
A meaning pressed only into breathing
Or illuminated by the speechless waters
That suck underground
Into the capillary rootlets opening beneath the feet
In the winding uncharted journey of footsteps
From one point of darkness to the next

The Zohar is a Kabbalistic commentary on Torah but also a fiction, a novel, the adventures of Rabbi Shimon bar Yochai, a second-century rabbi from the Galilee, and his small band of disciples who offer the commentary in discussions that take place as they wander around the Holy Land meeting various people. They usually discuss sitting outdoors by a brook or in a garden. A feature of the text is their constant delight in one another and in the various interpretations that they espouse. Almost certainly there was in thirteenth-century Spain a similar group of disciples surrounding Moses de Leon. A key theme of the Zohar is light, light and darkness: the disciples arose for study at midnight, a thin thread of light going out into the world emanating from their words and feelings. A "thread-thin ray of love" (Matt) that reverberates seven centuries later in Paul Celan's Holocaust-inflected "thread-suns," thin light rays of hope, that leak out of books and words even still.

The symbolic edifice of Kabbalism is prodigious and esoteric and I don't know enough about it to say much here. Suffice it to say that the system references the stage-by-stage emanations from Ayn Sof, the beyond beyond the beyond, into this world below through many supernal stages, the descent of the ineffable through light that illuminates this world: physical light, but also the light of human divinity and human goodness which is a reflection of the divine. Ayn Sof (which means "without end") is beyond light and dark, it is endless formless unknowable indefinable, beyond being and nonbeing. Yet within Ayn Sof, for no reason, there occurs an impulse toward light. This impulse creates an energy that leads to the first of the ten Sphirot (emanations) which is Keter, "crown," "circle," or Ayin, "nothing" (Ayn Sof being more nothing than nothing): a point of light that is completely surrounded by darkness, and this long before the world, even before what we call God (also an emanation of Ayn Sof) had come to be; a point of light that is, essentially, hidden. This becomes a key Kabbalistic theme, concealment, hiddenness. It led to theologies like those of the Marranos (Spanish secret Jews) and the Sabbatians (followers of the seventeenth-century "false messiah" who converted to Islam): to be a Jew concealed in the world is to manifest and imitate the concealed divine light. So that outward conversion to Islam or Christianity, while inwardly remaining Jewish, came to be viewed as the highest and most godlike of all paths!

In all this we can see germs of nearly all of avant-garde writing's chief themes: revolt against the polite, rational, Aristotelian order of things; focus on language not as conduit of communication but as infinitely suggestible medium that writes the world; concealment, hiddenness, obscurity, exile; intertextuality; resistance to closure and the univocal interpreting self. The world is hidden within language, words conceal rather then reveal meaning, meaning as meaning being essentially concealed, the not said contained in the said, the written writing the unwritten etc.

2.

The word zen is a Japanese transliteration of the Sanskrit word *dhyana,* which means meditative absorption. The Zen schools of Buddhism emphasize meditative absorption above all else. A cursory, or even a deeper, look at Zen literature and practice will surely suggest that language per se is not only irrelevant to Zen but that Zen is dismissive of, if not hostile to, language. A common early Chinese phrase to indicate the essential and unique position of Zen is usually translated "beyond words and letters." Language in Zen is "a finger pointing at the moon." In Zen it's silence, not language's constant noise-making, that gets to the heart of reality.

The most famous discussion of silence in Zen literature centers on a koan that is actually a quotation from the Vimalakirti Nirdesa sutra:

> Vimalakirti asked Manjushri, "What is the bodhisattva's method of entering nonduality?"
>
> Manjushri said, "According to my mind, in all things, no speech, no explanation, no direction, and no representation, leaving behind all questions and answers—this is the method of entering nonduality."
>
> Then Manjushri asked Vimalakirti, "We have all spoken. Now you should say, good man, what is a bodhisattva's method of entry into nonduality?"
>
> Vimalakirti was silent.

Manjushri's explanation that explanation, speech, representation are all to be let go of apparently doesn't go far enough, for he is still talking. Vimalakirti goes him one better by saying absolutely nothing. In Zen, Vimalakirti's silence is referred to as "thunderous," and there is much discussion about its nature. Though the word silence might suggest a singular experience, in fact there are many possible silences: passive silence, silence of withdrawal, angry silence, confused silence, enigmatic silence, manipulative silence. My silence is not the same as yours. Vimalakirti's thunderous silence is taken as an ultimate sort of silence, a silence which expresses, without expression, the highest, most complete, most inclusive, form of truth, beyond which there is no other.

The Jewish tradition, so wordy in all ways, also has a teaching about such an all-inclusive silence. When God gave the Ten Commandments on Mount Sinai the scene was, as depicted in the Bible, noisy and dramatic: the smoking blazing mountain, the terrifying presence, the deafening noise, thunder, horns blaring, and so on. But the rabbis of the Talmud explained that this deafening noise was actually a total and utter silence. They said that at the exact center of the noise was the most silent moment that had ever existed on earth: not even an animal stirred; there was no wind, and, most amazing of all, there was no human speech commenting on the silence.

Lest we frustrate ourselves in an effort to hear such a silence (are "silence" and "hearing" even compatible?) it will be good to remember two things: first, as John Cage famously discovered, it is impossible for a living human being to experience silence (there will always be, at least, the sounds of the breath and heartbeat); and second, that Vimalakirti's silence is a "nondualistic" silence, which is to say that it is not a silence opposed to noise, but, like the silence of the Talmudic vision of Sinai, a silence that defines not a particular object of listening (or absence of object) but instead points to something essential within any listening. It is a silence therefore which is not opposed to, or defined as different from, sound, and therefore language. It is the silence within rather than outside words and phrases. Like the vast spaces inside of atoms, without which what we call the "solid" world could not exist, silence makes words possible.

In fact the notion that language is in this sense beyond language (i.e., that it contains at its heart, of necessity, silence) is one of the chief insights and practice pathways of Zen. What is Zen koan practice, after all, if not the practice of discerning the silence within phrases; meditating, that is, not "beyond" phrases, but within and through them to meanings unrestricted by the apparent linguistic limitations of the words.

I think of koan practice as the practice of phrases. It is, on the one hand, the special province of the Zen school of Buddhism that has systematized it, and, on the other, a commonplace practice in all religions where scripture reading is conceived of as a meditative rather than an emotional or knowledge-based activity, and among poets and literary people who are attuned to the intuitive echoic possibilities of language. The practice of phrases consists of living with, being immersed in, meditating on, phrases, until they become large and strange and reveal themselves to us, which is to say, that through them we are revealed to ourselves. By phrases I mean literally phrases, words with meanings that are identifiable, explainable, conceptual; but phrases also indicate the silence, the larger, ineffable space, that we will find in the middle of and surrounding any word and concept if we contemplate it long and deeply enough. Zen meditation (zazen) can be a method for this. It involves breathing with phrases, inquiring of them, taking them beyond conventional styles of understanding. So that instead of trying to gain mastery over the phrase by interpreting or explaining it, the practitioner feels the phrase deeply, both with and beyond conceptual apparatus.

In Zen there are various traditions and methodologies for working with phrases, some more organized than others. In the contemporary Zen practiced in the West there are several koan traditions, all influenced by the Japanese Rinzai school. These traditions are very well organized, with koan curricula, and proscribed ways of responding to koans in a fairly regimented format. In the Soto Zen that I practice, working with phrases is fuzzy and somewhat disorganized. There is no curriculum and no particular format. Soto Zen also includes a wordless method of working with phrases. This is Zen mindfulness, which is not mindfulness of something, but mindfulness of the silence, spaciousness, or emptiness that is always at the heart of experience (a key point is the insight that language/silence and experience/emptiness are equivalents; experience is a form of language; language is a form of experience). This is practiced using the breath or whatever is in front of you (a person, a task, a physical object) as the phrase, the koan. Life becomes the phrase, not in the abstract, but as it appears uniquely, wherever and whenever you are. You pay close attention to it, avoid pegging it down to an explanation or an evaluation, and you wait with intense inquiry to see what will be revealed. The idea is, the hope is, that everything will illuminate you, everything will open you up, everything will surprise you. Although of course in real practice this doesn't always happen, it is a direction, an aspiration. It doesn't matter how it turns out. The main thing is to keep up a continuity of practice. It doesn't make much difference whether you are practicing with whatever's in front of you, or whether you are using a literal phrase, like "who is this?" or "what is love?" that may have arisen from the issues of your life; or whether you are using a classical Zen phrase. The more you contemplate the phrase, and maintain your contemplation of it through your activity, the more your practice can be continuous and the more will be revealed.

All this is to say that what at first may seem in Zen to be a bias against language in favor of "silence," or, in any case, activities (like meditation) that do not seem to be language based, is in fact a view of language, a practice of language.

Nowhere is this clearer than in the writings of the thirteenth-century Zen master Dogen, much appreciated these days by Western philosophers concerned with language. "The single most original and seminal aspect of Dogen's Zen is his treatment of the role of language in Zen soteriology. We moderns may pride ourselves on our acute language consciousness in the twentieth and twenty-first centuries, but Dogen was no less aware. He is similar to us in this regard" (Hee Jin Kim, *Dogen on Meditation and Thinking, a Reflection on His View of Zen* [New York: State University of New York, 2006], 59). Dogen was the rare Zen master who was as much a literary practitioner as he was a religious figure, and his text *Shobogenzo* (*Treasury of the True Dharma Eye*), a multivolume work, is considered a key text in Japanese literary, as well as religious, history. In his writings, Dogen constantly excoriates those Zen adepts who are critical of language, pointing to "silence" or other extralinguistic positions, as Zen's goal. Over and over, Dogen expresses his dissatisfaction with this essentially unsophisticated, dualistically unnuanced, and, in his view, religiously destructive, understanding. Like other Zen thinkers, Dogen saw language as the prison from which we seek freedom. But unlike them, he saw that the way out of this prison (from which there is no escape) is to be found within the prison itself. In other words, language's hold on us can be loosed only by language itself. For Dogen human beings must live within language, which is, as Heidegger put it, our "house of being," the constituent of essential humanness. The way out of the house is the full occupation of it, with awareness of its nature, so that in the end resistance is transformed into celebration. "The monastics of future generations will be able to understand one-taste Zen (ichimizen) based on words and letters if they devote their efforts to spiritual practice by seeing the universe through words and letters, and words and letters through the universe" (Kim 60, quoting Dogen). "How pitiful are they who are unaware that discriminative thought is words and phrases and that words and phrases liberate discriminative thought" (62).

In his discussion of Dogen's view of Zen, Kim delineates seven literary techniques with which Dogen endeavors to deconstruct conventional Zen and Buddhist language, so as to turn restrictive pious understandings inside-out. Like the Chasidic masters, who make liberal use of linguistic slights of hands (reference to word-roots; gematria; etc.), Dogen employs strikingly postmodern operations to produce texts so dense that they are from time to time incomprehensible. The seven techniques are (1) transposition of lexical components (an almost mathematical mechanical shifting of words or phrases in repetitive sentences, so that all possible, if sometimes apparently nonsensical, syntactic combinations are played out); (2) semantic reconstruction through syntactic change (often making use of the differences in grammar between Chinese—into which Buddhist texts that Dogen read had been translated—and the Japanese in which he was writing, to yield unique meanings); (3) explication of semantic attributes (making often punning or counter-indicated use of the multiple meanings possible within Chinese ideographs); (4) reflexive, self-causative utterances (in which statements and their opposites are identified, or the bald assertion of non sequiturs upon which arguments are based); (5) upgrading commonplace notions and using neglected metaphors (using obsolete meanings buried in contemporary words, leaning on ordinary expressions to yield surprising correspondences, emphasizing commonplace throw-away words); (6) use of homophonous expressions (not unlike Zukovsky's Catullus); and (7) reinterpretation based on the principle of non duality (in which clearly dualistic statements in the tradition are interpreted as though they were not dualistic). Through these and other methods Dogen relentlessly deconstructs the Zen and Buddhist traditions—as he believed they had been meant to be deconstructed—for the purpose of restoring to language and ordinary everyday reality the potential, dignity, and sense of wonder he believed they deserved. Dogen's project as a writer and religious teacher was to work against the perennial distinction religion (and language) inevitably wants to make between "holiness" and "the everyday." He believed this erroneous distinction to be the root of all human anguish.

"Language thinking and reason constitute the key to both zazen and koan study within Dogen's praxis-oriented Zen. The koan's and zazen's function is not to excoriate and abandon the intellect and its words and letters, but rather to liberate and restore them in the Zen enterprise. In short, enlightenment is not brought about by direct intuition (or transcendent wisdom) supplanting the intellect and its tools, but in and through their collaboration and corroboration in search of the expressible in deeds, words, and thoughts for a given situation (religious and secular)" (Kim 78).

3.

Where does all this leave language's capacity to describe reality? And where does it leave the possibility of a soteriologically efficacious understanding? That is, recognizing the silence of words, are we left speechless? And recognizing the impossibility of going beyond words, are we doomed to mouth them to our continued distress and confusion?

In a world in which we are all "dim-sighted" (Dogen's phrase) nothing could be more dim-sighted than to assert that one is not dim-sighted; and such an assertion could be none other than a projection of the very dim-sightedness itself. The way out of this trap would be to make use of the dim-sightedness (language, human perception) to see the nature of the very dim-sightedness, and in doing so, to proceed, with full appreciation of the process of becoming human—which always involves the practice of language.

It has often been remarked, and written about (I myself have written about it) that Jews frequently find themselves practicing in Buddhist centers, and that Buddhist centers are disproportionately Jewish. The foregoing understandings of language, light, and silence might provide a clue: that Jews (or at least some subset of Jews) have been spiritually and culturally immersed in language in a particular key: language whose tonalities bear the ineffable senses of light, of silence, of depth. Most modern Jews, long removed from traditional Jewish educational systems, can only dimly hear these tonalities, though they have become present, and perhaps have come out most strongly, in postmodern literary expressions, which, as we have seen, seem to be so basically Jewish in character. But for the average Jewish person, the tradition's riches are, so to speak, a closed book; deep and personal familiarity with Jewish texts and the sensibilities behind them have long been lost; and in any case it is likely that there never has been a deeply satisfying way of Jewish life and learning that was not inherently incompatible with modern cultural life, which is to say with a Judaism that was not of necessity cut off from the dominant culture in which it found itself. It is an odd historical fact that Buddhist meditation practice, appearing as it does in the West all but divorced from its Asian cultural contexts, and therefore to some extent a tabula rasa, to be filled in with whatever soul-stirrings that may be vaguely felt by those who access it, carries echoes of those ancient Jewish tonalities, so that the essentially Jewish linguistic moves can be activated within the "silence."

Silence is no weakness of language.
It is, on the contrary, its strength.
It is the weakness of words not to know this.
(Edmond Jabès, *Book of Shares,* 31)

On Yiddish Poetry and Translation of Yiddish Poetry

Kathryn Hellerstein

Let me start by saying that I learned Yiddish at Stanford University, before there was a Jewish Studies program there, believe it or not, but that is another story.[1] I have two quick comments to make just about things that have been said before I get into what I want to say. First, I want to touch on some of the comments that the other panelists have made about secular Jewish poetry by mentioning that there exists a very rich and variegated secular poetry in Hebrew in Israel right now. I think that Israeli secular poetry should be part of the conversation. My second comment is that there are as many shades and variegations of being a religious Jew as there are of being a secular Jew. We should not assume that there is an absolute dichotomy between these two terms. Third, I'd like to ask a question which some of you started answering in your presentations: Is there a secular Jewish poetry that is *not* a response to a subversion of or a rejection of Jewish tradition, however you might want to define that term?

In my presentation, I will focus on modernist Yiddish poetry and the translation of Yiddish poetry.

Beginning in 1907, a number of Jewish poets from Eastern Europe who immigrated to the United States (and many of whom settled in New York City) wrote and published avant-garde, modernist poetry in Yiddish. Rebelling against an earlier, convention-ridden verse expressing the political ideologies of the nascent Jewish Labor movement, the poets of Di Yunge (the Young Ones) published journals and anthologies of poetry exemplifying their new aestheticism and expressing the power they saw in a poetic voice that spoke for the individual rather than for the collective. In 1919, a second modernist movement arose in New York, when three poets who called themselves Di Inzikhistn (the Introspectivists) published an anthology of poetry that included a manifesto outlining the group's precepts of high modernism.

The works of the Yunge poets (Mani Leyb, Reuven Iceland, Zishe Landau, Joseph Rolnick) (all born between 1879 and 1889; all dead by 1955) embodied principles of musicality and romantic understatement, conveying mood or eroticism through quotidian detail. They experimented with prosody and form by importing and developing such conventional forms as the sonnet, rather than by fracturing the poetic line. What made their poetry appear radical was their subject, approach, and language, playing upon idiomatic Yiddish diction for unexpected melodious effect, excising rhetorical grandiosity or Germanic poeticisms (*daytshmerizms*), and relying on direct, sparse, concrete imagery.

One great poet briefly associated with the Yunge was Moyshe-Leyb Halpern (1886–1932), whose acerbic, ironic poems were characterized by their constant undercutting of poetic convention and readers' expectations,[2] as in his poem, *A Tfile Fun A Lump* (A Rogue's Prayer):

Nem mayn talent, un gib im op
An altn hund, tsi a balebos,
Vos vil abisl koved oykh,
Di libe shkheynem tsum fardros.
O, helf mir, helf mir, got

Take my talent, hand or toss
It to an old dog or a boss
Who also wants a little honor
To pique the envy of his neighbor.
Oh, help me, help me, God.

Oh, help me, God,
When in the middle of bright day
A roughneck tries to block my way,
Let my fist land on his chin
With the clang of bells resounding.
Oh, help me, help me, God.

Oh, help me, God,
Should my good friends discover,
Gritting their teeth, indeed uncover
With what and how I make my living;
Let me ever keep on loafing,
Oh, help me, help me, God

Oh, help me, God,
As burning and harsh
As fresh horseradish in a dish
Shall the pious hypocrite find pain
When he invades my small domain.
Oh, help me, help me, God.

Oh, help me, God,
Let my speech be disgusting
As a dead cat rotting in garbage,
Let every place where I set foot
Grow nothing and stay desolate.
Oh, help me, help me, God.

Oh, help me, God,
Let, as a whore's wild dance
In moral eyes, my impudence
Slap the cheeks of men with wives.
May they curse me roundly all their lives!
Oh, help me, help me, God.

Oh, help me, God,
Let me be the sickle blade
And let me be the stone that strayed
To break the blade. I shall spit
On You, on me, on the whole of it.
Oh, help me, help me, God.[3]

Halpern's poem is a prayer that implodes upon itself. It opens by denouncing the adversity encountered by the dramatic speaker in his gritty urban life in America. The speaker, here a poet, excoriates his own talent and his sloth, as well as the *grober yung* (roughneck) who blocks his way and the *frumak* (pious hypocrite) who imposes upon his *dalet-ames* (literally, "four corners" or "four ells or cubits," meaning, "domain, dwelling place"). The speaker then asks for God's so-called "blessing," in the most unholy of similes—that his own *reyd* (speech) be as disgusting as a dead cat and that his *khutspe* (impudence) with the wives of other men be as wild as *a vister hurn-tants* (a desolate dance of prostitution). The poem culminates when the poet works himself into a frenzy of self-destruction with the metaphor of the proverbial sickle blade and the stone that breaks it. In the end, the poet curses himself and the very God to whom he prays.

Although the poem calls itself a *tfile* (prayer) and takes the rhetorical stance of a prayer, addressing God, it is hardly a religious poem. In fact, in a typically Halpern style, the poem turns inside out the conventions of Jewish prayer and devotional Yiddish poetry. Even the *Got* of this poem is more generic, through His Germanic name, than particularly Jewish, as He would be if named by any of the many Hebraic names for the deity that Yiddish offers. Typical of Halpern, too, is the absence of Hebraic diction in the poem, except for the phrases *balebos* (boss), which here is written out phonetically, rather than in the standard Hebraic spelling, *dalet-ames* (domain) and *khutspe* (impudence).

The Inzikhistn, or Introspectivist poets—Yankev Glatshteyn (1896–1971), A. Leyeles (1889–1966), and Nakhum Minkoff (1893–1958)—especially Glatshteyn and Leyeles—aimed to take Yiddish poetry beyond the Yunge innovations. Their poetic principles opposed mimesis as the purpose of art and argued that poetry reflects an internalized social world, rather than acting as a vehicle for expressing a political mood or "man" in general. Their manifestoes urged poets to write poems that made the political personal and intimate through the individual's experience, to present the chaos of the psyche's experience through a "kaleidoscopic" fragmentation and synthesis, and to use poetic methods of association, suggestion, discontinuous composition, and alogical devices of language to express a particular moment in a particular psyche. Although the Introspectivists divorced themselves from any national or social mission, they proclaimed that "because it is art, it is Jewish anyway"[4] or, conversely, "A Jew will write about an Indian fertility temple and Japanese Shinto shrines as a Jew."[5] To these poets, Jewishness was the Yiddish language. Their poems were quite experimental in form, shifting rhythmic devices from free verse to traditional stanzas, even within the same poem, in order to avoid the monotony they considered poetically fatal.

Among the few women poets included in the Yunge publications, and later in those of the Inzikhistn (although many more women were publishing poems in those years), was Anna Margolin (pseudonym for Roza Lebensboym, 1887–1952). The poems in Margolin's single book of poetry, *Lider* (1929), are complex and rely upon dramatic personae that defuse the personal (and female) voice, as in the opening poem from that book, "*Ikh bin geven a mol a yingling*" (I Was Once a Boy):

Ikh bin geven a mol a yingling,
Gehert in portikos sokratn,
Es hot mayn bzem-fraynt, mayn libling,
Gehat dem shenstn tors in aten.

Gevezn tsezar, un a hele velt
Geboyt fun marmor, ikh der letster,
Un far a vayb mir oysderveylt
Mayn shtoltse shvester.

In royznkrants baym vayn biz shpet
Gehert in hoykhmutikn fridn
Vegn shvabling fun nazaret
Un vilde mayses vegn yidn.

I was once a boy, a stripling,
Listening in Socrates' portico,
My bosom-buddy, my sweet darling,
Had Athens' most stunning torso.

Was Caesar. And from marble constructed
A glistening world, I the last there,
And for my own wife selected
My stately sister.

Rose-garlanded, drinking wine all night
In high spirits, heard tell the news
About the weakling from Nazareth
And wild tales about Jews.[6]

Jewish life and ethnicity as well as religious forms and traditions are present, even in their deliberate absence, in both these secular, modernist Yiddish poems I have read you. As Halpern's poem transforms a prayer into a curse, it calls forth the prayer-form it negates. Margolin's poem identifies its speaker as a person as far removed from the poet herself as possible. The poem's persona is in the first stanza a Greek boy and, then in the second and third, a decadent Roman man, who knows of Jews (and Jesus, from whom Christianity will spring) only through drunken rumors, as creatures that inhabit the far outskirts of his cultural ken. Yet the poem, written in New York in Yiddish by a Jewish woman from Brest-Litovsk, calls up all that it leaves out—the situation of women in Yiddish poetry, who were classified by derogatory critics as mere writers of personal pettiness, and domestic and erotic poem, as well as the millennium-long clash between Hebraism and Hellenism and the cacophony of Jewish life in a Christian world.

Even Yiddish poems written in the United States during and after the World War II destruction of European Jewry, apparently in the form of prayers addressed to God, such as Kadya Molodowsky's famous "*Eyl khanun*" (God of Mercy) and Malka Heifetz Tussman's "*Tate ziser*" (Sweet Father), turn out, upon examination, to be narratives about praying, rather than direct supplications.[7] These poems, too, thus wiggle out from being literally "religious" poems.

Finally, I want to talk briefly about the significance of translating radical, secular Yiddish poetry into English. The word "radical" (as others tonight have or surely will point out) derives from the Latin word for "root." In my experience, such Yiddish poetry as I've read you and spoken briefly about here necessarily leads the translator back to the cultural roots, to those same religious traditions against which the poems have revolted. The translator needs to learn the traditions in order to understand the significance of the secularization of Yiddish culture in the twentieth century and therefore to be able to translate the poetry.

Not surprisingly, perhaps, that process of education affects the translator's own poems as well. I will conclude with one of my poems which takes on a religious Jewish theme, but ends up as a secular poem (if we look to the etymology of the word "secular" from a Latin word "akin to serere, to sow"), and which, conveniently for us, discusses a different kind of root. The poem is called "Rosh Hashanah," literally, "the head of the year," or the Jewish New Year. The poem contains three short lines in Yiddish, which I translate within the poem. They are based upon a very important pun. The Yiddish verb, "*mern*" means "to increase," as in God's injunction to Adam and Eve in Genesis, "to increase and multiply." At the same time, the Yiddish noun "*mern*" denotes the plural of the root vegetable, "carrot."

ROSH HASHANAH[8]
Sweet wine that burns, a round loaf
torn and dragged through
honey, an apple, honey-dipped
yet sour, a pomegranate
red as hands cupped in new snow.
It holds six hundred and thirteen seeds.
Once my grandmother counted them
as my grandfather named each *mitsve.*
We chew these jewels, hungry
for good deeds, greedy to obey
Law's numbers.

The pickled beets will keep
our enemies away.
We pass the bowls.
Our *bobe-loshn* makes us say,
Mir esn mern
kedey
unzere mayles zoln zikh mern,
and buttery sugared carrots
roll from the spoon to multiply
ever the more our merits.
Food becomes prayer.
Leeks and onions, pearls
that we unravel with our tongues,
by their very names
will confound nations.
And the puns are profound
as the roots are round.

Squash protects. The sticky date protects.
How mighty are Thy works, O Lord,
for with these first fruits on the circles of our plates,
the turning of earth and moon
makes sure and determined
what will come:
windfall apples
blown to the ground.[9]

On Rosh Hashanah, the Jewish New Year, the poem tells us, the speaker attempts to follow the 613 commandments of Jewish law, or *mitsves* in Yiddish, *mitsvot* in Hebrew, by eating and drinking according to her "*bobe-loshn,*" literally, "grandmother tongue," a phrase I made up to play on the common name for the mother tongue Yiddish, "*mame-loshn.*" Yet it is the root vegetables—beets and carrots—that bring the real blessings. The wheel-shaped slices of red pickled beets will cause our enemies to roll away from us. And the carrots—"*Mir esn mern / kedey / unzere mayles zoln zikh mern*" translates literally as, "We eat carrots / in order that / our merits shall multiply." Roundness comes into play again, as we consider the round shape of the slices of carrots cooked in brown sugar, which embody the cyclical year and the Yiddish pun that I mentioned just now, on the double meanings of "*mern*" as "carrots" "multiply." These homonyms bring together the roots of nourishment, time's continuous yet repetitive pattern, and the hope for increase and prosperity in the coming year. What more could one ask from radical, secular poetry?

Notes

1. This essay originated as a presentation at the panel discussion, "Secular Jewish Culture / Radical Poetic Practice," with Paul Auster, Charles Bernstein, Stephen Paul Miller, Marjorie Perloff, and Jerome Rothenberg, at the Center for Jewish History in New York, on September 21, 2004. The moderator Charles Bernstein asked us to address three questions:

1) What are the innovations and inventions of American Jewish poets over the past century? Can we say that there is a distinctly Jewish component to radical modernist and contemporary poetry? What is the relation of Jewish modernist and contemporary poets to the historical avant-garde and to contemporary innovative poetry?
2) How do Jewish cultural life and ethnic and religious forms and traditions manifest themselves in the forms, styles, and approaches to radical American poetry?
3) What role does a distinctly secular approach to Jewishness by poets and other Jewish artists mean for "radical Jewish culture?"

2. For fuller discussions of this background, see Kathryn Hellerstein, "Poetry, Yiddish" and "Halpern, Moyshe-Leyb," in *Jewish American History and Culture: An Encyclopedia*, ed. Fischel and Pinsker (New York: Garland, 1992), 220–221 and 497–503.

3. Moyshe-Leyb Halpern, "A Tfile Fun A Lump" (A Rogue's Prayer), trans. Kathryn Hellerstein, in *In New York: A Selection*, ed. and trans. Kathryn Hellerstein (Philadelphia: Jewish Publication Society, 1982), 28–31.

4. "Chronicle of a Movement: Excerpts from Introspective Criticism," in *American Yiddish Poetry: A Bilingual Anthology*, ed. and trans. Benjamin and Barbara Harshav, with Kathryn Hellerstein, Brian McHale, and Anita Norich (Berkeley and Los Angeles: University of California Press, 1986), 790.

5. Jacob Glatsheyn, A. Leyeles, Nakhum Minkov, "Introspectivism Manifesto of 1919," trans. Anita Norich, in *American Yiddish Poetry: A Bilingual Anthology*, 780.

6. Anna Margolin, "*Ikh Bin Geven Amol A Yingling*" (I Was Once a Boy), trans. Kathryn Hellerstein, in *Jewish American Literature: A Norton Anthology* (New York: W. W. Norton, 2001), 265.

7. These poems can be found in Yiddish and English as follows: Kadya Molodowsky, "*Eyl khanun*" (Merciful God), in *Paper Bridges: Selected Poems of Kadya Molodowsky*, ed. and trans. Kathryn Hellerstein (Detroit: Wayne State University Press, 1999), 353–355. Malka Heifetz Tussman, "*Tate ziser*" (Sweet Father), trans. Kathryn Hellerstein, in *American Yiddish Poetry: A Bilingual Anthology*, 614–615.

8. I dedicate this poem to Maeera Shreiber, who invited me to her Rosh Hashanah dinner table years ago, where I first encountered these foods and puns.

9. Kathryn Hellerstein, "Rosh Hashanah," *Bridges* 2, 2 (Fall 1991): 109.

An "Exotic" on East Broadway

Mikhl Likht and the Paradoxes of Yiddish Modernist Poetry

Merle Bachman

It's a little-known fact that in New York in the 1920s, Yiddish immigrant writers were participants in the internationalist modernist breakthrough, and like their colleagues in other languages and lands, gathered to debate literature in cafés and published their poetry in little magazines. Although these poets were fluent in English, they chose to write their poems in Yiddish. It was a choice made out of dedication and love that ironically guaranteed the poets' inaccessibility to a larger American audience and also cost them many of their Yiddish readers, who were unaccustomed to the challenges of modernist writing. The charge of *umfarshtandlekhkayt,* incomprehensibility,[1] dogged these intrepid poets among their readers; yet there was one poet whose experimentation drew that charge even from his fellow writers: his name was Mikhl Likht.

In approaching Likht, I have thought of him as an "exotic on East Broadway," after a line in one of his poems—only to reread the poem and realize I mis-remembered it, almost exactly opposite:

ah   rare still nights   with *shikse*-song
with *sheygets*-whistle   in my poor exotic wild
Ukrainian village
pray for your "prosperous" "all achieving" countryman
on Broadway

(*Gezamelte Lider* 130–131)[2]

It is Likht who (in however self-satirizing a manner) refers to his Ukrainian roots as "exotic." But to me, perhaps inevitably, Likht himself is the exotic, in the way that Moyshe Shifris describes Yiddish literature in America, in the 1920s: "like exotic flowers in a botanical garden" (Paver 98).

Modernist Yiddish poetry represents most intensely to me the paradoxes of Yiddish culture in America. It's the achievement of writers who see themselves as internationals, yet are most at home in Yiddish, a relatively minor language[3]; who indeed choose to write in Yiddish, yet are transparently engaged in American culture, the big city, its din of noise and alphabets. Yiddish modernism itself was an international phenomenon, with lively centers of writing in Warsaw, Kiev, and Moscow. My personal interest has focused on writers in New York, because of their choice to write in Yiddish, a choice that kept them in what I see as a "threshold" position, between their own language community, which did not fully accept or even understand them, and the potential community represented by American writers, who did not even know they existed. In 1937, twenty years after the inaugural issue of *Inzikh,* Leyeles complained about the Yiddish poets' obscurity and lack of translation, their abandonment by Jewish writers who went "uptown" into English and American recognition. "We must put an end to the situation in which, at the meeting between a Yiddish and an American writer, it is 'self-evident' that the Jew should have read all the works of the American and just as 'self-evident' that the American should have no idea whether the Jew writes mezuzahs, checks, or indeed 'real literature'" (Harshav, *AYP* 801). In 1919, when Leyeles, Yankev Glatshteyn, and Nakhum Minkov formed the *In zikh*[4] movement (meaning "inside one's self" or "introspective"), they set out to create a self-consciously modernist Yiddish poetry, a poetry concerned with "making it new," with pushing the boundaries of language. Yet even in 1920, when the possibilities of a threshold position were dazzling, one poet writes in *Inzikh:* "Does Yiddish literature have—a reader? . . . [It] already has writers. What is lacking, however, is the reader, and this is especially true for Yiddish poetry" (Harshav, *AYP* 791).

The poet was overstating the case. At that point, Yiddish poetry *did* have readers—but the poetry with which they were most familiar was of a far more accessible genre.

Yiddish literary development in the United States can be mapped tightly onto several overlapping "generations," from the 1880s through the 1920s, in an environment of close connections between writers and their readers.[5] The proletarian "sweatshop poetry" of the 1890s arose from the Yiddish immigrants' swift transformation into a working class. Leyeles comments that poetry then was a "helping tool (not to mention maidservant) of the [labor] movements" and that even labor leaders who had no literary background considered it "part of socialist duty to compose poems" ("Minkov" 115). Such poetry, with its strong, declamatory meters and rhymes, occupied a powerful public space in the Yiddish immigrant community, where it was available in newspapers, on picket lines, in cafés, and on the streets. Imagine the difficulties when around 1907, a new generation of writers—*Di Yunge* (the "young ones")—began publishing poetry based on more private conceptions of "beauty" and art for art's sake. When *Inzikh*'s modernists arose, twelve years later, with their individualistic, free-verse orientation, readers who bumped into them on the street or in the cafés argued with them about their work. Ruth Wisse, in discussing "the exceptional intimacy of American Yiddish culture in the 1920s," notes: "One can hardly imagine Ezra Pound trying to justify himself in the pages of a local daily for writing poetry beyond the grasp of its regular subscribers," as some poets were forced to do (*A Little Love* 128).

What happens when poetry moves from "an indispensable form of propagandizing" (Sanders 142)—a source of political sustenance and cultural strength—to a form of individualistic expression? a badge of identification with a cosmopolitan "high" culture? an exploration of language itself? Further, the young rebels of Yiddish modernism rejected the prevailing sense of communal responsibility. In Leyeles's March 1920 comments on "The Jewish Kingdom," L. Shapiro's story about anti-Jewish pogroms, he writes, "there is actually no special Jewishness in this work." It *could* be considered Jewish simply because "it is written by a Jew and in Yiddish. There cannot be and should not be any other Jewishness" (Harshav, *AYP* 790).[6]

Part of the radicalism of *Inzikh* poets lay in their even choosing to spell out all Hebrew source-words (which are normally retained in their Hebrew spellings) phonetically in Yiddish. As their manifesto states:

> "We are 'Jewish poets' simply because we are Jews and write in Yiddish . . . It is not the poet's task to seek and show his Jewishness. Whoever is interested in this endeavor is welcome to it, and whoever looks for Jewishness in Yiddish poets will find it.
>
> "We believe in Yiddish. We love Yiddish." (Harshav, *AYP* 780)

One has to ask: to whom did this poetry speak?

Leyeles writes in 1923: "I read English poetry in free verse, I compare their free verse with ours. And I maintain, with no hesitation whatever, that our free verse is better, more masterful, more rhythmically lucid and more profound . . . It may seem immodest, but I sincerely believe that the free verse of the Introspectivists is now perhaps the best in all languages" (*AYP* 798). Here Leyeles compares English verse with Yiddish, and "returns" to Yiddish, to boast about the quality of *Inzikh* poetry. There is an implied inattention to translation in his statement, without which no one other than Yiddish readers will ever know that *Inzikh* verse is "the best."

Poetry by *Inzikh* writers can be envisioned in double-exposure, their poems being mapped simultaneously onto Yiddish and American spaces despite their "Yiddish-only" address. Their own community had difficulty understanding their project, but the *Inzikh* poets seemed compelled to write both out of their enthusiasm for the poetic possibilities of Yiddish and their own grasp of "American," which they clearly understood, regardless of whether or not they chose it as the language of their poems. They understood, as poets, the kind of spoken language to which American writers were turning—"here," as Glatshteyn wrote, "where a poet walks unnoticed like a shadow through New York streets, is squeezed in subways and elevators along with everyone else" (Glatshteyn, quoted in Harshav *AYP* 786). What contemporary poet/critic Charles Bernstein says about the Jewish "Objectivist" poet, Charles Reznikoff, applies to these Yiddish poets as well: " 'America' [is] not so much a 'place' but an attitude toward language": that is, an embrace of the local, a "rejection of exile" (31, 14). Thus, Yiddish poets participate in the larger cultural environment: through identification with, and simultaneous ongoing difference from, America. Yiddish burrows into America, and its poetry rises "out of the American asphalt" (Landis 146). A 1920 *Inzikh* review of Vachel Lindsay's "Golden Wiles of California," comments: "Lindsay's language is indeed not English, but Americanish. A language that is sounded only on the American continent, that was created here, that will be mainly understood here" (Anon. 185). Since the Yiddish poets are on this continent, too—not in Europe—they understand Lindsay's "Americanish." Further, the degree of identification and reciprocality that the Yiddish modernists feel is expressed by Minkov in his "New York Letter," where he cites Malcolm Cowley as saying that "America is not a belief, or a style, or a conception, a way in which to think. America is 'a thing.' " Minkov adds, "The *THING,* I would emphasize." Later, he remarks: "We make the thing that's called America, we are the thing. Without us she is—nothing" (77). The materiality of America, its machine-like "thingness," enables immigrant poets, writing in Yiddish, to participate in it—and more than participate, to help *make* America. Further, Minkov reiterates, "America—'the thing'—begins with the newest period in Yiddish poetry, and those who can't grasp this, will also never understand and grasp us" (78).

The notion of alienating, modern urban space is one frequently associated with modernist literature, from James Joyce's *Ulysses* to Henry Roth's

Call It Sleep, and modern experience. William Boelhower describes a trip the young Frank Lloyd Wright makes into Chicago in 1887 as one in which “he is bombarded by signs, signs of all kinds and from every possible direction” (22). Using Wright’s experience as exemplary, the critic argues that “the city is an atopic space. The very notion of home is foreign to it. Nor can the urban dweller find philosophical repose in it, since it never sleeps . . . All this produces a loss, a sense of amnesia” (25).

In contrast, some Yiddish poems reenact the unhinging of letter from letter and crowding-in of “signs” as a celebratory, freeing re-genesis. Against the sense of alienation one can juxtapose Likht’s fertile

signs in space. gleam
  of wellings-up and rain.
  silhouettes of rivulets pouring out
  over an egg. once again—
(*Gezamlte* 63)[7]

or Glatshteyn’s playful

Metalheavy is airsong of fly
of a man who sings up and sinks down.
(*Kredos* 41)[8]

The Yiddish poets of course were not alone in finding New York to be the “crucible” in which social and political conditions were ripe for the language and visual experiments that later became known as “modernism” (Williams 46). From about 1908 until World War I, radical writers, socialists and anarchists, cultural nationalists and modernists mingled in Greenwich Village, creating a “little renaissance.” Among them were quite a few migrants from other parts of the United States, seeking a place to be free in the swirling, open currents of the metropolis. In the 1920s, African American writers and artists who were part of the “Great Migration” from the South made Harlem the site of their own cultural renaissance. But for the modernist Yiddish poets, whose personal points of origin lay scattered across Eastern Europe where war and political upheaval sealed the doors against any return, the anonymous city became the literal material for their sustenance and art. Their “initiation” into its chaos did not induce anomie, alienation, or amnesia: it produced poetry.[9] “From the driving, tumultuous pulses of jackhammers and spade—here is our poem. In the chaos of a dug-up foundation. In a plowed-up estate of the city. And as the wall is built and the tower is built, we must build our poem” (Kurts 11).

For *Inzikh* in particular, the chaos, fragmentation, and mechanical materiality of the city were to be embraced. In their manifesto they say: "In our age of the big metropolis and enormous variety in all domains, [the real life of the human being] becomes a thousandfold more complicated and entangled. We Introspectivists feel the need to convey and express it" (775).

As far as how much Introspectivist poems reflected this "platform," Glatshteyn himself admits that *Inzikh* poets weren't terribly consistent. "In 1920 or earlier, in 1919, when we began . . . we were hardly that familiar with American poetry. There were general tones at that time that one absorbed even if he read only one or two new poets in other languages. . . . We were groping. So we sat down, like big-city sophisticated poets, to create a discipline for ourselves, a theory without a program. But we were . . . only about fifty percent consistent with our made-to-order theory" (Tabachnik 47).

While *Inzikh's* founders were "groping" in 1919, Mikhl Likht was already publishing poems—in English (under a pseudonym). In 1926, the little magazine *Undzer Bukh* reports that Likht "knows excellently the field of American literature and is especially 'at home' when he talks about modern American poetry."[10] The poet who took chaos seriously was Likht.

Who was Mikhl Likht? He was described by Yiddish critics as: "The most solid Yiddish verse-and-word-virtuoso of the twentieth century" and as an "incomprehensible 'babbler' and mere 'scribbler' "; as an "individualistic rebel, [creeping] all the deeper into the extremes of modernism" and, framed positively, as someone who "doesn't go in the well-trod paths of most poets."[11]

Born in a Ukrainian village in 1893, he came to the United States in 1913 and died here at the age of sixty in 1953. At the time of his death, he hadn't been productive as a writer for nearly twenty years, because of a degenerative heart condition. His best work, according to Yitskhok Libman, appeared in the 1925–1930 issues of *Undzer Bukh* (which Libman edited), a modernist "little magazine" similar to *Inzikh.* Glatshteyn called Likht the "most forgotten" of Yiddish writers; yet at his death he received "poetic justice": an obituary in the *New York Times,* detailing his entire oeuvre (Glatshteyn "*Poetishe,*" first page).

Likht's colleague and close friend Minkov wrote in a foreword to the poet's translations of American verse: "American English poetry was very close to Likht. As a poet, he himself ripened during its renaissance. He began his poetic journey with poems in English, published in the most modern avant-garde journals. . . . Even after crossing over completely into Yiddish poetry, he still took a deep interest in every publication of American English poetry. . . .

[H]e read everything that was published in American poetry. What he liked, he translated (9)."[12] More than thirty of his translations from the works of poets as diverse as Carl Sandburg, Ezra Pound, Wallace Stevens, and Mina Loy, were published as a collection after his death (*Moderne Amerikaner Poezie*, 1954); many of them first appeared in issues of *Undzer Bukh* in 1927.

Likht "began" in English—was it his third, fourth, or fifth language? Russian, German, French, and Italian rumble around in his poems. He "crossed over completely" into Yiddish. It was his choice, as it was the choice of his colleagues from *Inzikh*, who had also attended college in New York and knew English quite well. Did he feel most at-home in Yiddish? "His poems read as if he's thinking in English and writing in Yiddish," a professor of Yiddish literature once told me. What does "home" mean, in a poetry like Likht's?

where does the Jew go
goy, where
somewhere echo nowhere

(somewhere) with 36 righteous volumes
crammed with hints one and zeroes in number
with astrological sign-shrouds
the whole kit-and-kaboodle in-the-beginning things
with pure reason thoroughly explicated
with history (the Rebbe with his leather whip)
with samovars ships
telephone and radio . . .

(*Gezamlte Lider*, 127–128)[13]

Even if all you know about Yiddish is that it's written in Hebrew letters from right to left, you notice something different about many of Likht's poems: there are blank spaces in the middle of lines; lines scatter across a page; some poems look like prose, others like an indented list. English words, citations, quotations, pop up here and there. No other Yiddish poets, no matter how "modern" their style, have poems that look quite like this.

Likht's words "somewhere 'echo' nowhere": the poet who wrote Yiddish in a force-field of English, who translated T. S. Eliot, Ezra Pound, Gertrude Stein, who best represents a *threshold poetics*, is also the "most forgotten." His poetic practice, his enthusiastic and dense essays on American literature, his translations, all bring him so close to the American word. Why aren't his poems found in English translation? Why is he (ironically) so unknown, on *both* sides of the threshold?

"They talked about Mikhl Likht's poetry around the [café] table. One threw out the well-known phrase: 'His poetry is not comprehensible.' . . . Colleagues defended him, not the way you'd defend somebody mediocre, but a great poet" (Tenenboym 475).

Imagine entering a Yiddish literary café, "the land of Yiddish writers in America" as it existed inside the twenty-foot by forty-foot space of (for example) Café Europa, on East Broadway in lower Manhattan. It's a transforming space, as Chaver Paver suggests; once you've been inside the café, it changes your relationship to the rest of New York, to America itself: when you go back outside, "you're already on the other side of the border, in an alien country" (Paver 178). Café Europa, Café Royale, Goodman and Levine's, Sholem's, the cafés gleam in memory (that is, in the memoirs of writers who are themselves just memory, right now, such as Khaver Paver or Ruben Iceland), each with its particular literary and political affiliations, a din of gabbing voices, all serving terrible food. The café is a place where "you might listen and discover something about poetry or stories, because the talk on literary topics never came to a stop" (Iceland 300). In Café Europa, where young, impoverished writers gather, you can eat "on credit," or linger for hours over tea with no one insisting that you order more food (Paver 183–184).

In Paver's memoir, the café is described as a place where poets hungry for culture flock, congregating as at the "rebbe's *tish*" (the rabbi's table). Avrom Reyzen's table, for example, was "the greatest yeshiva" (house of study); additional tables and chairs were often added to accommodate the young "students." There, one offered interpretations and engaged in hair-splitting Talmudic discussion, all about a poem or a story, and Reyzen dispensed approval and gentle criticism to the young writers (178–179). Paver adds that "other little tables were also like yeshivas. There were a lot of 'rebbes' in Café Europa, and each 'rebbe' presided over a separate table"—Zishe Landoy, at *Di Yunge*'s table and Glatshteyn or Leyeles at *Inzikh*'s (179).[14]

Come with me into the café, one I've constructed that gathers many writers together, so we can eavesdrop on their conversation and get a clearer understanding of their opinions of their colleague Mikhl Likht.

Here's what the poet Zishe Landoy has to say about Mikhl Likht's poetry. "When I receive a new number of *Undzer Bukh,* I stretch myself out on the sofa and start reading, first of all, of course, Mikhl Likht. True, I don't understand it at all, but it's still very good!" (Libman 27).

From a nearby table, Yankev Glatshteyn reminds us that "once Mikhl Likht was [nearly] famous for his unpopularity . . . His incomprehensibility was renowned. If one wanted to make fun of modern Yiddish poetry, one brought examples from his poems." Glatshteyn adds (you can imagine, with a superior sniff): "There was a lot of material in Likht's poems for easy laughs. The poet went his own way and it didn't matter to him that one used him as a stick to beat the new Yiddish poem over the head" (*"Poetishe"* second page). Yet Glatshteyn himself (now one of the sharper voices in the room) had not only been an innovator, he had even worked with Likht on an offshoot of *Inzikh*, a little magazine called *"Loglen"* that lasted for four issues.

A rush of other voices join in: "[Likht] didn't find his own way, he got lost in foreign paths"; "he . . . searched and searched and got drawn into his own searching. It didn't matter to him that he had ceased to find . . . He also didn't invite an audience to his search expeditions and he went alone."[15]

Where, in other words, is Likht's sense of responsibility to Yiddish poetry? Despite *Inzikh*'s proud denials on the subject of whether or not they cared that they had such few readers, there's still a feeling here that Likht, in his self-absorption, crossed a line. The charge of *umfarshtandlekhkayt*—incomprehensibility—stings. Tenenboym speaks up in Likht's defense: "Why should 'clarity' be the standpoint for judging poetry?" (476–477).

Leyeles, one of the originators of *Inzikh*, has much to say on the subject of incomprehensibility in poetry. The fact that he is talking at still another table about his colleague Minkov doesn't prevent us from drawing his words into the debate. He says that the whole question of whether a poet's work is comprehensible or not has no relation to a "deep" poet's work. Rather, "it's a question of the level of development of the reader, and also of the language. What seems hard to understand in one time will be self-explanatory in another time." Leyeles recalls how, in 1910, Dr. Chaim Zhitlovsky—"a serious and believable witness, no?"—said about the poets of *Di Yunge* that they wanted their poems accompanied by a commentary. "Without a commentary, that is, he found them incomprehensible. . . . Dear God, what could possibly have been incomprehensible about these poets?"

After the laughter dies down, Leyeles adds, "But let's not fool ourselves, every poet has incomprehensibilities . . . Incomprehensibility is in truth a very relative concept. To be understood by all is not at all possible. To reject a poet because one doesn't understand him is in one sense not always a charge against that poet." Poetry doesn't have a big circle of readers in any language, and in Yiddish this seems especially the case, where "the artistic word has developed quicker than the artistic sense of the Yiddish reader" ("Minkov" 113–115).

Leyeles adds, as he has so often in his writings, "the word itself is a piece of chaos" ("Minkov" 111). "Chaos" and a kaleidoscopic quality that refracts the world through the prism of the individual poet's consciousness are tenets of Introspectivism (see Harshav *Meaning*, 175–186). To the innocent eavesdropper, it seems that all Likht is "guilty" of is carrying out to the *n*th degree what *Inzikh* itself proposed, from its earliest manifesto on. To illustrate, here's an excerpt from "Procession One" (*Gezamlte Lider,* 68–69):

[G]
here a dot of fire presents itself: I
          lie helpless
          on my back:
diagonal.
Is velocity Einsteinian?
                    (I got a yen
                    to cause destruction
                    with my "knowledge."
Put it on my ego's account
[and it shows further
an egotistical ego
that I failed to record
in the right spot].—)[16]
a fire-twinkle twinkles fires:
it fires twinkles
                    more and more.

A bow of fire-twinkles twinkles:
fire fires fire-fire twinkles.
twinkle-twinkle-fire.
                    twinkles.
                    twinkling fire.
fiery twinkling twinkling twinkling—twinkling fire—fire
twinkles of fire: twinkles of fire: fire twinkles:
twink-twink-twinkling fire—fire—twink
fire-twinks twinkle twinkles

a whole ring enchained locks:
enflamed with fire on fire-twinkles.
a twinkle extinguishes itself somewhere: pure:
fire—twinkle—pure. twinkle. pure.
          pure fire. twink. pure. pure.
twinkle. pure. twink.
pure—
twink—
pure.
twink.
                              fire's out

How do you read a poem that *does* what this one does? I read it for its playfulness with language: a *pintl fayer,* a twinkle (point or dot) of fire (which recalls *dos pintele Yid,* the tiny spark of “Jew” in every Jewish soul), is here an “I”—an ego—helpless as Kafka’s Gregor Samsa, lying on its back. The only “velocity” I can find here is that of words, of nouns and verbs that change back and forth (in a way difficult for the translation to show), in a play of relativity. As Tenenboym comments, “There is time in [Likht’s poems]. Expansion of space, place is there” (481). Poet Yankev Stoldosky draws the comparisons: “In Science—Einstein. In English literature—James Joyce. In Yiddish literature—Mikhl Likht” (5; YIVO).

In Cynthia Ozick’s story, “Envy, or Yiddish in America”—whose subject, the volcanically frustrated Yiddish poet Edelshtein, is unable to find a translator for his writing (and who, some critics contend, was based on Glatshteyn himself, long after his youthful engagement with modernism), the poet complains: “Pour in symbolism, impressionism, be complex, be subtle, be daring, take risks, break your teeth—whatever you do, it still comes out Yiddish. *Mama loshen* doesn’t produce *Wastelands.* No alienation, no nihilism, no dadaism. With all the suffering no smashing! NO INCOHERENCE!” (82).

“It still comes out Yiddish”: on the level of language, my own native-English ear doesn’t—cannot—understand the comic/ironic implications. Coming to Yiddish as a learned language (like French, like Spanish), rather than one I was born into, I have found in Mikhl Likht’s poetry alienation, nihilism, Dadaism; in his nine-poem sequence of “Protsesiyes” (“Processions”), his version of the modernist long poem, I have found his *statement*—akin to Eliot’s “The Wasteland,” or Pound’s “Cantos.” Perhaps it’s lucky for me that Yiddish does not automatically possess the humble earthiness that distresses Ozick’s fictional modernist. Or that posed problems for the “real” poets, as Glatshteyn comments: “American Yiddish . . . had hardly a language of poetry. That language had to be created. And where was it created? In a country totally dedicated to payday and paycheck and Americanized Yiddish. . . . We Yiddish poets . . . were linguistically obstinate. We created the language of poetry along with our poems” (Tabachnik 44).

And even Glatshteyn wrote, in a poem published as late as 1929: “I would catalogue all that is *incomprehensible* / with the flutter of a word” (my emphasis; *Kredos* 39).

In the 1920s and even into the mid-1930s, Likht was not alone in engaging in language play, at the risk of the gradual alienation of an audience of readers. But larger issues loomed, as the world lurched to war in Europe; more was at stake in Yiddish poetry. Beginning around 1938, Glatshteyn’s poetic "seismograph" began to sense and record the "collective terror of a generation" in poems like his foreboding "*Vegener*" ("Wagons"), and his angry farewell to cosmopolitanism and re-embrace of the Jewish ghetto, "*A Gute Nakht, Velt*" ("Good Night, World") (Tabachnik 49). Likht's "crime," if any, was that he *persisted* in his poetic experiments long after the acceptable historical moment.

But to return to our imaginary café: from one corner, Fershlayser has more to say about Likht's keeping to his own course of "ultra-individualism" in pursuit of the "extremes of modernism." While Likht's companions—e.g., Glatshteyn and Leyeles—Fershlayser claims, "matured" out of "egotistical, introspective, individualist . . . experimentation"; they gained the consciousness that, by being a Jewish writer, "*one bears responsibility for the whole of Israel*" (102, 121; my emphasis).

The air in the café is darkening, like ominous clouds rolling across the skies of Europe. Yiddish modernist poetry, a rebellious upstart in a cultural milieu where a proletarian and certainly a religious collectivity had never dissolved, was always dancing on thin ice. "Obligation" was thrust back on Glatshteyn and other poets by circumstances in Russia and Poland, by Stalin and Hitler . . . What is the difference between a *Jewish* writer and a *Yiddish* writer? *Can* one split the two? They are the same, a single Yiddish word with a double meaning—and yet the "yoke" that Fershlayser mentions, and "*klal Yisroel* (the whole of Israel)" are freighted heavily toward the *Jewish* sense of Yiddish. In the café, the accusation is never directly stated, but present all the same: that Likht has betrayed his own people, by pursuing an exploration of Yiddish as a modern, intensely personal, artistic medium, in the face of the "modern" world, which persecutes Jews.

What's more, the activity of translation itself becomes suspect. In 1935, just three years after Likht's book of "Processions" appeared, Glatshteyn published an essay entitled "*Di Marsh tsu di Goyim*" ("The March to the Gentiles") in *Inzikh*, in which he criticizes in the harshest terms Yiddish writers who attempt to get themselves translated into English: they are "vulgar assimilators" (Wisse, *Language* 142). According to Wisse, Glatshteyn is arguing that "the greatest literature is essentially national, its greatness being that which is least translatable." "Incomprehensibility" comes amazingly full-circle here, as Wisse describes Glatshteyn's final volume of experimental poetry, *Yidishtaytshn*, published in 1937, as "poems that resist translation by seeking out the specificities of language . . . [b]urrowing into Yiddish" (143). The opacity of Yiddish, making it incomprehensible (let's say) to a prospective translation into English, is here applauded as an act of national resistance.

Likht's *umfarshtandlekhkayt*, at first a source of frustration and comedy, becomes by the late 1930s a transgression, because his "burrowing" participates in *multiplicity*—it assumes universality. As the historic moment of Yiddish modernist experiment recedes and Likht does not alter his poetics, he is perceived as having shaken off the "yoke" of Jewish responsibility. No matter how much he incorporates into his writing images and scenes from a Ukrainian village boyhood—his adherence to a modernist mode of writing, a style that thinks in English as much as it writes in Yiddish, ultimately makes him a target of disdain within his community and among his writing colleagues. And that is not the only realm in which he experiences isolation. Likht's engagement and identification with a larger Anglo/American modernism is evident in his active pursuit of translation, from English into Yiddish. The ironies of Likht's position, as he seeks to bridge American and Yiddish worlds, are painfully clear when one reads his correspondence with English-speaking poets, relating to translation.

In 1927, at age thirty-four, Likht writes a series of letters, in English, to poets who are Anglo-modernism's stars, requesting permission to translate some of their works into Yiddish. The letters are chatty a bit beyond what one might imagine would be the interest of the people receiving them. On February 7, 1927, Likht writes to George Platt Lynes, Esq., at The As Stable Publications in New Jersey, which publishes Gertrude Stein. I offer a long quotation from Likht's letter, interspersed with my own questions and comments:[17] "'Unser Buch,' the publication I am associated with presently, was ordered by me to be sent to you. I hope that its perusal by you through some intelligent Yiddish channels will render a satisfactory literary impression of its contents." Who were the "intelligent Yiddish channels" to whom Likht was referring here? Were they contacts that Likht provided to Lynes? Or did Likht expect Lynes himself to locate "intelligent" Yiddish readers? Likht continues: "However, there is a possibility of a new group-alignment. The publication that may thus result will probably be of a more exclusive nature. For years, we have been aiming at a stricter literary and critical vehicle. Once achieved, the work of Miss Stein in such a magazine should have even a more heightened effect." It is interesting that Likht feels the need to reassure Lynes, lest the publisher find the current magazine not up to critical par. Yet—one wonders why it would matter to Lynes that the magazine (already a modernist organ in the Yiddish community) be of a yet "more exclusive nature." In a sense, "Unser Buch" (Undzer Bukh) is highly "exclusive," because it excludes any non-Yiddish reader.

After two short paragraphs dealing with obtaining Stein's permission for the translations, Likht continues: "Description of Literature is in the writer's less dense vein. As a Steinite it gave me pleasure to read and re-read it. Meseems that your experimental activity with pamphlets of this kind is very laudable. It is to be hoped that you find no discouragement in your enterprise." It is only in this last paragraph that we (and Lynes) learn which Stein piece Likht is interested in translating. Likht's use of archaic English—"meseems"—and the passive voice "(It is to be hoped") give this part of the letter an exaggeratedly elevated tone (at least to my contemporary ear). The tone adds to the sense one gets from the letter as a whole, of the poet's attempting to approach Lynes colleague-to-colleague, an equal across the language threshold.

As a "Steinite," Likht was no doubt thrilled to received a letter dated March 1, 1927, direct from Paris, from Stein herself, consisting of three sentences and permission to translate "Description of Literature" and from *Geography and Plays* into Yiddish.[18] T. S. Eliot's response to Likht's inquiry, dated March 11, 1927, expresses "not the slightest objection to your translating ["Translation and the Individual Talent"] into Yiddish and printing [it] in your periodical." He adds: "I shall be very glad to see a copy of the magazine in which the essays appear, although I regret that I shall be unable to read it."

On March 15, 1927, Likht shoots off a two-page letter to American novelist James Branch Cabell, informing him of his translation of *Jurgen*. "You are doubtless interested in the 'who's who' instrumental in the bringing about of this version in book form," writes Likht. After a paragraph on the two figures who constitute the publishing firm, Likht describes himself as: "given to the infrequent fashioning of extremely unpopular, devoid of readership, Yidish [*sic*] verse." There's a note of (false) humility but also of a strange pride in this self-representation. But while his own poems are "devoid of [Yiddish] readership," Likht's translation into Yiddish of Cabell's book will also lack a certain highly important reader, the author Cabell himself. "I greatly deplore that the person who, under the circumstances, might have been my most sympathetic reader will, for obvious reasons, leave the translation unread," Likht writes, and adds: "Surely we who write in Yiddish are as human as the creators and re-creators in any other language. Yet to us is denied the satisfaction of sharing with our translated authors that intimate, unalloyed communion which author and translator of any other two languages enjoy."

When Cabell writes back to Likht scarcely a week later, returning to him a copy of the Yiddish translation that Likht has sent to him, "inscribed, I hope, at the correct end of the volume," he adds: "I only wish that I could congratulate you upon the good taste and the fidelity which I am sure your version maintains, but unluckily all I can read of it is the numerals in the chapter headings, a circumstance which deplorably limits the possibilities of praise.” Cabell’s remark has a comedic cast that Likht’s comment lacks (“Surely we who write in Yiddish are as human”). Layers of incomprehensibility lie between Likht and Cabell, and indeed between Likht and all his English-speaking correspondents. Their responses to Likht’s translating their work into Yiddish boil down to “thanks, and too bad I can’t read it,” displaying no curiosity in following up on anything Likht has said about himself, his own writing, or his lack of a readership in Yiddish. Yet while Likht complained bitterly about not getting a hearing from Yiddish critics, and ostentatiously dismissed the need for a “reader” (see *“Entfer af a Kritiker,”* Response to a Critic, 1956)—his correspondence betrays no complaints about any of the Anglo-modernist writers. Indeed, he seems eager to present himself to them, to give them a taste of who he is, as if to say: “You can’t comprehend my writing, because it’s in Yiddish: but I am more like you than you could imagine.”

As Likht reaches over the threshold of English/Yiddish, to draw modernist American poetry into Yiddish, one can recall the very different attitude of the editors of *Poetry* magazine in 1923, when they queried *Inzikh* as to whether their literary journal was written in Chinese (Harshav, *AYP* 798). Yiddish is “Chinese” to English readers—that is, utterly foreign and incomprehensible. Meanwhile, Likht’s own poetry is “Chinese” to Yiddish readers, as Tenenboym writes: “To upstanding, solid, conservative readers, Mikhl Likht’s poem . . . is—Chinese or Turkish” (481). Likht’s own poetry lacks readers in either Yiddish or English because of what it attempts, before stubbornly conservative readers, and because of its own stubborn Yiddishness.

At the same time, Likht’s writing imagines an audience of radical, English readers. “You are the audience to whom Likht was writing,” a Yiddish professor suggested, when he handed me a pile of Likht’s books, their pages not yet cut though they were published more than forty years earlier. At the time I was no more than a toddler in Yiddish—but then, as now, I was a poet, sharing with Likht the activity of a poetry that refuses easy “translation.” Likht labored over his translations of Marianne Moore, William Carlos Williams, Emily Dickinson. It’s time to return the favor, for his poems.

From Procession 3
for Yankev Beri

A1[19]

pindar pindar
rusty strings
from the old Jewish harp

to the Ukrainian lute[20]
with bloodshot eyes
cataract-eyes
pus-pouring
a fence for a hat
UZYALI BRATYA YAWSEFA
HAWTILI YAWKHAW ZABEETI[21]
pennies fall[22]

groshns hail down
with yellow rust
                        breadcrumbs in pants pockets

see
look through
through the
through the extraordinary fairs
gathered through lice-infested clothes
filthy with blood
            Dubno horse-fair
            Yarmelinitz diamond-silk-fair
the seller to the buyer
with a spit on the hem[23]
a copper coin
                        "it should all go well!"
the *shul* pulls with leaky walls[24]
prays the Afternoon Service[25]
prays   sings
multiplies, praying   singing
blesses God for surviving
        for misfortune's fortunate outcome
arm in arm with his God
(churchbells from mountain steeples)

stretches out hands
gropes in the dark
Jew   *goy*[26]

Jew   where are you going
goy   where

B1

where does the Jew go
goy, where
somewhere echo nowhere

(somewhere) with 36 righteous volumes[27]
crammed with hints one and zeroes in number
with astrological sign-shrouds
the whole kit-and-kaboodle in-the-beginning things[28]
with pure reason thoroughly explicated
with history (the Rebbe with his leather whip)
with samovars ships
telephone and radio

your hand brother misfortune (and how much have you collected already
for the Keren HaYesod?)[29]
the heavy doing-hand writes prescriptions chips away quartz[30]
plastered about somewhere echo nowhere
me to you entirely equal: somewhere-in-nowhere

child with mother-nipple in mouth
old man with pipe-stem in mouth
mother dies
old man dies
the young one hopes to educate death
to die to leave forlorn
the wormy raw earth[31]

C1

come come weak eagle come
wrapped in periphrases, rags
schematic hum[32]
hand over the mothers and fathers

conceal for a minute
a gas-bill demanding cents[33]
Atlantic? fine Pacific? good
any new ships?

I'm guilty   one sin:
bathing in slothful gossip[34]
not my neighbor's wife   not his ox
do I long for in my prayers

a bird   firedove   where
is Mother Rachel's grave?
Shabbes without delight   no weekly rest
the body's mystical members   one member[35]

the poor man by the door
must wait long hours
I am busy   one thought
lies in my head: customers bringing sales

my head lies in a caress
not on the *Shekhine*'s[36]   but foolish on my beloved's breast
a *shatnes* pants-belt   no pretty ritual sash[37]
divides heavenly from earthly

folds of scabrous night-nap
on a pillow white as down   black as pitch
ah!   I know my desolate offering[38]
my bulgar-with-beans feast

[Interlude]
my beloved little old village   on a rolling hill[39]
of the nearby Carpathians
tossed
a fatal handful of your poor clay huts
like a small bunch of horse-trampled field-flowers
now (no longer hearing) I see your stillness that trickles echoless
across the little river of the priest's orchard
across the school   up to the mountain with the spacious Christian cemetery[40]
like a pointed *yarmulke* on the mountain's head
now I see the little street where one *Pesakh* eve at dusk[41]

the urge seized me to pluck hair
from a horse's tail for a fiddle-bow
and I succeeded in getting my brow

into a sudden, bloody kiss with a horse's hoof
and spoiled my whole people's holiday
now I remember the old priest's burial
his heirs came running together from the ends of the earth
seeking a share of the poor village diocese:
the son from a great city with paved streets
in a godforsaken village rainstorm
one daughter the wife of a high-placed official
who lives off a great income
in a miasmatic village bureau[42]
another from somewhere else "a greater more beautiful life"
all:
after a share of the village diocese inheritance
and Vasil rascal:
wretched blundering thief
(caught him red-handed, she did, the Belizorke storekeeper, with a bit of unpaid-for soap in his goyish hairy bosom he didn't
argue too much answered back: "the demon
tempted me the cursed spirit not my fault
dear Hinde not my fault blame the devil

ah Vasil!

ah buried priest!

ah rare still nights with *shikse*-song[43]
with *sheygets*-whistle in my poor exotic wild
Ukrainian village
pray for your "prosperous" "all achieving" countryman
on Broadway[44]

Notes

1. "*Umfarshtandlekh*" is also defined as "unintelligible" in both Harkavy and Weinreich. Although Weinreich prefers "*nit tsu farshteyn*" for "incomprehensible," I use "*umfarshtandlekh,*" because it is the word that was commonly used by poets and critics in Yiddish literary discourse.

2. From "Interlude," in Procession Three. All translations of poems and prose passages are mine unless from Harshav's *American Yiddish Poetry* (AYP) and otherwise indicated.

3. "Minor" as distinguished from "major" in the commonsense meaning of the term.

4. Harshav notes that *"In zikh"* was eventually contracted into one word, *Inzikh.* The movement became known as *"Inzikhism"* and the poets as *Inzikhists* (*Meaning* 177). For ease of reading, I will use the contraction throughout this essay.

5. In his introduction to *Proletpen, America's Rebel Yiddish Poets* (edited by Amelia Glacer and David Weintraub), Dovid Katz puts two of the "generations"—*Di Yunge* and the *Inzikhistn*—into one "period" of "reaction against poetry for the sake of the labor movement, and the quest for genuine art" (6). He constructs the third "period" as running from the 1920s to the early years of the second World War and as encompassing writers for whom socialist politics was a predominant concern in their poetic art.

6. It's important to note that the word *Yiddish* means both "Jewish" and "Yiddish." The article from which this quote is taken is entitled *"Yidishe Kunst"*—or, as Harshav translates it, "Jewish Art." Harshav footnotes his translation: "Here, as elsewhere, it is impossible to translate the identity of the two notions, 'Yiddish' and 'Jewish,' in the author's argument, since in the original only one word is used for both" (790). Still, it is clear that of the two meanings of "Yiddish," the *Inzikhists* chose to foreground language and secular culture above religious or national identity.

7. From Procession One, section A.

8. From *"Faronfang"* ("Beforebeginning").

9. I do not know if this is the case for Yiddish modernists who remained in Europe. The New York-based poets had much in common with their European counterparts; some critics discuss the groups together, as exponents of an international Yiddish modernism (e.g., see Kronfeld 195). For more on the European Yiddish modernists, see Kronfeld, Wolitz (1987) and (1991), and Alt (1991).

10. Minkov cites Likht's poems in English in his introduction to Likht's translations, *Moderne Amerikane Poeziye* (1954). This latter comes from the contributors' notes for the January–February 1926 issue.

11. First set of quotes: Libman (25) and Sh. Niger (quoted in Libman, 26); second set, Fershlayser (102) and Tenenboym (480).

12. Minkov edited and published volumes of Likht's collected poems, essays, and translations after the poet's death.

13. From section B(1) in "Procession Three."

14. I should note that Paver is mixing separate streams in Jewish tradition, when he refers in one breath to the "rebbe's *tish*"—found among Chassidim—and "yeshivas," which are the traditional study houses of *misnagdim,* Orthodox Jews who reject the mysticism of the Chassidim.

15. Fershlayser (102); Glatshteyn *"Poetishe"* (first page).

16. Brackets and parentheses are as in the original Yiddish.

17. All correspondence excerpted in this section, whether from Likht or from writers who were corresponding with him, is found in the Mikhl Likht Archive at the YIVO Institute for Jewish Research in New York City.

18. Likht's translation of "Description of Literature" appeared in the September/October 1927 issue of *Undzer Bukh.*

19. Sections in the original are marked by a single letter: "*alef*" (A), "*beys*" (B), and so on. In order to distinguish the first set of sections from the set, similarly marked, that follow the Interlude, I also number them, as follows: A1, B1, C1.

20. Slavic word: Ukrainian "*kobze.*" Kobze is the Ukrainian name of this lute-like instrument.

21. Transliteration of these two lines, which appear in Ukrainian in the original and mean: "Then the brothers took Joseph / And wanted to kill him."

22. "*Deneshkes,*" which I have translated as "pennies," appear be a kind of coin, like "*groshn*" in the line that follows. I could not find it in the dictionaries, and my sources were not familiar with this word.

23. According to the late Dr. Eli Katz, it was a common Slavic folk custom at the fair, when completing a deal, to spit in one's hand. Spitting on the "lap or skirt of a garment" (which I have translated here as "hem")—"*shpay in pole*"—appears to be Likht's rendition of this custom (especially since it's followed by "*zol zayn mit glik*" (it should go well).

24. "*Shul*": synagogue, which I have kept in the original for the sound quality. "*Tselekhste vent,*" which I have translated as "leaky walls," could possibly be translated as "yearning walls." "*Lekhtsn*" means "yearn or long for" (Harkavy 28); "*tselekhste*" means "full of leaks; languid, faint" (Harkavy 432). A Yiddish reader would absorb both senses of the word.

25. In the version of the poem that appeared in "1925," there is an extra line:

di shul tsit mit tselekhste vent	the shul pulls with leaky walls
dem koyne onem shpay	the buyer without his spit
davent minkhe	prays the Afternoon Service

Here, "the buyer" is in the accusative case (*dem koyne*—instead of the nominative *der koyne*), meaning that he is the direct object of the *shul*'s "pulling."

26. Throughout, I choose to translate "*Yid*" as Jew and to retain "*goy*"—which means non-Jew, but has a negative cast. There is a different Yiddish word for "Christian," but Likht has chosen "goy" in creating an apposition to "Jew." Later in the poem, where Likht refers to female non-Jews as "*shikses*" and males as "*shkotsim*" (plural of *sheygets*), I have retained the Yiddish original—again to emphasize the sense of a difference that is not simply "gentile."

27. The number, which is represented by the Hebrew letters "*lamed*" and "*vav,*" also refers to the "*lamedvavnikim*"—the thirty-six righteous people who, according to legend, are born each generation, and whose existence prevents the world from being destroyed. Because "36 volumes" would not suggest any of this, I inserted the word "righteous."

28. "*Bereshisdike,*" which means literally "in-the-beginningish," Weinreich translates as "primeval." "*Breyshis*" is the Hebrew word meaning "in the beginning" and is the first word of the Jewish bible.

29. *"Keren haYesod"*: the Jewish National Fund, which financed the purchase of land in Palestine.

30. Thanks to Dr. Raphael Finkel, who found the meaning of *"kizels"* (quartz) from a colleague in Melbourne, Australia.

31. Footnote 2 in Likht's "1925" version appeared here, beginning with two Ukrainian words, which, according to my source, Slava Nedelin, refer to a small town in the Ukraine, famous for its fair and mentioned by many Russian writers: "Savrotchinkisi": "The cord connecting all folk writers since Gogol and his collegial contemporaries: and later: Gorvunov, Saltikov-Tshedrin. The first Yiddish storytellers, folkwriters: Mendeli, Dineson, Spektor. The first works of Ash, Reyzen, others. The *kheder* [Jewish religious school for young children] from the youngest years. Local literature, cheap (*'lubotshne'*) publications. [*Lubotshne:* a Russian word that Likht spells phonetically in the Yiddish. According to Nedelin, it means low-class, badly educated.] Calendars: folk sayings, fantastic stories. The line: 'and how much have you collected for the *Keren haYesod'* and the word 'radio' is [*sic*] the only little inlet from another environment and later time." [I have translated as "fantastic" Likht's expression: *"nit geshtoygn, nit gefloygn,"* an earthy saying that literally means "didn't ascend, didn't fly" but is used idiomatically to mean "never happened," or "isn't true" (E. Katz).]

32. Anglicisms: *"p*erifrazn" and "skematisher" in the Yiddish.

33. Anglicisms: "*gaz-bil*" and "*sentn*" in the Yiddish.

34. Dr. David Roskies points out that "Tuneyadevker" is a reference to the fictional town in Mendele Mokher-Sforim's *The Travels of Benjamin III* (personal correspondence, October 16, 2006).

35. From the Hebrew: *"remakh evrim,"* which I have translated as "all the body's members," is defined in Harkavy as "the 248 members (number of the members of the human body according to the belief of the ancients)" (479).

36. Jewish mystical term, from the Hebrew: *"Shekhine,"* the divine presence, manifestation of God; the word and its connotation are feminine.

37. Term from Jewish law, Hebrew origin: *"shatnes,"* is defined by Weinreich as "mixed linen and wool, forbidden to Orthodox Jews" (411). That is, they are prohibited by Jewish law from wearing garments that are *shatnes.* I have translated *"tekheles-gartl"* as ritual sash. *"Gartl"* refers to the sash or belt worn by Chassidic men, representing the division between "upper" (spiritual) and "lower" (physical, sexual) realms. Likht attaches to *"gartl"* the adjective *"tekheles,"* which is the Hebrew word for "light blue," but I am not aware of a specially colored *"gartl"* in Chassidic garb.

38. *"Vistik ruml"* ("desolate offering"): *"ruml,"* according to Harkavy, means "assortment" related to merchandise, such as staples of the (religious) book trade.

39. Slavicism: *"brodyevke bergl"* ("rolling hill"). *"Brodyeven,"* according to my Russian sources, means to roll or wander. In Harkavy, *brodzen* is to wander or ramble; *brodyage* is a vagabond or tramp. In Weinreich, *brodyen* means to wade or plod. But

brodevke (without the "*yud*") means—wart! *Brodyevke* could also be the name of a region. In the "1925" version, the word is: "*borodovke.*"

40. "*Tsvinter*" ("Christian cemetery") refers to a non-Jewish cemetery only. Ironically, Likht chooses an adjective based on a Hebrew root for describing it as spacious—"*rekhovesdike*"—and also compares it, in the next line, to the Jewish male head-covering, the *yarmulke.*

41. "*Pesakh*"—Passover.

42. Anglicism: "*miasmatishe*" in the Yiddish. Slavicism: "*Bayure*" ("bureau"). Not found in any of my written sources, and my Russian sources could not identify it. I use "bureau" for its sound-similarity and its institutional connotation.

43. A *shikse* is a female *goy*—non-Jew. *Sheygets* (actually, "*shgotsim*") in the next line, refers to non-Jewish males.

44. Footnote 3 in Likht's "1925" version: "Simple personal memoirs."

Works Cited

Anonymous. "Reflections" (Vachel Lindsay). *Inzikh* 1 (March 1920).

Bernstein, Charles. "Reznikoff's Nearness." *Sulfur: Literary Bi-Annual of the Whole Art* 32 (Spring 1993): 6–40.

Boelhower, William. "Ethnographic Politics: The Uses of Memory in Ethnic Fiction." *Memory and Cultural Politics: New Approaches to American Ethnic Literatures.* Ed. Amritjit Singh, Joseph T. Skerrett Jr. and Robert E. Hogan. Boston: Northeastern University Press, 1996.

Fershlayser, Emanuel. "*Leyendik Mikhl Likhtn*" (Reading Mikhl Likht), in his *Oyf Shrayberishe Shliyakhn.* New York: Farlag ha-soyfer, 1958.

Glatshteyn, Yankev. (Jacob Glatstein.) *Kredos.* New York: *Farlag Yidish Lebn,* 1929. Column, Prost un Poshet. "Poetishe Gerekhtikayt" (Poetic Justice). Tog-Morgn-*Zhurnal,* Sunday, June 21, 1953. Mikhl Likht Archive, YIVO Institute for Jewish Research.

Harshav, Barbara, and Benjamin Harshav. *American Yiddish Poetry, A Bilingual Anthology.* Translations with the participation of Kathryn Hellerstein, Brian McHale, and Anita Norich. Berkeley and Los Angeles: University of California Press, 1986.

Harshav, Benjamin. *The Meaning of Yiddish.* Berkeley and Los Angeles: University of California Press, 1990.

Iceland, Reuben. (Ayzland, Ruvn.) "At Goodman and Levine's." *Voices from the Yiddish: Essays, Memoirs, Diaries.* Ed. Irving Howe and Eliezer Greenberg. New York: Schocken, 1975. 300–305.

Katz, Dovid. "Introduction: The Days of *Proletpen* in American Yiddish Poetry." *Proletpen: America's Rebel Yiddish Poets.* Ed. Amelia Glaser and David Weintraub; translated by Amelia Glaser, with illustrations by Dana Craft and special editorial assistance from Yankl Salant. Madison: University of Wisconsin Press / Dora Teitelboim Center for Yiddish Culture, 2005. 3–25.

Kurts, Sh. "*Vuhin geyen mir?*" (Where are we going?) *1926* 1, 2 (January/February 1926): 11–16.

Landis, Joseph. "Yiddish Dreams in America." *Handbook of American-Jewish Literature: An Analytical Guide to Topics, Themes and Sources.* Westport, CT: Greenwood Press, 1988. 143–165.

Leyeles, A. Glants. "N. B. Minkov; Minkov, tsu fuftsik yor (to his fiftieth year)." In Velt un Vort: Literarishe un Andere Eseyen. New York: Tsiko, 1958.

Libman, Yitskhok. (Yitschok Liebman.) Column: *Boyer un Shafer fun Mayn Dor* (Builders and Creators of My Generation). "Mikhl Likht." *Nyu-Yorker Vokhnblat.* Mikhl Likht Archive at YIVO Institute for Jewish Research. (Date not available; probably 1954.)

Likht, Mikhl. *Gezamlte Lider* (Collected Poems). Edited with an introduction by N. B. Minkov. Buenos Aires: *Farlag Gelye,* 1957.

Minkov, N. B. "*Nyu Yorker Briv*" (New York Letter) (November 1922)." *Inzikh* 3 (December 1922): 76–78.

———. Introduction. *Moderne Amerikaner Poeziye. Lider Ibergezetst fun Mikhl Likht* (Modern American Poetry. Poems Translated by Mikhl Likht). Ed. Minkov. Buenos Aires: *Farlag Gelye,* 1954.

Ozick, Cynthia. "Envy, or Yiddish in America." *The Pagan Rabbi and Other Stories.* New York: E. P. Dutton, 1961, 1983. 41–100.

Paver, Chaver. (Gershon Aynbinder.) *Gershon in Amerike* (Gershon in America). Warsaw: Yidish Bukh, 1963.

Sanders, Ronald. The Downtown Jews: Portraits of an Immigrant Generation. New York: Dover, 1969, 1987.

Stoldoski, Jacob. (Yankev Stoldosky.) "Mikhl Likht" (undated). Mikhl Likht Archive, YIVO Institute for Jewish Research.

Tabachnik, A (Abraham). "A Conversation with Jacob Glatstein." Trans. Joseph Landis. *Yiddish* 1, 1 (Summer 1973): 40–53.

Tenenboym, Shay. (S. Tenenbaum.) "Mikhl Likht." *Shnit fun Mayn Feld. Eseyen, dertseylungen, minyaturen* (Harvest: Essays, Stories and Miniatures). New York: Passantino Printing Co., 1949. 475–482.

Williams, Raymond. *The Politics of Modernism: Against the New Conformists.* Ed. and introduced by Tony Pinkney. London and New York: Verso Classics, 1989.

Wisse, Ruth R. *A Little Love in Big Manhattan: Two Yiddish Poets.* Cambridge, MA: Harvard University Press, 1988.

———. "Language as Fate: Reflections on Jewish Literature in America." *Literary Strategies: Jewish Texts and Contexts.* Studies in Contemporary Jewry, An Annual (XII). Ed. Ezra Mendelsohn. New York: Oxford University Press, 1996. 129–147.

Revisiting Charles Reznikoff's Urban Poetics of Diaspora and Contingency

Ranen Omer-Sherman

Who or what is not ultimately diasporic in Charles Reznikoff's (1894–1976) emotively restrained but deeply compassionate rendering of the universe? From *diaspeirein,* the Greek (mis)translation of the *galut* of Hebrew Scripture, are constituted "seed," "sperm," "dispersal," "spore"—all these evocative cognates and even more inventive variations are expressed in Reznikoff's secular and humanistic poetics of twentieth-century struggle.[1] In the stern threat that "the Lord will scatter you among all the peoples from one end of the earth to the other, and there you shall serve other gods, wood and stone, whom neither you nor your ancestors have experienced" (Deuteronomy 28:64), there seems little consolation, but in Reznikoff's work the humiliating connotations of *galut* or exile (abject dispossession, insatiable yearning for territorial restoration, subjugation under hostile empires) undergo a substantially American transvaluation and are in fact supplanted by the joys of cosmopolitanism and the ingenuity of adaptability and renewed life.[2] Ultimately, he employs "Diaspora" in nuanced forms that deepen his powerful commitment to the neglected histories of other urban subjects, particularly in his caustic responses to the forces of industrialization, poverty, and violence. Born to working-class immigrants, he was also frequent witness to the arrival and difficult adjustments endured by family members and other new Americans. Their prodigious labor and struggle to adapt to the new inspired Reznikoff's poetry of empathy and solidarity.

Revisiting the newly reprinted works I was recently struck by how profoundly this essential paradigm begins with personal knowledge; intensely alive to his family origins in the Russian-Jewish Diaspora, Reznikoff's lyrics often explore the displacements, traumas, and exile of parents, grandparents, and other relatives. This awareness entails a further development, as from this vulnerability derives the lyrics' forceful empathy for such marginal figures as immigrants, those made homeless by the Depression, the wage-slaves and others who suffer the privations of America's rapid industrialization; through all this reverberates a recognition that instability and precarious transformations are, more often than not, the shared condition of humanity. In a postmodern age of readers who increasingly find cultural vitality and lasting value in uncertainty, destabilized subjectivities, marginality, hybridity, and fragmentation, Reznikoff, who faced severe literary neglect throughout most of his life, should be recognized as one of the most innovative voices of the past century of American poetry. In his rigorous interrogations of the ways that the nation meant danger and marginality to many of its inhabitants in spite of its claims to be a guarantee of safe haven and equal rights, he is a socially engaged poet for our own precarious times of xenophobia and anxiety. Fortunately, with the recent reissue of *The Poems of Charles Reznikoff: 1918–1975* (Black Sparrow, 2005), the attention of important studies by critics such as Norman Finkelstein, Stephen Fredman, and Monique Vescia as well as a progressively stronger presence in recent anthologies such as *The Oxford Book of American Poetry* (Oxford University Press, 2006), it seems more likely than ever that his unadorned and distilled language of testimony will find an appreciative audience for years to come.[3]

Though rarely uprooting himself from New York, Reznikoff was nevertheless a consistently peripatetic poet in the tradition of Wordsworth (substituting the Romantic countryside with the Jewish urban), an indefatigable walker fiercely devoted to a daily practice of traversing ten or twenty miles among the tenements from where he reported the gritty news of a struggle in which animals and humans alike seem ill-fated:

Scared dogs looking backwards with patient eyes;
at windows stooping old women, wrapped in shawls;
old men, wrinkled as knuckles, on the stoops.

A bitch, backbone and ribs showing in the sinuous back,
sniffed for food, her swollen udder nearly rubbing along the pavement.

Once a toothless woman opened her door,
chewing a slice of bacon that hung from her mouth like a tongue.

This is where I walked night after night;
this is where I walked many years. (*Poems* 29)

The final couplet of this 1921 poem forms the raw and wounded rationale for his poetic vocation to which the decades of poems to follow proved astonishingly faithful, whether documenting the privations of common labor or the atrocities of the Holocaust. But in the early years, aside from such raw images of poverty (which often linger with an aching afterlife in the reader's mind), what one finds most throughout the poems are permutations of scatteredness. While this occurs in many of the expected places—modern immigrants, the urban homeless, the historic expulsions and exiles that preoccupied him—this paradigm is also strikingly apparent in Reznikoff's myriad approaches to the natural world and the mysterious processes of growth and decay that beset all beings and elements.

Even in Reznikoff's often startling attention to the birds and beasts that flourish in the urban jungle, "Diaspora" indelibly emerges as the dynamic paradigm that best expresses what he learns about the hidden rhythms of Nature itself. Birds migrating, stars in their celestial movements, even falling leaves in the apparent chaos of their descent—all participate in this melancholic rhythm of an unseen order as 1934's "Lament of the Jewish Women for Tammuz: Ezekiel VIII:14" bears witness with an almost scriptural weight in spite of its quotidian observations: "Now the white roses, wilted and yellowing fast, / hang in the leaves and briers. / Now the maple trees squander their yellow leaves; / and the brown leaves of the oak have left Ur and become wanderers. / Now they are scattered over the pavements— / the delicate skeletons of the leaves" (*Poems* 102). There is much more than a witty exercise of Jewish intertextuality expressed in this poem that embodies Reznikoff's genius at compression. Whereas these lines are eminently representative of the poet's oeuvre, insofar as they present us with the unsparing revelation that all beings and entities prove frail and vulnerable under the stern onslaught of Time, natural exigency, and even violent history, the gesture to Abraham's self-exile from Ur and subsequent desert wanderings in a poem that ostensibly describes seasonal change seems strange. But this biblical allusion is also a characteristic marker of the poet's expansive poetic vision, hinting that he finds a note of redemption in the losses he recounts.

Where is the source of consolation in the cumulative losses and dispersals the poet reports? When thinking about the salient role of uprootedness and dispersals in Reznikoff's poetry it has often struck me as immensely helpful to consider the late Emmanuel Levinas, who illuminates just why Abraham's loss of home and departure for the unknown is the foundational movement of ethical monotheism: "Above all Abraham is the one who knows how to receive and feed men, the one whose tent was open to the four winds. . . .

Abraham's descendants are men to whom their ancestor bequeathed a difficult tradition of duties toward the other, which we have never finished fulfilling, an order from which we are never released, but where duty takes on above all the form of obligation toward the body, the duty to feed and shelter . . . Abraham's descendants are men of all nations: every man who is truly a man is probably a descendant of Abraham."[4] It strikes me that Reznikoff's lyrics, in which ethnic Others, their migratory histories, and urban struggles are sympathetically portrayed, are intriguingly congruent with Levinas's ethics in important ways. In a sense distinctly congruent with Levinas's post-Holocaust insistence on the primacy of the individual's inexorable thrall to the stranger, Reznikoff does not presume a loving deity or even one remotely interested in the human world. In the absence of such a caring deity, Reznikoff's artlessly spare and unassuming work relies instead on the reader's collaborative sympathy and urgent witnessing of the American urban environment and the vulnerable state of its displaced or destabilized inhabitants, as in this oft-cited exemplar of his empathy for the homeless in "Cooper Union Library": "Men and women with open books before them— / and never turn a page: come / merely for warmth / not light" (*Poems* 190).[5] Or in the visceral desperation portrayed in these excruciating lines from the stark Depression-era poems: "Old men and boys search the wet garbage with fingers / and slip pieces in bags. / This fat old man has found the hard end of a bread / and bites it" (*Poems* 19). Drawing from his poetic vocation as a walker in the city, his early poems, though often stressing personal loneliness, are never acts of self-enclosure or solipsism, instead revealing a modest "me" that is always subject to disruption and exposure to the disturbance caused by other beings living in peril or extremity.[6] This is a poetics of acute responsibility.

There is simply no getting past the sheer shock of many of these poems, the composition of which seem to have prepared him to confront the brutal statements of the Eichmann and Nuremberg trials, ultimately translating their dormant archived material into the wrenching narratives of *Holocaust* which impress Kathryn Shevelow for their "photographically vivid images" of atrocity.[7] But Reznikoff's insistence on extending the reader's perception through documentary poetry of witness of the horrific particulars of the European genocide as well as America's own predilection for violence and racism (*Testimony* [1934]) ultimately depend on his abiding faith in what poetry might actually achieve in that wounded world. As Monique Claire Vescia cogently declares, "Reznikoff discloses the potential . . . for mutually sustaining communities that transverse socioeconomic and racial barriers. The evidence exists and may be retrieved, ironically enough, from within the records of humankind's inhumanity to itself."[8] It has long been a common presumption, particularly among Reznikoff's earliest critics, that the highly ethical intersubjective mode of his poetry compensates for an apparent reticence toward adopting conventional formulations of political advocacy (the embrace of which might undermine his lyrics' role for the reader's moral autonomy). The observation that Reznikoff's verse is distinguished by compassion for the plight of strangers, particularly ordinary people—the *kleine menshele*—has rightly been the catalyst for much critical commentary. In a similar vein, Michael Davidson reads Reznikoff's magnum opus of American history, *Testimony,* as a radically political act, "a critical reappraisal of nationhood."[9] Like Vescia, Davidson persuasively situates Reznikoff as "part of a new documentary culture, that was trying to 'brush history against the grain' by reading American history not as a narrative of Adamic discovery and perfectibility but as a material record of diverse constituencies" (140).[10] For instance, a compelling case can be made for linking Reznikoff's counternarrative of American history (two of the thematic sequences of *Testimony* are designated "Chinese" and "Mexicans") and the radical social criticism of the iconoclastic Randolph Bourne, who challenged the solidarity of the "100% Americanism" of Anglo-Saxon culture in the 'teens by proposing a theory of "trans-nationalism" in which the diversity of ethnic identity and even cultural hybridity were elevated as values in themselves: "It bespeaks poverty of imagination not to be thrilled at the incalculable potentialities of so novel a union of men." Bourne asserted that hyphenated Americans (German-Americans, Jewish-Americans, Polish-Americans, Irish-Americans, and so forth) would create an anti-assimilationist culture: "America shall be what the immigrant will have a hand in making it, and not what a ruling descendant of those British stocks which were the first permanent immigrants, decides that America shall be."[11] Leslie J. Vaughan's meditation on Randolph Bourne's attraction to the urban spaces of modernity lends further support to my understanding of Reznikoff's own urgent rendering of the diverse groups that constituted American working-class life in the early twentieth century: "In the city, one reaches another state of consciousness, expressing oneself in ways not directly reducible to the past, in particularistic blends of current and past cultures and traditions. Modern urban transnationalism contained elements of diversity and a little disorder."[12] In this sense, Reznikoff's poetry is invigorated by the catalyst of diverse communities and histories in New York City, that most transnational of American metropolises.

Just as the poet seeks to enlarge America's understanding of itself, Reznikoff's portrays the urban stranger as a disruptive presence that compels the individual reader's ethical attention, transforming the self-assurance and wholeness of any insular identity into one bound to a sense of visceral interdependence. Such attention sometimes leads to small urban miracles of communion in which the poet's humanistic Jewishness fully merges with his New York milieu:

The young fellow walks about
with nothing to do: he has lost his job.
"If I ever get another, I'll be hard!
You've got to be hard
to get on. I'll be hard, all right,"
he says bitterly. Takes out his cigarettes.
Only four or five left.
Looks at me out of the corner of his eye—
a stranger he has just met; hesitates;
and offers me a cigarette. (*CP* II. 33)

Though Reznikoff's apparent confidence in the individual's capacity to retain their humanity when tried by dire circumstances rarely resorts to sentimentality, it is true that at times a certain sunny disposition emerges, which ultimately seems to be traced by the poet himself to early childhood, as these evocative lines from an early autobiographical sequence (written when the poet was only twenty-seven years old) ruefully report of his pertinacious response to a grim time during his parents' struggle in the millinery business:

His parents had lost their money. They sold the house and were to
move away.
He went up to his room for the last time.
The trunk of the tree, branches and twigs were still.
He thought, The tree is symmetrical . . . and whatever grows . . .
in shape . . . and in change during the years. So is my life . . .
and all lives.
He went down the stairs singing happily.
His father said, "There's so much trouble—and he sings."
(*Poems* 35; ellipsis are Reznikoff's)

Gently, insistently, Reznikoff's account of his precocious and nearly mystical apprehension that one must take the longest view of existence possible—namely, that the universe metes out catastrophe and redemption in its own mysterious way—would emerge as a surprisingly consistent ethos throughout his later career. Even in the absence of the divine, there is something almost liturgically uplifting, not at all incommensurate with the expansive wisdom of Ecclesiastes, borne by these lines. Still, the news the young poet brings us about human affairs in the early 1920s is often a great deal more dismal; capturing the brutality of modern existence without a glimmer of sentiment, the poetry can be remorselessly wounding in its effects: "The dead man lies in the street. / They spread a sack over his bleeding head. / It drizzles. Gutter and walks are black. / His wife now at her window, / the supper done, the table set, / waits for his coming out of the wet" (*Poems* 4). When it comes to witnessing the lonely fates that overtake Reznikoff's urban dwellers, it seems worth pausing to note that a strikingly analogous sensibility can be found in Annie Dillard's resolutely negative theology: "We do need reminding, not of what God can do, but of what he cannot do, or will not, which is to catch time in its free fall and stick a nickel's worth of sense into our days. And we need reminding of what time can do, must only do; churn out enormity at random and beat it, with God's blessing, into our heads: that we are created, created, sojourners in a land we did not make . . . Who are we to demand explanations from God?"[13] Dillard's bold conception presents a stark conception of divine transcendence, a paradigm that rebuffs all notions of immanence, or of immanent holiness. In other words, the world is determined by its internal causal structure alone, an ethos I find highly analogous with Reznikoff's poetry, which, though laden with biblical references and Jewish learning, is far more attuned to the consequences of historical process than to the conventions of religious piety.[14] The redemptive corollary of this grim condition is above all, adaptability.

In the city's confluence of diverse humans alongside other species the poet finds this manifested virtually everywhere he casts his gaze (the closer one reads him the more difficult it is to locate a clean demarcation between the human and "natural" worlds especially when it comes to this triumphal ethos of resilience) as in this comparatively late poem of *By the Well of Living and Seeing* (1969):

Please do not underestimate the starling:
it hasn't the beautiful feathers of the jay;
and its song,
to say the most for it,
is nothing to speak of.
But it has been doing pretty well
in numbers
and has taken over some of the handsomest houses of the city
to roost on. (*Poems* 250–251)

Over the years I have noted how, with notable consistency, whenever my Jewish students encounter such sardonic lines (and they are quick to observe that this lyric is truly representative of a staggering number of similar iterations) they immediately seize on the temptation to read these as displacements of what they see as Reznikoff's genuine preoccupation, as dutiful and pietistic allegories of the "Jewish condition" (I think I probably did much the same at one time). But that would be to ignore the concrete specificity of the poet's vision. The cumulative effect of reading the collected poems is to witness the poet repeatedly embracing a singular vision of all beings tested by an oppressive universe, responding with vigorous adaptability and small triumphs. This is not to say that these straightforward poems are devoid of interiority. Indeed, many of the lyrics reveal poignant hints of the loneliness and obscurity that Reznikoff endured during his most creative years. In the raw terms of his urban subjectivity, there are tangible indicators of isolation and loneliness but rarely bitterness because the poet always finds compelling ways to foreground how the essential nature of his estrangement is shared by most of humanity.

Reconciled to the inevitability of change, and facing the daunting challenge to prove his literary value in spite of a world that was largely indifferent to the voices of "ethnic" poets until near the end of his lifetime, Reznikoff presents a direct and unadorned poetry rooted in humility and concern for the disenfranchised that is never condescending precisely because it encompasses his own identity, achieving a tangible *mutuality.* In "Autobiography: Hollywood,"[15] he finds a certain solace in aligning his unease and uprootedness in the often unhappy years of his southern California sojourn (1937–1939) with an entire genealogy of upheavals and dispersions:

I like the streets of New York City, where I was born,
better than these streets of palms.
No doubt, my father liked his village in Ukrania
better than the streets of New York City;
and my grandfather the city and its synagogue,
where he once read aloud the holy books,
better than the village
in which he dickered in the market-place. (*Poems* 196)

In Maeera Shreiber's elegant analysis of the diasporic thrust of modern Jewish poetics, she asserts that what "begins as a liability becomes an asset; loss is recovered as gain . . . the question, 'How can we sing God's song in a foreign land?' is also itself the answer—as the song of exile becomes the master narrative in which all poems begin." For Reznikoff certainly, "radical displacement" is transformed into an "aesthetic boon."[16] In this lyric's suggestive concurrence of the disparate struggles of shtetl grandfather and urban American descendant (where it is the poet himself who must haplessly "dicker" in the banal commercial marketplace of movie studios),[17] Reznikoff offers a tangible sense of an utterly autonomous poet with an acerbic sensibility, and yet one who regards himself as a humble being within a far-reaching historic continuum.[18]

In his groundbreaking study of Reznikoff and his intellectual milieu, Stephen Fredman considers how both the *Menorah Journal* and the collegiate Menorah movement that launched it "made critical contributions to the negotiations between Judaism and the emergent cultural modernism" and "as someone who came of age during the rise of the Menorah movement, Reznikoff naturally looked to the *Journal* as a primary outlet for his writing, especially his works that examine Jewish history and the condition of betweenness."[19] (As a creative contributor whose poetry frequently expressed that intellectual community's overarching cultural vision for many years, Reznikoff's was never quite the solitary path that sympathetic critics often assume.) Like many of the Menorah intellectuals, Reznikoff resisted the grand organizing movements of Jewish destiny, Zionism, and Communism, and instead gravitated toward the nuanced cultural politics of the Russian-Jewish historian Simon Dubnow. Fully understanding the diasporic currents of Reznikoff's Jewish verse requires coming to terms with Dubnow's insistence that in the future all nations should depend no longer on a particular territory to express their "racial essence" but would be distinguished instead by their cultural and historical heritage. Dubnow saw world Jewry as a people bound by historical, cultural, and religious ties, no longer dependent on rootedness in homeland or contiguous territory. He passionately advocated a Jewish struggle for cultural and religious autonomy throughout the Diaspora.

In a highly influential essay that appeared in the *Menorah Journal,* Dubnow asserted that "only a very few, however, recognize the profound, moral content of the second half of Jewish history, the history of the Diaspora. Yet, by reason of its exceptional qualities and intensely tragic circumstances, it is beyond all others calculated to yield edification to a notable degree."[20] A kindred sensibility enlivens Reznikoff's poetic practice (especially in those lyrics that were published by the *Menorah Journal* over three decades) celebrated the myriad forms of "edification" of this heritage, an ethos committed to fully elucidate the deep core of this knowledge, not merely in Jewish history but in the construction of a modern Jewish sensibility. Hence, his explanatory notes for his 1944 story "Pharisee" revisit the ancient kingdom in terms that suggest he is most of all interested in the fact of its *destruction,* as the disembarking point for the ensuing epic of Jewish exile: "It is a time of war and civil war and the growth in power of the Pharisees. These, by their teaching and discipline, are to enable Judaism to survive the disasters and suffering of the twenty centuries that follow."[21] Reznikoff recognizes that some of the most central practices of Judaism, its ancient rituals of life and death, were formed in proximity to a landscape and people alien to it, transmuted into a Jewish historical and monotheistic key.

It seems highly revealing that the diasporic setting that most interests Reznikoff (apart from New York City) is Babylonia, which he seems to have understood as the archetypal site wherein Jews learned to assert themselves vis-à-vis Others as in the 1933 poem "Babylon: 539 B.C.E." where an elder prophesies:

We must build in Babylon
another Zion
of precepts, laws, ordinances and commandments
to outlast stone or metal,
between every Jew and the fury or blandishment of any land—
that shall keep up a man as much as bread
and swallows of water in his belly, strengthen him
like links of armor on his body.
Let other people come as streams
that overflow a valley
and leave dead bodies, uprooted trees and fields of sand;
we Jews are as the dew,
on every blade of grass.
trodden under foot today
and here tomorrow morning.

(*Poems* 127)

This is another one of the poet's powerful spatiotemporal juxtapositions, which imagines the still-precarious yet hopeful position of Jews in American society as joining the ancient evidence of Judaism's adaptive genius. Reznikoff knew that the displaced Judeans in Babylonia not only entered the mainstream of Babylonian culture but were even in a position to extend significant economic aid to those Judeans who returned to their homeland in 536 B.C.E. (much as Jewish Americans extended aid to Israel in his own lifetime). Similarly, a later work titled "Jews in Babylonia" does not "weep" for Zion but rather retains the everyday world of continuity and pragmatic activity, an exile of quotidian survival where the sun continues to shine and the rain falls: "Plough, sow and reap / bind the sheaves, thresh and winnow / shear the sheep / wash the wool / comb it and weave it" (*Poems* 349).

Reznikoff's diasporic perspective on the meaning of Jewish struggle contrasts one epoch with another until the reader begins to understand Jewish history as a personal lesson, broadening one's awareness of the phenomenal unfolding of Jewish—and in a broader sense, human—continuity across time and place. In *The Lionhearted* (1944), Reznikoff's novel of Jewish martyrdom during the Crusades, a character facing imminent destruction remarks wryly that, "The fire with which they attack is also a sign to those who will send us help" (106–107).[22] The ambivalence of this aphoristic declaration provides a direct conduit to the poet's lyrical visions of contingency, continuity, and restoration, even in the wake of seeming annihilation. Stripped of territorial ambition or the exercise of force, the Jewish imagination exhibits an awesome range of symbolic and theological strategies as here, where we find the poet struggling to respond to the alarming persecutions of the 1930s: "Though your tribe is the smallest and you are the least, / you shall speak, you shall drill, you shall war; / and, dying, / wheeled away so swiftly / you see the sun / no larger than the evening star, / their boots shall carry your blood— / its corpuscles / seeds / that will grow in the sandy lots, / between the cobblestones of alleys and on the pavement of avenues" (*Poems* 160). In the following decade, Reznikoff's simultaneous nod to both this spirit of the past—the enduring vitality of Judaism's textuality—and his incomparable struggle to look ahead, to a Judaism that might survive even the Holocaust (whose ghastly proportions were becoming more apparent), we find yet another lyrical utterance in the prophetic mode, one of the most dramatic declarations about the tenacity of his people in Reznikoff's entire oeuvre:

As when a great tree, bright with blossoms and heavy with fruit,
is cut down and its seeds are carried far
by the winds of the sky and the waves of the streams and seas
and it grows again on distant slopes and shores
in many places at once,
still blossoming and bearing fruit a hundred and a thousandfold,
so, at the destruction of the Temple
and the murder of its priests, ten thousand synagogues
took root and flourished

in Palestine and in Babylonia and along the Mediterranean;
so the tides carried from Spain and Portugal
a Spinoza to Holland
and a Disraeli to England.
God, delighting in life,
You have remembered us for life. (*Poems* 218)

Though its tone is somber, this lyric's confidence in recovery is undeniable. Depending on the reader's perspective, the allusive effect of the invocation of the Jews in the Diaspora as "seeds," "the sands of the sea," or "the stars of the sky"—in spite of their "death by gas, in trucks, in railway cars, in chambers hidden in the woods"—may be audaciously sanguine or simply heartbreaking. There is, at the same time, another layer of meaning that presses for our attention. For in the poem's fifth stanza we learn of the remarkably fecund properties that reside within the fertile soil of *dispersion.* The speaker asks: "Where is that mountain of which we read in the Bible— / Sinai—on which the Torah was given to Israel" then "Where was the Bible written?" (*Poems* 217), only to ultimately dismiss the significance of geography altogether. Ranging far and wide, the lyric underscores Reznikoff's persistent argument that there has never been one Platonic reading of Judaism that requires universal allegiance to secure Jewish continuity. Rather, Jewish history is one of constant tension as a new center of authority rises to wrest control over the shaping of tradition from its predecessor: hence Babylonia from Palestine; Spain from Babylonia; Portugal, Holland, and the rest in their turn. Furthermore, this modernist's reference to Spinoza tells us that, though tradition is engraved on one's subjectivity, the individual (like the Jewish people's role in history on a larger scale) also creates new patterns, in response to changing times.

The poet's unflagging interest in the presence of Others is even visible in his reworkings of traditional Jewish sources. For example, his acknowledged source for "Kaddish" (which appears as the introduction to the poem) is the *Kaddish de Rabbanan* as translated by R. Travers Herford in 1925, which appears as an epitaph in his translation of the Talmudic text *Pirke Aboth* ("Sayings of the Fathers"): "Upon Israel and upon the Rabbis, and upon their disciples and upon all the disciples of their disciples, and upon all who engage in the study of the Torah in this place and in every place, unto them and unto you be abundant peace, grace, lovingkindness, mercy, long life, ample sustenance and salvation, from their Father who is in Heaven. And say ye Amen" *(Kaddish de Rabbanan).*

Reznikoff's version is more complex. Since America is filled with homeless outsiders, then the outsider poet might introduce a new/ancient modal embodiment of moral authority. His sense of homelessness as an enabling concept is perhaps not so distant from Gramsci—it can be a civil and political space that hegemony cannot suture. For Reznikoff, homelessness seems to be a situation wherein a utopian potentiality endures: something can be learned from this condition and applied to something resembling "progress," though this is not construed as a linear movement free of catastrophic setbacks. The poet imagines himself as a being contented to be a guest and a stranger, committed to coexistence with other guests and strangers: and so in "Kaddish" (1936) he takes time to wish for *all:*

who live
as the sparrows of the streets
under the cornices of the houses of others,
and as rabbits
in the fields of strangers
on the grace of the seasons
and what the gleaners leave in the corners;
you children of the wind—
birds
that feed on the tree of knowledge
in this place and in every place
to them and to you
a living . . . (*Poems* 172)

In the original there is no explicit allusion to Others, but Reznikoff's alternative, while evoking the darkness that besets Jewish life in Europe during the 1930s, repeatedly beckons in every stanza to a reader with an uncertain identity: "to them and to you / peace." The xenophobic and racist shadow of fascism is all the more reason to resist an exclusively ethnocentric voice. On the one hand, it does no good to deny the need to belong to a community; in fact, it is futile to deny this claim of identity. There is nothing reprehensible about identity politics or about the desire to identify with a cultural tradition that has been responsible for some of the greatest products of human civilization. But for Reznikoff this does not mean that in our dealings with strangers we may neglect the principles of equity and equality. As "Kaddish" and other poems of the 1930s are acutely aware, rejecting these principles facilitates the deportations and exterminations of Others.

What the poetry so frequently reminds us, there are times when, to remain human, one must speak and act *outside* the interests of one's group. So rather than preserve the original text's emphasis on the singular burden of Israel's "chosenness," he prefers a liturgical form that yearns for an abundance that might be enough to go around to all the earth's deserving, an urgent address that might speak to the crisis of any moment. Since the dispersal of humanity into separate nations no longer serves the poet as a satisfactory paradigm, in Reznikoff's direct references to Jews, his lyric does not echo the traditional invocation of Jerusalem and "return," but rather pleads for a sovereign existence sanctified only by a living relationship with the Text. In his version of the *Kaddish de Rabbanan,* prayer is a direct address to a reader whose own identity remains an open question, rather than an assumption—something provisional and not reified. By failing to make any clear claims about who the Other is, Reznikoff wishes that the piety of the traditional prayer of Talmudic study might become an antidote not only to the fascism of the 1930s, but to any form of ideological imperative that culminates in territorialism and the persecution of Others.

For Reznikoff, the greatest value of Judaism's textual heritage is its capacity for doing a great deal more than serving the contemporary Jewish condition; it can also illuminate the identities and travails of others, precisely because of the lessons accrued from the centuries of struggle[23] as in these lines from "Jews in Babylonia" (1969), his aphoristic collage of Talmudic wisdom: "If the ship you are traveling on is wrecked / a plank may come floating your way / and on it you may ride wave after wave / until you walk again on dry land" (*Poems* 352). The poetry is filled with contingencies, but the recorded losses of history, no matter how unbearable, always contain the memory of hope. Moreover, the very condition of vulnerability can prove surprisingly efficacious, if only through the distant advantageous gaze of historical process. In thinking about Reznikoff's valuation of diasporic vulnerability as a catalyst for cultural regeneration, it is terrifically illuminating to consider Maurice Samuel's reflective analysis of Aleichem's ironic technique of reversal:

> It is more than a therapeutic resistance to the destructive frustrations and humiliations of the Exile. It was the application of a fantastic technique that the Jews had developed over the ages . . . to counter the torments and discriminations to which they were continuously subjected. It was a technique of avoidance and sublimation; also a technique of theoretical reversal. They had found the trick of converting disaster into a verbal triumph, applying a sort of Talmudic ingenuity of inter-

> pretation to events they could not handle in their reality. They turned the tables on their adversaries dialectically, and though their physical disadvantages were not diminished thereby, nor the external situation changed one whit, they emerged with a feeling of victory.[24]

Keenly self-conscious of his own textual debt to this powerful spiritual ethos, Reznikoff—though he layers his relationship to tradition with irony and discontinuity—enlarges on this paradigm again and again. In the following lines from a variation on a verse of Zacharia that anti-might ethos is plainly apparent even in these lines composed not long after the Holocaust:

Go swiftly in your chariot, my fellow Jew,
you who are blessed with horses;
and I will follow as best I can afoot,
bringing with me perhaps a word or two.
Speak your learned and witty discourses
and I will utter my word or two-
not by might or power
but by your spirit, Lord. (*Poems* 226)

It is a sad but inescapable irony for those with a deep acquaintance with Reznikoff's oeuvre that the otherwise admirable *Poems 1918–1975* is not truly "representative" insofar as it excludes any of the *Holocaust* or *Testimony* documentary poems that have been the subject of ever-increasing scholarly interest. But to my mind, it is equally regrettable that none of the long-unavailable *Nine Plays* (1927) are included, especially because these early works provide some of the liveliest evidence of Reznikoff's enduring interest in the historical conditions of exile and Diaspora in forming both individual identity and collective culture. Hence, to conclude this analysis of Reznikoff's fascination with this most ancient/modern of human circumstances it is essential to turn to what amounts to the rarest of his self-published works. Particularly with regards to the then-nascent role of Zionism in Jewish-American life, there is a great deal to be gained by considering one of these early poetic/political dramas, the foundational texts of his efforts to codify a linkage between ethics and the experience of dispossession.

In a 1922 letter to a friend, Reznikoff calculates the prospects for publishing his verse-drama *The Black Death*, a short work that examines medieval anti-anti-Semitism during the time of the bubonic plague, in a Jewish venue. An editor has "read it, and accepted it, but then hesitated because some of it seems anti-zionistic and the special issue is to be very zionistic."[25]

This is one of the rare moments in which we can catch Reznikoff speculating on the distance between his own conception of Jewish history and that of contemporary Zionist discourse. It is not difficult to locate the ways in which *The Black Death* would have aggravated the Zionist audience Reznikoff imagined. For example, in the first scene, which takes place somewhere in Western Europe at the beginning of the fourteenth century, two old Jews, the master of the house and his guest, converse pessimistically about the present. The uneasy host asks his guest: "Do you know that Christians, in debt to us / Say that we spread the plague?"[26] Their conversation abruptly shifts from the immediate prospect of persecution that faces them in the present, to a timeless exchange on the divine enigma of Judaism's extraterritoriality:

The Guest. Had Israel a land? Was Canaan ours,
Which we took a while and never held
Against Assyrian or Roman?
When Solomon was king was the land Israel's? (76)

The guest's speech exhibits Reznikoff's perversely cavalier attitude toward historical exigency; even while recognizing the distinct possibility of destruction, this speaker becomes more resolute in his embrace of a cultural vitality that outlives destruction:

Palestine was a halting place,
One of many. Our kin, the Arabs,
Wander over their desert. Our desert
Is the Earth. Our strength
Is that we have no land.
Nineveh and Babylon, our familiar cities,
Become dust; but we Jews have left
for Alexandria and Rome.
When the land is impoverished, as lands become,
The tree dies. Israel is not planted,
Israel is in the wind. (76)

If "halting" in the first line denotes uncertainty or hesitancy, it also suggests a stumbling, perhaps even a momentary lapse from a chosen path. At this juncture we might take stock of Reznikoff's ironic reversal of Zionist rhetoric, for the latter conventionally constructs Diaspora itself as a lapse, an aberrant exit from history. At the same time, it seems something of a paradox that Reznikoff chooses a well-known instance of one of the Jews' most futile struggles against a hostile environment in order to present his case for Diaspora. If he means to persuade us of something, why not argue it in the context of the numerous instances of benign coexistence? And is the case not weakened further by the fact that the guest's rather idealistic exposition of his belief in Judaism's viability is preceded by the reader's awareness that it is spoken just *prior* to the cruel massacre?

Perhaps this apparent self-entrapment may best be understood as Reznikoff's determination to fully acknowledge the very events of Judaism's dark history, which were so often the privileged references of the Zionist polemicists, in order to produce an argument that could not possibly be accused of utopianism. In fact, the guest's speech is intertextually linked to Jewish literature's traditional symbiotic relation to catastrophe. For Reznikoff, the collective memory that recounts this grim history is understood as an emphatic affirmation of continuity. A keen knowledge of this literature of lamentation privileges the poet to argue: "Take no threats to heart / This may be the end of you and me / But for all the grains of sand blown / From the desert, the desert is" (76). For Reznikoff, "Israel is in the wind" signifies diasporic "geography"—the movement of Jewish civilization through time and space. In this regard, Reznikoff's alteration of his original title for a 1934 volume of historical poems seems significant. Originally, the typescript that includes the full-length versions of "Babylon," "The Academy at Jamnia," "The Synagogue Defeated," "Spain," "Poland," and "Russia," bore the title "If I Forget You Jerusalem: In Memoriam, 1933." But in the final revision—faithfully reproduced in all subsequent appearances in print—only the second phrase is preserved, and in two additional places, the phrase "If I Forget You, Jerusalem" has been vigorously crossed out by Reznikoff's hand. In this boldly diasporic effacement we know that Reznikoff made an important choice. In spite of the growing crisis in Europe and Palestine (not to mention the severe admonition of the psalm), he elects to affirm the radical autonomy and creativity of Jewish dispersal, not its hopelessness. The fracture produces a radically individuated voice and sensibility that is uncertain of regaining the uncomplicated piety of the poem's pre-text.

Reznikoff's diasporism, however ardent, never denies or diminishes the scope of evil in the universe. Hence it is entirely consistent that, some years after the Jews have been massacred for their "guilt" in the plague, two characters speak of the likelihood of future atrocities:[27]

The Guest. Evil to Man—like the plague—and
  evil men do,
  Like sores upon a healthy body,

Scab and fall off.
The Host. If the body is healthy—sores?
The Guest. Those at least are gone, your city once
more crowded.
The Host. The disease is in the blood to break out
again. (84)

As he would continue to affirm even in the aftermath of the Holocaust, though historical persecution indeed poses a severe threat, far from discrediting the Jewish presence in Europe, more often than not, it actually strengthened Jewish civilization by acting as a stimulus for its spiritual and political imagination. His lyrics visibly avoid any suggestion that the trauma to which Jews have been subjected justifies or necessitates an embrace of nationalist identity.

Many years after writing *The Black Death* Reznikoff would make several remarks to interviewers that greatly clarify his idiosyncratic attitude toward anti-Semitism and the entire tragic history of persecution: "occasionally you have situations like the Holocaust or during the Crusades, where there were lots of killings, or during, say, the Black Death, where they were blamed for the Black Death in Europe . . . my own feeling about it is, that the effect of anti-Semitism is double; in one case you have assimilation, and in the other, you have a strengthening of whatever the person thinks is Judaism."[28] Looking back on the past century's rich experiments in Jewish American life, the phrase "Whatever the person thinks is Judaism" exhibits a dramatic openness to the unpredictable ways in which American Jews have accommodated the challenges of modernity while yet drawing from a genuine wellspring of Jewish textual traditions and belief systems. At the end of his life he tells an interviewer that "you know, anti-Semitism can sometimes bring out the best in you. In my case I know it strengthened my identity and my resolve. Americans are often spurred to do more precisely because of prejudice—blacks are a good example."[29]

Nine Plays cleaves to a Diasporic ethic that somehow remains intact even when the poet examines the ancient Jewish relation to the Land. The epiphanies that he evokes for his readers might occur anywhere, but "Genesis" is inflected by the fact that, in twentieth century Palestine, the "peoples of the Book" are poised to devour one another in order to possess the Land. It would be difficult to imagine a verse that would be less palatable to a territorial ideology than Genesis 26:15–31, a strange account of a series of submissive accommodations and withdrawals that Isaac makes to resolve disputes with local tribes over the rights to various wells and grazing lands. Reznikoff's midrashic rendering of the biblical text is typically understated:

The Eldest of the Herdsmen. If Ishmael
  were the master, they would not dare this.
The Eldest of the Shepherds. How gentle
  Isaac was beside Ishmael,
  When he was here to bury Abraham:
  Isaac has lived in booths and tents,
  His clothing woven from the hair of goats and camels;
  Ishmael was in the skins of the wild deer he has killed.
  Isaac's face is like honey, Ishmael's
  Like the black rocks among which he hunts;
  Ishmael's hair and beard are two bushes,
  His glances arrows and his hands fists;
  Isaac's eyes are like a father's on his grown son,
  His palms open as if to help or bless—
  Here he comes. (110–111)

For the modernist poet this narrative represents a critical juncture in which the ancient Hebrew writers (possibly composing the text in exile) examined their relationship to God, the Land, and Others. Reznikoff interprets Isaac's refusal to act aggressively as a radical resistance toward the seductive power inherent in exercising control over the land. After the desert chieftain, Abimelech, demands that he remove his flocks and herds from the very land God has promised to his father Abraham, Isaac instantly surrenders. The biblical text does not explain why. But in Reznikoff's lyric, "Isaac" seems to be a surrogate for the poet's modernist Jewish soul. The characteristic sense of "apartness" is also present in "Isaac's" Bourne-like idealism, which is clearly incomprehensible to his herdsmen and shepherds:

Isaac. My wealth is the wealth of the land in which
  I am,
  In a time of hunger yours as well as mine;
  My men in a time of need are also yours.
  My father, Abraham, took no man's, but if one said of
    his,
  This is mine, he answered, It is yours;
  Nevertheless, he grew richer.
  And this my father did, not out of fear—

  Abraham gave because of friendliness.
  I am my father's son in this:
  That I wish all men well;

Surely the stars send them sorrows enough.
But if you say that there is no room for us,
My father, Abraham, and his father, Terah, wandered
far;
The Earth is wide,
And as they prospered, their son may hope to prosper. (112)

Undoubtedly, the ethical vision articulated in Reznikoff's lyrical drama was intended to be applied to contemporary Jews and Arabs, as if to suggest that these groups need to recover Isaac's diasporist skills to achieve accommodation and yet preserve difference. In suggesting this, I am reading Reznikoff against the grain of what has lately been dubbed "Settler Judaism"—whose adherents so distort Judaism that they not only believe that God gave them the West Bank as an eternal inheritance, but that whatever is done to hold on to it is also right. After digging a well, an action that declares sovereignty, Isaac's herdsman enters to complain that the men of Gerar have claimed its water as their own. The patriarch responds simply, "Let them have it." A second herdsman soon enters, to declare that he has gone on a "day's journey" from the first contested site only to have his rights to the well also challenged by the valley inhabitants. Isaac announces that this well too should be abandoned. The play concludes with the arrival of another herdsman who observes: "We dug a well / beyond the valley and are not troubled" (113). Reznikoff transforms this ambiguous moment in the ancient narrative into a triumphantly universal appeal: The Land must be shared by peoples with competing claims, rather than possessed. Whatever the biblical source's original intent, Reznikoff has written a midrash about the cost of ideology in the present.[30] He imports an anachronistic strategy of diasporic adaptation, rather than the force justified by divine intervention on behalf of a favored tribe.

Where Zionists of his day stressed the minimal fact of ancient Jewish life in Palestine, Reznikoff enunciated the *how*—the original text's special attention to the moral nature of that presence in the land, as in Isaac's patient willingness to wander to the next valley: Land-loss does not mean the end of history or identity. Whenever Reznikoff turns to the past of the sacred text, he does so with a particular moral imperative situated in the present. What he observed in the American city reflected his Jewish modernism and vice versa: a sense of homelessness (literal and metaphysical). A belonging to nothing and therefore everything feeds the humanity that persists in his poetry. The Jewish diasporic experience is deeply embedded in the way he imagines the economic, political, and cultural struggles of other human beings. The American urban experience suggested the liminality of a new way of thinking about Jewish identity, the paradoxical condition of organic continuity coexisting with ultimate estrangement. As such, his vocabulary of alienation is actually a profound claim to being-at-home. Reznikoff's historical poems invite the reader to interrogate the relationship between the Jewish ethical tradition and the moral limitations of an identity founded solely in the nation or the tribe. Though Reznikoff is rightly appreciated as a poet of immediacy and the present tense, the poetry written in this period suggests that in his construction of the domain of personal identity, he could not but imagine himself as cast from the past. History is personalized: in reconstructing the past he fashions himself in the present, a mode of writing that enables him to relate to others on the basic ground of humanity.

Notes

1. The term "diaspora" first appears in the Septuagint, the Egyptian Jewish translation of the Hebrew Bible into Greek in 250 B.C.E. The literal translation, "to be scattered" (like seeds) derives from the Hebrew of Deuteronomy 28:64, *v'hefitzcha* ("you will be scattered"). Today it is most often used in the Jewish context by those for whom the condition of exile does not necessarily engender a feeling of exile.

2. Recently, non-Jewish theorists such as James Clifford and Paul Gilroy have transvalued diaspora from a negative form of displacement to a positive condition of multiple location, temporality, and identification, while not effacing the violent histories that engender it. Both theorists offer nuanced readings of diaspora across black and Jewish histories. See James Clifford, *Routes: Travel and Translation in the Late Twentieth Century.* (London: Harvard University Press, 1997); Paul Gilroy, *The Black Atlantic: Modernity and Double Consciousness* (Cambridge, MA: Harvard University Press, 1993).

3. I embrace the crucial insight of Rocco Marinaccio, one of Reznikoff's most recent critical admirers, who asserts that the poet deserves a new canonical status "as an early and significant innovator of modernism, whose adaptation of foundational imagist principles for a socially engaged poetry complicates the canonical representation not only of his work but also of the relationship of literature and politics in the modern era," and ultimately concludes that Reznikoff pioneered a unique "fusion of crusading journalism and Poundian imagism," a poetics that embraced the loftiest values of Progressive Era journalism. Reznikoff studied at the University of Missouri's journalism school in 1910, which, together with his later training in the law, would combine to create what I argue amounts to the most concentrated and consistent poetry of testimony and witness yet produced in any generation of American poets. See Rocco Marinaccio, "'The Sight to See and the Will to Do': Charles Reznikoff and the Poetics of Exposure," *Literature Interpretation Theory* 17, 2 (April–June 2006): 105–135. Quotations appear on 108, 127.

4. Emmanuel Levinas, *Du sacré au saint. Cinq nouvelles lectures talmudiques* (Paris: Minuit, 1977), 19. I discuss this passage and other aspects of Levinas's thought that have bearing on contemporary Jewish literary imagination in *Israel in Exile: Jewish Writing and the Desert* (Chicago: University of Illinois Press, 2006), 11–14.

5. All poetry citations refer to *The Poems of Charles Reznikoff: 1918–1975*, edited by Seamus Cooney (Boston: Black Sparrow Books / David R. Godine, 2005), unless stated otherwise. This is a revised edition of the Black Sparrow Press collection titled *Poems 1918–1975: The Complete Poems of Charles Reznikoff* (1989). I am grateful to Brandeis University Press for their permission to reprint material that appeared in earlier and substantially different form in *Diaspora and Zionism in Jewish American Literature: Lazarus, Syrkin, Reznikoff, Roth* (Hanover, NH: Brandeis University Press / University Press of New England, 2002), 110–190.

6. It is important to stress that Reznikoff always saw the success of his poems as dependent on the degree with which they stimulated the reader's own moral imagination.

As he once told an interviewer, "The world is very large, I think, and I certainly can't testify to the whole of it. I can only testify to my own feelings; I can only say what I saw and heard, and I try to say it as well as I can. And if your conclusion is that what I saw and heard makes you feel the way I did, then the poem is successful." See L. S. Dembo, "The 'Objectivist' Poet: Four Interviews," *Contemporary Literature* 10, 2 (1969): 193–202. Quotation appears on 195.

7. Kathryn Shevelow, "History and Objectification in Charles Reznikoff's Documentary Poems, *Testimony* and *Holocaust*," *Sagetrieb* 1, 2 (Fall 1982): 290–306. Quotation appears on 290. Charles Reznikoff, *Holocaust* (Los Angeles: Black Sparrow Press, 1975).

8. Monique Claire Vescia, *Depression Glass: Documentary Photography and the Medium of the Camera Eye in Charles Reznikoff, George Oppen, and William Carlos Williams* (New York: Routledge, 2006), 62.

9. Michael Davidson, *Ghostlier Demarcations: Modern Poetry and the Material Word* (Berkeley and Los Angeles: University of California Press, 1997), 138.

10. In *Diaspora and Zionism in Jewish American Literature,* I make a case for a consistent correlation between what Davidson sees as the rejection "of a unified national [American] story" in Reznikoff's epic treatment of marginalized nineteenth-century Americans, and my sense that the poet was alarmed by Zionism's debasement of the multifarious history and ethical heritage of the Diaspora. For Reznikoff, the linked concepts of race, homeland, and state fundamentally undermined the ethical possibility of dialogical openness and the realm of poetry itself. In that study, I assert that openness to otherness and radical particularity—the poet's voice—are fatally compromised by the rhetoric of autochthony surrounding Zionism in its early decades.

11. Randolph Bourne, "Trans-National America," *The Radical Will: Selected Writings, 1911–1918* (New York: Urizen Books, 1977), 249, 255. Bourne later claimed to have borrowed the term from Jewish intellectuals. See also Randolph Bourne, "The Jew and Trans-National America," in *Menorah Journal* (December 1916).

12. Leslie J. Vaughan, "Cosmopolitanism, Ethnicity and American Identity: Randolph Bourne's 'Trans-National America,'" *Journal of American Studies* 25, 3 (1991): 443–459. Quotation appears on pages 457–458.

13. See Annie Dillard, *Holy the Firm* (New York: Harper and Row, 1977), 45.

14. In this regard, I fully embrace Norman Finkelstein's assertion that for Reznikoff, "history, not Torah, is the arbiter of Judaism. Jewish history, not Jewish belief or tradition, is what Reznikoff draws upon to maintain himself as a Jew." See Norman Finkelstein, "Tradition and Modernity, Judaism and Objectivism: The Poetry of Charles Reznikoff," in *The Objectivist Nexus: Essays in Cultural Poetics*, ed. Rachel Blau DuPlessis and Peter Quartermain (Tuscaloosa: The University of Alabama Press, 1999), 191–209. Quotation appears on 199.

15. Beset with financial woes, Reznikoff joined his friend Albert Lewin, a successful producer at Paramount Pictures, for whom he reviewed scripts. This was the only extended period that Reznikoff left his beloved New York City during his adult life. Though often morose over his prolonged separation from his wife, Marie Syrkin, and his familiar haunts he used the time to great advantage, completing the first draft of his historical novel about medieval Jews, *The Lionhearted* (1944). As Stephen Fredman explains, "Reznikoff's Hollywood" is where the Jewish poet must always be vigilant that "the most important tasks of the day consist of acknowledging the invisible people, 'the man at the door' and 'the man polishing the stairs,' who have been rendered as insignificant as flies by the aristocracy of glamour that rules their world." See Stephen Fredman, *A Menorah for Athena: Charles Reznikoff and the Jewish Dilemmas of Objectivist Poetry* (Chicago: University of Chicago Press, 2001), 116.

16. Maeera Y. Shreiber, "The End of Exile: Jewish Identity and Its Diasporic Poetics," *PMLA* (March 1998): 273–287. Quotation appears on 273.

17. His preference for struggle is evident in his dismissal of his wasted months among the rich and privileged in what he called "Lotus-land": "very little, if anything is done here." See *Selected Letters of Charles Reznikoff 1917–1976*, ed. Milton Hindus (Santa Rosa, CA: Black Sparrow Press, 1997), 174.

18. In the last decade of his life, Reznikoff would express this relation with even starker urgency; in these lines from a 1969 poem it is clear that he perceives himself as an essential conduit for a past that speaks only through the poetic mediation of his urban present in which the Jew's relation to an inhospitable terrain is still not fully resolved: "My grandfather, dead long before I was born / died among strangers; and all the verse he wrote / was lost / except for what / still speaks through me / as mine" (*Poems* 249). By continually rehearsing themes of temporal rupture, geographic displacement, and the almost uncanny intrusion of an exilic sensibility on the self's present sense of belonging, this poetry refuses a seamless assimilation that supplants diasporic vulnerability.

19. Stephen Fredman, *A Menorah for Athena*, 8, 53.

20. Simon Dubnow, "An Essay in the Philosophy of History," reprinted in *Ideas of Jewish History*, ed. Michael A. Meyer (Detroit: Wayne State University Press, 1987), 250–269. Quotation appears on page 255.

21. Charles Reznikoff, "Introductory Note for 'Pharisee,'" June 1944 ts., Henry Hurwitz Memorial Collection, American Jewish Archives.

22. Charles Reznikoff, *The Lionhearted* (Philadelphia: The Jewish Publication Society of America, 1944).

23. As I write these lines, I am struck by the prominent role of Jewish students (rabbinical and secular) on campuses across America in demanding urgent attention to the suffering in Darfur, where genocide is once again putting to shame the post-Holocaust slogan of "Never Again." Jewish organizations such as The Union for Reform Judaism (the largest synagogue movement in the United States) and the Jewish Fund for Justice have recently launched major initiatives to stir the country to more vigorous action on behalf of the refugees.

24. Maurice Samuel, "The Tribune of the Golus," *Jewish Book Annual* 25 (1967–1968): 54.

25. Charles Reznikoff, "Letter to Albert Lewin" (September 16, 1922), *Selected Letters*, 27. The *Menorah Journal* published the verse drama two years later and Reznikoff would later privately print and publish it within his other German-Expressionist inspired works as *Nine Plays* (1927).

26. Charles Reznikoff, "The Black Death," in *Nine Plays* (author's edition, 1927), 74–84. Quotation appears on 75. Hereafter cited parenthetically.

27. As Linda Simon points out, such a haunting prognosis might "have less impact . . . if the play were staged realistically as if it occurred" in the time and place indicated in the first scene. "But he allows time and place to fade, so that in the final scene, 'Years later' intrudes into our own time." See Linda Simon, "Reznikoff: The Poet as Witness," in *Man and Poet*, 233–250. Quotation appears on 247.

28. Interview, "Charles Reznikoff and Reinhold Schiffer: The Poet in His Milieu," *Man and Poet*, 109–126. Quotation appears on 120.

29. Ruth Rovner, "Charles Reznikoff—A Profile," 16. In these days of deteriorating black-Jewish relations it is worth noting that the *Menorah* Jews often referred to the plight of blacks, including the problem of lynchings in the South and their unfair treatment in the labor market in the urban North, many years before most Jews had entered the American middle class.

30. *Midrash*, a term I often invoke to describe Reznikoff's poetics, derives from the vast tradition of creative commentaries, parables, and other rabbinic reflections on the five books of the Torah. This form of textual argumentation and filling-in-the-gaps has lately proven attractive to progressive movements within Judaism, particularly among Jewish feminists such as Alicia Ostriker, in *The Nakedness of the Fathers: Biblical Visions and Revisions* (New Brunswick, NJ: Rutgers University Press, 1994).

Looking at Louis Zukofsky's Poetics through Spinozist Glasses

Joshua Schuster

No one so far knows what a poem can do. That might be "Objectivist" poet Louis Zukofsky's response to the famous challenge launched by Spinoza in his *Ethics*—"no one so far has determined the limits of the body's capabilities"[1]—which is quoted by Zukofsky in his poem "A"-12. Yet Spinoza, a lens grinder by profession who never wandered outside of a few cities in the seventeenth-century Dutch Netherlands, is not a guru urging people to strain their bodies to new sexual or survival limits. Spinoza means approaching the limits of knowledge of what is an ethical connection of the body to the mind, with both being embedded in the world. No one has pursued the affective range of the human body to its fullest capacities, no one knows the extent of how it may tune the mind by its feelings to intuit love.[2] The utopian potential of such an ethics might tempt a reader of Spinoza such as Zukofsky to charge the poem with a surfeit of ethical feelings that lead to happiness and love. But the end result is likely to elicit a false conflation—a philosophy of ethics unfolds through the natural potential of affective bodies, but do poems even have a nature or a body? Yet does anyone so far really know what a poem can do?

Spinoza is arguably Zukofsky's favorite philosopher—he writes that "Spinoza may be said to be the last great Western philosopher. He based his *Ethics* on a single definition that was integrated in the manner of Bach's *Art of Fugue*"[3]—and the reasons for Zukofsky's lifelong involvement with the early Enlightenment philosopher are indisputably crucial to understanding his poetry and poetics. Here I analyze how several key moments in Zukofsky's poetry and poetics intersect with Spinozian thought; this culminates for Zukofsky, often considered the most painstakingly intellectual of poets, instead into an affective poetics and a sensuous metaphysics. Zukofsky's avant-garde experiments with poetic form represent a high-water mark for

American modernism, stretching a period from the early 1920s to his death in 1978. He is most known for his long poem titled "A" written over the span of forty-six years. His work exemplifies a patient, enduring creation of poetry at the intersection of ethical form and affective form, a combination he finds urged by Spinoza. In this essay I offer a brief summary of Spinoza's philosophy and consider how it informs Zukofsky's aims to show an ethics and poetics in touch with how one lives in a complex, interconnected environment. In what follows I trace an overall arc in Spinoza's *Ethics* that moves *from substance to affect to knowledge*—and I argue there is a similar movement at work in Zukofsky's poetry. Additionally, a close examination of the relation between Zukofsky and Spinoza as it concerns the relevance of Judaism (rejected by Spinoza and mostly considered at a distance by the secular Zukofsky) opens onto a sharper sense of what radical Jewish poetics can mean, and could even suggest how to approach a future of secular Judaism.

Zukofsky's poetry still has not achieved widespread critical attention, though his work has been gaining steadily in readership in recent years, such that one could say he is read more today than at any other previous time. Zukofsky's poetry stayed remarkably intense and focused on experimentation with poetic forms, new and old, from his earliest poems in 1928 that mixed multiple languages and rhythms to his later work in the 1960s and 1970s where he created rigid forms such as five words per line that brought out new levels of virtuosity in his wordplay. Zukofsky was as likely to invent new forms as he was to invest old ones with new twists, such as transforming the renaissance poet Guido Cavalcanti's canzone about love by adapting his heavily coded meter and rhyme scheme into a canzone on Marxist economics. This makes for a rewarding reading that goes beyond the satisfaction of deciphering difficulty—Zukofsky has an extraordinary touch in transforming density into intensity, keeping his forms curious enough to attract a rereading that encourages a reliving or reexperiencing the multiple connections a poem has to its environments. But the time-delay it takes to overcome difficulty, along with the fact that Zukofsky had been passed over by most major printing houses and that he kept himself out of the limelight by not courting personal heroics or scandal, has kept his work less known. It is only in the last few decades that Zukofsky's writings, with consistent publishing and active public reading and interpretation, has come to take its place as one of the most important modernist oeuvres alongside those of the more commonly known poets Ezra Pound, Gertrude Stein, T. S. Eliot, and William Carlos Williams.

Zukofsky's masterwork is the long poem "A," which amasses enough history to qualify for Pound's definition of an epic but is more apt to be called an anti-epic in its attention to everyday experience and quotidian detail than to so-called great historical events associated with heroic names and deeds. After all, the poem only has one letter as its name, inhibiting any grandiose title and insisting on any old particularity rather than poetic aristocracy. Zukofsky calls for a writing "which is the detail . . . of thinking with things as they exist" (*Prepositions* 194). Thinking and living with things as they exist involves a more subdued idea of the role of the poet, who is not necessarily spreading revolution, but exemplifying what it means to live out a particular form of radicalism. The poem is divided into twenty-four sections or "movements," which foregrounds a sense of time (twenty-four hours in a day; also the age at which he started writing the poem) that Zukofsky layers in multiple ways rather than simply setting forth a linear progression. For example "A"-22 begins: "AN ERA / ANY TIME / OF YEAR" (508), which layers inside the word *anno* for "year" in Latin and also foreshortens the notion of an era that could fit inside a moment of any year. Following this opening, Zukofsky keeps to five words per line, a constraint he uses to effect both condensation and stretching out. This gives "A"-22 a variable rather than a flat time sequence, a stratified rather than de-stratified language, as in the first few lines: "Others letters a sum owed / ages account years each year / out of old fields, permute" (508). Tempo fluctuates also as an effect of the variable length of "A" sections: "A"-12 takes up over a hundred pages, while "A"-16 is one page with four words. Since the poem took nearly five decades to write, plenty of world history accumulates throughout the poem, including the section "A"-8 that captures debates during the Depression over capitalism and communism, a lament for the fall of Paris in WWII in "A"-10, the assassination of Kennedy in "A"-15, and the Vietnam War in "A"-18. But the poem is as much punctuated by local and personal moments of time, including the suicide of Zukofsky's friend Ricky Chambers in "A"-3, and a section "A"-20 comprised almost wholly of Zukofsky's son Paul's twelve music composition titles. By not monumentalizing time, or casting epochs in enormous molds of ancient, classical, or modern, Zukofsky creates an impression overall that is antiheroic (no one person or ego spans the whole poem, though there are particular favored persons that span the work, most notably Bach, Aristotle, Spinoza, and Zukofsky's family) and anti-tragic (there are moments of tragedy in the poem but they are not depicted as fatalistic and the poem tends toward an optimism of the transformative effects of poetic language).

Zukofsky's evaluation in modernist poetics takes another twist in consideration of how he fits in as a Jewish modernist. To be considered a Jewish poet, one would have to have some engagement with Jewish content, form, or history—Zukofsky does touch all these bases although only sporadically in

"A." These issues are inseparable from Zukofsky due to his personal history, being born in New York in a Yiddish-speaking household and having tremendous admiration for his Orthodox father. Yet Zukofsky remains remote from Judaism as an organized religion, and even though he addresses concerns of secular Judaism, including anti-Semitism, Yiddishkeit, and past Jewish poets, he does not position himself as a torchbearer for a secular Jewish movement. After an early attempt at publishing an essay in the culturally Jewish *Menorah Journal* is rejected, Zukofsky steers clear of trying to relate his work to any specifically Jewish institution. In this essay I will not detail all the ins and outs of Jewishness in Zukofsky,[4] but I am interested in how Zukofsky's interest in Spinoza intersects the Jewish history of Spinoza and Zukofsky's own secularism. What I see in common between Zukofsky and Spinoza is how they take part in a long tradition of Jewish secularism that *uses Judaism to get out of Judaism,* a means of extrication that is typically Jewish nonetheless. I will address Spinoza's history with the Jewish community in a moment, but since the notion of cultural Judaism did not exist as a distinct way of life separate from Judaism, it could be said (as is argued by the scholar Yirmiyahu Yovel) that Spinoza is trying to invent the very notion of secularism out of Judaism. For Zukofsky, what seems to motivate his radical Jewish poetics is a deep interest in assembling modern Jewish poetic works, disdainful of religion or not, into an affirmatively cultural Jewish consciousness. Zukofsky does not feel guilty or regretful of his distance toward Judaism but instead approaches Jewish culture through his own confidence in poetic experimentation. Zukofsky's approach to Spinoza is similar, in that he is looking at Spinoza's ethics as an affirmative approach to living—wondering what the body and the poem can do, and how living and writing with things as they exist can be an ethics.

While reading the relation of Zukofsky and Spinoza, I also want to consider if it would be possible to think of Zukofsky's poetic experiments as a model for how to affirm a future secular Judaism. Still today we are dealing with the problem of how secular life should be motivated—by ethics, pleasure, power? Moreover, how should we motivate Jewish cultural life beyond the institutional staples of museums and Jewish inflected entertainment complexes (comedy, cinema, media houses)? I think that part of this future secular Jewish consciousness involves the waning of the feeling that exile is at the foundation of Jewishness. Indeed, *the age of Jewish exile is closing.* I do not mean in the religious sense of separation from God, but in the way in which Jewish otherness or outsiderness is no longer the core characteristic of Jewish secular life (irrespective of whether one views the state of Israel as a homeland or not). The primary problem of being Jewish now is not in feeling a secure belonging to a state or institution or even a fixed identity, but in how to affirm one's Jewishness in a world dominated by alienation that is generalized as a way of living. Certainly Jewish religious practice needs continual motivation, but so does secular Jewish practice. Whether religious practice increases or decreases, one must not lose the multiple ways of secular Jewish being, including reading Jewish authors, knowing cultural history, and creating future experiences for Jewish "amateurs" and "professionals" alike. But how does secular Judaism motivate itself? To take one example, Jonathan Boyarin draws attention to a continued creation of Jewish "folklore" that exists within the tensions of an American Jewish community that is aware (mostly) of the illusion of its wholeness.[5] Boyarin's ethnographic and cultural approach to diversified Judaism is one example of the interest in secular renewal. The creation of Jewish folklore should be an ongoing and inventive activity, even if there is no stable notion of the "folk" to back it up. Although there is still much to be said about the condition of exile and Judaism, there is a pressing need to address what an affirmative secular Jewish experience of the future might look like. For Zukofsky, one way to affirm this secular experience was to spend a lifetime with Spinoza. Zukofsky's poetry is not one of exile but of an affirmative experimentation of radical poetics. The philosopher Gilles Deleuze remarks that, "Spinoza's philosophy is a philosophy of pure affirmation."[6] What if Spinoza of all people could provide some indications of how to be Jewish at a time when Judaism is suffering, among other things, a lack of motivation? Perhaps even a bit of Jewish Nietzscheanism is necessary to avoid Jewish nihilism.

Among religious Jews there is still a shock of admitting to Spinozism: even today there remains a dose of rebellion in taking on Spinoza in the face of rabbinic Judaism—"see if you can take this!" a reader of Spinoza cracks at the generally indifferent Jewish community today. Of course, in current times this attitude probably will not bring accusations of heresy, but Spinoza still stands dissonant toward the Talmud's rabbinic-centered teachings of Judaism. For Zukofsky, the turn to Spinoza involved at least something of a personal rebellion in a Jewish context. Zukofsky writes in "Poem beginning 'The,'" his first major poem (written in 1926 and first published by Pound in 1928) where he numbers each line:

54 Let me be
55 Not by art have we lived,
56 Not by graven images forbidden to us
57 Not by letters I fancy,

58 Do we dare say
59 With Spinoza grinding lenses, Rabbaisi,
60 After living on Cathedral Parkway?[7]

Zukofsky is refusing to be hypocritical by openly admitting his wanting to live by art, grinding it into the rabbis (or "Rabbaisi," a diminutive term said with a smirk) that Zukofsky is launching an open transgression in his native New York City, living on the unkosher-named "Cathedral Parkway." Spinoza certainly symbolized being outside even the outsiders. As a Sephardic Jew from a Portugese family expelled from their native country, Spinoza began as an outsider from the day he was born in Amsterdam, which was later compounded by his own excommunication from the Jewish community (and thus scorned by his family, though both his parents had already died) at the age of twenty-four.[8] Yet I would argue that while it may be the Jewish question that hooked Zukofsky to Spinoza in the first place, Zukofsky is gripped more by the philosophical tour-de-force of Spinoza's *Ethics,* a work that pertains little to direct issues of Judaism and that claims to consider philosophy *more geometrico,* in the manner of geometry.[9] While Spinoza attracts outsiders, he does not offer a philosophy from the outside. One of Spinoza's basic propositions is that "God, or Nature" (*Deus sive Natura*) is an infinitely perfect substance, which immediately drew charges of naturalist pantheism rather than fidelity to any overtly Jewish religious tenets. *The philosopher in exile from the Jewish community does not really offer a philosophy of Jewish exile.*[10] Ultimately, the building blocks of Spinoza's *Ethics* that are philosophical and naturalist rather than religious receive the most attention by Zukofsky in his poetry and poetics. After all, Zukofsky's "A" begins with an image of the passion of Christ provoked by Bach's quasi-liturgical music (Zukofsky is attending a performance of Bach's *St. Matthew Passion,* and as he notes laconically, "It was also Passover" [3]).

It is clear that Spinoza is already present at the beginning of Zukofsky's poetry and poetics in the late 1920s, an affinity that stands out more so considering that Spinoza had few dedicated readers among poets or philosophers at the time. Spinoza's philosophy has gone in waves of popularity and disdain among philosophers and poets. Several countries banned Spinoza's work in his lifetime and generally his name was invoked by his contemporaries only to be instantly denounced. A resurgence of Spinoza occurred among the Romantics, who saw Spinoza's fusion of nature and desire as a way out of Kantian duties and restrictive categories, with Goethe, Novalis, Coleridge, and Heine leading the way. Hegel writes in *History of Philosophy,* "If one begins to philosophize, one must first be a Spinozist."[11] In opposition to the Romantic spiritualization of nature, Spinoza also plays a major role in Marx's turn to a hard-nosed materialism. Marx uses Spinoza to help him integrate his early political philosophy with his later attention to economics and science, an issue I will return to. Yet Spinoza's importance fades thereafter from the forefront of intellectual currents, albeit with notable exceptions. He reappears in French philosophy of psychology from Maine de Biran and Henri Bergson and in the philosophy of science of Alfred North Whitehead and Albert Einstein (who once wrote a poem on Spinoza in 1920). Another great exception is Nietzsche, who was bowled over when he read Spinoza midway in his own career, as he writes in a letter to Franz Overbeck in 1881: "I am utterly amazed, utterly enchanted. I have a *precursor,* and what a precursor! I hardly knew Spinoza: that I should have turned to him just *now* was inspired by 'instinct.' "[12] Nietzsche adds that "his over-all tendency [is] like mine—making knowledge the *most powerful* affect" (105). But by Zukofsky's generation, the controversies that dogged the legacy of Spinoza had receded and been coated with a layer of dust, and his philosophy appeared only at the periphery of university activity.[13] One of the few major texts on Spinoza of the time was the Harvard philosopher Harry A. Wolfson's *The Philosophy of Spinoza* (1934), a dense, scholarly work that historicizes Spinoza as a reader of other Jewish philosophers and Scholastics, not at all touching on the issue of his work in relation to contemporary life. My sense is that though Zukofsky was aware of these legacies of Spinoza, his main interest in Spinoza was in an attempt to live and write with him, to experience his ethics directly as a poet. That is why the focus here will be more on what it means to live and write with Spinoza's ethics.[14]

Permit a brief summary of Spinoza's philosophy in his five-part *Ethics* (published posthumously in 1677). In Part I, Spinoza begins with nature, imbued or embedded with God; actually Spinoza does not posit anything to begin with but assumes that the universe posits itself, is self-causing (*causa sui*). Nature is the realm of substance, conceived in and through itself (the definition of immanence), where God is nothing if not material. This is a physics and a metaphysics interlaced, a universe where substances are their own essences. But Spinoza is quick to distinguish his materialism from the then-popular Cartesian model that equates substance in a mechanical fashion to what does not change, conceiving of matter as that which remains a static and objective presence. The major difference for Spinoza is that substance includes change, interactive processes, and creation—Spinoza's nature is a step forward in conceiving an organic universe that changes and grows. Nature, as Spinoza defines it, has an infinite number of attributes connected to it, though humans are only aware of two: extension or a body, and intellect or thought (but perhaps there is a secret sect of Spinozians experimenting on ways to access more attributes?). Part I closes with a consideration of the determination of action in nature that will be key for Zukofsky. Spinoza makes a distinction between two types of causality in nature, free cause and necessary cause, which he describes with the concepts *naturing nature* and *natured nature:* "by '*Natura naturans*' we must understand that which is in itself and is conceived through itself; that is, the attributes of substance that express eternal and infinite substance; or, God in so far as he is considered a free cause. By '*Natura naturata*' I understand all that follows from the necessity of God's nature, that is, from the necessity of each one of God's attributes" (EI Sch.Pr.29, 51–52). The terms of this distinction were first proposed by Latin translations of Averroes in the twelfth century. In Spinoza's usage, God or nature fits *natura naturans,* as the essence of both is to be always in the process of creating through their own powers of self-causation. The human mind would be *natura naturata* since it is always attached to the human body, which has its own limited nature and is also always exposed to outside influence by other bodies.

In Part II, Spinoza turns to focus on the human body and its parallel relation to the mind, both of which are modes of substance. Denying Descartes dualism of the separation of mind and body, Spinoza proposes that the mind perceives variety in proportion to the range of states or affectations of the body. "The mind does not know itself except in so far as it perceives ideas of affections of the body" (EII Pr. 23, 81). Without the body's sensory input, there would be no ideas in the mind. The body is constantly being affected, and it feeds this data to the mind to be processed into an idea. Spinoza's universe is therefore a *sensuous metaphysics,* where bodies are constantly sensing or coming into contact with other bodies and substances, stimulating consciousness. For humans this means that motions are constantly being translated into emotions; dynamics of feeling are the fuel or resources that are driving or feeding the body and the mind. The psychologist Silvan S. Tomkins once remarked that affects are our "primary motivators."[15] The neurologist Antonio Damasio, who has written extensively on Spinoza as a precursor for contemporary scientific models of the brain/body connections, commented that "feelings index the state of life within each living human organism."[16] In Part III, Spinoza launches a direct inquiry into the nature of human affects, which Spinoza divides into positive, pleasurable affects that increase the body's power and negative, painful ones that decrease it. "By emotion (*affectus*) I understand the affections of the body by which the body's power of activity is increased or diminished, assisted or checked, together with the ideas of these affections" (EIII Def. 3, 103). Positive affects like love and joy enhance the mind and body while negative affects like pain and fear subtract and immobilize the body. In many cases this is correct biologically and psychologically, but I want to add a wrinkle in this positive/negative binary and remark that there are times when the body needs or is empowered by negative affects (which, it is fair to say, are intended to lead to a later positive outcome). Examples of this are numerous, and I'll say more about this in Zukofsky's poetry, but consider how mourning is a painful affect that the mind/body needs to deal with in a patient way or else a trauma risks spreading. Or take for example how rage can be a correct and ethical reaction to visible injustice occurring in one's presence. Unhappy revolutions are just as necessary as happy ones.

Spinoza's ethics begins in nature and then shifts to considering the relation of the mind to the body, both of which are inseparable from nature. It continues through the principle that there is no inherent contradiction between ethics and power. Spinoza would say that his philosophy comes from experience of and reflection on nature, and that since human nature includes good and bad affects, Spinoza does not naively eliminate bad human nature from reality. Moreover, desire and truth are not exclusive; the mind needs the desire of the body to supply it with experience, such that pleasure and pain are not dissociable from conceptual thought. The question then is: what to do with all these affects? This is where an ethics of affects enters. Spinoza counts three main affective drives: pleasure, pain, and desire (from these he derives up to forty-five other affects such as pride, anger, shame, and so forth).[17] In this respect, Deleuze calls the *Ethics* "a typology of immanent modes of existence."[18] We know that we can only hold a few ideas in our head at any given moment, and, according to the theory of our *conatus* (our ontological drive for self-preservation), pleasure empowers our body while pain immobilizes it. So Spinoza argues that the job of the mind is to filter through the affects and seek out events that encourage positive affects. Spinozism requires a micro and macro attention to sensations. Yet the critical upshot of the *Ethics* is that one cannot completely overcome the passions, but one can learn to live with them and use them for good if the intellect has knowledge of what is good for the body. Freedom is not in liberation from nature but through our capacity to understand nature and find the best affective correspondences to human nature. However, in the final Part V, Spinoza claims that while bodily based affective knowledge is temporary, there is an eternal knowledge that can be gained in intuitive understanding that the mind, in the form of love, seeks to contemplate God's infinite perfection. Sensual pleasure is a lower form of knowledge, whereas intellectual pleasure is said to touch the eternal knowledge of the original infinity of God and nature. Yet the way to this *amor dei intellectualis* is still through immanent knowledge of how nature exists: "The more we understand particular things, the more we understand God" (EV Pr. 24, 214). Spinoza's knowledge is always accretive: the more we understand our bodies, our minds, substances, modes of nature, and so on, the more pleasure we have and the closer we get toward an intellectual love of God/nature.

In a radically brief summary: we descend from infinity of God in causality, to world, to body, to affect (a point of particularity, one could call it the point of the event), and then from there, Spinoza takes us back out again, as affect connects body to mind, increases the power of the mind, stimulating the mind to perfect itself back into pleasure in knowing God's infinity of causality. Visually this might look like two cones extending to infinity that touch or affect each other at their point of apex.[19]

There is an ethical unfolding of substance-affect-knowledge that is paralleled in Zukofsky's poetry and poetics. Form and content each partake of these three aspects: form and content are attributes of the same substance (words in the world), are both engaged in affective systems, and both pertain to knowledge of existence in the world. Enhance or obliterate, intensify or erase these attributes and you change the world. It could be argued that this formula applies to any poetry, so what makes Zukofsky stand out from other modernists, for example? I should note that this is not a proprietary model for writing poetry—it can easily be adopted by others, and the only way to make an argument for Zukofsky's uniqueness is to look at how this ethical understanding appears in a given poem. Most of Zukofsky's poems are written in clusters or patches with short patterns (measured formally as stanzas or thematically as concept-units) that are sometimes strung together for longer narratives or collected in series to make lengthier sections of poems. The rhythm is closer to Pound's *The Cantos* than, for example, Stein, who is more concerned about the narrative/antinarrative structure of individual sentences, or Williams, who generally opts for the lyric in short stanzas or longer narratives held together by lyric threads (his later work *Paterson* is more like patchwork and seemingly more influenced by the younger Zukofsky). I think he prefers these strategies of sectioning because it allows for an experience, image, or object to appear quickly in a complex of substance-affect-knowledge but also allows for a layering of these effects over time and in between stanzas. This compositional method, I would argue, is how he seeks to achieve living-with-things-as-they-exist. And ultimately the way we live with something is a form of knowledge. Let's look closer at how this unfolds in Zukofsky's poetic paradigm.

For Zukofsky, the world is comprised of "historic and contemporary particulars" (*Prepositions* 189). Materialist reality is a given for the poet, though Zukofsky actually locates two forms of materiality that are always intertwined: historical materiality (of a Marxist and social basis) and natural materiality. I'll look closer at the Marxist aspect in a moment; the notion of natural materialism is in direct confirmation of Spinoza's notion of nature as substance. The first quote of the *Ethics* in Zukofsky's "A" appears in "A"-6 (written in 1930) and is significant in this case:

Natura Naturans—
Nature as creator,
Natura Naturata—
Nature as created.
He who creates
Is a mode of these inertial systems—
The flower—leaf around leaf wrapped
Around the center leaf,
("A"-6, 22–23)

The image here of leaves wrapped around a center that is also a leaf suggests nature creating a model out of itself (the center leaf patterns the rest of the leaves). Zukofsky's somewhat strange use of the word "inertial" may refer to the totality of nature, but it is important to account for the fact that substance is a process and that nature is always and endlessly creating. Naturing nature is self-causality or autonomous creation through immanence, while natured nature—which includes human mind and body, as well as poetry—is open to secondary or external causes (other minds, other poems). Poetic creation is a "mode" of the two-fold process of natural creation. We can detect a subtle reasoning of Zukofsky, who admits it is nature that is the primary creator while the poet is in a somewhat secondary position, as a mode. Being a mode of nature means working within its ways and means as tied to history; yet nature is at work whether the poet notices or not. Although one gets the sense that Zukofsky—whose long poem gives us many reconstitutions of its own materials, as for example the letter "A" reappearing as the first letter of eleven sections of the poem, or "A"-24 being an intertwining of four previous writings by Zukofsky with musical arrangement by Celia Zukofsky—wants poetry to aspire to the power of naturing nature. There is a kind of material substrate of Zukofsky's formal experimentation whereby he seeks this naturing effect—call it a *social naturalism.* Zukofsky is after a mode of thinking that does not divide nature from history. Accordingly, Zukofsky is attracted to repetitive forms that could produce a variety of poems in the same way that nature creates one leaf and arrays additional leaves around it. In the language of biology and physics, this is called "self-organization," whereby matter achieves higher complexity by integrating simpler patterns of new information into a learning process that effects a greater degree of autonomy (involving a jump from linear to nonlinear progression). A prime example would be DNA, which has achieved a high level of self-organization over a long evolution. Another example would certainly be the patterns of a leaf whose design maximizes a flower's "learning" potential in its environment. Zukofsky taps into a kind of poetics of self-organization when he layers his poems with previous writings and prepares for further extensions and experimentations of form. Zukofsky's *Catullus* as translating translation and *80 Flowers* as naturing nature can be read as late career attempts at this as well.

Returning to historical materialism in Marx's conception here is not unwarranted since Marx conceived of the dynamics of capital precisely on the model of *naturans/naturata.* However, Marx is interested in this concept as it relates production to social forces, not forces of nature. The substance of nature becomes social in human hands, and human labor participates in the creation and recreation of the social. Thus human labor is both "naturing" and "natured"—we can just say producer and produced. Marx references Spinoza in the opening pages of the *Grundrisse,* noting that Spinoza's system helps one to conceptualize the reciprocal relation between production and consumption, the way production (re)produces consumption and consumption (re)produces production.[20] Production however is the primary object/process that Marx is after—*Capital* is really the first sustained attempt by anyone to give a history, a language, and expose the exploitative "laws" of production (previous economists focused on what they thought was most "objective" in economics such as money, land, and specialization of labor). Zukofsky is certainly attracted to the synergy of Spinoza and Marx, their cohabitation in rebelliousness and shared materialist outlook. "A"-8 begins with the juxtaposition apparent in the lines "Labor as creator, / Labor as creature" (43). Most of "A"-8, written as the nation was pulling itself out of the Depression, is an interweaving of left economic theory with the discourse and dialect of workers and their historic and contemporary particulars. There is no dialectic without dialect—work brings out its own language and vice versa. Though perhaps the dream of every communist poet is that language might overcome the machine, one also detects that Zukofsky wants to use his epic poem to *expose* the language and lyric of labor in the same way that Marx exposes production. Zukofsky calls history and economy "the material clef of the music" (49) and tries his best to make music out of economics and labor-speak, with stanzas of the poem jumping from work ballads to quotes from Marx's *Capital* to brief looks at nineteenth- and early-twentieth-century sites and types of labor, from the factory worker to the craftsman. Ultimately Zukofsky stays within the parameters of a rather common view of leftist economic theory that privileges the artisan; his best skill lies in matching the wordsmithing of regional speech codes and the high cosmopolitanism of modern advertising with coded leftist language. Not incidentally, in considering the relation of Spinoza and Marx, it is interesting to note that while Spinoza does have a politics (liberalist and democratic), he does not have an economics, a discourse which was only in its early stages in Spinoza's lifetime, though Spinoza's family were merchants and Spinoza excelled at the family business before his exile. Spinoza also fits Zukofsky's ideal laborer as an artisan grinding lenses, who also refused extensive patronage, only accepting tiny sums of money offered by friends. Zukofsky wrote in a letter to the poet Lorine Niedecker, "the Marx is in Spinny, but without (in Spinny) the hell in it"; Barry Ahearn explicates that, "One thing that 'hell' might be is the hell of factories, but it also might be Marx's rage. Spinoza has no such rage, possibly because he lived before the Industrial Revolution, possibly because his philosophy aims at paradise."[21] It is fair to say that Marx also "aims" at paradise. The "hell" might also refer to Marx's argument that the pain and dissatisfaction of the proletariat will inevitably press them into revolution, while Spinoza seeks a world of concordance in happiness that need not pass through affects of extreme negativity. But then again Spinoza was never a labor organizer.

The apex of the Marx/Spinoza dialogue occurs obviously in "A"-9, which consists of two canzones, each with six stanzas. Much has already been said by critics regarding the remarkable eight-year gap between the end of the first half (dated 1938–1940, and whose primary source text is *Capital*), and the beginning of the second half (dated 1948–1950; the primary text is *Ethics*) of the poem as reflecting a shift from Marx to Spinoza. Considering that Spinoza abounds all over "A," I do not think there is a shift or break between Marx and Spinoza. Both sections use Cavalcanti's canzone form from "Donna Mi Prega" and draw from its "music and emotion of intellect,"[22] Zukofsky writes. In a short essay on the form of the poem, Zukofsky cites the authority of Pound, who twice translated the canzone (and printed it in Canto XXXVI): "The canzone was to the poets of this period what the fugue was to musicians in Bach's time" (37). Pound goes on to explain the rhythm and rhyme scheme of the canzone, derived from a troubadour form, which commanded a technical mastery of versification from a poet. Cavalcanti's poem, one of the crown jewels of this renaissance form, sings of the meaning of love at the behest of a non-named "lady [who] asks me" ("Donna mi priegha," in Cavalcanti's spelling). Cavalcanti, who was atheist, then elaborates a beautiful materialist psychology of the meaning of love, which he described as awash among the affects and culminating in a sparkling light. Spinoza probably never read this poem but its stress on following the subtle and complex variations of sensations as they pass through an emotion certainly vibrates in concordance with his own philosophy.

The two canzones of Zukofsky's "A"-9 form a diptych whose connectivity is like a Möbius strip where recto relies on verso rather than two sliced halves. The first part is composed formally according to a heavy dose of mathematical precision based on an elaborate and nearly impossible to follow proportion of rhymes and repetition of "n" and "r" letters, and the second seems to have a similar precision with the letter "l"; one could say that both reflect Spinoza's thought as *more geometrico* and Marx's mathematically inflected dissection of capital. In the first half of "A"-9, things do most of the talking. In the middle of the first stanza, things begin their discourse to try and define what went wrong, whereas by comparison in Cavalcanti's poem, the poet launches into a detailed account of love's skills and situations, where it is found and how it is sustained. Zukofsky's first half of "A"-9 is the case where the world of love is inverted, and even things are complaining of lack of affection. Zukofsky gives the things words—"So that were the things words they could say:" (106)—so they can tell their story. A similar conversation with things, letting them speak while humans listen, is staged by Marx at the end of the first chapter of *Capital,* titled "The Commodity," after Marx has revealed the fetish character of the commodity.[23] Marx writes, "If commodities could speak, they would say this: our use-value may interest men, but it does not belong to us as objects. What does belong to us as objects, however, is our value. Our own intercourse as commodities proves it. We relate to each other merely as exchange-values" (*Capital,* 176–177). Here *exchange-value* (an inherently social form that Marx often just calls "value") is the language commodities speak in the market-place, when they hang out among one another and try to stand out and look good to attract the buyer's eye.[24] *Use-value* is the language commodities speak in the hands of humans, who want to extract something useful for them. As exchange-value, commodities tell the story of quantity (money) rather than quality. They also bemoan the increase of the speed of labor at the cost of their own prestige. Zukofsky writes, "The labor speeded while our worth decreases— / Naturally surplus value increases" (107). Commodities seem to want to testify to the human effort invested in them, but their false identity as "exchange-value" prevents this story from being told since it erases the history of labor in the object once it circulates and leaves its maker. Zukofsky's commodities mourn their masters:

Hands, heart, not value made us, and of any
Desired perfection the projection solely,
Lives worked us slowly to delight the senses (107)

It's nice to know that things aren't too happy about this situation either; they would rather delight the senses than be dulled by abstraction. Zukofsky's poem is a dense prismatic of the "congealed" discourse of commodities that are striving to show their better half.[25]

There seems to be a Hegelian-like dialectical movement to the whole of "A"-9—the positive thesis is Cavalcanti's poem on love, the negative antithesis is the labor in alienated form in the first half of "A"-9, and the sublation is through love via Spinoza's message of blessedness in the second half of "A"-9. The question of value in the second half of "A"-9 becomes inextricable from affect. For Zukofsky and Spinoza, love is the fullest affective integration of ethics with the mind and body, and the pursuit of love is the point of ethics. Value now is defined not in terms of exchange-value, but in terms of richness of affect: "Virtue flames value, merriment love" (109). Zukofsky's "A"-9 has shown how to use the twisting, inter-wrapping movements of the form of a canzone to thread together an ethical and affective response to the problem of labor. As love casts away negative emotions (hate, pain, furor), the things that were debased as commodities return to speak as objects midway through the fourth sonnet-stanza:

Love acts beyond the phase day wills it into—
Hate is obscure, errs, is pain, furor, torn—a
Lust to adorn aversion, hope—love eyeing
Its object joined to its cause, sees path into
Things the future or now, that poorer bourne, a
Past, a step, a worn, a voiced look, gone—eyeing
These, each in itself is saying, "behoove us,
Disprove us least as things of love appearing
In a wish gearing to light's infinite locus,
Balm or jewelweed is according to focus.
No one really knows us who does not love us,

Time does not move us, we are and love, searing
Remembrance—veering from guises which cloak us,
So defined as eternal, men invoke us." (110)

Thus intimate knowledge of things "each in itself" is not a matter of epistemology—Zukofsky later scoffs at the term—but a matter of the ethical understanding brought out by care toward affective resonance: "love eyeing / its object joined to its cause." Objects speak here as "things of love," showing their connections to the infinite energy of light, a positive power in Zukofsky's eyes, and to the program of the Objectivists who work "according to focus." The jewelweed is a natural balm for poison ivy, a promise of the free and useful good that nature offers, hence the value or "jewel" attached to its name.

In the coda of Cavalcanti's poem, the poet bids farewell to the canzone, letting it out like a bird to fly wherever it pleases, the poet's assuredness resting in the confidence that his skills have lavished his song with enough ornate quality that it would not bother to be sullied by lesser company. In Zukofsky's coda, love gets the final word, but leaves the reader with a twist, somewhat less assured of perfection:

Love speaks: "in wracked cities there is less action,
Sweet alyssum sometimes is not of time; now
Weep, love's heir, rhyme now how song's exaction
Is your distraction—related is equated,
How else is love's distance approximated." (110–111)

Love's first concern is for the wave of violence that has hit "wracked cities" in WWII. Love commands its heir, poetry, to weep for this loss first. The immediately following poem "A"-10, though written in 1940, well before the end of "A"-9, is nonetheless placed after as a poem in the midst of weeping for the fall of Paris to the Germans. The sweet alyssum, a flower that blooms continuously throughout the growing season as if overfilled with joy, is not timely in the face of such pain—the word "asylum" always stands out in "alyssum," as does "Elysium." Finally I want to make a remark on the eloquent line "related is equated," which appears three times in the poem (first with "as" instead of "is"). When it first appears in the second line of the poem, it is a negative condition, prompted by a Marxian outlook on how the equation process levels all social values. Commodities in the marketplace are related only by equations of cost, profit, and loss and thereby lose their specific labor history. But in the second half of "A"-9, the same line refers to the positive condition of how love makes bonds and bridges distances. For Spinoza, ethics is the constant search for positive relatedness, elective affinities and common notions that give pleasure. Not to say that Zukofsky is a nominalist here, but as previously noted in an earlier example of how the word "other" is susceptible to various and perhaps opposed meanings, here Zukofsky uses the same line to refer to opposite modes of existence. The *poetics of relation,* in Edouard Glissant's phrase, is a tightly contested experience.

"A"-9 captures the interrelated arc of substance-affect-knowledge compressed into a canzone and the section stands in for the continuity of this relation throughout "A." In "A"-12, Zukofsky works at length to set Spinoza's *Ethics* into poetry, quoting and interpreting Spinoza primarily on the relation of ethics to affects and the power of love. In the space remaining I also want to note briefly a similar arc (substance-affect-knowledge) in Zukofsky's poetics statements. In Zukofsky's sense of language, words partake of all three categories. Words have a substance in his poetic paradigm as he allots particular attention to the shape and sound of letters. Words in action are always emitting affect or detailing experience in Zukofsky's poem—and the ability to find these substance-affect resonances is a kind of knowledge.[26] Zukofsky claims in a late interview with L. S. Dembo that "so much of the word is a physiological thing" (*Prepositions* 231), a statement he thinks will get him in trouble with resident linguists who only see words as substances. Zukofsky tended in his earlier writing to take the symbolic function of language at face value, such as in his flagship poetics statement, "Sincerity and Objectification," written in 1931: "The economy of presentation in this writing is a reassertion of faith that the combined letters—the words—are absolute symbols for objects, states, acts, interrelations, thoughts about them. If not, why use words?" (*Prepositions* 198). Skepticism is a canard for Zukofsky, which Mark Scroggins details in his nicely titled *Louis Zukofsky and the Poetry of Knowledge.* Zukofsky does not seem to be too interested in Spinoza's problem of nominalism here either (or rather, Zukofsky seems to have an *affirmative nominalism,* which is also apparent in poetry by Clark Coolidge, for example). Less important is whether such things as "absolute symbols" exist—Zukofsky's reference to symbol is somewhere between Charles Peirce and Whitehead's theories of symbols[27]—than that language is conceived of as "a reassertion of faith" in words. Zukofsky's favorite term for this is *sincerity.* For Zukofsky, sincerity is attention to and care for particularity in words and images, a "preoccupation with the accuracy of detail in writing" (*Prepositions* 199). Sincerity invites a trust rather than skepticism in writing. It is a kind of fidelity to the detail, or as the philosopher Alain Badiou calls it, a fidelity to the event.[28] *Suffice it to say, after the revolution, language will be inherently sincere.* And the opposite of sincerity is not irony but cynicism.

The poetics of sincerity move Zukofsky to search for a form of expressionism in language. In one of Zukofsky's broader claims for poetry (also made in 1931), he writes, "the order of all poetry is to approach a state of music wherein the ideas present themselves sensuously and intelligently and are of no predatory intention" (*Prepositions* 214). Sensuously and intelligently—that is the body/mind complex we saw in Spinoza. A poetics of sincerity is also a poetics of affect. However, at this point, I think a contemporary reader might grow skeptical to claims of a physiological-symbolic language by Zukofsky, if one has not already dismissed his poetics as minor or not applicable to the poetry. If one has had training in structuralist linguistics of the Saussurian and Jakobsonian kind, one no longer believes in motivated signs, symbols that correspond directly to objects—and that since a signifier is endlessly differential, it never gets us too close to the thing, or the real, except perhaps by shock or short circuit. It is tempting to apply a kind of structuralist linguistic paradigm to Zukofsky's poetry—visually it looks like he's peeling apart the ideology of the sign and carousing openly with signifiers, or as Zukofsky puts it in "A"-6, "Outwriggling the wriggly Wrigley boys" (21). Writing is wriggling through an already wriggly language (writing as writhing). Yet structuralist linguistics is not the dominant paradigm for Zukofsky. Rather, he is motivated in developing an affective language theory combined with a musical pattern. Language is embedded in an affective relation to the world. At stake is overcoming a kind of ahistoricism of relational word value and instead opening a new relation to history, of being inside the historical, of generating agency through poetic sincerity. Zukofsky quotes Wittgenstein's statement, "ethics and aesthetics are one."[29] A radically affective language leads to a radical ethics. I think this different language theory is largely neglected, with few exceptions, by the contemporary poetry and theory scenes today, but it is one that will have growing importance in generating an *intensive* poetics to come.

Plenitude of affect means increased mental ability for Spinoza: "In proportion as a body is more apt than other bodies to act or be acted upon simultaneously in many ways, so is its mind more apt than other minds to perceive many things simultaneously" (EII, Sch.Pr. 13, 72). An affective poetics would be a poetry of serial simultaneity, combinations of affect and intellect in many ways. The culmination of the poem, "A"-24—a gift from Celia Zukofsky that sets four different writings of Louis's (called "thought, drama, story, poem" [564]) to music—is an excellent example of this synesthetics. I began this essay with the combined question: what can a poem and a body possibly do? Poetry is the place where one experiments on a response to this question. From the essay "Sincerity and Objectification," here is Zukofsky's imagining of that new poetic body: "poets who see with their ears, hear with their eyes, move with their noses and speak and breathe with their feet" (*Prepositions* 212).

Earlier I remarked that there is a long tradition of Jewish secularism that uses Judaism to get out of Judaism. A traditionally Jewish way of trying not to be Jewish. Love of Jewish irony, great fear of Jewish cynicism. Zukofsky sent a poetics essay in 1931 that included in-depth readings of fellow "Objectivist" poet Charles Reznikoff to the *Menorah Journal*, a secular and literary publication that sought to encourage a flourishing Jewish American intellectual scene. The journal rejected the essay, and though Reznikoff wrote on Jewish themes, perhaps Zukofsky's reading was not Jewish enough, or did not espouse the assumed tenets of Jewish American consciousness. This too is a classic Jewish story. An ethics started by Spinoza and lived and written through what Zukofsky calls, in the final line of "A"-23, the "z-sited path" (563) of his poetry touches on the relation of *feeling* Jewish to being Jewish. The letter "w" of Jewish marks the up-and-down experience in its midst, a w-sited path.

Notes

I want to thank Heather Love, Charles Bernstein, Bob Perelman, and Louis Cabri for help and inspiration on this paper.

1. Baruch Spinoza, *The Ethics; Treatise on the Emendation of the Intellect; Selected Letters*, trans. Samuel Shirley (Indianapolis: Hackett, 1992), EIII Sch.Pr. 2, 105, translation slightly modified. The "Part" of Spinoza's *Ethics* along with the page number in Shirley's edition will be cited hereafter. Zukofsky used the edition Baruch Spinoza, *Ethics and On the Correction of the Understanding*, trans. Andrew Boyle (New York: Everyman's Library, 1910).

2. Research on affects of the body, with contributions from philosophers, psychologists, and neuropsychiatrist, has blossomed in recent decades. Four writers have influenced my approach to this issue in particular. They would be cited in many places in this paper if I had more time. Silvan S. Tomkins's breakthrough research on affects as a "feedback system" and emotions as our primary motivators has been a primary motivator in my own work to ask many of the questions in this paper. See Silvan S. Tomkins, *Affect, Imagery, Consciousness* (New York: Springer Publishing Co., 1962). Antonio Damasio's *The Feeling of What Happens: Body and Emotion in the Making of Consciousness* (New York: Harcourt, 2000) and *Looking for Spinoza: Joy, Sorrow, and the Feeling Brain* (New York: Harcourt, 2003) offer a current, science-rich

look at the issue of affects. I follow his distinction between *emotion* as the bodily reaction and *feeling* as the combination of body and mind, where the mind recognizes and reads the activity of the body. *Affect* would be the term for this entire process. Gilles Deleuze also focuses on ethics and affects and the link both have to "common notions" in Spinoza's philosophy. See Gilles Deleuze, *Expressionism in Philosophy: Spinoza,* trans. Martin Joughin (New York: Zone Books, 1992), and *Spinoza: Practical Philosophy,* trans. Robert Hurley (San Francisco: City Lights Books, 1988). One of the best recent books in reading modernist poetry through affect and Spinoza's philosophy in particular is Charles Altieri's *The Particulars of Rapture: An Aesthetics of the Affects* (Ithaca, NY: Cornell University Press, 2003).

3. *Prepositions + : The Critical Essays* (Hanover: Wesleyan University Press, 2000), 55.

4. For a closer reading on the issue of Jewishness in Zukofsky, see Stephen Fredman, *A Menorah for Athena: Charles Reznikoff and the Jewish Dilemmas of Objectivist Poetry* (Chicago: University of Chicago Press, 2001), esp. 124–139, and Mark Scroggins, *Louis Zukofsky and the Poetry of Knowledge* (Tuscaloosa: The University of Alabama Press, 1998), esp. 121–139.

5. Jonathan Boyarin, *Thinking in Jewish* (Chicago: University of Chicago Press, 1996).

6. Deleuze, *Expressionism in Philosophy: Spinoza,* 60.

7. *All: The Collected Short Poems 1923–1964* (New York: W. W. Norton, 1971), 14.

8. The Spinoza scholar Yirmiyahu Yovel sees Spinoza's rejection of Judaism as mutual. Yovel's summary of Spinoza's stance toward Judaism is worth quoting at length, though since an affirmative secular Jewish culture did not really exist in Spinoza's time, it is impossible to say for sure how Spinoza would react to other ways of being Jewish and to the ethical impact of his writing and rebellion on other Jews. Yovel writes: "Spinoza's view of Judaism has two main components. First, he makes Jewish history—and, following it, human history at large—a thoroughly *secular* phenomenon determined by rational and natural causes alone. Second, Spinoza construes the Mosaic religion as the *political constitution* of the ancient Jews (the Hebrews), created by a social contract in which the Jews decided to make God their political sovereign. The first component abolishes the notions of miracle, providence, the 'chosen people,' and *historia sacra* (sacred history) in general; the second component leads Spinoza to view Jewish life in the Diaspora as outdated because it has lost its political *raison d'être,* and explain the Jews' continued survival . . . as the result of perfectly natural causes: the other nations' hatred toward the Jews (caused by the Jews' willful seclusion and disdain for Gentiles) and the power of the Jews' religious faith (which Spinoza, who left the Jewish community in a scandal, calls their 'superstition')." In Yirmiyahu Yovel, *Dark Riddle: Hegel, Nietzsche, and the Jews* (University Park: Pennsylvania State University Press, 1998), 7–8.

9. For a specific cultural history of Jewishness as it relates to the Objectivist poet Charles Reznikoff, and also to some of Zukofsky's experience with this issue, see Stephen Fredman, *A Menorah for Athena.*

10. In Spinoza's *Theological-Political Treatise*, he insisted on separating faith from philosophy. Spinoza had a deft eye for reading scripture and certainly knew the Talmud, yet he used these skills to mount a critique of the rituals and hierarchies of religion. Spinoza wrote a study of Hebrew grammar to teach friends and others how to read the original language of the Torah in order to be more analytic about language and authorship issues. Though Spinoza read Jewish religious philosophers like Maimonides and Isaac Abravanel, and also read Kabbalist texts, he tended to interpret such writings out of religion and into philosophy. Yirmiyahu Yovel suggests he is "the first secular Jew" for his insistent social and philosophical critique of irrational faith in religion. See Yovel, *Spinoza and Other Heretics,* vol. 1 (Princeton, NJ: Princeton University Press, 1992).

11. "Wenn man anfängt zu philosophieren, so muss man zuerst Spinozist sein." *Geschichte der Philosophie,* in *Werke* (Frankfurt: Suhrkamp, 1971), 20: 165.

12. Quoted in Yirmiyahu Yovel, *Spinoza and Other Heretics, Vol. 2: The Adventures of Immanence* (Princeton, NJ: Princeton University Press, 1992), 105.

13. Not until the 1960s did another major wave of Spinoza studies break out, starting largely in France, including Gilles Deleuze's Nietzsche-inflected reading, a renewed Marxist-materialist reading promoted by Louis Althusser, Pierre Macherey, and Etienne Balibar and Antonio Negri, and a densely philosophical reading by Martial Gueroult.

14. I am advocating a type of ethical reading of Zukofsky along with Spinoza, but I want to be careful to distinguish this approach from other ethical readings of Zukofsky, most notably from the pairing of twentieth-century French philosopher Emmanuel Levinas and Zukofsky in Tim Woods's book *The Poetics of the Limit: Ethics and Politics in Modern and Contemporary American Poetry* (New York: Palgrave MacMillan, 2002), especially chapters 4–5.

Woods's reading is effective in his connection with Levinas's insistence on the Abrahamic side of Judaism that is continuously in a condition of wandering and being confronted by otherness to Zukofsky's constantly shifting poetic environments that eschew the notion of a stable self. Yet Woods overlooks the problem that Levinas carried a lifelong distaste for Spinoza and would trash his notion of *conatus essendi* (Spinoza's term for the power that seeks to preserve one's being) as often as he could. "Spinoza is guilty of betrayal," writes Levinas; "We cannot ignore the harmful role Spinoza played in the decomposition of the Jewish intelligentsia" (Emmanuel Levinas, *Difficult Freedom: Essays on Judaism,* trans. Seán Hand [Baltimore: Johns Hopkins University Press, 1990], 108). There is no communication without excommunication! Levinas accuses Spinoza of pushing Christian doctrine by devaluing the authority of the prophets and rabbinic writings, reading the Torah along with the New Testament, and reducing philosophy to the more Christian themes of charity and love. If Zukofsky's preferred philosopher is Spinoza, there must be some dissonance in a Levinasian reading of Zukofsky. That is not to say that Levinas's ethics of attention to the Other is not embedded in Zukofsky's writing. But there is no ignoring the principled difference between Spinoza's philosophy of immanence and

Levinas's philosophy of transcendence. Still, can there be a combined Spinozian and Levinasian ethics? I am convinced that this would be to break the conventional norms and expectations of traditional ethics in the name of a much more potent ethics.

There is not room for an extended critique of Levinas here, but consider a brief problem. Levinas argues that since the self is always encountering others in the world, and one can never fully predict or control the action of another, the self is always in a position of passivity and response-ability or responding to the other. My being, my *conatus,* is never fully my own since the other penetrates my being and makes demands on me. Because the other can always make demands on me, I am always accountable for responding to the other's call for help. Levinas insists that otherness has been systematically obscured by Western philosophy, yet he claims it is otherness that puts into action the whole drama of being and the categories of knowing. Moreover, according to Levinas, otherness cannot be conceptualized solely with philosophy, but actually precedes comprehension, knowledge, and the concept—again, we do not know what to expect from an encounter, the other interrupts the self, so preexisting concepts are no good. Levinas's "ethics as first philosophy" is not so much an argument or a proof for ethics as it is an attempt to account for the condition of interhuman relations that fundamentally already presuppose a basis for ethical action. But in side-stepping critical argument and concepts, in favor of an ethics as encounter that can only come from the other, there may arise a problem that does a disservice to ethics. For how do we know that the demand from the other is an ethical demand? If we are always passive and responsible for the other, how do we adjudicate between the vast range of demands made by the other on the self, some which are ethical, some which forestall ethics (father knows best), and some which could demolish the possibility of ethics (an objective of war)? In that case one would need a critical philosophy that reinforces the ability of the self to distinguish what responses improve ethical action.

But there is a more pressing problem at the level of distinguishing how one interacts with the other at the outset. Should one not precondition oneself for encounters with others that will maximize the potential for ethical action? Is the knock at the door that interrupts me someone who needs help or someone who is harassing me—shouldn't I organize my existence to the best I can to know the difference? What if the "other" abuses my hospitality, ruining it for later others—shouldn't I try to avoid these unfortunate encounters as a kind of ethical self-knowledge? Ultimately, the "other" is just a word or a title given to the encounter as a generic title; we cannot control the distribution of the term otherness to make sure that only the "worthy" others fall into its parameters. We cannot say from the outset that whoever fits the term "other" is a pure good; we can only say that attention to the other should be foremost, such that positive ethical action can occur and destructive action with others avoided. This is not ethical relativism but ethical relationism. No signifier is an absolute good: "negation" or "revolution" works just as well for right-wing radicals. Again, it is not about relativizing terms but rather resisting pinning absolute hopes on this or that element of language. As a nominalist, Spinoza suggests we drop this uncritical attitude to terms and language; there have been "others" in history that have sought to systematically destroy the capacity for being "other," and it is a waste of time and effort to elaborate an ethics that would theoretically have to include this destructive ability. Spinoza argues that it is the nature of a body (*conatus*) to seek positive encounters and avoid negative ones. Spinoza claims that even if for selfish reasons helping others may make us feel good, that is fine since pleasure and ethics are reinforced as they really are in God's universe (where like seeks like and there is pleasure in finding affinities among bodies). Ethical action is something that increases the ability of the self to act positively, and pleasure occurs when the self is realized or expanded according to its nature. More true to real life, it is not altruism but knowledge and power that motivate humans toward ethical action. Since we would rather live in a world in which mutual appreciation ensures the greatest security and collective power to act and defend ourselves, ethics is reinforced by the natural pleasures that our body seeks. Spinoza's immanence of the self can be compared to Levinas's transcendental ethics of the other, but not without eliminating the dissonances of Spinoza's privileging of the natural self and Levinas's distrust of the self that broods in its being. Both ethical philosophies are necessary, even as critiques of one another. A Levinas in the streets, manifesting desire; a Spinoza dialoguing with rabbis, searching for a way to strengthen ethics and Jewish culture.

15. See Silvan S. Tomkins, *Affect, Imagery, Consciousness.*

16. Damasio, *Looking for Spinoza,* 165.

17. There is continued debate among neurologists, psychologists, philosophers, and artists on how to subdivide the affects into categories. Tomkins proposes eight main affects, distinct from drives of pleasure and pain. Damasio draws a multiply branching tree that puts regulative affects at the base and more subtle affects at the finer, higher regions of the affect system.

18. Deleuze, *Spinoza: Practical Philosophy,* 23.

19. Since these cones extend to infinity, they are actually the same cone. The point of contact, the chiasmus, could be compared to a synapse. In a similar model, Henri Bergson draws a geometric model for consciousness that shows a cone (point of perception) that touches a plane (field of potentiality)—though the topology proposed here is two cones (two beings or two substances) touching each other.

20. *Grundrisse,* trans. Martin Nicolaus (New York: Penguin Books, 1993), 90.

21. Barry Ahearn, *Zukofsky's "A": An Introduction* (Berkeley and Los Angeles: University of California Press, 1982), 114.

22. The citation is in Zukofsky's self-published *First Half of "A"-9* (New York, 1940), 1.

23. Karl Marx, *Capital,* trans. Ben Fowkes (New York: Penguin Books, 1990).

24. In a curious aside in the same chapter, Marx notes that commodities can speak in many dialects: "Let us note, incidentally, that the language of commodities also has, apart from [biblical] Hebrew, plenty of other more or less correct dialects" (*Capital* 144). Perhaps this line is winked at in Zukofsky's "A foin lass bodders me," a dialect rendering of "Donna Mi Prega" contained as a study in *First Half of "A"-9.*

25. In a similar comparison, consider the Spinozist inflected language of desire in the philosophy of Guy Debord, who writes, "Consciousness of desire and the desire for consciousness together and indissolubly constitute that project which in its negative form has as its goal the abolition of classes and the direct possession by the workers of every aspect of their activity. The opposite of this project is the society of the spectacle, where the commodity contemplates itself in a world of its own making." Guy Debord, *Society of the Spectacle*, trans. Donald Nicholson-Smith (New York: Zone Books, 1994), 34.

26. This issue resonates with T. S. Eliot's notion of "objective correlative," where a word is said to conjure a specific thing or emotion. Zukofsky seems not to be totally opposed to such a proposition, but Zukofsky wants nothing to do with the proprietary and aristocratic function that Eliot attributes to language. For Eliot, emotions give way to feelings of authenticity that are steeped in classical hierarchies and ritualistic dramas. Zukofsky aims at the labor and life of words, enjoying a mixture of sincerity and playfulness. Language does not pivot around objective correlatives, but collections of lived-through correspondences.

27. Here is Whitehead on the poetics of symbols: "The poet is a person for whom visual sights and sounds and emotional experiences refer symbolically to words. The poet's readers are people for whom his words refer symbolically to the visual sights and sounds and emotions he wants to invoke. Thus in the use of language there is a double symbolic reference:—from things to words on the part of the speaker, and from words back to things on the part of the listener." In Whitehead, *Symbolism: Its Meaning and Effect* (New York: Capricorn Books, 1927), 12. Whitehead also uses the term "objectification" in several places in this book, a few years before Zukofsky latched on to the term. It is possible that Zukofsky had read Whitehead prior to writing "Sincerity and Objectification."

Peirce argues that words are the fundamental units of symbols: "All words, sentences, books, and other conventional signs are symbols. . . . The word itself has no existence although it has a real being, consisting in the fact that existents will conform to it." In *Philosophical Writings of Charles Peirce*, ed. Justus Buchler (New York: Dover, 1955), 112. But ultimately, the pragmatist Peirce resists both affective and poetic potentialities of language: "My pragmatism, having nothing to do with qualities of feeling" (272); as well as this anti-poetic screed: "But the time is coming when there shall be no more poetry, for that which was poetically divined shall be scientifically known." In *Charles S. Peirce: Selected Writings*, ed. Philip P. Weiner (New York: Dover, 1958), 13.

28. Alain Badiou, *Ethics: An Essay on the Understanding of Evil*, trans. Peter Hallward (New York: Verso, 2002).

29. Quoted in Louis Zukofsky, *Bottom: On Shakespeare* (Wesleyan University Press, 2002), 83.

“Can a jew be wild”

The Radical Jewish Grammar of Gertrude Stein’s Voices Poems

Amy Feinstein

During and after World War One, Gertrude Stein combined the strange and the familiar in a poetic style that consisted of conversational excerpts by unattributed voices.[1] In these “voices” poems, habitually unmoored from any static context save the human voice, short statements with varying degrees of sense follow one another creating “voice-montages” that make it difficult to ascertain where sense-continuity begins and ends (Moad 1). Successive voicings may indicate semantic breaks and one puzzles over the juxtaposition, or they may indicate continuity and one attempts to make meaning between them. The conventional critical reading of Stein’s nonrepresentational and voices texts argues that their purposeful openness to interpretation forms a libratory and “thoroughly democratic” language practice (Quartermain 43).[2] Such claims, however, often rely on assumptions regarding Stein’s marginalized and queer “Jewomanish” subject position, which stereotype Stein’s sense of her identity as lesbian, a woman, and a Jew (Damon, “Gertrude Stein’s Jewishness” 502). When Maria Damon argues, for example, that “Stein creates makeshift homelands in books comprised of language that itself is not stable, but. . . . enacts the instability that necessarily informs a Jewish notion of home” (499), her thinking dovetails with the general narrative of displacement in modern Jewish history and with Stein’s biography: Stein had lived in three countries by the age of five and lost both of her parents when she was still in her teens. While instability was a discernable quality of her youthful home life, Stein nonetheless consistently figured the middle-class Jewish home as an ideal of domestic stability, worthwhile because of the strictures of conventionality it engendered. Even if Stein did partake in some kind of early-twentieth-century Jewish *gestalt,* the evidence from Stein’s early writing is at best contradictory: at times Stein endorses fin-de-siècle theories of Jewish primitivism, dogmatism, and deviance, and at times she reappropriates such associations to bolster notions of Jewish chosen-ness, superiority, and genius. In any case, critical assumptions about Stein's identity that draw conclusions about her metaphorically Jewish textual practice have tended to overlook the explicit, nonmetaphorical Jewish content that appears in her voices writing. Against the desires of critics to read Stein's Jewish identity as a solely revolutionary impulse, I argue that Stein figures Jews as icons of both convention and singularity, inflecting personal stories and the histories of peoples with the longevity and authority of Jewish practice and biblical and literary traditions, while also using heterogeneous Jewish voices to call such authority and traditions into question.

Beginning in 1915, Stein makes her first direct references to Jewish people, ideas, and history in writing aimed at publication.[3] Such references find little context in early modernist writing, where the closest comparable Jewish presence would have been Ezra Pound's prosaically anti-Semitic verse in *BLAST,* "Let us be done with Jews and Jobbery, / Let us SPIT upon those who fawn on the JEWS for their money"(45), or the handful of Jews scattered about Joyce's *Dubliners,* both from 1914. By 1919 one could have read of "Rachel née Rabinovitch" with her "murderous paws," who inaugurates the London publication of T. S. Eliot's *Poems* and is joined in 1920 by the "spawned" and "squatting" Jews of the New York edition (13). Only in the twenties and thirties would Stein's references to Jews have coincided with the much more notable Semitic presence in many of the seminal works of the modernist era.

If a primary concern is arguably identifiable in the voices compositions, it is not, by and large, with things Jewish. Stein peppered these writings with the names of specific locales, newsworthy figures and events, and, from time to time, a Jewish lexicon predominated by the words "Jew" and "Jewish." These words appear as abruptly as lightning striking, as it does on the preceding stanzaic "Page" of the poem quoted in my title, "Have They Attacked Mary. He Giggled. (A Political Caricature)," published in *Vanity Fair* in 1917:

Page VIII

Lighting.
We can see to the lighting.

Page IX

Can a jew be wild.[4]

Stein incorporates a Jewish lexicon into the voices poems, and, as in this example, that lexicon maintains a surprising sense of abstraction due to the strange fabric of the texts in which it appears. Such explicit references to

Jews and Jewishness resonate nonetheless with the gradually accumulated if often-enigmatic meanings about Jews and Jewish identity that had appeared in Stein's earlier writing in a more veiled form. Stein's "jew" allows the word's long history as a racial epithet to be heard while also blithely ignoring it. Later, in *Everybody's Autobiography* (1937), Stein affirms this reappropriation, insisting that Jews should be called Jews: "I dislike it when instead of saying Jew they say Hebrew or Israelite or Semite, I do not like it. . . . Well its name is Negro if it is a Negro and Jew if it is a Jew and both of them are nice strong solid names and so let us keep them" (206). Stein even puns on the sound of the word *Jews* and their reputation as a chosen people when asking readers to *choose* between sound and sense and among various significations in this persistently indeterminate writing: "I choose Christmas and I choose an education. And I choose a robust jew. And I choose, I choose mending glasses" ("As Fine As Melanctha" 267). Such choices emphasize the methodological determinacy of the voices poems in maintaining simultaneous and multiple significations and frustrating the possibility of choosing a single meaning.[5] Whether Jews are superstitious ("A horse shoe soothes a Jew"), a people to be bothered en masse ("she annoys every Jew"), or merely tricksters ("he was terribly deceived about the Jews"), Stein registers uncertainty over the nature of Jewish difference and whether "Jew" or "Jewish" have real meaning in describing cultural, racial, national, or biological character ("Reread Another. A Play" 352; "Saints and Singing: A Play" 393; "Geography" 240). Similar to the "peculiar tension between conventional symbols . . . and [more] stylized images of reality" that Marjorie Perloff sees in Cubist painting, Stein's Jewish lexicon in the voices poems points to the resistance of the word "jew" to a singularity of meaning and to the difficulty with which it sheds its cluster of historical and cultural associations (72).

Stein had, previously, purposefully omitted the word "Jew" from her work, despite the importance of implicitly Jewish character in her early fictions. Indeed, my archival research reveals that for the first decade of Stein's life as a writer, she consistently neutralized all references to Jews when writing for publication. Stein's character studies—recorded in notebooks written at the same time as her revisions to *The Making of Americans* (1906–1911), for example—refer explicitly to "Jewish" nature as one of the two major sides of human character. Racial understandings of human difference soon lost some of their explanatory power for Stein, and, in the novel itself, Stein references Jewish nature only metaphorically, using behavioral terms that mark a clear shift away from "scientific" racial classifications of Jewish nature. Ulla Dydo dubs Stein "a master of neutralizing the language" and indicates that Stein used the word "decontextuate" to describe her attempts to erase the particularities of proper names and other nouns with their attendant historical and cultural associations (Dydo 6–7).

In a seeming reversal of the process of decontextuating her diction, however, Stein makes notable Jewish references in the voices writing, with an explicitly Jewish lexicon that functions in three ways. First, as the above examples demonstrate, Stein asks qualitative questions about Jewish nature, such as "Can a jew be wild," which in turn suggest ontological questions about Jews individually and as a group. Secondly, Stein merges private and public discourses by writing about a love relationship whose language of affection has a familial Jewish accent, affirming her sense of the clannish comfort and support of the conventional bourgeois Jewish family. This romantic Jewish lexicon focuses on the possession of a Jewish noun, the love-object, in domestic relations. In contrast, Stein's third use of a Jewish lexicon focuses on the international relations concerning the proper nouns "Zionist" and "Palestine" in the aftermath of World War One. Grammatically, speakers in these poems exploit the diplomatic personification of nations as individuals inhabiting relationships of independence and possession, and semantically, these voices call into question the very nature of nations and national identities. In each of these lexical uses, Stein's "jew" becomes a wild card of modern identity, remaking romantic, diplomatic, and nationalistic discourses, while also confirming conservative poetic, political, and social traditions.

In her lecture, "Poetry and Grammar," Stein states that "Poetry is doing nothing but using losing refusing and pleasing and betraying and caressing nouns. . . . really loving the name of any thing" (*Lectures in America* 231–232). As critics have observed, one finds ample evidence of this metaphorical merging of writing and loving throughout Stein's career.[6] In the first voices poems, written in what she later referred to as her "romanticism" era, beginning in 1914, Stein names the love of her life, Alice B. Toklas, sometimes using a Jewish lexicon ("Composition as Explanation" 501). On or about 1910, Stein and her brother Leo were joined in their Paris apartment by Alice Toklas and, once Leo departed in the summer of 1913, Stein and Toklas began a domestic arrangement that they considered to be a marriage and that lasted until Stein's death thirty-three years later.[7] Stein wrote frequent love notes to Toklas, such as one addressing her as "my little Hebrew" and, in numerous voices poems, turns these private love letters into public, publishable language within the poems themselves (qtd. in Dydo 27).[8] References to pearls, rosebuds, weddings, and honeymoons, as well as constant "cooing," declaim the romantic and often connubial context of these poems ("A Sonatina Followed By Another" 4–7). A voice in one poem observes outright that the poem is made up of "Eighty pages of love and blandishment and small handwriting," revealing its romantic methods to be those of traditional love poetry whose function, as blandishment, was a persuading or cajoling flattery ("A Sonatina Followed by Another" 4). In poems whose voices are by turns epic, choral, epithalamial, lyrical, doggerel,[9] and sexual, Jewish nature serves as a kinship marker of the marital bond between Stein and Toklas, typically with Stein as husband or baby to Toklas's wife and mother. *Lifting Belly* (composed 1915–1917), for example, one of the earliest and longest of the romantic poems, includes the exchange: "Say how do you do to the lady. Which lady. The jew lady. How do you do. She is my wife" (100). And in another long voices poem, "A Sonatina Followed By Another" (from 1921), one hears that "Little Alice B. is the wife for me" from a speaker who repeatedly exclaims, "I love her too my little jew" (12, 31), a possessive endearment that evokes the idealized cohesiveness and affection of the middle-class Jewish family.[10] Stein thus articulates her relation, as husband to Toklas's wife, in Jewish terms of endearment that invoke traditional poetic methods of blandishment, while radically departing from traditional poetic forms and objects.

Some feminist critics frown on Stein's frequent use of this conventional and often chivalric poetic husbandry, while others interpret it as a transgressive reinterpretation of gender roles.[11] Gender transgressions (or lack thereof) seem secondary, however, to the transgressive allusions to Jewish household traditions in "A Sonatina Followed By Another":

> I took a piece of pork and I stuck it on a fork and I gave it to a curly headed jew jew jew.
> I want my little jew to be round like a pork, a young round pork with a cork for his tail.
> A young round pork. I want my little jew to be round like a young round pork. I do. (13–14)

In this passage, which parodies a Mother Goose rhyme, a speaker feeds "my little jew" with parental affection that echoes the fattening of Hansel and Gretel by the witch. The speaker's concern over the Jew's diet accords with Kay Turner's well-documented account of Stein's unremitting expressions of concern for Toklas's digestive health (Turner 25–30). Such concern here transgresses Jewish dietary laws, juxtaposing the speaker's role as the best kind of Jewish mother with the worst (or witchiest), by having the caregiver flagrantly break those traditions by feeding pork to a Jew.[12] And yet the passage concludes with a rhyme that affirms traditional family ties by binding "my little jew" to the speaker with the wedding vow, "I do."[13]

The amatory context of the Jewish references in the poem highlight the peculiarity of "Jew" as a name that had not before been dared to be spoken as an object of affection in English poetry. By calling attention to the speaking of and the very sound of the word "jew," the romantic lexicon of the voices poems radically breaks from tradition; it "unfreezes" the word "jew" from its history as a demon or epithet in English literature (Nielsen 3). The main speaker in "A Sonatina Followed By Another" repeatedly refers to the very recital of her love, prompted it seems by her Jewish lover, as revealed in a two-voiced exchange in the poem's opening lines: "And what would you have me do. / I would have you sing songs to your little Jew" (4). The voice serenading this "little Jew" sustains the vocalization of the word "Jew" through rhyme (with "do" here) and repetition (such as "jew jew jew" in the passage above). Near the end of the poem, the speaker reprises the annunciatory framework:

> I say it to you and I say it to you I say it to you how I love my little jew. I say it to you and I say it to you. I say it to you and I say it to you. I say it to you.
>
> How can I have the air of here and there and I say it to you I say it to you I love my own little jew. How can I have the air and I do care I care for her hair and there for the rest of her too my little jew. I love her too my little jew. (31)

The repetition of the phrase "I say it to you" advertises to both a general audience and the specific love object "how" the speaker "loves my little jew" and demonstrates the ease of rhyming "you" with "jew," perhaps suggesting that in this context they are synonymous. The speaker's interest in the sound of the voice ("I say it"), furthermore, recalls the poem's titular form, the musical composition "A Sonatina," which shares its root in the word for *sound* with the sonnet, a traditional poetic form for avowals of love. The vocal sounding of a Jewish noun punctuates this and other voices poems with a radical grammar; the "little jew" addressed by the speaker is not a traditional love object in English poetry but instead serves as a harmonic counterpoint to the conventional serenades and blandishments of traditional love poems.

Stein's romantic voices poems coincided with World War One and its aftermath and many of the poems merge the poetical, personal, and familial language of blandishment with the political, general, and national rhetoric of patriotism (and diplomacy), commonly symbolized by flowers. As a voice somewhat impatiently instructs in "A Sonatina Followed By Another" (1921): "A poppy, need I say a red poppy. A poppy by its color is a symbol of the decoration a grateful country gives you in recognition of your devotion to duty and the daisies are a humble expression of a husband's love. Now take it" (10). This voice demonstrates the long-standing symbolic relationship—in terms of poetic grammar—that flowers have as "expressions" of either personal affection, as in the case of a daisy, or national appreciation, as in the case of the poppy, which came to symbolize the contributions made by WWI veterans. Despite symbolic similarity for expressing romantic and international relations in the voices poems, when considering the Jewish noun as a nation or a nationalist, unblushing blandishment gives way to a more temperate and indeterminate lexicon.

Following the Paris Peace Conference of 1919, where a treaty for Palestine was signed and where discussions of the formation of the League of Nations began, Stein wrote what she called her "world series,"[14] consisting of the poems "Land of Nations," "IRELAND," and "The Revery of the Zionist," and perhaps the poems "A League," "More League," and "Land Rising."[15] These works express a titular concern with current international affairs, however various or indeterminate their topical foci. Amid explicit references to the continuing Irish War of Independence and the diplomatic negotiations concerning British colonial possessions in Africa, Asia Minor, and the Levant, several voices poems mention Jews and Palestine and, in the case of "The Revery of the Zionist," consider the question of Jewish nationalism. As Barbara Will notes in "Gertrude Stein and Zionism," Stein later recalls the politics of the time in *The Autobiography of Alice B. Toklas,* where she writes about the Paris Peace Conference with a familiarity gleaned from Alfred Whitehead's daughter, Jessie, who "had come over with the peace commission as secretary to one of the delegations" (*Autobiography* 189). Stein continues, "Of course we were very interested in knowing all about the peace. It was then that Gertrude Stein described one of the young men of the peace commission who was holding forth, as one who knew all about the war, he had been here ever since the peace" (189–190). This reference—"it was then that Gertrude Stein described"—alludes to "The Revery of the Zionist" (1919), which begins with one voice's account of this young man's speech. Despite the poem's titular reference to a Zionist (the only work in Stein's oeuvre to mention a Jewish topic in its title), it is difficult to firmly establish who or what in the poem expresses the Zionist's revery. Here is the poem as it appears in Stein's bound volumes of typescripts:

The Revery of the Zionist

I know all about the war I have been in France ever since the peace. Remember what was said yesterday.

We can think and we know that we love our country so.

Can we believe that all Jews are these.

Let us remember that the little bird of all is not the one that has the singing doll. It sings and it sings and a great many people say it is not pleasant. Is it likely that there is real grief. Anywhere there are beards and everywhere there are girls and all about there is a wealth of imagery.

I saw all this to prove that Judaism should be a question of religion.

Don't talk about race. Race is disgusting if you don't love your country.

I don't want to go to Zion.

This is an expression of Shem.[16]

It is difficult to distinguish between the knowing "I" of the first line, likely "one of the young men of the peace commission who was holding forth," and the voices that follow. While Will is convinced that this man speaks from a Zionist point of view, there is no evidence to support such a claim. The first speaker may be Jewish and a Zionist or merely an example of someone "holding forth" in a provocative manner. Either way, the voice unwittingly provokes mistrust of his "know-all" claims to authority about a war from which he has been absent.

Stein expresses a similar concern over claims to expertise in the short voices poem "A Radical Expert" (1918), quoted below in its entirety, where one voice calls into question the idea of expertise and where, for another voice, authority ambiguously rests on the "saying-so" of "a great many Jews":

A Radical Expert

Can you please by asking what is expert. And then we met one another. I do not think it right. Marksman. Expert. Loaf. Potato bread. Sugar Card. Leaf. And mortar. What is the meaning of white wash. The upper walls.

That sounds well.

And then we sinned.

A great many jews say so. (198)

In this poem the opening questioner challenges the expert's authority and the very idea of expertise by inquiring about it, implying that it might not be "pleasing" to the so-called expert for others to ask "what is expert." As is typical in voices poems, sequential lines are indeterminately related by sense, disarming even the expert reader, and making it difficult to determine the semantic context for the mention of Jews in the poem's final line. The concluding triplet first expresses an affirming judgment ("That sounds well"), then a confession ("And then we sinned"), and then perhaps a justification for the judgment, an attribution for the confession, an attribution of the authority according to which "we sinned," or merely the unrelated observation that "A great many jews say so." The final line implies that large numbers may authorize expertise and, in the case of large numbers of Jews, this may allude to biblical authority in which, Genesis-like, the saying makes it so. Jewish declarations may be considered suspect, however, if one considers the literary reputation of Shylock's merciless steadfastness or the popular reputation of the alleged degeneracy plaguing the genius of fin-de-siècle Jewish nature. The last line may thus call into question the validity of these judgments or confessions, not just as hearsay, but untrustworthy precisely because "a great many jews say so."

In another "world series" poem, "Jews" once again have their say in the final line, but in this case, the plural reference masks the voice of a character penned by the Jewish writer and English politician Benjamin Disraeli. Stein alludes abstractly to a passage from Disraeli's 1870 novel *Lothair,* in which the heroine is asked if she is conventional, and she answers, "Well, I live only for climate and the affections" (105). Stein concludes the poem "Land of Nations" with the lines, "What do we live for. / Climate and the affections. Jews quote that" (408). By abstracting the famed Jewish source of the quotation, Stein renders the voice anonymous. It maintains its authority, however, as part of a Jewish plurality. In both poems there is an ambiguous relationship between an unidentified first-person plural speaker ("And then we sinned" and "What do we live for") and the third-person plural Jewish speakers. Whether by "saying so" or "quoting that," Stein highlights the plural articulations of Jewish expression to assert Jewish authority as a broadly unified voice.

"The Revery of the Zionist," in contrast, disperses Jewish expression.[17] Although the poem concludes with a reference to the thoughts of a single Jewish speaker, "This is an expression of Shem," not only does "this" remain indeterminate as the referent for Shem's expression but who Shem is and his relationship to other voices in the poem remains indeterminate as well. Syntactically, Shem's "expression" might refer to the titular "Revery," perhaps embodied by the entire poem, or merely to the desire not to go to Zion voiced by the speaker of the penultimate line. Shem, the Hebrew word for "name," is commonly used in Jewish tradition to refer to God without using the name for God. If the poem's contents in whole or in part are "an expression of Shem," the name of the one who, according to the Bible, named and created, then Shem's authority is authorial and poetry assumes a divine function for

Stein as it names and "caress[es] nouns," something Stein may allude to with the two definite articles in the poem's title. Or, by way of the Bible, Shem's "expression" might refer more semantically to the nature of Judaism and the Jewish people as a race, nation, or religion, topics debated by voices in the poem. In Genesis 10:5, Shem was one of Noah's sons who, with his brothers Ham and Japheth, was considered to be one of the progenitors of world peoples, differentiated, as later commentators understood it, by racial phenotype: Ham as progenitor of those with black skin, Japheth with white, and Shem with the yellow-brown or red of those people from the Levant now called "Semitic" after him.[18] So an "expression of Shem" might indicate more colloquially a "Semitic expression," not unlike "Jews quote that," and thereby affirm, through allusion to the story of Noah, a Jewish racial difference.

Years before, in a college essay, Stein had argued that Jews were a race whose spiritual foundation was a morally purposeful religion of endeavor. She suggested that Jews should remain racially distinct to preserve their strength of moral purpose and other beneficial Jewish character traits, since the familial bond of race "does not in any sense clash with the loyalty of a man to his nation" ("The Modern Jew" 426). Although the Jews may have been a nation in ancient times, Stein reassured her collegiate readers that the Jews were no longer a nationality: "the Jew's loyalty to Judaism is not that of obedience to any temporal power, not to a formation of any kind of government" ("The Modern Jew" 426). Some of the voices in "The Revery" seem to echo Stein's collegiate urgings for Jews to maintain a racial separatism through endogamous marriage and to avoid Jewish nationalism. These voices insist on a differentiable if interdependent notion of race and nation and may mock the Zionist's revery by disavowing Zionism in lieu of diasporic patriotism. Once Zionism is equated with racialism, it becomes a nationalism gone awry, something expressed by the three negative imperatives "don't" near the end of the poem: "Don't talk about race. Race is disgusting if you don't love your country. / I don't want to go to Zion."[19] Similarly, the patriotic sing-song of the third line may be diasporic or Zionist—"We can think and we know that we love our country so"—although, if this *is* the song of the Zionist rallying a unified Jewish citizenry, the next line inverts the "we can" surety of the previous by asking, "Can we believe that all Jews are these." This question emphasizes the grammatical abuse of power when someone purports to speak for "all" by using the first-person plural "we," even if the questioner uses it too, perhaps ironically, to make the point that there might be more than one "we." In this vein, the young man unpleasantly "holding forth," who claims to "know *all* about the war," may likewise be mocked when another voice tells of "the little bird of *all*" whose singing "a great many people say is not pleasant" (emphases added). Despite a "wealth of imagery" and one speaker's "all"-encompassing empirical proofs—"I saw all this to prove that Judaism should be a question of religion"—the nature of Judaism and Jewish identity remain indeterminate in "The Revery of the Zionist," even as various voices affirm separable racial, national, and religious Jewish identities. Given the heterogeneous voices in the poem, "all" Jews may not be Zionists interested in tying Jewish identity to the land of Palestine.[20]

The opening lines of the voices poem "Coal and Wood" (1920), which describe "a ridiculous authority" (3), may, like "The Revery," be referring to a dubious voice "holding forth" at the Paris Peace Conference. Unlike the voice in "The Revery," however, this one plausibly sounds like a Zionist despite the lack of specificity of his proclamation, since he expresses interest in an unspecified "land." He states: "This is an introduction to a description of an incident which will interest all of us in the land which interests all of us and where we all would like to be" ("Coal and Wood" 4). If the "we" in question refers to Jews, this voice sounds like a Zionist, who energetically if undiplomatically exhibits what a voice in another poem calls "the rising tide of national enthusiasm" ("Painted Lace" 2) about a place where, in the perfect future, "we all would like to be." The voice's pronounced use of "all," insists that his listeners are of one mind, a rhetorical tic that unintentionally implies that Zionism (or any nationalist fervor) may *not* "interest all of us," even if a "great many" "Jews *are* these." Instead, the call for a Jewish state in Palestine, a specifically Zionist reverie, ironically provides Stein with the opportunity to cement her understanding of a heterogeneous racial and religious Jewish identity exclusive of nationality. With these voices, she affirms the idea that Zionism or any nationalist movement could not exist without rhetorical, diplomatic, or other "enthusiasms."

What then is the specific significance of Stein's several references to Palestine in these and other voices poems?[21] The wider scope of the much longer poem "Coal and Wood" gives a clearer sense of Stein's thinking of Palestine as part of Britain's imperial endeavors, which were decidedly on the upswing in the wake of the Paris Peace Conference of 1919. Britain may have been losing Ireland to independence but maintained its sway as a great power, winning territories through the diplomatic proceedings at the Peace Conference and in the League of Nations.[22] In order to provide fuel for its immense navy, Britain was determined to assure its access to oil concessions in the lands of the former Ottoman Empire from Baku to Mosul.[23] As the war ended, it quickly moved armed forces to maintain and establish colonial administrations in several newly mandated lands in Asia Minor, Palestine, Mesopotamia, and even portions of the former German Cameroon (to be administered as part of Nigeria). Resistance to the occupying British-led Allied forces helped spark Turkish nationalist movements "all over Anatolia," which "reached a crisis stage by late 1919" (Gokay 51). The formal makeup of Stein's voices poems domesticates (and pacifies) international affairs to the level of salon conversation—the point of intersection between the public and private realms—and confirms Stein's attention to both the diplomatic proceedings in Paris and to news of events taking place outside the diplomatic arena. The often-indeterminate voices in the poems also convey her sensitivity to the limitations and often-masked purposes of diplomacy. As one voice says, "I can exist in conversation. So can the Turk" (5).

The politesse of the diplomatic rhetoric rehearsed by many voices in "Coal and Wood" veils a greed for the natural resources to be procured in British colonies and protectorates, including Palestine. Implicitly and explicitly the poem is concerned in large part with natural resources (such as those named in the title) and the often-fraught international dynamics of acquiring and maintaining those resources in the face of national struggles for possession and independence. Voices in the poem debate, for example, whether "We need to conquer the British Empire" or whether "The British Empire conquers" (8). Voices also question the merits of independence struggles like the one in Ireland: one asks, "And what do you believe should be done by independence" (4), and another, "Can you tell me how to protect possessions" (7), and another, "But why should Ireland be free" (7), and another, "He feels it necessary to offend Ireland" (7). These and other questions, such as "How many nations make a country" (5), openly trouble "country" and "nation" as names for people and places to suggest the constructed and often consolidated nature of empire. The following voice-montage, furthermore, sounds as though countries are conducting diplomacy at a tea party:

Let us call countries.
How often are you exasperated. We are exasperated very often.
A great many meanings are respected.
We respect the other.
Thank you politely.
Let us call their countries.
Little country to a big country. Split in two you. You split in two. I excuse you.
Let us regret Sylvia.
I dare not use another name.
How many nations make a country.
A country is tall.
Very tall. Not small.
Let us call a country. (5)

Like the lover in Stein's romantic poems who likes to mention having things said aloud, one of the above voices in "Coal and Wood" repeatedly refers to the "calling" of countries by name, even though no country names are mentioned in the first third of the poem. Instead, when "calling countries," a voice names "Sylvia," a name that looks and sounds like Syria and echoes through other place-names like Transylvania or Pennsylvania, exposing the artificiality of diplomatic conventions of personification, according to which things may not necessarily be called by their real names. Indeed, the very next voice asserts, "I dare not use another name," an allusion to the famous concluding line, "I am the love that dare not speak its name," of Lord Alfred Douglas's poem "Two Loves," which ironically couches the ceremonious discourses of diplomacy's calling of countries in the romantic lexicon of desire. The nature of the allusion is ambiguous, however, for the voice may "use" a name not dared to be spoken, or, like the speaker in Douglas's poem, the voice may dare "not use another name" than the one allowed by convention or propriety.

The conversational diplomacy in "Coal and Wood" nonetheless maintains copasetic relations through semiotic openness, as when "A great many meanings are respected" and "We respect the other." Perhaps this openness even encourages the bluntness of directives that might "exasperate" or "offend," such as "Split in two you. You split in two. I excuse you." Another voice in the poem calls on Palestine in a series of colonial lands plagued by diplomatic and personal offenses. Echoing an earlier call to "Come together colonies" (6), a speaker rallies these "dear" and "offended" lands into a kind of colonial counterpart to the League of Nations: "He feels it necessary to offend Ireland. Defend Ireland. Offend Arabia. And Palestine. Dear Palestine. Arouse yourself dear Nigeria. Arouse yourself dear Southerland. Arouse yourself you are dormant. Arouse yourself land of promise. Be proud of oil, olive oil, wood oil, ground oil, cotton seed oil, ginger oil, palm oil, and gushing oil. Be proud of yourselves all of you together and sing peaceably. Gather yourselves together for an education. Read the notices. Decide the parts. And be gracious. If you must do it do it graciously" (7). By including Palestine in a litany of English colonial possessions in Europe, Africa, and the Levant, Stein confirms her sense of Palestine as part of the larger diplomatic conversations about international relations, rather than solely a question of Jewish nationalism. A voice with a hint of divine authority does, however, distinguish Palestine from the others with the biblical allusion to the "land of promise." And yet, the context of the passage frustrates attempts to fix the referent and renders the significance of the allusion indeterminate, since the voice may allude to the Promised Land to signify not just Palestine but, more broadly, the "promise" that Nigeria, Southerland, *and* Palestine have as British protectorates rich in natural resources. In this passage the rhetorical caresses of a condescending blandishment (the repeated use of "dear") seem to sooth the "offenses" of empire (enacted by a representative "he") but it is impossible to determine whether the addresses to these colonies are examples of offensive remarks (by "he") or rebuttals to such offenses. However ambiguous, the rules of this vocal game follow the thinly veiled imperialism of European diplomacy and suggest a reading of Stein's interest in Palestine as a land among other lands "chosen" for exploitation by Europe.

The "voices" poems remain one of the most enigmatic works of modernist writing and, in their use of a Jewish lexicon, reveal the abstraction present in seemingly non-metaphorical language. Persistent ambiguity and abstraction would seem to tend toward the asemantic and hermetic, but instead the voices poems are fascinating for their simultaneous voicing of plain-spoken quotidian concerns. For Stein, there may be something Jewish about the modernist determination to frustrate the surety of interpretation while persistently encouraging it. In the poem "Geography" from 1923, Stein associates such resistance to semantic fixity and surety with "the Jews":

> He was terribly deceived about the Jews about Napoleon and about everything else.
>
> If you do not know the meaning of such things do not use them. That is all. Such phrases. ("Geography" 240)

The first voice clearly states that an unspecified "he" had not realized how much he misunderstood "the Jews," "Napoleon," and "everything else;" it is not clear, however, whether the deception was caused by his own reluctance to accept the truth about "the Jews," et al., or whether someone else had deceived him "terribly" about them. The subsequent lines complain about someone's dubious usage of "such things" the meaning of which one may not know. The "things" in this case might be words, since there is a voice earlier in the poem that seems to be looking up a word in the dictionary—"Looking up under fairly see fairly looking up under as to movement" (239)—or groups of words, since a voice says with possible exasperation, "Such phrases." "The Jews" in the passage, possibly indicated by one of "such phrases," are elusively meaningful, as a group of people, who are as imperiously and singularly evocative as Napoleon and yet as diffusely identifiable as "everything else."

Stein's Jewish lexicon figures both indeterminacy and fixity in these poems that trace the possibilities and limits of modern poetry. "The Jews" might inhabit a concretely geographic place or verifiable dictionary definition and also be "terribly deceiving." Jewish identity, for Stein, thus inhabits a "meaning" that may individually name Jewish history, tradition, place, ideology, and people, while also affirming a multiplicity that renders abstract, ambiguous, and anonymous the words and phrases "Jew," "Jewish," "a Jew," and "the Jews." By summoning the wild heterogeneity of modern Jewish identity, Stein expresses a paradoxical marriage of convention and singularity, such that Jews *are* wild: whether as frozen metaphors for stranger or lover, for religious tradition or semantic apostasy, they remain abstract, representative pretenders and symbolize the ever-separating but never absolutely distinct nature of words and meaning.

Notes

1. Unidentified voices dominate the overarching structure of the pieces, which is why Marianne DeKoven dubs them the "voices" style. Rosalind Moad elaborates on this characterization and describes them as "voice-montages" in which Stein experimentally attempted to "catch ephemeral voices in literary forms" (Moad 1).

2. In addition to Peter Quartermain, see Shari Benstock, Marianne DeKoven, Elizabeth Fifer, Lisa Ruddick, and Neil Schmitz. Notably, Lorna Smedman calls this libratory reading into question by looking at Stein's use of black racial epithets and Wanda Van Dusen argues the opposite extreme (of Stein's fascism).

3. Stein's 1913 composition "Yet Dish," from the "lively words" style that directly preceded the "voices" style, is often read as a transyllabification of the word "Yiddish." Although this may be the first time Stein *pronounces* a Jewish topic in her work, it is still visually veiled by the punning homophones.

4. The appearance of the word "jew" in the poem likely provoked the editor to introduce Stein not only as a "Cubist writer," with an intellectually daunting oeuvre of "greatly misunderstood masterpiece[s]," "who is immensely famous in France," but also as "a Jewess, once of San Francisco, but now of Paris." In the version later published in *Selected Writings* the "J" in "jew" is capitalized even though it was not capitalized in Stein's manuscript notebook nor in *Vanity Fair.*

5. DeKoven sees such semantic openness as forming a "comic contrast" with the "absolute assurance of th[e] tone" of such declarations (86).

6. Julie Abraham argues that Stein's love life and her writing life were intimately intertwined and Dydo claims that "Stein likens the creative act to the sexual act" (Abraham 87; Dydo *Gertrude Stein* 28).

7. See Mellow 149–150. Moad gives the dates as 1909 and 1914 (238).

8. Many of these notes appear in her drafting notebooks where, as Dydo argues, they were used to communicate Stein's affection and sometimes served as incantation-like dedications to mark the beginning of a new composition. See also Kay Turner's publication of Stein's love notes, a selection that includes at least three Jewish references (100, 143, 148).

9. See Damon's "Gertrude Stein's Doggerel 'Yiddish': Women, Dogs and Jews."

10. Stein's familial Jewish vocabulary extended to her close relations outside the home as well; in correspondence, for example, Stein notes that she is "rather pleased" that Picasso considers her to be "a real Jewish mother" to his children (Gertrude Stein, Letter to Robert and Diana Abdy, c. 1938).

11. Blanche Cook, Penelope Engelbrecht, and Gilbert and Gubar frown on what they see as Stein's embrace of stereotypical gender roles while Turner, Benstock, Norris, DeKoven, and Ruddick are encouraged by it. Stimpson outlines Stein's simultaneous repudiation and reconstitution of heterosexual and patriarchal norms ("Stein and the Transposition of Gender").

12. In another poem, "As Fine As Melanctha," Stein has voices discuss fattening another Jew with butter: "Waves of heat in cold weather make steam, I do not know why they call it a dream. I really do not know how to dream. Do you. Fill the jew. With what. With butter. Thank you so much for all that good butter" (263).

13. The following year Stein corroborates the connubial context of this poem by writing in another poem that, "A sonatina followed by another is a honeymoon" ("Mildred's Thoughts" 364).

14. On October 16, 1919, Stein sent the poems "The Revery of the Zionist," "IRELAND," and "Land of Nations," to Ellery Sedgwick, the editor of the *Atlantic Monthly* as part of what she called her "World Series" (Letter to Ellery Sedgwick, YCAL MSS 77, Box 15).

15. The poem "More League" also appeared as one of "Two Cubist Poems. The Peace Conference" in the *Oxford Magazine* (see Dydo 94n).

16. The poem was composed between January and October 1919. I am quoting from the corrected typescript of the poem from Stein's Bound Volume 15 (YCAL MSS76, Box 90, Folder 1701, page 300), rather than the version published in the posthumous volume *Painted Lace* (94). On the typescript "Revery" is spelled with a "y" instead of an "ie" and has a "singing doll" rather than a "singing dell."

17. As Damon argues, "The piece appears to be shot through with contradictions. . . . [that] enact the internal heterogeneity, the contentious pluralism that comprises the Jewish interpretive community ("Gertrude Stein's Jewishness" 503). Will, too, points to the way that the "voices" style "emphasizes heterogeneity rather than agreement, pluralism rather than univocality" ("Gertrude Stein and Zionism" 440).

18. See Stephen R. Haynes, *Noah's Curse: The Biblical Justification of American Slavery* (New York: Oxford University Press, 2002).

19. As Barbara Will usefully notes, this voice's claim "that '[r]ace is disgusting if you don't love your country' . . . open[s] the door for the argument that racialist or racist thinking is acceptable if you *do* love your country" (451). Will warns that despite its ambiguity, such thinking—which she attributes to Stein—hints at a linguistic congruity between Stein's diction and the nationalistic creeds of fascism: "What Stein seems to want to get away from in 'Reverie,' 'Land of Nations,' and other texts of the time is the absolute *injunction* to belong that a racialist nationalism demanded. . . . Ten years after 'Reverie,' . . . Stein's terms would indeed begin

to resonate in unfortunate ways with emerging discourses of fascism. Her insistence upon 'lov[ing] your country' would seem not dissimilar from fascist arguments about the difference between natives and 'foreigners' " (450–451).

20. A literary inspiration for this kind of heterogeneity might have been the Philosopher's Club roundtable of voices debating a proto-Zionist answer to the Jewish question in chapter 42 of George Eliot's *Daniel Deronda.* Given Stein's interest in Jews and as a great admirer of Eliot, she likely read the novel.

21. Other references to Palestine appear in "Nest of Dishes" from 1921 (*Painted Lace* 100) and "Natural Phenomena" from 1925 (*Painted Lace* 202).

22. Stephen Stillwell claims that Britain "used the League of Nations apparatus ... to forward the aims of their imperial policy" (67). In the treaty signed in the Paris suburb of Sèvres in August 1920, the British acquired mandates in Iraq and Palestine. See Stillwell's *Anglo-Turkish Relations in the Interwar Era* (Lewiston, NY: Edwin Mellon Press, 2003).

23. In late 1918, British forces followed the Ottoman army to occupy the Baku oil fields (Gokay 39) and, as Marian Kent argues, "By 1920 Mesopotamian oil . . . had come to occupy a major place in British diplomatic and military concerns in the Middle East" (Kent 157). See Kent's *Oil and Empire: British Policy and Mesopotamian Oil, 1900–1920* (London: Macmillan, 1976).

Works Cited

Abraham, Julie. *Are Girls Necessary?: Lesbian Writing and Modern Histories.* London: Routledge, 1996.

Benstock, Shari. *Women of the Left Bank.* Austin: University of Texas Press, 1986.

Cook, Blanche. " 'Women Alone Stir My Imagination': Lesbianism and the Cultural Tradition." *Signs* 4, 4 (Summer 1979): 718–739.

Damon, Maria. "Gertrude Stein's Jewishness, Jewish Social Scientist and the 'Jewish Question.' " *Modern Fiction Studies* 42, 3 (Fall 1996): 489–506.

———. "Gertrude Stein's Doggerel 'Yiddish': Women, Dogs and Jews." *The Dark End of the Street: Margins in American Vanguard Poetry.* Minneapolis: University of Minnesota Press, 1993. 202–235.

DeKoven, Marianne. *A Different Language.* Madison: University of Wisconsin Press, 1983.

Disraeli, Benjamin. *Lothair* [1870]. London: Longmans and Co., 1882.

Dydo, Ulla. With William Rice. *Gertrude Stein: The Language That Rises (1923–1934).* Evanston: Northwestern University Press, 2003.

Eliot, T. S. *Poems.* Richmond, England: Hogarth Press, 1919.

———. *Poems.* New York: Knopf, 1920.

Engelbrecht, Penelope. " 'Lifting Belly Is a Language': The Post Modern Lesbian Subject." *Feminist Studies* 16, 1 (1990).

Fifer, Elizabeth. *Rescued Readings: A Reconstruction of Gertrude Stein's Difficult Texts.* Detroit: Wayne State University Press, 1992.

Gilbert, Sandra M., and Susan Gubar. *No Man's Land: The Place of the Woman Writer in the Twentieth Century, II: Sexchanges.* New Haven, CT: Yale University Press, 1988.

Gokay, Bulent. *A Clash of Empires: Turkey between Russian Bolshevism and British Imperialism, 1918–1923.* New York: Taurus Academic Studies, 1997.

Mellow, James R. *Charmed Circle: Gertrude Stein and Company.* New York: Avon, 1974.

Moad, Rosalind. *1914–16: Years of Innovation in Gertrude Stein's Writing.* Ph.D. dissertation. University of York, 1993.

Nielsen, Aldon Lynn. *Reading Race: White American Poets and Racial Discourse in the Twentieth Century.* Athens: University of Georgia Press, 1988.

Norris, Margot. "The 'Wife' and the 'Genius': Domesticating Modern Art in Stein's *Autobiography of Alice B. Toklas.*" *Modernism, Gender, and Culture: A Cultural Studies Approach.* Ed. Lisa Rado. New York: Garland, 1997. 79–99.

Perloff, Marjorie. *The Poetics of Indeterminacy: Rimbaud to Cage.* Princeton, NJ: Princeton University Press, 1981.

Pound, Ezra. "Salutation the Third." *BLAST* 1. [1914]. Ed. Wyndham Lewis. Santa Rosa, CA: Black Sparrow Press, 1992. 45.

Quartermain, Peter. *Disjunctive Poetics: From Gertrude Stein and Louis Zukofsky to Susan Howe.* Cambridge: Cambridge University Press, 1992.

Ruddick, Lisa. *Reading Gertrude Stein: Body, Text, Gnosis.* Ithaca, NY: Cornell University Press, 1990.

Schmitz, Neil. *Of Huck and Alice: Humorous Writing in American Literature.* Minneapolis: University of Minnesota Press, 1983.

———. "Portrait, Patriarchy, Mythos: The Revenge of Gertrude Stein." *Salmagundi* 40 (1978): 69–91.

Smedman, Lorna. "'Cousin to Cooning': Relation, Difference, and Racialized Language in Stein's Nonrepresentational Texts." *Modern Fiction Studies* 42, 3 (1996): 569–588.

Stein, Gertrude. "As Fine As Melanctha." *As Fine As Melanctha, 1914–1930.* New Haven, CT: Yale University Press, 1954. 255–269.

———. *The Autobiography of Alice B. Toklas.* 1933. New York: Vintage, 1990.

———. "Coal and Wood." *Painted Lace and Other Pieces, 1914–1937.* New Haven, CT: Yale University Press, 1955. 3–11.

———. "Composition as Explanation." *A Stein Reader.* Ed. Ulla Dydo. Evanston: Northwestern University Press, 1993. 493–503.

———. *Everybody's Autobiography.* Cambridge, MA: Exact Change, 1993.

———. "Geography." *Painted Lace.* 240.

———. "Have They Attacked Mary. He Giggled. (A Political Caricature)." *Vanity Fair* 8, 4 (June 1917): 55.

———. "Land of Nations." *Geography and Plays.* 1922. Madison: University of Wisconsin Press, 1993. 408.

———. *Lectures in America.* 1935. Boston: Beacon Press, 1985. 209–246.

———. Letter to Ellery Sedgwick. October 16, 1919. Yale Collection of American Literature (YCAL), Beinecke Rare Book and Manuscript Library, New Haven, CT.

———. Letter to Robert and Diana Abdy. c. 1938. YCAL.

———. "Lifting Belly." *Bee Time Vine, and Other Pieces, 1913–1927.* New Haven, CT: Yale University Press, 1953. 63–115.

———. "Mildred's Thoughts." 1922. *A Stein Reader.* 364.

———. "The Modern Jew Who Has Given Up the Faith of His Fathers Can Reasonably and Consistently Believe in Isolation." Ed. Amy Feinstein. *PMLA* 116 (2001): 416–428.

———. "Painted Lace." *Painted Lace and Other Pieces.* 1–3.

———. "A Radical Expert." *Bee Time Vine.* 198.

———. "Reread Another. A Play. To Be Played Indoors Or Out. I Wish to Be A School." *A Stein Reader.* 352.

———. "The Revery of the Zionist." Stein's Bound Volume 15, YCAL.

———. "Saints and Singing: A Play." *A Stein Reader.* 393.

———. "A Sonatina Followed By Another." *Bee Time Vine.* 4–32.

———. "Yet Dish." *Bee Time Vine.* 53–60.

Stimpson, Catharine. "Stein and the Transposition of Gender." *The Poetics of Gender.* Ed. Nancy K. Miller. New York: Columbia University Press, 1986. 1–18.

Turner, Kay, ed. *Baby Precious Always Shines: Selected Love Notes Between Gertrude Stein and Alice B. Toklas.* New York: St. Martin's Press, 1999.

Van Dusen, Wanda. "Portrait of a National Fetish: Gertrude Stein's 'Introduction to the Speeches of Maréchal Pétain' (1942)." *Modernism/Modernity* 3, 3 (1996): 69–92.

Will, Barbara. "Gertrude Stein and Zionism." *Modern Fiction Studies* 51, 2 (Summer 2005): 437–455.

Remains of the Diaspora

A Personal Meditation

Michael Heller

If the diaspora is my ground of no-ground, and yet the place where both signification and metaphor operate, then what does a term like "radical poetics" mean to me? If the diaspora is geographic and physical, it is also psychic and emotional, rife with constantly agitated language and even more agitated silence. Scattered, scatterings. I can only speak of it via some indirection, speak of it as remains, as traces left by encounters with others, encounters with my surroundings. My thoughts then are modified by a diaspora that never totally exists for me, and (to place my thought properly) never totally does not exist. Texts and textuality, allegiances and disavowals. Pressures. Every thought, every word should be useful, ripe with both fullness and negations, and depending on context, every word should sputter and decay toward silence. The ground of the diaspora that is not a diaspora is the place where this happens to words, where the pressure on language is at its utmost.

The Hebrew poet Haim Nahman Bialik, who saw himself as a creature of endless exile, wrote in his essay "Revealment and Concealment", that "the most dangerous moment—both in speech and in life—is that between concealments, when the void looms" (23). Let us say this writing, these words, are a concealment, and that the territory and act of the poem are always begun "between concealments." Or, as Bialik puts it: "no reply to the question of essence is ever possible in the process of speech" (21). As soon as a word is deployed as poetry—or, better, and more generally, as soon as a word is or becomes part of a figure, it has forsaken or supplemented its conventional referentiality to become something other, different, more, even something less. Bialik ascribes the impossibility of answering the question of "essence" to the perpetual dynamic of language where "a word or system declines and yields to another, not because it has lost the power to reveal, to enlighten, to invalidate the enigma . . . but for the very opposite reason—because the word or system has been worn out by being manipulated and used." The word, Bialik says, "can no longer divert mankind momentarily." A "crack" is opened, terror ensues, and the "void" looms, a void that must immediately be covered with a new word (22). Lorca had his *duende,* and the poet who is in touch—allied in some fashion—with Judaism's speculations on language has as his animating creative goad primarily his awareness of the "between," of the space of the diaspora.

This "between" is, in a sense, foundational. It exists in the relational sphere between the law of religious observance and secular life. Robert Alter, commenting on Walter Benjamin's reading of Kafka, sees it as operative in the decay of "traditional" tradition (if I may use an oxymoron), the loss of Halakic Judaism to Aggadic Judaism. What is left, according to Alter, is "lore in quest of Law, yet so painfully estranged from what it seeks that the pursuit can end in a pounce of destruction, the fictional rending the doctrinal" (*H* 53). Alter could as well be speaking of the poetic, for Kafka's 'graven' images are imagistic and allegorical constructs, already caught in the "between" of Law and lore, and demanding to be read across the two genres.

Another Israeli thinker, Ari Elon, whose thoughts in *From Jerusalem to the Edge of Heaven* inform my discussion here, writes movingly of what he calls the *ribboni* individual, the secular Jew whose activity he contrasts with the *rabbani,* the follower of the Halakic tradition who sees in Judaism's spiritual literature primarily Law. Elon speaks to the religious/secular crisis in his native country, but that crisis mirrors the conflicting pulls that animate American intellectual life as well. The central question to be asked about this crisis is put by way of a parable of doubleness, in which Elon's narrator performs a kind of mercy killing on a holy man (as Elon makes clear, this is his other self) who has been walking the streets of Jerusalem muttering that "it is Shabbat today . . . it is forbidden to put on tefillin . . . it is forbidden to tear the strings that mark the Shabbat boundaries . . . it is Shabbat today . . . it is forbidden to throw stones at dogs today." What the holy man fears most is that the dogs will run off to the edge of town and tear the strings of the Shabbat boundaries, "and then Jerusalem will not be marked off from the rest of the world" (1). Elon's parable concerns the struggle within, the act of near self-murder he must undertake to release himself from a constraining religious orthodoxy.

The *ribboni*'s mission, Elon implies, is to "turn the Torah of Israel from a source for authority to a source for inspiration" (35). "Law" into "lore." The *ribboni* must take a walk into or over the void, at which point he or she is suspended between the religious and the secular worlds, but there, according to Elon, the *ribboni* must try to hang in suspension. The "Shabbat" boundary signifies not only the limits of the theocratic dispensation but is also the edge beyond which *labor must continue.* If "shabbat" poetics sanctify rules, strategies, even moments where labor is no longer governed by thought (in the sense that it is rule- and precedent-driven), the poetics of the space beyond the Sabbath's broken string boundaries, requires endless questioning and testing. Nothing is established as final. No clean break, no new totalizing embrace. The *ribboni* is not a new person; rather, he must live with Shabbat memory, the time and space of sancity that, like a mother's embrace, offered answers and comfort. He is governed by this history, by his textual origins. For the poet of the diaspora, then, all yearnings, even those seeking to recover a lostness, involve, even if only *sub rosa,* a sense of felt opposition, of yearning against as well as for. And "innovation," warns Elon, "without tradition creates alienation and sows a short-lived field of rootless symbols doomed from their inception" (36).

But isn't this a condition of all poem making? For example, the Syrian born poet Adonis, in his *Introduction to Arab Poetics,* a book written while under his own diaspora and exile from his homeland, tells us that "legislation and codification go against the nature of poetic language, for this language, since it is man's expression of his explosive moods, his impetuousness, his difference, is incandescent, constantly renewing itself . . . always a disrupter of codes." This is not a particularly unconventional view. But he goes on: "It [poetic language] is the search for the self, and the return to the self, but by means of a personal exodus away from the self" (33). Adonis's words entail "exodus" as dynamical, in a sense, always about being in motion, but always about being in some relation between the place of departure and the place of arrival.

With Adonis, we could say that the diaspora only has meaning in terms of the exodus one has made from a homeland, or that homeland only has meaning in terms of an exodus. The poet participates in just such a movement between the capacity of language to render certainties and at the same time to undermine them, to carry a reader of the poem away from the familiar to the unfamiliar.

Whatever I have to say, then, never stands alone, never makes of itself an entity without referencing an elsewhere, an elsewhere that remains invoked and yet undefined. If, like Adonis, I search for the self, I also seek that exodus from it. And this very movement will express a kind of return to the other term, the other side of the in-between. (I would admit here to a resonance with Eliot's doctrine of the impersonal, which he saw as an "escape from personality.") And in fact, mustn't it be that as soon as I find a border or contour to something I label the self, I am already looking over the perimeter toward the non-self? Thus, I do not see the whiteness of the page or screen on which these words are placed as something neutral but as a part of the Heisenbergian motion of uncertainty, as itself a real fiction, an element in what a Buddhist would call the "as if" illusion of the real. I am not alone, certainly not in this realization.

From the *ribboni*'s standpoint—my standpoint—there is little difference between the governed utterances of the *rabbini* and those potentially freestanding ones of the purely secular (if such an utterance could even exist). For the *ribboni*, language is never determined nor free. Rather, he finds it lying between the sacred space of Israel or religion or belief and the purely secularized and mechanical spaces of the outlyings. Bialik, in his essay, constructs the fable of a word's birth, its winning of articulation from fear and confusion, and also how it is at first full, then hollowed out, then filled (if differently) again in the course of usage in time. In the sacred space, the word has already assumed its fullness of meaning; to utter is to partake of the language of God, of scriptural authority. In the outlyings, in its phases of emptiness, it has reduced itself to a husk, even to a manipulatible purity: music, *art pour l'art*, a signifier without need of its signified. (This standpoint came early to me. In the statement I made for the back cover of my first book, *Accidental Center*, published in 1972, I noted that while I tried to "pose something as language which gives more force to a human argument of the world," I also insisted that "I would not want to call it a 'fine art.'")

Bialik, in his meditations on poetry, seem to continually worry such points. His thoughts lie along the border not only of concealments but of our reifying tendencies. "If the empty word enslaves," he writes, "how much more is this true of the full word?" (15). "No word," he continues, "contains the complete dissolution of any question. What does it contain? The question's concealment" (16). Bialik's thoughts are not only a great defense against literalism but also, in the most curious way, a defense against the autonomy of language. For "concealment" can only occur referentially. That is, something before the poet must be at stake, something like the sacred nature of an object or idea, something—if we follow the kabbalists—containing within itself the Creator's intent. The boundary lines of emptiness and fullness are only the markers of a region where pressure exists for something to fulfill its function in transcendence or to "lapse" toward the profane. The word's existence, by its very nature, is always signifying a signified. But, it is also performing another more mysterious function, as Bialik notes, "by virtue of the process by which it closes up the small aperture of the void—constructing a barrier to prevent the void's darkness from welling up and overflowing its bounds" (17).

Poetry, as I sense it, as I find confirmation in Bialik and in my reading, covers the underlying void and exposes it at the same time. One of my tutors here has been Oppen's late poetry, which I read not as fragmentary or discontinuous but as a place of *agon* where void and concealment struggle with each other as Oppen strives for a complete utterance, an utterance, he is at great points not to have confused with any idea of the Rimbaudian "derangement of the senses." Oppen referred to this desire as "speaking the estranged" (254).

It is true that signifying—pointing at an object, for instance—is one of the word's more complicated strengths. The shifting dynamism of language, of syntax and meaning often make the act of signification a secondary power. Bialik admits as much, remarking that "no reply to the question of essence is ever possible in the practice of speech" (17). Essence, if I may borrow from Oppen, is always "estranged," always beyond possession. But from another perspective, to ignore or even eliminate language's signifying function—assuming this could ever be done—is to strip it of all power, to reduce it to mere sound or clever fancy. For at all times, the fullness of language must remind us of the void it conceals.

Concealment, as Bialik suggests, is always related to fear and uncertainty. Our urge to write or speak (our logorrheic disposition) comes, as Bialik points out, from "man's atmosphere of knowledge," an atmosphere that "must never for a single moment be rid of words, crowded and consecutive like the links in a great suit of armor, without so much as a hair's breath between them" (19). Long before I had read Bialik, in a gesture of my own, in my memoir *Living Root,* I had speculated in the poem "The American Jewish Clock" on the fact that my grandfather's Old World European first name Zalman was translated into "Solomon" on his arrival into the United States. What did it mean to have that added extra syllable? The Book of Genesis has this passage, which I quoted in the memoir, in which God speaks to Abraham at one of the most crucial points in the founding of Judaism: "As for me, behold my covenant is with thee, and thou shalt be a father of many nations. Neither shall thy name anymore be called Abram, but thy name shall be Abraham, for a father of many nations have I made thee" (*LR* 66, 67) The onomastic moment, in which the named one is renamed, has struck me as the singular poetic act of the Judaic sensibility, the act that contains all the empowerments of faith, psychology, and self-determination. In my speculations on the poem in the memoir, I too, somewhat like Bialik, had imagined that for a Jew, the universe was constructed of an immense brick wall of words and wordings and that the introduction of so much as a new syllable would indeed, like forcing a brick into such a wall, create a shattering and crumbling of what was there. If man's atmosphere of knowledge were a seamless armor of language (and surely this image has a monstrous paranoia about it), a continuous intoning of words, like the mumbled dovening by rote in *shuls* and *yeshivas,* wouldn't it be the poet's task to intervene, to wake one's self and others from the sleep of such "holy" verbiage?

My thought here turns speculative, poetic perhaps. What intervenes in the drone of language is the name because the name is surrounded not by more language but by silence. For a name to be a name, it must arise from, it must fall back into the space of soundlessness. A further speculation, as I hinted at in my book on the Objectivists, *Conviction's Net of Branches,* was that the poem, conceived of as a name, is in effect a stand-in for personage (*CNB* 106). This idea is ancient, rife with mystical and spiritual aspects. Gershom Scholem, in *On the Mystical Shape of the Godhead,* seems to infer exactly this sense of naming. In the book, he refers us to a key passage from Marcus, one of the early Gnostic teachers, whose work is associated with kabbalah. Marcus writes: "When, in the beginning, the fatherless father, who is neither grasped by the mind nor has a substance and who is neither man nor woman, wanted to express His ineffable being and make His invisible being visible, He opened his mouth and produced a word that resembled Him. In coming to him, it showed him that it was thereby becoming manifest as the shape of the invisible" (*TMS* 26).

If, to remind ourselves of the Gospel of John, that in the beginning was the word, Marcus's scenario is something like the Big Bang of primordial naming. Its physical structure, in Judaic terms, seems to undergird all subsequent acts of naming. Here God's unconcealment, his visibility is made possible by the production of a word that "resembled Him." The word "in coming to Him" seems to be a gathering of His attributes, which function like an empowering toward the word's utterance. They are traceries of powers and qualities. The sounding of the word will not display these attributes but will manifest as the "shape of the invisible." It is as though revealment and concealment, Bialik's terms, were simply the two sides of the same coin. The name both posits God and preserves His mystery, that is, preserving as well, the invisibility of the "fatherless father."

Walter Benjamin writes, in the spirit of Bialik's "revealment and concealment," that "the theory of proper names is the theory of the frontier between the finite and the infinite," the conditions of his "void," transposed onto something like a mathematical plane. Not only does name reside alongside the use of number (finites and infinities) in a range of poetics, but, like mathematics itself, poetry is very much the carrying of ratios into articulation. I would add to this, that the proper name and the poem point to similar entities, specificities created by language that cannot be reduced solely to genre or class. Benjamin says elsewhere that "a speaker who is poetic in the literal sense of the word—namely a maker whose activity is that of producing a new meaning, a maker who is creative—is someone who at the same time compels language to take on his/her individuality" (Frank 68).

Neither "expression" nor "art" seem like adequate terms for this Benjaminian concept of naming. Nor, in my personal experience, did the workings of a programmatic avant-garde or "experimental" poetry answer adequately to the challenge of the name. I had gone through a phase of looking at poetry in this way (see my work in Richard Kostelanentz's *The Young American Writers*, 1970) and then thought further. For what struck me as self-evident was that the "experimental" modality, as I have written in "Avant-Garde Propellants of the Machine Made of Words" (*UP* 205–223), despite its claims, offered no serious challenge to the constructs of language that actually governed and empowered individuals, societies, institutions. The "experimental" as it was then for the most part conceived, seemed to me to remain always in the realm of "art," in the realm of a "consumerist" culture of planned obsolescence and inflated political claims, whereas the activity of naming—always an intervention—returned language to the social realm, to questions of identity and nonidentity.

For a poet, then, the "danger" Bialik speaks of, the one that exists between revealment and concealment, can be rethought as being at the very heart of poetic practice. Bialik continually explores the dynamics of this danger zone: "The profane turns sacred, the sacred profane. Long established words are constantly being pulled out of their settings, as it were, and exchanging places with one another. Meanwhile, between concealments, the void looms" (25).

How to take Bialik's thought? At points, its dualism is instructive. In his essay, "The Sacred and the Secular in Language," he writes that "the whole purpose of Hebrew speech, that is to say, the rule of language over life, is to turn the sacred into the profane. That is the point of secularization—we had a sacred language and we're turning it into a secular language." He is, of course, describing what has been occurring with Hebrew in Israel, but he means something more universal, in that every country has, as he put it, "a sacred and a secular language."

Scholem's commemorative poem on Bialik, translated by Richard Sieburth, brings to the fore in a disguised form some of the troubling ambiguities of the sacred/secular nexus. Here is the poem in full:

BIALIK
So communicative was he that his words
were almost anonymous in their reach
So close was he to the people's world
that each meeting deepened his speech.
His death is but a pause in the conversation
in which, lost in thought, he still perseveres—
Ah, who could break this cursed silence
which carries him off, screaming in our ears.
17 July 1934 (*TFOT* 107)

The words "communicative" and "anonymous" suggest that in Scholem's reading of the poet, the hieratic and religious nature of Hebrew, its coming from "on high," are brought earthbound, made demotic and secularized to the level of the "people's world." And yet, Bialik's death, the "pause in the conversation," further exposes the void or concealment underlying this newly secularized speech. Steven Wasserstrom, in his introduction to Scholem's poems, remarks of this poem that "a spare two quatrains, this lament drew its agonizing theme from Bialik's other major essay, 'Revealment and Concealment in Language,' which contains the following lines: 'for man shall not look on me and live,' says the void, and every speech, every pulsation of speech, partakes of the nature of a concealment of nothingness, a husk enclosing within itself a dark seed of the eternal enigma" (*TFOT* 26).

Scholem sensed this very dichotomy between a perfunctory usage of language (husk) and the mysteries (enigma) of sacred text. He asked, in *Jews and Judaism in Crisis*, "who knows the limits of sanctity? . . . Perhaps a double way is possible, secular and holy, toward which we are evolving? Perhaps this holiness will be revealed at the heart of the secular, and the mystical is not recognized because it appears in forms which are new to the concepts of tradition." Scholem, as Susan Handelman describes it, goes on to offer up as an example, Walt Whtiman, "a writer," she says, "whose song of America emanated from," and here she cites from Scholem's discussion that describes Whitman as having: "*a feeling of the absolute holiness of the completely secular*" (my italics) (*H* 167).

An aside: Scholem's words above bring to mind Hugh Kenner's comment in *A Homemade World* that the motto of poets like Oppen, Reznikoff, and Zukofsky, might have been "no myths" (187). If we define the mystical as having a quality of "absolute holiness," then can we conjecture that the holiness of the completely secular is achieved in such poets by a powerful *via negative*—something I was alluding to throughout my study, *Conviction's Net of Branches*—testing each word for its truth-quality, weighing its history until that word is tuned anew to our time? I began *Conviction's* with the example of Whitman, I realize, not only to elaborate the Objectivists but to shed light on my own poetics. In answer to Scholem's question above, "who knows the limits of sanctity?" we might, like good Jews, answer his question with a question, one of Whitman's that I quoted in my book:

Was somebody asking to see the soul?
See, your own shape and countenance, persons
substances, beasts, the trees, the running rivers,
the rocks and sands
from "Starting From Paumanok" (183)

Bialik tells us that "the word receives its full vitality only within its existence in its country, that is, within the work as a whole" (90). Let us assume that the ambiguity between "country" and "work" is either a problem in translation or that Bialik is pointing to a sense in which the categories of residence are subsumed under the larger, more encompassing sense of one's writing. While the ambiguity poses problems, let us shift the discussion and ask, what does "full vitality" mean if one's "country" is the diaspora, if the sensibility of the poet, in this case the "Jewish-American" poet is always aslant the "America" making up a piece of that hypenated term (I mistyped "hyphenhated"). Alter's formula of "lore in quest of Law" seems to precisely define the exilic poet's dilemma and desiring. It suggests, as well, that the attempt to conceive of the diaspora as a new kind of homeland runs against the tensions of the self's poetic "exodus." It would be unfaithful, in other words, to turn diaspora into a new kind of Law.

I confess that in my sense of a poetics I have always been more loyal to certain desires and abstractions than to land, or to flag or to naïve patriotism. For me, the diaspora and the not-diaspora that I inhabit is the place pregnant with poetic possibility. I take heart when I read what Emmanuel Levinas writes: "Is it certain a true poet occupies a place? Is the poet not that which, in the eminent sense of the term, loses its place, ceases occupation, precisely, and is thus the very opening of space, neither the transparency nor the emptiness which (no more than night, nor the volume of beings) yet displays the bottomlessness or the excellence, the heaven that is possible" (63).

The French poet and novelist Marcel Cohen writes: "If we have seen the values of a civilization blown to pieces, a corollary of this is that over the same period, in war as in peace, we have seen the 'self' surrender any real grasp on its destiny" (*WLT* 55). "Destiny" here is a very loaded word, one that at its "fullness," if I may borrow from Bialik, might very well point toward a heavily nationalistic or theologically based concept of the individual; at its most empty, it may simple mean the inalienable right to "do your own thing." Somewhere, in between the nationalist and the free spirit, is a more common "surrender" of political and social will to forces or pressures of seeming inevitability, cultural, linguistic and intellectual. Surrender of the "self" in this middle place is more subtle as the individual allies himself with forms of group-think, with making a bet on the zeitgeist or its ethos. On the surface, such a surrender seems freely chosen. However, in a secular intellectual culture (I use this phrase to distinguish the primarily literary and academic culture in which I live from the increasingly sectarian saturation of American cultural life), while the old gods are dispensed with, it seems clear to me that new ones in the form of critical ideologies take their hold. I believe, with Levinas, that it is part of my work as a poet to try not to occupy such a place, whether in a camp or within a theoretical construct or within a belief structure of how and what poetry ought to be. I still want to grasp my destiny or, as Alon says of the *ribboni,* to be master of myself, "not the master of the world or of other people" (26).

Daniel Stern, in his essay "Midrash and Indeterminacy," describes the spatial aspects of polysemy as conceived in various interpretative traditions. Meaning in traditionalist "logocentric" readings of texts is defined as located "behind" the text; in postmodern or deconstructionist readings, as being "in front" of the text. In the case of Rabbinic Judaism, the divine guarantee of meaning is described as "coming from above." Above, not only from a divine presence but also in the physical sense, as given on a mountaintop, from Mount Sinai. (In this far from positive description of polysemy, I hear echoes of Scholem's plaint in his poem to Bialik.) The secular poet of the diaspora might well sense that meaning comes to him not from any unitary direction, but surrounds and even overwhelms him, and mostly comes to him "through" other texts, entrained by other meanings and surfacings. And, as Scholem reminds us, even the religious poet must acknowledge that the imageless God of the Jews manifests almost exclusively as speech. The texts of the world (and His-self as text too) arrive as traceries. They are not works, but linguistic representations of works. The ear cannot not hear, and the poet has no dispensation save as a kind of stand-in for the palimpsest on which the traceries do their work. His "place" is, in a sense, to be experimented on by meanings, by culture, tradition, history, personal circumstance.

Such a poet may well go in fear of instrumental technique, of any procedures that release him from the burden of meaning's tasks. (At least, this is how I took my sense of being a poet, less a maker than a recorder.)

This understanding implies a method. Caught between numerous texts and cultures, and as a figure of many cultures, the poet can turn to commentary because commentary is the place of engagement, of both synthesis and confrontation as products of a poetico-rhetorical stance with tradition. Commentary, the practice of *midrash*, or something like it, defined by Daniel Stern as "avoiding the dichotomized opposition of literature versus commentary," is the path that most appeals to me because it is true to the spirit, the "inbetween" of being. To take up midrash, as Stern says, is to live in "the dense shuttle space between text and interpreter" (132), what I have described above as "the surround" of meanings offered by texts. Alon, in speaking about his *ribboni* figure above claims that such activity, because it is always in relation to both its origin and its destination, creates "organic symbols." Such symbols can only be "cultivated" by midrash (37).

The midrashic condition for the poet amounts to a situation in which no issue of language is finally settled. Caught at every point in language's endlessness, in the web Bialik describes, he finds his environment cocoon-like, ever-circling into self-referentiality. This is a "condition" but, surely, it is not yet poetry. What then?

Revault D'Allonnes, in his marvelous book *Musical Variations on Jewish Thought*, gives a clue: "The major artfulness—not to say astuteness—of Jewish thought has been, on this very point, to approach everything by writing, above all, by the names of things" (47). Writing, and its punctuating corollary, naming, are the products of time and are also its consumers. Revault D'Allonnes lays the importance of these practices in the Judaic cultural matrix to the shift in early Jewish religious thinking away from Yahweh, the god of tribal geography and its spatialness, to Elohim, the "God of the nomads . . . the universal divine principle who is linked neither to a people nor to a land . . . a god of time" unlike Yahweh "a god of space," of territory. For Revault D'Allonnes, Elohim is the "true Jewish god," and the "entire ideological history of the people of Israel can be presented as dominated by the conflict between Elohim and Yahweh, between the nomadic and the sedentary life . . . between internal morality represented by time, nomadism, fidelity, and by external power "represented by space, sedentarization, the State" (41).

For me, the Ark is portable. Especially if inwardness is central. The Ark's interior place, as Revault D'Allonnes points out, is signified by the Hebrew word *kerev*, the same word for the interior space of the human body, the body cavity which "each person conveys everywhere with him or herself" (40, 41). Indeed, time and nomadism so predominate those who inhabit the Elohimist ethos, that according to Revault D'Allonnes "writing... constitutes their sole possible monument" (44). The state religion of the avant-garde, with its rule-bound products, its strictures and group demands strikes as foreign to the Elohimist position (or non-position, as I would have it).

The poetics I reach for would be one that was receptive to limit, to closure. The awareness of time made manifest not by its ongoingness but by fits and starts, its stuttering coalescences in naming. Susan Handelman rehearses such a poetics in her discussion of Benjamin, pointing to *The Origin of German Tragedy,* where Benjamin writes that "truth is not a process of exposure which destroys the secret, but a revelation which does justice to it." Such a style will exercise the "art of interruption in contrast to the chain of deduction" (*H* 63). Put another way, the aim of such a poetics would be something like Oppen's "limited, limiting clarity."

In Talmudic and midrashic perspectives, clarity is virtually synonymous with truth and revelation. If, for a poet like Oppen, they were the words which "could not not be understood," for the midrashist, they are incitements. In Stern's essay on midrash, we find the following: "The words of the wise," says Rabbi Eleazar Ben Azariah, "are like goads; like nails well-planted are the words of the masters of assemblies; they were given by one shepherd" (137). For Rabbi Ben Azariah, the shepherd may have been God or the intelligible face of creation. Geoffrey Hartmann, quoted in Stern, has seen that this process, the love of truth, is close to commentary itself "the taking away, modification, elaboration of previous meanings" (141). Hartmann I think is referring to the relational aspect of Jewish thought, the I Thou-ness, within the sacred and the poetic, to the back and forth course of its motions. The temple's question and response, a conversation held under the roof of the *kerev,* the interiority of self and Ark, is to me the model of the poetics I am after. (In "Avant-Garde Propellants of the Machine Made of Words," I called this notion "counter-continuities . . . works which, even as they construe new networks, necessarily deconstruct the old 'mind-forged manacles' of formerly held continuities" (*UP* 218).

Revelations are the momentary end process of a poetic practice—they are announced through time; to be cognized, to register, they invoke an awe-filled pause in language. They expose the void underneath the very words that construe them. My sense is that revelation, as both secular and nonsecular Judaic traditions understand it, is bound to the ethical, and therefore to vulnerability. What makes poets and their poetry vulnerable is not so much newness or uniqueness but communicability, an opening to being verified or falsified by experience. Levinas, as Handelman tries to show us, supplies a mild corrective to both Benjamin and Scholem, thinkers who have invoked "the mystery of language beyond meaning" (Benjamin) or "pure language" (Scholem). All thought, even its most theoretical or poetic utterances, is, according to Levinas—as Handelman reminds us—"an address to another, it must be *told*" (*H* 224). While communications eventually pass from truth into a kind of falsehood or nonrelevance, the revelations stand. "Man," Bialik asserts, "has the ability to declare that any day is a holiday. . . . This is not merely a matter of will. The power of the day is great because many memories are attached to it that are not attached to other days, and this day thus receives, as it were, an extra soul" (91). Day by day, poem by poem, the poet makes and commemorates revelations. As such they constitute the remains of the diaspora I speak of.

Works Cited

Adonis. *An Introduction to Arab Poetics.* Translated from the Arabic by Catherine Cobham. Austin: University of Texas Press, 1990.

Bialik, Haim Nahman. *Revealment and Concealment.* Miscellaneous translators, and with an Afterword by Zali Gurevitch. Jerusalem: Ibis Editions, 2000.

Cohen, Marcel. "Notes." *World Literature Today.* Translated by Steven Jaron. (Summer/Autumn 2001.) 54–62.

Elon, Ari. *From Jerusalem to the Edge of Heaven.* Translated from the Hebrew by Tikva Frymer-Kensky. Philadelphia-Jerusalem: The Jewish Publication Society, 1990.

Frank, Manfred. *Common Knowledge* 1, 1 (2002): 68.

Handelman, Susan A. *Fragments of Redemption.* Bloomington: Indiana University Press, 1991. (Abbreviated *H.*)

Heller, Michael. *Accidental Center.* Fremont, MI: Sumac Press, 1972.

———. *Conviction's Net of Branches.* Carbondale: Southern Illinois University Press, 1985.

———. *Living Root: A Memoir.* Albany: State University of New York Press, 2000.

———. *Uncertain Poetries.* Cambridge: Salt Publishing, 2005.

Kenner, Hugh. *A Homemade World.* New York: Murrow, 1975.

Levinas, Emmanuel. *Proper Names.* Stanford: Stanford University Press, 1997.

Oppen, George. *New Collected Poems.* Introduced by Michael Davidson, and with a Preface by Eliot Weinberger. New York: New Direction, 2002.

Revault D'Allonnes, Olivier. *Musical Variations on Jewish Thought.* Translated by Judith Greenberg, and with an Introduction by Harold Bloom. New York: George Braziller, 1984.

Scholem, Gershom. *The Fullness of Time.* Translated by Richard Sieburth, and introduced and annotated by Steven M. Wasserstrom. Jerusalem: Ibis Editions, 2003.

———. *On the Mystical Shape of the Godhead.* Translated by Joachim Neugroschel, edited and revised by Jonathan Chipman, and with a Foreword by Joseph Dan. New York: Schocken Books, 1991.

Stern, David. "Midrash and Indeterminancy." *Critical Inquiry* 15, 1 (Autumn 1988): 132–161.

Whitman, Walt. *Complete Poetry and Collected Prose.* New York: The Library of America, 1982.

Secular and Sacred

Returning (to) the Repressed

Alicia Ostriker

> My intuition was then, as it is now, that valid poetry comes to be only when the man or woman with work to do has exhausted all means other than poetic for doing the work that needs to be done.
>
> —Allen Grossman, *The Long Schoolroom*

In this essay I speak as a poet who was raised as a third-generation atheist socialist Jew, who began wrestling with the Bible and Jewish tradition in the middle of the journey of her life. In connection with my book *The Nakedness of the Fathers,* I discuss the fact that the being we in the west call God the Father swallowed God the Mother in prehistory and proposing that—as in the story of the wolf swallowing grandmother—God the Mother remains alive in the belly of the beast (aka what William Blake calls "the Human Imagination") awaiting rebirth, or as the Freudians would put it, the Return of the Repressed. In Jewish tradition her name is Shekhinah. I go on to discuss my recent book *The Volcano Sequence,* an experimental work in which the poems were channeled more than planned; the poet functioned as aperture. The book's voice(s) address a slippery "you" that is sometimes God, sometimes Mother, sometimes Shekhinah. As Celan says: "Only in the space of this dialogue does that which is addressed take form and gather around the I who is addressing it." The essay asks: can parallel lines converge?

The topic proposed is radical poetics / secular Jewish culture. My first response is to raise my hand. Call on me, teacher. Call on me. I'm Jewish.

My second response is to wonder why "secular." As opposed to what? Who needs this polarization between "secular" and "sacred?" Who profits by it?[1] Before I built a wall I'd like to know what I was walling in or walling out. It is true that the academy as I have experienced it over forty years is allergic to religious thought or feeling unless penned up in a "religious studies" department where it can be counted on to be harmless. It is also true that feminism in most of its forms sees religion as its sworn enemy. Gays, lesbians, and transsexuals ditto. There are excellent historical reasons for this. Politically, religious orthodoxy—Jewish, Christian, Muslim—is the whale that wants to swallow the world. The Enlightenment was right about religion. Voltaire was right. Our forefathers Marx and Freud were right. Religion gives us sexual repression, self-righteousness, ignorance, intolerance, and war. I too dislike it.

But poetry? Does not poetry always plant one foot in this world, one in the world of the spirit? Is not poetry the very cusp or cup of language where sacred and profane mingle? It seems odd to me to insist on the "secular" in a collection of essays about poetry, especially since we are speaking of Jewish poetry, with all those glinting threads of biblical and liturgical phrasing tangled into its DNA. Is there some dread that if a nonsecular Jewish poet appears, he or she will somehow infect the whole barrel? It feels like the old-style restricted country club ethos, you know, if you let one of them in . . .

I wish I could write like Charles Reznikoff. I am not sure if he is secular or not. How about Rukeyser? I am so confused. How about Ginsberg? Does Buddhism count as secular? How about the author of *Angels in America*, that gorgeously Jewish mess of a play? Is Kushner or is he not a secular writer?

An old friend once warned me to beware hardening of the categories. I love that line.

And then there is "radical poetics," which could be code for poetry that avoids sentences. Or looks like prose on the page, nice blocky right-hand-justified shapes, or mixes prose and verse. Or doesn't use uppercase. Or has spaces instead of punctuation between its words. Is Gerald Stern's poetry radical? What of the poetry of Adrienne Rich? What of Marilyn Hacker's lesbian sonnets? Is the poem radical if the poet feels she is feeling her way in the dark while she is writing it? Crawling into a cave? Swinging on a star?

Or does "radical poetics" refer only to the poet's political positions? Radical: Far out. Far in. Far down. Rooted, or pertaining to a root or foundation. Extreme or thoroughgoing. One who advocates widespread governmental and social change designed to benefit the powerless. Ah. This I understand. All this. I am and am not secular, but surely I would like you to see me as radical.

I

I was born and raised in America as a third-generation atheist socialist Jew. My religious training consisted of being told that religion was the opiate of the people. My pride in being Jewish was always a cultural pride: Jews stood for learning, for cultural accomplishment, for the brotherhood of man, for tolerance and for justice, and against war, poverty, and injustice. Jews fought against prejudice and against bosses. Because my parents despised what they called superstition, I do not think they were aware that their passion for social justice derived, ultimately, from the Hebrew prophets. But I am aware of it. When I hear the phrase "speak truth to power," I think: Isaiah. Jeremiah. Amos.

~

Reading the Bible for the first time in college, reading for pleasure rather than instruction, I identified with laughing Sarah and with Jacob wrestling with the angel. The line "I will not let thee go except thou bless me" brings tears of delight to my eyes even today. From the first moment of contact, I experienced this book as mine, its men and women as my mothers and fathers, its God as my God—atheist though I was and am. Do I contradict myself? Very well, then. Like many another Jew, I wrestle with the text for reasons I cannot wholly explain. Sometimes I think that every value by which I live, as well as every value against which I struggle, has its origin in that book. As a woman, as a seeker, as an old leftist, as a feminist, as a poet, I attempt to wrestle a blessing from it. It resists; I persist.

The first book in which I found myself erasing the division between secular and sacred came about as a result of my wondering how Job's wife liked having her ten children, the ones God let Satan kill off on a bet—to see if Job would still worship him—replaced in the ostensibly happy ending of the Book of Job by ten new children. The experience of asking this question precipitated what felt like a ten-thousand-year-old silent scream, followed by a spell of automatic writing, in which my pen attempted to imagine what the wife of Job knew about her husband's God when she told him to "curse God and die," and what this woman (who is all of us) would/will say to God when she acquires the courage to challenge God as her husband did. This piece became the germ of *The Nakedness of the Fathers: Biblical Visions and Revisions.*

The book is part midrash, part autobiography. The "I" is included because, as Thoreau says, it is always the first person who is doing the writing; because interpretive objectivity is a myth that deserves to be exploded; because to read the Bible with one's own I's and one's own eyes, without what Harold Bloom calls the varnish of pious commentary, transforms the texts completely, particularly if one is a woman. I say: "To the rest of the world the Jew is marginal. But to Judaism I am marginal." I say women "have to enter the tents / texts, invade the sanctuary, uncover the father's nakedness." I say that I enter these compelling stories and that they enter me; I say that (speaking of roots, origins, the past) at times I remember a beginning before the beginning, when my name was woman of valor, when my name was wisdom. On the page the book shifts between verse, prose, and prose-poetry. In this respect it resembles the Bible, the original multigenre experiment. *Nakedness* is, then, formally "radical."

It is commonly assumed that if a woman writes about the Bible, she writes about "women in the Bible." That is to say, it is assumed that a woman writer will confine her speculation, her imagination, to her side of the mehitzah, as it were. Another ghetto. But why should a woman not reimagine the lives of the patriarchs? Why should she not reimagine the motives of warriors, judges, and kings, as well as their occasional mothers, sisters, daughters, wives? *Nakedness* therefore pursues the arc of biblical narrative from the Garden to Job and beyond. Resting on the assumption that the Bible is both deeply archaic and entirely contemporary, and that every portion of it speaks to something in my life and the life of those around me, the book naturally includes political as well as psychological and theological drama. Noah, the first alcoholic, suffers survivor guilt. How curious that no commentary has noticed this. How interesting that Primo Levi called one of his last books *The Drowned and the Saved.* Isaac, the man whose father tried to kill him, becomes the first Jewish stand-up comic. I wish my readers to comprehend the logic without my having to explain it. Hagar is the mother of an intifada fighter:

I call him Ishmael, I whisper to him
Fight to your dying breath (74)

Moses is God's pack animal, Samson is a psychopath, David is the world's smoothest politician. Solomon makes trade not war, and lets his many wives and concubines worship the goddesses of their choice. Esther and Mordecai are (of course) Ishtar and Marduk.

If Judaism is half tribal and half universalist, the bias of *Nakedness* is toward the latter.

If Judaism has a future as well as a past, *Nakedness* has some suggestions. (Does Judaism have a future? Does it have the capacity for growth and change as well as for memory, memory, memory?) Here the intervention of the so-called secular—the secular voice that feels itself called and commanded to remind the so-called sacred voice of what it has forgotten, the margin crying out to the center, asking it to forget the distinction between margin and center—is essential.

After the sections of poetry and prose in which *Nakedness* reimagines the tales of the shepherd-patriarchs, after Moses and Aaron and the problematic conquest of the Land, with God commanding both genocide and the love of the stranger (does he contradict himself?), after the warriors and kings, along with the occasional mothers, sisters, and wives of all these, after the sexy summit meeting between Solomon and Sheba, after the invocation of Wisdom, the female hochmah, and after a section that wonders what the wife of Job will say to God when she screws her courage to that sticking point, and what she will require as reparation, we arrive at a piece called "Intensive Care." It is the book's penultimate section. Here we find the Holy One surrounded by balloons and candy, television cameras and reporters asking him irritating questions. Has he named his successor? No. He is evidently in severe pain, but refuses to speak. Two women reporters, Chloe and Olivia, whom I have lifted from Virginia Woolf's *A Room of One's Own,* come to the realization that God is not dead, not dying, only pregnant and in labor.

> But my God, says Chloe, did you see how bloated he looked there. He looked pregnant. Perhaps he's having a baby instead of a cancer.
>
> Olivia inadvertently laughs, dribbling coffee and making a rude noise. O right, she says after swallowing. Pregnant. What a riot. God in labor. Believe that? She punches Chloe on the shoulder.
>
> I believe because it is absurd, says Chloe. . . . Well, burn my bush, says Olivia. (251)

This is what I think. It is not a joke. The being whom we in the West call God the Father swallowed God the Mother in prehistory. That is to say, as the religions associated with patriarchy advanced throughout the ancient Middle East in the fourth through third millennium B.C.E., "he" absorbed the attributes that had been "hers" through millennia of Goddess-worship, attributes such as control over fertility and the promulgation of law.[2] The consequences of male divinity include not only the subordination of girls and women, of course, but also the subordination of anything culturally gendered "female." Combat and conquest trump compassion and nurture, for instance.

However, as in the story of the wolf swallowing grandmother, God the Mother remains alive in the belly of the beast. An old story, very old. From time to time, in the text, one can see her kicking. She awaits rebirth, with a little help from her friends. Since gods emerge into existence through what William Blake used to call "the Human Imagination," artists have a certain responsibility in this area. We have certain choices. To be a feminist writer (whether one is male or female) is to open the imagination, to be a midwife of repressed femaleness, to assist the collective process of the return of the repressed, including repressed divinity. For repressed power is of a piece; you cannot have the secular kind without the sacred kind to back it up, and vice versa. They are not chicken and egg, they are connected faces of latent reality, one existing in the material world, one in the spiritual—but really, there is only the one world.

The Goddess, as we know, has numerous names. In Jewish tradition she is the Shekhinah, whose name derives from a noun meaning dwelling. In the Bible the "presence" of God in the world is referred to by this term; since the word is a feminine noun, it becomes personified over the centuries. In the Zohar the Shekhinah is the final emanation (sephirah) of God. In Lurianic kabbala, at the explosive moment of creation which is so very like the Big Bang, when the divine energy burst the vessels that contained it, and the divine sparks descended into the material world, God and his Shekhinah were blown apart. It is the goal of history to reunite them. When one performs good deeds, one aids in the process of tikkun olam, mending the world, which also means mending the rift in the godhead. When a Jewish man and his wife make love on the Sabbath, they model that reunion. When secular or semi-secular Jews labor for social justice, they model it too. Or so I believe.

Do I oversimplify? Very well then, I oversimplify.[3]

The final piece of *The Nakedness of the Fathers* is a prayer to the Shekhinah. It borrows its language in part from the Book of Proverbs, in part from Jewish liturgy, in part from Steven Dedalus's declaration in *Ulysses* that "history is a nightmare from which I am trying to awake." It begins to imagine:

When she wakes from her long repose in us
When she wipes the nightmare
Of history from her eyes
When she returns from exile
When she utters her voice in the streets
In the opening of the gates. . . .
When she enters the modern world
When she crosses the land
Shaking her breasts and hips
With timbrels and with dances
Magnified and sanctified
Exalted and honored
Blessed and glorified
When she causes tyranny
To vanish
When she and he meet
When they behold each other face to face

When they become naked and not ashamed
On that day will our God be One
And their name One
Shekhinah bless us and keep us
Shekhinah shine your face on us
Shekhinah turn your countenance
To us and give us peace

Until this day, as numerous feminist theologians have observed, those who worship a God made in the image of masculinity worship an idol. But is it in fact possible for a closed system that has lasted thousands of years to be opened?

II

To be radical is to go to the root of a matter. To be radical is to be extreme. Politically, to be radical is to support the powerless. When I finished *Nakedness,* I thought the next thing I needed to do was have a goddess-vision: to imagine her body would mean to help bring her forth into the world. I read volumes of women's spirituality, most of which were too sweet for my taste. I read Gershom Scholem, Raphael Patai, and Daniel Matt's beautiful translation of the Zohar. I read H.D., Denise Levertov, Anne Sexton (not the "confessional" poems but the *Psalms* and *The Awful Rowing Toward God*),[4] Lucille Clifton. To each of these profoundly intelligent and profoundly spiritual women poets the goddess had, if only as a glimmer, appeared. I waited for her to appear to me.

Nothing happened. Nada. No vision. In fact, no poetry. There is an amusing moment in *Henry IV,* part I, when Glendower announces to his fellow rebels, "I can call spirits from the vasty deep," and Hotspur replies, "Why, so can I, and so can any man. / But will they come when you do call for them?" Often I thought of this line and was not amused. Although well aware that writer's block signifies something under the rock, that we do not wish to look at, I failed to lift the rock; apparently it was too large and heavy for me. Apparently it also contained some sort of magnetic material, since I was unable to walk away.

The advent of *The Volcano Sequence* was not what I expected. Its opening poem arrived in December 1998 as I was looking at photographs of Thera, also known as Santorini, the volcanic Greek island whose explosion in prehistory is supposed to have produced the tsunami that drowned Atlantis, Plato's ideal state. As I admired a particularly austere photograph of its white limestone crust, the island spoke in a way that told me its voice was mine—the voice of an extinct volcano that had caused irreparable destruction in the world. Ironically, this voice noted, "the tourists come, oh they come / to stand where the lava flew," to look for an hour "at where the tidal wave began / that drowned Atlantis." Tidal wave? The story of a lifelong tendency toward anger, perhaps inherited from my mother, which had damaged the lives of myself, my husband and children, and my mother herself, lifted itself urgently from under the rock. Here were some poems, not pleasant but informative. "Who cares if afterward / everything is dead," the poems asked. Emotionally, I swallowed hard. I made a deal with the poems: if you agree to keep arriving, I agree not to tell you what to say.

For a year then, I allowed my self to become an aperture, and received, intermittently, the poems of *Volcano.* Almost all were complete and precise in the first draft. Their shifting voices speak to a slippery "you" who is at times God, at times the Mother, at times, ah yes, the Shekhinah. Its tones are the Jewish tones of despair, irony, and accusation. In a poem entitled "psalm,"

I will not make a joyful
noise to you, neither
will I lament
for I know you drink
lamentation, too,
like wine (13)

The accusation appears to circle around images of God's "ruthless radiance." In one poem it remembers God's failure to protect his various chosen peoples, in another it remembers first being embraced by God, and then being called whore, k'dosha, while God was called kaddosh, holy. It meditates on the consequences of a Lord God who keeps saying, "keep my law," who is a consuming fire, a man of war, a sponsor of murderous zealotry among Jews, Christians, and Muslims alike:

One of these days
oh one of these days
will be a festival and a judgment

and our enemies will be thrown
into the pit while we rejoice
and sing hymns

some people actually think this way (34)

Gradually the voice registers some recognition that its remote and punitive God is an icon, an imagined thing, not the creator of heaven and earth. Its tone toward God alters; it does not cease to challenge but begins to expect a response. Perhaps this seems shocking. The topic of what we think we are doing when we address God is a fascinating one. Fascinating and absurd. Celan describes it succinctly: "Only in the space of this dialogue does that which is addressed take form and gather around the I who is addressing it." The same Celan addresses God as "No one" and makes clear that the "I" and what it addresses are equivalent fictions. At some points the dialogue perhaps ceases to be a dialogue of the deaf.

the suffering of love
the love of suffering
that too is a spectacle
or do you feel it too
God, do you
feel it too

~

have you not guessed
your desire is mine your pain is mine (51)

The idea that God is in pain appears to intersect with the idea at the close of *Nakedness* that God is pregnant, yet the poems do not pursue that idea. From time to time, instead, the poems address a mother. In fact, the poems keep sliding unpredictably between the theological and the personal. My own mother, or generic mother, or Mother Nature? Difficult to say. Difficult to distinguish either theology or autobiography from politics. It is important to recall that the standard images of the Jewish mother in our culture are unappealing: someone who cooks and shops and is all matter, maternal matter, mutter, no mind. A smotherer. A worrier. A joke. A madwoman. In *Volcano,* the arrival of the line "honor your mother / what if it commanded only that" precipitates a cascade of resistance:

unasked for disappointing hateful life
it is the mother's fault

we fall from her space into the world
webs of organs helpless

what a pity she does not eat us
and be done with it

rats do
lions do

in dry times (11)

A harsh picture of the relation between Jewish mother and Jewish daughter emerges, becoming gradually particularized. This mother. This daughter. This impossible relationship in which the daughter laments that "it has tortured me that I cannot save you . . . / and that I do not love you enough // what is enough / nothing is enough,"(20), while mother claims that "people, you know, are like ants / relentless / bite whatever they need"(21). When the Shekhinah is invoked as a potential mediator, she is exiled, amnesiac, mute. In Jewish lore, she is "the king's daughter, all glorious within," which is usually taken to mean that she is only to be found through study of torah or through kabbalistic meditation. It may also mean that she is divine immanence as God-the-father is divine transcendance. The poems announce that the Shekhinah is locked inside our mothers, but that our mothers cannot tell us this:

they cannot say seek me
they teach us cooking clothing craftiness
they tell us their own stories of power and shame
and even if it is she who speaks through their mouths
and has crawled through ten thousand wombs until this day
we cannot listen

their words fall like spilled face powder (64)

The verses here convey a partial idea of what the voices do in *Volcano,* but only a partial one. The process was, it must be repeated, radically undetermined, radically uncontrolled by the author. One section includes remarks by the poet Toi Derricotte, originally made as marginal comments on the manuscript-in-progress. So here is another instance in which the marginal becomes the central. There is also digression, an inevitable consequence of the open aperture. In the course of the book, as the poems wrestle with the power of God and the powerlessness of the mother, other matters interrupt: a visit to Crete, the bombing of Kosovo, a beggar on a New York City sidewalk. It is speculated that the unconscious is a sort of geniza in which everything threateningly divine or demonic is stored. Two-thirds of the way through the book the geniza explodes: it becomes a scene of birth scattered over the page. The poems stand in the book in the order of writing, its sections dated by month. A final section, including some psalms and addresses to the mother in a tone more of yearning than irony, remains undated. Formally, with the exception of the geniza poem, the poems are typically short-lined and brief. The white space on the page represents whatever they cannot say. The use of lowercase and the absence of punctuation suggest the stillness of their interior voices. Meandering, they edge very slightly forward. They do not arrive anywhere.

III

Were I to address a group of Jewish feminists, women and men, I would say that we share a task. I would define the task as radical, and I would define it as one in which the "secular" and the "sacred" cease to mock each other. We know that the human need for God (or god-figures) is not disappearing. Our species is religion making as it is culture making. Human beings apparently require divine beings to address, to invoke, to explain the universe, to guide us, to inspire, to commend, to command, to punish, to console. Lives that lack some spiritual dimension are shallow lives; something essential is missing from them. We know also that the God of male monotheism is an idol more permanently dangerous than any human dictator. I trust that in today's political climate this statement needs no proving. If we who are engaged in tikkun olam and hope for a less self-destroying planet do not invent/imagine/create a somewhat more benign divinity, who will? And if not now, when? All deities reside in the human breast, Blake rightly claims. The difficulty is to open the doors of our breasts. To discover what exists behind or beneath the stone. The granite of denial. What desire lies beneath anger. What trust might lie on the other side of bitterness. What might come after irony. The dominant postmodern response to suffering, one's own and others', is indifference. Calculated indifference, hardening the rock. As Yeats says, "Too long a sacrifice / Can make a stone of the heart." We see this stoniness in the culture all around us. I find it unacceptable, impossible, un-Jewish.

Do I imagine a cultural shift that may require centuries? Very well then.

A portion of the task involves actually honoring our mothers. That is: ceasing to attempt to escape them. Turning around at last, facing them, our biological mothers who not only fail to be ideal beings but are in many ways monsters. How could they fail to be monsters? To turn and face them, to perceive the force that is the Shekhinah in them—exiled, amnesiac, mute—and honor it. Is this possible, in our lives, in our language, in our art? If we have the art to do so, we make it easier for others; we hasten the distant day when the concept "god" includes whatever genders there may be, and when the sacredness immanent within matter is as significant culturally as the sacredness that transcends matter. I can tell that the task is important because when I suggest it to other women intellectuals or poets they look at me blankly or recoil in dread. "If the doors of perception were cleansed, man would see everything as it really is, infinite," says Blake. "For everything that lives is holy, life delights in life." However, none of my colleagues wants to undertake this difficult thing. They would rather talk about Levinas and the face of the Other than look, look, at their mothers' faces.

Theoretically, the parallel lines of "God," "my mother" and "the Shekhinah" converge at infinity—the infinity which is a prophet's or a mystic's imagination, and which is also here and now. Theoretically these three are one, just as the man, the woman, and the blackbird in Stevens are one. As for myself, I lack the imagination to make real this abstraction. Unable to perceive experientially what I conceive theoretically, I leave the task to others.

Allies do exist, have existed. Of women poets engaged in the task I have already mentioned H.D., all of whose late work involves the attempt to reimagine the mother/goddess construct, as well as Denise Levertov, Anne Sexton, and Lucille Clifton. These are Christian women. Jewish women poets have not tilled the same ground, with one possible exception: in Louise Glück's *The Wild Iris,* the god-voice is gender neutral, neither male nor female. Prayed to, it does not or cannot respond with anything but a cold and melancholy distance. Most readers assume this voice to be paternal, but perhaps it is the voice of the poet's mother. Surely part (though not all) of what we need is the ability to imagine a divine Mother who is as indifferent to our needs as the Father seems to be.

Jewish women essayists on the other hand have been immeasurably helpful. Adrienne Rich in *Of Woman Born* first opened my eyes to the fact that our culture ostensibly respects but actually requires rejection of the mother, and that mothers are the crippled agents required to cripple their daughters. The instance Rich uses is footbinding; today we might speak of genital mutilation, by which the maternal generation to which sexual pleasure has been denied must deny it to the generation of daughters. It has been the role of the mother to bind the daughter—a role that goes unmentioned in Genesis, while the binding of Isaac is the Black Hole of Judaism, sucking in endless commentary. A daughter who craves liberty will naturally be repelled by her crippled mother, yet when we fail to see the holy one, the Shekhinah, the life energy boiling within the frustrated mother, pouring its joy and grief from womb to womb down the generations, we are to that degree lost. We replicate her frustration in the fashion mandated by the whole weight of our society. The psychologist Dorothy Dinnerstein, in her neglected masterpiece *The Mermaid and the Minotaur,* brilliantly and elaborately tracks the consequences to ourselves and to history of the fact that the overwhelmingly carnal mother is every infant's earliest object of blissful worship, dread, and rage; see especially the chapter "The Dirty Goddess."[5] Dinnerstein, in her possibly correct conviction that "the male-female conspiracy to keep history mad has become impossible to sustain" and might be ameliorated if infant care were equally shared by fathers and mothers, almost but not quite endorses the idea that "goddess" is a term human society could profitably use. The Algerian Jew Helene Cixous, writing as she says with mother's milk, writing in exile and in a style of fearless ecstasy that fuses sexuality, politics, and mysticism, declaring that "nothing compels us to deposit our lives in these lack-banks . . . to endlessly bail out the father's religion," is able to propose mother as goddess threatened yet powerful: " 'You!' the voice says 'you.' And I am born!—'Look,' she says, and I see everything!—'Touch!' and I am touched. There! The voice opens my eyes, her light opens my mouth, makes me cry out. And I am born from this."[6]

Jewish men whose work feels adjacent to my own include the Ginsberg of "Kaddish," and before that of "Howl." Naomi is the beloved mourned monster of "Kaddish," but she is the muse of "Howl." One might go so far as to say that Naomi's presence as madwoman-muse is closeted in Ginsberg's first major poem, and outed in his second. Were it not for Naomi, his flinching/unflinching loyalty to Naomi, Ginsberg could never have brought into poetic existence his community of holy outsiders "driven by madness." By insisting on the beatitude of the beat, Ginsberg implicitly recasts his mother as a form of divine energy. Another example is Allen Grossman, whose oracular poetry "is, in the most literal sense, the speech of my mother, or rather, the completion of the speech of my mother. . . . who was restlessly and in some sense destructively dissatisfied with the world around her. The prolongation and, as it were, consummation of her will toward a golden world is as veracious an account as I can give of my motive to art."[7] Rodger Kamenetz's prose memoir of his mother's life and death, apparently entirely secular, was according to the author triggered by a sequence of dreams, and comes close at its close to acknowledging a power more spiritual than psychological, speaking of the ambiguousness of his mother's love: "A love that never set me free, a love that bound my voice to hers in confusion. Even in my most powerful dreams I could not tell whose voice was speaking, hers or mine."[8] Perhaps there are other Jews scrambling to the other side of Mrs. Portnoy? In the quest for God the Mother we need whatever help we can get. We may certainly turn to the goddesses of the ancient world, or to Kali, or Innanna, but they are not our own mothers. If God the Mother is not transcendent but immanent within the material world, she has been traveling down the millennia to us through the womblike, tomblike, fleshy bodies of women. We should be able to encounter the physical selves of these women, glorious and horrible as they are, to experience them as embodying that which we lack. That which we seek. It is a difficult task. May many of us undertake it. May the mind become a cervix. May her awful beauty be reborn to us and to the world.

Notes

1. Jeffrey Stout, *Democracy and Tradition* (Princeton, NJ: Princeton University Press, 2004), argues that we are increasingly confronted by two "very abstract, oppositionally constructed positions," an antisecular religiousness and an antireligious secularism, each of which "thrives mainly by inflating the other's importance" (10).

2. Cf. Gerda Lerner's excellent summary, *The Creation of Patriarchy* (New York: Oxford University Press, 1986), 145: "The observable pattern is: first, the demotion of the Mother-Goddess figure and the ascendance and later dominance of her male consort/son; then his merging with a storm-god into a male Creator-God, who heads the pantheon of gods and goddesses. Wherever such changes occur, the power of creation and of fertility is transferred from the Goddess to the God." Male monotheism is the end product of this process. What Lerner omits is the fact that the transition is never quite complete, that the repressed is always in danger of returning. See my discussion of this, and the way it inflects biblical storytelling, in Ostriker, *Feminist Revision and the Bible* (Cambridge, MA: Blackwell Publishers, 1993), 27–55.

3. For more scholarly accounts of the changing roles of the Shekhinah in Jewish mysticism, see Raphael Patai, *The Hebrew Goddess* (New York: Avon, 1978), Gershom Scholem, *Major Trends in Jewish Mysticism* (New York, Schocken Books, 1971), and Scholem, *On the Kabbalah and Its Symbolism,* trans. Ralph Mannheim (New York: Schocken, 1965).

4. Anne Sexton is best understood not as a "confessional poet" but as a devotional poet with links to Christopher Smart and Gerard Manly Hopkins, whose poetry increasingly struggles with religious issues, and who had some excellent glimpses of god the mother, but who was unable to imagine a father-god she could both believe in and be loved by. See my essay, "That Story: The Changes of Anne Sexton," in *Writing Like a Woman.*

5. Dorothy Dinnerstein, *The Mermaid and the Minotaur* (New York: Harper & Row, 1976).

6. Helene Cixous, "'Sorties,' The Newly Born Woman," trans. Betsy Wing (Min-

neapolis: University of Minnesota Press, 1975), 85; "Breaths, (Souffles)," *The Helene Cixous Reader,* ed. Susan Sellers (London: Routledge, 1994), 50.

7. Allen Grossman (with Mark Halliday), *The Sighted Singer: Two Works on Poetry for Readers and Writers* (Baltimore: Johns Hopkins University Press, 1992), 61.

8. Rodger Kamenetz, *Terra Infirma* (Fayetteville: University of Arkansas Press, 1985), 115.

Midrashic Sensibilities

Secular Judaism and Radical Poetics (A personal essay in several chapters)

Rachel Blau DuPlessis

> Meanings accumulate as one "other thing" (davar 'ahar) brings up "another."
>
> —Michael Fishbane

> How simple and how difficult to be Jewish. Difficult simplicity, I would say. But how come the Jew does not hesitate a second to answer "Jewish" to the question of his identity. . . . How come the non-believer as much as the believer can claim, can presume on the same Judaism? Is it because their past and future are alike? Is there such a thing as Jewish destiny?
>
> —Edmund Jabès

Chapter I

In 1998, I participated in a panel on the Objectivist poets with Michael Heller, Jenny Penberthy, and Carl Rakosi (1903–2004) at a summer session at the Naropa Institute in Boulder, Colorado. A student had just asked Rakosi a very good question about the Jewishness of the four central players in the first "Objectivist" formation of the late 1920s and early 1930s. Reznikoff, Zukofsky, Oppen, and Rakosi were all, quite variously, of Jewish origin and background, and she wondered what import this had, did it matter, how did it matter, and so on. . . . Rakosi's response? Off-handed, discounting, deflecting; that their religious background was a coincidence. "These things happen."

On either side of him, without exchanging a glance, Heller and I simultaneously and loudly said: "You're wrong, Carl." It was a startling moment, confronting several generations of assimilated secular Jews with each other. The implied debate was invested with many meanings. Rakosi (a lively ninety-five years old in 1998) wanted to avoid dwelling on an affiliation that seemed to anchor people in a community of particularity, even peculiarity, one not in the mainstream, even resistant to the mainstream, patronizable, and, notably susceptible to prejudice. Rakosi was well aware that if you claim an equal playing field of meritocracy and secular participation, it can then seem provincial, indeed logically inconsistent, to call attention to a Jewish heritage. He could have felt this was having it both ways, and therefore nobly renounced an easy social contradiction (having it both ways) for the sake of principle. He was also probably aware of what else he was resisting in denying meaning to the "coincidence" of Jewishness: that is, the canard "clannish." This charge used against the Jews—they stick together, they plot against others—can lead to conspiracy theory all too fast—and has. Rakosi had, in his professional career as a social worker, assumed a mainstream, even WASP, name, Callman Rawley, to avoid potential prejudice and to avoid the mangling of "foreign" names (Heller, ed. 1993, 81). This heteronym or pseudonym does, however, encode suggestive elements of pain and resistance in its "beck and call" and "raw" allusions.

Rakosi was of the generation born to overcome the shetel narrowness of pre-Enlightenment Jewish culture, when Jews were legally ghettoized and did not have full civil rights. He was still fighting the struggles for Haskalah—the Jewish Enlightenment, and thus may have felt that our fascination with this "coincidence" of Jewishness was misguided. Why would we want to call attention to something that should not be noticed? This is similar to the response of certain professional women in the 1940s and 1950s; far from "feminism" (or sociopolitical identification with one's gender), individualist pride and affirmative exceptionalism were the rule (as in, "we are not women like those other women"). It was at least unhelpful and at most professionally dangerous to call attention to particularity.

Speaking from our distinct forms of adhesion or relation to Judaism, and benefiting from the pioneering generation to which Rakosi belonged, Michael Heller and I, in contrast, wanted to notice, to discuss, to be curious about the (really various) "Jewishness" of the nonetheless generally secular Objectivists. Heller and I had also benefited from a recent historical moment involving intense discussion of identity and social location by all sorts of groups, including women. With respect for localisms and the specifics of social formation, and with a lot of interest in the differences among the Objectivists regarding their Jewish culture, Heller and I still saw the possibility of discussing ways in which their poetries and poetics were invested in aspects of the religious culture from which they had, variously, emerged. For us, the gains of Jewish Enlightenment were a given; it was where we were formed, no matter our degree of adhesion to practicing or religious Judaism. Not to mention: this adhesion is potentially quite different in structure and import for a man and for a woman. I am alluding to some of the legalistic customs sanctified by text and woven into particularism that are characteristic of formal orthodoxy (e.g., blood taboos around menstruation and childbirth, "purity" law and mikvah cleansing, absence from the definitionally all-male minyan). These customs are so arcane and tribal, in my view, that I can barely credit my alleged "place" as female within their pietistic strictures, nor honor, with even a tinge of atavistic nostalgia, their damaging binarist mythography. So, at any rate, as Yosef Hayim Yerushalmi remarks: "In the often turbulent process of social and cultural change that accompanied or succeeded the Haskalah, there emerged that modern species of 'gottloser Jude' [godless Jew] whom we know as the secular Jew" (Yerushalmi 1991, 9). I certainly won't speak for Heller, but that's pretty much a description of me.

Chapter II

Once—when? maybe in the mideighties (I think at the H.D. conference in Orono, Maine, 1986, perhaps at the 1950s conference a few years later)—I asked Robert Creeley why, in his view, the Objectivists were so under-known and so under-acknowledged. He replied, "Anti-Semitism." "Anti-Semitism," he replied.

Chapter III

The precise relationship different Objectivists held to Judaism as structure of feeling, as a religious culture, and as an ethical context is a question opened by the essays on Charles Reznikoff in *The Objectivist Nexus.* ("Structure of feeling" is a phrase from Raymond Williams 1977, 128–135.) Both Norman Finkelstein and Charles Bernstein insist, importantly, on the necessity for a general cultural literacy in Jewish material (comparable to critical literacy in Christianity as a set of ideologies, practices, and iconographies that appear in visual art and written texts). Such terms as diaspora, nomadism, exile, messianism, the holiness of the ordinary, textual study as worship, the quarrel with God are among the repeated, although not atemporal, topoi in Judaism, while historical practices—whether this means assimilation, secularization and the attenuation of Jewish tradition (discussed in Finkelstein's essay), or the impact of the Holocaust as a startling, almost unassimilable fact within modernity—have all been important not only to Objectivists as poets drawing on, or approaching Jewishness, but to many poets. Steven Shoemaker has recently suggested that Objectivist poetics "drew on an awareness of Jewish history and a core of Jewish identity" certainly present at the beginning of the movement but becoming "more important with the rise of fascism in the thirties" (Shoemaker, in Scroggins, ed., 41). We can see that Jewishness (and its various modes, including secular Jewishness) is not static, but like all social locations and cultural products, it is mobile, self-different, in continual debate, and inflected with pressures and interests from history and politics. No identity is unmediated by historical specificity, and Jewish history / the history of Jews in the modern period could not be, and is not. It is in this generally antiessentialist spirit that I proceed.

Chapter IV

In Oppen's letters, a moment counterpoising Charles Reznikoff against T. S. Eliot illuminates Oppen's suspicion of the Christianization of literary culture in the 1940s through the 1960s. Responding to Reznikoff's *Inscriptions: 1944–1956* after it was published in 1959, Oppen singles out the section dealing with Hanukkah in "Meditations on the Fall and Winter Holidays" as something striking "even to as simple an H.G. Wellsian atheist as myself"; he continues "The lines beginning 'penniless, penniless' render Eliot simply absurd. The critics would have made these things famous if they [the poems] were Christian: there is no statement in literature near them" (Oppen 1990, 34).

Penniless, penniless, I have come with less and still less
To this place of my need and the lack of this hour.
(Reznikoff 1962, 91)

Oppen hears the cadence here that parallels *Four Quartets,* and the humility, sense of loss, the almost posthumous voice, the reverence and resignation combined with tempered hope that characterizes this poem. He hears all this as particularly Jewish, even if he resists what is central to this poem: an intimate, if also somewhat weary address to the Lord and His complex blessings. "Remember us / as the servants / You have inherited" (Reznikoff 1962, 90). The way Oppen praises Reznikoff shows that he identified normative poetic and literary culture with a Christian ideology and ethos—and was prepared to resist this. The ways that modern literary culture for more than thirty years (covertly and overtly) embodied a Christianizing structure of feeling still needs careful investigation. Was the hegemony of Eliot's increasingly callow mix of universalist-yet-exclusionary aims that compelling? In the postwar period, was this affirmatively Christian literary culture involved with the strange shadow cast by the Holocaust, a desire to find some redemptive ideology in the unredeemable? I say this in the spirit of John Felstiner's withering moral assessments of postwar critics and theorists commenting on the Holocaust, writers whose Christianizing metaphors of suffering are repeatedly revealed to be sanctimonious pieties (Felstiner 1997). In the prewar and in the postwar periods, were Christian ideology and ideogogues an anti-communist hedge? Was New Criticism's emphasis on climaxes in epiphany, the unveiling of Presence, and dissecting literal/figurative distinctions in poetic texts not secular methods only but ones with a Christianized aura? (Handelman 1982, 120, 55; the application to lyric is my own). These are rhetorical questions; they imply affirmative answers.

Chapter V

Despite the "Episcopalianism" of his upbringing, his lack of a bar mitzvah, his claim to have entered a synagogue only once (out of curiosity, probably in the 1970s), despite all this and more, George Oppen identified as Jewish, and increasingly so after a 1975 trip to Israel, sometimes marked in his later poems.[1] This allegiance is made clear in several of his letters, one droll and one lyrical, separated by a number of years. One is a shtick-like moment, characteristic of his flashing wit. He remembers, apropos of reading some Reznikoff to Charles Humboldt in 1961, that once upon a time, asked to produce a definition of a Jew for Humboldt, he quipped: "A Jew is what you and I are" (Oppen 1990, 48). The tautology, the paradox, the drollery, the fantastic circular "proof"—none of this should make the reader ignore the centerpiece—Oppen's personal identification (not really an identity) which certainly had some contrapuntal function given their shared Marxist context. Some years later, in 1976, Sharon Olds asked him whether he were Jewish; she was preparing a course on Jewish American writers. Oppen responded in a letter that recapped Molly Bloom's soliloquy in *Ulysses:* "yes, I will say, yes, I am yes (I am)" (Oppen 1990, 323). The intricacies of this, its passage from determined will to affirmation, its uses of the modernist representation of the Irish feminine to make this aroused declaration are all of note. Oppen made other quips around Jewishness—which seems for him to have been at once a topic of some seriousness and the provocation for his antic wit. He characterized himself and Mary, for instance, as "a stiff-necked people." This is God's epithet about the contentious Jews who always had an objection or a modifying question and would not simply submit, without queries, distinctions, and quibbles, to the Monotheist Voice. Oppen transfers this biblical phrase to their little family, making them (at the time of the remark) a mongrel tribe of two. (Only one, that is, was Jewish in origin.)

But was Oppen a Jewish writer? Or rather—what is it to be asking that question; what is contained in it? And how many ways can one answer it? Did he, and when did he write from a Jewish cultural identification? This is still a question for criticism, and there are poems of significant import to consider, including his resistant, heartbroken, enraged discussion of Pound. "TEST it by poetry, Ezra: write about the gas chambers, write of the children in the gas chambers" (Oppen 1989, 22). Can we say that he was a Jew writing—that formulation being a statement of agency and praxis, of choosing? Rakosi was wrong that this "Jewishness" of certain Objectivists is a "coincidence" but he is right that there is no one-size-fits-all concept of Judaism or of the secular, much less of their radical poetics. One might be a writer and a Jew, but not a Jewish writer. This is a formulation from Edmund Jabès, said in conversation with Rosmarie Waldrop, and told me by Waldrop, in conversation.

Chapter VI

In *The Secrets of Creation*, Gershom Scholem says that in Judaism "Every word is a name of God" (cited in Felstiner 1997, 106). There are similar, moving aphorisms in Jabès. The way the words come, oblique, sparse, intense, oddly linked in later Oppen makes one take these aphorisms to heart.

Yet evocations of "God" as in this rather absolutist but in-group statement of Scholem ignores other moments in other religious cultures when approximately the same thing can be said. The statement tends to take that "thing" of Judaism's notable textuality as something that simply exists, absolutely, rather than a set of multiple relationships that are changing, in motion. (For instance, even the secular Jews working in radical poetics have chosen different relationships to textuality: gematria as Jerome Rothenberg uses it is different from notarikon as Anne Blonstein uses it and different from midrash, as—and I'll get to this—I use it.) I want to argue against the static, absolute, and unchanging concept of any part of religion; I want to argue for chosen and investigated relationships to one's religious culture.

Many religions yearn to be static, claim they are, get fixed by dogma, have fundamental, fixed, permanent Truth handed down from some On High (or so the story goes), overlook their own customs and syncretisms (like the Easter Bunny and the crucified Christ within the same holiday; like Santa Claus mixed up with the birth of the Christian Messiah). But to change the terms from religion (and the up-down/ yes-no adhesion it apparently demands) to religious culture and its influence, we have to see any religion (itself an amalgam of myriad historical layers and practices) as a set of cultural and spiritual relationships in motion, historical, malleable. Making a systems analysis of the cultural impact of pressures on one's formation and of one's choices of affiliation is truer to the terms of my experience. One also gets to winnow and choose.

Chapter VII

I participate in Jewish religious and textual culture, but I am not Jewish by religious affiliation. I am an atheist and a humanist by ethical affiliation. By choices of affiliation I mean something like what Harryette Mullen has noted in relation to her masterful use of African American slang, diction, cultural allusions, song titles, folk performances, rhymes, and jargon in *Muse & Drudge.* Simply put, Mullen had to choose to learn about certain aspects of blackness. She states in an interview that, when growing up, she'd not been saturated in any "oral tradition" or "lowdown" part of black culture. Because of her own social class of origin, not only had this not been part of her actual upbringing, but that knowledge had been taboo or resisted in her family of origin.

Although it was not her cultural possession in any easy or assumed way, she decided to research these materials as a deliberate project of commitment for her artwork and community. She researched aspects of African American culture in order "to make ourselves, our knowledge, more complete. . . . This poem [*Muse & Drudge*] is a performance of that knowledge. It's a very hard-won knowledge that I treasure, because I did not want to be ignorant of my culture" (Mullen in *Callaloo* 1996, 669). Mullen had consciously to learn some of the things she deploys by attentiveness to the folklore of her own putative, identificatory, and culturally assigned group. It was social learning, chosen deliberately by herself as a cultural act, an act of self-fashioning, and a choice of affiliation. I could say some parallel things about Jewish culture and my poetry. At some point early in *Drafts,* key stories from Hebrew Scripture entered my work; I wondered, in the tonality of the time, "what is *that* about," and chose to pursue the implications of a surprising turn by some reading, some gleaning, some cultural attentiveness and study.

The more I pursued, the more I became convinced that a relationship to textuality and textual practices, latent in me (by familial osmosis? certainly as a form of social learning) had been first unconsciously activated and then consciously chosen. The operable concept, however, is "religious culture," not religion. These traits would be (but are not limited to) skepticism, a reverence for textuality so intense it moves into an antic quality within the seriousness, an exilic, nomadic sensibility, a certain kind of humor (Yiddish humor—the litotes of self-mocking/group-mocking fondness), a quarrel with the negative space some call God, a particular, actually somewhat skeptical, somewhat hopeful attitude to fulfillment and messianic hope. These I take to be cultural/historical structures of feeling imbedded in myself, some activated in my poetry, that do not depend on formal adhesion to official Jewish communities. I think the proper term is elective affinity.

Chapter VIII

In her essay "Toward a New Yiddish" Cynthia Ozick contrasts the fates-in-canon of G. K. Chesterton and Israel Zangwill, of Charles Lamb and Isaac D'Israeli—all minor writers of parallel generations and careers. Ozick argues that those forgotten in English letters are in both cases the Jews (Ozick 1983, 166–167). Her argument is that assimilation in literature does not work. "The fact is that nothing thought or written in Diaspora has ever been able to last unless it has been centrally Jewish. If it is centrally Jewish it will last for Jews. If it is not centrally Jewish it will last neither for Jews nor for the host nations" (Ozick 1983, 168–169). "The secular Jew is a figment: when a Jew becomes a secular person he is no longer a Jew" (Ozick 1983, 169). This is certainly a devastating, passionate argument, anti-assimilationist in every fiber.

By that criterion, what shall we do with Oppen? He is not thereby a Jewish writer. Neither are the rest of us. This is because we are figments, being secular Jews. Or, conversely, the trace of Jewishness that we have, and that some of us are manifesting here, in this anthology, is the proof that she is right, but we are continuing in our wrong, as we have failed by not understanding our real place; we have not affiliated adequately and are cut at the root. Ozick emerges from a particular cultural conservatism, even an enraged place, angry not only at what she sees as the corrosive loss of affiliation, but also, like a prophet denouncing back-sliding in Hebrew Scriptures, she is angry at a loss of exemplary holiness (what Jews are Chosen for). The whole tone of her argument reminds me of a moment when a (female) scholar of religion and a fully affiliated Jew confronted me with my non-Hebrew, my non-attendance at synagogue, my secular Judaism (indeed, she might have denied that the word "Judaism" was properly applied in this instance), possibly even my "mixed" marriage. She demanded: "What did your parents name you 'Rachel' for, if you are not going to be Jewish?" The astonishing aggressiveness of that question—a question that sweepingly criticizes my origins, assumes some knowledge of my parents' choices and affiliation (wrongly, as it happens), as well as undercutting my bearing in the world—is duly registered. The judgmental attacks on my authenticity, loyalty, heritage, on my honoring father and mother, and on my standing in the world were deployed to devastate; it is a good example of the quarrels—and intolerant passions—in the Jewish community. It's like the desert island joke—a man has survived on a desert island, and his rescuers were surprised to find that he had built not one but two synagogues. "Why two?" they asked. "One I go to and the other I would not be caught dead in." Secular Judaism is the site that some Jews would not be caught dead in.

Chapter IX

In the summer of 2005, someone told me I was on the "SHIT" list. This list (searchable on the web) whose initials stand for Self-Hating and Israel Threatening [Jews], is notably antigay and verbally vulgar; those who construct it have had the nerve, for instance, to put "Rabbi" in quotation marks to indicate disagreement with a particular rabbi's intellectual and political positions or sexual preference. These self-styled defenders of the faith, with their bullying tactics, represent a lot of things that could be analyzed (or pitied), but whoever they are, they certainly have taken the trouble, obsessively, to list, for example, all the names of signers of certain peace-process petitions from Brit Tzedek v'Shalom (The Jewish Alliance for Justice and Peace). Of what use is such a list? It is to take the free speech rights and political choices of others as the occasion to accuse them of heresy.

When I run across situations like this, I realize my secular position is not part of religion. It is not a weak or sniveling religion, nor a bleached-out religion. It is antireligion (though not antireligions—that would be patently ridiculous). I resist religion, so often deployed as a club to beat others, as a fundamentalist intolerance. That is, I am secular not because I am a bad or lacking or ignorant Jew, but because I think religions as social practices are basically retrograde, exclusionary, controlling, and morally—if not politically—supercilious. I am a cultural Jew not by default, but by choice. It is not because I cannot improve myself, get better at Judaism (according to the lights of others), learn Hebrew, or otherwise shape up, but because I think that religious practices that do not acknowledge modernity have led, are leading, and will lead to the religious wars we are now again inside of, as if there never had been "modernity" or "enlightenment." I am a secular Jew as a positive choice, not because I have failed to understand something, or have not chosen correctly, or need others aggressively, rhetorically to confront me.

Religion, religious adhesion as humanly practiced, seems to lead to religious wars and/or to other forms of human sacrifice. History and the present combine to teach us this striking and unbearable lesson; so-called modernity has not (yet) stopped this practice for one second. Certainly, religions have their versions of ethics and these can be a source of positive or appropriate structures of feeling and action. Religion might organize and focus human yearning, senses of mystery, awe at the general oddness of life, plus death; it is not the only way to do so, and its explanations are often simplistic, but it has certainly served to channel and shape the ineffable spiritual sensation people may experience at being in this world. Religion also has given rise to some of the most astonishing and desirable human products: texts, music, ritual, buildings, paraphernalia, mythologies, concepts. But religions are fundamentally a source of all-or-nothing authority claims concerning a set of invisible and unprovable premises said to be absolute. It apparently doesn't take much of this kind of absolutist, fundamentalist, and fervent thinking to want forcibly to convert people, or to kill them for "their own good" (often coterminus with the killers' desire for power), or to extirpate their kind from the face of the earth, or to purify an apparent "taint" that the others carry, or to take over their land and livelihood because you are "saved," "sanctified," plus more "civilized," or to force them into "Final Judgment," or to protect "our kind" from their heretical influence, or to hyper-control a particular gender (guess which . . .), to fulminate against a particular sexual preference (guess which . . .), or otherwise to use the exquisite resource religion (whichever one) has always provided—the sword. That the sword (burning alive, torturing to death, beheading, and so forth) often encodes material and political struggles in the ideological name of "Faith" hardly excuses religion; it shows that for all the apparent high-mindedness of this ideological practice, religion has always participated willingly and eagerly in hideous struggles over secular power and territory, using "God" as an excuse and manifestations of the "will of God" as a cudgel.

There is no single bad religion; all religions can and have behaved this way, and all have this potential. Religion as a practice can, presumably, be reformed and reformulated in such ways as the potential for grievous harm not be activated. That is, religions can continue to evolve in historical time. One can idealize certain religions, or certain aspects of religion (polytheism rather than monotheism has, curiously, offered convenient possibilities for those who want to think of salvaging this general situation). But reform is not my personal path. For me, religion is a rich cultural resource (a little like a museum or a library, to say this very coolly), on which I draw, and in which I wander, one that evokes some feelings from me (from puzzlement to joy to fascination), but to which I do not, can not, and will not adhere either as faith or as practice.

However, by one of these rubrics I am called. I am a secular Jew, a cultural Jew. That is, I am secular, and nothing but a Jew, although some Jews would reject and revile my self-characterization, and might even get quite angry about my claims of any Jewishness whatsoever, since I adhere, in an institutional sense, to none of it.

Chapter X

What is secular Judaism? Yosef Yerushalmi traces an array of possibilities: the loss of practices, so that, in order to be Jewish, you don't have to be religious and follow the variety of legalisms (e.g., kosher laws, laws around purity) or observances (festivals), or rituals, injunctions to prayer and study of sacred texts, and their modes and gender-laden norms. Other "surrogate" choices are an investment in historical scholarship usually about Judaism (this would be what my father did), also "varieties of Jewish nationalism, socialism, philanthropy, fraternal organizations, Hebrew or Yiddish culture" (Yerushalmi 1991, 10). What holds these together is the disinterest in, withdrawal from or lack of the particularities and practices of Judaism as a religion and way of life, by people who "have felt themselves to be somehow irreducibly Jewish nonetheless" (Yerushalmi 1991, 10). This is a perfect description of my affiliation. Prayer, I do not do, but the injunction to study, I have followed.

My Jewish heritage involves both a minor, not at all fluent, Yiddishkeit, a spoken word, through my mother, and allegiance to the Book, a written word, through my father and grandfather. My grandfather, who died in 1927, was a rabbi, fairly inspired, but also arrogant, by all reports, and my father (who died in 1986) a pretty distinguished scholar of American Judaism and American philosophy and religion, and a great believer in the separation of Church and State. (I have listed a few of his books in my bibliography.) However, my religious training was absolutely universalizing, not particularist, and my upbringing included no Hebrew, no services, no celebrations, no official synagogue-based religious training, no bat mitzvah, no holidays. RE: Je-wish, *je* do not *wish* to be any more of a Jew than I am. Yet I am irreducibly Jewish.

I was raised in that syncretic, late-nineteenth-century invention, the comparative-religion oriented "Ethical Culture Movement," a post-particularist, Emersonian humanist kind of faith. This rational-intellectual religious affiliation desired (with a serious utopian will) a universal sense of ethics without the particularist "trappings," the rituals and divisive theologies of religion. Extract the best and most noble from religious thought, they argued, and leave behind the worst—fundmentalisms, religious wars, burnings at stakes, and "ignorance/superstition." That this movement also left behind liturgy, stained glass, and the mysticism and sensuousness of religion (except as art appreciation) was a low price to pay, in their view. Ethical Culture was an uplifting, progress-oriented, socially conscious religious movement.

I had all my religious training under this aegis, which meant that Sunday School was one long course in comparative religion for kiddies, with "festivals" (e.g., Winter Festival) at punctual times of the year. However, I was also raised in a [Jewish] patriarchal family, granddaughter of a dissenting but conservative rabbi and a father who was a professor of philosophy and then of religion at Columbia University. Attenuations of Judaism occur across three generations in this family. (Incidentally, some members of the fourth generation have chosen to reaffiliate and reaffirm Judaism as a religion and daily practice.) My father was a Jew *malgré lui,* one might say; he might have truly disagreed, as Judaism was his past, not our collective future. As for me, I would never be anything but a Jew, if I am anything at all, except a secular atheist. That is, my specific Jewishness is a thinned-out, but very powerful, intellectual and even religious culture that I picked up by an osmosis so delicate as to be impalpable.

Chapter XI

How do I define my creolized Jewishness? Not the least in my skepticism, resistance, intuitive exilism, and quarrel with that curiosity called God. And in my deep commitment to the book and to textuality. "Is there such a thing as Jewish destiny?" If it exists, the Jabès I cited above suggests it is in and of "the book." In my writing, in my poetry. I have a fundamentally midrashic sensibility and a serious thematic play with the problematics of memory. I have been very drawn to a number of "Jewish" themes in recent work, including meditations on the Holocaust. The Holocaust, it should be said, was not "Jewish," but Nazi-fascist in its origins, justifications, implementations, and successes. It is only "Jewish" (and that mainly, but not solely) in its outcomes. So while I hardly think that certain things are unique to Jews, nor essential/intrinsic to Jews, I know as "authentic" within Jewish culture certain "discourses of memory, resistance, and liberation" (Boyarin 1992, xvii). It is these with which I identify. There are certain kinds of relationships to hegemony, relationships from minority and a specialness from being a resistant, nonhegemonic religious practice that saturate Jewish culture. There are also practices and traditions out of the relationship with a diasporic and ghettoized historical situation as well as practices and traditions that come from a relationship with textuality.

Chapter XII

Since 1986, I have been engaged in the writing of a long poem, in cantos, called *Drafts.* The Poundian reference is quite deliberate. As I have pointed out in *Blue Studios,* given some of Pound's damaged and damaging opinions on Jews and their historical roles:

> Mine is a poem that—how to say this right—speaks of the dilemma of writing upon, or after, the deaths of those to whom Pound addressed the possibility of "antisepsis" or a "cleansing" social purgation. My work begins in the long aftermath of the destructive underside of modernity.
>
> (DuPlessis 2006, 250–251)

In these works (by 2006, there are seventy-six cantos and one unnumbered work sportively called "Précis") there is a lot of mourning as well as leaps of amazement. Recurrent motifs and materials in many of these works are: home, homelessness, and exile, the death and the dead linked to the living, political grief and passion, including an attempt to look at the many corpses of the twentieth century. There is also silence, speaking and crying out, the sayable, the ineffable or unsayable. In many of these poems I speak of the enormousness of the universe, and the enormities of what has happened in our milky corner of it. I feel, increasingly, as the work goes on, that I am being spoken through, almost as if I were single-handedly building into existence some of the works of the lost. That this idea is arrogant, unseemly, astonishing, and shattering does not make it any less palpable, and sorrowful.

Chapter XIII

The "Jewishness" of *Drafts* occurs in several different modes, all of which perform cultural tasks. First, there is a little use of Hebrew or Yiddish words, and some allusion to ceremonies and religious practices. "Little" in this context is just a little comic: I know only so much of these issues, far less than even many other secular Jews. But "little" is also deeply serious. I figure this dot, imagined as the smallest Hebrew letter "yod," as a pinhole through which "it" all enters. The questions of the "itness" of the world, its flooding plethora, are central to my poetry.

Every so often, there is an allusion to Passover, the only Jewish holiday

I know with any attentiveness (and this by choice, learning more about it and celebrating, in a minor, potchkered-together, way, as an adult). I wrote a passage about making a particular seder dish called maror and about how I add, to the mix of apples, honey, raisins, nuts, the South Asian mixed spice called *garam masala.* This play with a traditional recipe indicates my actual tendency toward creolization. (This creolizing tendency occurs elsewhere in the poetry. For example, when I talk about *kol isha,* the Orthodox forbidding of the songs of liturgy to women when men might be listening, this gets all mixed up with the almost lost achievements of Sappho, in "Draft 43: Gap," DuPlessis 2004, 45.) This passage about Passover customs, the final lines from "Draft 34: Recto," refers to my precise Jewishness, the exact identification:

And afterwards,
        after words
                with the door shut,
should I let Elijah's winecup—
        a whole goblet, so hopeful—
just go to waste?
                  Not a chance.

You can see at a glance
        how I take my place
in a lineup of unbelieving
        Jews who
took the cup   and drank.
                ("Draft 34: Recto," DuPlessis 2001, 240)

These "Jewish allusions" are often diasporically dispersed (appropriately!)—that is, not all in one poem—and often mixed with other questions of tikkun olam (or the failure thereof) and various compromises of social justice. (And although it could seem, from this essay, that Jewish motifs are all that *Drafts* contains, this is not so.)

Chapter XIV

My poetry does deploy recurrent allusions to some key stories in Hebrew Scripture—the call of Samuel with its strange positionality ("here am I"), the pillar of smoke in Exodus (now read as a signal of disaster and burning bodies), baby Moses set adrift (as my dying mother, incidentally), Noah and the ark, Rachel escaping from her father's house to marry her cousin and pilfering crucial tribal icons from her father (what, in the name of monotheism, was that about? Laban was "Aramaic" but Rachel was, supposedly, Jewish). A central story is the one about the struggle between Jacob and the Angel. When one enters such a gigantic task as a long poem, it is difficult not to think of being called and of struggling with something large, multidimensional, and fundamentally unknowable by which you have been touched. Jacob and the angel is a story suggestive in this situation. Thus (from "Draft 8: The"):

staring into the eyes of the past
that grapple back all night,
Angel, angel, what shall we name this place?
Pouring oil down the ladder
bone to bone

plenitude and grief; of wordy words,
of wording words, I am
logy from touching the site.

"Let me go, for day is breaking"
I have forgotten what I am.
("Draft 8: The," DuPlessis 2001, 50–51)

Of these materials, aside from Jacob, angel, and their astonishing struggle, by far the most startling, repeated, vital story in *Drafts* as a whole is that of "Mt. Moriah" as it is antiseptically known (Genesis 22: 1–19). This is the near sacrifice of Isaac by his father Abraham, the son saved by the intervention of an angel as the father's knife descended to kill him, as commanded by God.

It is very difficult for me to sum up the full dimensionality of this story for my work. But the near-sacrifice of Isaac has some of these aspects for me: the driven father who puts the will of God above all else and, incidentally, chooses not to quarrel with God about this particular command, something quite interesting to examine and to fathom. Or perhaps it is unfathomable. Abraham, in other stories, is found quarrelling or discussing His commands with God, as per the discussion with God, prior to this episode, about the destruction of Sodom (Genesis 18–19). That the fates of both of the human protagonists in the Mt. Moriah episode are in the "hands of God" (through His angel) is of course a pious recognition, for those willing to entertain it.

Further, one might ask how God could be so cruel? He was in effect demanding that Abraham be stronger than He himself, since at that point, He had no son, only the fecundating power to give or not to give sons, a power appropriated from the Mother Goddess religions which He replaced, unevenly and with great difficulty (at least to judge from the vicious forays onto polytheistic Canaanites and others in Hebrew Scriptures). To "test the faith" of the hapless Abraham seems shallow, unworthy of a Concept whom one needs consider worshipping. That God grows up and matures in Hebrew Scriptures is a pleasant, if condescending, thought, but the price is high. That His people tend to grow up is a more pleasant developmental trope (a bit Christianizing in its implications). However, this (common) insight about the tribal godhead, Yaweh, and the dialectic of that God and that People does indicate the tremendous historicity of Judaism. Its claims about specific interventions made by this God into historical time, and the dialogue between God and his creation are startlingly exciting, for me a fascinating and profound aspect of Judaism: its basis in debate and skepticism, in endless interpretation rather than Incarnation (this latter point from Handelman 1982). Incidentally, this changeability and maturing of God, the willingness of the central biblical Jews to argue, talk back, discuss, quarrel with God, is part of the dialectical and historical heritage of Judaism. I continue this heritage here.

The Abraham-Isaac story is ambiguous in its demand for trust of the patriarchal, especially of the immature patriarch: does one trust *that* God, the God of *that* command? Indeed, one might find that one's nearest emotion is contempt. Does one trust the broken, pre-bereft father who is nonetheless willing to believe and obey and carry out a human sacrifice? Does one trust the already fissured son? For Isaac had an elder half-brother named Ishmael, cast out by Abraham with his mother Hagar because in Hebrew Scriptures two sons are trouble—Cain/Abel; Jacob/Esau; only one son is chosen to be Chosen: certainly an ambiguous cultural heritage consistent with monotheism. Ishmael is, in contrast, central to Muslim tradition. This Abraham-Isaac story was once explained to me as the moment, in this religious history, that human sacrifice was (institutionally, theologically) rejected. Unfortunately, it was not historically rejected.

The shadow of the Holocaust now falls over this story for me, and for others: in the myth God "saved" the two Jews, but here, in our near history, "He" did not save the eight million. Plus many more. The question where there is God becomes germane, not to speak of whether. In any event, all those killed by Nazi-fascist faith in the political nightmare of Nazi-fascist logic are very much on my mind when contemplating this story. And elements of this story (including the angel and the knife) appear repeatedly in *Drafts* (in "Draft 25: Segno"; "Draft 32: Renga"; "Draft 34: Recto," for example). Two places stand out in their intensity: "Draft 25: Segno" and "Draft 52: Midrash." But generally in *Drafts* there is a good deal (to pun, perhaps unforgiveably) of "Holocause. And effect" ("Draft 38: Georgics and Shadow," DuPlessis 2001, 266).

I speak of the feeling of moving through a landscape of doom to Mt. Moriah—or to any specific historical doom:

No matter who was walker,
who was not,
all moved along the toxic
path shrouded in silence
twigs bound up in ragged canvas,
fuel incipient . . .
("Draft 25: Segno," DuPlessis 2001, 163)

The key element of "Segno"—the question of the "ram in the thicket" found and substituted, just in time, for Isaac—comes out as an outcry of an elegy for those, precisely not me, yet just like me, the Jews and the others, who did burn in the Holocaust.

The claim that for "I" or "you"
would come the substitute
"lamb" or "ewe."

Yet in effect it was
"you" snarled in the barbèd site
who burned in place of "I."
("Draft 25: Segno," DuPlessis 2001, 164)

The fact that one must confront this story emerges at the end of the poem; the poet comes:

posing moments of gloss
on the text of loss
that has been long set
and has been set long:

one conjuncture of ash,
one girder of smoke,
hovering, still,
over rubble also of smoke.
("Draft 25: Segno," DuPlessis 2001, 165)

Chapter XV

Paul Celan and his example concerning the historically necessary task to write a post-Holocaust poetry entered *Drafts* from the first. In "Draft 1: It," my vow parallels his, citing his clear aesthetic choice: "no sandpoems" ("Draft 1: It," DuPlessis 2001, 9). Taking poetry with extreme seriousness as an ethical intervention meant, in some ways, rejecting a good deal of a more decorative and pleasant kind of poetry, although not rejecting an acerbic kind of wit. Then the Holocaust entered abruptly, in the first of the six poems called "Gap" in *Drafts:*

Low late pre-dawn freight
moans, or seems to
"J-w"
as it rushes the grade crossing

its track shining ahead
and away into unfillable

space.
("Draft 5: Gap," DuPlessis 2001, 30)

Using the visual formula for the unspoken name of "G-d" as some Orthodox Jews do, and applying it to the unspeakable event for the "J-w," the convoys lying behind my very American freight train as a shattering echo makes a condensed comment on this situation. When that sound entered the poem, the thematics of the Jew in the twentieth century followed.

Paul Celan says that the Beyond is inside us, immeasurable and imponderable. We are the ones who are burning. We are those who have been burnt, in the identification of, and with disaster. And we are living the aftermath; we live inside the thing that exudes from us. We know the situation that surrounded Celan, part of every air he breathed.

Burnt
fumes of Beyond
leak thick from our pores.
(Celan 2001, 301)

Our situation is more diffuse. I do not want to be misunderstood in invoking the Holocaust and all the immeasurable strains that conjures. There is a contemporary politics and nationalism that claims the shocking rip and wound in the human fabric that the Holocaust represents as endless justification for its actions, no matter what they are. I reject this position. It is not what I am talking about.

Chapter XVI

Indeed, I say very directly exactly what my balancing between Jewish specialness and human tragedy came to mean in "Draft 17: Unnamed." This work contains a long passage about people about to be shot by the Nazis, who threw down their names on pieces of paper as talismanic evidence. A local person who saw these scraps decided not to gather them up; many years later, she was haunted by her moral failure and calculation. This material comes from a news story and corresponds to many of the themes of loss that *Drafts* as a whole contains.

But what I meant is this.
She stood at the pit
where, this 50 years,

155 Jews were shot.
There, near a field of rye,
she'd found dozens of notes and addresses

tossed away
moments before their deaths.
To this day,

she regrets
that, out of fear,
she did not pick them up.

The poetics seems plain.
Since then
there are many people spend their time

picking up the notes.
But they are not there.
They are as gone as possible to be.

So the gathering
is impossible.
But still the shapes are bowed,

and search
this otherwhere of here.
Yet had they actually

been there
that time
being remembered,

it is equally possible
they too would have left
all of them where they lay.

What illusion, what delusion, what disillusion
writes these gaps?
tries these missing bits and scraps?

It is not elegy
though elegy seems the nearest category of genre
raising stars, strewing flowers. . . .

It's not that I have not
done this, in life or wherever I
needed to

or throwing out the curled tough leather
of the dead
the cracked insteps of unwalkable shoes,

but it is not the name or term
for what is meant
by this inexorable bending.

And it is not "the Jews"
(though of course it's the Jews),
but Jews as an iterated sign of this site.
("Draft 17: Unnamed," DuPlessis 2001, 110–111)

This passage, in Williams's implacable three-step line, is a locus for *Drafts;* it has been commented on movingly by Walter Kalaidjian in his chapter "The Holocaust at Home."

Chapter XVII

With the allusions at the end of "Draft 25: Segno" cited above, all—Exodus, the Objectivist "girder" amid "rubble" (simultaneously Reznikoff and Oppen), and the Holocaust—become linked up with the necessity for endless gloss. Thus another element of "Jewishness" in my work emerges as the textual practice of midrash. Amid the many literary genres alluded to in the titles and aspects of these works, from Renga, Haibun, Eclogue, Cento, Georgics, and Epistle to Doggerel, Ditties, Intellectual Autobiography, Bildungsgedicht, Rebus, Dialogue and (One) Lyric, the key genre animating *Drafts* is a textual strategy from Hebrew interpretive practices called midrash. Midrash originally meant a continuous and generations-long commentary on sacred texts by those—males, in Orthodox tradition—invested with the spiritual authority to discuss them. It takes its impetus from the incompletion of law, and the double gift of written and oral Torah, which necessitates the creation of an explanatory elaboration and continuous interpretation of text, an "extension" of the text (Handelman 1982, 31, 39). *Drafts* as a whole project alludes to—but secularizes—this genre of serious commentary and continuous gloss. Midrash is continual interpretation and reinterpetation, never completed, and never fulfilled. It is expressed in my folding these poems over each other on a periodicity of 19; it is expressed by tactics of citation and continuation, which are ways of resituating and interpreting materials.

There are some bizarre and fascinating forms of interpretation—what Susan Handelman calls the "outlandish techniques of interpretation" in "rabbinic hermeneutics," that have penetrating analogues with the work of radical poetics (Handelman 1982, xv). There is the mystical/lettristic reading of the "crowns" on individual letters of the Hebrew alphabet so like aspects of visual poetics today. This migrates into MacLow's and Cage's mesostic procedures. There is the way words open and make other words characteristic of notarikon, which is the making of new words based on the spelling of a specific source word. There is the secular gematria and numerical playfulness and productiveness that Oulipo, in our time, has pursued; there is the endless intertextuality, so that "texts echo, interact, and interpenetrate" without ever being set in the teleological time of fulfillment—that last is midrashic for me (Handelman 1982, 47). There is the fact that "the text continues to develop each time it is studied" for it is "a self-regenerating process" (Handelman 1982, 49). I am interested in the continuities and debates within textual commentary, the historically situated necessity for interpretation and reinterpretation, the dialogue and arguments over meaning, the layering of the results in multiple, ceaseless writing. All of these activities are also terms for a radical poetics, especially the notion of an endless, unrolling of writing as its own poetics, the disinterest in resolution, and the sense of ethical commentary posed as a necessary writing. This midrashic sensibility, in my imperfect comprehension of it, nonetheless has an ontological necessity for me.

This midrashic mode takes shape in *Drafts* as a secular composition strategy of self-citation and recurrent reflection upon the poems' themes and images. The endless unrolling of elaboration via gloss, self-reading, reconsideration, recontextualization, citation and debate, central to the structure of *Drafts,* is a way of living in textuality characteristic of a Jewish heritage. For in Jewish traditions, the mark of reverence for the book is something quite beyond the merely literary; it is the practice in which debates about ethics and Being travel down multiple generations. Midrash, etymologically, means search or inquiry, and, as Handelman argues, there is never "one single interpretation to which all understanding of the text aims, but a continuous production of multiple meaning" (Handelman 1982, 75).

This midrashic attitude to structure seems, as I said, to be part of "radical poetics" in several particulars. In midrash, closure and finality are deferred, although each comment has authority; in midrash, interpretations clash or pull in different directions. My midrashic sensibility treats the texts I make as openable, never fully closed. It makes of form a kind of self-skepticism and praxis, not an iconic object. It resists epiphany, which, as a narrative structure, is to some degree associated with Christianity, although, of course, God "appears" and is spoken with in several stories of the Hebrew Scriptures (though the Messiah does not). Or, more accurately, if there is a sense of the climactic shining forth characteristic of epiphany, this is immediately transposed, for closure is not permanent, and statement is always open to its own modification and self-quarreling. If epiphany, it is a manifestation thereupon subject to doubt and senses of loss rather than the fullness of presence. Epiphany as a Christian structure of feeling (like the closures in kinds of lyric poetry) is associated with fulfillment, with an achieved messiah. What I am talking about is a non-messianic (or pre-messianic) structure of feeling, something that has deep formal and structural implications for radical poetics. I inhabit a poetics of negativity and I am happily transported in the dialectics between presence and absence. The Jewish structure of feeling in which I participate is deferral intermingled with a helix of hope and doubt. Religiously speaking, it is that stiff-necked resistance to accepting an achieved Messiah (in Jesus) that enrages those who want, with a patronizing assiduity, to convert us. But it is clear that certain elements of radical poetics draw on this Jewish structure of feeling, this Jewish sense of textuality involved with endless writing, multiple commentary and vectors, endless deferral.

Chapter XVIII

My poem "Draft 52: Midrash" is a locus of the concerns both for the Holocaust and for the question of midrash. This poem makes an endless, unresolved gloss on Adorno's dour, moving sententia, "After Auschwitz to write a poem is barbaric," taking his statement as an important spiritual talisman concerning this ethical-political nightmare and its challenge to art. This poem has twenty-seven sections, one more than our alphabet, and each section directly approaches and reapproaches Adorno's challenging statement in a myriad of ways, agreeing, disagreeing, acceding, identifying with, resisting, facing, and trying to get around, to avoid his incredibly grief-stricken, enraged comment (Adorno 1981, 34). This poem contains the following section based, in part, on a depiction of the Abraham-Isaac-angel story by Caravaggio:

16.
Making such rules about how who what why and whether
to make art is useless, quixotic. Why then did he do it?
Why *poetry* that it has been singled out, chosen (named: like
Jews, first and foremost, faceted jewel, Gypsies, gays, leftists, dissenters,
activists, nationalists, resistants, handicapped children, and more,
hanging pendants):

It is an act of mourning
to cut off
what is important to him—
poetry—
as if to sacrifice Isaac
to walk the choked road
to bind one's closest bond,
who that, once realized,
will blubber, snotty and noisy
screaming with fear—the knife goes up
to strike the poem, held down by
the driven father, in transfixed

obedience to higher command
whilst the angel (who looks just like
doomed son "poetry" but isn't blubbering;
in fact is lucid, pretty, and removed
without an ounce of human empathy)
tells the dazed,
shattered Abraham
to desist.

Adorno! desist!
put down your knife!
Have I been taken in the role of angel?
Perhaps I should not write poetry.
("Draft 52: Midrash," DuPlessis 2004, 150–151)

Note

1. When she read this essay in draft, Linda Oppen wrote me a rich and interesting response, which I have, with her permission, cited here in full. This from an email of April 3, 2006.

> Speaking of fathers, I end with some notes on George, since you write about his familial Jewishness. George's search for identity was the greater since he was motherless, I think his identification as a Jew was a loyalty to her [to Elsie, the mother who killed herself in 1912], a distancing from George Sr and Seville [Oppen's stepmother]. I'm guessing about that, but in any case, George's parents were married in an Ethical Culture ceremony, his mother's family [the Rothfeld family] were intimately involved in its causes, funding and world from its beginning. You know that world far better than I, and its Jewish loyalties. Of course, George Sr and Elsie could not have stated their assimilation more strongly than they did in naming both their children after their living selves! Their circle as far as I know was among German Jews. I don't know whether George Sr. had much to do with that choice but he seemed not to care about Seville's Episcopalian veneers or even her decision to shorten his name; they did fund San Francisco Jewish causes and moved within Jewish social settings.
>
> Yet when George Jr met Mary he announced solemnly that he was a Jew. To skip to the other end of his life, he was hugely pleased that Hamburger (Michael?) introduced him to others in Britain as a Jewish poet. I'm always a little surprised and pleased when I'm included as a Jew [said Linda Oppen]; I think he found the same.

Bibliography of Works Cited or Mentioned

Adorno, Theodor. *Prisms,* trans. Samuel and Shierry Weber. Cambridge, MA: MIT Press, 1981.

Bernstein, Charles. "Reznikoff's Nearness." In DuPlessis and Quartermain, eds. 1999. 210–239.

Blau, Joseph L. *Modern Varieties of Judaism.* New York: Columbia University Press, 1966.

———, ed. *Cornerstones of Religious Freedom in America.* Boston: Beacon Press, 1949; revision, Harper & Row, 1964.

Blonstein, Anne. *Worked on Screen.* Salzburg: Poetry Salzburg, University of Salzburg, 2005.

Boyarin, Jonathan. *Storm from Paradise: The Politics of Jewish Memory.* Minneapolis: University of Minnesota Press, 1992.

Celan, Paul. *Selected Poems and Prose of Paul Celan,* trans. John Felstiner. New York: W. W. Norton, 2001.

DuPlessis, Rachel Blau. *Drafts 1–38, Toll.* Middletown, CT: Wesleyan University Press, 2001.

———. *Drafts. Drafts 39–57, Pledge, with Draft, Unnumbered: Précis.* Cambridge: Salt Publishing, 2004.

———. *Torques, Drafts 58–76.* Cambridge: Salt Publishing, 2007.

———. *Blue Studios: Poetry and Its Cultural Work.* Tuscaloosa: The University of Alabama Press, 2006.

——— and Peter Quartermain, eds. *The Objectivist Nexus: Essays in Cultural Poetics.* Tuscaloosa: The University of Alabama Press, 1999.

Evans, George, and August Kleinzahler. "An Interview with Carl Rakosi" (1988), in Heller, ed. 1993. 61–92.

Felstiner, John. *Paul Celan: Poet, Survivor, Jew.* New Haven, CT: Yale University Press, 1997.

Finkelstein, Norman. "Tradition and Modernity, Judaism and Objectivism: The Poetry of Charles Reznikoff." In DuPlessis and Quartermain, eds. 191–209.

Fishbane, Michael. *The Exegetical Imagination: On Jewish Thought and Theology.* Cambridge, MA: Harvard University Press, 1998.

Handelman, Susan A. *The Slayers of Moses: The Emergence of Rabbinic Interpretation in Modern Literary Theory.* Albany: State University of New York Press, 1982.

Hartman, Geoffrey H., and Sanford Budick, eds. *Midrash and Literature.* New Haven, CT: Yale University Press, 1986.

Heller, Michael, ed. *Carl Rakosi: Man and Poet.* Orono, ME: National Poetry Foundation, 1993.

Jabès, Edmund. "The Key." Trans. Rosmarie Waldrop. In Hartman and Budick, eds. *Midrash and Literature.* 349–360.

Kalaidjian, Walter. *The Edge of Modernism: American Poetry and the Traumatic Past.* Baltimore: Johns Hopkins University Press, 2006.

Mullen, Harryette. *Muse & Drudge*. Philadelphia: Singing Horse Press, 1995.
———. "The Solo Mysterioso Blues: An Interview with Harryette Mullen by Calvin Bedient." *Callaloo* 19, 3 (1996): 651–669.
Oppen, George. *New Collected Poems*. Michael Davidson, ed., preface by Eliot Weinberger. New York: New Directions, 2002.
———. *The Selected Letters of George Oppen*. Rachel Blau DuPlessis, ed. Durham, NC: Duke University Press, 1990.
———. "The Circumstances: A Selection from George Oppen's Uncollected Writing." Rachel Blau DuPlessis, ed. *Sulfur* 25 (Fall 1989): 10–43.
Ozick, Cynthia. "Toward a New Yiddish." In *Art and Ardor: Essays*. New York: Alfred A. Knopf, 1983. 151–177.
Reznikoff, Charles. *By the Waters of Manhattan*. New York: New Directions / San Francisco Review, 1962.
Rothenberg, Jerome. *Gematria*. Los Angeles: Sun & Moon Press, 1994.
Scroggins, Mark, ed. *Upper Limit Music: The Writing of Louis Zukofsky*. Tuscaloosa: The University of Alabama Press, 1997.
Shoemaker, Steven. "Between Contact and Exile: Louis Zukofsky's Poetry of Survival." In Scroggins 1997. 23–43.
Williams, Raymond. *Marxism and Literature*. Oxford: Oxford University Press, 1977.
Yerushalmi, Yosef Hayim. *Freud's Moses: Judaism Terminable and Interminable*. New Haven, CT: Yale University Press, 1991.

Secular Jewish Culture and Its Radical Poetic Discontents

Norman Finkelstein

1. Moses, Zusya, and Me

> The very first task of each man is the actualizing of his unique possibilities, without precedent and never renewed, and not the repetition of something that someone else, were he the greatest person of all, would already have accomplished. It is this idea that Rabbi Zusya expressed shortly before his death: in the other world I will not be asked, Why were you not Moses? I will be asked, Why were you not Zusya?
>
> —Martin Buber

The question has been posed; the books surround me. I have been asked to reflect upon the relationship between secular Jewish culture and radical poetic practice, or more broadly, how Judaism and experimental poetry relate to each other. As is my wont, I prepare for the task by turning to my bookshelves, seeking the new texts with which I am currently engaged as well as the old, reassuring works that have guided me in the past. As I dutifully read and research, I come upon Buber's anecdote about Zusya in Marc-Alain Ouaknin's *The Burnt Book: Reading the Talmud* (and it's familiar; I've encountered it before, but I cannot recall the original context). Ouaknin then takes us to a commentary on Buber by Emmanuel Levinas: "This suggests that the totality of truth is made up of the contributions of multiple persons: the uniqueness of each reaction bearing the secret of the text: the voice of Revelation precisely inasmuch as it is inflected by the ear of each person, would be necessary for the Whole of Truth!" After which Ouaknin himself comments: "The same idea is expressed in the texts of Hasidism in the following manner: each man is a letter or a part of a letter. The Book has been completely written when there is no longer any letter missing. Each man must write his letter, must write himself, that is to say, create himself by renewing a meaning: his meaning" (60).

I am both encouraged and dismayed: encouraged because my immersion in the world of the text leads me to understand that it is my own meaning, my unique contribution that ultimately counts; dismayed because, paradoxically, it is only through that very dutiful, habitual, obsessive immersion, that I am led to this discovery. Because I am so much a creature of the Book, I am able to learn that I am myself. Yet I am myself only insofar as I am a part of the Book, completing something infinitely greater than myself. Where, I wonder, am I to be found? Where does my practice—my reading, my writing—begin, and those of others end? How will the textual play in which I constantly engage answer the question that awaits me (whether I really believe it will be posed to me or not): Why were you not Norman?

But wait: "Rabbi Nachman does not like answers. In that respect he is faithful to the whole Talmudic and Cabalistic tradition that defines man-Adam as a 'what?' (*Mah?*). Man is a 'What is it?' As Jabès remarks very well: 'The Jew not only asks questions: he has himself become a question.' He is a question without an answer" (Ouaknin 281). Needless to say, I read this with some feeling of relief. Furthermore, have I forgotten the Talmudic adage which I have encountered and repeated now in so many contexts, but which still remains my goad and my comfort?: "You are not required to complete the work, but neither are you free to desist from it" (*Aboth* II: 21). Each of these passages stresses the radical incompletion of human being in the work of understanding the Word. None can encompass the whole, yet it is in the spirit of the whole that the work goes on. Furthermore, the Talmud insists upon the equal importance of each individual in his devotion to the Book and to his scholarly responsibility, which in turn represents a communal responsibility. Hence another famous passage: "If I am not for myself, then who is for me? And if I am only for myself, then what am I? And if not now, when?" (*Aboth* II: 14).

Called to ask the existential question, Who am I?, but also charged to participate in an endless textual community and a process of culture through which I take responsibility both for myself and others, I am led to wonder at my conduct and my stance as Jew, as poet, as Jewish poet.[1] To pose the question of Jewish culture is to enter into the process of Jewish culture. To pose the question of poetry is to enter into the experiment of poetry. If I do not pose those questions, however unanswerable, then what will I answer if asked, Why were you not yourself?

(And yet I already anticipate what my answers might be. This premonition comes in the form of an allergic reaction to the reference, in almost any intellectual context, of *experimental* poetics or of *secular* Jewish culture. I reach for an antihistamine. Stevens: "All poetry is experimental poetry" [*Opus Posthumous* 187]. Derrida: "the intelligible face of the sign remains turned toward the word and face of God" [13]. Ah, I feel better already. It would follow then that Jewish poetry is always experimental poetry; and that Jewish poetry—if not Jewish culture in general—can never be fully secular. Perhaps. Let us see . . .)

2. Cadaverization and Undeadness

In the Talmudic tradition, the work of self-actualization, of discovering the integrity of the individual, the person, takes place in the vertiginous world of endless textual play, a world of total hermeneutical and exegetical freedom bound only by the fact of divinity: "And the tables were the work of God, and the writing was the writing of God, graven upon the tables. Read not *charuth* (graven) but *cheruth* (freedom), for no man is free but he who labours in the Torah" (*Aboth* VI: 2). Recent accounts of traditional Jewish textuality present compelling analogies to poststructuralist theories of reading and writing, which we may relate in turn to modernist and postmodernist poetic practices.[2] Thus, to stay with Ouaknin for a while longer, "*Mahloket* [controversial or polemical discussion between Talmudic masters about the same subject] produces an interruption into which is introduced a waiting, a suspension, which measures the irreducible distance between the two masters. *Mahloket* research is not unifying; on the contrary, it seeks separation, a breach, the interval, which are the other's possibility of being" (282). What interests me about these disruptive and deconstructive practices is the Talmudic notion that they do not undermine a sense of identity or personhood, as in the case of some versions of postmodernism, but rather help to reveal and affirm the place of the person, both in the text and in the world at large. What might be the modern Jewish poet's inheritance from this religious tradition? For me, it is just this notion: that the linguistic indeterminacy and extreme hermeneutical procedures of traditional Jewish textuality may lead us to a deeper and (dare I say it?) more genuine or authentic sense of self. We live in a world that is increasingly characterized by totalizing modes of thought and discourse, facile and manipulative cultural production, insidious forms of political coercion, and institutionalized violence. Perhaps what we think of as experimental poetry, radical or avant-garde writing, at least as practiced in a Jewish context or in a self-conscious relation to Jewish scriptural tradition, can provide access for us today to personal and social truths opposed to such administered forms of modern life. How can this be the case?

(I pause, led to reflect upon my last two sentences. First: whom do I mean by "us today"? Obviously not observant Jews who still follow the Law fully and lead a more prescribed way of life than most. Broadly speaking, I suppose I mean readers of poetry, or readers of Jewish poetry, or readers of poems by Jews [*all poets are Jews,* whispers a ghostly voice], or those who seek to become, as Jerome Rothenberg would say, a "connoisseur of jews" [*Poland/1931* 12]. But I also mean, more specifically, nonobservant Jews, *secular* Jews—though for the moment, I set aside the question of whether such Jews really take part in what is an identifiably *secular* Jewish culture. Second: do I honestly believe that poetry of any sort, in relation to any tradition or set of beliefs, can lead us to self-understanding and to truths that oppose or even dispel the violence and illusion of modern life? To which I can only respond, in the words of George Oppen's "The Building of the Skyscraper," "It is the business of the poet / 'To suffer the things of the world / And to speak them and himself out'" [149].)

We think of innovative writing as providing a liberating perspective on reality—otherwise, why "Make It New?" In his discussion of Rabbi Nachman's contribution to Jewish hermeneutics, Ouaknin focuses on Nachman's interpretation of the concept of divine *tsimtsum* (contraction or withdrawal) that is fundamental to Isaac Luria's kabbalistic theory of creation. According to Ouaknin, Nachman's concern is with the process of textual innovation, how it is possible and how it may be encouraged, since in Talmudic interpretation, "the plural speech of *Mahloket,* room is left for each person to create his own world" (284). Nachman associates innovation with *tsimtsum:* "When someone wishes to innovate new words (new meanings), he should limit his knowledge (literally: accomplish the *Tsimtsum* in his mind), that is to say, evacuate, not hurry into the known preliminary considerations that confuse his mind and are not necessary for innovating. He should act like someone who does not know and only then can he progressively, and in order, innovate new meanings" (285). The rationale for this procedure implies a critique of institutional thinking and of the status quo. As Ouaknin puts it, "Man has to withdraw from 'himself' in order to attain himself. The first 'self' is not the real one; it is constructed, prefabricated by institutions" (285). *Tsimtsum* is thus a process of *designification;* the innovative reader (or writer) "attacks the semantic actuality of a speech, or, in other words, rediscovers for himself the power of words through their 'designifying'" (287). Withdrawal from conventional signification transforms one into a "simple man," one who says, "I know nothing"—a notion that I cannot help but see as analogous to Keats's negative capability, which went on to inspire ideas of open form composition in poetry over a century later.[3] Ouaknin asserts that "The 'I know not' of designifying removes language and the text from a sort of cadavcrization where the words would no longer have the power to signify an affective or emotional actuality" (287). Against this condition, innovative writing organizes a repertory of designifying or defamiliarizing techniques—poetic techniques—in the production of new meaning.

Ouaknin's emphasis on the writing self's withdrawal and his use of the term "cadaverization" to denote the stultifying force of institutionalized language have extraordinary resonance for me, for they relate directly to some of the most important insights in Eric L. Santner's *On the Psychotheology of Everyday Life: Reflections on Freud and Rosenzweig.* On one level, this magisterial book is an analysis of the ways in which two of the greatest modern Jewish thinkers have reconceived (but by no means "secularized") Judaism so to redeem us from the "undeadness" imposed by the surplus power of social institutions, those "sites that endow us with social recognition and intelligibility, that produce and regulate symbolic identities" (26). The *"too much of an address"* (32) by these sovereign powers leads in turn to a defense mechanism producing a condition that Santner names "Egyptomania," a " 'too much of demand,' [that] most powerfully captures life, undeadens it, makes it rigid with energy" (64). Freud and Rosenzweig variously offer the therapeutic means necessary for us to enact an "Exodus" from this condition, renewing our capacity to love and allowing us to open to the Other whom we previously feared. This, for Santner, constitutes "Revelation": "an opening of a space in human possibilities organized around the claims made upon me by the Other insofar as he or she is singularly out-of-joint with respect to the social intelligibility produced by this inscription in law" (105). Indeed (at this point Santner opposes Rosenzweig to Freud), "Judaism, this first religion of revelation, can rather be understood as a kind of therapy directed precisely against the fantasmatic pressures of the superego and its tendency to keep the subject at a distance from his or her answerability within the world" (104).

For Santner, one of the most potentially effective human creations through which we may overcome our undeadness is *poetry.* "What poets establish," he argues, "is not some sort of vision or consciousness of the All; rather they introduce into the relational totality of social existence—into the social body divided into parts—the perspective of 'non-all' " (142). Like Ouaknin's view of innovative writing as a designifying practice, Santner understands artistic production (i.e., "the beautiful") "conceived not as a harmonization of parts within an ordered whole but rather as the representation of an interrupted whole—or better, a *self-interrupting whole*—one animated, as it were, by a 'too much' of pressure from within its midst. . . . beautiful objects are *disarming* not in the sense of releasing us, and once for all, from the 'too much' of excitation that is, at some level constitutive of human life, but rather in the sense of loosening our defenses, opening beyond our stuckness in the especially rigid and defensive organization of this pressure" (136). As in the case of Ouaknin and Nachman, here we see some form of negativity, some sense of the "non-all" intervening in a totalizing structure of signification. Of particular importance for me is the notion of the poem as *self-interrupting whole,* for Santner's formulation startlingly resembles my own reflections while working on *Track,* my long serial poem. I quote the first of my "Statements for *Track*":

> *Track* is a series of controlled discontinuities, the self-conscious dilapidation of the structuralist's dream as it ascends toward the transcendental signifier. The poem as "field of action" or "park of eternal events" applies to my work only insofar as the action or events can be both determined *and* left open to happenstance. Linguistic and experiential pressures brought to bear on the writing (and again, this is a matter of deliberation *and* accident) set off "articulations of sound forms in time," or lyric moments arising in spite of themselves. *Track* is the lyric of disaster, the disaster of lyric. It inoculates itself through measured sequences of verbal shocks, which then reveal themselves as parts of a larger pattern. It becomes a totality in spite of itself, and it is under this condition that it continues to be conceived and composed. Always at odds with itself, it requires a grandiosity that must be continually punctured, sufficiently punctured in an act that is still a shaping, still formal. Its place in the course of my work in general is thus inevitable and extreme.

Although I was not thinking in specifically "Jewish" terms in this passage (my reference points are drawn from the "radical" poetics of modernism and postmodernism), I would argue that the sense of form I was attempting to articulate is related in principle to what I was later to learn about Jewish writing from the authors I have been discussing here. In *Track* itself, I frequently have recourse to Jewish content or references, sometimes engaging in what amounts to full-blown poetic midrash, even on biblical passages. But regardless of the particular matter or content under hand, *Track,* as a *"self-interrupting whole,"* operates through what I now conceive to be not only "experimental" but also "Jewish" textual procedures.[4] And as a serial poem in the tradition of such poets as Oppen, Creeley, Duncan, Spicer, and perhaps further back, Whitman and Dickinson, it is contoured to the shape of a life lived, taking on the search for definition of that life's path or track. Here again, I find congruence between Jewish textuality and "radical" poetic composition. The designifying procedures we associate with both traditions constitute the open work of self-discovery, the renewal of meaning and answerability, the overcoming of undeadness. Again, from my "Statements for Track": "The incursion of a certain kind of pleasure/terror, akin to the strong incursions of eros into one's life, is registered through a shift in the verbal patterning, until it potentially becomes a part of the patterning." Or as I put it in one of many such passages in the poem itself:

#
Sometimes there are numbers
and sometimes there are ruptures

Sometimes the rules
break the continuities

And sometimes the continuities
break the rules

Sometimes a seventh is added much later. (*Track* 67)

As I think of the movement from one point to the next in *Track,* the incursions, ruptures, discontinuities, and abrupt revelations, I recall Franz Rosenzweig's words at the end of *Understanding the Sick and the Healthy:* "The world's assurances should prevent one's eyes from closing. Nor do they close. They peer ahead to find what the hands must grip next and where the feet must step" (102).

3. Language, World, and Thought

What Rosenzweig lovingly calls "the world's assurances" come to us through language, "the companion of everything, including every event which takes place in the world, and yet is external to them all: the Word." Language is "a bridge between the world and these other things. . . . To utter a word is to affix a seal as a witness of man's presence. The word is not part of the world; it is the seal of man" (*Understanding the Sick and the Healthy* 71). Through our engagement with language, we span the gap between self and world. Rosenzweig's model of being is tripartite: world, man, and God. Thus, he goes on to tell us that "language stamps the sign of God and man upon all the things of this world. . . . The thing is and as such immediately acquires a name. Its name bears it into the flow of things" (73–74). The power of the word to bear the thing into world, to secure it in the cognizance of the subject, whether human and divine, calls to mind one of the most significant qualities of modern poetry, as one finds, for instance, in Rilke, or in a different register, in Stevens, Oppen, or Bronk. I am thinking of a poetry of worldly presence in which language in its naming of things grants them (or unveils in them) a sense of the numinous, even when the work generally tends toward the agnostic. Bronk: "This tree! This tree! Look, there are parts of the world / not ever wounded, within whose light, the world / is always changed with light. This tree, this tree" (57). Oppen: "The small nouns / Crying faith / In this in which the wild deer / Startle, and stare out" (99).

For Rosenzweig, poetry, more than any other art, holds out what is in effect a redemptive promise through the aesthetic experience that it has to offer. As he explains, "Poetry is not a kind of art of thought, but thinking is its element as space is that of the plastic arts and time is that of music; and from thinking, it ends also by putting at its service the world of inner and outer intuition, space and time, the extensive 'epic' breadth and the intensive 'lyrical' depth. It follows that it is the living art in the proper sense" (*Star of Redemption* 263). "Because it is the most alive," Rosenzweig declares, "poetry is the most indispensable art . . . every man who is fully man must have a sense for poetry" (263).

But although poetry is indispensible, its power and ultimately its redemptive significance lies in its relation to thought, not what Rosenzweig calls its "tonality" (i.e., musical qualities) or the "language" (i.e., style) of the individual poet. "It is only the 'idea' that gives life to the poem," he insists; "it is that which is perceptible from an aesthetic point of view for the senses, that which is actually real and effective in the work. . . . The idea is that which 'speaks' in the poem to the spectator, like the melody in the musical work and the plastic figure in the visual work. The idea is not somewhere behind the poem, it is in it" (*Star of Redemption* 265). This certainly poses a problem for any sort of formalist or language-centered poetic, including those which posit their "radical" nature in the play of the sign. We have already noted that the designifying practices of traditional Jewish textuality function as a means of self-determination: language may be regarded as indeterminate, but that indeterminacy renews, rather than disperses, the unique meaning of each individual. Now we observe that for one of our most important Jewish philosophers, language in its formal capacity, however much it makes manifest the poem—indeed, constitutes the poem—is ultimately subordinate to the idea of the poem, which, as Rosenzweig concludes, is that element "where life itself stirs most of the time" (266).

It is very much in this spirit that Michael Heller, one of our best commentators (in prose and in verse) on Jewish thought and modernist poetics, criticizes the formalism of language-centered writing. In "Avant-Garde Propellants and the Machine Made of Words," Heller argues that the problem of this work lies in its "fetishizing not reality but language, as though language were now suddenly capable of becoming an object where all else had failed" (213). By contrast, he proposes that "the power of poetry . . . is that it puts a word back into the voice of an Other, that it is a power for him or her and so confronts my particular empowerment of it. The word again becomes an object of thought." And in "Diasporic Poetics," an essay on his relation to the Objectivists that also draws from Rosenzweig and Levinas, Heller writes of the Jewish poet "as transmuter of a worked-upon physiology into language, the re-namer. Implicit in this line of thought is that the poet is not perceived as an experimenter with language *per se,* for there is nothing more confident than the experimenter in the laboratory who can objectively manipulate materials (language in this case) in a fanciful manner. On the contrary, Levinas's poet is anguished and exposed . . . does not perform but is performed upon by experience, by adversity, by love and history" (171–172).

Both Heller's critique of experimentalism and his own position (which he likes to speak of as offering a "counter-history," or "counter-memory," producing "countercontinuities") stem from a strong belief in the primacy of thought, the product of a thinking subject that both mediates and is mediated by language. In Heller's nuanced and dialectical view, language, self, and world are constantly assayed, valued, recalibrated at the site of the poem. And when he asks himself "how a particular Jewishness informs a poetry" (173), his answer takes much the same dialectical form, in which the poet both performs and is performed upon in a continuous process of becoming, and poetry is both revelation and commentary: "becoming begins in exposures and antecedents: those poets that I read, the life their words lead me to. This is very much in keeping with the Jewish notion of revelation which begins in overhearing the revelatory nature of the text before one's eyes, its imports and prophetic hopes" (174). In terms of both content and form, thought and language, I am reminded of another instance in *Track,* when passages from Oppen and Bronk, two poets who mean a great deal to me, suddenly take on a force akin to revelation, and the poem acknowledges its status as commentary, and the responsibility that lies therein:

#
Gathering, arranging
the endless repetitions

At risk of ending
at any moment

Any moment suffused
with ending or beginning

"*Now* that tremendous
plunge"

#
Any moment suffused
with endless quotation
Quotation as translation
beyond all strategies

Lifting the text
in and out of time

"these certainties against
the all-uncertain" (*Powers* 51)

(Once again I pause and reflect. "Quotation as translation / beyond all strategies"? The procedures or strategies we associate with modern and postmodern poetry, insofar as they relate to Jewishness, must take up the risk, the challenge, of revelation: revelation of the self, of the world—and of God? Inevitably we are led back to the question of divinity, in terms of poetic practice and Jewish culture. But I am not quite ready to deal with the question head on, which would not, in any case, be a particularly Jewish move. Let's engage in commentary just a little longer . . .)

4. Rothenberg *contra* Grossman; Or, the Secular and the Holy

More than any other recent Jewish poet, Jerome Rothenberg has self-consciously appropriated traditional religious writing procedures and formal strategies for the production of secular poetry. As he explains in the "Post/Face" to *Gematria*, one of his most radical experiments along these lines, "Unlike the traditionalists of gematria, I have seen these coincidences/synchronicities not as hermeneutics substantiations for religious and ethical doctrines, but as an entry into the kinds of correspondences/constellations that have been central to modernist & 'post' modernist experiments over the last century & a half" (165). Note the ease with which Rothenberg moves from "religious and ethical doctrines" to "modernist and 'post' modernist experiments." As he sees it, the complexity, variety, and dizzyingly contradictory nature of Jewish culture and history is best understood as an evolving continuum of creation, of *poesis,* which means that "religious and ethical doctrines" are not, ultimately, the driving forces behind traditional Jewish writing. This view is elaborated in the "Pre-Face" to *A Big Jewish Book* (reworked as *Exiled in the Word*), his monumental anthology of "Poems and Other Visions of the Jews from Tribal Times to Present." For me, this Pre-Face remains one of the most important documents in the annals of Jewish literature. At the center of the text, Rothenberg tells us that

> Work for this book has accordingly been drawn from both "sacred" and "secular" sources, with the link between them *my* stress on a poetic/visionary continuum & on the mystical & magical side of the Jewish tradition. And since poetry, in the consensus of my contemporaries, is more concerned with the "free play of the imagination" than with doctrinal certainties *per se,* I've made no attempt to establish an "orthodox" line or to isolate any one strain as purer or more purely Jewish than any others. Instead my assumption has been that poetry, here as elsewhere, is an inherently impure activity of individuals creating reality from all conditions & influences at hand. (9)

Not only does this account for the remarkable heterogeneity of the material in the anthology, it also definitively establishes Jewish *poesis* as a sort of visionary secularism, since Rothenberg disregards the fundamental distinction in normative Judaism between the sacred (or more accurately, the holy—*kadosh*—difference or separation) and the profane. The resulting "promiscuity" (6) (a term Rothenberg himself uses) in regard to Jewish writing allows for previously repressed linkages and filiations in apparently contradictory traditions and ideologies to reveal themselves, so that kabbalistic spells and Dadaist performance pieces, passages from Torah and from heretical messianic texts shed light on one another in an immense modernist collage. From this perspective, the shaman, the prophet, the Talmudist, and the poet are all engaged in the same activity, whether the cultural artifact is presented as a spell, a sermon, a scriptural commentary, or a "word event." Under the aegis of modern ethnography and religious historiography (remember, Rothenberg is the inventor of the term "ethnopoetics"), we discover "the poetic *mainstream* . . . magic, myth, & dream; earth, nature, orgy, love; the female presence the Jewish poets named Shekinah" (5). The marginal and the avant-garde, in Rothenberg's antiauthoritarian and decentered view, reveal themselves to be the hidden or repressed center of the culture: all Jewish writing participates in an endlessly evolving process of experimentation which is, to reiterate, "an inherently impure activity."

As Rothenberg well knows, this inherently impure activity poses a serious challenge to any sense of normative, not to mention orthodox, Judaism. Thus, Jewish poetry, indeed, Jewish cultural activity of any sort, regardless of how it understands itself in regard to traditional Jewish belief, is ultimately secular, profane, *treyf* [unclean], *asur* [forbidden]. If it is to be understood as having any relation to the "sacred" (as in the invocation of "magic, myth & dream; earth, nature, orgy, love"), it is an understanding of that term that could actually be *opposed* to the fundamental Jewish concept of holiness. As Levinas explains in his severe Talmudic essay "Desacralization and Disenchantment," "The sacred is in fact the half light in which the sorcery the Jewish tradition abhors flourishes. . . . Sorcery, first cousin, perhaps even sister, of the sacred, is the mistress of appearance. She is a relative slightly fallen in status, but within the family, who profits from the connections of her brother, who is received in the best circles" (141).[5] This is why, as Levinas puts it, "I have always asked myself if holiness, that is separation or purity, the essence without admixture that can be called Spirit and which animates the Jewish tradition—or to which the Jewish tradition aspires—can dwell in a world that has not been desacralized" (141). And in Levinas's view, the sacred tends not toward desacralization, but toward degeneration, and in its degeneration, becomes sorcery: "That is why the sacred is not sacred, why the sacred is not holiness" (152).

Much as I admire Levinas's brilliant integration of Jewish tradition and modern philosophy, I would simply note in passing the tension between his view and that of Rothenberg were it not for another crucial poet who adopts much the same view as Levinas in his understanding of Jewish poetry. I refer to Allen Grossman, whose poetry and poetics I regard as equally significant as Rothenberg's, but who stands, it seems to me, diametrically opposed to the ethnopoetic position that Rothenberg represents.[6] Rather than take an anthropological perspective on Jewish culture, in which the Jewish writers, however they define themselves, are ultimately *bricoleurs* ("individuals creating reality from all conditions & influences at hand"), Grossman assumes that Jewish culture is, by definition, a *culture of holiness:* "the supreme human work (man's service and creativity) is the voluntary performance of the transactions of holiness, which reciprocate and complete God's creation of the world by restoring it day by day, fact by scattered fact, to his nature. The specifications of such work, as in the 613 *mitzvot,* or commandments, defines a *culture of holiness,* a system of transactions by which through the mediation of holiness man and God come to be included within the precinct of the same term" (180).

This passage comes from "Holiness," originally published as a chapter in a volume called *Contemporary Jewish Religious Thought.* Grossman focuses on a number of basic Jewish prayers, but it's clear that he has poetry in mind when he notes that "from the point of view of human experience, therefore (the point of view of language), *holy* is not in the ordinary sense a predicate, a word that asserts something about a term, but a sign of the withdrawal of all reference into its source, a determinator of the radical disablement of metaphor and the absolute preemption of the truth of discourse at the supremely privileged moment of reference to reality" (180). Thus holiness, as the signifier of ultimate difference between creator and creation, is that which simultaneously inspires but also shuts down linguistic production. In Jewish culture, "transactions of holiness," especially linguistic transactions, enable humanity to interact with the Absolute, for God both constitutes and creates reality. This is why, as Grossman tells us in his great essay "Jewish Poetry Considered as a Theophoric Project," "The Jew's word, strictly speaking, is One (holy, sacred, *Kadosh*), and is unlike all other words in that it does not signify by difference [as does gentile poetry] but rather serves the Master who is difference—which is to say, existence itself" (162).

According to Grossman's paradigm, although poetry has always been associated with the sacred (that is, the holy), "for the Jew *there is always a sense* (a profound understanding beneath all other understandings) *that the category of the sacred and the category of the poetic repel one another*" (161). Yet Jewish poetry still strives to be a "theophoric" or God-bearing enterprise. And with remarkable irony, the mediating power that Grossman names as the inspiration for Jewish poetry, the power through which the transaction of holiness, of *purity,* between God and the Jewish poem takes place, is the Shekinah, the very figure that Rothenberg identifies with the *impurity* of poetic activity: "The Jewish poet who invokes the Shechinah has an obligation to construct the place where 'Light and Law are manifest,' to which the nations may come because it is where they are. The obligation is the same as the obligation to the intelligibility of experience, the covenant" (166). In other words, that figure which for Grossman distinguishes Jewish poetry from the poetry of other peoples is the same figure that for Rothenberg aligns Jewish poetry with the poetry of other peoples. For Grossman, the Shekinah assists the Jewish poet in approaching a covenental state of holiness. For

Rothenberg, she leads the Jewish poem into what he calls in regard to his own *Poland/1931*, "some supreme yiddish surrealist vaudeville" of the utmost heterogeneity.[7]

Although Rothenberg is usually associated with "avant-garde" modernism and postmodernism, both in terms of technique and affiliation, while Grossman is seen as a more "academic" poet with roots going back to romanticism via such precursors as Yeats and Crane, what I would argue is that both practice versions of a radical Jewish poetics. I say this because although their styles and theoretical positions are diametrically opposed, both are radical in their *idea* of the Jewish poem. Both formulate their approach through a deep and sustained engagement with Jewish beliefs, Jewish history, Jewish traditions of writing and discourse. This in turn manifests itself in each poet's style, technique and attitude toward language, though as we observed with Rosenzweig in section 3, beneath style, technique, and attitude lies the idea, the concept, derived from a Jewish worldview. Modern Jewish poets, like Jewish writers and thinkers in the past, enter into dialogue with that worldview. Even when they struggle against it, perhaps even seeking to negate it, it remains foundational to the Jewish poem.

5. "My Secularism is not secular": Tentative Conclusions

In an interview originally published in 1975, Gershom Scholem was asked to account for the varying responses of religious and secular students to his classes on kabbalah at the Hebrew University. The secular students seemed to be seeking for "some living spark," while the religious students saw kabbalah "as no more than a chapter in the history of religion that had no significance for their own faith." Scholem's response led him to reflect on his own stance:

> I don't consider myself a secularist. My secularism fails right at the core, owing to the fact that I am a religious person, because I am sure of my belief in God. My secularism is not secular. But the fact that I addressed myself to *kabbalah* not merely as a chapter of history but from a dialectical distance—from identification and distance together—certainly stems from the fact that I had a feeling that *kabbalah* had a living center . . . Something unknown of this sort must have motivated me beyond all the philological games and masquerades at which I excel. I can understand that something of this sort inspired my secularist listeners the way it inspired me. (*Jews and Judaism in Crisis* 46)

Scholem raises a number of points that I find very helpful and personally appealing. The first is the "dialectical distance" in his immersion into a deeply Jewish subject, which at the time he began his research was either dismissed or repressed. This may be close to the attitude that appears in all my work, not only in regard to kabbalah, or to Jewish religious matters in general, but to all matters involving issues of religion, faith, and spirituality. Yet my very ambivalence, or sense of identification and distance, has led me to some of the most challenging and rewarding moments in my poetry and criticism. This leads me to the second point, which is the idea of Scholem and then his *secular* students being attracted to a living center or some living spark in the Jewish mystical tradition, as is certainly true for me as well. Unlike Scholem, I am not at all sure in my belief in God: if one were to ask me, nine times out of ten I would probably say that I'm an atheist. But if what I profess can be called atheism, it is an atheism that circles around some living center, perhaps an *absent* center which still has compelling power. Elsewhere, Scholem comments on the kabbalistic *tzimtzum,* comparing it to the "emptying of the world to a meaningless void not illuminated by any ray of meaning or direction [that] is the experience of him whom I would call the pious atheist. The void is the abyss, the chasm or the crack which opens up in all that exists. This is the experience of modern man, surpassingly well depicted in all its desolation by Kafka, for whom nothing has remained of God but the void—in Kafka's sense, to be sure, the void of God" (*Jews and Judaism in Crisis* 283). In this respect, at least, I think of myself as more of a modern rather than postmodern writer.

The third point with which I identify is Scholem's sense of something unknown motivating him "beyond all the philological games and masquerades"—and let us recall that Scholem was a serious if not prolific poet as well as a great scholar.[8] Jews, of course, have excelled in language games and masquerades for a very long time. But as we have seen (pace Rothenberg), they are usually put in the service of some religious or ethical idea, if not doctrine. Whether we cast it in religious or secular terms, we continue to yearn for some form of transcendence, some experience of the numinous, with which poetry has been traditionally associated. Scholem remains a paradigmatic figure for me partly because the volatile categories he explores (messianism, gnosis, counter-history, redemption through sin, nihilism, and so forth) continue to manifest themselves today, not only in the frightening versions of religious fundamentalism that so dangerously shape global politics, but even in the most apparently secularized of cultural formations. Steven M. Wasserstrom notes that for Scholem, "Secularization revealed novel religious forces. . . . The crisis of tradition is still tradition, both remaining within its spirit and yet leaving its current form behind" (*Religion after Religion* 61, 62). About Scholem and his colleague Henry Corbin, Wasserstrom tells us, "What they championed as the most 'traditional' theosophy appears as an expression of a curiously emphatic modernism: antinomian, individualistic, and secular. One may call their paradoxical approach *religion after religion*" (65).

The figure of Scholem as a paradigmatic modern Jew of culture, engaged in *religion after religion,* is in some respects even more attractive to me than the more well-known "non-Jewish Jew" first identified by Isaac Deutscher nearly fifty years ago. Akher, the Talmudic heretic still revered by his former rabbinic colleagues, and Spinoza, whose philosophy led to his excommunication by the Jewish religious leaders of Amsterdam, are Deutscher's models for a tradition which includes Heine, Marx, and Freud: "They all went beyond the boundaries of Jewry. They all found Jewry too narrow, too archaic, and too constricting" (26). The marginal status of non-Jewish Jews, their being "in society and yet not in it, of it and yet not of it" (27), their dialectical determinism, their understanding of "reality as being dynamic, not static" (35), their rejection of moral absolutes, their revolutionary optimism despite their acceptance of the tragedy of Jewish history—all these qualities remain relevant to any discussion of secular Jewish identity and culture. And yet when we study individual figures or specific intellectual or artistic tendencies in what is broadly called secular Jewish culture, we often discover it is precisely the volatile, dialectical engagements of "non-Jewish Jews" with "narrow," "archaic," or "constricting" aspects of Jewry that lead to their most bold, radical, and innovative contributions. The transformations of this sort—one sees them throughout modern Jewish literature, including the most innovative Jewish American poetry—may, on one hand, be considered instances of "secularization," insofar as they constitute, to use Rothenberg's term again, "an inherently impure activity." On the other hand, we may think about Jewish culture in the way Scholem thinks of the Jewish religious tradition: "Tradition undergoes changes with the times, new facets of its meaning shining forth and lighting its way. Tradition, according to its mystical sense, is Oral Torah, precisely because each stabilization in the text would hinder and destroy the infinitely moving, the constantly progressing and unfolding element within it, which would otherwise become petrified" (*Messianic Idea* 296).

This passage, from Scholem's "Revelation and Tradition as Religious Categories in Judaism," has provided a guiding principle for my understanding of Jewish culture—and for my understanding of myself as a Jewish writer—ever since my "return" to Judaism over twenty years ago. The indeterminacy, the designification, the dialectical play of this concept has repeatedly helped me negotiate matters of belief and practice. My secularism is not secular—and my religion is not religious.

Nowhere is this more true than in the combinations and permutations of *Track:*

#
But to profane
this sacred history

But to sacrifice
this deserted writing

To call and call
knowing he will answer

To answer
not knowing if he calls. (*Columns* 10)

In *The Burnt Book,* Ouaknin quotes Henri Atlan: "The primary preoccupation with biblical teaching is not the existence of God, theism as contrasted with atheism, but the fight against idolatry. In all theism there is the danger of idolatry. All theism is idolatry, since expression signifies it, thereby freezing it; except if, somehow, its discourse refuses itself and so becomes atheistic. In other words, the paradoxes of language and its meanings are such that the only discourse possible about God that is not idolatrous is an atheistic discourse."

"The Text," declares Ouaknin, "which is the primary relation to God, must not turn into an idol" (65). Hence Rabbi Nachman, whose belief in God was as tortured as his textual innovations were inspired, seeks to write a book "that is written in the margins, the one which, through its writing, becomes margins. The book is burnt; it becomes margins, empty space—*Hallal hapanui*—which creates the absolute separation between man and God" (299). That separation, that space, is the space in which Jewish writing occurs. It is the space that defines a radical Jewish poetics.

Notes

1. For an earlier autobiographical reflection on these matters, see "'The Master of Turning': Walter Benjamin, Gershom Scholem, Harold Bloom, and the Writing of a Jewish Life."

2. In addition to Marc-Alain Ouaknin, *The Burnt Book: Reading the Talmud,* especially 57–99, see Susan Handelman, *The Slayers of Moses: The Emergence of Rabbinic Interpretation in Modern Literary Theory,* 27–82.

3. "You must become an ignorant man again," says Stevens to his "ephebe," his initiate into poetry, at the beginning of *Notes Toward a Supreme Fiction* (*Collected Poems* 380). In a different register, Olson names Keats as one of his influences at the start of "Projective Verse" (239).

4. Cf. Joseph Conte in regard to serial poems and discontinuity: "But the discontinuity of elements in the series, as Creeley's volume *Pieces* demonstrates, disrupts any internal development or progression of its materials. The sections of a series are not hierarchical. There is not initiation, climax or terminus precisely because there can be no development. In the sequence, the reader must, so to speak, enter through the front door and exit through the rear; but in a series such as Robert Duncan's *Passages,* the reader is encouraged to select any of these 'passages' as an entrance. The reader does not require the information of any one section in order to comprehend the others" (22–23).

5. Levinas defines sorcery as "looking beyond what it is possible to see. It is to go beyond the limits within which one must stay when truth approaches, not to stop in time. . . . Sorcery is the curiosity which manifests itself when the eyes should be cast down: indiscretion regarding the Divine; insensitivity to Mystery; clarity projected unto something the approach to which requires some modesty . . . Sorcery does not come about because of bad influences; it is the excess of knowledge itself, that which is beyond what can be borne in truth" (145).

6. In *Not One of Them in Place,* I present separate discussions of Rothenberg's and Grossman's work, but do not actively contrast them as I do here. I refer the reader to my expositions in that book.

7. To see this difference in specific poems, one need only compare such poems by Rothenberg in *Poland/1931* as "The Wedding," "The Bride," or "Galician Nights" to Grossman's "The Law" (in his first book, *A Harlot's Hire,* and unfortunately never republished) or his much more recent "Rose of Sharon" (one of the "Old Man" poems in *Sweet Youth*).

8. See Steven M. Wasserstrom's illuminating introduction to Scholem's *The Fullness of Time: Poems.* Wasserstrom calls Scholem "a link in the golden chain of poets from Heine to Nelly Sachs and Celan" (28), and, after observing his influence on numerous figures in literature and the arts, concludes that "secularized 'Judaic' high-culture of the twentieth century is for all intents and purposes Gershom Scholem" (36).

Works Cited

Bronk, William. *Life Supports: New and Collected Poems.* San Francisco: North Point Press, 1981.

Conte, Joseph M. *Unending Design: The Forms of Postmodern Poetry.* Ithaca, NY: Cornell University Press, 1991.

Derrida, Jacques. *Of Grammatology.* Trans. Gayatri Chakravorty Spivak. Baltimore: Johns Hopkins University Press, 1976.

Deutscher, Isaac. *The Non-Jewish Jew and Other Essays.* Ed. Tamara Deutscher. London: Oxford University Press, 1968.

Finkelstein, Norman. *Columns: Track, Volume II.* New York: Spuyten Duyvil, 2002.

———. "'The Master of Turning': Walter Benjamin, Gershom Scholem, Harold Bloom, and the Writing of a Jewish Life." *People of the Book: Thirty Scholars Reflect on Their Jewish Identity.* Ed. Jeffrey Rubin-Dorsky and Shelley Fisher Fishkin. Madison: University of Wisconsin Press, 1996. 415–426.

———. *Not One of Them in Place: Modern Poetry and Jewish American Identity.* Albany: State University of New York Press, 2001.

———. *Powers: Track, Volume III.* New York: Spuyten Duyvil, 2005.

———. "Statements for *Track.*" The Cultural Society. www.culturalsociety.org.

———. *Track.* New York: Spuyten Duyvil, 1999.

Grossman, Allen. *A Harlot's Hire.* Cambridge, MA: Walker-de Berry, 1961.

———. *The Long Schoolroom: Lessons in the Bitter Logic of the Poetic Principle.* Ann Arbor: University of Michigan Press, 1997.

———. *Sweet Youth.* New York: New Directions, 2002.

Handelman, Susan A. *The Slayers of Moses: The Emergence of Rabbinic Interpretation in Modern Literary Theory.* Albany: State University of New York Press, 1982.

Heller, Michael. *Uncertain Poetries: Selected Essays on Poets, Poetry and Poetics.* Cambridge, UK: Salt Publishing, 2005.

Levinas, Emmanuel. *Nine Talmudic Readings.* Trans. Annette Aronowicz. Bloomington: Indiana University Press, 1990.

Olson, Charles. *Collected Prose.* Ed. Donald Allen and Benjamin Friedlander. Berkeley and Los Angeles: University of California Press, 1997.

Oppen, George. *New Collected Poems.* Ed. Michael Davidson. New York: New Directions, 2002.

Ouaknin, Marc-Alain. *The Burnt Book: Reading the Talmud.* Trans. Llewellyn Brown. Princeton, NJ: Princeton University Press, 1995.

Rosenzweig, Franz. *The Star of Redemption.* Trans. Barbara E. Galli. Madison: University of Wisconsin Press, 2005.

———. *Understanding the Sick and the Healthy: A View of World, Man, and God.* Trans. Nahum Glatzer. Cambridge, MA: Harvard University Press, 1999.

Rothenberg, Jerome. *Gematria.* Los Angeles: Sun & Moon Press, 1994.

———. *Poland/1931.* New York: New Directions, 1974.

———. "Pre-Face." *Exiled in the Word: Poems and Other Visions of the Jews from Tribal Times to the Present.* Ed. Jerome Rothenberg and Harris Lenowitz. Port Townsend, WA: Copper Canyon, 1989. 3–14.

Santner, Eric L. *On the Psychotheology of Everyday Life: Reflections on Freud and Rosenzweig.* Chicago: University of Chicago Press, 2001.

Scholem, Gershom. *The Messianic Idea in Judaism.* New York: Schocken Books, 1971.

———. *On Jews and Judaism in Crisis: Selected Essays.* Ed. Werner J. Dannhauser. New York: Schocken Books, 1976.

Stevens, Wallace. *The Collected Poems.* New York: Vintage, 1982.

———. *Opus Posthumous.* Ed. Milton J. Bates. New York: Vintage, 1989.

Wasserstrom, Steven M. "Introduction." Gershom Scholem. *The Fullness of Time: Poems.* Trans. Richard Sieburth. Jerusalem: Ibis Editions, 2003.

———. *Religion after Religion: Gershom Scholem, Mircea Eliade, and Henry Corbin at Eranos.* Princeton, NJ: Princeton University Press, 1999.

Radical Relation

Jewish Identity and the Power of Contradictions in the Poetics of Muriel Rukeyser and George Oppen

Meg Schoerke

> : What are you now? If we could touch one another,
> if these our separate entities could come to grips,
> clenched like a Chinese puzzle . . . yesterday
> I stood in a crowded street that was live with people,
> and no one spoke a word, and the morning shone.
> Everyone silent, moving. . . . Take my hand. Speak to me.
>
> —Muriel Rukeyser, "Effort at Speech Between Two People"

> How shall we say?
> In ordinary discourse—
>
> We must talk now. I am no longer sure of the words,
> The clockwork of the world. What is inexplicable
>
> Is the 'preponderance of objects.' The sky lights
> Daily with that predominance
>
> And we have become the present.
>
> We must talk now. Fear
> Is fear. But we abandon each other.
>
> —George Oppen, "Leviathan"

"Effort at Speech Between Two People," first published in 1935, and "Leviathan," first published in 1962, raise questions not only about the challenges of communication between people, but also about the possibilities of intertextual dialogue between two poets who, although contemporaries, have rarely been considered in relation to each other. The poems articulate central concerns that occupied Muriel Rukeyser and George Oppen throughout their respective careers: Can individuals escape their isolation and make contact with other people and the world around them? Does language serve as a gateway to such interactions, or an obstacle, especially if it lacks clarity and freshness? Although both poems are anchored in ordinary experience, they also implicitly voice political concerns, especially about whether people in a century wrenched by world wars and capitalist exploitation can overcome barriers of social conditioning, fear, and self-interest. Yet the drama of communication that both poems enact could just as well be applied to the dialogue they establish with each other. Simple, declarative sentences predominate in each poem, but Rukeyser writes in a loose blank verse augmented by gaps in her spacing and the ambiguous colons that introduce each stanza, while Oppen's enjambed free verse announces his affiliation with William Carlos Williams, whose work he published in the 1930s through his funding of To Publishers and the Objectivist Press. "Effort at Speech Between Two People" and "Leviathan" speak to each other, yet also serve as reminders of how literary culture in the United States became so divided as the twentieth century unfolded that some readers may consider the poems' stylistic differences more significant than their thematic similarities. In particular, readers who champion an American avant-garde tradition may not view Rukeyser's poem as sufficiently experimental, despite her unconventional spacing and punctuation; while readers of a more traditionalist bent may dismiss Oppen's poem as too experimental and likely deplore the liberties that Rukeyser takes with blank verse.

Ironically, the poems are most radically experimental not in their styles, but in their incorporation of contraries: each poem advocates the importance of communication between people and clear apprehension of what Oppen calls "the preponderance of objects," while recognizing how difficult these goals are to attain. Oppen's last line abruptly announces a separation, even as the "we" show their kinship by their act of mutual abandonment, while in Rukeyser's poem the two speakers, who alternate stanza by stanza, crave recognition but describe only their own experiences and fail to acknowledge the other speaker's revelations. In contrast to Oppen's bleak ending, "Speak to me" seems upbeat, but in context of the full poem there's no evidence that the two speakers will ever exchange speech that is truly reciprocal. Both poems are, paradoxically, utopian and realistic.

As literary experimentalists, Oppen and Rukeyser cultivated such unconventional ways of incorporating their political and ethical convictions into their writing. The two poets were so dedicated to those convictions, and so successful in realizing them not only in their work, but also in how they conducted their lives, that they became models for many poets who came of age in the 1960s and 1970s. But because of their stylistic differences, and the very different groups of poets who championed their work, their many "meeting-places," to borrow a term from Rukeyser, have not been adequately recognized. Certainly, critics who write on the 1930s have acknowledged their Leftist politics,[1] but have not commented on some of the similar aesthetic positions they took, particularly their frequent meditations on the complex relations between the individual and the community; their devotion to material facts and the importance of seeing them clearly; and how such goals led them to experiment with the language and poetic forms that they deploy in their work.

Despite their skepticism about whether language can serve as an adequate vehicle for communication, both Oppen and Rukeyser remained dedicated to the utopian ideal that poetry is not useless, that it can reveal ethical and perceptual truths about our relationship with the world and with one another. In "Oppen Then," the preface to the *New Collected Poems,* Eliot Weinberger claims, "Over and over Oppen emphasized that the function of poetry was a test of truth; he must have been the last writer in the West to use the word 'truth' without irony" (ix). But Oppen was certainly not the last, for Rukeyser also used the word straightforwardly, as in her well-known lines from "Käthe Kollwitz": "What would happen if one woman told the truth about her life? / The world would split open." Rukeyser's unapologetic use of "truth" here and in other poems, and her lifelong effort to break through silences about women's experiences, made her a model poet and activist during the 1960s and 1970s to feminist readers, who celebrated her forthrightness. The feminist framing of Rukeyser as primarily an assertive truth-teller still reverberates today, for she is not well known for her experimentation with form and the skepticism that she sometimes voices about language and its capacity to reveal the truth—and how she made such concerns themes in her poetry. Oppen's advocates have mainly been among the community of avant-garde poets, especially the Language poets, and their supporters in the academy, who tend to value his skepticism toward language and his experimental approach to form, and sometimes downplay his equal dedication to truth and clarity, except in reference to his politics. The literary spotlight that such critics shine on Oppen's difficulty, and their tendency to consider him primarily as a member of an avant-garde coterie (whether as an Objectivist, or as a forerunner of the Language poets), may be among the reasons why his work is underrepresented in anthologies and still not well known among readers outside of the academy.[2]

Both Rukeyser and Oppen are radical enough, and complex enough, that their work defies categorization. Their poetry constantly mediates between the perceptions of the isolate self and appeals for community, between difficulty and clarity, silence and speech, and between linguistic experimentation and direct assertion. For both poets, such mediation resulted in a poetry of process, in which the orientation constantly shifts between these various poles, and in which the poets remain ethically committed to maintaining a balance, as best they can. Oppen and Rukeyser refused to settle for an "either/or" model, but preferred "both/and," and their probing of language and form, as well as their acceptance of doubt and failure as necessary consequences of their high aims, attest to the moral ground of their aesthetic. Thus, their poetry is revelatory, even spiritual in its intentions, yet profoundly anti-transcendental, due to its focus on the material world and on relations with others.[3] Oppen and Rukeyser's radical juxtaposition of seemingly antithetical positions is an elegant, hard-earned solution to the challenge they faced as second-generation Modernists who came of age in the 1930s: how to adapt and extend the conventions and extraordinary vitality of Modernist poetry, while also creating work that was socially responsible, yet not propaganda driven or sentimental. Their radical strategy of mediating between but not reconciling oppositions, however, may also have derived from their efforts to negotiate the pull of different identities, especially between the demands of secular American culture, with its emphasis on the individual, and Jewish culture, with its stress on community bonds.[4] As Oppen suggests in a Daybook entry, "somewhere half-way between the fact of being singular and the fact of being numerous is the fact of being Jewish" (*The Germ* 14).

There are, in fact, a number of striking biographical parallels between Oppen and Rukeyser.[5] Born in New York at the outset of the Modernist revolution (Oppen, New Rochelle, 1908; Rukeyser, New York City, 1913), both poets were raised by wealthy, second-generation, assimilationist Jewish parents. They both lived sheltered childhoods, buttressed by all the privileges wealth brings, including servants and private schools. Yet each poet experienced emotional trauma during childhood as well. Rukeyser endured the repercussions of her parents' unhappy marriage; while Oppen was scarred by his mother's suicide when he was four, his father's remarriage in 1917, the family's move to San Francisco a year later, and physical and psychological abuse from his stepmother. Both poets reached adulthood determined to distance themselves from everything they associated with "home": not only from the conjunction of material privilege and emotional violence that they had experienced but also from their families' Jewishness. Although Rukeyser eventually embraced Judaism more openly than Oppen did, she nonetheless rejected the Reform version practiced by her parents, noting in "Under Forty" that their congregation sought "a religion of reassurance; they listened to the muted organ, and refused to be involved in suffering that demanded resistance. . . . If they had a mission as a responsible and inspired people, they did not want it"

(6). Oppen, in summing up his attitude toward his parents, was more blunt in his dismissal: "No, I don't value my background, neither its wealth nor its Jewishness, I value only my rejection of it—" (*Sulfur* 26, 151). For both poets, the radicalism they practiced as adults, whether through writing or social activism, had its roots in a spirited rejection of their bourgeois family upbringings, a rejection predicated on resistance to the status quo.

They both began to practice such resistance in earnest during the 1930s, through their political engagement and their refusal to compromise their attitudes toward poetry. As young adults, both poets were restless—eager to experience the world and devote themselves to writing and activism, while remaining suspicious of programmatically activist writing. Neither finished college. Shortly after matriculating at Oregon State University, Corvallis, Oppen dropped out when Mary Colby, whom he later married, was expelled and he was suspended after they stayed out all night on their first date. Rukeyser left Vassar after only two years as a result of her father's bankruptcy, yet she was also anxious to pursue a career as a poet and political journalist. Both poets traveled extensively in the United States and also spent time in Europe and Mexico. Both published their first books early: Rukeyser's *Theory of Flight* (1935) appeared as the winner of the Yale Series of Younger Poets series when she was only twenty-one, and Oppen published *Discrete Series* (1934) at age twenty-six.

Rather than reject Modernism altogether, as many of their comrades in poetry did, Rukeyser and Oppen adopted Modernist techniques, with Rukeyser initially finding inspiration in the examples of Hart Crane and T. S. Eliot and Oppen grounding his work on the Pound-Williams axis; Rukeyser, especially in her early books, leans toward a Symbolist derivation of Modernism, while Oppen's *Discrete Series* works off of an Imagist model. And, while both poets committed themselves to political activism in the 1930s—Rukeyser through journalism, and Oppen through organizing—neither of them were willing to denounce Modernism as bourgeois or to write the sort of propagandistic poetry that extreme Leftists such as Mike Gold demanded. Oppen's commitment to political activism and refusal to compromise his art were so thoroughgoing that he stopped writing after 1935, the year that he joined the Communist party, and did not start again until 1958. He wrote to his sister, June Oppen Degan, in 1959, "—Maybe I admire myself more for knowing what is one thing and what is the other and what are the levels of truth—that is to say, for simply not attempting to write communist verse. Poetry has to be protean; the meaning must begin there, with the perception" (*SL* 22). Rukeyser, too, valued the process of poetry more than the product, and, although her work was more message driven than Oppen's, it was never instrumentalist enough to satisfy her critics on the Left.[6] Like Oppen, she felt leery of poetry that draws more attention to the poet's noble motives than to the subject matter. In *The Life of Poetry* (1949), she clarifies her position: "A good deal of the repugnance to the social poetry of the 1930's was caused by reactionary beliefs; but as much was caused, I think, because there were so many degrees of blood-savagery in it, ranging all the way from self-pity—naked or identified with one victim after another—to actual blood-lust and display of wounds, a rotten sort of begging for attention and sympathy in the name of an art that was supposed to produce action" (211). Rukeyser objects not to instrumentalist poetry *per se,* but to the literary and moral problems of sentimentalism and sensationalism that can too easily taint a political poem if the writer's ego takes precedence over the aim "to produce action."

Yet Rukeyser did not strictly partition her activism from her writing, as Oppen did. Oppen's long silence, in which he wrote neither poetry nor prose, began after he joined the Communist Party in 1935; he served the party not through writing but though organizing for the Workers' Alliance, and then opposed fascism during World War II by prompting his induction into the U.S. Army and fighting in France, where he was severely wounded. In contrast to Oppen, Rukeyser did see her poetry and journalism as a form of social activism—something that can, ideally, inspire readers to work toward changing themselves or existing conditions. Rukeyer embraced radical politics in the 1930s, but refrained from becoming a party member. As Tom Dayton reports in *Muriel Rukeyser's The Book of the Dead,*

> while she never joined the Communist party as a member, she did travel in party circles, worked briefly for the *Daily Worker,* and appeared with reasonable frequency in the pages of *New Masses.* In a tellingly ambivalent statement in a letter dated December 20, 1936, Rukeyser wrote to John Wheelwright: "When I was there [Catalonia] I wanted to join the C.P.—came back, and didn't, again." . . . Clearly, Rukeyser felt the appeal of the Communist party, yet . . . she was not one of those for whom the Communist party *was* the Left. Rukeyser was certainly attracted to it (in particular, to its progressive stance on labor and civil rights and its antifascism), but at the same time found it necessary to maintain some distance from it. (11–12)

That distance enabled her not only to continue writing, but also to experiment—most successfully through the documentary form of "The Book of the Dead" (1938)—with different ways to combine her poetry and radical political convictions while still maintaining her allegiance to the Modernist tradition.

In the 1940s and 1950s, Oppen and Rukeyser held fast to their radical political ideals, even as, like many activists of their generation, they distanced themselves from the organized Left and staunchly supported the war effort: Oppen through his service in the army; Rukeyser through addressing the war in her poetry.[7] Unlike many of their peers, Oppen and Rukeyser did not abandon their leftist convictions, and their opposition to fascism was rooted not only in their egalitarian politics but also in their Jewish identity. In *Meaning a Life,* Mary Oppen describes the evolution of her and her husband's politics in the late 1930s—and of their charged status as a "special kind of couple," a Jew married to a gentile:

> George and I had been unaware of our being a special kind of couple until Hitler and fascism made being Jewish a pointed issue of survival. Our interest had been to understand a class not our own and to be part of sweeping changes in the United States. We held close a belief in ourselves as artists, and we intended to find our way back to a life in poetry and the arts. If there had not been a clear need for people like us to defeat fascism, we would probably have dropped the politics as the depression eased, and we would have resumed a life in the arts. But fascism, socialism, or a more liberal form of republicanism were the choices. . . . Events moved us with them, and we believed that fascism meant death to us along with the other Jews of the world, and death to millions who would be caught in the war which actually came to pass. Communists were still, at the end of the Depression, the ones who warned most consistently against this danger. (158)

The Oppens were actively involved with the party until 1941; their only child, Linda, was born in 1940, and George was inducted into the army in 1942. After his return, they moved to Redondo Beach, California, and while they did not join the local branch of the party there, they did not break with the party altogether by turning in their membership cards (Duplessis *SL,* xv). Harassed by the FBI, which had kept a file on George since 1941, and unwilling to subject themselves to investigation by the House Un-American Activities Committee (HUAC), they fled to Mexico in 1950, where they remained in exile for the next ten years.

Rukeyser, too, was investigated by the FBI and pursued by HUAC. In *The Poetic Vision of Muriel Rukeyser,* Louise Kertesz notes that "her 118 page dossier . . . shows that the FBI gathered information about her and her family beginning in the thirties. 'They knew more about the circumstances of my father's bankruptcy than I did,' [Rukeyser] says. Beginning in the forties, if not sooner, her phone was tapped and both letters she wrote and letters she received were opened or acquired and examined" (273). Despite her suspicions that she was watched, Rukeyser in 1944 ended her essay for "Under Forty," on her sense of Jewish identity, with a bold condemnation of European—and American—versions of fascism:

> To live as poet, woman, American, and Jew—this chalks in my identity. If the four come together in one person, each strengthens the others. Red-baiting undercuts at the position of women, anti-intellectualism and anti-imaginative drives such as Congress has recently been conducting—these are on the same level as the growing storm of anti-Semitism.
>
> One questions oneself when all these attacks arrive, and one looks at the Jews. The Jews I knew as a child, the Jewish professionals who were able to get out of Europe and come here as refugees, the Jews who could put up with fascism as long as it left them alone, the Jews who objected to a poster against discrimination because it mentioned Jews and Negroes together. The Jews that so many Christians, fighting fascism and all its implications, look sideward at. And then one thinks of the men and women in the Warsaw ghetto, standing as the Loyalists stood in Spain, weaponless against what must have seemed like the thunder and steel of the whole world; one thinks of the men and women, Jews moving freely in Russia; one thinks of the men and women, planting Palestine and taking a fierce oath never to put down their arms.
>
> To me, the value of my Jewish heritage, in life and in writing, is its value as a guarantee. Once one's responsibility as a Jew is really assumed, one is guaranteed, not only against fascism, but against many kinds of temptation to close the spirit. It is a strong force in oneself against many kinds of hardness which may arrive in the war—the idea that when you throw off insight, you travel light and are equipped for fighting; the idea that it is impractical to plan and create, and that concrete construction and invention are the only practical things, apart from killing. Organized religion has not been able to take a strong stand about these things, any more than it has been able to stand with the Jews in Warsaw, or against the disguised Fascists at home. (8–9)

Rukeyser posits not a unitary form of Jewishness here, but distinguishes between varieties of moral courage, as well as cowardice and racism, that she has observed among different Jewish communities, even as she condemns organized religion (Jewish or Christian) as itself having little power or incentive to resist fascism. In particular, she attacks the spiritual and civic complacency that she witnessed in her parents' Reform congregation and explicitly links it with the inaction that enabled fascism to gain power in Europe. Nevertheless, she applauds the courage of Jews who fought against fascism, especially those of the Warsaw ghetto, and finds in them the inspiration to maintain her own resistance, creativity, and sense of ethical commitment despite the intense pressure that she faced in the 1940s to conform politically and as a writer. That pressure continued through the 1950s, culminating in a 1958 HUAC censure of Sarah Lawrence College for continuing to employ her despite her inclusion in an American Legion investigation into "subversives" in West Chester country.

Such pressure, as well as the demands of single motherhood (her son, William, was born in 1947) and of teaching at Sarah Lawrence (where she was employed during the 1950s and 1960s), contributed not to the total abstention from writing that Oppen maintained until 1958, but to a significant diminishment in her production. As Kate Daniels notes in her preface to *Out of Silence:*

> [Rukeyser] referred to the years between 1947 and 1958 as 'the intercepted years,' and the dramatic and immediate decrease in her literary production testifies to the labor-, time-, and energy-intensive project of childrearing. From 1935 to 1948, she published five full-length books of poetry, a full-length biography, a three-act play and hundreds of articles, essays and reviews. From 1949 to 1964, when her son entered college, she published two volumes of previously published selected poems, a biography-in-verse, and one collection of new poems. While it is true that her great prose meditation, *The Life of Poetry,* appeared in 1949, the work on that book had been almost all completed by the time her son was born. (xiii)

The lessening of her responsibilities as a parent, as well as the reorientation of the cultural and literary milieux toward social activism and egalitarian causes such as civil rights, feminism, and opposition to the Vietnam War, contributed to Rukeyser's late career renaissance in which, along with a biography, translations, and a play, she published a series of important poetry books: *Waterlily Fire* (1962), *The Speed of Darkness* (1968), *Breaking Open* (1973), *The Gates* (1976), and her *Collected Poems* (1978). Rukeyser also rededicated herself to social activism, which included getting arrested in civil rights and antiwar protests, as well as engaging in high-profile endeavors such as traveling to Hanoi, Vietnam, in 1972 with Denise Levertov to protest U.S. bombing and visiting South Korea in 1975, as president of the

PEN American Center to protest the imprisonment of the poet Kim Chi-Ha. Yet these productive years were also challenging, for she suffered a stroke in 1964 that "struck at her powers of speech" and resulted in "her struggle to regain language" (Levi 284); additional strokes seriously compromised her health in the late 1970s. By the time of her death in 1980, she had become a major influence on a new generation of poets, especially feminists for whom Rukeyser served as a friend, model, and mentor. The poems of her late period were often spare—much leaner, stylistically, than her work of the 1930s and 1940s—and sometimes juxtaposed references to her personal experiences, such as single motherhood, or her relationship with another woman, with political insights—a strategy that resisted Confessionalism and the pure instrumentality of protest poetry.

The trajectory of Oppen's career in the 1960s and 1970s parallels that of Rukeyser. After his daughter matriculated at Sarah Lawrence in 1958, Oppen began writing again, and he and Mary moved to New York two years later, and then relocated to San Francisco (where Rukeyser had lived in the 1940s) in 1966. Oppen's late productive phase gained momentum from the ripening of his poetic consciousness during his twenty-five years of silence, and, as with Rukeyser, his new poetry sometimes interpolated references to personal experience—of his shared life with Mary or of being wounded in France—with meditations on the nature of reality, which, in their focus on scenes of urban isolation and decay, often raise implicit political questions. In *The Materials* (1962), *This in Which* (1965), *Of Being Numerous* (1968), *Seascape: Needle's Eye* (1972), and *Primitive* (1978), he developed a poetry simultaneously personal and public and succeeded in avoiding the excesses of Confessionalism and of the message-driven political poetry he opposed. Like Rukeyser, he received recognition for his achievements during the last twenty years of his life through awards, such as the 1969 Pulitzer Prize for Poetry, and invitations to do high-profile readings, including a month-long residency in 1975 at Mishkenot Sha'ananim in Jerusalem. And, like Rukeyser, in the late 1970s he struggled to write against the debilitations of old age: the gradual onset of Alzheimer's disease, from which he died in 1984.

Of course, their lives and careers were not identical. While both of them had a financial cushion (Oppen in the form of an inheritance from his mother's estate that he could fall back on, if necessary; Rukeyser through the occasional support of a patron), only Oppen had steady companionship. From age eighteen until his death, with the exception of his army service, he and Mary were inseparable. She saw herself not simply as a spouse, but as an intellectual and artistic partner in all of Oppen's endeavors. In contrast, Rukeyser had a series of relationships with men and was briefly married to a painter in the mid-1940s (who was not the father of her child); late in her life, she committed herself to a woman. In addition to her lack of a life partner, Rukeyser also never allied herself with any particular group or school of poets, until late in her career when she was hailed as a foremother by feminists. Oppen, in contrast, was sustained as an artist not only by his relationship with Mary, but by his connections with the Objectivists, especially Louis Zukofsky and Charles Reznikoff. Although in his late career, he disagreed with elements of Zukofsky's and Reznikoff's work, his poetry nonetheless remained true to the Objectivist goal: "to keep the poem open to the entire domain of fact, and simultaneously to keep it a thing made of words, which have their own laws" (Kenner 164). And, as John Taggart argues in "Walk-Out: Rereading the Poetry of George Oppen," he established an artistic ground for himself in complex relation to the achievements of Zukofsky and Reznikoff—a relation that involved both agreement and difference and reflected his own equally contradictory understanding of his Jewishness:

> As with Zukofsky, so with Reznikoff: a yes of recognition and a no of difference even as the degrees of the one and the other are, respectively, much more positive and much less confrontational. Oppen's position of poetics is no one "position," but rather a dialectical movement working to create a tensioned space of *between, between* Zukofsky and Reznikoff. If there is no such space, then there can be no middle, no voice, or the voice only an echo either of recognition or difference, each sort of echo a kind of death.
>
> As with poetics, so with Jewish identity. If that motion cannot be maintained, if that space of between cannot be maintained, it becomes only a tension, a knot. The poet becomes a "Jew most strange / to myself," the ray becomes a "ray of strangeness ray / of exile" ("To Find a Way," *Ironwood* 5 [1975], 28). If a space of between cannot be maintained, if movement within that space cannot be maintained, the poet becomes a knot of self-estrangement, a knot of self-exile. (53–54)

Although Oppen defined himself, both as an artist and as a Jew, in part through his differences with the two senior poets, his affiliation with them, and as a core member of the Objectivists, gave him a sense of artistic stability that Rukeyser, as a woman poet who stood outside of such group identification, lacked throughout most of her career. In a sense, sustained as he was by Mary and his ties with the Objectivists, Oppen was secure enough to explore the radical "betweenness" that Taggart describes.

Yet Rukeyser also cultivated betweenness, as she proudly proclaims in the "Under Forty" essay: "To live as poet, woman, American, and Jew—this chalks in my identity. If the four come together in one person, each strengthens the others" (8). The "four come together," yet neither do they cancel one another out, for their combinations established Rukeyser's complex identity, predicated on difference. Throughout her life, Rukeyser believed in the paradox that contraries can exist in concert without canceling each other or losing the attributes that make them distinct. This idea serves as the foundation for her "relational poetics," which she articulated during her career with remarkable consistency.[8] She advocated "a poetry of meeting-places, where the false barriers go down" (*LP* 20); defined poetry in terms of process, as "a gathering-together of elements so that they move together" (*LP* 19); and insisted that poetry, especially modern poetry, depends on "ways of bringing-together, . . . arrangements" of disparate elements (*LP* 19), including those that many of her critics found incompatible: the literary and the political; poetry and science; free verse and formal verse. Unlike so many of her peers who felt compelled to choose sides in the recurring American poetry wars that pitted writers of free verse against advocates of traditional rhyme and meter, Rukeyser included in each of her books poems in a variety of forms: from sonnets, ballads, and an often loose blank verse, to different styles of free verse.[9] She also defied convention in her biographies: offering meditations on the American Transcendentalists in her life of the late-nineteenth-century physical chemist, *Willard Gibbs* (1942); including both poetry and prose in *One Life* (1957), her book on Wendell Wilkie, the 1940 Republican presidential candidate; or spending as much time considering the gaps and silences in the biographical record as she does examining the life in her third unconventional biography, *The Traces of Thomas Hariot* (1972). As my description of these books suggests, she opposed specialization and celebrated the lives and work of outsiders who crossed disciplinary boundaries, as she herself did (and took fire for it from reviewers) when writing these biographies and her poetry. As she argues in *The Life of Poetry*, "Our education is one of specialization. We become experts in some narrow 'field.' That expertness allows us to deal with the limited problems presented to us; it allows us to face emotional reality, symbolic reality, very little" (17–18). She sees such a destructive tendency toward specialization as a product of the American desire for uniformity, which, interestingly, she attributes to an assimilationist mentality:

> Margaret Mead describes us as a 'third generation society.' She does not mean, of course, that we are all the grandchildren of pioneers and immigrants; but she does mean that our parents shared the attitudes

> of the children of foreigners, who because of their strange families, with their old-country ways, their effusive gestures, the flavor of their speech, leaned over backward to rule out any foreignness, any color at all.
>
> We suffer from that background, with its hunger for uniformity, the shared norm of ambition and habit and living standard. The repressive codes are everywhere. (*LP* 17)

Rukeyser, in opposition to such uniformity, envisioned a form of unity (for American poetry, and also for American culture and politics) in which individual differences are not erased, but instead conjoin to create dynamic energy: a dialogic meeting, in which the differences ceaselessly play off one another, rather than a dialectic predicated on synthesis.

As the Mead quotation from *The Life of Poetry* suggests, Rukeyser's radical poetics of process and relationship developed, in part, as a reaction against the assimilationist uniformity of her parents' household. In "Under Forty," she invokes Mead again, this time on a more personal level: "Most of the younger Jewish writers in America are the children of immigrants, and I am not representative of that generation. It has the qualities which Margaret Mead points out as a 'second-generation'—split with the parent culture, leaning over backward to be 'American' at its most acceptable" (4–5). She goes on to describe her mother and father as reacting against their immigrant parents and laments that "the young man my father and the young woman my mother had no cultural resources to strengthen them. There was not a trace of Jewish culture that I could feel—no stories, no songs, no special food—but then there was not *any* cultural background that could make itself felt. . . . There was no mark of Judaism in my childhood home except for a silver ceremonial goblet, handed down from a great-grandfather who had been a cantor, and a legend that my mother's family was directly descended from Akiba" (5). Yet, despite her conviction that she lacked exposure to Jewish culture during her childhood, she was more thoroughly steeped in Judaism than Oppen was as a child. She attended religious school ("Under Forty" 5–6), heard Yiddish spoken by her parents (Kaufman 49), and, during dull services found inspiration in the English (rather than the Hebrew) Bible, which she felt was truer to reality, especially to the stark contrasts that she observed growing up in New York City, than anything else she experienced at Temple ("Under Forty" 7). In "'But Not the Study': Writing as a Jew," Janet Kaufman confirms that, while Rukeyser only erratically attended services as an adult, she nonetheless saw her Jewishness as "a guarantee": a source of moral courage and spiritual strength, and her two major poems that invoke Judaism—her sonnet from "Letter to the Front," "To Be a Jew in the Twentieth Century" (1944), which became part of the Reform liturgy, and "Akiba" (1968)—voice optimism, even while acknowledging the challenges facing modern Jews. As Kaufman argues, "while Rukeyser resisted formal identification with organized religion, her poetry nonetheless reiterated the theme from 'Letter to the Front': refusing the gift of being Jewish means turning away from one's heritage and one's own self, denying one's spirit" (50). Kaufman demonstrates how Rukeyser, "in both her political action and her writing," is a type of "non-Jewish Jew," who turns away from traditional religious practice, and instead works for human solidarity and social justice on a broad scale (50). In linking Rukeyser's relational poetics with her Jewish identity, Kaufman, through noting correspondences between Rukeyser's ideas and the philosophy of Martin Buber, emphasizes how she negotiates a position of betweenness:

> By the time Rukeyser came into knowledge of Buber's writing, she had been writing for nearly 25 years about the importance, to both poetry and politics, of relationship and dialogue. It is not surprising that, when Rukeyser did begin reading Buber, he seemed familiar to her. Like him, she worked to find a way of describing the unity she discovered among otherwise disparate arenas such as politics and spirituality. Religion for Buber carried no overtones of exaltation or ecstasy but referred to "all that is lived in its possibility of dialogue" (*Between Man and Man* 14). Buber wrote extensively of the *meeting* that occurred *between* "I" and "Thou," and some of his primary terminology recurs throughout Rukeyser's poetry: meeting, meeting-place, I, Thou, It, between, binding, signs, change. *Meeting*, for Buber and Rukeyser, does not remain stable over time but occurs in process, in the *between*, in the effort to go out toward an Other and recognize its full presence. (55; emphasis Kaufman's)

For Rukeyser, the "process, in the *between*," developed not only in her evolving identity as a Jew, predicated on a tense combination of opposition to organized religion and acceptance of a rich spiritual and moral heritage, but also in the themes of her writing: the dialogic interplay (which often withheld resolution) of "I" and "Thou"; individual and community; the subjective experience of the self and the objective reality of the world; and the formal tensions between Modernist experimentation and moments of clarity designed to move a reader (or, in Rukeyser's terms, a "witness") toward action—not necessarily political action *per se*, but action that could also involve a change in the self or in one's perception of the world.

Although Oppen felt much more conflicted about his Jewishness than Rukeyser did, his experience of betweenness, and its influence on his poetry, was similar, especially in his sense of having multiple, contradictory identities, as he explains to Donald Davie in 1972:

> (Several million Zionists wish to tell me that, being Jewish, I am not quite American, and that being not quite Jewish—with two passionately assimilationist generations behind me—I am not quite either
>
> about which I sometimes think that, being not quite American since I am a Jew, I am the MOST American—and essentially an uneducated man. It is true. (*SL* 245)

Jewish and American, yet feeling like an outsider in both cultures, Oppen shares Rukeyser's understanding of an identity predicated on contradictions, which in his case include his mixed-class affiliations (as a child of the upper class who earned his living, in adulthood, as a tool-and-die cutter and furniture maker) and his keen awareness of being "uneducated" (in terms not only of a university education, but of religious training as well). In "Walk-Out," Taggart explores the poet's "ambivalent spirituality," in which, lacking any religious instruction or experience of Jewish culture as a child, Oppen identified himself in adulthood as a "self-chosen Jew" (31)—an oppositional designation that flagrantly rebuffs the core belief of a people being chosen by God.[10] Yet Taggart demonstrates how Oppen's ambivalence resulted in persistent feelings of guilt, which rose to a crisis point after his "disastrous" visit to Israel in 1975: "The poet's daughter suggested that her father may have undergone in Israel something akin to her own experience as a child and young adult: she felt herself to be Jewish but in the company of other Jewish persons somehow not Jewish enough. She thought the visit made her father defensive about his self-chosen identity" (32). Taggart later claims that Oppen was, like Joyce's Leopold Bloom, "a Jew by opposition/difference" (36): Oppen felt Jewish when he encountered opposition in the form of anti-Semitism, even as he himself took an oppositional stance toward religious practice and opposed Israeli nationalism.

Throughout his letters and his Daybooks, Oppen tacks back and forth, sometimes accepting a Jewish identity (usually with qualifications), and other times distancing himself from it. Thus, when he writes about Reznikoff's work, he not only frames it as Jewish, but uses that frame as a contrast to his own poetry: he writes, for example, in 1959 to his half-sister, June Oppen Degan, "And Rezi has the solid Hebrew voice behind him. But I have got to loosen up somehow" (*SL* 20); and, in a 1961 letter to Mary Ellen Stolt about tradition and the Objectivists, he denies himself any foundation besides family and his historical understanding of the things he observes: "[The Objectivists] had a very strong sense of their own histories. Rezi's awareness of the Jewish past, Williams' strong sense of America and its roots, Louis' relation to Bach and other 'sources we tide from,'——I am sort of short-winded historically, but not blind. I remember my father and my grandfather: I think of my daughter. I'm aware that the subways are pretty old . . . and that the Queen Mary is fairly new. The ground seems very old to me. I write about nothing else" (*SL* 47). For Oppen, the world—the physical universe of objects and other people—becomes the ground (literal and metaphorical) of his writing. As Taggart argues, Oppen's position is both antinomian and antitranscendentalist: "Insofar as Oppen's work may be considered Jewish, it is a differing Jewishness, or, to adopt one of Oppen's own terms, it is an antinomian Jewishness. . . . The ground of Oppen's poetry is not the scriptural covenant experience but rather that experience reread and inverted . . . so that what is revealed is the undeniable and finally unreadable physical universe" (40).

Yet, despite his lack of religious training, Oppen was drawn to biblical stories; he had a religious temperament, one high-minded enough that, like Rukeyser, he had little patience for organized religion, yet sought spiritual sustenance in religious writings. His antinomian bent shows in his ecumenical reading habits: quotations from Christian philosophers—Plotinus, Saint Augustine, Aquinas, Meister Eckhart—occur with far greater frequency in his poetry and prose than those from Jewish writers. Citing lines from Saint John of the Cross that he reworked in "Route," Oppen admits in a 1969 letter: "Words of desire which bring one to tears: word of reality which brings one to 'religion' religion in quotes because if it retains its root meaning and if the 'bond' means a bond tying a people together, it is nowhere in my experience——a descendent of a number of generations of German Jewish merchants, two generations behind me at least powerfully assimilationist and argumentatively atheist, Christianity and Judaism are about as exotic to me as Zoroastrianism——and yet I stumble over these stories, the Christian and Jewish stories, the Christian writings——increasingly for many years" (*SL* 408–409 n. 16). Oppen here denies any bond, any religious ties, with Judaism; instead, for him "religion" inheres in the writing, the "word of reality," which he feels that organized religion denies: "Both the Eastern and Western religions are filled with hatred of the world I don't share that" (*Iowa Review* 4). In a 1973 letter to John Crawford, he sets his poem "Chartres," and the materiality of the cathedral, beyond religious conventions: "what the world cried out above the mountain was I Am What Is the marvel of the fact, the marvel of the real, not the whole of Christian or Hebrew orthodoxy" (*SL* 254).

In the poems and the Daybooks, Oppen repeatedly tries to acknowledge the world for what it is, even as he recognizes that "confining" the world in language is impossible, as he notes in the following Daybook entries: "The absolutely incomprehensible, which pierces any possible structure of the mind: will not be confined in language" ; "The poems: I put forward a primitive and an extremely dramatic philosophy. : that the world is there, that infinity is the most obvious fact in the world" (*Iowa Review* 12).[11]

Oppen's poetic practice sprang from this contradiction, which was, in turn, grounded on his oppositional attitude toward his Jewishness: his utopian conviction that the world could be apprehended in words and his equally strong belief that words could never, finally, do justice to the world. This paradox led to the compression of his poetry—the fragmentation of syntax, the active enjambments that throw a fulcrum onto nouns, function words, and open-ended verbs such as "is"—and contributed to his twenty-five-year silence. As he admits in his 1980 interview with Burton Hatlen and Tom Mandel, the silence arose not only as a political stance, so that he could initially focus on activism and avoid writing instrumentalist poetry, but also as a gesture of humility, an acknowledgment that he lacked experience—enough knowledge of the world—to write: "when the crisis [of the Depression] occurred we knew we didn't know what the world was and we knew we had to find out so it [the silence] was a poetic exploration at the same time that it was an action of conscience. . . . And I thought most of the poets didn't know about the world as a life" (*Man and Poet* 25). Characteristically, Oppen speaks of his poetic and political life as something that he and Mary ("we") pursued jointly, and he defines his long silence not in terms of lack (the absence of writing), but as a poetic exploration in and of itself.

The power of silence in George Oppen's work, whether his years of "exploratory" silence or the intense compression of the poems, may seem to be what separates him most from Muriel Rukeyser—and may be one of the main reasons why these two writers are more likely to be seen as antithetical to one another, rather than as sharing so many aesthetic and political ideals. She wrote and published prolifically, and her poems are often wordy, capacious, modeled on a Whitmanesque ideal of inclusiveness—something from which Oppen instinctively recoiled, as he confesses in a 1960 letter to Williams, "Whitman has been no use to me. Perhaps arriving after you I didn't need him. I always feel that that deluge and soup of words is a screen for the uncertainty of his own identity" (*SL* 39). Like many of Rukeyser's reviewers, Oppen would likely have seen her poetry as "word soup"; yet he was also capable of accepting a profusion of words if he thought it was well earned. Thus, he admires Ginsberg's *Kaddish,* but disparages "Howl" (*SL* 20, 57, 78) and observes in a Daybook entry: "Duncan's copiousness: almost the meaning of the work That so many words are present for him. In mere honesty I have had to make a virtue of the contrary—few words are present for me" (*Iowa Review* 15).

Oppen's stylistic purity, and the consequent paring down of individual poems and each of his books to a spare perfectionism, contrasts sharply with Rukeyser's impulse to fill each of her books not only with poems in a wide range of styles, but also with poems of varying quality. Rukeyser was the kind of process-oriented writer who felt that experimentation and progress toward a goal illuminated—and were therefore equally important as—perfectly achieved results. Her description in *Willard Gibbs* of the creative process applies just as well to her own writing as it does to scientific thought:

> Creation is a delicate and experimental thing. The process of combining depends on experimentation. Knowledge and effective action here become one gesture; the gesture of understanding the world and changing it.
>
> This combined power does not call for a knowledge of types alone, but for a search among deviations. The expression of turning-points, of new groupings and rhythms observed for the first time, leads to new analogies, new holy families. (32)

Rukeyser's relational poetics encompasses a radically expansive concept of poetic form; in search of "turning-points, of new groupings and rhythms," she develops eclectic combinations of forms in her books, even crossing conventional genre boundaries through the documentary form of "The Book of the Dead" and through mixing prose and poetry in *One Life.* Even when she adopts traditional forms such as ballad, sonnet, or blank verse, she often takes an experimental approach to them—so much so, that critics who expected tight perfection accused her of failing to master her craft. At root, such experimentation, and its combinations of different forms and genres, was a political gesture, for it reflected a principle that, in *The Life of Poetry,* Rukeyser associates with Whitman, whose "fight for reconciliation . . . was the essential process of democracy; to remake and acknowledge the relationships, to find the truth and power in diversity, among antagonists; and a poet of that democracy would have to acknowledge and make that truth emerge from the widest humanity in himself, among the horizons of his contradicted days and nights. The reconciliation was not a passive one; the unity was not an identification in which the range was lost" (78). For Rukeyser, Whitman—as a person and in his writing—exemplified the unity in diversity that she saw as the core principle of democracy. Her own lived experience of that principle sprung from her contradictory identity (including, along with her Jewishness, her bisexuality) and gained expression in her experiments with different poetic styles and crossing of genre boundaries.

Oppen, despite the comparative austerity of his published work, also based his writing practice on a process-oriented approach in which he mixed poetry and prose and cycled through the kind of self-repetition and recasting of lines and phrases that drove critics crazy in Rukeyser's published work. Since the publication, beginning in 1985, of excerpts from Oppen's working papers ("the Daybooks") and the *Selected Letters,* readers of Oppen have seen his achievement as encompassing not only the exactions of his published poetry, but also the interpenetration of the poetry with his prose meditations. Oppen did not keep separate notebooks for drafting poems, writing a prose journal, or transcribing quotations, but mixed all three, sometimes in single notebooks but also on sheets of paper fastened together by homely devices such as safety pins or pipe cleaners (*Ghostlier Demarcations* 76–77). As Michael Davidson demonstrates through close readings of several pages of the Daybooks, early incarnations of Oppen's published poems interact in the working papers with exploratory prose musings and quotations from other writers (64–78). Davidson argues that the "larger conversation" of Oppen's material text characterizes his work as process oriented, rather than focused on the lyric moment, and allies him with epistemologically centered poets such as Creeley, Olson, Ginsberg—and, I would add, Rukeyser[12]—for whom "writing is a form of knowing" (70). Davidson concludes that, for Oppen, such an approach is political; as with Rukeyser, his aligning of contraries—whether genres or themes—reflects the unfolding of his thought and intertwines the poem in a web of concerns: "As he meditated on contradictions in American politics, so he drafted poems; as he drafted poems, so he thought about the relation of old age to love. The manuscripts do not suggest someone working toward the perfect lyric, but one struggling for a vision of society in which the poem plays an instrumental role" (78).

Thus, Oppen's deep suspicion of instrumentalist poetry did not mean that he believed poetry could never "play an instrumental role" for an audience; Oppen aims to alter the perception of readers, rather than to drive them to the barricades. At the conclusion of his 1968 interview with L. S. Denbo he argues that one goal of poetry is "to bridge certain gaps between temperament to reach common ground, in spite of differences in temperament. After all, it's one of the difficult and crucial questions of that poetry, whether within these differences in one's personal vision, etc., one can reach common ground. One always finds that one can—that's the very wonderful thing" (*Man and Poet* 212). This declaration seems to counteract the version of Oppen promulgated by many of his commentators: the high-minded avant-gardist who cultivates difficulty, eschews a wide audience, and writes for a small group of like-minded cohorts. In keeping with his contrarian nature, Oppen was equally comfortable with—and equally skeptical of—audience-oriented, populist poetry and narrow avant-gardism. In the Daybooks, he meditates often on how popular culture increasingly diminishes the power of language and therefore of thought:

> Pop art to rescue the self-love of the people The characteristic of pop art, and therefore the rock singers, is that it must say what the audience already agrees to It is incapable of saying anything which its audience does not believe in advance TO SHOW, TO PERFORM, TO PUBLISH WORKS WHICH WILL CREATE A SELF-LOVE OF THE MILLIONS—A PEOPLE'S ART. (you may dance and dance to the most popular band of the moment until you go mad with cliché and sentiment and lies and self-love) (*Iowa Review* 13)

His criticism here is, of course, a moral one—a complaint that echoes his opposition to "communist verse" in the 1959 letter to June Oppen Degan on the grounds that the language and ideas of such poetry are predetermined rather than discovered through the process of writing (*SL* 22). The spareness of his published work derives from his efforts to cleanse and reclaim language, as he argues in the following Daybook entry, with its implicit jab at consumer culture: "We are consuming the language, and it is only by great labor that one can restore a word" (*Iowa Review* 30). Although he was far more sympathetic to the avant-garde tradition than to the depredations he attacked in popular and populist poetry, he felt equally wary of how poetry may also become dangerously predetermined when avant-garde techniques harden into convention:

> "avant garde": I have no liking for the word and no need of it One does not need the word, it is obvious enough that there is little use in repeating what has been adequately said before. I am concerned with 'thinking' (involuntary thoughts) that requires the poem, the verse. The turn and the turn
>
> thinking within the poem truth comes forth?
> Thinking within the world. (*Iowa Review* 2)

> 'avant garde'—the distinction between the avant garde and anything I could wish to be is the distinction between writing stylishly and the attempt to say with lucidity some part of what has not been said—but

> to be anti-avant garde is what? to write Yeats over again? (*Iowa Review* 2)

Even while acknowledging his affiliation for the avant-garde—his aversion "to write Yeats over again"—he remains skeptical of avant-garde writing driven more by fashion—"writing stylishly"—than by thought. Oppen's mode of "thinking that requires the poem, the verse" and "the turn and the turn" not only plays off the root meaning of "verse" but also gains vitality through contrariness: turning toward populism and away from it; turning toward avant-garde modes and away from them. As with his attitude toward being Jewish, he takes an oppositional stance, by situating himself between populist *and* avant-garde poetry. Oppen establishes a radical space for his work through his betweenness: his poetry is both populist and avant-garde, lucid and difficult, and aims to resist reductive, either/or paradigms and preestablished patterns of thought and perception.[13]

Rukeyser, too, situates herself between different poetic modes. Throughout *The Life of Poetry,* she insists on the need for poetry to move readers, whether emotionally or through impelling them toward some form of change. Yet she opposes the erosion of language through advertising and mass-produced sentiment and warns poets against adopting such predetermined language. Listing impoverishments of the imagination that may ensnare a poet, Rukeyser therefore condemns "the weakness of cliché, which is a product of corruption of consciousness and contempt for the audience: its mask is laziness" (53). Yet she also decries "the weakness of the 'intentionally obscure' who have formed groups: these groups, you will discover, after the first few years of a fashion, are using the same expressions" (53). But even as she warns against the pitfalls of fashionable obscurity, she also notes that much of the best modern poetry has been automatically dismissed as obscure by people unwilling to make the effort to approach it (*LP* 54). Like Oppen, Rukeyser feels equally suspicious of false, manipulative forms of populism and fashionable obscurity, while not denying the value either of reaching an audience or of difficulty as a viable poetic strategy.

Thus, despite their stylistic differences, Oppen and Rukeyser favored poetic forms that enabled them to articulate and embody the "betweenness" they advocated. Both poets often developed poems in series, a form—as the title of Oppen's first collection, *Discrete Series,* suggests—in which poems may stand discretely, as individual entities, but are also inextricable from a group. Both poets are, in fact, difficult to anthologize because so much of their finest work is in series form. But even on the level of the individual poem, Oppen and Rukeyser cultivate expressive silence, often through fragmented syntax, spacing on the page, or leaving gaps within a line. For Oppen the serial poem gave him increased opportunities: "SERIAL POEM—SPACE, SILENCE The serial poem permits the use of space, of silence" (*Iowa Review* 3). Process oriented and suspicious of any predetermined type of language, Oppen and Rukeyser saw poetry as a way of saying—or, better, an effort at saying—the unsayable. Oppen observes in a Daybook entry, "because there is something we cannot say, cannot grasp, the poem is an attempt to work it out, to find its form" (*Iowa Review* 3); and adds in another entry, "Poetry—a poem—succeeds in meaning what the words have never meant before—and this creates a strangeness of words" (*Iowa Review* 16). And Kate Daniels points out in the preface to *Out of Silence*, "One of [Rukeyser's] favorite assignments for her poetry writing students was to begin a poem with the words *I could not say*" (xv). While Daniels rightly places this assignment in the feminist context of breaking cultural silences about women's experiences, the assignment also corresponds with Rukeyser's view that poetry, as a genre, can articulate things that a writer would be unable to say in any other context. Oppen, as many commentators have documented, envisions silence as equally important as language—as, in fact, a necessary means of cleansing language by concentrating the reader's attention on linguistic process. Several Daybook entries insist on silence—gained by enjambment or gaps in a line—as a crucial poetic resource:

> I am concerned with   a thinking that requires the poem in order to be tight it is not a thinking outside of language: the linebreak is as much a part of language as the comma, the period, the paragraph
>
> The spacing is a part of the drama of the poem
> (visible as much as audible) (*Iowa Review* 17)

Likewise, Rukeyser in *The Life of Poetry* also considers silence a viable form of expression: "At this juncture, I wish to defend the wordless—the mute act, which proves itself without speech, which declares and insinuates in silence, and is stamped on memory. Even in concern for poetry, we realize the life of the unspoken. . . . There is no better place than a book about poetry to praise the untold" (*LP* 122). Silence is important to Rukeyser, both as something from which to escape (poetry as a form of combat against silences of various kinds—about emotions, about the body, about political truths) and also as something that heightens the power of language: "in the arts of speech . . . —in poetry and song and the dramatic arts—while silence may be even the climax, it is language and the relations of language with which we deal" (*LP* 123). Silence helps us perceive the relations of language—and that's often how the spaces in Rukeyser's poems function, as gaps that may or may not be bridged by the words surrounding them.

Silences create hesitations, approximate the pressure of thought, whether a headlong leaping from point to point without transition, or an extended pause that registers the difficulty of breaking through to the next insight. Predictably, the spaces and gaps in both poets' work never mean the same things in every instance, but shift in implication depending on context, even as they open out a poem's syntax toward multiple possibilities. Michael Heller's insights on Oppen's syntax are equally applicable to much of Rukeyser's work, especially her late series such as "Breaking Open" or "The Gates": "Oppen's radical use of syntax, while bordering on the disjunctive effects of much experimental poetry, never quite loses, never seems to want to lose, coherence. Rather, it is a constant struggle for coherence mounted against dispersal and disintegration. . . . The fragmentary character of Oppen's poetry is, essentially, not a postmodern sign, not a device, but embodies a yearning, an expression of the pressures and difficulties of articulating an idea or experience" ("Speaking the Estranged" 139). For both poets, the gaps and spaces (and, for Rukeyser, her unconventional adaptations of the colon) embody the contingencies of writing: the impulse toward communication and relation qualified by recognition of the barriers (social, political, linguistic) that impede the goal.

Muriel Rukeyser and George Oppen, despite their affiliations with different poetic schools, exhibit the same integrity: the uncompromisingly high moral and aesthetic standards that gave them the flexibility to practice a radical nonconformism in their lives and writing. Their ability to accept contingency, and their refusal to abide by an either/or approach to the world or to their work, arose in part from their oppositional, contradictory understanding of their Jewish identity. As experimental poets, they were perhaps most radical for developing a poetics of betweenness which allowed them to encompass—but never to resolve—so many contradictions in their writing: subjectivity and objectivity, isolation and connections with others; difficulty and clarity. However opposite their poetry may seem—with Rukeyser the poet of expansion and prolixity, Oppen the poet of concentration and spareness—they complement each other and have much to teach a current generation of poets who feel they must choose among various styles and schools of writing. As Oppen muses in a Daybook entry, "truth perhaps reached by going down, a sinking down, into the contradiction" (*Iowa Review* 3); Rukeyser affirms in *The Life of Poetry:* "the oppositions turn to music" (67).

Notes

1. See, for example, Michael Heller's "Utopocalypse: America Poetry in the 1930s" and Michael Davidson's *Ghostlier Demarcations: Modern Poetry and the Material World.* Both Heller and Davidson acknowledge Rukeyser and Oppen as important writers who share many convictions born of the political and aesthetic ferment of the 1930s, yet consider the two writers in completely separate sections of their studies.

2. For astute discussions of how Oppen and Rukeyser resist fitting into the highly polarized canon of twentieth-century American poetry, see Oren Izenberg's "Oppen Silence, Crusoe's Silence, and the Silence of Other Minds" and Richard Flynn's "'The Buried Life and the Body of Waking': Muriel Rukeyser and the Politics of Literary History."

3. For a discussion of the anti-transcendental bent of twentieth-century Jewish American poetry, see Jonathan N. Barron's "Commentary in Contemporary Jewish American Poetry," especially pages 233–240. The view espoused by Barron and many of the other contributors to *Jewish American Poetry: Poems, Commentary, and Reflections,* that Jewish American poetry often defines itself through quotation and commentary, also applies to Oppen and Rukeyser.

4. An additional influence on Oppen and Rukeyser's conviction that contraries can coexist without canceling each other out is William Blake; both poets were lifelong readers of his work, and they absorbed many of his ideas about politics and aesthetics. Moreover, Oppen and Rukeyser's contrarian poetics also reflect the conclusions of twentieth-century physics, particularly quantum mechanics. In "George Oppen's Silence and the Role of Uncertainty in Post-War American Avant-Garde Poetry," Burt Kimmelman develops this analogy between Oppen's poetics and post-classical scientific thought. A quotation from Stephen Carter that Kimmelman adapts to Oppen's aesthetics could apply equally well to Rukeyser, given her interest in science (as a founder of San Francisco's interactive science museum, the Exploratorium, and as the biographer of Willard Gibbs, the nineteenth-century American physical chemist): "complementarity describes a system or systems of mutually interdependent and irreconcilable relations. As a scientific way of knowing, it denies strictly classical notions of contradiction, either/or, and binary (digital) oppositions" (146). For an analysis of how some of Rukeyser's writings on science reflect her literary approach, see my essay, "'Forever Broken and Made': Muriel Rukeyser's Theory of Form" 27–29.

5. I base my discussion of the two poets' lives primarily on the following sources: Michael Davidson, "Introduction" to the *New Collected Poems;* Rachel Blau DuPlessis, "Introduction" to *The Selected Letters of George Oppen;* Jeffrey Peterson, "George

Oppen"; Mary Oppen, *Meaning a Life;* Kate Daniels, "In Order to Feel," the Preface to *Out of Silence;* Louise Kertesz, *The Poetic Vision of Muriel Rukseyser;* "Introduction" to *The Collected Poems of Muriel Rukeyser,* ed. Janet E. Kaufman and Anne F. Herzog, with Jan Heller Levi; Muriel Rukeyser, "Under Forty" (4–9), "Craft Interview," and "The Education of a Poet"; and Jan Heller Levi, e-mail correspondence. One question that my essay will naturally raise: did Oppen and Rukeyser know each other? Unfortunately I have not been able to find documentary evidence. The finding aids of the poets' archives, at UCSD (Oppen) and the NYPL's Berg Collection (Rukeyser), don't offer any record of correspondence, so it's probable that if Oppen and Rukeyser had met (whether in the 1930s, or in the late 1950s–early 1960s, when the Oppens had moved to Brooklyn and their daughter attended Sarah Lawrence, where Rukeyser was teaching), they did not feel enough of a kinship to write to each other, especially after the Oppens moved to San Francisco in December 1966.

6. For analysis of reviewers' assessments of Rukeyser's poetry, see Tim Dayton's chapter on "The Critical Reception of *The Book of the Dead*" (118–130); Kate Daniels, "Muriel Rukeyser and her Literary Critics"; and James Brock, "The Perils of a 'Poster Girl': Rukeyser, *Partisan Review,* and *Wake Island.*"

7. Rukeyser, likely still stung by the critical attacks on *Wake Island,* omitted the long poem from her 1978 *Collected Poems.* Justifying their inclusion of it in their new edition of the *Collected Poems,* Janet E. Kaufman and Anne F. Herzog note: "As both Jim Brock and Louise Kertesz have argued, while the poem does not represent the zenith of Rukeyser's poetic talent, it is consistent with her lifelong vision that poetry should respond to questions of social justice and freedom, as well as to the historical moment, not only locally, but globally. Perhaps now that the moment is less charged, readers will be interested in reconsidering this poem in the trajectory of Rukeyser's writing and as part of the writing to emerge from World War II" (xxvi).

8. Rukeyser's "relational poetics" is foundational enough to her oeuvre that most of her commentators address her concept of relation to some extent. The most detailed treatment is Anne F. Herzog's "Anything Away from Anything: Muriel Rukeyser's Relational Poetics."

9. For a demonstration of how Rukeyser's verse forms don't fit into conventional categories of "formal" and "free," see my essay, "'Forever Broken and Made.'"

10. Along with Taggart's detailed essay, other considerations of Oppen as a Jewish poet include Paul Lake's "The Archetypal Gesture: Myth and History in the Poetry of George Oppen"; Shirley Kaufman's "The Obvious and the Hidden: Some Thoughts about 'Disasters,' which examines his 1975 visit to Israel; Stephen Fredman's brief consideration, which owes much to Taggart, in *A Menorah for Athena: Charles Reznikoff and the Jewish Dilemmas of Objectivist Poetry* (77–80); and Michael Heller's inclusive discussion of the Objectivist poets and Jewish tradition in "Diasporic Poetics."

11. Despite Oppen's obsession with "the marvel of the real," it's important to recognize, as Susan Thackrey argues, that he is not a "simple realist," but instead enacts the process of perception, as it arises side-by-side with the recognition of elemental reality as both unavoidable fact and supreme mystery: for Oppen, "thoughts, in the

sense of whatever might arise in one . . . are part of what is perceivable, part of the world, in which mind is" (20). Thackrey convincingly argues that "George Oppen was afraid he would be read as a simple realist—someone not only kicking stones to prove the point that they exist, but then talking *about* the experience of kicking stones" (17); instead, "in Oppen's poetry it is a *given* that cultural norms render perception impossible—this is one of the things that makes his series 'Of Being Numerous' so intensely tenuous; how is it possible to find relation in existence as it is embodied in other human beings, when so many are embroiled and entangled in a network of rigidly defined perceptions—if an attempt to perceive without prior definition is one's basis for truth?" (19). Rukeyser shares this concern: how to establish relations with other human beings, when all people are limited by, entangled in, their own subjectivity.

12. Given her presence in San Francisco in the 1940s and the ties that she forged then with key figures such as Kenneth Rexroth, Robert Duncan, and Charles Olson, it is surprising that she is rarely cited as one of the members of the San Francisco Renaissance despite her dedication to a process-oriented poetry and her profound opposition to the New Critics. Michael Davidson, for example, doesn't even mention her in *The San Francisco Renaissance: Poetics and Community at Mid-Century*, a study that many critics accept as definitive. As Louise Kertesz notes, "she is not associated with the San Francisco Renaissance because, she says, she has never been a group person and because she was 'pushing a baby carriage' much of the time" (371).

13. Michael Davidson, discussing *New Collected Poems* in an online interview, demonstrates how Oppen's readers are divided about how to categorize him; the problem lies in the readers' insistence on seeing him as either a difficult poet or a lucid one, rather than a poet capable of combining both modes, often in the same poem:

> I don't think that Oppen has received adequate recognition from the major literary establishment, nor has he been as thoroughly discussed, critically, as have many younger (and lesser) poets. But he does command enormous respect among poets in a variety of different areas. Of the Objectivists, he is the poet who seems to cross-over into multiple camps, earning the praise of Sharon Olds, Shirley Kaufman, Robert Hass, and Robert Pinsky, as well as Charles Bernstein, Rachel Blau DuPlessis, and Susan Howe. I note, however, a tendency among some poets and critics to make Oppen into a considerably more user-friendly poet. At a conference on the Objectivists in Royaumont, France, some years ago, a spirited debate was launched over Charles Bernstein's remark that Oppen was a "difficult poet" whereupon Carl Rakosi piped up, challenging Charles's claim. The French in the audience largely saw Oppen as "difficult" in the way that Zukofsky is, but many Americans in the audience, spurred-on by Carl's remark, defended the "plain style" Oppen. In subsequent reports on this conference in Poetry Flash, respondents lined-up on different sides of the fence, alternately claiming Oppen as a predecessor of language-writing or as a populist poet like Sandburg. The fact that Oppen has generated such widespread debate suggests that he can be read from a number of different optics.

Works Cited

Barron, Jonathan N., and Eric Murphy Selinger, eds. *Jewish American Poetry: Poems, Commentary, and Reflections.* Hanover: Brandeis University Press/ University Press of New England, 2000.

Barron, Jonathan N. "Commentary in Contemporary Jewish American Poetry." In Barron and Selinger, 233–249.

Brock, James. "The Perils of a 'Poster Girl': Rukeyser, *Partisan Review,* and *Wake Island.* In Herzog and Kaufman, 254–263.

Daniels, Kate. "Muriel Rukeyser and Her Literary Critics." In Dickie and Travisano, 247–263.

———. "Preface: 'In Order to Feel.'" *Out of Silence: Selected Poems of Muriel Rukeyser.* Evanston: TriQuarterly Books, 1992. ix–xvii.

Davidson, Michael. *Ghostlier Demarcations: Modern Poetry and the Material World.* Berkeley: University of California Press, 1997.

———. "On Collecting George Oppen's Poems." Online interview. *Poets&Writers:* http://www.pw.org/mag/dq_oppen.htm.

———. *The San Francisco Renaissance: Poetics and Community at Mid-Century.* Cambridge: Cambridge University Press, 1989.

Dayton, Tim. *Muriel Rukeyser's The Book of the Dead.* Columbia: University of Missouri Press, 2003.

Dickie, Margaret, and Thomas Travisano, eds. *Gendered Modernisms.* Philadelphia: University of Pennsylvania Press, 1996.

Flynn, Richard. "'The Buried Life and the Body of Waking': Muriel Rukeyser and the Politics of Literary History." In Dickie and Travisano, 264–279.

Fredman, Stephen. *A Menorah for Athena: Charles Reznikoff and the Jewish Dilemmas of Objectivist Poetry.* Chicago: University of Chicago Press, 2001.

Hatlen, Burton, ed. *George Oppen: Man and Poet.* Orono, ME: National Poetry Foundation, 1981.

Heller, Michael. "Diasporic Poetics." In Barron and Selinger, 216–229.

———. "Speaking the Estranged: Oppen's Poetics of the Word." *Chicago Review* 50, 2 (Winter 2004–2005): 137–150.

———. "Utopocalypse: American Poetry in the 1930s." *A Profile of Twentieth Century American Poetry.* Jack Meyers and David Wojan, eds. Carbondale: Southern Illinois University Press. 84–101.

Herzog, Anne F. "'Anything Away from Anything': Muriel Rukeyser's Relational Poetics." In Herzog and Kaufman, 32–44.

———, and Janet E. Kaufman, eds. *"How Shall We Tell Each Other of the Poet?: The Life and Writing of Muriel Rukeyser.* New York: St. Martin's Press, 1999.

Izenberg, Oren. "Oppen's Silence, Crusoe's Silence, and the Silence of Other Minds." *Modernism/Modernity* 13, 1 (January 2006): 41–65.

Kaufman, Janet E. "'But Not the Study': Writing as a Jew." In Herzog and Kaufman, 45–61.

Kaufman, Shirley. "The Obvious and the Hidden: Some Thoughts about 'Disasters.'" *Ironwood* 13, 2 (Fall 1985): 152–158.

Kenner, Hugh. "Oppen, Zukofsky, and the Poems and Lens." *Literature at the Barricades: The American Writer in the 1930s.* Ralph F. Bogardus and Fred Hobson, eds. University: University of Alabama Press, 1982. 162–171.

Kertesz, Louise. *The Poetic Vision of Muriel Rukeyser.* Baton Rouge: Louisiana State University Press, 1980.

Kimmelman, Burt. "George Oppen's Silence and the Role of Uncertainty in Post-War American Avant-Garde Poetry." *Mosaic: A Journal for the Interdisciplinary Study of Literature* 36, 2 (June 2003): 145–162.

Lake, Paul. "The Archetypal Gesture: Myth and History in the Poetry of George Oppen." In Hatlen, 113–122.

Levi, Jan Heller. "'Too Much Life to Kill': Some Thoughts on Muriel Rukeyser." In Herzog and Kaufman, 282–286.

Oppen, George. "The Anthropologist of Myself: A Selection from Working Papers." Rachel Blau DuPlessis, ed. *Sulfur* 26 (Spring 1990): 135–164.

———. Interview with Burton Hatlen and Tom Mandel. "Poetry and Politics: A Conversation with George and Mary Oppen." San Francisco, June 1980. In Hatlan, 23–47.

———. Interview with L. S. Denbo. "Oppen on His Poems: A Discussion." May 1968. Rpt. in Hatlen, 197–213.

———. *New Collected Poems.* Michael Davidson, ed. New York: New Directions, 2002.

———. *The Selected Letters of George Oppen.* Rachel Blau DuPlessis, ed. Durham, NC: Duke University Press, 1990.

———. "A Selection from 'Daybook One,' 'Daybook Two,' and 'Daybook Three,' from The Working Papers of George Oppen." Stephen Cope, ed. *The Germ* 2 (1999): 192–253.

———. "Selections from George Oppen's Daybook." David Young, ed. *Iowa Review* 18 (Fall 1988): 1–17.

Oppen, Mary. *Meaning a Life: An Autobiography.* Santa Barbara: Black Sparrow Press, 1978.

Peterson, Jeffrey. "George Oppen." In *Dictionary of Literary Biography, Volume 165: American Poets since World War II, Fourth Series.* Ed. Joseph Conte. New York: Bruccoli Clark Layman/Gale, 1990. 188–206.

Rukeyser, Muriel. *The Collected Poems.* Ed. Janet E. Kaufman and Anne F. Herzog; with Jan Heller Levi. Pittsburgh: University of Pittsburgh Press, 2005.

———. "Craft Interview with Muriel Rukeyser." In *The Craft of Poetry,* ed. William Packard, 153–176. Garden City, NY: Doubleday, 1974.

———. "Education of a Poet." 1976. In *The Muriel Rukeyser Reader,* ed. Jan Heller Levi, 277–295. New York: W. W. Norton, 1994.

———. *The Life of Poetry.* 1949. Ashfield, MA: Paris Press, 1995.

———. "Under Forty: A Symposium of American Literature and the Younger Generation of American Jews." *Contemporary Jewish Record* 7, 1 (February 1944): 3–36.

Schoerke, Meg. "'Forever Broken and Made': Muriel Rukeyser's Theory of Form." In Herzog and Kaufman, 17–31.

Taggart, John. "Walk-Out: Rereading the Poetry of George Oppen." *Chicago Review* 44, 2 (1998): 29–93.

Thackrey, Susan. *George Oppen: A Radical Practice.* San Francisco: O Books/The American Poetry Archives, 2001.

Weinberger, Eliot. "Preface: Oppen Then." *New Collected Poems.* vii–xii.

"Yes and No, Not Either/Or"

Aesthetics, Identity, and Marjorie Perloff's *Vienna Paradox*

Daniel Morris

In her splendid memoir, Marjorie Perloff defines the Vienna Paradox. The paradox concerns the sad fate of the sophisticated upper-class Jews of Vienna (circa 1930) who perceived themselves as Austrians, not as Jews, because they revered Germanic high culture, Goethe especially. Being Austrian, for these non-Jewish Jews, had nothing to do with the racial mythology that, under Hitler, became the defining category of national belonging. Of course, with the Anschluss of March 1938, families such as the Mintz's (Perloff's name was then Gabrielle Mintz) were defined as the undesirable Other—the Jew—and forced to flee their country with few belongings. Death was the other option. In the end, with Hitler defining key terms such as "Jew" and "Austrian," it did not matter that friends of the Mintz family had accepted baptism to advance in their careers, or that no other Austrians were more devoted to the culture that would expel or destroy them. As George Steiner has concluded, after noting the failure of European humanism to protect Jews from "the face of bestiality," "The Muses knew how to goose-step."

Trained from youth in the German classics, and then at graduate school in High Modernism during the heyday of the New Criticism in America in the 1950s, the memoir shows how Perloff in the early 1960s begins to rework her relation to her hyphenated identity as a highly cultured, immigrant American Jew during her early teaching career. In the memoir, she does not dwell on her Jewish background as an influence to her rise to becoming a successful American academic whose topics of study from the modernist Yeats to the postmodernist O'Hara have not tended to be Jewish, but she also does not deny the indelible fact of her Jewishness. Perloff counters her Viennese forebears' dissociation from their Jewishness as a significant identity marker. She also qualifies the contemporary trend in cultural theory to perceive all identity markers as antiessentialist, and thus to view the self as a performance in which Americans, ala Gatsby, or, more to the point, Barbra Streisand as the cross-dressing Yeshiva girl in the film version of I. B. Singer's story "Yentyl," have the freedom to compose and recompose their character. Perloff writes: "Jewish identity can never be merely expunged, for the simple reason that, as the refugees from Hitler were forced to learn the hard way, one is always a Jew in the eyes of the Other" (2004; 234). She continues: "Given this state of affairs, one cannot stop being a Jew, whatever one's response to the Jewish religion and however strong one's rival affiliations, whether professional, intellectual, national, or familial. It is a reality the upper class Viennese Jewish refugees were reluctant to face: many remained staunchly in denial even after they came to America" (2004; 236). We may read Perloff's endeavors as critic and scholar as a conversation about identity formation that pivots between essentialist and constructivist modes.

In the memoir, Perloff addresses with subtlety her relation to Jewishness as a mature adult, as well as her feelings about defining herself via national citizenship and toward High Culture. Her version of Jewishness, citizenship, and Kultur are more nuanced, ambivalent, and circumspect than would have been the case with her Austrian forebears, who in part defined their identity via their ability to distinguish Kultur from Kitsch. Her memoir, then, offers a model of what it might mean to define oneself as Jewish in the postmodern, transnational context in which a Viennese girl, Gabrielle Mintz, becomes a celebrated American intellectual, Marjorie Perloff, who decided on her first name because it "was the name of the most popular girl in my class at the Fieldston School" in New York in the 1940s (1996; preface xi). This new version of Jewishness, which seems at times related to "queer" understandings of identity—the link between "Jewishness" and "gender troubles" is a theme explored by such theorists as Daniel Boyarin, Sander Gilman, Marjorie Garber, and Eve Sedgwick—but at other times is critical of antiessentialist ways of thinking about identity, suggests the author's willingness to balance different markers of personal affiliation (Jewish/not Jewish, high/low culture, American/European, essentialist/constructivist) without the need to settle into one or another category of personal identification.

In this essay, I will read Perloff's scholarly works in a Nietzschean manner, which is to say as displaced autobiography.[1] Her experience as a transnational citizen whose thoughts about the fluidity of identity were formed through the experiences of refugee displacement, name change, immigration to the United States as a young girl, as well as her desire to discover a flexible relationship to Jewishness that her Viennese forebears denied at great peril, are mirrored in her changing attitudes toward literary scholarship as an American academic from the 1960s to now. Perloff champions a postmodern aesthetic that is marked by the qualities of indeterminacy, constructivism, anti-absorption, assemblage, disorientations in representations of time frames and spatial locations, interchangeable or opaque pronoun referents that suggest the protean nature of personal identity, and the breakdown of the modernist value distinction between "High" and "Low" culture. Her aesthetic is informed by her biography as a transnational, diasporic figure, a story that denounces traditional understandings of national identity as well as religious or ethnic association. Perloff's ambivalent relationship to being a Jew in contemporary America, and her wish to dissociate herself from the rejection of Jewishness altogether of her Viennese forebears is subtly expressed in the postmodern aesthetic that Perloff has developed in over a dozen books on such avant-garde (and, intriguingly, queer) Americans as the poet Frank O'Hara and the polymath John Cage. In advocating for their aesthetic sensibility, she is also imagining for herself *a* new relationship to the previously discarded terms of her Viennese forebears (Jewish and Kitsch), while at the same time not simply reifying the essential value of the previously discarded terms.

As a distinguished American literary critic for the last four decades, and recent president of the Modern Language Association, Perloff continues to specialize in high cultural analysis, but of a kind that breaks down rigid categorizations of "high" versus "low." Similarly, Perloff openly defines herself as Jewish, but not as a religious Jew. "Raised as I was on Christmas and Easter pageantry, on notions of Christian ethnics and the religion of Kultur, Jewish observance and ritual remain alien to me. In my case, then, Jewishness was to become an ethical, cultural, and political complex, an identity (among other identities) that I take quite seriously" (2004; 238–239). In an e-mail response to an early version of my essay, Perloff has elaborated on what being Jewish, but not observant, means to her now:

> On the Jewish issue: I find that ETHNICALLY I do identify with the Jews and therefore when I hear anti-Semitic and anti-Israeli remarks, I am troubled. Much as I disapprove of the settler movement in Israel and many other features of their politics, I still find myself emotionally on their side rather than the Palestinian side. But for me this does not translate into observant Judaism. My grandson is about to have his Bar Mitzvah and the actual ritual of these things (and money spent!) is not something I can get very interested in.
>
> So it remains for me a cultural and ethnic identity rather than a religious one. But now things get complicated: why Frank O'Hara and John Cage rather than various Jewish poets or artists? I suppose be-

> cause the overt Jewishness of a Saul Bellow or Philip Roth in "realistic" fiction doesn't appeal to me. It is also the Jewishness of Eastern European background that is quite different from mine. But I do relate to the more avant-garde German (or Austrian) Jewish writers from Kafka and Joseph Roth to Elfriede Jelinek and Paul Celan (whom I've just written on).

On one level, Perloff remains her parents' child. Her career as an advocate for avant-garde movements in the United States may not have gotten off the ground had it not been for the Mintz family devotion to art, music, and literature in Austria. Author of books on subjects such as Yeats, Lowell, O'Hara, Wittgenstein, Cage, and the "language" poetry of Susan Howe and Charles Bernstein, Perloff's fascination with hermetic trends in late-twentieth-century poetics and literary theory speaks to a dedication to examining culture at its most esoteric levels. In the memoir, Perloff relates stories about the extraordinary work habits and intellectual curiosity of her parents, including a poignant reflection on how her father, who became a successful CPA in New York City, would return home after a long day at the office, only to engage in painstaking correspondence on the fine points of political theory with Erich Voegelin, another expatriate Viennese, then teaching at Louisiana State University. A brilliant and dedicated student who won a scholarship to the Fieldston School of Ethical Culture, and later succeeded at Oberlin and Barnard before earning a doctorate at Catholic University, where she was quickly tapped to teach as an assistant professor, Perloff's initial training was as a modernist in formalist poetics and critical theory. Exposed to the vibrant popular culture of 1940s New York City in the form of radio, movies, and Broadway, she was at first unable to shake off the rigid categories of Kultur versus Kitsch that defined her parents' national affiliation in Austria. Even *Death of a Salesman,* Perloff reports, was considered Kitsch!

The story of Perloff's shift from a modernist to a postmodernist aesthetic begins in Washington, D.C. Encouraged by senior professors to pursue a formalist analysis of Yeats in the early 1950s as a graduate student at Catholic University, Perloff chafes against such restrictions, both of topic and approach. "When I became more speculative and looked at the way rhyme (sound) and trope (meaning) are interrelated, [her advisor and senior professor] demurred. I was now in an area not amenable to empirical evidence and hence in a suspect gray zone. What he couldn't bear, I think, is that my work, technical though it was, showed that I was not a full-fledged disciple." In the memoir, discussion of her early teaching career (she was fired for "insubordination" before being rehired and then leaving for another university) becomes allegorical of her declaration of independence from the small-c catholic distinctions between Highbrow and Kitsch that dominated her upbringing in Vienna:

> I started writing on problems of genre and convention and issues of literary history that blurred boundaries. More important: I wanted to become a different kind of Modernist: no longer the student of Anglo-American poetics from Yeats to Robert Lowell [the subjects of her first two books], but of the larger, early 20th-century world called the Avant-Garde. Joyce certainly played a central role in that world, but the Joyce not of *Portrait of the Artist,* Exhibit A at Catholic U., but of the more experimental sections of *Ulysses* and *Finnegan's Wake.* (2004; 234)

Where parents and senior professors defined their cultural positions by excluding terms that "blurred boundaries" in between forms of representation, or existed in what she calls the "suspect gray zone," Perloff specifically dwells in the ambivalent realm in between sanctioned and unsanctioned (taboo? transgressive?) cultural productions. The shift in focus from Yeats to the Joyce of *Ulysses* with Leopold Bloom among its main characters and with its emphasis on such earthy subjects as food and sex and body organs may seem to be a slight transgression of taste according to a modernist sensibility, but Perloff's subsequent embrace of the "I do this, I do that" poetics of Frank O'Hara, and the "sound" compositions based on "Chance Operations" performed on a "prepared" piano by John Cage suggest a more radical disaffection with the definition of cultural achievement based in exclusion of material once understood to be "low" or "popular" or "mass produced" or "profane" or "Kitsch."

In O'Hara and Cage—two queer American men, neither Jewish—Perloff discovers groundbreaking contemporary artists who developed their compositions out of the detritus of everyday life, the kinds of sights and sounds that the Jewish Austrian theorist Theodor Adorno would have lambasted as Ground Zero of the mass media's "Culture Industry." The critic remains in love with the work of the Viennese Jew Arnold Schoenberg (1874–1951), whom she describes as "the Ultimate Modernist Composer, solitary, serious, and dedicated" (2004; 242). But she increasingly attends in her writings to the "wide-ranging and eclectic" career of Cage, Schoenberg's student when the modernist master had himself become an expatriate living in Los Angeles after World War II. Cage's emphasis on sound and silence, rather than harmony, suggests a radical dismantling of the traditional idea of musical composition in the West, and his collaborative work process undermines the High

Modernist mythos of the artist as solitary culture hero (2004; 243). "Far from being wedded to the notion of individual masterpiece, [Cage] frequently collaborates with composer (e.g. David Tudor), dancers (Merce Cunningham), and artists (Jasper Johns)," Perloff writes.

In " 'A duchamp unto my self': 'Writing through' Marcel," Perloff interprets Cage through the lens of his ambivalent admiration for Marcel Duchamp. She writes: "The real appeal of Duchamp for Cage ("I love him and he . . . changed my life") may have had less to do with Marcel's work than with his enticing presence—the exotic image of the man smiling enigmatically over the chessboard or appearing in drag as Rrose Selavy" (1994; 102–103). In linking Cage to Duchamp as *Rrose Selavy* (1924)—the title of which translates into English as "Eros is Life"—Perloff is highlighting elements of Cage's practice that disrupt rigid hierarchies of aesthetic value in part by connecting the fine arts to the "queer," or nonheteronormative, body. Her essay demonstrates how Cage grasped Duchamp's "commitment to the renunciation of the ego in art" through the antiessentialist play of gendered identity in the image of Duchamp in drag, Perloff also argues that Cage admired how Duchamp breaks down the difference between work and play, as well as the blurring of the difference between art and life, as well as the use of humor and parody as a way to mock aesthetic pieties, as in Duchamp's putting a mustache on the Mona Lisa and calling the new "art work" *L.H.O.O.Q.* Of course, Duchamp's ready-mades, which offer, as Perloff writes, the "presentation of everyday—and frequently ugly and tasteless—commercial objects" as museum pieces are a precursor to Cage's generation of texts via chance operations (1994; 109). "For the notion that any object can be considered "art," if it is looked at properly, is not so much Duchampian as Cagean. Duchamp, after all, held that the very idea of "art" is bogus, that at best what the "artist" makes should be called "craft" and be denied reverence on the part of the public" (1994; 113).

In "Pound/Stevens: Whose Era?" a key essay in the 1985 study on "poetry of the Pound tradition," *The Dance of the Intellect,* Perloff develops a manifesto for modern and postmodern poetry. She emphasizes the importance of Pound's aesthetics in the *Cantos* over and above the influence of Wallace Stevens, whose work had been championed by leading critics such as Helen Vendler and Harold Bloom for continuing the line of visionary Romanticism into the twentieth century. Whereas Stevens's aesthetic privileges such Romantic ideals as subjectivity, interiority, and the notion of the artist as individual genius engaged in private meditation, Perloff argues that Pound's *Cantos* break out of the lyric mode through a disorienting collage technique that challenges fixed ideas about poetry as a form of individual expression.

As in visual cubism, Pound juxtaposes bits and pieces of "found" material in ways that cause readers to question the idea of authorial point of view, lyric coherence and closure, as well as the lines between poetry and prose and between private expression and political discourse. Perloff traces Pound's development of a style that favors constructionism over expressionism to the writings of postmodern American authors such as O'Hara and John Cage. She demonstrates how these authors challenge the association of poetry with lyric subjectivity, as they move away from the meditational strains of a Stevens and toward writings that defy easy generic classification. Narrative, collage, fragmentation, hybridic modes that incorporate varieties of social text and, as in John Ashbery, that tend to shift time frames and pronoun referents "often within the space of a single sentence or sentence fragment" (1985; 146) become prevalent.[2]

What Perloff finds intriguing about Pound's *Cantos,* Picasso's cubism, and the avant-garde poetry, art, and music that follow in their wake by postmodern Americans such as the proto-Pop artist Robert Rauschenberg, New York School poets such as Ashbery, and polymathic author-performers such as Cage, is that relationships between modes of representation and modes of being become radically destabilized. She writes: "For is the newspaper fragment in, say, a Picasso collage to be read as a compositional unit, a luminous plane juxtaposed to the neighboring planes (or, from another angle, the outline of a table leg), or are we to read it as a block of newsprint and focus on its content? 'the situation,' as John Cage, himself a great *collagiste,* puts it, 'must be Yes-and-No, not either or'" (1985; 183). Even more so than would be the case with a Picasso collage, Perloff finds (however unselfconsciously) in the postmodern assemblages of the queer Jewish artist Rauschenberg a visual metaphor for the unstable, fluid construction of identity as experienced by the displaced Austrian Jew in America.

Perloff quotes art critic Rosalind Krauss on the difference between Cubist collage à la Picasso and how "real" pieces of material culture (such as newspaper clippings, pieces of bedding, and street signs) are put together in a work by Rauschenberg: "[In Cubist collage] a bit of newspaper absorbed in to the shape of a wine glass can identify itself as a piece of the real world only from within the depths of a whole network of ambiguity. Caught up in the process of mapping, it is on the way to being absorbed, it has already been absorbed, into the transformational mesh of the image" (Krauss quoted in Perloff, 1985; 63). By contrast, Perloff writes that in Rauschenberg: "The objects to be collaged are not transformed by their absorption into the pictorial design or tone; they are simply transferred, taken out of the space of the world and embedded into the surface of the painting, never at the sacrifice of their density as material . . . By never transcending the material world, the image is unambiguously identified with the material world" (1985; 63). In Rauschenberg, Perloff argues, the canvas becomes "a kind of memory-space, for only in memory does such leveling [of various objects] occur: an image of a scene from a film or from a novel may be just as vivid as something that has really happened to us" (1985; 63).

I want to highlight the issue of absorption and resistance of material elements to incorporation into the imaginative space of the picture plane in Rauschenberg because it is important to my understanding of Perloff's situation as a displaced transnational Jew working in America as a successful academician under the name of Marjorie Perloff, not Gabrielle Mintz. The poet David Antin has written that collage "operates in a middle space between representation on the one hand and the kind of constructional game of Mondrian on the other; and its operation oscillates between the two possibilities of representational reference and compositional game" (quoted in Perloff, 1985; 183). It is my sense that Perloff has come to dwell in a comparable "middle space," comparable to what Homi Bhaba calls "liminality," in which the answer to such questions as "Are you a Jew?" or "Are you an American?" or "Is it fine art?" are not to be answered in terms of "yes" OR "no," but rather in terms of "yes" AND "no." Perloff/Mintz is physically transferred to the new spaces of New York, Washington, and, eventually California, where she has taught for many years, first at the University of Southern California and then at Stanford. Her memoir reveals the failure of that space to completely absorb her into it as a home that is not also what Freud called "unheimlich," unhomelike, or uncanny. For Perloff, there remains in the American landscape a spillage, a trace of a part of the displaced Viennese self from the 1930s that cannot be completely erased or ignored, but that also cannot be fully translated or transferred onto American soil.

Where Perloff appreciates Cage's challenge to traditional Western ideas about compositional technique, she welcomes Frank O'Hara's questioning of the line between High and Low cultural materials. "Imagine making poetry out of the Mayflower Shoppe, across from Bergdorf Goodman's on Fifth Avenue, out of Juliet's Corner on Times Square!" she writes of O'Hara's "A Step Away from Them," where the speaker famously stops for a cheeseburger and to eye the "laborers in yellow helmets" as they "feed their dirty glistening torsos sandwiches." Perloff continues: "Flexibility and attentiveness, these poems [by O'Hara] tell us, are the qualities needed to enjoy such city pleasures as Neon in Daylight. It was a matter, as O'Hara put it, of 'Grace to be born and live as variously as possible.' But in 1941 I could not yet articulate this notion, and although I carefully studied each item in the Horn & Hardart windows, I always chose the same three or four things" (2004; 149). In *Lunch Poems,* named as such because the author jotted the lyrics down during breaks from his job at the Metropolitan Museum of Art, O'Hara is the master of mixing, as he does in "A Step Away from Them," the realms of sophisticated discourse (he speaks in the poem of the writer Edward Denby, for example, as well as of Fellini, Jackson Pollock, the Armory Show, and the poems of Pierre Reverdy) and the Joycean realms of the body and food and the carnivalesque street life shared by millions of New York pedestrians everyday (the view of hardhat construction workers and the taste of cheeseburgers at a corner lunch counter). O'Hara's willingness to confuse categories of perception and their value in the representational space echoes Perloff's interest in finding alternative versions of Jewish identity. Her embrace of his "flexibility and attentiveness" to life on the border in between different forms of personal identity illustrates her process of overcoming the denial of any relationship to the previously discarded terms of her Viennese forebears, while at the same time not simply reifying or affirming the essential value of the previously discarded terms.

Reading Perloff's criticism in light of the back story provided by her memoir, we begin to appreciate how her key themes and aesthetic predilections are informed by her background as a displaced person, a refugee of European fascism whose experience as the daughter of Viennese intellectuals in the 1930s, *and* as an American immigrant who has remade herself into a critic of the false equation of High Cultural affiliation with a sense of national belonging that proved so destructive to the Jews of Austria in the 1930s. A study of Perloff's scholarship reveals her championship of terms and concepts that are all about breaking down aesthetic categories that, in modernism, signified the terms of cultural and social belonging. Instead of cordoning off High Cult works of art, music, and literature from everyday life, Perloff champions an art of indeterminacy. She describes how material objects often resist absorption into the artwork in her celebration of collage, as well as the breaking down of what Andreas Huyssen calls the Modernist "discourse which insists on the categorical distinction between high art and mass culture," and the favoring of the "working of Kitsch into art" that "can result in high quality works" such as those of Andy Warhol and Robert Rauschenberg (quoted in Perloff, 1991; 10).

Perloff's challenge to the "great divide" between cultural realms defined by Huyssen has recently animated her rethinking of what constitutes the legitimate space of cultural productions. Her interest is in juxtaposing, as she does in *Radical Artifice,* "what really happens on the video screen, at the computer terminal, or in the advertising media, and then to see how poetic or art discourse positions itself vis-à-vis these powerful new environments" (1991; 15). Playing off Richard A. Lanham's treatment of the experimental possibilities of graphic production on the computer terminal, Perloff theorizes the production of creative writing in the age of computer technology. Unlike the printed book, in which Lanham argued that the page was "not to be read aesthetically; that would only interfere with purely literate transparency" (quoted in Perloff, 1991; 266), the computer screen as compositional surface will dismantle such fundamental categories of distinction as the written surface and the "picture elements," the "dots which electronically paint the letters onto the computer screen" (1991; 16). Further, electronic composition tends to upset distinctions between poetry and prose, creator and critic, and the difference between the verbal and the visual realms. She writes: "I can 'transform' what is usually thought of as prose into what is usually thought of as poetry, simply by hitting the 'indent' key and lineating the text. I can illuminate the text in various ways, use different colors, reformat it in italics or capitals, and so on. The textual surface has, in other words, become what Lanham calls 'permanently bistable'" (1991; 16).

When Perloff does, textually speaking, return to Vienna in 1996, it is to discuss, in book-length form, the social and historical contexts for the language theory of Ludwig Wittgenstein, as well as his influence on, or common cause with, such other experimental authors (and displaced persons affected by World Wars) as Gertrude Stein and Samuel Beckett. Considering that Perloff is not a trained philosopher, and that her scholarship has been, almost without exception, in contemporary American studies since at least 1970, one wonders, why a book on Wittgenstein? And which Wittgenstein does she choose to draw upon? And how does Perloff's return to Vienna via Wittgenstein inform my thesis that her scholarship reflects upon her own autobiographical concerns? In her "Preface" to *Wittgenstein's Ladder: Poetic Language and the Strangeness of the Ordinary* (1996)—a title that refers to the philosopher's famous statement on the final page of the *Tractatus* comparing his propositions to a provisional ladder that readers may discard once they have "climbed out through them, on them, over them" (xiv)—Perloff admits that her study of Wittgenstein, "while not some sort of autobiographical memoir," "is probably more personal than any" of her other books (Preface xi). Like Wittgenstein, Perloff belonged to a wealthy family of Viennese intellectuals whose lives were rocked by World War (the First War for Ludwig, an Austrian taken "prisoner of war on the Italian front" in 1919, the Second War for Marjorie, "transported to the U.S. in 1938 as a refugee from Hitler" [xi]). Wittgenstein's contextual analysis of language, which suggests that personal identity is the product of historical and cultural forces beyond the scope of the individual will, are certainly mirrored in Perloff's biography, as well as in her admiration for Cage, whose aesthetics of "Chance Operations," often determined by a reading of the Tarot deck, enact a Buddhist acceptance of "what is," as the greatest indication of the outcome to human endeavors such as making art.

Like many in Perloff's circle, "Wittgenstein was a Jew baptized in the Catholic church" (1996; 7). Although Wittgenstein was a non-Jewish Jew, Perloff argues that his "ethnicity" does influence his philosophical disposition.

> Wittgenstein has little to say abut the Jews (and when he does, as in *Culture and Value,* his derogatory tone suggests a certain self-hatred, typical of his class and milieu), but Jewishness is, for him, a kind of subtext of difference. Only someone who is not fully at home in the world will talk as much as Wittgenstein does about "the language-game which is [one's] original home." The reference to "foreign traditions" and "foreign country" refers not only to Wittgenstein's foreignness on English soil but also to his "foreignness" as a Jew, in the Vienna of his birth. (1996; 76)

In *The Vienna Paradox,* Perloff shows that the Mintz family and its circle learned the hard way that being Jewish may itself be a characterization "foreign" to the self for it may be defined by others. Although they celebrated Easter and Christmas, snubbed their noses at the Eastern European Jews who practiced Orthodoxy, Perloff writes that Jewishness, not national identification, defined the Mintz family. Similarly, she writes of Wittgenstein: "The writings of the Investigations, we must remember, took place in precisely the years when Wittgenstein was forced to recognize that, despite the baptism and Catholic upbringing that generations of Wittgensteins had undergone, from the perspective of the Nazi regime, they were simply Jews. In this context, even the 'mastery' of his 'country's language' cannot eradicate the sense of difference Wittgenstein speaks of above" (1996; 76). Like Perloff herself, Ludwig was an exiled, nomadic figure. His writings attest to the slippery relationships between language, translation, grammar, and personal identity when perceived as a fluid construct subject to the vicissitudes of international political and historical events far beyond the scope of the individual person to alter or control. "For Wittgenstein comes to us as the ultimate modernist outsider, the changeling who never stops reinventing himself, who never really 'belongs,' and whose presence is nevertheless so overwhelming that we can immediately identify it as Wittgenstein's" (1996; 7–8).

Just as I am reading Perloff through the lens of her autobiography as a displaced person who is suspicious of those who fetishize high culture as a sign of their cultural or national belonging, Perloff reads Wittgenstein's philosophy as the cryptic autobiography of a stranger in a strange land. Wittgenstein echoed "Victor Shklovsky's famous doctrine of "making it strange" or "defamiliarization, with its emphasis on the 'artistic' removal of the object from its usual surroundings so as to recharge its potency" (1996; 11) in his examination of the elusive meanings of the most ordinary language as a form of interpersonal communication. Wittgenstein's obsession with the strangeness of ordinary words and the interrogation of grammar as a site of semantic ambiguity, Perloff argues, is a product of "war discourse" (1996; 25). By "war discourse," she means the traumatic upsetting of social and personal norms. Perloff thus reads Wittgenstein's sentence, "I am completely powerless," from his *Notebook* against the fact that he wrote it only one week after he engaged in the "heavy fighting of the Brusilov offensive" on June 4, 1916 (1996; 29). His critique in the *Tractatus* of the logic of cause and effect, as well as his emphasis on difficulty, pain, and the arbitrary nature of how things are, are all for Perloff the result of personal upheavals and cultural displacements brought about by war trauma and expatriation. She speaks of his years in Cambridge as "the exile of teaching the mysteries of ordinary language in a country and language not his own" (1996; 48).

Wittgenstein is often represented as a product of Viennese art and culture prior to World War One—a book entitled *Wittgenstein's Vienna* by Allan Janik and Stephen Toulmin makes this case. But Perloff in effect removes Ludwig from his national origins in order to place him in a line with transnational artists and thinkers who influenced postmodern movements in American culture such as "language" poetry and Pop Art. "Indeed, the enigmatic *Tractatus* may be closer to the language games of Duchamp or Gertrude Stein than to the erotic exhibitionism characteristic of Klimt and Schiele, much less the witty, amoral ironies of Schnitzler. The avant-garde connection is, in any case, the one I now want to consider," she writes (1996; 37–38).

With this comment, we have come full circle. Wittgenstein's Vienna becomes Perloff's New York and California, primary sites of "postmodern movements in American culture such as 'language' poetry and Pop Art." Jewish Vienna is no longer characterized exclusively by the tastes of upper-class sophisticates. Wittgenstein survives, Perloff suggests, in the sensibility of Rauschenberg, of Cage, of O'Hara, of Charles Bernstein and Susan Howe. Wittgenstein was a survivor, Perloff also suggests, because he accepted the idea of language as a foreign country, as itself a space of estrangement. Perloff's experience as a transnational citizen whose thoughts about the fluidity of identity were formed through the experiences of refugee displacement, name change, immigration to the United States as a girl, as well as her desire to discover a flexible relation to Jewishness that her Viennese forebears denied at great peril, are mirrored in her changing attitudes toward literary scholarship as an American academic, but also in her version of Wittgenstein as a resilient figure, one whose sensibility compares to Perloff's open-minded attitudes toward personal identity, citizenship, religious affiliation, and aesthetic predilection.

Notes

1. Since it is true that Nietzsche criticizes the notion of the "ego" or the "I," the true autobiography of someone, so to speak, is always the rather hidden story of their drives.

Here are a couple relevant passages: "They [philosophers] claim it is a question of 'the truth'—when at bottom it is only a question of themselves. Or rather: their most violent impulse is brought to light with all the impudence and innocence of a fundamental impulse: it makes itself sovereign and, if possible, the aim of every thing and every event. The philosopher is only a kind of occasion and chance through which the impulse is finally able to speak" (quoted in Pierre Klossowski, *Nietzsche and the Vicious Circle,* Chicago: University of Chicago Press, 4–5). "I have tried to show, on the other hand, what instincts have been active behind all these *pure* theoreticians—how they have all, under the spell of their instincts, gone fatalistically for something that was 'truth' *for them*—for them and only for them. The conflict between different systems, including that between epistemological scruples, is a conflict between quite definite instincts" (*Will to Power* Sec. 227).

2. Perloff defines collage as "the setting side by side or juxtaposition of disparate materials without commitment to explicit syntactical relations between elements" (*Dance of the Intellect* 183).

Works Cited

Boyarin, Daniel, Daniel Itzkovitz, and Ann Pellegrini. *Queer Theory and the Jewish Question.* New York: Columbia University Press, 2003.

Perloff, Marjorie. *The Dance of the Intellect: Studies in the Poetry of the Pound Tradition.* London: Cambridge University Press, 1985.

———. *The Poetics of Indeterminacy: Rimbaud to Cage.* Princeton, NJ: Princeton University Press, 1981.

———. *Radical Artifice: Writing Poetry in the Age of Media.* Chicago: University of Chicago Press, 1991.

———. *The Vienna Paradox: A Memoir.* New York: New Directions, 2004.

———. *Wittgenstein's Ladder: Poetic Language and the Strangeness of the Ordinary.* Chicago. University of Chicago Press, 1996.

———, ed., with Charles Junkerman. *John Cage: Composed in America.* Chicago: University of Chicago Press, 1994.

"Sound Scraps, Vision Scraps"

Paul Celan's Poetic Practice

Marjorie Perloff

> Thirty-four years after his death, Paul Celan's status as the greatest German-language poet of the second half of the twentieth century seems assured. His oeuvre—roughly 900 pages of poetry distributed over eleven volumes, 250 pages of prose, more than 1,000 published correspondence, and nearly 700 pages of poetry translated from eight languages—has by now received massive critical attention. . . . And yet the work continues to be to a great extent terra incognita.
>
> —Pierre Joris[1]

Paul Celan's reception, at least in the English-speaking world, has always been connected to his status as great Holocaust Poet, the poet who showed that, Adorno's caveat notwithstanding, it was possible to write poetry, even great poetry, in the German language, after Auschwitz. As "Poet, Survivor, Jew" (the subtitle of John Felstiner's groundbreaking study of 1995),[2] Celan has become an iconic figure: continental philosophers from Hans-Georg Gadamer to Phillipe Lacoue-Labarthe have read Celan's poetic oeuvre as a post–World War II Book of Wisdom. The result, ironically, has been to place Celan in a kind of solitary confinement, a private cell where his every "circumcised word" (Jacques Derrida's term)[3] can be examined for its allegorical weight and theological import, even as, so Pierre Joris suggests in the excellent introduction to his new *Selections,* its actual poetic forms and choices are largely ignored. "Perhaps the greatest risk for the reading of Celan in our time," writes the poet Charles Bernstein, "is that we have venerated him, in the process of removing him not only from his own time and place, but also from our own poetic horizon. . . . [A] crippling exceptionalism has made his work a symbol of his fate rather than an active matrix for an ongoing poetic practice."[4]

It is that ongoing poetic practice I want to consider here. What follows is thus an experiment in reading Celan, not as exemplary Holocaust poet or as philosophical thinker, but quite simply as a mid-twentieth-century poet. What, to begin with is Celan's radius of discourse? Is he a Modernist? A postmodernist? Does he believe that language can *signify* a reality outside itself? What is Celan's relationship to the various poetic currents dominant when he came of age? Is his a self-contained semiosis in the vein of John Ashbery? Or is Celan perhaps a proto-language poet? However unique a poet we take him to be, Celan does, after all, write out of a tradition, a culture, a history.

Suppose we take a poem often cited as conveying Celan's basic sense that the *ground* of language has become an *abyss,* that language is forced to speak the unspeakable. I am thinking of the title poem of *Sprachgitter* (1959), a title whose translation can only be reductive: *sprach* (past tense of *sprechen*) means "spoke," *Sprache* refers to both individual speech and language: in other words, to both *langue* and *parole.* As for *Gitter,* the noun designates "grate," "gate," "fence" and "mesh" as well as "grille." "For fishermen," Anne Carson points out in her study of Celan and Simonides,[5] "it means a net or trap. For mineralogists, the lattice formation of a crystal." Whether fence or net, *Gitter* is always associated with some sense of blockage or obstruction. Here is the poem:

Sprachgitter

Augenrund zwischen den Stäben.

Flimmertier Lid
rudert nach oben,
gibt einen Blick frei.

Iris, Schwimmerin, traumlos und trüb:
der Himmel, herzgrau, muß nah sein.

Schräg, in der eisernen Tülle,
Der blakende Span.
Am Lichtsinn
errätst du die Seele.

(Wär ich wie du. Wärst du wie ich.
Standen wir nicht
unter einem Passat?
Wir sind Fremde.)

Die Fliesen. Darauf,
dicht beieinander, die beiden
herzgrauen Lachen:

zwei
Mundvoll Schweigen.

Speech Grille

Eyeround between the bars.
Flitterbug lid
rows upward
sets a glance free.

Iris, swimmer, dreamless and dim;
the sky, heartgray, must be near.

Slanting, in the iron spout
the smouldering splinter.
By its lightsense
you guess the soul.

(Were I like you. Were you like me.
Did we not stand
under *one* Passat?
We are strangers.)

The flagstones. On them,
right next to each other, the two
heartgray puddles:
two
mouthfuls of silence. (my translation)[6]

Poststructuralist theorists have consistently taken "Speech Grille" as representative of Celan's post-Holocaust estrangement from language, an estrangement that culminates in what this particular poem refers to in the inscrutable *zwei / Mundvoll Schweigen.* In Jacques Derrida's famous essay "Shibboleth for Paul Celan," "Speech Grille" is cited in a discussion of the poet's "witness[ing] to the universal by virtue of absolute singularity," the singularity of the *Shibboleth,* that "word used as a test for detecting foreigners, or persons from another district, by their pronunciation," more loosely, "a catchword or formula adopted by a party or sect, by which their adherents or followers may be discerned, or those not their followers may be excluded."[7]

The original *Shibboleth,* as the OED notes and as Derrida reminds us, was the Hebrew word used by Jephthah in Judges 12:4–6, as a test-word by which to distinguish the fleeing Ephraimites (who could not pronounce the *sh*) from his own men, the Gileadites.[8] *Shibboleth,* Derrida argues, thus "marks the multiplicity within language, insignificant difference as the condition of meaning" (31). And that mark of difference or trace, which becomes comprehensible only in relation to a particular site or place," is, for Derrida, the key to Celan's poetic language. His is a "ciphered singularity: irreducible to any concept, to any knowledge," a "singularity which gathers a multiplicity *in eins,* and through whose grid a poem remains readable. . . . The poem speaks, even should none of its references be intelligible, none other than the Other, the one to whom it addresses itself. . . . Even if it does not reach and leave its mark on, at least it calls to, the Other. Address takes place" (35–36).

The Shibboleth must also be understood as a "circumcised word." The poet witnesses the universal—the wounding emblematized by circumcision, the Holocaust, (death in general) "by virtue of absolute singularity, by virtue of and in the name of the other, the stranger, you toward whom I must take a step which, without bringing me nearer to you, without exchanging myself with you, without being assured passages, lets the word pass and assigns us, if not to the one, at least to the same. We were already assigned to it, dwelling beneath the same contrary wind" (35). The reference is to the fourth stanza of "Sprachgitter," with its reference to the strong Atlantic wind called Passat:

(Were I like you. Were you like me.
Did we not stand
under *one* Passat?
We are strangers.) (Derrida 55)

Strangers because we cannot speak the Shibboleth, the lost word (Holocaust, Jew, the exterminated family, death). The stanza above is thus one more instance of the inability of language to render the unspeakable, except as trace structure. *Circumcision,* Derrida posits, "designate[s] an operation, the surgical act of cutting, but also and equally the state, the quality, the condition of being circumcised" (63). The poetic word is opened only to be closed again; it names only to withdraw the name as soon as it is given. "The circumcised word is *first of all* written, at once both incised and excised in a body, which may be the body of a language and which in any case always binds the body to language" (67). More specifically it is also the German language that must be "circumcised," given that it had been debased by its status as the language of the Nazis (67). In Celan's own frequently cited words:

> No matter how alive its traditions, with most sinister events in its Memory, most questionable developments around it, [German poetry] can no longer speak the language which many willing ears seem to expect. Its language has become more sober, more factual. It distrusts “beauty.” It tries to be truthful. If I may search for a visual analogy while keeping in mind the polychrome of apparent actuality: it is a “greyer” language, a language which wants to locate even its “musicality” in such a way that it has nothing in common with the “euphony” which more or less blithely continued to sound alongside the greatest horrors.[9]

In its “circumcised” version of the German language, Derrida suggests, Celan’s poetry becomes an offering of something that the reader can never fully understand, a cipher of a language that can never quite speak the unspeakable and is hence a speaking silence. As Dennis J. Schmidt puts it, Celan’s “‘Two mouthfuls of silence’ (*zwei / Mundvoll Schweigen*) . . . mark the place of the poem for Celan . . . such silence is not to be confused with mere quiet but needs to be heard as the unvocalized voice of the poem. . . . a voice estranged from language, rendering the effort to listen to language in the poem rare, demanding, and painful at once.”[10] And the classicist poet-philosopher Anne Carson reads *Sprachgitter* (in her translation, “Language Mesh”) as “a word Celan uses to describe the operations of his own poetic language, in a poem about strangeness and strangers.” And she asks: “Does Celan use *Gitter* to imply passage, blockage or salvaging of speech? Mesh may do all these. Celan may mean all of these . . . The German language offers Celan a qualified hospitality, a murderously impure meal. . . . Celan can make himself at home in his mother tongue only by a process of severe and parsimonious redaction. . . . Mesh limits what he can say but may also cleanse it. As crystal it cleanses to the essence. As net it salvages what is cleansed” (Carson 30–31). The “action of estrangement [that] takes place in this poem,” Carson concludes, “represents, in some part, the condition of intimate alienation that obtained between Celan and his own language” (33).

The alienation of the poet from his own language, the status of a given word in that language as Shibboleth, designed to be misunderstood even by the Other addressed, the “mouthfuls of silence” the poet proffers the reader—these analyses of Celan’s poetic are based, we should note, on a very particular set of assumptions about the way Celan’s poetry—or, for that matter, any poetry—works. For Derrida in particular, a given poem is no more than an entrance into a larger poetic universe where particular thematic motifs can be traced. Indeed, the book jacket copy for *Sovereignties in Ques-*

tion: The Poetics of Paul Celan, the recently published book from Fordham University Press (2005) that brings together the 1984 "Shibboleth" with a number of later Derrida essays and interviews concerning Celan, contains the following description:

> Central themes include the date or signature and its singularity; the notion of the trace; temporal structures of futurity and the "to come"; the multiplicity of language and questions of translation; such speech acts as witness, promise, and testimony, but also lying and perjury; the possibility of the impossible; and, above all, the question of the poem as addressed and destined beyond knowledge, seeking to speak to and for the irreducible other. . . . Derrida's approach to a poem is a revelation on many levels, from the most concrete ways of reading—for example, his analysis of a sequence of personal pronouns—to the most sweeping imperatives of human existence.

It is true that Derrida's "Shibboleth" contains some discussion of personal pronouns, of dates and place names, and of particular events commemorated in the poems, even as no single poem is discussed as a whole. From start to finish, Derrida mines the poems, short as most of them are, for particular lines or even single words that point to his larger interpretation of Celan's oeuvre. The "circumcised word," it seems, is one that is regularly taken out of context and linked to other related words so as to produce a coherent account of Celan's poetics. Moreover, in this discussion of lyric poetry—and here Derrida is representative of philosophical critics in general—nothing is said about sound structure, rhythm, lineation, syntax, or the actual organization of the poem in question. Such reading, we might say, is more properly a reading *for.* Having found the phrase, *Nach /dem Unwiederholbaren* ("After / the unrepeatable") in *A La Pointe Acérée* (*Gedichte* 146), the strategy is to find echoes and analogues of *Das Unwiederholbare* and its relationship to the *Herzgewordenes* ("what has become heart"), never mind the surrounding details.

As such, the name Celan has become a cipher for profundity, for the true voice of the Holocaust in all its horror and pain—a voice that of necessity presents what Werner Hamacher has called "a language which appears at odds with itself" (Hamacher xi). Celan, writes Anne Carson "is a poet who uses language *as if he were always translating*" (28). Pierre Joris similarly remarks that "Celan's language, though German on the surface, is a foreign language, even for native speakers. . . . The Celanian dynamic . . . involves a complex double movement . . . of love for his mother tongue and of . . .

strife against her murderers who are the originators and carriers of that same tongue."[11] This emphasis on double movement is even more prominent in Adorno: "Celan's poems," he notes, "want to speak of the most extreme horror through silence. Their truth content itself becomes negative. They imitate a language beneath the helpless language of human beings, indeed beneath all organic language: It is that of the dead speaking of stones and stars."[12]

A language beyond all organic language, a language that looks like translation rather than "original," a language at odds with itself, Shibboleth, circumcised word, and so on. How do we reconcile such views with Celan's own insistence that "This language, notwithstanding its inalienable complexity of expression, is concerned with *precision.* It does not transfigure or render 'poetical'; it names, it posits, it tries to measure the area of the given and the possible" (*Collected Prose* 16)? In what follows, I want to explore that "precision"—what Ezra Pound called the "luminous detail"—by reading Celan, not as the "special case" he is usually taken to be, but as a sophisticated postwar European poet, whose native language and culture were German—more specifically the German of the Austro-Hungarian Empire into which he was born—but whose mature years were lived in France, with his wife Gisèle de Lestrange, a woman from an aristocratic, Catholic background, and his son Eric. His real last name *Antschel* had become, by a kind of anagram, the French-sounding Celan.

2. On the Fence

In a draft for "The Meridian" (the speech Celan gave on the occasion of receiving the Georg Büchner Prize in 1960), the poet notes, "The pictorial (*Bildhaftes*), that is by no means something visual; it is, like everything connected to speech, a mental phenomenon . . . a manifestation of speech as something derived from writing, therefore from something that is silent." And he adds the parenthetical note (*Sprachgitter, das ist auch das* Sprechgitter, *macht das sichtbar* ["Speech-grille, that is also speak-grille, makes that evident"] *Gedichte* 643). The German word *Sprechgitter* is not a neologism. On the contrary, it refers to an object to be found at hardware or electric stores: namely, the transom above or below the doorbell, used in apartment or office buildings to announce one's arrival and desire to be buzzed in (figure 1). As such, a *Sprechgitter* serves as the conduit from a speaker's voice to that of an unseen (and perhaps unknown) addressee—-a situation that, as we shall see, is indeed germane to Celan's poem.

But *Sprechgitter* is also an architectural term, relating to the medieval church. In the notes to the Suhrkamp *Gesamtausgabe* (*Gedichte* 652–653)

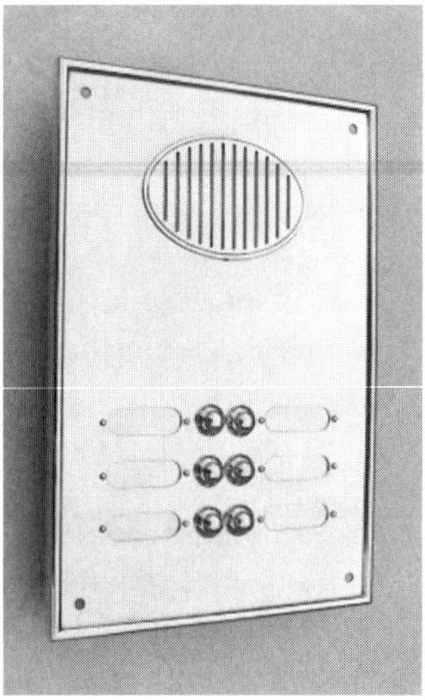

1. "Milano" doorbell with *Sprechgitter*. Firma Replicata, Germany.

Barbara Wiedemann informs us that *Sprachgitter* was written in response to a picture postcard Celan received from the author and publisher Günther Neske, with whom he planned to publish his next collection.[13] The card, dated *Pfingsten* (Whitsuntide) 1957, bears the image of the fourteenth-century *Sprechgitter* or Confessional Screen (figure 2) of the former convent church (1300) called *Klarissenkloster* at Pfullingen in Württemberg (figure 3). The *Sprechgitter* pictured on the card was, according to the official guide to the Visit of German Monuments, "the only contact the convent's nuns had with the outside world."[14]

The *Klarissenkloster* itself was named for Santa Clara of Assisi (1194–1253). According to legend, the aristocratic eighteen-year old Clara, having fallen under the spell of Saint Francis's preaching (see figure 4), secretly left her father's house in the dark of night, and "proceeded to the humble chapel of the Porziuncula, where Saint Francis and his disciples met her with lights in their hands. Clara then laid aside her rich dress, and Saint Francis, having cut off her hair, clothed her in a rough tunic and a thick veil, and in this way the young heroine vowed herself to the service of Jesus Christ."[15] From then on, no one in the outside world saw Clara again. As foundress of the Order of Poor Ladies, also known as Poor Claras, she lived in the strictest poverty. In her later years as Abbess, Clara helped the blind and ill Saint Francis by erecting a little wattle hut for him in an olive grove close to the monastery; it was here that he composed his famous "Canticle of the Sun." Another time, Clara defended her convent from the troops of Frederick II, who were trying to enter by a ladder placed against an open window of the abbey. She raised

2. Confessional Box, Church at Oradour, fourteenth century.

3. Klosterkirche, Pfüllingen, Germany. Thirteenth century; restored 1539.

4. Santa Clara of Assisi as a little girl with St. Francis.

the ciborium bearing the Host so high that the soldiers fell backward as if dazzled, and the others who were ready to follow them took flight. Both these stories—the transfiguration of the blind Saint Francis and the dazzling of the invading army of Frederick II—fostered the belief that the Holy Water of the Church of Santa Clara in Assisi could cure those with eye-diseases, and it was hence referred to, in a nice pun, as *aqua clara.* The abbess was canonized in 1255. In 1958, a year before the publication of Celan's *Sprachgitter,* Pope Pius XII also declared Santa Clara to be the patroness of *television* because of her legendary ability to see into the distance.[16]

Celan's poem, prompted by Neske's picture postcard, contains a network of references to the eye and its inability to see. The opening line *Augenrund zwischen den Stäben* ("Eyeround between the bars"), presents the image of the poet's eye (or is it the priest's behind the confessional screen?) trying to penetrate the bars so as to *see* what is on the other side. The coinage *Augenrund* can also refer to the round made by the poet's eyes making a circle as they take in the scene and try to penetrate what is *behind* or inside the *Stäben.* The theme is carried on in the next two stanzas: the "shimmering" eyelid "rows" upward, stealing a glance at the ceiling. And beneath that lid, "swims" the iris, dreamless and dim or drab. A "swimming" iris means a watery or blurred eye; indeed, it can be the sign of the detachment of the retina.

In Greek mythology, Iris is the Goddess of the Rainbow, the swift- footed messenger of the Gods, who often assumed the shape of a mortal, known only to those who received her message. When a quarrel arose among the gods, Zeus sent Iris to the river Styx in the Underworld to bring back the golden jug of sacred water, which signified the oath of the gods. But in "Speech-Grille," the blurry iris beneath the flickering lid suggests that the message of the Gods, like the healing *aqua clara* of the Abbey, cannot penetrate the speech screen. There is no response from its other side. Hence the poet posits that a "heartgray" sky, its gloom reflected in the dark, dim iris, must be near—a sky in which the rainbow of the Covenant is nowhere to be glimpsed.

The fourth stanza introduces a new image, but one which metonymically relates to the eye. *Schräg in der eisenern Tülle, / der blakende Span: Tülle,* meaning spout, also brings to mind the silken fabric called Tüll (*tulle* in French); *Span is* a shaving or splinter. What is this smoldering splinter, slanting in its silken or silvery container? If we assume that the speaker facing the grille, a speaker whose eyelid "rows" upward to take a glance at what is above, has entered a church, the iron spout, seen at an angle, is probably a censer, hanging from the ceiling (figure 5). The roundness of the censer matches the "eyeround" of line 1, even as the smoking splinter within it is analogous to a mote in the poet's eye—the mote that evidently makes the iris swim, the dream fade, and the lid shimmer or flicker. The conclusion drawn in lines 9–10 thus seems nothing if not logical: it is the "lightsense" experienced by the churchgoer that animates the soul, the "lightsense" Clara could offer to the blind St. Francis and the invaders at the abbey's gate. But here there is no light: the soul remains in darkness.

What the poet is suggesting is that for him, there is no grace of God, not only not in this Christian church, but perhaps nowhere. His companion, however, mentioned for the first time in line 11 (and most probably a veiled allusion to Celan's French Catholic wife Gisèle de Lestrange) may be reacting differently. Hence the question:

Were I like you. Were you like me.
Did we not stand
Under *one* Passat?

These lines (placed in parentheses, of which more below) express the poet's painful desired to be *at one* with his wife, to *share* with her as his other. But

5. Smoking censer in medieval church.

the recognition (line 14) is that this is not the case: "We are strangers." Hence, on leaving the church, the flagstones are always and only flagstones, and these, in turn, are covered by two "heartgray" *Lachen* (note the repetition of the adjective used in line 6). *Lachen,* in this context, has the primary meaning of puddles or pools: two gray pools of water blot the flagstones. But *Lachen* also means "notches"—the stones are notched with the sign of the two unknown strangers—and in the singular, the noun "Lachen" is the common word "laughter"—in this case, a mirthless, hollow chuckle of sorts. In all three cases, the flagstones reflect the "heartgray" condition of the lovers: the desire for communion—with hidden priest? God? and especially the "you" who is his beloved—has failed. All that remains are their two mouthfuls of silence. The poem's conclusion links sight and speech: both are, at least for the moment, suspended. As Celan wrote his friend Joachim Seng, "I tell myself that in *Sprachgitter* the existential, the difficulty of all speaking (to one another) and at the same time the structure of that speaking is what counts" (*Gedichte* 643).

To say, as does Hamacher, that a poem like "Speech-Grille" embodies a "language at odds with itself," or that, in Anne Carson's words, *Sprachgitter* represents "the condition of intimate alienation that obtained between Celan and his own language," may well be true as a generality, but it doesn't get us very far. For here—and this is usually the case in Celan's work—the issues are quite specific. To be literal: the poet and his wife have evidently wandered into an unnamed abbey church; the poet eyes the confessional screen or barred side chapel, ruminating on whether he can, in Wordsworth's words, "see into the life of things," if he can make contact with God or at least with his companion. But there is a mote in his eye, figured by the splinter in the swinging censer, as by the tick in his eyelid and the "swimming" of his iris; this poet is neither a reliable messenger nor does a message from outside come through to him. It is not so much speech but vision that fails and the heart that shuts. Does his companion feel the same way? Evidently not, so that separation occurs: the watery eyes of the suppliants are replaced by two gray puddles, or again, the mote in the poet's eye becomes the "heartgray" notch on the stone. Blockage prevents both vision and speech.

Sprachgitter can thus be read, first and foremost, as a poem about failed love, failed communion, both between lovers and between the poet and his God. As in the case of Santa Clara, the outside world—what Yeats called the "emperor's drunken soldiery"—recedes. And that failure of communication, critics like Joris and Carson have noted, spells out a necessary alienation not only from the poet's *intimates* and friends but from the German language itself. In "Memory of Words" (1990), the poet Edmund Jabès maintains that "the German language, though it is the one in which [Celan] immersed himself, is also the one which for a time those who claimed to be its protectors had forbidden him. If it is indeed the language of his pride, it is also that of his humiliation. . . . There is something paradoxical . . . to totally invest yourself in the language of a country that rejects you."[17] But, strictly speaking—and here I think we must be strict—Germany had never been Celan's country, and his language, as deformed and unsituated as it seems to be, should perhaps also be understood as the language of Karl Kraus and Robert Musil, rather than primarily that of the poet's "humiliation." True, "Speech-grille" contains a number of elaborate neologisms, beginning with the title—*Sprachgitter, Augenrund, Flimmertier*—and unusual compounds such as *herzgrau* and *Lichtsinn* as well as exotic references like "Passat" (the standard, but foreign-sounding German term for trade wind). But on the whole the syntactic locutions, if not the diction, seem familiar enough, especially to an Austrian ear like mine. And here we must remember that Celan's German was never that of Berlin or Frankfurt but the German of Vienna, which was the center and magnet of the Austro-Hungarian empire, into which Celan was belatedly born in 1920 two years after its dissolution. For his parents, the "official" German of Vienna was the necessary language of the educated class: Paul's mother Fritzi always spoke German to her son and taught him the German classics. Such colloquial locutions as *gibt einen*

Blick frei, der Himmel muß nah sein, errätst du die Seele, or *Wär ich wie du. Wärst du wich ich,* testify to the naturalness, if only an intermittent one, of Celan's speech-base. He was, in other words, more at home in German—his particular variant of German—than he or his readers were given to admit. Then, too, we must remember that Celan lived in Vienna from 1947 to 1948 before moving to Paris—and that he had an intense affair—and drawn-out correspondence—with the Austrian writer Ingeborg Bachmann.

Indeed, the difficulty of Celan's lyric has less to do with word choice or even word order than with the absence of any and all connective tissue, whether causal, temporal, or even paratactic, in his poetic discourse. What is missing, for starters, are the pronouns. *Augenrund zwischen den Stäben:* we surmise that the eye is the poet's own but we cannot be sure, and lines 2–4 provide no clues. In line 5, "Iris" is represented in the third person, as "The Swimmer" (female noun), and hence evokes the goddess as well as the poet's eye. The abrupt introduction of "du" in line 11 thus comes as something of a shock: here, suddenly and parenthetically, is an address to another person. But after the announcement that "We are strangers" in line 14, the poem lapses back into its blank, subjectless third-person mode, culminating in those mouthfuls (whose?) of silence.

In the same vein, a given line rarely prepares us for the next. It is not a foregone conclusion, for example, that because the iris is a swimmer, "dreamless and dim," that the sky must be equally drab and grey. Again, the perspective of the smoking splinter in lines 7–8 does not explain why or how the "Lightsense" allows us to guess the soul's status. And there are no signals to indicate the shift from indoors to outdoors between lines 14 and 15. This is, in other words, an extremely oblique lyric, stripped of temporal and spatial markers that might explain what is going on. Then, too, pun and allusion produce great density: "Iris" is both the colored part of the eye and the Greek Goddess, "tulle" suggests cloth as well as spout, "lightsense" can be the yearning for light (think of Saint Francis) but also the unbearable lightness of being, which may define the soul. And the Passat wind looks and sounds like *Passah,* German for Pesach or Passover;[18] it thus interjects a Jewish note into the otherwise Christian imagery.

Other poets—Mallarmé in French, Hölderlin in German, Emily Dickinson in English—have written lyric as obscure and condensed as Celan's. Dickinson, for that matter, introduces at least as many neologisms as does Celan, and her syntax is equally complex and disjunctive. Like Dickinson, Celan uses extensive sound patterning to relate what is otherwise disparate. Consider the internal rhyme of *Flimmertier—Schwimmerin—Himmel,* the alternate alliteration of *Dicht beieinander die beiden,* the alliteration of *traumlos und trüb,* of *Himmel, herzgrau,* and of *darauf, / dicht.* The dominant rhythm of line 1:

/ x ∧ / x x / x
Aúgeͯnrûnd´ zwíscheͯn deͯn Stábeͯn

where a dactyl, whose third syllable has secondary stress, is followed by trochee and ambiphrach, is repeated in truncated form in line 2:

/ x ∧ /
Flímmeͯrtiêr Líd

And with variations throughout. The penultimate line with its \break after the monosyllabic *Zwei,* produce the final tongue twister:

/ ∧ /
Múndvôll Schwéigên

Here the heavy consonants sound as if the words are hard to spit out, as indeed they are. Sounds of silence would be one thing, but mouthfuls of being silent, of refusing or being unable to speak, have a sinister edge, drowning the poignancy of those eight monosyllables of the utmost simplicity—

/ x x / || / x x /
Wár îch wiͯe dú. wárst dû wiͯe ích.

—a conditional that cannot be satisfied despite the rhythmic identity between the two hemistychs.

Finally, a word about punctuation. Celan's opening line, a suspended noun phrase, would seem to need no punctuation, yet Celan concludes it with a period, thus emphasizing its separation from what follows. Similarly «Wär ich wie du» ends, not on a note of question, as the intonation may suggest, but again with two periods, the punctuation itself implying that there is no match between the first conditional and the second. Indeed, the short nonsentences closed by periods retain their separate identity. More important, the whole fifth stanza is placed in parentheses, as if to suggest that the actual conversation between «I» and «you» occurs only in memory or perhaps in supposition; it stands outside the main frame, itself a kind of *Augenrund* ("eyeround") between the bars that separate the poet from his interlocutor. Confession, that is to say, cannot take place.

Such overpunctuation becomes a Celan signature, as in *Engführung* ("Stretto"), where we find passages like the following:

Asche.
Asche, Asche.
Nacht.
Nacht-und-Nacht.—Zum
Aug geh, zum feuchten.
Zum
Aug geh,
Zum feuchten—
(*Gedichte* 114–115)

Ashes.
Ashes, ashes.
Night.
Night-and-night.—To
the eye, go, to the moist.
To
the eye, go,
to the moist—[19]

Here the poetic tension arises from the simple repetition that should be incantatory but is just the opposite because of the passage's line-breaks and punctuation, creating a feverish rhythm. I am reminded of such Wallace Stevens titles as «How to Live. What to Do—» a title whose poignancy surely has a lot to do with the period rather than expected comma after the word «Live.» The comma would supply continuity, the drive toward a way of being. But the period suggests that the poet feels there is no way to live. The sentence merely stops. Similar effects are found within Stevens's later poems: for example, in «No Possum, No Sop, No Taters,» the couplets are overpunctuated, as in:

It is deep January. The sky is hard.
The stalks are firmly rooted in ice.

And in «Debris of Life and Mind» the final couplet reads:

The most gay and yet not so gay as it was.
Stay here. Speak of familiar things a while.[20]

Late Modernist poetry—Celan's, Stevens's, or, for example, Beckett's poetic prose, is characterized by such condensation and reduction of its symbolist base, its dissolution of the speaking subject into the fragmented world it inhabits. But it remains, I would argue, a «high» mode of lyric discourse, avoiding the popular culture references, verbal-visual disjunctions, shifts from comic to serious, and found text of the poetry to come in the later twentieth century.

Then, too, this is a poetry that still respects—as later poetry will not—the emblematic status of the natural and human world. Celan's imagery—eye, mouth, grass, stone, flower, tree—is the imagery of Dickinson and Stevens as well; but for Celan, the natural world always bears the imprint of technological invention as well. Consider the late minimalist poem in *Atemwende* ("Breathturn," 1965) that gave Celan's 1967 volume its title:

FADENSONNEN
Über der grauschwarzen Ödnis,
Ein baum-
Hoher Gedanke
Greift sich den Lichtton: es sind
Noch Lieder zu singen jenseits
Der Menschen. (*Gedichte* 179)

THREADSUNS
above the greyblack wastes.
A tree-
high thought
grasps the light-tone: there are
still songs to sing beyond
mankind.[21]

Apollinaire's great 1913 poem "Zone," concludes with the startling image of the setting sun as a cut throat: *soleil cou coupé.* But for Apollinaire, the sun still existed, a perfect sphere, an orb of light, or ball of fire that might be perceived as cut off. For Celan, by contrast, there is no more single sun—no center, no point of origin—only a multiplicity of threadsuns—thin slivers of sun or light rays, fragile and breakable. The poet's life hangs, so to speak, by a sun-thread above the gray-black wasteland in which he dwells. But in line 3 a tree-high thought counters his despair, for it "grasps the light-tone." The English translation, which suggests that the German noun means no more than a "light tone" or "tone of light" is deceptive, for *Lichtton* is a technical

6. Welte *Licht-Ton* or Light Organ, 1936.

term from the annals of early sound film. The *Welte* Light-Tone or Light-Organ, invented in Germany in 1936 (figure 6) was an electronic instrument using electro-optically controlled tone generators. As the Welte web site informs us, "A glass disk was printed with 18 different waveforms giving three different timbres for all the octave registers of each single note. The glass tone wheel rotated over a series of photoelectric cells, filtering a light beam that controlled the sound timbre and pitch."[22]

If we thus think of "light-tone" as a controlled sound pitch mechanically produced on celluloid film, the poem's thrust becomes obvious. Like Stevens's "palm at the end of the mind," "stand[ing] on the edge of space," in "Of Mere Being,"[23] Celan's "tree-high thought" grasps for the sound pitch that allows his own particular film strip to come to life. "There are," it seems, "still songs to sing beyond / mankind." A *Sprachgitter,* let us recall, is not an impenetrable language wall; its openings allow the threadsuns of song to come through, even as "The wind moves slowly in the branches," of Stevens's palm. Indeed, to read Celan against the late Stevens is to become aware that, by midcentury, Pound's Imagist credo that "The natural object is always the adequate symbol," had given way to a curious sleight-of-hand whereby an image like *Lichtton* ("light-tone") can morph into an obscure—but highly specific—reference, in this case to the new technology of the period.

Such odd shifts are by no means unique to Celan: his contemporary

Samuel Beckett, for example, was fond of introducing arcane words like *ravanastron* (an Indian stringed instrument played with a bow) into the texture of otherwise flat, sober descriptions by his protagonists, in this case, Watt. But just as Beckett's ravanastron hangs on an ordinary wall in a "large bare white room,"[24] so Celan's «threadsunned» *Lichtton* is found among the "heartgray" puddles on the paving stones. It is this tension between the Imagist-Symbolist model of the early century and the "illegible" texts to come that makes Celan's lyric poetry so challenging—a pivot in the tradition that takes us from Hölderlin, Dickinson, and Mallarmé to the elliptical fragments of Wallace Stevens, George Oppen and Susan Howe. I conclude with the following seven-line poem from *Lichtzwang* (*Lightduress*):

Was es An Sternen Bedarf
schüttet sich aus,

deiner Hände laubgrüner Schatten
sammelt es ein,

freudig zerbeiß ich
das münzenkernige
Schicksal.

What's Required of Stars,
pours itself out.

your hands' leafgreen shadow
gathers it in.

joyfully I bite in two
coin-powered
fate. (*Gedichte* 287, my translation)

Here syntax seems uncomplicated, the only obscure word being *münzenkernige*. This compound combines *Münzen* ("coins") with the adjective *kernig* for "robust," "strong," "powerful," the neologism formed on the analogy of the epithet "high-powered." But, as in the case of such related texts as Beckett's *Imagination Dead Imagine* (which, incidentally, has often been said to refer to a crematorium), we know what the words "say" well enough, but not what they mean. "What's required of stars" is surely their light—a light that is "gathered" or collected into the foliage-green or "leafgreen shadow" of "your hands." But does such gathering dissipate the shadow or vice-versa? And does biting one's coin-powered destiny in half mark resignation to one's fate or the triumph above it? "You know," we read in Stevens's "Of Mere Being," "that it is not the reason / That makes us happy or unhappy." But the speech-grille remains open, poised to receive those words that pour themselves into the waiting shadows.

Notes

1. Pierre Joris, "Introduction," Paul Celan, *Selections,* ed. Pierre Joris (Berkeley and Los Angeles: University of California Press, 2005), 3.

2. John Felstiner, *Paul Celan: Poet, Survivor, Jew* (New Haven, CT: Yale University Press, 1995).

3. Jacques Derrida, "Shibboleth for Paul Celan," trans. Joshua Wilner, in Aris Fioretos (ed.), *Word Traces: Readings of Paul Celan* (Baltimore: Johns Hopkins University Press, 1994), 3–72.

4. Charles Bernstein, "Celan's Folds and Veils," *Textual Practice* 18, 2 (Summer 2004): 200–201.

5. Anne Carson, *Economy of the Unlost (Reading Simonides of Kios with Paul Celan)* (Princeton, NJ: Princeton University Press, 1999), 30.

6. Paul Celan, *Die Gedichte, Kommentierte Gesamtausgabe,* ed. with commentary by Barbara Wiedemann (Frankfurt: Suhrkamp, 2005), 99–100. All further references to the German text are to this edition. Compare to the following three published translations:

(1) Joachim Neugroschl, in Joris, Paul Celan, *Selections,* 63–64:

Speech-Grille
Eye-orb between the bars.

Ciliary lid
rows upwards,
releases a gaze.

Iris, swimmer, dreamless and dim:
the sky, heart-gray, must be near.

Skew, in the iron socket,
the smoldering splinter.
By the sense of light
you guess the soul.

(Were I like you. Were you like me.
did we not stand

under *one* tradewind
We are strangers.)

The tiles. Upon them,
close together, the two
heart-gray pools:
two
mouthfuls of silence.

(2) John Felstiner, translator, *Selected Poems and Prose of Paul Celan* (New York: Norton, 2000), 107:

Speech-Grille

Round eyed between the bars.

Flittering lid
paddles upward,
breaks a glance free.

Iris, the swimmer, dreamless and drab:
heaven, heartgray, must be near.

Aslant, in the iron socket
a smoldering chip.
By sense of light
you hit on the soul.

(Were I like you. Were you like me.
Did we not stand
Under *one* trade wind?
We are strangers.)

The flagstones. On them,
close by each other, both
heartgray puddles:
two mouthfuls of silence.

(3) Anne Carson, *Economy of the Unlost*, 31–32:

Language Mesh

Eyeround between the bars,
glimmeranimal lid

rows upward,
sets a look free.

Iris, swimmer, dreamless and dismal:
the sky heartgrey, must be near.

Slanted, in the iron socket
the smoking splinter,
By its lightsense
you guess the soul.

(Were I like you. Were you like me.
Stand we not
under *one* tradewind?
We are strangers.)

The pavingstones. On them,
tight by each other, the two
heartgrey pools:
two
mouthfuls of silence

I have taken the liberty of retranslating the poem because all of the above have some rationalizations or slightly misleading renditions. Neugroschl's "orb of light" (line 1), for example, seems an overtranslation of "eyeround." Again, Carson's "dismal" for *trüb*" is too emphatic in the context. And the verb in line 12 must be in the past tense, as in the original. And so on.

7. See *Oxford English Dictionary* (161), Vol. 9, #2; Derrida, "Shibboleth for Paul Celan," 55.

8. See *OED,* 1; Derrida, "Shibboleth for Paul Celan," 24–25.

9. Paul Celan, "Reply to a Questionnaire from the Flinker Bookstore, Paris, 1958," in *Collected Prose,* trans. Rosmarie Waldrop (New York: Sheep Meadow Press, 1986), 15–16.

10. Dennis J. Schmidt, "Black Milk and Blue: Celan and Heidegger on Pain and Language," in Fioretos 110–129; see page 110.

11. Pierre Joris, Introduction, Paul Celan, *Breathturn,* trans. Pierre Joris (Los Angeles: Sun & Moon, 1995), 42.

12. Theodor Adorno, *Aesthetic Theory,* 322.

13. *Gedichte* 632. In the event, the volume was published by S. Fischer instead.

14. See http: tag-des-offenen-denmals.de/laender/bw/reis_reutlingent/pfullingen.

15. See entry on "St. Clare of Assisi," *Catholic Encyclopedia,* http:www.newadvent.org/cathen/04004a.htm.

16. See the *Catholic Encyclopedia* online: http://www.newadvent.org/cathen/ (accessed January 28, 2006).

17. Edmond Jabès, *La mémoire des mots* (Paris: Fourbis, 1990); trans. Pierre Joris, in Joris, *Celan Selections,* 217–223; see page 217.

18. See Felstiner, *Celan,* 107.

19. Robert Kelly, trans., in Joris, *Celan Selections,* 69.

20. *The Collected Poems of Wallace Stevens* (New York: Alfred A. Knopf, 1961), 293, 338.

21. *Gedichte* 179; Celan, *Breathturn,* trans. Pierre Joris (Los Angeles: Sun & Moon, 1995), 84.

22. See Lichtton website: http://www.obsolete.com/120_years/machines/light_tone_organ/ (accessed January 25, 2006).

23. Wallace Stevens, "Of Mere Being," *The Palm at the End of the Mind: Selected Poems and a Play,* ed. Holly Stevens, 398 (New York: Archon Books, 1984).

24. Samuel Beckett, *Watt* (1953; London: John Calder, 1976), 68.

Language in the Dark

The Legacy of Walter Benjamin in the Opera *Shadowtime*

Charlie Bertsch

"Is it possible to forget without remembering that one has forgotten?" The words ring out clearly, in stark contrast to the ones that precede and follow them, forming an island of sense in a sea of sonic confusion. The woodwinds and horn notes that punctuate the preceding minutes of the score, distracting from the singing, have fallen away. And for once, only one voice is heard. Even so, the words don't sound right. There's a trace of a lisp in the voice. The pronunciation of "remembering" is askew, with a delay on the second syllable, creating an aural hyphen. The strings in the background underscore the vocalist's mannered delivery with a tension that holds no promise of release. If Lewis Carroll's *Alice in Wonderland* had been properly set to music, this is what his hookah-smoking caterpillar would have sounded like. Yet this remains one of the more accessible moments in composer Brian Ferneyhough's 2004 opera *Shadowtime.* Most of the time, even when a phrase or two can be discerned without difficulty, the overwhelming impression is anarchy, voices and instruments so at odds with one another that the music sounds more like an orchestra warming up than an actual performance.

Indeed, it's hard to imagine more uneasy listening. For those music lovers who keep their home or car stereo tuned to a frequency that plays a steady stream of Bach, Mozart, and Beethoven, *Shadowtime* is bound to be off-putting. Whereas the music of the masters creates a bubble of comfort that wards off everyday pressures, Ferneyhough's composition stabs violently into the personal space of its audience, savaging the illusion of serenity promoted within the world of mainstream classical music. But because *Shadowtime* reflects on the life and work of the leftist Jewish thinker Walter Benjamin, noted for the density of his melancholy, and focuses in particular on the tragic circumstances of his passing, as he was trying to flee German-occupied France in September 1940, the work's edginess is understandable. The burden of hearing *Shadowtime* serves a purpose. This is art that refuses to let you forget what you should always bear in mind. That means the Sho'ah, first and foremost, but also loss more generally.

The most obvious loss with which the opera confronts the listener is the meaning of the words it contains. The score's mannered cacaphony plays havoc with the poet Charles Bernstein's libretto, which uses Benjamin's fate as the starting point for a rich engagement with his ideas about language, time, and spirituality. Considered apart from the music, the text superbly demonstrates the poet's ability to balance theory and craft and could easily be considered one of the crowning achievements of his rich literary career. Drawing upon a startling variety of techniques, the text manages to be both accessible and esoteric, channeling the populist cadence of the Beats and the avant-garde silence of OUILIPO with equal aplomb.

As impressive as the libretto is, however, reading it in isolation is deceptive. Bernstein's words function differently when placed within the context of Ferneyhough's unapologetically avant-garde score. In many cases, they do not function as words at all. Indeed, the opera casts the bulk of the libretto in shadow, making the quest for comprehension feel futile. And that's no accident. Ferneyhough likes to layer voices, often presenting different portions of the text at the same time, until it becomes a palimpsest in which language is liberated from meaning. Even the portions of the opera that play the libretto "straight" tend to obscure meaning through the interplay of word and music.

Interestingly, Bernstein has expressed complete approval for the violence Ferneyhough's score does to the libretto, emphasizing the importance of, "the different things that you can't hear, that are not audible," and those, "that become audible at the price of other things not being audible." From his perspective, it is crucial that "you can't hear everything all at once in crystal clarity." Indeed, the very title of the opera testifies to the impossibility of full comprehension, drawing our attention to the interplay between what can and cannot be discerned. "The idea of the shadow or the echo is crucial to the whole meaning of the opera. And it's played out in this very issue of only partial legibility at any given time. When you move to another mode, you gain something and you lose something."[1] What is lost in the passage of his words into music is as important as what survives the journey.

Someone unfamiliar with Bernstein's poetry might imagine that he is merely being polite in defending the opera. How could a writer of his stature be happy about having the majority of his words hidden? The truth, though, is that he has devoted much of his literary career to promoting the approach to language that *Shadowtime* puts into practice. A passage from "The Lives of the Toll Takers," the long first poem in his 1994 collection *Dark City,* provides evidence, not only for his interest in a language of the shadows, but for the connection he perceives between this language and the political circumstances that led to Benjamin's untimely death. "The hidden language of the Jews: self-reproach, laden with / ambivalence, not this or this either, seeing five sides to / every issue, the old *pilpul* song and dance, obfuscation," he writes, highlighting the religious and ethnic underpinnings of the preference for indirection, "clowning as ingratiation, whose only motivation is never / offend, criticize only with a discountable barb: Genocide / is made of words like these."[2] The speaker's point here is, like that "hidden language of the Jews," hard to determine. Is he praising the capacity to see "five sides to every issue," or suggesting that the Holocaust may be the result of a refusal to see danger for what it is?

As the passage unfolds, however, it becomes clear that, whatever fault may lie with Jews "whose only motivation is never offend," the biggest problem with refusing to make things simple is how others perceive this tendency to obfuscate. "Pound laughing (with Nietzsche's gay laughter) all the way to the canon's bank spewing forth about the concrete value of gold," he continues, "the 'plain sense of the word,' a people rooted in the land they sow, and cashing in on such verbal usury." The motivation that Jews may have for avoiding the plainspoken does not matter to someone like Pound, who is willing to make use of centuries-old stereotypes in order to make his point that authentic communication must arise in a rootedness and clarity of purpose that can never be achieved in the diaspora.

The speaker in Bernstein's poem recognizes the extent to which the figure of the Wandering Jew gets conflated with the reluctance to take a stand in language. But, even as he recognizes the peril in indirection, he cannot bring himself to advocate its renunciation. "There is no plain sense of the word, / nothing is straightforward, / description a lie behind a lie: / but truths can still be told."[3] In the end, intellectual honesty wins out. Because pretending that there are not "five sides to every issue" in order to refute pernicious stereotypes would still represent "ingratiation" and in a particularly self-reproaching form, the only dignified solution for Jews caught in this dilemma is to take a stand *on* language, insisting that the ambivalence they discern derives, not from an instinct for deviousness, but the realization that there never has been, and never will be, a linguistic gold standard of the sort Pound longs for.

Bernstein's remark that there is "only partial legibility at any given time" looks rather different in light of this passage from *Dark City* and others like it in his work. Although he is referring to the status of words within the score for *Shadowtime,* it is hard not to impute allegorical significance to his statement as well, reading it as a gloss on the status of words within *any* act of communication. From this perspective, the poet has good reason to defend an opera that seems, on first hearing, to make his own impressive labor largely irrelevant. By preventing most of the words in the score from being understood, Ferneyhough is able to reveal something about the nature of language itself and, as a consequence, help make a point Bernstein has repeatedly sought to make.

Of course, we are only able to recognize the extent of that labor in the first place because the libretto was published separately. Budget considerations prevented it from being included with the recording of *Shadowtime,* as is typically the case with operas. And, although the use of supertitles could help audiences to hear some of Bernstein's words in performance, the overlapping of voices at many points in the score makes it impossible to display them in the proper order. Knowing that he can rely on the printed record to demonstrate both the beauty and power of his words and the fact that they are clearly preoccupied with the same "idea of the shadow or the echo" as the score gives Bernstein the sure footing that the opera itself denies.

While a closer look at Bernstein's libretto makes clear the extent to which its philosophical concerns coincide with those of Ferneyhough's score, it also reveals some important differences. First and foremost, the words convey a dark levity largely absent from the austere, discomfiting music. "Pools of Darkness," the scene mentioned at the beginning of this essay, is an excellent example. The character of Walter Benjamin converses with three giant mouths in the scene's first section, a headless ghoul in the second, "the two-headed figure of Karl Marx and Groucho Marx"—the source of the quotation about forgetting without "remembering that one has forgotten"—and Kerebus in the third; Pope Pius XII in the fourth; Joan of Arc in the fifth; "Baal Shem Tov Disguised as Vampire" in the sixth; Adolph Hitler in the seventh; Albert Einstein in the eighth; a border guard in the ninth; four furies in the tenth; and "Golem" in the eleventh.

Although these exchanges are full of weighty philosophical speculation, the rapid succession of interlocutors gives the scene an absurd cast. Or at least it does so on the page and in performance. Ferneyhough's score makes little distinction between speakers. While this trait does an admirable job of furthering the confusion that Bernstein's aesthetic welcomes, it undercuts the care he takes to assign dialogue to the appropriate character. It is not an accident, for example, that Groucho Marx's head says, "A duck was crossing the strasse and the peacock said, Why a duck? Why a rabbit? Why a pipe? Why a carousel?" Nor is it coincidence that Albert Einstein repeats a single question over and over: "What time is it *now?*"

Perhaps responding to criticism of his treatment of the libretto for *Shadow-*

time, Ferneyhough has sought to emphasize that, although the singing of different characters in this scene may sound alike, the mode of their singing serves to individuate them. Each of the conversations, he notes, "adopts the conventions of a particular historical musical genre (rondo, passacaglia, isorhythmic motet, quodlibet, etc.), whereby the succession of interrogations on the stage is paralleled by an overview of the development of occidental musical forms from the 11th to the 19th Century."[4] This means he echoes the allegorical quality of Bernstein's libretto in the score, transforming it into a sort of "pilgrim's progress" through the history of music. But the *telos* of that journey is a place where the conventions of both genre and characterization are subordinated to the innovations of the avant-garde.

Ferneyhough begins the piece in which he explains his intentions for *Shadowtime* with a general discussion of his approach to vocal work, for which he admits to having "a certain amount of trepidation." Collaborating with another artist means risking a loss of control over his art, something he is not happy to countenance. "Since it is usually music (as the aptly named 'setting') which is imagined as faithfully serving the text by displaying it to best advantage, the composer not prepared to accept this ritual self-effacement is constrained to formulating and realizing quite complex work-specific strategies. In effect, he must accept, re-inscribe and thus empower this fundamental fracture of communicative discursivity as the price of creative liberty."[5]

Recognizing that "the demands of 'standard received' textual conventions—sentence structure, accentuation, case agreements and the like—relentlessly conspire to undermine optimal deployment of musically immanent parsing devices," he sets out, not to conceal the "text-music discontinuities" that are inevitable in any coupling of libretto and score, but to exaggerate them.[6] It is telling that both of the examples he provides of music that achieves this goal are works of Arnold Schönberg. This helps to explain why what seems, on the face of it, to be a stereotypically postmodern move—referencing different musical genres and the periods with which they are associated in rapid succession—ends up sounding like a sincere tribute to the apex of musical Modernism. When Ferneyhough concludes his discussion of the "Pools of Darkness" scene from *Shadowtime* by conjecturing that "the larger temporal scale involved in music theatrical projects demands a more excessive or, at any rate, explicit, form of fracture," he is implicitly arguing for the merits of his approach.[7]

Although Ferneyhough makes an articulate case for his decision to dismember and disguise the libretto, the fact that his "trepidation" derives from a reluctance to be seen "faithfully serving" the text indicates that his aesthetic motivations are complicated by professional interest. Simply put, he wants to preserve mastery over the opera that bears his name and, having invited an artist of Bernstein's stature to collaborate with him, must work especially hard to achieve that goal. The score's refusal to imbue the voices in the "Pools of Darkness" scene with distinctiveness serves as an apt metaphor for the liberties it takes with the text more generally. While the violence done to the integrity of the libretto may coincide with Bernstein's overarching intentions, it is hard to see how taking the duck out of Groucho's mouth does his work any favors. By depriving the many characters in the text of their human specificity—even the most learned listener is unlikely to hear a rondo and think, "Oh, this must be Adolph Hitler"—the score risks depriving the libretto itself of its character. In the end, Ferneyhough's long-standing devotion to a disciplined avant-garde aesthetic with origins in early-twentieth-century composers' experiments with dissonance and serialism drowns out the libretto's subtle nuances, even if it manages to put its theoretical speculations into practice. In stating that "when you move to another mode, you gain something and you lose something," Bernstein delicately addresses the aesthetic compromise necessitated by having a minority share in the construction of the opera. And he seems, as previously noted, to be at peace with the fate of his words.

But there is another aspect to *Shadowtime* that makes Ferneyhough's musical approach more troubling than it might initially seem. Although he draws upon postwar innovations in the use of rhythm and meter, as well as playing off the vocal and narrative conventions of Baroque opera, which he turns into a kind of "negative space," his allegiance to the "New Music" developed by Schönberg, Alban Berg, and Anton von Webern is never in question. In self-consciously demonstrating the continued vitality of their musical bloodline, Ferneyhough simultaneously pays those composers tribute and conjures a sonic landscape that calls the heady atmosphere of early-twentieth-century Middle Europe forcefully to mind. Since that was also the world that Walter Benjamin inhabited, it could be argued that the music of *Shadowtime* does an excellent job of capturing the intellectual milieu from which he emerged and wrote so insightfully about. After all, Benjamin's close friend and eventual literary executor Theodor Adorno was one of the New Music's staunchest defenders, promoting it well into the post–World War II era.

The paradox of this music's novelty is that, while it was already dismissed by many for being dated when Adorno took up its cause as a music student in the 1920s, it continues to sound more cutting edge than much newer work. To the extent that the musical avant-garde is still associated with a kind of sonic punishment, in which the listener is forced to confront the ideological implications of pleasure, the New Music remains the standard-bearer for progress. This is why it functions as the *telos* for the allegorical journey through musical history that Ferneyhough constructs in the "Pools of Darkness" scene. To someone steeped in the tradition of the New Music, the answer to Albert Einstein's rhetorical question, "What time is it *now?*" might well be "the first decade of the twentieth century," when stunning breakthroughs in the natural sciences were mirrored by stunning breakthroughs across the arts. By contrast, the decades that followed have often seemed like a return to the New Music's past.

Over time, the innovations of the New Music were incorporated into pieces that also made use of traditional octaval melody and harmony. In the work of Kurt Weill and Hans Eisler, the two composers who worked closely with playwright Bertolt Brecht, traces of Schönberg's most radical work give an edge to a sensibility that derives as much from the cabaret as the concert hall. Despite the overwhelming evidence of serious music's need to breed with popular culture, however, Adorno never relented in his insistence that such hybridization represented the worst reactionary tendencies. When he set out to write his own short "song-play" in the early 1930s, a piece based on Mark Twain's fiction called *The Treasure of Indian-Joe,* he composed vocal parts that refused the conventions of nineteenth-century bourgeois opera and their modern continuation in the work of Sergei Prokoviev, Richard Strauss, and Stravinsky. The two extant songs from this unfinished project sound a great deal like Schönberg, not to mention the Ferneyhough of *Shadowtime.*

This is where the problem with Ferneyhough's musical approach in *Shadowtime* manifests itself most forcefully. Eager for the approbation of his intellectual elder, Adorno sent the libretto for *The Treasure of Indian-Joe* to Benjamin, who managed not to comment on it, despite several requests, until he grudgingly provided his assessment in a letter. Lamenting the text's "reduction to the idyllic," Benjamin compared it unfavorably to Jean Cocteau's novel *Enfants terribles.* He also indicated his lack of interest in Adorno's struggle to defend the New Music. Benjamin writes that "the range of material itself—quite apart from the musical question about which I cannot venture any opinion whatsoever—appears to me to be an unpromising one."[8] For someone who wrote so widely on modern culture, it is truly startling how little Benjamin had to say about music. Despite the fact that Adorno repeatedly refers to music in their extensive correspondence, Benjamin preferred to discuss other matters, mustering only the occasional perfunctory response such as this rather condescending profession of ignorance.

Given the severe critique that Adorno went on to levy against portions of Benjamin's Arcades Project—for all their shared interests and the spirit of friendship animating their correspondence, they disagreed strenuously on many topics—there is something disturbing, then, about an opera on Benjamin's life and work that largely conforms to Adorno's more rigid aesthetic standards.[9] Although Benjamin was no cultural reactionary, the modern art that he preferred was far more accessible and popular than the New Music: Charles Baudelaire, Marcel Proust, Franz Kafka, Bertolt Brecht. And he was also more optimistic than Adorno about the popular culture of his day, arguing in his essay "The Work of Art in the Age of Mechanical Reproduction" for the revolutionary potential of the cinema. Even though Benjamin's temperament may have been better suited to the secular cloister of the library than either the concert hall or the cabaret, he made a concerted effort to experience the popular culture of his day firsthand.

A fan of the bestselling detective stories of the French writer Georges Simenon, Benjamin walked the world and the fast-paced modern city they documented with an open mind and heart.[10] By experimenting with hashish, he was able to magnify his perceptiveness and see and feel things that his intellectual training might well have concealed. "I make it my policy to head straight for the suburbs so as to learn my way around the outskirts. I soon discovered the rightness of this principle in the case of Marseilles. Never had the first hour been as profitable as the one I spent in and among the inner port and dock installations, the warehouses, the poorer neighborhoods, the scattered refuges of the destitute. Outlying districts are, in fact, the town in a state of emergency; they are the terrain upon which the great decisive battles between town and country are continuously being fought out."[11] It is no coincidence that these suburbs were the domain where mainstream popular culture's sway was strongest in Benjamin's day and where, in most cases, it currently remains. Needless to say, they were also inimical to the rarified Modernism of the New Music and its equivalents in literature and visual art. In a sense, Benjamin sought these areas out in a bid for temporary freedom from his own background.

On one of his drug-enhanced excursions, Benjamin even found himself temporarily living what can justifiably be described as his friend Adorno's worst nightmare. "The music, which meanwhile kept rising and falling, I called the 'rush switches of jazz.' I have forgotten on what grounds I permitted myself to mark the beat with my foot. This is against my education, and it did not happen without inner disputation."[12] Significantly, although he is reluctant to let his body give in to the music, he has put himself in the position to do so by performing an experiment *on* his body that reduces his inhibitions. In the process he has also forsaken the aesthetic purity of the narrowly circumscribed domain of mandarins like himself and Adorno for the impure sensations of a wider world in which cultural miscegenation is taken for granted.

Whatever the intellectual merits of Benjamin's controlled use of mind-altering substances, his decision to take that path marks him as a thinker more interested in exploring the messy complexity of modern everyday life than the refined reaction to it that gave rise to "high" Modernism. Indeed, like American contemporaries such as William Carlos Williams and Louis Zukovsky—both crucial influences on the post–World War II poetry scene from which Charles Bernstein emerged—Benjamin was never willing to forsake the energy of mainstream culture. His examination of contemporary German society in *One-Way Street,* his memoir *Berlin Childhood Around 1900,* and his massive and sadly uncompleted Arcades Project, on which he had been working throughout the last decade of his life, all testify to the value he discerned in the attempt to redeem the mass-produced and therefore dismissively tended material culture that developed in the wake of the Industrial Revolution. The scope and depth of his investment in this material thus begs the question of whether a more populist approach to the composition of *Shadowtime* might have been preferable. After all, during the same period in which Adorno is writing Benjamin about *The Treasure of Indian-Joe,* Benjamin is praising Brecht in reply, almost as though he wanted to raise his friend's ire.

Reflecting on the appropriateness of a musical aesthetic at odds with its subject's own tastes and, more importantly, work, Bernstein acknowledges that "in terms of Benjamin's interest in popular culture, there doesn't seem to be a sampling or an engagement with certain aspects of what people would consider to be popular music within the Ferneyhough score. That's something many people mention to me, even if they don't say it in those terms."[13] What *Shadowtime* loses, in other words, by prioritizing the New Music over newer, less pure musics, is this engagement with the popular. In asserting his mastery over the score, Ferneyhough not only obscures much of Bernstein's contribution to the opera, but also the legacy of the man who inspired it. *Shadowtime* ends up giving us the Benjamin that Adorno wished for and, through relentless criticism of his friend's populist tendencies, sought to produce, rather than Benjamin as he actually was, a supple thinker torn between incompatible worldviews.[14]

The principal reason to temper this critique of the opera, aside from Bernstein's strong declaration of support for the project, is that, while Benjamin's tastes inclined toward more accessible fare, he was also intrigued by the sort of questions the score raises. Although Bernstein's interest in obfuscation and its identification with Jewish thought long predates his work on the project, it is clear that *Shadowtime* inspired him to revisit the topic with new vigor. As the scenes "The Doctrine of Similarity (13 Canons)," "Seven Tableaux Vivants Representing the Angel of History as Melancholia," and "Stelae for Failed Time (Solo for Melancholia as the Angel of History)" indicate, the libretto makes active use of Benjamin's titles and tropes.

Bernstein borrows inventively, both from well-known passages in his work and less familiar material, such as the essay "Hashish in Marseilles." Sometimes he quotes bits and pieces verbatim, rearranging them into collages that relate to their sources the way that costume-clad carnival-goers relate to their normal appearances, inviting the game of recognition but making it difficult to play. At other junctures he paraphrases, paring Benjamin's famously hypotactic prose into lapidary formulas that might fit on a bumper sticker. Liberal use of repetition makes noteworthy phrases resonate through the text. Interestingly, the effect Bernstein achieves in the printed libretto comes surprisingly close to the experience of reading the Arcades Project or the many short pieces Benjamin wrote in the early 1930s, in which the same ideas—and sometimes even the same sentences—appear over and over in different contexts and to different ends. The absence of this quality, one of the libretto's most impressive achievements, from the score may be the hardest loss to bear of the many that Ferneyhough's approach forces upon the listener.

But the perception of that loss also points the way toward *Shadowtime*'s redemption. Even if Ferneyhough inclines too far in Adorno's direction, by presenting the bulk of Bernstein's libretto as if it were in ruins, he makes the listener feel Benjamin's premature demise instead of merely thinking it. Although Bernstein thematizes loss and the possibility of making it good in a time yet to come, his borrowings from the source make Benjamin's presence palpable. Indeed, by breaking his sentences into pieces and then rearranging them in new combinations, Bernstein sometimes gives the impression that he has found a lost text by his subject, perhaps even the one that Benjamin was supposed to be carrying with him as he headed for the French border. At these junctures, the libretto seems, however fleetingly, to have brought the dead back to life. As appealing as this messianic quality may be to devotees of Benjamin's work, however, it risks making too palatable the incomprehensible loss that his death metonymically figures: the Sho'ah.

Ferneyhough's score provides no such comforts. By turning the libretto for *Shadowtime* into a shadow of its printed self, he reminds the listener that, while it may be true that "you gain something and you lose something" in making the passage from one world to the next, the conservation of matter presumed by that formulation does not capture what matters. A compensation in quantity is not a compensation in quality. There may be a specificity to loss that simply cannot be made good through the logic of substitution. While Ferneyhough's reasons for doing violence to Bernstein's words surely are, as already suggested, multiple and not reducible to abstract artistic intention, the fact remains that his score gives the text a power it would otherwise lack, the power, ironically enough, *of* lack. Nor is this an effect achieved in spite of the composer's intentions. Though self-interest was, as he freely admits, a factor in his treatment of the libretto, he also had Benjamin's work in mind. Playing off "The Work of Art in the Age of Mechanical Reproduction," which argues that expanding access to art diminishes its aura proportionally, Ferneyhough states that the scene "The Doctrine of Similarity (13 Canons)," concerns itself, "not with presentation but 're-presentation', and it is this dimension which permitted me to continually re-initialize the power of auratic distance from movement to movement." In other words, he consciously sought to deny the listener access to the scene that would have compromised the opera's aura. Because "The Work of Art in the Age of Mechanical Reproduction" welcomes the aura's demise, this comment demonstrates that Ferneyhough is reading the essay "against the grain," the very practice advocated by Benjamin in its celebrated coda. Preserving the aura in spite of the forces seeking its dissolution means barring the door to ease.[15]

It is the rigor with which Ferneyhough undertakes this task that inspires Bernstein's strongest praise for his aesthetic. He contrasts him to "a John Adams or a Philip Glass or any number of other contemporary composers that are doing opera, who make many more concessions to a certain aspect of popular music." Bernstein notes, "I like popular music quite a lot. And I'm not a composer. Probably if I were a composer I'd be more like Kurt Weill than I would be like Brian Ferneyhough."[16] Although he recognizes this crucial difference in temperament between himself and his collaborator on *Shadowtime*, that does not stop him from expressing admiration for the composer. On the contrary, he regards Ferneyhough's rejection of the popular as a bracing alternative to culture that is too willing to conform with the demands of the marketplace. "That's what he does. A lot of people don't like severe, atonal music. You never hear it on the radio either. Not just Brian's music, but the whole twentieth-century tradition of it rarely comes on the radio, even on the satellite radio shows. It's almost like spinach or something. I love that music. I find it very engaging."

In likening Ferneyhough's music to "spinach," Bernstein selects a particularly apt metaphor. Recalling both the bitter herbs of the Seder and Popeye's secret weapon, the image fuses religious and popular culture, the gravity of remembrance and the froth of childhood delight. To be sure, it is not the way that Ferneyhough would choose to characterize his aesthetic. But that is precisely what makes it so revealing. Bernstein's relation to Ferneyhough proves to be a great deal like Benjamin's relation to Adorno. Just as the sprawl of the Arcades Project becomes more coherent in light of Adorno's unsparing critique, the libretto for *Shadowtime* benefits from Ferneyhough's radical musical treatment. In the end, the loss of control to which Bernstein consented in signing on to Ferneyhough's project gave him the opportunity to achieve effects that his printed work, for all of its brilliance on the page, is unable to achieve. Conversely, in warding off the populist impulses of both Bernstein and Benjamin himself, Ferneyhough was forced to transform the austerity of his aesthetic into a commentary on the poverty of loss. The libretto and score for *Shadowtime* illuminate each other by casting shadows over their respective limitations, making them a great deal richer in the process. Sometimes language communicates more effectively in the dark.

Notes

1. Charlie Bertsch, "Bitter Greens: Walter Benjamin Goes to the Opera," *Tikkun* (July–August 2006): 78. The quotation comes from a long interview I conducted with Charles Bernstein for the article in question, in which we discussed *Shadowtime,* its relation to the work of Walter Benjamin, Modernism, the emigration of Jewish intellectuals to the United States in the 1930s, and the reception of American culture in the contemporary European art world.

2. Charles Bernstein, "The Lives of the Toll Takers," in *Dark City* (Los Angeles: Sun & Moon Press, 1994), 23–24.

3. Ibid.

4. Brian Ferneyhough, "Words and Music," *The Argotist Online* http://www.argotistonline.co.uk/Ferneyhough%20essay.htm. It is worth noting that Charles Bernstein links to this article in the website he set up about *Shadowtime,* which is an excellent resource for considering the opera: http://epc.buffalo.edu/authors/bernstein/shadowtime/ (accessed March 30, 2009).

5. Ibid.

6. Ibid.

7. Ibid.

8. Henri Lonitz, ed., *Theodor W. Adorno and Walter Benjamin: The Complete Correspondence 1928–1940* (Cambridge, MA: Harvard University Press, 1999), 23.

9. Adorno's critique is most sharply articulated in his letters to Benjamin from March 18, 1936, and November 10, 1938, included in Ronald Taylor, editor, *Aesthetics and Politics: Debates Between Ernst Bloch, Georg Lukács, Bertolt Brecht, Walter Benjamin, Theodor Adorno* (London: NLB, 1977), 120–133 (123 in particular).

10. See Gershom Scholem, ed., *The Correspondence of Walter Benjamin and Gershom Scholem, 1932–1940* (New York: Schocken Books, 1989), 76.

11. Walter Benjamin, *On Hashish* (Cambridge, MA: Harvard University Press, 2006), 107.

12. Ibid., 125.

13. Charlie Bertsch, "Bitter Greens: Walter Benjamin Goes to the Opera," 79.

14. Again, see Adorno's letters to Benjamin from March 18, 1936, and November 10, 1938, included in Ronald Taylor, ed., *Aesthetics and Politics*, 120–133.

15. In Adorno's letter to Benjamin of March 18, 1936, he writes, "Certainly Schönberg's music is not aural." Ibid., 124. Ferneyhough clearly subscribes to Adorno's line of reasoning.

16. Charlie Bertsch, "Bitter Greens: Walter Benjamin Goes to the Opera," 79.

Danger, Skepticism, and Democratic Longing

Five Contemporary Secular Jewish American Poets

Thomas Fink

The five Jewish American poets whose work I will discuss (in reverse chronological order) alert us to various dangers, practice similar modes of skepticism, at times in divergent ways, and use different strategies to imply or articulate some form of democratic longing. While David Shapiro (b. 1947), Charles Bernstein (b. 1950), and Stephen Paul Miller (b. 1951) are close in age, Joseph Lease (b. 1960) and Joanna Fuhrman (b. 1972) are not. All of the poems analyzed here were produced in the last decade and a half, and most were written in the current decade. Generational distinctions seem less important to me than the notion that all of the writers are actively engaged in socially and formally acute exploration that characterizes innovative poetry in the United States at this time.

Although David Shapiro has influenced younger experimental poets who write explicitly about Jewish issues, references to Judaism in his work coexist among so many different elements that it is difficult to consider them part of a sustained engagement with Jewish concerns in a single poem or a poetic sequence. And yet there are illuminating exceptions. In "Voice," the first section of the sequence of the same name, Shapiro includes his most direct reference to the Shoah. This 1994 poem begins with an allusion to rabbinical interpretation:

A woman's voice
is a sexual organ
according to the Rabbis
I would draw your voice
photo of a sketch for
reproduction (not for sale)

A woman's voice
is a body part
again washed to the beach
like a bloody misogyny
Cold light
is misunderstood
Do the firefly
lights up from inside
a children's song.[1]

The first two unpunctuated sentences occupying the first six lines can be read as a male lover's celebration of his beloved, bolstered by the authority of Jewish tradition's admiration of women's vocal beauty. "Organ" punningly includes a synesthesia of embodiment *and* an evocative musical instrument. The lover's desire to re-present the voice in an artwork, allowing the voice to undergo multiple mediations ("photo"/"sketch"/ "reproduction"), is an act of homage, but "reproduction" is also a pun; perhaps the Rabbis affirm women's sexual allure as insurance that the Jews will survive from generation to generation. But in the poem's third sentence, Shapiro eliminates the ambiguity in "organ" by replacing it with the much less lyrical "body part," and "bloody misogyny" challenges the assignment of a celebratory tone to the first six lines and may suggest that dangerous, antidemocratic tendencies within the rabbinical tradition would contain women's sexuality with the excuse that it is a danger to men and to the Jewish people. The idea that "cold light / is misunderstood"—indicating a relay of synesthesia from "voice" indicates that interpretation is a problem, but it does not help us choose between the conflicting views in the first and second six lines. And the "enactment" (imitation) of the firefly's light in the "children's song" is a reminder of illusion built into the fiction of representation. At this point, an indirect allusion to the Shoah enters the poem:

Friend meets Waldheim
Temple of Hypermnesia
are you in the
"forgetting movement"
Kitsch and poetry
No I'm in the remembrance
movement and poetry
is fire in the house. (55)

Kurt Waldheim was secretary-general of the United Nations from 1972 to 1981, and between 1986 and 1992, when he was president of Austria, it was discovered that he had lied about his participation in the German army during World War II. As it turns out, Waldheim was tied to major war crimes. In his friend's "meeting" with Waldheim, Shapiro envisions an intense recognition of the Holocaust's dangerous impact on the present.

"Hypermnesia" is not merely a prodigious memory, but one so troubling as to be linked with psychological illness. "Temple of Hypermnesia" connotes a religious calling for the extremely difficult exertion of memory to abhor past horrors as a means to democratic vigilance. This "remembrance / movement" is pitted against " 'the forgetting movement' " exemplified by the tendency at the time for some "revisionist" historians to minimize or even deny what occurred during the Holocaust.[2] For Shapiro, such forgetting includes the aesthetic failure of kitsch, which misunderstands the "cold light" of tragedy by imposing sentimental representations of it. Instead, as "fire in the house," poetry of acute remembrance bespeaks emergency and disturbs complacency. If we also consider this "fire" a psychological or spiritual "hearth," it can be said to promote solidarity against oppression. Because they are juxtaposed in "Voice," the conflict within Jewish tradition between a positive view of female sexuality and the danger of a "bloody misogyny" is comparable to the struggle between the anti-kitsch, "hypermnesiac" democratic ethos and " 'the forgetting movement' " that could be used to justify murderous anti-Semitism in the past and present.

Questioned by Tom Beckett about a prose-passage from "The Lives of the Toll Takers," Charles Bernstein responds in verse and articulates a critique of what he considers dangerous and reductive forms of Jewish identity.[3] Bernstein traces the references in the passage "to Sander Gilman's *Jewish Self-Hatred*" and identifies the condition represented by the title as one "in which a person internalizes the racist / stereotype that their true language is not the one / they speak but an imaginary 'hidden language of the Jews' " (*My Way* 188). According to "the anti-Semite," "the Jews can never be 'native' / or even competent speakers of their own language" (189); assimilation into non-Jewish culture is seen as impossible. Against these concepts, Bernstein speaks of his

        preoccupation
with the radical morphogenerativeness of language
and its related instability and ambiguity, its
unsettling and polydictory logics, which constitute,

rather than impede, our mutual grounding in language
as a grounding in each other that forms the basis not
of nations or ethnicities or races but of polis.

I take this as an aesthetic practice that repudiates the moral
discourse of a right to speak as a racial or national
patrimony, and also a right way to speak. This is a lesson I
learned not from Pound and Eliot, exactly, but from Stein,
from Reznikoff and Zukofsky, and also from Groucho Marx
and Lenny Bruce. (189)

For Bernstein, the perils of anti-Semitism and Jews' internalization of that pathology both involve the illusion of a linguistic "racial or national / patrimony." Therefore, to subject the concept of an original "unity" of language-use to severe skepticism and to expose "unsettling," fundamental heterogeneity within a language's deployment by various ethnic groups challenges anti-Semitic ideology and "Jewish self-hatred" in the name of democratic inclusiveness. But it goes farther: it indicates serious problems with *positive* formulations of Jewish identity that do not admit for "polydictory logics" within Jews. In an essay on Gertrude Stein, Bernstein notes that this writer triply marginalized by "gender, sexual orientation, ethnicity,"[4] like other "Jewish-American modernists" such as Louis Zukofsky, "turned away from Yiddish or other overt markers of ethnicity" (143) without embracing assimilationism: "Stein celebrates her suspension of identity, this holding off naming to see what otherwise emerges" (144).

Bernstein's mention of the Jewish comics Groucho Marx, whose dizzily decentered wordplay unraveled many a conversation with a linear-minded foil,[5] and Lenny Bruce as influences on his critique of identity-discourse seems especially apt, because the American-Jewish-sounding comic bounce in his poetry is a prime element in how he names excessively and elusively in order to "hold off" limiting "naming." Section 3 (the first section) of "The Manufacture of Negative Experience" begins: "My bread has some nerve. No / sooner does it come out of the oven / than I have to slap it for being / so fresh. My head has some / curve."[6]

A boast is one way to assert one's stable identity or to compensate for self-doubt and uncertainties posed by competition and prejudice. But the "boast" of Bernstein's first speaker (of many voices) undoes itself through the pun on "fresh" in relation to "nerve" and "slap." If the metonymic use of food (or, to acknowledge more punning, money) is supposed to serve as an index of someone's accomplishment, then consciousness of linguistic play seems to upstage this aim, and this is further emphasized by the fact that the third sentence is a repetition with a doubly rhyming difference that conveys information too unusual and vague to impress its audience. Whose "head" doesn't "curve"? What would constitute a remarkable "curve"? Or is "head" yet another pun—an obscene one?

One way of bypassing the boasting game and yet reaping its rewards is for the comic poet or standup comic to play the *schlemiel* (fool): self-deprecating humor that "manufactures" a "negative experience" not only has positive entertainment value for others but also underscores linguistic inventiveness and disruption of audience expectations as evidence of intelligence. The appreciation of this evidence "wins" affirmation of his identity for the comic. However, Bernstein's strategies of discontinuity and his foregrounding of words' materiality are far more extreme and relentless than those of, say, Groucho Marx, who could at least rely on a picaresque plot structure to comfort his movie audiences with some sense of "order." The next sentence of the poem, which first indicates where the "head" travels and then details supposed consequences, gives ample proof of Bernstein's departures from his Jewish comic predecessors:

> No sooner does it run for
> the patio than the lights begin
> to jam, the commotion dies down
> in the corridor outside the
> farm administration building,
> Randy & Billy & Bob grab a Diet
> Lite with a side of slope,
> the nerve doctors convene for
> an all-night session on breaking
> the self-help habit, I'm okay
> you're not worth the paper you're
> printed on, or I'm in deep
> trouble but you never came up
> to the surface after that dive,
> lo these many years ago. (28)

As if the synecdoche of the "head" dashing "for / the patio" were not absurd enough, except perhaps in a cartoon, the spectator becomes too dizzy to forge connections between the "running" and the ambiguous problem with the lights *and* the quieting of the "commotion" in an unexpected location, as well as the "actions" of "characters" that abruptly follow. Odd touches like the repetition in the fake product-name "Diet Lite," the "side" order of a visual property vaguely suggesting psychological instability, and the repetition of the word "nerve," indicating the slippage from *chutzpah* in the first line to neurological *or* psychological professionals engaging in a dubious group ritual in the eleventh, all displace attention from the unfolding of a drama featuring a self-advertising self to language as the medium in which identity-formations—an alternative way of interpreting the popular phrase "self-help"—are "broken," scrambled, dispersed, and scattered. The "I'm OK, You're OK" pop psych ideology is parodied by the supposition that self-esteem is constituted, not by empirical truth but by textuality and, like Ashbery and the Oulipians, Bernstein perverts another cliché to suggest that the substance that enables a text's material existence is more valuable than an unsatisfactory (dangerous?) idea about the self represented in the text. The last three clauses of the sentence make light of "depth" psychology by juxtaposing a reference to psychological surface/depth with an apostrophe describing an actual physical danger involving spatial depth.

The effects of displacement and disorientation in the section I have partly discussed are intensified by their complex relation to the twelve other numbered sections in the poem. Like most of Bernstein's longer poems, this one includes many kinds of discourse to be found in U.S. culture, and this illustrates what Bernstein in the interview with Beckett calls the primacy of "polydictory logics" over the concept that a single kind of language stands as a marker of selfhood. In the fifth section, 41, the premise of unified intentionality and "communication" are subject to riotous divisions:

"When I say 'no' I mean
maybe, probably not, what's
the matter with you?, do I
make myself clear?, is anybody
out there?, do you serve a
no-doze with your lecture?,
how's the water?, are you
insensitive or just emotionally
challenged?, brace yourself
I'm going to write a memo! . . .
possibly I could rephrase
that but from the look of things
you'd be even more likely

to take it the way it was
intended! (30)

If "anyone" is "out there" (in both the sense of present and bizarre), that "one" embodies a multiplicity of influences, and, if the poet would encourage us to read the clichéd question in the third and fourth lines freshly, the achievement of temporary "clarity" involves exerting an effort to compose "oneself" "clearly" for others. The last five lines in the passage above offers the kind of jolt that a defamiliarizing Groucho Marx insult "communicates"; one who understands the danger of being pinned down by another and losing some aspect of freedom simultaneously appears to posit and evade communication.

The notion of identity, not quite obliterated in the poet's varied efforts to "manufacture negative experience," is complicated to the extent that its raving multiplicity—and the inability to sort definitively what it is inside and outside the self—cannot be apprehended and will not stand still. And Bernstein's general skepticism about the readability of individual and collective identity and about the capability of language (bypassing ambiguity) to disclose it corresponds to the specific questioning of determinate forms of Jewish identity that he voices in his interview with Beckett.

Stephen Paul Miller, author of *The Seventies Now: Culture as Surveillance* (1999), has written a great deal of poetry that is simultaneously cultural criticism or even scholarship. His 2002 poem "Row" braids together treatments of various seemingly disparate cultural phenomena while developing a triangular relationship among the Holocaust, computers, and U.S. suburbs. (Here, I will ponder the connection between the first two items, since I find the link between the third and the others underdeveloped.) Within the first page of "Row," Miller cites his first and most crucial of many sources at the end of a story placing Bob Dylan's character Mr. Jones in Nazi Germany *and* speaking to the poet:

Jones tells me "I'll sue
        If Dylan uses my first name *too*,"
then Jones tells a kapo (Jew working
        within the vast German concentration camp
                system including ghettoes and work
            and transit camps)
to check the wrist band
against the punch card

(they really only tattooed concentration camp
victims in Auschwitz and Bergen Belsen)
that initially corresponded to it.
Edwin Black's IBM and the Holocaust
(Crown, NY, 2001)

explains the human bar codes.

IBM finessed its punch card system
to accommodate
the advanced sorting requirements of handling
Social Security and the holocaust.

It's just that things were coming together.

Okay, Black stretches it:
Manual Nazi census taking
might have been more efficient
than Black would wish

and IBM didn't make the *only* punch cards, but

still

if it were all true
would you be surprised?[7]

The strangeness of IBM's complicity in the *Shoah* is intensified by the mention of their work on the great New Deal safety net *and* the most profound danger to a particular people. Miller goes on to dramatize the corporate giant's separation of basic morality from the drive for profit in such a matter-of-fact way that the reader can develop righteous indignation on her own: "Last spring my mother gave my son some IBM stock, / a company merely helping Hitler who was just a client / looking for 'Jewish bloodlines,' and that was / difficult, what with rampant assimilation and conversion. / Lots of Jews felt safe. You really couldn't tell who / was and who wasn't" (17). But it turns out a few pages later, based on evidence from Paul E. Cerruzi, *The History of Modern Computing* (MIT Press, 2000) and not Black, that "Nazi scientists develop / Random Access Memory," and "IBM appropriates RAM / from [these] German scientists / and Ram allows IBM / to annihilate its competitors" (22). Therefore, IBM repays Germany for the benefit of this capitalist "annihilation" by enabling it to achieve literal annihilation, and yet the repayment results in further profit.

In emphasizing the reification *and* commodification of Holocaust victims, the shocking trope of "human bar codes" in the long passage above emphasizes Miller's point that the murder of the six million was not only tied to psychotic, racist totalitarianism but to the dynamics of capitalism. Exploiting the statement that "capital comes from / the late Latin for cattle" in "Hernando de Soto's *Mystery of Capital*" (Basic Books, 2000)(19), and the fact that cattle and Holocaust victims are "branded," Miller suggests that, for the Nazis, "the mystery of capital"—their mystification of Jews as an "undetectable" source of what we would now call a pandemic—is the supreme danger that must be "perfectly identified," immobilized by classification, and, ultimately, eradicated:

> ... de Soto has this notion of "dead capital"—
> The Nazis called Jews "life unworthy of life"
> and were intrigued with Jews as capital, dead capital.
> Their uniqueness, their aura, was considered undetectable,
> contagious, and all-powerful. Unconsciously,
> the Nazis saw Jews as the mystery of capital
> and, in the worst possible way,
> wished to uncompute them,
> dead end them,
> treat them like cattle
> that do not need to be cared for or
> invested in, that is
> treat them like dead capital, or nearly dead cattle.
>
> The mystery, the inside secret, of capital
> is property with perfectly identifiable ownership
> so that wealth can be leveraged
> and used in every which way. (19)

The Nazis' drive for certainty about the alien other is tied not only to extreme psychological insecurity but to material greed; greed and paranoia feed off each other. Thus, Miller, fascinated throughout the poem by how "realities converge / and no logic / is consistent" (16), implies that the IBM executives' greed bears some relation to that of Nazi leaders. Further, the poet uses his and others' conjectures about a variety of historical materials in the poem to goad those currently in power within the realm of U.S. and multinational capitalism and others who have benefited to acknowledge, first to themselves, their denial of how social/political/ economic "realities" have "converged": "People / can't talk to themselves / about stuff they can't admit" (17). The poem, in part, constitutes a taunt for "people" to "admit" this disheartening "stuff," or at least to entertain it as a possibility.

In "Row," Miller discusses how the computer not only allows the Holocaust to occur but how the computer is also used to finish off the Nazi regime and thus end the Shoah. He credits "Alan Turing's infinite-laid backness" as a computer theorist/programmer with being "able to relax logic, / universalize applied mathematics, / break the German code, / and win World War II / by turning Nazi war strategy on its head" (23). While Miller hyperbolically claims that Turing "invents the computer" as he "deprograms the Nazis," his findings were revolutionary. One aspect of the gay British computer scientist's motivation to stop the Nazis was his awareness that Hitler, whose army was expected "in Britain soon" (24), also sought to exterminate homosexuals.

No Luddite, Miller stresses how the computer's capabilities can support both totalitarian and democratic purposes. Also, the totalizing classification that the Nazis utilized is countered by "Turing's queer logic," which

> does not fear or dislike wrong answers.
> His logic doesn't need to prove its answer.
> It rather needs a base of virtually every possible answer
> within the problem's range and a way to specify
> which answers work. Suitability replaces provability.
> Each time-consuming shuffle of physical punch cards
> is a question or a search through a
> quickly generated set of lame answers. (26)

For Turing, "computation" should be "infinitely ongoing" (31), and he strives for a complex, relativistic, open "system." When Miller observes that "a Jew comes up / with relativity and / a campy queer thinks of the computer" (26), he reiterates the common claim that "outsiders" develop perspectives that break new ground and are threatening to a mainstream and its status quo:

> Nazis hate relativity
> less for its Jewish roots
> than because it feels queer
> and that's the *only* reason
> we beat them to the bomb.

They can't even imagine the *possibility*
of Brits decoding the Enigma,
let alone its more complex version. (26)

Emotionally invested in a closed, "pure" system, Nazis erroneously consider it impenetrable by "queer logic"; what the poet calls their failure of imagination involves a clinging to "Truth" as imaginative limit and limitation. In various parts of "Row," Miller shows that he is concerned with ways in which such limits undermined political freedom and expansive imagination *after* the Nazi era: "To say we're on a holocaust continuum *because that's what this poem / grapples with, with all its idiosyncratic connections, / because I felt a little of my soul robbed by the 2000 election / even if I don't know what punch card machines had to do with it*" (15). In a persistence of thinking that, ironically, is comparable enough to Nazi "logic," "after the war, British and American / homophobes undo Turing" (24) leading him to commit suicide in 1954: "When Turing dies he's working on / curves of biological growth. // He's anxious to find non-military / computer uses. // With Turing's loss of security clearing, the Cold War seizes the computer" (25). Not aiming to work within the tradition of elegiac texts on the Shoah, Miller in "Row" links the contexts of this tragedy with those of the computer in a critical poetry that posits skepticism and imaginative amplitude as fuel for resistance to whatever antidemocratic coercions must be confronted.

Concern with the representation of the Shoah and the significance currently assigned to it has been an important and sometimes a central part of various poems by Joseph Lease. Elsewhere, I have written about how Lease elaborately and compelling treats these issues in the long "Slivovitz," a poem published in 1998 and dedicated to David Shapiro.[8] In "'The Jew with the hole in his voice,'" published three years later, Lease implicitly confronts the argument that Jewish-Israeli leaders have used the Holocaust to justify oppression of the Palestinians. The prose block that opens the poem features uncanny repetitions that are not unlike a relaxed pantoum:

First we killed them, then they killed us. The wind is steel wool.
Then, first they killed us, then we killed green. Sunlight lathers
blonde, oiled wood. Light from the hole that keeps unfolding
under his stomach. She'll hear or not hear snow walking on the
rooftop. She'll go for long walks at night when the town is
sleeping. She'll hear or not hear history walking on the rooftop.
Families drowning, dancing in loops, singing words they loved.

Families drowning, singing words they loved, dancing in loops, in
green and blue water curved in a circle. Dream they can breathe.
First we killed them, then they killed us. Dream they can breathe.
Open their mouths. Those to whom evil was done did evil again as
ghosts. Dream they can breathe. Open their mouths.[9]

If "the Jew with the hole in his voice" is the speaking or writing subject, the chronological structure of the first sentence seems to indicate that, after World War II, Israeli Jews killed Palestinians, and then members of the latter group began killing the former. The second sentence could be a non sequitur, and the concept of "a hole" or gap in the articulation of Jewish identity tied to the traumas of Jewish history makes this plausible. However, since "wind" has long been a trope suggesting prophecy and large political trends, the poet is probably reinforcing a sense of general, proliferating abrasiveness in the relations between Jews and Palestinians—or Jews and Moslem Arabs. "Then," the Holocaust is posited as a "first" preceding the temporal chain of the poem's opening sentence, and this is as an antecedent for either environmental damage or economic waste or both ("we killed green").

While luxuriant images are "lathered" by "sunlight," such ostensibly pleasure-giving light only reinforces the psychic ulcer affecting the communication (and probably the sense of identity) of the Jew mentioned in the title. Switching his focus to an equally haunted woman's "long walks at night," the poet stresses the intermittent presence of difficult historical memory and the "snow" of welcome or unwelcome forgetting; the "hole" in an ear does not always prevent her from "hearing" the past, including "families drowning." From Lease's reiterated imagery, one may surmise either that the families "drown" because they are so attached to Jewish tradition that they do not pay enough attention to how to survive in the modern world *or* that this tradition is the only consolation in their encounter with invincible opponents. The "dream" of "breath" in a situation of suffocation comprises the hope for survival, and it can be said that such hope did contribute to the thwarting of Hitler's plan to exterminate *all* the Jews.

In considering the reiteration of the poem's first sentence near the end of the paragraph, we should take into account its proximity to the male and female figures who, I believe, reflect on the Shoah from some temporal distance. Therefore, "we" might be contemporary Jews who have figuratively "killed" the Holocaust victims ("them") by misinterpreting or being unable to interpret their historical "truth" or the extremity of their deaths *exceeding* incomplete truths. "As ghosts," "they" have haunted the contemporaries to the extent that the latter's spiritual or psychic life is depleted. However,

American Jews of this time are also witnesses to the protracted destruction of the Israeli-Palestinian conflict, and they are divided about the issue. U.S. Jews, mostly on the left, who have not approved of the dominant Israeli posture toward the Palestinians—and this, of course, is now very much in flux—may believe that Jews in Israel who have been responsible for injustices against the Palestinians were so haunted by the atrocities committed against their forebears in Nazi Germany that they do not function as rational, ethical human beings (in keeping with Jewish beliefs about justice and equality) but as vehicles for "ghostly" repressive ideology based on revenge.

The poet does not intervene to "settle" the conflict of interpretation caused by his deliberately ambiguous language with some "key" "statement"; instead, as the poem continues for six challenging strophes of one or two lines each, new angles of focus emerge and bear comparison with the paragraph preceding them:

Our cheap history keeps smiling.
"you've been disliked for three thousand years: do you ever look in
the mirror?"

stains on the wall, mattress on the floor, November night—

Is he a monster? No more innocent than a hydrangea or a
beagle—or the grass by the prison door—

"we have determined that you are different; we have decided that we
will eat you—"

Our cheap history keeps smiling. (23–24)

Jewish history, not necessarily valued by others, continues with a smile or grimace. The adjective "cheap," though, also alludes to the stereotype of Jewish stinginess, derived from the fact of racist European Christian communities' confinement of Jews' employment to moneylending. "Cheap history" is a metonymy for ungenerous (inherently morally defective) people. The perpetuation of the stereotype "smiles" favorably on those, like neo-Nazis and the Ku Klux Klan, who seek justification for making the world unsafe for Jews. The quoted strophe which follows, deprived of the dignity of a sentence with a small letter beginning the first word, excuses attempted genocide with the warped logic that, if a people repeatedly face the hatred of others for a long period, then the victims themselves must be at fault for it, whereas occasional persecution might not be a reflection on the group. Of course, the anti-Semite himself avoids looking in the mirror.

Whether or not the image of "stains on the wall" represents after-effects of slaughter in a concentration camp, the line as a whole can be read as a response to the anti-Semite's prior admonition through identification of a sullied environment rather than a victim "needing" further punishment. The "he" in the question about whether someone "is . . . a monster" could refer to Hitler or a prototypical Nazi, but it may also be the figure of a Jew "disliked for three thousand years," *or* an Israeli politician or soldier who has persecuted Palestinians, *or* a Palestinian suicide-bomber who has wreaked havoc in a Jewish-Israeli neighborhood.

By keeping the identity of the individual maddeningly open, Lease seems to be asking us to consider what it means to call anyone a monster for ethico-political reasons. The comparison he introduces is strange but not absurd. Although it seems obvious that a person does not exceed a flower or a dog or "grass" in "innocence," the poet's phrasing allows for the hypothesis that an individual's innocence is potentially equal to that of an animal or insentient being. The "hydrangea" was first cultivated in Japan and has been transplanted to Western areas. In this sense, it bears comparison to the diasporic Jews, who have lived in many places, and the fact that the hydrangea can change colors resembles Jews' adaptability to host cultures. The change of colors may also be a trope for the potential of all human beings, depending on a complex array of environmental circumstances, to behave in ways that are generally considered highly unethical or monstrous.

While, from the perspective of logical argumentation, there are various "holes" in the "voice" of this ensemble of images and abstractions, the strophe seems to criticize ahistorical interpretations of human turpitude—ones that indicate that certain people are born inherently evil and could never be influenced to deviate from their monstrous trajectory. A similar critique is implied when Lease puts a typical fascist expression of horror and rage at others' "difference" in ironizing quotes. Those who magnify cultural differences into absolute moral "Difference" fail to perceive how cultural factors and values are historically constituted, evolved, and are transformed through both the separation and interaction of diverse groups. The simplicity of "First we killed them, then they killed us" turns out to be a "cheap history" of the Shoah and of its relation to the ongoing Israeli-Palestinian conflict. Lease's careful juxtapositions demonstrate—without preaching or shrillness—that such inadequate historical reasoning needs to be replaced by investigations of intricate causal chains and an emphasis on possibilities that foster negotiation, promote human rights, and turn away from the reading of "Difference" as apocalyptic.

Joanna Fuhrman's "Return to Normalcy," a poem alternating brief verse and prose sections, is dated "9/25–10/03, 2001" and was published in 2003. Ruefully ironic, the poem's title refers to Warren G. Harding's call for U.S. citizens to trust him to understand how to heal the psychological, social, and economic damage of World War I, which ended a little over a year before his successful campaign for the presidency. (Further irony stems from the fact that Harding's major "accomplishment" was the egregious political corruption that characterized his peacetime administration. Whether this should be considered "normalcy" is open to question.) Fuhrman gives every indication that she was aware, just weeks after 9/11, that the call for a "return to normalcy" was merely a front for the beginning of war. She is skeptical about efforts to continue business as usual while acknowledging the tragedy: "Every multinational corporation / adds a U.S. flag to their sign // while our President grits his teeth to cover / the sound of malfunctioning palm pilots."[10]

In the poem's second section, Fuhrman, who lives in New York City and was there on 9/11, draws a connection between her emotional response to the event and the Shoah:

It's thundering at 1 am which reminds me of the sound of the crash
which I thought was thunder. I'm shaking and alone—half sleeping
at the door of a nightmare. Then I convince the dream terrorists
that if they let me walk back home in the bottomless shopping cart
they use for hauling people to their death, I'll tell everyone who
passes I'm already dead. They acquiesce to my request and I think
to myself that I'm like one of the Jewish guards, guiding the other
Jews, whom I don't know at all, to their death. When a thin woman
approaches I say to her, "I'm a metal railing. I'll help to keep you
in." (67)

Disruption of the "normalcy" of mainland U.S. invulnerability to foreign invasion elicits anticipation of a long-term state of emergency and the threat of extermination. For a Jewish American like Fuhrman, the Shoah is a primary reference point for emotions occasioned by such a disruption. So fundamental is the survival instinct that the poet has an anxiety nightmare about how such extreme conditions could override her ethical standards to an unprecedented degree, as the Holocaust did for "Jewish guards" who took other Jews to the gas ovens or "showers." The dream-paradox of the speaker telling passersby that she is "already dead" suggests that, in a time of violent social chaos during which basic human rights are thrown aside, one can experience a death-in-life, a loss of ethical and psychological existence despite the continuation of physical existence. Fuhrman's allusion to some Jews' complicity in the Holocaust—horrible behavior in victimizers bringing out only slightly less horrible conduct in victims—can be read as analogous to the concern that the U.S. Government will suspend ordinary morality in waging the war on terrorism.

In the poem's third section, the poet represents an encounter she had in Brooklyn that alludes chillingly to the origins of the Holocaust and of 9/11:

On Fulton, a man in purple
is giddy with apocalyptic hope.
"White devils. Jews." Blah blah blah.
I ask "Can't you see how hating
people causes death?" He says
"No men flew those planes.
That was God. God loves to hate." (67)

In the days following 9/11, bizarre rumors held that Jews masterminded the attacks to frame Moslems and promote hatred against them and support for Israel; while the rumors died down, Fuhrman had reason to believe in the weeks following the tragedy that such absurd interpretations of the event could trigger a new wave of anti-Semitism in the United States. Embracing "apocalyptic" thinking comparable to the terrorist pilots of 9/11, the "man in purple"—perhaps assuming a royalty that his society would not recognize—reiterates Fuhrman's logic while reversing her moral position. For him, despising "Jews" and other people he wishes to demonize is congruent with "God's" will, since he regards the human pilots as no less instruments of God's rage than their aircraft or the "malfunctioning palm pilots" mentioned in Fuhrman's first section. How far is this "logic" from *Mein Kampf* or from fundamentalist readings of *Jihad* in the Koran? Not merely a supposition of God's passionate hatred, the sentence "God loves to hate" can be parsed, "God loves *some people in order to* hate *other people.*" As a secular Jew, Fuhrman does not seek counterevidence in the Old Testament, Talmud, or Midrash to refute the man's apocalyptic irrationality, but she represents how "God" is deployed as a tropological resource for a precritical, pathological ideology that clashes with ordinary humanist ethics.

In the poem's concluding prose part, Fuhrman considers various domestic ironies and then moves to ironies involved in official U.S. responses to dangers posed by 9/11: "It takes a long time to fold the map of tragedy into a paper hat. Blood keeps getting in the way of the crease" (68). However typical, the practice of "wearing" one's tragedy and ignoring surrounding contexts is problematic, and the mention of "blood" as an obstacle to the utilization of the "paper hat" indicates the irony of rushing to violent action as a response to violence whose aim, ultimately, is peace. From the proliferation of war, as the U.S.'s second Iraqi war would demonstrate starting in the year of the poem's publication, complications that *defer* opportunities for peace routinely surface.

Fuhrman's task here is not to deny the inevitability of interpretation and contextualization of a tragedy within the framework of an interpreter's major interests, including national security, but to encourage readers to exercise skepticism about egregiously condensed, excessively emotional reasoning: "Already, the Speaker is holding a press conference to change the name of the war. Already, the ads for the new fall programming are in. Soon it will start raining again on the children whom our army doesn't even need to kill in order to let die" (68). In actuality, Secretary of Defense Donald Rumsfeld, and not Speaker of the House Dennis Hastert, announced that the name of the war in extremely impoverished Afghanistan would be changed from "Operation Infinite Justice," which offended Moslems, to "Operation Enduring Freedom," but the poet is emphasizing how rhetoric ("ads") by politicians are "the new fall programming" of citizens to accept military actions like that particular campaign. The closing ironies in Fuhrman's poem suggest that a delay in selecting a single interpretation of 9/11 and in implementing a particular set of solutions to the problem of "homeland security" would not signify a lack of nerve or foolish indecision but would be a prudent acknowledgment of world affairs' complexity and an effort to develop an approach that would minimize long-term dangers and would have optimum long-term effects.

Among the fears that the five poets articulate, the limiting or misapprehension of Jewish identity is common to all. Whereas Shapiro calls attention to a misogynistic strain within Jewish religious tradition, Bernstein laments the reductiveness and exclusion of salubrious possibilities and even, at times, internalization of anti-Semitic beliefs that results from some Jews' tendencies to postulate a narrow range of identity formation and to ground it in a theory of linguistic unity and purity. Miller, Lease, and Fuhrman focus instead on addressing the possible resurgence of Nazi or Nazi-like demonization of Jewish identity when they make these horrific concepts palpable through poetic means.

The representation of the Shoah is a central danger zone. Shapiro's warning in "Voice" about relative amnesia regarding the Holocaust and "kitsch" depictions of it are heeded in Miller's "Row," which vigorously combats the notion that genocide's abject extremity bears no relation to the "normal" development of modern capitalism (and computer technology). Lease, however, is preoccupied with Zionist Jews' use of the Shoah to justify oppression of Palestinians and *also* with a wholesale dismissal of the Holocaust's horror (sometimes tied to this kind of critique) and a "blame the (Jewish) victim" syndrome. Fuhrman elucidates several related dangers: 9/11 as a rupture of national security, the spread of apocalyptic thinking with an anti-Semitic cast, and anticipation of the proliferation of violent injustice (on the part of various groups/nations) arising from the nightmare of 9/11.

The poets press varied aesthetic resources into service in their elaboration of poetic skepticism. With lyric concision, Shapiro's poem marshals subtle allusions, uncanny images, and spare narrative elements linked with a play of binary oppositions to enable readers to detect a call for a non-authoritarian, affirmative view of female sexuality and painstaking, unsentimental remembrance of the Shoah. Building on a tradition of Jewish comic entertainers' defamiliarization of the social and foregrounding of language's "polydictory" potential, Bernstein, on the one hand, relentlessly pursues a fragmenting of nearly every continuity involving self-representation ("voice"), narration, logical development, and straightforward communication. Miller, on the other hand, writes conversational poetry that switches subjects, casually returns to them, and mixes abstract critical speculation with brief historical and personal narratives and with realistic and surreal imagery in an effort to draw links between Nazism and coercive forms of capitalism and to trace implications of computer science's evolution in these contexts. Through lyrically charged prose and poetic strophes that feature juxtaposition of multivoiced interpretive gestures, evocative images, and tropes conveying states of extremity, Lease enacts a critique of interpretations of Jewish identity and the Holocaust and of their uses. "Leaps" between sentences encourage the reader to tease out salient historical connections and ruptures in a way that resembles Miller's more casual development of analogies. Fuhrman, like Lease, includes poetry and prose sections; dream-narrative, "realistic" narrative (including dialogue), allusions to current events, and ironic, intricate troping play against one another to produce a skeptical encounter with common individual and collective strategies for facing (or evading) the difficulties of the 9/11 tragedy.

"Democratic longing," of course, is the affirmative flip side of the representation of danger and skeptical questioning in these poets' texts. While Bernstein in his verse-retort to Beckett's question celebrates a dialogical multiplicity and respect for unpredictable process ("morphogenerativeness") in the uses of language as evidence of how democratic "polis" can take precedence over racial/ethnic separation, Miller advocates a critical pluralist tolerance and antihierarchical approaches to the flow of information, especially in his descriptions of Turing's open systematizing. In his affirmation of "the remembrance / movement" and "poetry" as "fire in the house," Shapiro implies that vigilance is a precondition, not only for the elimination of anti-Semitism, but for an overall advance of tolerance. In both Lease and Fuhrman's poems, criticism of emotion-saturated and oversimplified ways of reasoning about history (especially apocalyptic ones) and about race is designed to promote the eventual transcendence of violent political polarization and its frequently tragic consequences. Although some poets have different emphases than others, all five could probably agree substantially about general democratic aims.

Notes

1. David Shapiro, "Voice," *After a Lost Original* (Woodstock, NY: Overlook Press, 1994), 55. Further quotation from "Voice" is located in the text and is accompanied, when necessary, by page citation.

2. See Deborah Lipstadt, *Denying the Holocaust: The Growing Assault on Truth and Memory* (New York: Free Press, 1993).

3. Charles Bernstein, "From an Ongoing Interview with Tom Beckett," *My Way: Speeches and Poems* (Chicago: University of Chicago Press, 1999), 188. Further quotation from Bernstein's interview with Beckett is located in the text and is accompanied, when necessary, by page citation. "The Lives of the Toll Takers" is published in Charles Bernstein, *Dark City* (Los Angeles: Sun and Moon Press, 1994), 9–28.

4. Bernstein, "Stein's Identity," *My Way: Speeches and Poems,* 141. Further quotation from "Stein's Identity" is located in the text and is accompanied, when necessary, by page citation.

5. See Charles Bernstein, "Comedy and the Poetics of Political Form," *A Poetics* (Cambridge, MA: Harvard University Press, 1992), 218–228.

6. Charles Bernstein, "The Manufacture of Negative Experience," *With Strings* (Chicago: University of Chicago Press, 2001), 28. Further quotation from "The Manufacture of Negative Experience" is located in the text and is accompanied, when necessary, by page citation.

7. Stephen Paul Miller, "Row," *The Bee Flies in May* (New York: Marsh Hawk Press, 2002), 14–15. Further quotation from "Row" is located in the text and is accompanied, when necessary, by page citation.

8. Thomas Fink, *"A Different Sense of Power": Problems of Community in Late-Twentieth-Century U.S. Poetry* (Madison, NJ: Fairleigh Dickinson University Press, 2001), 111–123.

9. Joseph Lease, *My Sister Life* (Jersey City, NJ: Jensen/Daniels, 2001), 23. Further quotation from "'The Jew with the hole in his voice'" is located in the text and is accompanied, when necessary, by page citation.

Various phrases from "'The Jew with the hole in his voice'" are reiterated and transformed in a three-page section of Lease's *Free Again* (Oakland, CA: Xantippe, 2005), a chapbook-length poem that mostly explores social and economic conditions in the contemporary United States without other substantial references to Jewishness. "Free Again" is published in Lease's full-length collection, *Broken World* (Minneapolis: Coffee House Press, 2007).

10. Joanna Fuhrman, "Return to Normalcy," *Ugh Ugh Ocean* (Brooklyn, NY: Hanging Loose Press, 2003), 67. Further quotation from "Return to Normalcy" is located in the text and is accompanied, when necessary, by page citation.

Works Cited

Bernstein, Charles. *A Poetics.* Cambridge, MA: Harvard University Press, 1992.

———. *Dark City.* Los Angeles: Sun and Moon Press, 1994.

———. *My Way: Speeches and Poems.* Chicago: University of Chicago Press, 1999.

———. *With Strings.* Chicago: University of Chicago Press, 2001.

Fink, Thomas. *"A Different Sense of Power": Problems of Community in Late-Twentieth-Century U.S. Poetry.* Madison, NJ: Fairleigh Dickinson University Press, 2001.

Fuhrman, Joanna. *Ugh Ugh Ocean.* Brooklyn, NY: Hanging Loose Press, 2003.

Lease, Joseph. *My Sister Life.* Jersey City, NJ: Jensen/Daniels, 2001.

———. *Free Again.* Oakland, CA: Xantippe, 2005.

Lipstadt, Deborah. *Denying the Holocaust: The Growing Assault on Truth and Memory.* New York: Free Press, 1993.

Miller, Stephen Paul. *The Bee Flies in May.* New York: Marsh Hawk Press, 2002.

Shapiro, David. *After a Lost Original.* Woodstock, NY: Overlook Press, 1994.

Relentlessly Going On and On: How Jews Remade Modern Poetry without Even Trying

Stephen Paul Miller

What is Jewish poetry, or,
at least
one kind of Jewish poetry?[1]

Putting aside all-encompassing definitions and
tautological-"Jewish-poetry-is-as-Jewish-
poetry-does"-responses,
I find myself
examining my own experience,
asking
"What sounds Jewish?"
or, more to the point,

"What does 'Jewishness' sound like?"
I'm not sure, of course, and thankfully
there's no simple answer,
but while driving I entertain
my 90-year-old ma by
turning the radio to
Steve Somers'
Yiddish nuanced sports-talk schtick.
She immediately
identifies him as Jewish and is happy
(though she cares nothing for sports).

I ask how she
so quickly

picks up "Jewishness" in his voice
and she eventually says

the Yiddish accent comes from dovening,
the Yiddish word for prayer sharing Indo-European
roots with "divine."

Dovening as praying doesn't exclude silent prayer,
and my mother knows this, but thinks nonetheless of
dovening
as a rhythmic recitation of Hebrew liturgy
while nodding and rocking back and forth.
Since dovening is not a Hebrew word,
in her experience rhythmic dovening
reflects
how Yiddish-and-English-speaking peoples process
Hebrew,
and she sees dovening as an important link between
Yiddish and Hebrew,
noting cadences of dovening in Yiddish.

Okay, I'm not an expert,
and my mother's theory could be
wrong, and even if it's true,
it might concern only Eastern European Jews.

And yet it might point to something
even further back than Yiddish.

When I think of dovening, I think of an anapestic rhythm:

unstress—unstress—STRESS

An anapestic rhythm is generative, propelling us
through language
as dovening does through prayer, and indeed
ancient Jews
see time as linear,
not cyclical

            or restarting with each new king
but thrusting endlessly from creation
              ceaselessly as a
      distinctive way of reckoning time,
I mention this to my young son
  on Rosh Hashanah, when I tell him why
  it's 5765. "Do some people still rewind time?" he asks.
There's an ambiguity to Rosh Hashanah.
It moves you to the start of creation,
clearing
space to move forward.

  I won't pretend to know anything about Hebrew—
or even Yiddish—
            or for that matter
        the Aramaic in which Kaddish is chanted,
but I think it's notable that Kaddish
begins in the future tense
anapestically,
constructing motion even
from death:

yisgadol
yiskadosh—

which are reflexive future
third person singular verbs,
so I think they mean something like:

May He magnify Himself.
May He sanctify Himself.

I'm not sure but the point is it's in the future tense
and so is the word Israel, or Yisrael, meaning something
                                                                                         like

He will struggle with God and he will succeed,
suggesting a constantly edgy relation with God.

When I think of a Yiddish accent and the anapest
                                        and a certain Jewish drive, I

think of somehow finding myself chatting
with Jackie Mason on 57th St and 6th Ave.
His last words to me are

It's a PLEASure to TALK to an *inTELL*igent PERson."

I think this sort of anapest lends itself to a
direction indirection surprise!
. . . direction indirection surprise!
or
unstress unstress stress
ho hum wow
ho hum wow
rhythm. Rhythm is perhaps a better word
than meter here since when performing Jewish
liturgy
dovening imposes something rhythmic on other possible
metric readings,
though it could of course be in the meter of
the text too, and a poem can be enriched by
possibilities of differing meters
in the same passage—this richness of possibility
maybe a mark between a good poem and
less good one, between say, "of man's first disobedience"
and "once upon a midnight dreary."
Therefore, I do not mean overly to emphasize the
anapest, or exaggerate its place in the Bible.
The anapest merely indicates, in part through
dovening, a tendency to stress a more
generative and dynamic, rather than referentially
reflective,
poetic m.o.,
m.o.s that can accommodate the pace of say
the Marx Brothers' *Duck Soup*
or a Charles Bernstein or David Shapiro poem.
The Yiddish accent
might owe
something to both
dovening and
biblical poetry,

perhaps more than to Hebrew itself.
Hebrew lives so much through poetry
that dovening and what I'll call
the dynamic and parallel structures
of biblical poetry influence Yiddish,
and other languages Jews use, such as English, AND
Ladino, Arabic, Judeo-Persian,
Rumanian, Judeo-Arabic,
Judeo-Italian, Judeo-Provencal,
Judeo-French, Judeo-Greek,
Judeo-Crimean Tatar, and Jewish Neo-Aramaic——
my evidence is very
Eastern-Euro-American, and I think it would be cool if
someone looked into some of these other languages for biblical
poetic influences within their respective
literatures.

Robert Alter finds "the structure of biblical poems is
determined not by any substantive impulse of narration, but by
a steady progression of image or theme, a sort of mounting
semantic pressure which is to say a structure of

intensification."
What I say about the anapest
concerns a way to make
dynamic poesis
indicating something like
the intensities and
drives
of biblical poetry as Alter characterizes it
more than valuing
any particular meter,

more of a twin phenomenon with
breaking the back of iambic pentameter
then replacing it with another meter,

perhaps relating the new ethnicities
of modern America with modern poetry,

perhaps something "other." Eliot after all says he needs
Paris, a mix of English and not English
to write "Prufrock."
While vetting this paper with a friend
who probably experiences Judaism much
more directly than me, she says
    Kaddish, for her, is its trance-like rhythm:
chanting with extremely flat intonation
with a fairly even if at times anapestic delivery.
For her (Ilana Abramowitz), the meter seems part
of a bigger linguistic *dynamic.*
Maybe I shouldn't,
  but I think of Eliot's flat rhythmic quality.
In her *21st Century Modernism* book, Marjorie
Perloff talks of
                how
  important Eliot and Pound are in promoting
"generative" and
dynamic poetic models.
Frankly, I haven't been drawn to Eliot and Pound since I
                                was a teenager.
Rigidities and pretensions in their dictions and their
differing brands of anti-Semitic and fascistic leanings
      grow as turnoffs
and yet my teen attraction seems valid.
They're important to what poetry is becoming here.
I find their ambivalence toward
                        Whitman
  instructive because American
diversity
  inflects Whitman's parallelisms. I use the plural, "parallelisms,"
since there are many different kinds—
                    ones of usage, syntax, word
choice, syncopation, and all manner of linguistic constants
    changing within fixed structures.

      Whitman
      remakes poetry
      in a Jewish tradition

that's
unavoidable thereafter.

Certainly Eliot and Pound take parallelism in more
odd, syncopated directions, using different parallelisms and intensities like
the Bible sometimes does. Note "Prufrock"
repeating "let us" to initiate—
"Let us go then, you and I"—
responding—
"Do not ask 'what is it?' Let us go . . ."
And each time Pound's *Canto 45* repeats "with Usura" it refers to both
Usura's previous and following examples.
This kind of dynamic is used in JOB (where, for
example, "do you know?" parallels other "do you"
questions: "Do you know the time when the mountain goat
gives birth, / do you mark the birth pangs of the gazelles? /
Do you number the months till they come to term? / Do you
know the time when they give birth?" Check out the Bible and the *Cantos*
for more complex interactions among parallel structures. Similar modes are
available to Pound and Eliot
in poetic devices such as the villanelle and the sestina, and in musical
forms, (the use of these sources in itself demonstrates a push to the "something else"
of modern poetry) but, when the edge of epic
becomes poetry, Whitman
and biblical poetry cannot be ignored/get more of their due.
I can't say on what level Eliot and Pound adapt a
Jewish model of poetry
but perhaps it's
difficult to avoid,
especially
after Whitman unleashes it.
And, obviously being subjective,
Eliot and Pound sometimes seem
more Jewish than Whitman.
Well, sometimes anyway.
A secular Jewish poet like Kenneth
Koch organizes much work around
parallel structures *and* a sense of intensity *and*

relentlessly
ongoing discourse.
By ongoing discourse, I mean talk
flowing to and fro like dovening yet also
hurtling
endlessly forward.
Perhaps parallelism, discourse, and intensity
are hallmarks of
something like Jewish poetry. Its parallelisms and
intensities dovetail with argumentative, narrative,
and/or referentially abstract, linguistically
reflexive
poetry that, as Duke Ellington puts it, swings. Ellington,
backstage following a concert in Lincoln Center,
wearing pajamas and a bowler hat, signs my
Confucian Odes Pound translation

near where it says "the Duke rings true"
and close to

"everything comes to the Duke"
(though not exactly those words)

and around 1930 James Weldon Johnson says

Jews only among white folk can sing
black, and from the Andrews sisters
to Andy Statman, Klezmer and jazz
rhythms and melodies
blend easily. Lenny Bruce,
living perhaps in a more innocent time
says black people are, after all, Jewish.
David Antin is Jewish, but Spalding Gray
says he thinks of himself as Jewish too. He might not sound
Jewish though he composes that way through ongoing discourse.
Maybe his neurosis helps.
The generative feature I'm describing might not
dominate all Jewish poetry, but

describes some I like.
Perhaps Jewish poetry is concrete and
probing, like the anti-fascism as strong as
fascism that Benjamin tells Brecht he feels taking shape within
him—odd to say when speaking of Eliot and Pound, but I'm not
saying there aren't other workings in both, and perhaps that's
why their obscurities and rigidities
sometimes seem out of place.

One might expect a healthy dose of skepticism
from Jewish poets Pound influences, and skepticism
isn't totally unrelated to the poets we
associate with Objectivism,
so many of whom are secular Jews.
Zukovsky and other so-called Objectivists
desire oddly externalized sincerity
virtually embedded in words. Also preferring
sense and reality, my mother often says
"I'm from Missouri."
I wish she could vote there
(It's a swing state). Objectivism might
concern
what for me is Theodore Herzl's
most compelling reason for a Jewish state—and of course I'm
talkin' a century ago—and for me the
reason the United States at its best might be
a secular Jewish state, that is, a state in which Dreyfus would
theoretically get a fair shake
and the truth get direct presentation.
(The French right never acknowledges
the persuasive case for Dreyfus.
You'd think the truth would be more convincing.
Or at least entertainable.
What am I blocking?)
Of course a direct presentation's difficult to achieve, but the
desire's real and sheds light on
how Objectivism paradoxically also
involves subjective qualities such as
sincerity when verbally constructed. Note Jerome
Rothenberg's "Poland/1931":

“if there are men who ride the train to lodz / there are still
jews / just as there are still oranges / & jars / there is still
someone to write the Jewish poem—others to write their
mothers names in light.” Norman Finkelstein says
“Poland/1931” is distinctively “Jewish” because it is as
“objective in its identity as a jar or an orange, an
utterance . . . circulating,”
making me think of God promising
Jacob a home as He tells him
of perpetual Diaspora.
The Jewish imagination is not necessarily
grounded in a nation; Jewish poetry
needn’t be by Jews, and Jewish poetic
imagination isn’t limited to poetry.
Much of Harold Bloom’s fierce rap starts
with the *Kabbalah* but, in a less overtly Jewish
fashion, the urge to stress language, to experience what makes
us see language-as-language *as poetry* is central in Roman Jakobson’s work;
knowing cultures as languages is
of course advanced by Claude Lévi-Strauss,
and Derrida makes clear that language is
more than anything else a generative if painstaking “sense
of itself.”

That perhaps the preeminent Formalist,
founding “Structuralist,” and most philosophically
influential “Post-Structuralist” are secular Jews
suggests, as secular Jews, they
extend a
close attention characteristic of traditional Jewish scholars
to secular texts that
magnify
our sense of what texts
can be. Similarly, secular Jewish figures
such as Lenny Bruce and Bob Dylan and, hey, my son just asked
if Simon and Garfunkel are two people, and I don’t know,
Rodgers and Hammerstein and Einstein and
Irving Berlin and Lerner and Lowe—okay,
forget Lerner and Lowe, not because they’re not Jewish, but no, I
like them too, and I think they’re Jewish—secular Jewish figures s t r e t c h

linguistic, critical, and poetic substance
          through swinging
                    spiels.

Note

1. Based on talk at "Secular Jewish Culture / Radical Poetic Practice," Center for Jewish History / American Jewish Historical Society, September 21, 2004.

Azoy Toot a Yid

Secular Poetics and "The Jewish Way"

Eric Murphy Selinger

To begin, an old joke—a canonical joke, I suppose, since it's in the *Norton Anthology of Jewish American Literature.* The young rabbi of an old congregation found himself in a pickle. Week after week, when the Shema was said, half the congregants would stand, and half would stay seated. Each group yelled at the other to sit back down or get up on their feet. Baffled, the rabbi turned for advice to the housebound elder of the *shul.* "Is the tradition to stand during the prayer?" he demanded.

> The old man answered, "No, that is not the tradition."
> "Then the tradition is to sit during the Shema!"
> The old man answered, "No, that is not the tradition."
> Then the rabbi said to the old man, "But the congregants fight all the time, yelling at each other about whether they should sit or stand."
> The old man interrupted, exclaiming, "*That* is the tradition!" (*Norton* 325)

The Jewish sensibility, this little tale suggests, prefers argument to harmony, disputation to accord. Even at the moment in the service when everyone bears witness that God is One, "the tradition" endorses human bickering.

We cannot claim endless debate to be an exclusively Jewish value. Romantics like Blake and Schlegel embraced it; one thinks also of the "quarrel with ourselves" that produces poetry in the Yeats, and of the "YES & NO" of James Merrill's Ouija-board.[1] Likewise, as Daniel Boyarin has argued, this ideal of dissensus is no Jewish universal. It arises in particular texts and historical circumstances (the Babylonian Talmud in the Stammaitic period, roughly 450–650 C.E.), and plays out within clearly defined, albeit unspoken boundaries.[2] The joke I have quoted never hints that the congregants might choose not to say *Shema* at all, for example. One notes as well that all the characters are men.

Im kol zeh, the Jewish passion for "disputation without telos" remains a noteworthy phenomenon, one that can encompass a remarkable variety of tones and genres (Boyarin 161). If the joke from the *Norton* embodies it as comedy, a tale from the Babylonian Talmud captures its pathos:

> Resh Lakish died, and Rabbi Yohanan grieved greatly.
> The *talmidei hakhamim* said, "Who will go and revive him? Let Elazar ben Pedat go, whose *shma'atas* are so sharp."
> He went and sat before him. To everything that Rabbi Yohanan would say, he would say, "Here is a tannaitic passage that supports you."
> He said to him, "You are [supposed to be] like Ben Lakish?! Ben Lakish, whenever I said anything, would pose twenty-four questions, and I would give him twenty-four responses and the *shma'ata* would expand. You answer 'Here is a tannaitic passage that supports you.' Don't I know that I am speaking well?"
> He would walk tearing his clothes, crying, and saying, "Where are you, Ben Lakish? Where are you, Ben Lakish?"
> He cried until he lost his mind.
> The *talmidei hakhamim* asked mercy for him:
> He found his rest (he died). (BT Bava Metzia 84; qtd. in Elon 108–109)

The former bandit, Resh Lakish, and his teacher, Rabbi Yohanan, may have been rivals. But their battles were more life-giving, and more expansive of the text at hand (the *shma'ata*) than the hapless affirmation supplied by Elazar ben Pedat. Even the Holy One, the Talmud attests, would rather lose an argument than hear mere assent. "My children have defeated me," God famously laughs on finding that divine intervention—a voice from Heaven declaring one side right—does not settle a fractious halakhic debate. Rather, His authority gets trumped by a rabbi quoting scripture: "it is not in Heaven," says the rabbi, twisting words that originally referred to the Torah itself to mean that the power to settle the argument rests among humans alone (Baba Metzia 59b, quoting Deut. 30:12).[3]

Among Jewish American poets, the notion that God likes a lively opponent has proven deeply inviting. Consider the use that Alicia Ostriker makes of this idea in *The Volcano Sequence,* a serial poem that gives voice to the divine in order to let Him / Her / It—the gender and degree of anthropomorphism shift throughout the text—respond to the poet's questions, quotations, and other forms of address. "Only in the space of this dialogue does that which is addressed take form," she quotes from Paul Celan in an epigraph, "and gather around the I who is addressing it." Through this imagined colloquy, the secular "nothing" that marks the absence of a God becomes a mystical "nothing," an apophatic no-thing of a deity, and thus an addressable, if still unembraceable, You.

In the book's "addendum to Jonah," Ostriker casts herself as the pouting prophet and hears an italicized response from the Mouth of Mouths:

a dead gourd
one of your jokes

are you very angry
be serious
your heartbreak is not interesting
it is your rhetoric that beguiles me
I liked your performance at Nineveh
just as I liked your song by the waters of Babylon
your legal brief at Uz
I want you to praise me hotly but more than that
I want you to save the world
by any means necessary
your word against
mine

The twist at the end of this passage from end-paused free verse to jarring enjambment—"your word against / mine"—draws our attention to the complexity of the thought. This God loves human rhetoric, longs for our human "word" to contest, as well as report, divine decrees. He quotes Malcolm X, "*by any means necessary,*" as though to suggest that divine rule is no more natural or inevitable than white supremacy. As the linebreak hints, however, our human word may also belong *to* God—"*your word against / [is] mine*"—, which makes our resistance part of an argument within the Godhead: a new twist on the Talmudic precept that "these and these [two opposing rulings] are the words of the living God" (BT Eruvin 13b).

Among secular Jews—again, a fuzzy category, so let's say, among those Jews who recite the Shema less frequently and reverently than they tell Jewish jokes—the Judaism of disputation has been put to a variety of uses. Some are political. When Sarah Ironson tells her grandson Louis, in Tony Kushner's

Angels in America, "As er darf ringen mit zain Libm Nomen" ("You should struggle with the Almighty") since *"Azoy toot a Yid"* ("It's the Jewish way"), her injunction has little to do with theology, and everything to do with fighting the Powers-That-Be and the Way-Life-Is, on Earth much more than in Heaven. That she gives the admonition in Yiddish, the language of Jewish *sotsyalizm,* lets Kushner stake two claims, one religious and one secular, to resistance as the "Jewish way." Kushner credits Harold Bloom as an influence, and in Bloom's *Ruin the Sacred Truths,* the critic describes "Jewish dualism" in terms that echo Kushner's "Jewish way," but strip it of its lingering theistic rhetoric. A "ceaseless agon within the self," Bloom calls it, "not only against all outward injustice but also against what I have called the injustice of outwardness, or, more simply, the way things are" (*Ruin* 162). Like Marlon Brando in *The Wild One,* the secular Jew is ready to rebel, however inwardly, against whatever you've got. (Is this such a leap? The film's director, Laszlo Benedek, was a Hungarian Jew smuggled to safety by Louis B. Mayer in 1939.)

Of Rabbis and Debates

Religious, ambivalent, and thoroughly secular Jewish poets have all made good use of this figure of the Jew-as-mental-rebel: the one who will, in Jerome Rothenberg's words, "refuse consensus, [and] thus become . . . the model for the Great Refusal to the lie of Church and State" (7). They have cast this figure in a variety of costumes, however, and done so in a variety of forms. (A "ceaseless agon" could hardly find rest in a single genre or mode!) Some will strike the reader as "Jewish," because of their rich and varied association with Jewish religious texts, Jewish humor, or Jewish fiction. Others will prove equally familiar, but from non-Jewish sources: proof of their author's refusal of any consensus about the boundary between the Jewish and the non-Jewish. (As Charles Bernstein puts it in the "Commentary" to his poem "Solidarity is the Name We Give to What We Cannot Hold": "But is it Jewish? / —I think, probably, maybe so / But it could also be not Jewish / —Exactly" (35).

The poetic structure one could derive most easily from the traditions of rabbinic argument would be, well, a rabbinic argument—or at least the report of one, reframed for secular use. "Rabbi José the Angel," the opening poem of Jay Ladin's *Alternatives to History,* illustrates this move. The poem recounts a legend confected by Ladin herself—the story of Rabbi José, born with wings, and his eventual murder by the Romans—by conflating the Latino-looking transliterated name of a real Talmudic rabbi (Jose the Galilean) and the Very Old Man With Enormous Wings from the Gabriel Garcia Márquez story of that name. Here's how the poem begins:

"A miracle is an embarrassment,"
Rabbi José the Angel said. His parents
were human—we know that.

The Talmud preserves a single discussion
of the wings that sprouted from his shoulders.
Rabbi José said they meant

that even to reach the Earth
he needed to ascend;
Rabbi Pinchas cited Daniel;

Rabbi Asher laughed;
Rabbi Tarfon taught, in the name of his teacher,
that a winged one is born in every generation

to see if the Flood has receded
and history can begin.
Flight was painful to him.

His wife, Tzipporah, a Moabite prophetess
with turmeric eyes, said
as much as she loved his wings

she preferred the rest of him.

In these opening stanzas, the miraculous fact of Rabbi José's wings serves as the "text" or *shma'ata* to be expanded. Notably, the "reading" of those wings by Rabbi José himself opens, rather than concludes, the discussion, and his experience of them ("Flight was painful to him") does not supply its closing cadence. That right belongs to his wife, Tzipporah ["Bird"], whose identity hovers between Jew and non-Jew and whose commentary grounds the others' hermeneutical flights. (Ladin offers a range of such little jokes. Rabbi Asher laughs; his name means "Happy." Rabbi José has wings; his namesake, R. Jose, argued that chicken was not "meat" and could therefore be simmered in milk, in the style of his home town [Hul. 113a, 116a].)

As the poem continues, Ladin weaves additional legends, tales, and scholars' debates into it, filtering the story of Rabbi José's life and possible martyrdom ("no source preserves the end") through an array of voices and speakers. The multiplicity of such reports, arguments, and interpretations, the poem suggests, does not clutter our path back to an original, self-evident revelation, a "miracle." Rather, the dispute itself is the stuff of Jewish knowledge. This idea may be familiar, not least from Gershom Scholem's magisterial essay "Revelation and Tradition as Religious Categories in Judaism," but Ladin stages it memorably, especially in the poem's closing cadence:

Rabbi Asher argued

that since José didn't know Latin
his death was miraculous;
Pinchas agreed with reservations;

Tzipporah the prophetess wept.

Rabbi José the Angel said
life is a seal on a letter.
The wax is broken.

We have reached the text.

The efforts of Rabbi Asher to give a single, "miraculous" import to his colleague's execution falter in the face of Pinchas's "reservations" and Tzipporah's tears, which insist on the plurality of its meanings. (The line about Tzipporah echoes John 11:35, "Jesus wept," as though to draw yet another tradition into the dialogue.) Ladin ensures, too, that the poem's closure will be open to "disputation without telos." Does the final line belong to Rabbi José? If so, "the text" would mean some sort of meaning beyond this world, this life, only reachable through death. Or does the last line belong to the poet himself, and send us not outward, into blessed assurance, but merely onward, into the necessity of further commentary, further debate, and further reading?

By writing his poem of dialogue in rabbis, Ladin situates his work primarily within Jewish tradition. There are, of course, other traditions of poetic argument: medieval debates between body and soul; Renaissance arguments between duty and pleasure ("Ulysses and the Siren," by Samuel Daniel, for example); and, in the modern period, Yeats's dialogues between self and soul, self and anti-self, Solomon and Sheba, and so on. To write a poem of the "Jewish way" that hearkens back to such texts would mean, at the very least, to place the poet on both Jewish and non-Jewish sides of a cultural divide; more dramatically, it might mean to "Judaize" those antecedents, or at least offer them Jewish affiliation.

Both meanings can be found in Howard Nemerov's "Debate with the Rabbi," a witty poem whose speaker plays Crazy Jane to the Rabbi's smugly confident Bishop:

You've lost your religion, the Rabbi said,
  It wasn't much to keep, said I.
You should affirm the spirit, said he,
And the communal solidarity.
  I don't feel so solid, I said.
. . . .
We Jews are creative people, the Rabbi said.
  Make something, then, said I.
In science and in art, said he,
Violinists and physicists have we.
  Fiddle and physic indeed, I said. . . .

Nemerov's Rabbi speaks not simply for normative *faith* (Judaism as a religion), but also for the normative *identity* imposed by "communal solidarity." Nemerov's speaker demurs from both. His "religion" was never "much to keep," he shrugs—a swipe at his own upbringing or, perhaps, a reminder that Judaism has only recently been, and can only reductively be, thought of as a "religion" *per se.* As for solidarity, this speaker feels too fluid, too shifting or multiple to affirm his membership in something as stable as The Community. Like Kafka, perhaps he feels like he has little in common with himself, let alone with "the Jews."

The wordplay in the poem's penultimate stanza suggests one agent that has dissolved those bonds of solidarity. When he hears "violinists and physicists," this speaker doesn't think of Jascha Heifitz and John von Neumann, or even of Albert Einstein (famously both). Rather, he thinks of slang ("fiddle and physic" plays off "fiddle-faddle," for trifling nonsense), of Shakespeare, Pope, and other English poets (in whom "physic" is medicine), and of Marianne Moore (whose "Poetry" scoffs at "all this fiddle"). The speaker's fluent immersion in English—the English language, and Anglo-American culture—supplies this range of reference, and its current leads him to a set of "creative people," fellow makers, who are not notably Jewish. As for that, how "Jewish" *are* the scientists, artists, and musicians lauded by the Rabbi, really—and how "Jewish" their work? To cite them as reasons for communal pride is so much nonsense and patent medicine, Nemerov suggests. In the poem's final stanza, however, Nemerov's speaker steps into the communally identifiable role he has heretofore refused.

Stubborn and stiff-necked man! the Rabbi cried.
   The pain you give me, said I.
Instead of bowing down, said he,
You go on in your obstinacy.
   We Jews are that way, I replied.

For the first time, he speaks in the first-person plural, and does so to embrace an identity based on multiple biblical precedents. From Exodus to Chronicles, a series of authority figures (God, Moses, Jeremiah, Nehemiah, and others) lament that the Jews are a "stiff-necked" people. If to be a Jew means to be stiff necked, the speaker concedes, he will be one. If it means to bow down, forget about it. The Rabbi now plays Haman to Nemerov's "obstinate" Mordecai, or "Mordecai the Jew," as the Book of Esther periodically calls him. To be "that way" is to follow Kushner's "Jewish way": to follow an obstinate, rebellious *halacha* (a term which means, of course "the path" or "the way").

Although "Debate with the Rabbi" offers us a debate-poem on English models, then, rather than rabbinic ones, it ends by endorsing debate itself as *more* Jewish than religious faith or communal affiliation. This endorsement allies the poem with many formally "radical" poems in which "the Jewish way" of resistance trumps any more obedient Judaism as a marker of identity. In these, as in Nemerov's poem, figures from the Jewish past underwrite the Jewishness of the contemporary poet's scoffing or obstinacy. In David Antin's talk-poem "writing and exile," the sponsoring figure is the poet's biological ancestor Wolf Kitzes, the Hasidic master and comrade of the Baal Shem Tov, who answers a question from God—"how is it with my people"—not with a petition for mercy but with a question of his own: "so how should it be?" In Charles Bernstein's "anaffirmation," a paraphrase of Gertrude Stein's line "I am I because my little dog knows me" signals the Jewish ancestry of what is otherwise a culturally nonspecific poem about refusing "the corrosive ardency / of blinkered identification." "[M]y growling / Zebra knows me just / enough to tip / her hat," this poem ends, replacing Stein's dog with a dapper, paradoxical animal that is both black and white.[4]

If Nemerov's poem leads us outward to these other, more radical poems, it can also remind us that many a Jew, without being a poet, has defined him or herself as (in John Taggart's phrase, describing George Oppen) a "Jew by opposition / difference" (5), and that Nemerov's poem now offers itself as a resource for such Jews to draw upon, just as Nemerov draws upon the Bible or Bernstein on Stein. Were Jewish American poetry better known, "Debate with the Rabbi" might well find mention of the work of the Israeli "religious secularist" Ari Elon. Nemerov's Rabbi embodies what Elon calls *rabbani* Jewish culture, which looks to Torah and its official interpreters as sources of authority, while the speaker embodies a *ribboni,* free-thinking Jewish identity that sees once-sacred texts and communal decrees as touchstones for new creation, but never as determinative.

My Way; or, The Other Within

Once we hear the two voices of "Debate with the Rabbi" as *rabbani* and *ribboni* strands within Jewish culture, we are not far from hearing them as two voices within a single ambivalent Jew: impulses toward affirmation and "anaffirmation" (in Bernstein's neologism), or *t'shuvah* and aversion. Two radically different Jewish American poets, Jacqueline Osherow and Norman Finkelstein, have repeatedly staged the *agon* of the Jewish way within a single self, or at least within the various materials that *make up* a self. Osherow rebels both against the normative (the "pious," as she sometimes calls it) and against her own bravado of refusal, unwilling to give up the restless, passionate, zig-zag motion she identifies with *poesis* for the security that either stance would bring. By turns proving points in prose and disputing them in verse, staking out poetic voices and abandoning them in subsequent volumes, and deploying assertion, contradiction, and paradox within individual poems, Finkelstein too has carried on a series of arguments with himself about the role of nostalgia in secular Jewish culture, about the relationship between religion and *poesis,* and about the place of the Jewish poet vis-à-vis any normative Jewish community.

Let me begin with Osherow's long poem "Views of *La Leggenda della Vera Croce,*" which enacts its Jewish debate within the self in Dantean terza rima. In the poem's opening pages, Osherow alternately loses herself in rapt contemplation of Piero's "Legend of the True Cross" and finds herself troubled by the casual anti-Semitism of panels like *The Torture of Judas*—which turns out, in Italian, to have a slightly longer name, "*The Torture of the Jew who wouldn't reveal / The location of the true cross*" (6). This argument between art and history, ethics and aesthetics, carries Osherow into fresh debates with herself. Why can't she stop looking? What explains, or excuses, her "breeziness about the Temple's destruction, / This complete inability to feel its loss" (10)—and, given that breeziness, why does she fast each year at Tisha b'Av?

As she wrestles such questions, Osherow's speaker proves herself at once richly knowledgeable about Jewish texts and practices and thoroughly skeptical, "stiff-necked" in her scoffing and refusal. "Don't be too shocked, I'm often blasphemous," she shrugs.

It's a deal I have with God; at least I pray.
Though he may have a plan—I'm not impervious—

In which I'm expected to wake up one day,
Go to synagogue, recite the psalms,
And convince myself with every word I say.

Beggers can't be choosers; these are godless times;
Let Him hold on to His illusions.

A moment later, since "the way things are" now includes her skepticism, Osherow pivots to turn against it—and, like so many Jewish poets, to find a Jewish precedent for her claims and retractions:

Besides, maybe I do have a few qualms

About my persistent heretical allusions
To Someone who is—after all—a Deity. . . .
You'll find I'm a jumble of confusions.

Besides, I'm not sure God much cares for piety;
My guess is—since David was His favorite—
That He's partial to passion, spontaneity,

And likes a little genuine regret.
True, David lost his ill-begotten child—
But what did the pious ever get? (10–11)

That eyebrow she cocks at "the pious" is less skeptical than regal, and the Jewish identity it enacts suddenly looks less secular than Davidic, recalling the imaginative and active freedom of that "giant-hearted, // if somewhat errant, poet-king" as Osherow calls him in another long poem in terza rima, "At the Art Nouveau Synagogue, Rue Pavée."

Because David is poet, as well as king, Osherow can use his "errant" Jewish practice as a model for the Jewish poet's dialectical relationship to the normative community. On the one hand, this relationship is one of participation in and appreciation of rabbinic Judaism. Few Jewish American poets have been so able to represent, without treacly sentiment, what Osherow calls "the elaborate grace // available only to the hidebound" (*TK*). But as that pun on the leather straps of *tefillin* suggests, Osherow also views rabbinic Judaism from the ironic distance of one who has been called to a separate path. Davidic straying, royal liberty, antedates the rabbinic "way" of halakha, and although they may cross paths, they never intersect for very long. "Look what care they take of my belongings," Osherow thus smiles with regal indulgence at the end of "At the Art Nouveau Synagogue":

when I, myself, have all but let them go.
They'll even keep safe for me my Sabbath day
while I'm off ogling the Paolo Uccello

and pray the daily prayers I never pray.
I absolutely count on their intransigence;
I wouldn't want all of us to go astray.

You never know. One day, I might learn reverence
or simply need a perfect word to say
or even to overhear as some believer chants
before I continue on my way.

Unlike the rabbinic "way" envisioned by this poem, in which much (the order of the service, the weekly *parasha,* the endurance of the covenant) is always already known, the poet's trajectory careers between the known and the unknown ("you never know"). "My way," she calls it, with *halacha* and Sinatra held equally in mind.[5]

If "At the Art Nouveau Synagogue" presents the poet's "my way" as Davidic, Norman Finkelstein's "Acher" offers a contrasting model from the Jewish past. The speaker of this persona-poem, the eponymous "Acher," wears the mask of rabbi Elisha ben Abuya, the apostate dubbed "The Other" (*acher*) by the Talmud. Despite this condemnation, ben Abuya's opinions and acts remain in the text, which makes him a figure within rabbinic Jewish tradition for the Jew who stands at once inside and outside of the boundaries of community and halacha. Isaac Deutscher thus makes ben Abuya the original "Non-Jewish Jew": "a prototype of those great revolutionaries of modern thought: Spinoza, Heine, Marx, Rosa Luxemburg, Trotsky, and Freud," all of whom "went beyond the boundaries of Jewry" because they "found Jewry too narrow, too archaic, and too constricting" (207).

Finkelstein's Acher bears some resemblance to Deutscher's, and the Talmudic story that Deutscher cites about ben Abuya reaching "the boundaries of Jewry" shows up in the third stanza of the poem, clinching the connection. But Finkelstein takes his cues even more from Gershom Scholem's and Harold Bloom's accounts of the enigmatic rabbi. (Finkelstein cites "The Meaning of the Torah in Jewish Mysticism" and *Poetics of Influence* as his source texts.) The poem begins with a haunting Talmudic parable (Hagigah 14b) drawn from Scholem's essay, as though to insist, first and foremost, on Acher's inextricable place among the texts and heroes of rabbinic Judaism—and, by extension, on the reader's fluency, or at least familiarity, with those texts and names. It takes a certain amount of background knowledge to plunge into a poem that begins like this:

It was like this in the garden:
  Ben Azzai looked and died,
  Ben Zoma looked and went mad;
  Akiba and I went forth in peace,
but they said I cut down the young plants.

What is the reader to make of this? What "garden" does the speaker have in mind? Who are these rabbis, and why should it be that although two of them escape madness and death, one of the survivors stands accused of "cut[ting] down the young plants"? (A naughty thing to do in any garden, certainly—but the phrase is heavy with implication.) Who, finally, are the accusatory "they"?

To answer these questions, you need to look to Finkelstein's sources, or at least to the poet's own commentary on "Acher." In the process, you enter into the poet's dissent from those sources: an argument he pursues at first through a simple shift in perspective. Because the Other speaks in this poem, reporting the stories about him, he calls those stories into question; thus, for example, the Talmudic charge against ben Abuya that he seduced the young away from Judaism ("cut down the young plants") sounds in this poem more like a charge of petty vandalism back in "the garden," one which "they" cannot have witnessed, and which Rabbi Akiba, who was there, does not support.

As the poem goes on, Finkelstein makes Acher seem more and more appealing, even as the normative "they" seems more and more hypocritical, projecting on to him their own doubts and errant desires. "I said that one is two," he explains, "and they answered if two why not a thousand: / so they cast me from the congregation / —but they still come to hear me teach." With that pivot into the present tense—not "they still *came*," but "still come"—Finkelstein marks his first major departure from the model of the Jew-as-rebel we saw in "Debate with the Rabbi." In this poem, the Other does not simply contest the members of his former congregation. He continues to teach them, *at their desire*, from outside the boundaries of their community. (Our reading of the poem might well stand as one such moment of instruction.) The truth that he teaches, "one is two," seems less theological here than structural: it's the truth that sets dialectic—any dialectic—into motion. "One is two" describes the Jewish community in the poem, divided by the expulsion of Acher; it describes the micro-community of rabbis who survived their excursion in the Garden, and of those who did not; more broadly, it describes the core impulse of the "Jewish way" described by Kushner, Bloom, and others, with its love for a "ceaseless *agon*." Acher himself, then, has a stake in his own exclusion, at least as long as that exclusion is partial, provocative, and pedagogical.

When Finkelstein reaches his second anecdote about ben Abuya, then, he invites us to read it as a parable of this mutual dependence:

Meir went with me to the boundary;
  I rode and he walked by my side
until I reminded him that he could go no further
  since he honored the Sabbath and the Law.
But he longed to hear me finish the argument,
  and he waited there till I returned.

For there to be an argument, like the one Meir "longed to hear me finish," there must be contrasting possibilities: two, not one. Return demands departure; dishonor, honor; companionship, difference. Ben Abuya may not have read Derrida or Blake, but Finkelstein has; his Acher and Meir illustrate the infernal proverb "opposition is true friendship" as well as any couple in the Talmud.

I drift into anachronisms—but then, so does the poem. In its final stanzas, "Acher" invokes Freud, Gnosticism, modern Hebrew, as well as biblical material to flesh out and articulate its vision of the dialectical "Jewish way." Finkelstein begins by reminding us of sexual difference, and through sex, of Freud's account of both civilization and the individual mind as irredeemably divided against themselves. "I went on to visit the fairest of my disciples," Acher recalls, "but I will never see her again, / for she spoke for civilization / and I for its discontents." His response to her reminds us that the rabbis of the Talmud, too, faced irresolvable disputes—and did so often enough that their shrug of deferral, "*Tishbi yetzaretz kushyot u'avayot*" [Elijah the prophet—who heralds redemption—will resolve questions and problems] has been turned into an acronym and adopted in modern Hebrew as the noun *teiku,* meaning a tie score. Some disputes are endless, and perhaps are best so, the poem concludes: those between opposed desires within the self, between soul and body, between the normative and the antinomian. The real question, then, is how we treat that unyielding, necessary interlocutor. Appropriately, the poem's final lines set up opposing possibilities:

> *Teku* I said, and so we parted,
> for the dispute cannot be resolved.
>
> This is how it must be
> for one who cannot reconcile his desires:
> the soul is a spark that consumes the body:
> let no one seek to rest.
> There is a Law beyond the Law and we may not know it
> except through all our wanderings.
>
> I said do not look for the book nor its author,
> Elisha ben Abuyah, called Acher,
> the other, the stranger in your midst.

On the one hand, this poem might be said to suggest that the other, the Acher, is to be loved as oneself. That's what we learn in Leviticus 19:34—"the stranger who resides with you . . . you shall love him as yourself, for you were strangers in the land of Egypt"—a verse that this poem extends, through Freud, to include the other within the self. On the other hand, the Torah repeatedly also commands that "stranger in your midst" should be subject to the same laws as "you" are, and this stranger breaks and refutes those, in search of that "Law beyond the Law." A love that elides the boundaries between other and self, Acher and Meir, joining two into one, imposes a false, messianic, inhuman unity that cannot help but damage both. (Again one thinks of Blake: "one law for the ox and the ass is oppression.")

Although it speaks in a single voice, "Acher" gathers and juxtaposes several different discourses. One hears echoes of Talmud, Freud, of Gnostic writing, of Robert Duncan ("there is a Law beyond the Law"), the Bible, and more.

Finkelstein makes no effort to imagine his way into the voice of the historical Elisha ben Abuyah; if this is a dramatic monologue, the character it dramatizes is almost ostentatiously textual. "For Jews in particular," the poet has written, " 'the Vale of Soul-Making' (Keats's term for the world as the place of imaginative self-discovery) is composed of others' texts." The texts in question may be Jewish or non-Jewish, in prose or poetry, by others or even by one's younger self. To conflate a number of allusions, one might say that for Finkelstein, "our wanderings" in search of that "Law beyond the Law" add up eventually to the onward, zig-zagging trajectory that Osherow calls "my way," and they take us through the textual "Vale of Soul-Making," where some Thou is always with us, rod and staff at hand to comfort or threaten, as the case may be.

Let me take a moment to trace how Finkelstein turns the "Jewish way" of argument, including argument with oneself, into a sojourn in the Vale of Soul-Making. In *The Ritual of New Creation: Jewish Tradition and Contemporary Literature* (1992), Finkelstein speaks of modern Jewish poetry and fiction, at least in the Diaspora, as "associated with loss and deprivation" whatever pleasure it may bring (128). "The current act of writing," he observes, "is marked by the imagination of past wholeness, a melancholy longing for irretrievable conditions that were somehow more conducive to the writer's task, and a nagging sense of diminishment or inadequacy. The work, in short, is premised upon nostalgic remembrance. Like Benjamin's angel, it is always looking backward toward Paradise, from which a disastrous wind hurtles it into the future" (128). In a later essay, "The Master of Turning," Finkelstein recasts this pronouncement as an autobiographical reflection. "Ineluctably modern and ineluctably Jewish," he writes, "I realized that both of these dimensions of myself embodied an uncertain longing for versions of an idealized past which I had never really experienced, for to a great extent they were imaginative constructs. Yet these constructs inspired my best writing; indeed, it was in some of that writing that these image worlds came to be constructed" (419). In this later account, loss and deprivation bring a recompense that outweighs any sense of "diminishment or inadequacy." Nostalgia this may be, but it proves, as the critic observes, a "strangely productive version" of that sweet sadness.

This second account of a "productive" nostalgia marks Finkelstein's debt to Romanticism far more than to Jewish thought. Emerson, for example, understood that a poet's cultural deprivation could turn out to be rewarding, and this dialectic of loss and gain recurs in Robert Frost and Wallace Stevens, each a master at turning nostalgia to discovery. Think of Frost's "Directive," where the clutter of the present ("all this now too much for us") leads us to search for renewal in an imagined past and in the imagined home, the fictive "grail," of the poem. In Stevens, too, loss tends to produce a compensatory influx of imaginative possibility. "To see the gods dispelled in mid-air and dissolve like clouds is one of the great human experiences," he proposes in "Two or Three Ideas." "It was their annihilation, not ours, and yet it left us feeling that in a measure, we too had been annihilated." This sense of being returned to the *nihil,* the uncreated or pre-created state, does not last long—indeed, its rebuttal arises "at the same time," in Stevens's account. "At the same time, no man ever muttered a petition in his heart for the restoration of those unreal shapes," he observes. "There was in every man the increasingly human self, which instead of remaining the observer, the nonparticipant, the delinquent, became constantly more and more all there was or so it seemed; and whether it was so or merely seemed so still left it for him to resolve life and the world on his own terms."

The post-Christian nostalgias of Frost and Stevens may seem odd company at first for a Jewish poet. The "Acher-poet" in Finkelstein, however, does not hesitate to weave them into his texts. Consider "A Poem for the Little Shoemakers," the opening poem of *Restless Messengers.* The poems in this collection, Finkelstein has written, arose "simultaneously" with *The Ritual of New Creation,* and the two books share the project of putting a Jewish identity into practice through textual commentary that writes "both with and against . . . with audacity and respect in equal measure" (424). The text this poem comments on, at least ostensibly, is Isaac Bashevis Singer's short story "The Little Shoemakers." Implicitly, however, Finkelstein also brings Frost, Stevens, and Keats into his sights, using them to limn a Jewish Romantic poetics.

The poem begins on a promising note. "The sunset opens against the horizon," Finkelstein writes, "like a book in which are inscribed / the deeds of a thousand generations—." Readers familiar with "The Little Shoemakers" will recognize a nod to Abba Shuster's comfortable vision of the summer skies. "He could virtually see the Almighty seated on His throne of glory, the earth serving Him as a footstool," Singer writes early in the story. "Satan was vanquished; the angels sang hymns. The Book of Memory in which were recorded all the deeds of men lay open" (44). In Finkelstein's poem, however, this dream of accord between human deeds and heavenly memory vanishes by the fourth line. The pages turn out to be "blank," and when the poem pans upward, as if in search of consolation, it finds "Nothing but sentiment / among the hosts of heaven, / while here on earth / the black smoke rises / as the villages are consumed."

The next stanza responds to this loss—both of homes and of faith in redemption—by turning farther back into history. To be a Jew, it imagines, once meant to choose whether "to be scattered among the nations / and to seek through codes of piety / to raise the sparks of creation"—the normative myth of post-Lurianic Jewry—or conversely "to follow some leader / in to the maw of the abyss," the Sabbatean attempt to end history as such, or "force the end," in the traditional phrase. The poem holds these choices in their infinitive suspense only a moment, again, before they slip away. "The choices are dashed on the rocks / and the rocks are worn into dust," Finkelstein sighs, but this loss plunges him back, again, into an imagined past mediated by Singer and by religious tradition. "There is nothing to be learned from patience," the poem now declares,

> except for the most minute of wonders:
> toadstools around the door
> and moss growing softly in the rafters,
> a halo of clouds around the moon,
> stars when the moon is new.
> And then to turn and worship the invisible,
> creation wrenched once more from a book,
> an alphabet of living forms.

For a moment, the poem edges into Abba Shuster's pious, halakhic worldview—a way of seeing that insists on "patience" (as he waits for redemption) and that fosters natural observation (as one watches the heavens for stars or a new moon)—only to back away from that sympathy. A cry to the heavens—"Why are we held back, oh Lord?"—pivots the poem into a fast-break through diaspora, American-style. One moment we are in "workshops and kitchens" dining off chipped plates, mismatched silverware; the next, we find ourselves, like Singer's Abba, disoriented, walking on "carpet" as "wealth suddenly breeds and thrives" in "an exile wrought in gold." Held back no longer, at least materially, the voice of the poem still imagines itself and its readers as anxious, in exile. What reassurance can it provide?

First, Finkelstein offers nostalgia *tout court.* "So lean back into the past," the poem advises:

> Somewhere is a house that is the navel of the world.
> In winter the wolves come down out of the mountains,
> and in spring the goats seek the higher pastures,
> but the shoemaker sits at his bench forever

and the people walk back and forth upon the earth.
For this is merely the story of a passage
not from one land to another
nor from one world to the next,
but into the living structure of memory,
as that alone must suffice.

That suite of folkloric details, all drawn from the Singer story, lures us into increasingly dangerous territory. How ominous is it, after all, that "the people" in this stanza "walk back and forth upon the earth" like Satan in Job 1:7? Yes, memory is more comforting than history, and a "living structure of memory" is what normative Jewish tradition has long offered its members—but in that tradition, covenantal promises sustain the people, so that memory does not have to "suffice" all on its own.

In the poem's final lines, Finkelstein's ambivalence snaps into focus. "The books are submerged in a great repository," he writes, "or consumed by braided flames." In either case, these supplements to memory lie out of reach, as distant as Prospero's drowned books of magic or as Shabbat once the Havdalah candle is lit. Help from above will not come, nor did it ever. ("The Throne of Justice is vacant," Finkelstein observes, "as it was always meant to be.") But all is not lost, thanks not to memory, but something deeper, more generative:

—but the sun is warming the shoemaker's shed
and his hammer, striking the worn sole,
seems to make the sparks fly up into the light.

How can we explicate this extraordinary figure? Even when the books are drowned or burned, and even if we're writing after Havdalah, radically immersed in the ordinary, and even if the Throne is empty and always has been, a Stevensian "sun" remains. (The poem began, you may recall, at "sunset": after stanzas of anxiety, loss and rupture it ends with *more* energy pouring in from that source than when it began. Finkelstein thus echoes Stevens's assertion, in "Notes Toward a Supreme Fiction," that despite the death of Phoebus "There was a project for the sun and is.") The sun warms the shed of "the shoemaker," a name at once for the poet as Romantic, engaged in soul / sole-making, and for the poet more specifically as *Jewish* Romantic, engaged in remaking an already "worn sole" through a dialectical "hammering." Finkelstein strikes Stevens against Keats, Keats against Singer, and each of them against the anvil of Mani Leyb, the "poet who makes shoes," as he famously called himself in the Yiddish poem "I Am . . ." (220). Such Jewish Romantic poesis "seems to make the sparks fly up into the light." It continues, or at least resembles (the hedging is deliberate), the old Kabbalistic task of gathering "the sparks" of deity and returning them to the Divine, even as it remains fully human, and not free of *tsuris.* (Man is born to trouble as the sparks fly upward, says Job; these lines remember that, too.)

Juxtaposition and Its Discontents

Over the course of "A Poem for the Little Shoemakers," Finkelstein brings us from smoke to sparks, from sunset to darkness to warm sunlight, from deprivation to a freshly imagined, now enabling poverty. Finkelstein the poet, we might say, has taken up the same set of texts from which Finkelstein the critic derived his "melancholy longing . . . and a nagging sense of diminishment or inadequacy," and in the best rabbinic fashion has engaged in a life-giving argument that makes those texts expand. To witness that argument, however, we have had to re-assemble the texts involved, to gather (quite literally, in my case, on my desk) Finkelstein's works in verse and prose, those of Stevens, Frost, and Keats, translations of Mani Leyb's "I Am" and Isaac Beshavis Singer's "The Little Shoemakers," and a fistful of other works I have left on the cutting-room floor. In the hands of another poet, this great assembly might produce but a textual assemblage, rather than a single allusive lyric: a poem whose arguments are juxtapositional, not hammered out but cut and pasted, collaged.

At its simplest, such a poem might look like Jay Ladin's "Heaven's Gate": a two-column text in which versified newspaper stories from the Israeli/Palestinian war—one from *Ha-aretz,* dated May 16, 2002, and the second from the *New York Times,* January 6, 2003—recount stories of violence and its aftermath. Turn to the right, and you read about Mohammed:

When he went to claim the bodies
He fainted
Soldiers who killed
His wife and two children
Tied his hands
And removed his pants
He sat for hours
His son crying and dying
Beside him . . .

Turn to the left, meanwhile, and the neutral tones of *Times* coverage detail a second set of deaths:

A pair of suicide bombers
Blew themselves up
Seconds apart
Killing 23 other people
Injuring 100 more
In the deadliest attack
In 10 months
The first attacker
In front of a bus stop, the second
Next to a money changer, in a pedestrian mall
Teeming with Sunday evening shoppers . . .

Depending on his or her sympathies, the reader might well conclude that such suicide attacks are in response to the brutality of the occupation—or, conversely, that the killings by the IDF reported in *Ha-aretz,* although lamentable, are the inevitable collateral damage of fighting the sort of enemy whose work we see in column B. Ladin refuses to pass either judgment, not least in order to dramatize, compositionally, an American Jew's despairing helplessness in the face of what she calls elsewhere the "bitter rhythm" and "self-perpetuating slaughter" of "*ha-Matzav,* the Situation."

To end "Heaven's Gate," Ladin adds a third text to the mix: the Hebrew Bible, which she quotes from to fill out the right-hand column, the story from the *New York Times.* These quotations provide the poem's moral center, and come as a considerable relief to the reader, who can see the otherwise utterly banal apology from an IDF officer in the left-hand column ("'Look at my daughter and my wife' // 'We're sorry,' the officer said") as pregnant with implications from the tag from Jacob in Genesis 28:17 that lies across from it ("*This is Heaven's gate*"). Like Nemerov's speaker quoting the Bible against the Rabbi, Ladin quotes the phrase in a "stiff-necked" way to challenge orthodoxies: not only any Zionist orthodoxy that would explain away the IDF's killing, but also presumably his own liberal orthodoxy, which would excuse the suicide bomber, and any form of religious orthodoxy, liberal or conservative, that looks for traces of divine grace or plan in this slaughter. An apology from the killers—a *real* apology—might well open "Heaven's gate" for both sides, as it did in a sense when Jacob finally faced Esau. But as Ladin the Jew surely knows, that moment comes years later in the story—and as Ladin the American surely knows, "Heaven's Gate" has grimmer associations, not least the cult of that name who committed mass suicide in 1997, at the coming of Comet Hale-Bopp. The poem is as laden with bitter irony as it is with any hope of *t'shuvah.*

A recent book-length poem by Ammiel Alcalay, *from the warring factions,* employs collage to even more radical ends. Unlike "Heaven's Gate," *from the warring factions* does not address a specifically Jewish subject. Framed by two dates—December 1, 1993, during the siege of Sarajevo, and August 2, 2001, when Serbian general Radislav Krstic was convicted for war crimes—the poem centers on the Bosnian war of the early 1990s, although other ancient and modern wars press their way into the pages as Alcalay juxtaposes texts from a remarkable range of sources. As in *The Waste Land,* the allusive collage of *from the warring factions* enacts a sense of endless, hopeless repetition; here, too, we find a remarkable variety of source-texts to consult, or at least note in passing. (The afterword to the book lists "the letters of Sacco and Vanzetti, Jane Harrison, Carl Sauer, Thomas Nashe, Hannah Arendt . . . Hippocrates, Empedocles, Herodotus, the Quran, pre-Islamic poetry, the *Zohar,* Ibn 'Arabi, Chaucer, Dryden, Emerson, Melville's *Clarel,*" and pages more.)

Unlike Eliot, however, Alcalay offers the reader no trace of a transcendent, redeeming order, no "alternative to history" (in Ladin's phrase) that can be glimpsed either in a text or in the gaps between them. Rather, *from the warring factions* insists a secular ethic of responsibility for and to the Other, indeed a willingness to see the ethnically, historically, and linguistically Other as inextricably part of the self. As Alcalay explains in the interview bound in at the end of the book—effectively an additional section of the poem, in dialogue with the rest of the text—"by using the words of others, I was opening up a way of taking greater responsibility for them than if they were 'mine' " (187). And then, in words that oddly recall Finkelstein's "Acher," Alcalay says this: "Inhabiting the world means there is no 'other' not already in us, no capacities outside the human that can be attributed to anything outside what we ourselves are individually and collectively capable of" (187). The poet, then, must step back from the "self" to take responsibility for the *ger toshav,* the other within him, whose words are all-but all we possess. To do otherwise, the poem suggests, is to enact on the individual and aesthetic level the sort of ethnic cleansing and murderous pursuit of a monoculture that underwrote the Bosnian wars.

Is this a Jewish ethic, a Jewish poetic? The first five sections of Alcalay's book, the poem proper, make none of the overt Jewish references we have come to expect from texts of "the Jewish way." The interview that closes the text, however, allows the interviewer Benjamin Hollander to draw Alcalay out on his work as an essayist, translator, anthologist, and cultural theorist in ways that suggest how narrow our sense of the "Jewish" often turns out to be. A descendent of Sephardic Jews, Alcalay has biographical and cultural ties to the Balkans; just as crucially, he has been a rigorous leftist critic of Zionism, a movement whose dream of a Jewish state is silently mirrored by this book's depiction of Serbian and Croatian nationalism. In *from the warring factions,* then, and in his still more obdurate *the cairo notebooks,* Alcalay offers his readers the chance to see in literary practice a version of Jewish identity that is not simply polyvocal and internally multicultural, but dramatically at odds with the normative identities, both Ashkenazi and Zionist, that dominate late-twentieth- and early-twenty-first-century Jewish America.

"We are all multiple, and cannot pretend to be exclusively this or that," the poet explains in his essay "Why Israel?" "My Arabic last name tells me that much" (208). In *the cairo notebooks* a list of thirty-six numbered declarations that mix east and west, the known and the forgotten, dramatizes this internal multiplicity. "I had thought of writing a play based on the following facts," the poet writes by way of introduction.

1. I now live in Nahlaot.
2. From the end of our street I can see Gan Sacker and the stone wall enclosing the graveyard where my grandmother is buried.
3. Gan Sacker used to be wheat fields farmed by the villagers of Sheikh Badr.

. . . .

6. The villagers of Sheikh Badr used to pray at the mosque that's now on Strauss, in back of the Edison Theater.
7. The Edison Theater was built in 1932 by M. Y. Mizrahi and Sons.
8. I have a great aunt who lives in Istanbul but now she spends half the year in Athens with her daughter's family since being evicted by a developer. We've never met.
9. A relative on my mother's side, Shlomo Almuli, published a book called *The Interpretation of Dreams* in Constantinople in 1530 which was first quoted by Freud in 1899.
10. Another great aunt, whom I know well, was a patient of Freud's for a brief period after being sent from Belgrade to study in Vienna.
11. Sheikh Badr, who had a feud with Sheikh Jarrah and was sanctified for his power of answering prayers for rain, is buried under the Hilton, to the right of the graveyard.

Collectively, these facts set Jewish identity into motion through both space—Jerusalem, Istanbul, Vienna—and time, with subsequent entries reaching back to the Roman Tenth Legion and forward to the end of the British Mandate:

17. Sima Kedmi, now a resident, said: "The first thing I remember from Sheikh Badr was seeing a building blown up and 10 Arab women expelled. Their hands were raised and their children were on their shoulders—they said 'The Jews are attacking us.' I'll never forget those words."
18. The evacuation of Jewish families from neighborhoods in the North of the city was not carried out without some resistance. Housed on mattresses in a school, they refused to leave for the empty houses of Sheikh Badr. Sanctions imposed against them, including cutting off the money they were getting for sustenance, didn't help. The few belongings they'd managed to salvage were finally piled into trucks by the National Guard. The people protested to the Neighborhood Committee and tried to resist the National Guard, but they too were piled into trucks and taken to Sheikh Badr. After they arrived, even the British had to be called in to restore order. (60–62)

I would love to attribute my impulse to rebut these paragraphs—an impulse I feel even now, rereading them with some familiarity—to the "Jewish way" of argument. Alas, I suspect that religious-school training in advocacy for Israel account for that instinct far more than the exilic traditions of disputation. The paragraphs themselves imply that the "Jewish way" was more in view among the Jewish residents who resisted being forcibly transferred to the Sheikh Badr neighborhood than it was among the members of the "National Guard," presumably the Haganah, who took them to their new homes.

It may seem grim or polemical of me to end with Alcalay's poems. How much happier and more satisfying it would be to end with Finkelstein's vision of the sun warming the shoemaker's shed, or with Osherow heading off to ogle paintings by Paolo Uccello, with Nemerov's victory over the Rabbi, or even with Rabbi José leading us to "the text"! But the arguments that each of those previous poems worked through are, for me as a reader, entirely easy to savor—*too* easy, as though I had no real stake in their outcome, or as though there were some fence of agreement that all parties stayed safely inside. Alcalay, by contrast, leaves me uncomfortable, as though the quarrel at last were in earnest, the stakes both sharpened and high. And the collagist form of *from the warring factions* and *the cairo notebooks* raises crucial issues as well. Such texts ask for multiple readers, multiple voices to engage in argument both with and around them. (This isn't simply a matter of politics: the same holds true, for example, for Finkelstein's searching and poignant long poem *Track.*) Real debate entails both intertextual and interpersonal practice: communities of study, however secular or provisional.

May this collection spur such study into being, with actual debate around the texts it brings into view—and, as long as we're praying, may these come with participants who "fight all the time, yelling at each other about whether they should sit or stand," in the words of the joke where I began.

That is, after all, the tradition.

V'nomar:

Notes

1. Stephen Yenser introduces Merrill's work through this gate of doubling and dialectic, with some reference to its Romantic foundations; see *The Consuming Myth,* 4–7.

2. "This pluralism is pluralism only when looked at from a very particular, rabbinic insider's perspective," Boyarin observes. From outside, it can be read as "a highly efficient means for the securing of 'consensual' orthodoxy" (152); see Boyarin 157–201, especially 172–173, and 223–225.

3. Although this story is often cited as evidence of rabbinic pluralism, or even "protodeconstruction," Boyarin reads it, persuasively, as reflecting "the production of an exclusivistic institution of orthodoxy," marked in this case by the harsh punishment (excommunication) of Rabbi Eli'ezer, who asked for and received that confirming voice from Heaven. See Boyarin 168–174.

4. Since the 1990s, Bernstein has repeatedly allied himself with a tradition of specifically Jewish refusals to identify oneself as Jewish, often by invoking Stein as a precursor. See, in particular, his essay "Stein's Identity."

5. In *My Way: Speeches and Poems,* Charles Bernstein offers a cultural-nationalist reading of such straying into the unknown. It signals, he writes, a particularly American impulse, or at least it can be read this way, "if, following Stanley Cavell's reading of Emerson, we take America to be a movement away from given identities and toward something new, unapproachable, unrepresentable, and unattainable" (*My Way,* 143). That the Jewish poet makes this case in an essay on Gertrude Stein's Jewishness, however, and that to make it, he cites a Jewish philosopher, suggests that the American / Emersonian "movement away from given identities" has a particular importance for Jewish American writing and identity, whatever its place in the broader national context. Cavell has read Emersonian romanticism as a home for precisely the forms of self-production, self-transformation, and play with identity that a heterodox Jew who wishes to preserve his heterodoxy, against and within all cultures, might most desire.

A Jew in New York

Bob Holman

Like everybody else, I wasn't a Jew
Until I came to New York. In Portland, OR,
The other day, a young Latina asked me
If I were Jewyorican. Papa and Bubby
Came from Ukraine, landed in Brooklyn,
Settled in Harlan, KY, and named my father
Benjamin Franklin. My mother, the offspring
Of a coalminer, married Ben, the only Jew
In town. He didn't last. Ma remarried.
In kindergarten, in Cincinnati, instead
Of moving to the afternoon session the second

Semester, I stayed in Morning and changed my name.
This is the year 5755. In Chinese it is Year
Of the Dog. I just learned that the time between
Rosh Hashanah (Jewish New Year) and Yom Kippur
(Day of Atonement) are the Days of Awe. Moody
And gray, with dashes of absolute clarity, I love
These days. Cleansing summer's sweat from the streets
Of New York, I always think of the year beginning in
September. "That's when school starts." A holdover
from Youth. This year, for the first time, woo,
It's the real New Year, and I am a real Jew.
A real Jew, and a real coalminer's son, too.

Imp/penetrable Archive

Adeena Karasick's Wall of Sound

Maria Damon

> And, as the welcome of a welcome,
> (incarcerated or deported, persecuted, traumatized
> and obsessed), i am writing a writing that opens from its own
> threshold, erupts in withdrawal in carnal-soaked
> codes, naked liaisons rapt with all that is trivial,
> tragic suffocating
>
> and oppressive. all that is sacred and
> elliptic resting in jagged syntax breeks
> irrupts
>
> (from http://www.adeenakarasick.com/poetics.html)

> Nothing that has ever happened should be regarded as lost for history.
>
> —Walter Benjamin, "Theses on the Philosophy of History"

> . . . kitsch allow[s] us to look outward from within objects.
>
> —Walter Benjamin, "Some Remarks on Folk Art"

In the 1960s (the Jewish) Phil Spector pioneered his famous Wall of Sound, which he employed to greatest effect with his famous girl groups, most notably the Ronettes, a trio of (Black-Puerto Rican) cousins, but also Tina Turner, the Righteous Brothers, and even the Beatles. The Wall of Sound was an effect of thick, sonorous resonance, a kind of echoic "fat sound" achieved through dense layering of orchestration, often featuring unusual instrumentation for pop music, against which a powerful vocal soloist or group would hold his, her, or its own. The technique was this: many musicians on diverse instruments, ranging from standard rock-and-roll fare (drums, electric guitars, bass) to the symphonic (violins, harp) to icons of other genres (acoustic guitars) would crowd into Spector's small studio space and turn it into an enormous, reverberating echo chamber. All playing the same melody, the instruments would nonetheless subtly retain their differences in timbre, effect and affect, and their minute differences in timing, thus creating a polyvocal dis/unity, that is at the same time a fretful, multidimensional swirl of unrest and self-difference that stimulates, simulates, represents, and embodies emotional charge, which, given the banality of most of the song-lyrics, is necessary to add texture and interest, as do the singers' vocal qualities, which are often rough and/or complex though appealing (Tina Turner, Veronica Bennett). The hum of the (human) universe can be discerned in the Wall of Sound, and though compelling it ain't necessarily pretty. The oceanic expansiveness of the sound, though acclaimed for its super-resonance, is also a site of dissonance, terror, displacement, and loss that is "river deep, mountain high."

A few not-so-digressive notes on this loss: listen to Tina Turner on "River Deep, Mountain High," a paradigmatic instance of the Wall of Sound in action. In the opening lines of each verse Spector wrote, "When I was a little girl I had a rag doll / the only doll I ever owned" and "When you were a young boy did you have a puppy / who always followed you around?" the voice ascends from the lower pitch to higher registers—"If I lost you, would I cry?" as if whipping itself from fear to assertiveness, from vulnerability to toughness, from childhood to premature adulthood that palinodically ("we're not orphaned children anymore") reinvests transitional objects with animistic life ("oh yes we are"). Turner's voice is mournful, palpably full of tears over loss of . . . childhood, innocence, love, self, home . . . ? As the verses progress, Turner's voice rises to her famous rough howl; her protests of the depth and height—the insurmountability and submersive dangers not only of her own emotions but those of diasporic histories (the Red Sea, the Middle Passage, Mount Sinai, the River Jordan, the mountaintop from which freedom can be glimpsed though the prophet may not get there). According to rock and roll legend, Tina Turner became so overwrought in the recording booth that she tore her shirt open as the song reached its climax. More fundamental to the entire edifice of the sonic empire of the "first teenaged tycoon" (a common epithet for Spector at the time of his emergence), the title of Spector's big hit, "To Know Him Is to Love Him," was taken from his father's epitaph; Benjamin Spector, a Russian emigré, committed suicide due to financial difficulties in 1949, when Spector was eight years old. Further, as Paul Gilroy has analyzed in a discussion of the gender standoff in popular African American musical idioms, the violence visited upon diasporic family structures reinscribes itself as self-mutilating gender relations in a displacement of these communal and familial traumas. Both Tina Turner's and Ronnie Bennett Spector's memoirs detail the physical and emotional abuse they suffered at the hands of their musical-genius husbands; and Phil Spector, now in his sixties, was tried recently for his role in the shooting death of an actress at his home.

Thus one can read the Wall of Sound as an aural cenotaph for those lost in diasporic lines of frightflight, submerged in "all that is trivial," to cite my first epigraph—in this case, the many near-kitschy recorded artifacts of a brilliant-though-troubled career of a popular music producer and his star musicians who were more often than not people of color. The Wall of Sound is an instance of diasporic (in Spector's case Jewish) excess, an instance in which the creator cannot bear to leave anything out, cannot let anything that has ever happened be lost for history, which in this case is acknowledged through the sonorous temporality that is part cacophony, part melodious unification of effect—a secular, popular cultural, multivocal Jewish counterpart to the subaural registers of the cathedral organ that are said to induce visual/visceral feelings of oceanic awe in listeners of Reformation church music. This subaural force is so powerful it is believed to cause, if not actual visual hallucinations, at least a strong sense of a spatial/spectral presence, a visitation from a being who is/is not there, the transitional objects of "River Deep Mountain High"—rag doll, puppy—banal in themselves but the focal points of desperate attachment for the orphaned that stand in for an intuited but ungraspable and irreparably lost state of wholeness.

In what follows I examine the creative world/work of Jewish Canadian feminist Kabbalah scholar and poet Adeena Karasick, especially the tour-de-force "The Wall," which forms the centerpiece of her book *Dyssemia Sleaze* (2000). "The Wall," in which the Western Wall of Jerusalem becomes, like every other apparent topic toward which Karasick turns her deconstructive imagination, a trope for Jewish female relationship to language, history, and spirituality, is, like Spector's Wall of Sound, an oxymoronically spectral monolith, a seemingly solid edifice that on exploration and closer experience reveals fissures, discontinuities, roughly striated and textured differences, competing threads of narrative, dissonant sound and conflicted history, an archive of turbulent feelings delivered in a maelstrom of kitschy grandiosity and dazzling style. Perhaps the Wall/poem is more than a trope; it is a space that Karasick's imagination inhabits, as one inhabits an animated spiritual object in order to see how it contains the entire cosmos. One can look outward from within its animated (coded-feminine) interiority. If not one scrap of history is to be lost, as Walter Benjamin implored his intellectual heirs on the eve of his death, the habitués of this echoic world, like Veronica Bennett and her cousins singing outward from within the raggle-taggle orchestra's overwhelming buzz, must be *scrappy:* tough/vulnerable, street/glamorous, gamine/gamy, derivative/authentic survivors making life strategies out of exaggerated eye makeup and beehive hairdos and voices as grainy as they are melodic.[1] This fractured, bubbly compendiousness, as well as the sense that one is being spoken to from within a condition of overwrought (hysterical, coded-female, teetering on the banal) expressiveness, characterizes all of Karasick's work (not to mention Spector's): a title like "dyssemia sleaze" and the cover of *MêmeWars* (itself a mockery of the self-disclosing genre associated with feminine mass culture), which shows Karasick, a foxy babe with face half-concealed by hair and defamiliarized alphabetic lettering, in boxing stance and gloves, amply carry forth the combined urgency and triviality of a post-diasporic, feminine Jewish logomania. The "structure of feeling" of her performative persona and of the volumes of poetry is, to repeat, *scrappy:* simultaneously earnest and ersatz. Like Spector's pop masterpieces, "The Wall" (as does all of Karasick's work) teems and swarms with excess; in this case, an excess of history, sonically (as well as architecturally and visually) embodied in the ambiguously female "voice," not only the poet's but the Wall's itself, as it represents a similarly ambiguously feminine principle. A semiotic analysis cum poetic paean addressing the many issues embedded in and performed by Jerusalem's Western Wall, the piece collects the detritus of almost two thousand years of diasporic history (and, of course, a much longer history as a people-in-more-or-less-place, albeit one that includes slavery, exile, and what is now termed "internal displacement," though that term suggests, anachronistically, that there is an "externality") and sets it into stormy relationship with and within itself; the poem is itself a "storm from paradise," even as its topic is the pile of wreckage upon wreckage, the putatively monolithic Wall caught in the storm. As the embodiment/dwelling of the Shekhinah, the in-dwelling Spirit of whispering/listening, the Wall is the pile of self-different wreckage, the roaring windstorm, and also the Angel of History it is buffeting away into the future.[2] The poem "The Wall" itself, of course, is all these things as well: a tsunamic wall of words and images bearing down on the reader, a chaotic pile of junk, a roaring whirl and whisper, a messenger frightened of its prophetic task approaching the future butt-first, Chaplinesque. Yes: what if Benjamin's angel of history, based on Paul Klee's drawing "Angelus Novus," were, in fact, ambiguously female: the Shekhinah as comic gamine? What would be the ramifications of recognizing the angel of history as the breath of life, of language, of poetry, in a feminine principle that is not strictly speaking female? For while images of bound and gagged-or-open-mouthed women and praying men fill the pages of "The Wall" and *Dyssemia Sleaze* more generally, the opening passage of the former reminds us, in cut-out, punk, ransom-note lettering, that the binding/sacrificing and family violence foundational to Judaism is not only not restricted to women but takes the form of cruelty to children and fratricide as well:

ACCORDINGTOANCIENTISRAELITE
TRADITIONSTHEWESTERNWALL
STANDSINFORTHEBINDINGOF
ISAAKAKEDATYITZHAK
ACCORDINGTOMAIMONIDES
ITISALSOTHESITEOFARAVNAHS
THRESHINGFLOORISTHEPLACE
WHEREABRAHAMBUILTANALTAR
TOSACRIFICEHISSONISAACAND
WHERENOAHEMERGEDFROMHISARK
WHERECAINANDABLE[*SIC*]OFFERED
SACRIFICEISTHESITEOFTHEARKOFTHE
COVENANTANDTHE
SYMBOLOFTHEDWELLINGPLACE
OFTHEDIVINEPRESENCE

Gender is a central concern for Karasick, but not in a binaristic way that would simplify the history our angel represents, any more than the Shekhinah, a universal capacity (as everyone has indwelling spirit) that is figured as female, is only present for or in women. Angels are ungendered but generally presumed to be male; Benjamin's comment on the ephemerality of a print journal of his time suggested that angels are ephemeral as well: "according to a legend from the Talmud, even the angels are created—new ones at every moment and in countless hosts—simply to sing their hymns before God, then to cease to be and disappear into nothingness" (Broderson 118 citing Benjamin, GS II, 243.) It should not be impossible to shift the perspective, then, and imagine an ungendered but feminine-inflected counterpart to this tragicomic figure: Chaplin's gamine, like him a scrap of expendable humanity in the eyes of an instrumentalist majority culture. If the Wall is a pile of rubble, the wreckage of the past, it is necessarily an archive; the angel, also, is this archive, is this mountain of refuse away from which s/he is being driven by the whirlwind. A whirlwind, by the way, within which there is no still small voice but a babel of cacophonous girl-grouped dys/harmonies: a whirlwind that is a Wall of Sound. The poem is likewise a cacophony of fonts, formats and voices, illegible print superimposed on photographs, visual and verbal puns, prayers, send-ups, and equivocations.

Of all the things the Western Wall and this poem about it are, the archive is a useful if somewhat arbitrary metaphoric point of entry. An archive, as we all know, is a repository of significant documents and meanings, importantly centralized as its etymology—*government, town hall, rulership*—implies: any historical edifice saturated with cultural significance could be called an archive: this Wall, for instance. An archive is also, as we also know, and as we wish government and rulership were, a site continually productive of knowledge; it swarms with activity; it is an arch-hive. Its business—its feverish buzziness, one could say, is impressive, vibrant with both regally official document and semio-detritus ranging from the quotidien to the eccentric; from the mundane to the otherworldly; from the constant to the ephemeral. This Wall that doubles as a hive (and triples as a poem in Karasick's rendering) is full of, erotically athrob with, plant and animal life as well as its more famously noted spiritual and national life, and the attendant affective, literary, and expressive aspects of Jewish life; one page of the poem shows, in a repeating image symmetrically organized, doves perched on the ridges of the stone blocks making up the wall, over which a Star of David is superimposed; tufts of grass growing from between the Wall's cracks, and the unevenness of the stones themselves, cast shadows that look like writing.

In Karasick's ADD-MTV-ish world, it's hard to distinguish movement from stasis, organicity from inorganic material, human "writing" from accidental tracery, the significant from the less so. What counts as knowledge, what counts as a "find" in an archival quest, in a descent into the teeming underworld of source material? Which of the myriad competing factoids or docu-fragments in the rubble-heap of information and human culture is the philosopher's stone, the holy grail, the nectar of the fountain of youth, knowledge or redemption, the centrifugal funhouse map of the thru-the-looking-glass promised land? We make it up as we go along; knowledge on this path thru uncertain space—the poem, the sound, the Wall—is always becoming even in its brash effrontery. Each of these archives is a divine and human comedy and each has its multiple points and paths of entry, its orifices, its tunnels of love, its birth canals. The steppingstones on one of its paths of access are the letters of the alphabet, that great, mystical, dynamic ecosystem that has held us in its web since premodern times; every letter is an archive of feeling, of meaning, of specific spiritual insight, as the Kabbalists have elaborated. The interaction between the archivist and the contents of the archive (or here, the orant orifice and the oracular edifice: the page facing the dove-Star of David Wall is entirely taken up by an enormous, wide-open, sensually lipsticked female mouth—probably Sandra Bernhardt's—both aggressive and vulnerable) speaking to each other across time within the "container" of materials is productive and continual, and changes the materials and the container as it changes the archivist. The body likewise is an archive continually reproducing itself, a repository repositioning itself at every turn, a body in performance remade, remaking itself in poeisis and autopoeisis in every context. The Wall, with its multitude of cracks and fissures stuffed or unstuffed with paper, reads like a female body whose orifices have been dammed up with a range of never-quite-effective "feminine hygiene products" intended to ward off danger both internal and external—precisely in that liminal space where blood emerges, where speech emerges, where seed and succor penetrate. (On the other side of the Wall, of course, is the Dome of the Rock, a political danger in the nationalist narrative but also a graceful, hovering image of androgynous architecture.) The female performance poet (Karasick, but also Ronnie/Veronica Bennett—and now Amy Winehouse—with their enormous beehive hairdos, and with her multiple ethnicities in constant conversation within the Wall of Sound) embodies all of these: the archive, the interactive site, the (coded-female) reproductive body spew-*shpritz*ing verb-effluence as if it were a bodily fluid (which it is) . . . all that material set in diasporic orbit around the flailing stuttering body, a world unto itself but sited among other worlds in chaotic interdependence, transience and tangence . . . Adeena Karasick, Jewish Canadian feminist performance poet and author of *this* "Wall," a chaotic, palimpsestic meditation plastered on the see-thru semiotics of the Western Wall (all over it, as we say, like a cheap-sleazy-suit), is an arch-ark-hive of activity whose manic mellifluid production fuels this inquiry into the beehive-archive, the honey in the cavern, the crevices of walls honeycombed with writing, the queen of the drone of barely distinguishable syllables bubbling malleable as beeswax. Archiving "modernism"? In this postmodern performative medium and with this premodern thematic material, modernism is archived by being sandwiched between the pre and post cursors to which it has given its name; it is the content that announces itself as substance ripe for redefinition, ready to be put in its place (twixt the twin thin walls of pre and post), though that place is noplace. (Nationalized Jewishness as modernism sandwich?) In fact, Karasick's overstuffed archive could be figured not only as sandwich spilling over with organic matter but also as a teenage girl's jewelry box, chaotically ajumble with bright baubles and genuine treasure, kitsch transfigured by sheer juxtaposition and effect, a shimmering disorganization of syllables and letters vibrating against each other in a pageant of sublimity that is, at the same time, "touchingly primitive." You name it, we can trope it.

Since the year 70 C.E., the date of the burning and destruction of the Second Temple (rebuilt on the site of the first, which had also previously been destroyed), the Western Wall—or, more colloquially (but disavowed by formal definitions as tinged with anti-Semitism), the "Wailing Wall"—is the primary site around which the Jewish history of displacement and diaspora is organized; it is the sole remnant of that rebuilt temple and hence both a simulacrum and a token of an "authentic" past, a past that encompasses Isaac and Abraham, Cain and Abel, Noah's ark. The Wall comprises premodern forms of writing whose cultural significance was established during the modern era using the narrative strategies of modernity (the rise and fall of great civilizations, the coming to consciousness of individuals against that backdrop, the "right to a homeland," etc.). Now under a deconstructive/performative aegis, those forms of writing become postmodern. The forms of writing comprising the Wall, a bricolage of eras, civilizations, religions (it comprises one side of the Dome of the Rock Mosque), materials (grass, stone, mortar, paper, animal life, and the shreds of paper containing prayers in many languages that are stuffed so pastiche-ishly into those crevices and fissures that are within human reach) also comprise Karasick's performances. The Wall appears to be static, a stable referent, a literal monolith in that it is built of stone—and it has certainly been a symbol around which acute if belated (perhaps particularly anguished and acute *because* belated) battles of nationalism have been pitched, just as millenia earlier, violently destructive battles of imperial and religious rivalry and/or dominance created the absence that is now filled with a plenitude of melancholia, resentment, and other toxins, as well as the wellsprings of grief, sustenance, consolation, and meaning that have been attributed to it. Karasick offers a version of Jewishness and of the Wall that provide something of an alternative (though also ambivalently continuous) narrative to the scene of permanent exile and/or desperate and/or triumphant return to a point of origin, a teleological trajectory that ratifies the modernist tale of rising and falling, coming and going and going and coming and, in the case of Jewish nationalism as ratified in 1946, always too late (pace Mel Brooks). Instead, Karasick proposes, or intuits in Jewish thought and particularly in its mystical underpinnings as made explicit in the Kabbalah, a form of diaspora that remembers but does not fetishize a point of origin; that entertains the possibility of an originary moment or site but does not posit one as fact; that recognizes such a hypothetical point of origin as useful and dangerous a fiction as all others, and that sees language itself, rather than a lithic edifice, as the terrain in which this flux of departure, return, circumvolation, orbit, diasporic fragmentation and fables of origin and exile perform themselves: "all that is sacred and elliptic resting in jagged syntax." The Wall is itself a linguistic structure, and language itself multilithic; the Wall's importance has not only been narrated into being, but its crevices and crannies are literally filled with tiny bits of writing, scraps of paper on which supplicants have confessed their deepest desires, which are then shoved into the Wall to literalize a verbal offering—which is both gift and request—to the God whose absence and presence is embodied and negated in this porous, penetrable rockface. Language can be lithic and static as we see in the nationalist narratives that have dominated the modern era and that are trying so hard for a last-ditch comeback right now; Karasick's job is to unbuild it, to reinject it with short-fuse phrase fragments and swirls of expressive deliquescence, to limber it up and dismantle its aggressive mask of rooted stasis to show the (s)warm insides—its archival aliveness, its anarchival, rhizomic exuberance. Karasick aims for an ex-stasis, the ecstatic outside of, within and beyond formal fixity, an ex-ile or ex-ilium, a repudiation of isolation (island) and of Ilium, the Trojan war that set in motion, through exile and diaspora, a narrative of empire that enslaved the Jews. For Karasick, the Wall is also an archive of race, ethnicity, gender, sexuality, nation—as Jewishness and its relation to space, place, time, and the broad and narrow socii it has been and been embedded in has been variously figured over the millenia of its emergence and evolution; her task is to demonstrate—to perform through both the multimedia text and her own performative style, i.e., through her body—its instability and downright volatility, its permeability, its corporeal and theoretical vulnerability. Karasick's descriptions of the Wall as a fluidly interlinking series of systems—including: as a regulatory mechanism of knowledge, a psychic system of memory and forgetting, a governing figure of subjectivity, and a space of embodied experience—have enlivened some of the possible ways in which we might conceive of hypernationalized, hyperpoliticized, hyperspiritualized, hypertextualized locations in relation to cultural critique. At the same time, her exploration of its significance in contemporary culture in its social, political, historical, and material contexts raises vexing questions about the Wall as a set of practices, as an apparatus, and as a discursive network (ho-hum!).

This notion of language spatialized—which can't help but assume political dimensions—is forecast in an earlier Karasick video-poem, *Alphabet City*, which dramatizes the gridded lettering of Manhattan's Lower East Side, or Loïsaida as it is known by its largely Spanglish-speaking population; home to the Nuyorican Poets' Café, Alphabet City is currently the site of great verbal and artistic creativity as well as urban ethnic hybridity. Though this grid of Avenues A, B, C, and D constitutes, at first glance, an entirely different kind of space, historically, aesthetically, and culturally, from Jerusalem's Western Wall, Karasick finds in both sites a rich but fluid wellspring for lingual poeisis, down to the level of letters themselves; a poeisis which she in turn mediates through her bodily, textual, and oral performance as she herself claims a space as a wellspring for poeisis, not as Author capital A but more as focal point for irruption, as the dramatic narrowing of a flowing body of water increases its power and spectacularity. Likewise, *Mumbai Ya,* another video-poem, plays with over-the-top silly puns and opulent images of South Asian/Hindi kitsch: "Hello Dahli," "kiss my sari ass," and so forth, in a disorienting and shape-shifting send-up of orientalism and identification. Her performances as well as some of the visuals in her printed work enact aggressive displays of sensuous femininity—fashionable, borderline commodifiable but joyously assertive in their foxiness—reminiscent, perhaps, of Ronnie Spector née Bennett in the Ronettes' heyday as Spectorized spectacle as well as auracle, and certainly of Tina Turner, with an umbral edge of diasporic tragedy. Like the Ronettes; the post-Ike, 1980s comeback Tina Turner; as well as, more recently, Amy Winehouse, Karasick uses her hair to construct a relationship with her audience; in her case, her face, in both the video and book-cover photographs, is never fully visible. The look is alluring rather than shy, because the one visible eye is looking directly into the viewers'; the human veil is a turn-on, what Alfred North Whitehead has called a proposition: a "lure of feeling," coaxing the reader/viewer into direct engagement. In order to facilitate such a bodily performance there must be an investment in the aestheticized self which is generatively open—generous and risk taking. The danger of "falling flat" is always present in such specifically corporealized work and this lends it some of its interest—as in (I can only hope) the overload of corny puns with which I tend to freight my essays. The very willingness to incur charges of excessive self-regard a woman faces when she performs, her looks, her body, her need to be seen, to be read, indicates a certain urgency and vulnerability; the visceral discomfort it can engender in an audience is often one of identification gone awry, a skewed empathy that reacts against itself as judgment of the Other. While much of her work is undisguisedly Jewish in content and methodology (as she has put it, Kaballah is not defined by its religious content; it is an interpretive strategy), her performances, which draw on a heavily Brooklyn-ese spoken-word intonation, and her video-poems, which do not address Jewishness directly but rather use linguistic and performative strategies of displacement and cultural/geographical transformation, nonetheless undermine assumptions that there is a "Jewish" essence, identity, or quality that preexists the act of writing (the major argument of "The Wall" is that the most holy site of Judaism is an ongoing self-construction that "writes" itself in the historically layered words of its supplicants, celebrants, and critics). Her performance in *Mumbai Ya,* moreover, intimates that ethnicity is no, uh, forgive the expression, sacred cow; that is, Jewishness itself might be characterized by "an aversion to identification— . . . a practice of dialogue and . . . an openness to the unfolding performance of the everyday."

From *Alphabet City* to "The Wall," Karasick returns narratives about space and place embedded in material sites to the linguistic realm, be it sonic or visual, disorienting the concept of sitedness in the meanwhile. Is a Jew a traveling, corporealized archive functioning in modernity to preserve the premodern and foretell the postmodern? Or, to rewrite our earlier trope, is a modern Jew a modernism sandwich in reverse, all modernism on the outside which protects (i first wrote protests) an inner anachrony, a defiant simultaneity that gives the lie to the neat linearity embedded in the "pre>non-prefixed>post" continuum whereby we arrange our relationship to time? Whatever; perhaps this modern Jewish exhibitionist/self-concealer is our Angelus Novus, our celestial trampette blown backward, robe billowing in Marilyn-manquée clumsiness-cum-grace. Of course a Jew is no more simultaneous than any other person—anyone can be an archive!, but Jewish thought and the current Jewish cultural studies can bring a useful perspective to these contemporary musings. At the very least, Karasick's work multiply how "Jewishness" might look, sound, act, and interact; how it might be *read*.

Moreover, the notion of architecturalized lettering is a distinctly Kabbalistic one, with deep roots in Jewish exegetical tradition and the special place occupied therein by textual materials in the most literal sense; this tradition, compounded with the prohibition against pictorial representation, means that letters themselves become descriptors; they are their own illustrations. "A" doesn't stand for "apple;" "apple" stands for "A." Karasick's commitment to the materiality of language down to its smallest elements, letters and phonemes, is also at work in a later post-Wall project: an English-to-English homophonic translation of the Sefer Yetzirah, the first and oldest book of the Kabbalah, which has been published in her most recent volume, *The House That Hijack Built.* "Homophonic translation" is a serio-comic genre formalized by the Jewish American Objectivist poet Louis Zukofsky, in which sound rather than meaning is the connection between source text and target text, or product. As the Sefer Yetzirah is the Book of Creation, it and Karasick's distressing of it (that is, her subjecting it to chemically transformative processes as Marc Jacobs might distress fine fabric for a punk-sleaze look, her, ahem, hijacking of this sacred text) constitute creatively deconstructive processes rather than merely products, a recreation of language and of the text which reveals new meaning (and hence new realities beyond those bound by ethnocultural specificity) through the slippages such homophony incurs. Thus one might use the term "radical Jewish poeisis" rather than "poetics," to emphasize the incompleteness, and the desirability of such incompleteness, of a poetic becoming-process. Hinting at the textually violent, mutilating aspects of the project as well, Karasick, in her words, "[carves] out ways in which this text could be dislodged from a socio-religious and historically-limiting hermeneutic." Thus, this morphously polyverse, self-inflicted and seemingly purposeless—an i.e. English-to-English homolinguistic trans'elation, as she puts it—translator's task is actually a monumental—though de-monumentalizing—undertaking of reworlding or unworlding, and one which stays true to the import of the book itself, as its "focus," as Karasick explains, "is on the 22 letters of the Hebrew alphabet" (how they were formed, how they interrelate, how they make meaning). The text itself is inscribed through slippage, elision, rupture, and undecidability, and language is foregrounded as "a continuum of letters, names, mathematical equations, gates of meaning." Here are the first several lines of the piece, with the "translation" in boldface above the already-translated source-text:

With dirty tombs, sticky pathos official isms
With 32 mystical paths of wisdom
riveted, Yeah
engraved Yah
The Horde of Ghosts
the Lord of Hosts
a Grid of serial
the God of Israel
lifting, Gedichte
the living God
connaisses or verse
King of the universe
Of shady
El Shaddai
Mercy, flanged rations
Merciful and Gracious
Honeyed Exiles . . .
High and Exalted . . .

(*THTHB* 95)

If one did not know of Karasick's serious and long-standing commitment to Kabbalistic scholarship one might take this as an attempt at sacrilege, but this intertextual rend(er)ing is an homage, albeit a feisty, "cheeky," and daring one that takes eye-opening ludic liberties. Reinventing a sacred text, it is also re-creational activity in another sense as well; it is pleasure and eros. "I do it because it makes me feel good," Karasick says. "It soothes me." It is also a process of recreation as self-creation as doubling; we know from Gertrude Stein that English, or any language, is never the same when it is revisited: you can never utter the same word twice. English to English, ashes to ashes, sweets to the sweet, taste my honey honey, it's never the same anguish, the same lashes, the same master-suite; and the archivist, the poet, is never the same poet as she was, will be or even is. Archive and archivist, poet and poetry, angel and rubble-heap change places and become each other fluidly, seeping into each other through active cerebral and bodily—bawdy—engagement. Kabbalistic study itself has been, for Karasick, an exercise in self-creation. When she began this self-initiated apprenticeship to her culturally specific language mysticism at age eighteen, no one would teach her, as Kabbalistic study is traditionally an activity reserved for men over the age of forty; the local yeshiva, when she turned to it for instruction, gave her a diluted version. Since then she has sought out teachers to work with her one-on-one, and has cobbled together a diasporic patchwork of mentors and teachings in a praxis well in tune with her penchant for palimpsest and bricolage, and one mimetic of the Wall itself as it emerges in her altervision—an architectural, historical, and textual crazy-quilt (constructed by a swarm of quilting and spelling bees) whose bristling textemes and rough surface materialize letters, meaning, sound and the word, testifying to their livingness, interdependent mutability, textilic/exilic multiplicity.

As beekeepers in an arch-hive of activity, it B-hooves us readers to understand something about the bee herself, that tiny un-pin-downable archive residing tumultuously under the sign of bee-coming, who guards her living, glistening trove with maternal ferocity. The an/archive is alive with materials self-created by bees, its geometrically perfect walls dripping melus. In our approach, we must understand the danger to which our investigations commit us; all beekeepers die of anaphylactic shock sooner or later; instead of becoming immune one becomes more sensitive to it: you don't assimilate it, it assimilates you. Human becomes antihuman or inhuman or posthuman as your allergic reaction is written on your body; hives and rashes, welts and archive fevers; page 54 cites Richard Avedon's eerie image of a naked man covered with crawling bees (flies?) and a line-drawn stringwig for maximus-creepoid X-Files effect. You are marked as and by the archive, you *become* the archive, and not voluntarily at that; contrary to your original foraging intentions, you are the prey and the archival material is the predator; the material becomes the archivist acting violently on you and you become its source material, the burning welt world words written on your flesh are yielded up to be mined, explained, exploited. Lanced, your boils and welts ooze viscous language, a bodily fluid symptomatic of illness, invasion, corruption. Honey is gall and must be transubstantiated once again by any means necessary—through extrusion, expulsion, abjection, exile, reproduction, birth, mothering. Your archival sputum gums and gels into a web of language, that prison-house where you catch and are caught, the labyrinth of labial excretion that turns mortar into honey and walls into wombs, permeable and bruised, endlessly generative in their degenerative uncontrollability. The bee, a natural alchemist, excretes or secretes (sexcretes?) its own gold, its own shelter, its own workshop, its own book as portable homeland where it conceals or reveals its own secret, "a secret that bleeds, is infected, swells and pusses in the gaps. Is always already a secret within a secret that only another secret can explain" (60).

Moreover, its beeswax commands a venerable place in the history of Western writing and domesticity, as fuel, energy, sealing wax, writing, printing, unit of monetary exchange or tribute payment, modeling, casting, and painting material. Wax itself, medium for earliest phonograph sound, has been invoked as a liminal material, a becoming-material, as in recent critical comparisons between wax museums and cinema, media that interface between animate and inanimate, creation and dissolution—transitional media that hardens, softens and then melts thoroughly, becoming in turn opaque, translucent and wholly clarified. To play out the relation between wax and cinema a little further, the "dissolve shot" in French is *"fond enchainé,"* or sequential melting (enchained melting, a vividly erotic image); and we are reminded by its etymology that a "ghetto" is an archive and an ark-hive: a foundry (place of melting and casting) where Jews were sequestered during the Italian Renaissance. Both a melting-place and a foundation (from fundere and fundare respectively), the Wall and the body of the performing female poet are citational non-sites of transformation, exile, elixir, palimpsests, and gridded griddles where heat solidifies and liquifies. The techniques of the essay-poem "The Wall" also enact the "dissolve shot" in the sense that there are close-ups so close up that they become grainy or fuzzy in their detail, and there are layered sequences in which one layer of meaning and medium melts into or through another (one might also say they "bleed" into each other, emphasizing a family resemblance between wax and blood that foregrounds the female abject).

Honey, need it be said, on the other end of the abject-idealized continuum from wax, is a primary metaphor for eros, treasure, beauty, sensory delight both internal (taste) and external (visual pleasure)—as we learn most notably from the Song of Songs, the most holy book of the Hebrew Bible according to the Kabbalists. Honey wine, or mead, is the premodern Anglo-Saxon kenning for poetry: it is the mead of Odin, who stole it from a giant, who stole it from an elf, who killed a nomadic sage made from the combined spit of gods and men, mixed into honey his blood, which became mead, the poetic motherlode. (In other words, the feminine abjection theorized by Kristeva the Bulgarian Jew would not be so different from the divine poetry of the hypermacho Nordic gods, if history did not teach otherwise.) In contemporary as well as premodern and modern Ethiopia, as in pre-Christian Norse culture where poetry was known as "Odin's mead," copious consumption of mead and honey-beer accompanies poetic cutting sessions, where spontaneous oral poetics are spun by competitive cognoscenti. To speak with honeyed tongue, though, honey, simultaneously suggests deception, dis-simulation as in disingenuous simulacrum and danger, as poetry, a gift, is also a toxin (gift being, etymologically, poison); the bee's venom is indistinguishable, at some register, from its honeyed legacy, its exilic elixir. Honey, venom, and wax are ranged along a transubstantial continuum saturated with anthropophagomorphemic signification. Forgive the Christian vocabulary (transub etc.); Spector's Wall of Sound can also be said to be crafted to resonate with a "gospel" sound, sneaking a diasporic Jewishness in under the heavy cloak of sonic buzz as a stranger, in Edmond Jabès's title, smuggles into his host city a "tiny book" snuggled in the crook of his arm. Perhaps an appeal to the Kristevan body-fluid resonances of these viscous materials—sound, honey, venom, bile (gift as sacred potion/poison)—would be more appropriate, but I want to hit on the orality and consuming/devouring notes of this transub/succubus bouquet as well. These sticky substances are produced in the (myth-mouth-mother) ark-hive, house of the bee and home of the scripture, beit, the letter b, the bosom of family valuables.

And further: we need, in this belle-letteraturistic Kabbalistic world we enter when we enter Karasick's honeycomb, to understand that B, Beit, the little house of the second letter, the tiny arkhive residing in mysterious fulsomeness under the sign of B-coming, the shelter (the ark) that clothes and covers the sacred words of history and spirit. Though it is the second letter of the alphabet, Beit is the B-ginning, as it is the first letter of the Torah; it is with this letter that God created the world. The belatedness of B, its deferral, implies a second-rate standing, woman created from man, or a b-grade movie, so Karasick implicitly participates in a feminist project at the most atomized level when she elevates the standing of the B in her oeuvre. While alef, the first letter, is silent, encompassing all sounds, beit as a consonant introduces form without which all would be chaos; it is thus a domesticating, Apollonian, aesthetic ordering principle, just as the Wall signifies in its materiality a world of affect, history, time/space unmoored. Like an arch-hive, Beit is an arched structure or a shelter, like the absent temple, already the Second

Temple, a replica of the first, at which the Wall's partiality gestures; and like the Dome of the Rock "behind" it, a graceful haunting present shored up by the pastness of the Wall; the B references a structure which is not there, like an ultimate signified or an inaccessible, invented and infinitely inventable and inventive, past—one wall of the Beit is missing, creating an opening for full circulation of the universe or, in other terms, of the Real; that wall, one could say, is next year, i.e., never and always already the wall in Jerusalem.

Having thus taken to heart Benjamin's exhortative description of/to the historian that s/he leave not a scrap of the past uncollected, Karasick exults in scraps and detritus, verbal, material, and otherwise, and unbuilds a wall by showing how scrappy and disheveled the Wall actually is, made up of shards and debris, a collage of verbal ghosts and letters to God, love-letters to letters of the alef beit, every alphabet an archive, every letter within that alphabet an archive, that is, among other things, a space of embodied experience, so that words written in stone are not fixed at all but just as fulsome and living, as ghostly and shimmering, as ephemeral and elusively persistent as words inscribed on flesh, wind, water, or other physical elements, as sound; stone is as permeable and vulnerable as flesh, as skin, as spirit or other animal/human elements; history as malleable, evanescently alive and performative as culture, as art, as dreams or any other imaginative zone or body of activity. "And, just as the stones of the Wall (layers upon layers) are not whole, but broken, cracked and weathered, they are structured like a language (mimic the ideological cracks in the surface of a complex and inaccessible, nonlinear grammar). A language marked by fractures, contaminations, durational spaces, chronic mochery, crutches, leeches, ruptures" (*DS* 43). *Fond enchainé* indeed: the photographs in the poem dissolve harshness into grainy softness, staunchness into permeability, stone into paper which trumps rock which trumps scissors which trumps. . . . In an interview conducted before the work's publication, Karasick explains how this artifact of origin and fixity becomes a kind of sacred, ritualistic girl-child's play, feminized and kinked up through its means of production and reproduction. She describes the then-work-in-progress as "an extensive full colour poetic essay on how the Wall (the Wailing Wall) is structured like a language. And I find that working with different typefaces, fonts, layering letters upon letters in a very physical way . . . to foreground[s] language as a material body . . . And, all the collages, assemblages, graphic intrusions are all constructed with purple gluestick, manicure scissors & transparencies. Some people go to fetish bars. I go to Kinko's."[3] As suggested at the outset of this dyssemic oddessay, part of what animates this recovery of the Wall as multiform unconscious, as a site of polymorphemic and heteroglossolalic per- and multiversity, is the coded-feminine Shekhinah: breath, and poetic inspiration; our Holy Ghost, our kitschy Muse with manicure scissors in hand, an animating visitation associated with the interior, with air, wind, and fire, with feminized (interior) pink-bedroom space, but also with the adolescent angel-tough voices lofted by the Wall of Sound. Ronnie Bennett Spector as (non-Jewish) Shekhinah as Angel of History? This realm of culture is the B-side, the B-girl, the B-lated archival matrix, Eve the second human, in which nexus nests and rests the next rest of the language and all verbal imp/possibility. The beehive—Adeena herself—the "poem itself"—the Wall itself—becomes B-Eve, that tatterdemallion in tattered medallions garnered from the war of bleeding words; like a Joanie-come-lately of ark she leads the holy war against forgetting and language loss, the restoration and preservation of all archives, all bodies which are archives which is all bodies. Though Jewish linguistic tradition is at the center of this investigation and practice, the above description of a gaminesque liberty-lady of language (Wall as Statue of Libertine?) should not be understood to be the sole domain of any one group of people, ethnically or otherwise determined. Multiple ironies abound that cannot be lost on anyone reading this volume; anyone, that is, invested in poetics, pre- and postmodernity, Jewish cultural life, radical, secular, etc. Not only was the 2002 invasion of Iraq (arguably the birthplace of modern alphabetic writing), undertaken with an eye toward "stabilizing the Middle East," accompanied by archival destruction that beggars description; but the uncertainty and conflicting reports about what archaeological, artistic, and textual treasures were lost and/or retrieved are themselves symptomatic of conflicting desires to forget, remember, destroy, retrieve, remake, declare solidarity, repudiate connection. Not intending an indecorous aestheticization of serious and volatile political matters, I want to call attention to the weird way that, at the time, archive fever seemed to grip the *New York Times* and other major mainstream U.S. news venues over the supposed looting of the Baghdad archives and museums while less was said about loss of Iraqi life, medical supplies, water, food, civil and civic life and infrastructure, etc. (Years later, though the anxiety about archival damage has been much allayed, the focus continues to be on lost American life as the main tragic outcome of the war.) Moreover, a new wall is being built in Israel/Palestine, harshly political in this go-round, to cordon off and reify nationalist intentions, to interfere with Palestinian daily life, underscoring and shoring up a duality (us/them) on which modernity has already foundered. There are urgent and immediately contemporary political undertones to be deciphered from the Wall, though one can read it without going there. While other pieces in *Dyssemia Sleaze* touch upon the political suffering of Israel's current Others-Within, especially "Mehaneh

Yehuda" ("Jewish Market," site of a Hamas bombing in Jerusalem in 1997) in which the word "HAMAS" is multiply glossed, the Wall stays within a Jewish context; eruptions and challenges come from within, from feminism, from a diasporic take on place and space, rather than from an investigation into the Wall's precarious proximity to Muslim worship, its role in sustaining, physically, a holy site of Islam, and what that Janus-role might say about current anguish on the other side. Perhaps Karasick's dual approach—an intentionally dysfunctional hyperglossic outpouring combined with lovingly careful attention to the minutiae of the letters to which *Dyssemia Sleaze* is dedicated

(" . . . these letters which t/ravel together,
mysteriously united, one stretched towards
the other, one emerging from the other's side, one
suckling the other; folding in on these letters i belong to
that carry me and dance both within the pages
of this text and as social, historical
effects of reference")

(*DS* 5)

—can offer tools for processing all of these losses, and perhaps this essay is a tiny bioverbal thread pulsating, penetrating, and interlacing the constitutive body of freedom (an Invisible Wall), working athwart its political closure, running sonic sustenance across the lines. Perhaps, and more likely, this is wishful thinking; a radical poetic practice within the world of "Radical Jewish Poetics," "The Wall," not allowed an oppressive materiality, does not explicitly extend beyond/behind the Wall to embrace that Wall's political, linguistic, sonic Others, nos semblables, nos soeurs trapped behind a Wall of Sound.

Notes

1. Ronnie Spector, with Vince Waldron, *Be My Baby: How I Survived Mascara, Miniskirts, and Madness or My Life as a Fabulous Ronette* (New York: HarperCollins, 1990). See especially the first five chapters. It seems clear that Amy Winehouse is a natural "extension" or merging of Karasick and Bennett.

2. The "storm from paradise," the pile of wreckage, and the angel of history are all drawn from Walter Benjamin's oft-cited image in "Theses on the Philosophy of History," *Illuminations,* translated by Harry Zohn (New York: Schocken, 1969), x.

3. Interview with Nada Gordon.

In the Shadow of Desire

Charles Bernstein's *Shadowtime* and Its Kabbalistic Trajectories

Adeena Karasick

According to Kabbalistic thinking, the world is strewn with fragments of light, sparks of desire that are continually scattered and bifurcating. And though we are constantly trying to create *Tikkun* (reassimilate the shattered fragments), as *Shadowtime* points out, "this is an impossible task." Journeying through its ghostly portals, through spectral voices, nursery rhymes, dialogues, homophonic translations, numerical systems, blues riffs, anagrams, invented languages, sociopolitical aesthetic and mystical debates, we can "imagine no wholes / from all that has been smashed."[1] Intuiting a kind of Kabbalistic hermeneutics, *Shadowtime* erupts as a heteroglossic arena where conflicting texts collide, intersect, overlap, and any overarching notion of Totality, Authority, Truth, Translation, or Closure is called into question.

Like *Shadowtime,* Kabbalah (the "umbrella term" for a complex assemblage of mystical teachings and codification techniques embedded in the Jewish arcana) presents itself as a non-unified, non-containable discourse. Composed of mystical *Midrash, Targumim, Halakhah,* Torah, and prayer, it is strewn with short commentaries, extensive disquisitions, *Aggadic* legends[2] (essentially "creative exegesis" that is often polyvocal, ambiguous, and indeterminate), homilies, which take the form of arguments or dialogues between rabbis set in the framework of travel stories, anecdotes, anonymous expositions, and conjectural confabulations. Exposing an exegetical, homiletic character, Kabbalah (like *Shadowtime*) moves from legal topics, liturgical matters through interpretation, interpolation, poetry, philosophy, biblical commentary, lexicons and codes with "[little] internal connection between them."[3] Through this infusion of otherness, Kabbalah foregrounds language and meaning as a contagion agency of multiple subjectivities inscribed along shifting axes of influence, ever-circulating systems of difference.

This sense of defamiliarity, polyvocality, and ambiguity pervades *Shadowtime.* This is particularly evident in that, throughout the text, Benjamin (both as historical figure and as trope) becomes a generative process of production. In Scene 3, through hysterical monomania, anagrams of Benjamin's name are layered upon each other,

I'm a lent barn Jew
A mint bran jewel
A barn Jew melt in
A rent Jew in balm
A Jew lamb intern[4]

Contracted into an alchemical cocktail of the letters of his name, "walter-benjamin" becomes a s/cite of pulsional incidents, which inhabit multiple and conflicting positions.

As the signifier of reference slips, the text performs itself through a hyper-absorptive orbit which infuses subjectivity into it, and as such, metonymically acts out a hybridity of meaning, forbidden transparency, and impossible univocity.

Each anagrammatic syntagm is another name, an alter name, a pseudonym, an eponym, or a hidden name. Understood in this way, it is similar to how the *Zohar* speaks of how the single all-inclusive name separates out into its individual elements and the different combinations all designating different forces of emanation. Or how G-d is referenced through a seventy-two-letter name, or forty-two-letter name or a four-letter name; each hidden, concealed, unpronounceable. Thus, "The Name" becomes the name of the name; the name that exceeds the name in an ever-mnemonic process of renaming.

And just as subjectivity is acknowledged as an unassimilable slippage of shades, shards, in *Shadowtime*, time is renegotiated as disjunctive, coexistent, and synchronic. Kabbalistically, the world was said to be created *illo tempore;*[5] and is re-actualized in every ceremonious act. Time is regenerated in every trope, letter, graphematic axiom, and thus in mimetic mutation functions as a simulacra of "the creation of the world." Similarly, in *Shadowtime*, Bernstein points out that each utterance is "releasing the sparks inside the words."[6] Every letter, word, sound, breath, generates meaning both *in* and *out* of time. So it seems, both within *Shadowtime* and Kabbalistic poetics, time is renegotiated" as contemporaneous (as in *cum tempus: with time*), or *jetzszeit* ("now time"),

for now time is lost, now time is
cracked, now time is empty, now
time is framed, now time is lived,

now time is hollow, now time
is smoked, now time is stolen[7]

or swollen—

This sentiment, however, is not a revolt *against* concrete, historical time in favor of a "mythical time" or a "Great time" or a "Pure time," but through repetitious reproduction, time is regenerated as an irreplaceable time. A historical moment that comes and keeps coming, *becoming*. Pulsing in radical discontiguity, *Shadowtime* is not stable, but functions through a process of temporal disjoining.

This is particularly foregrounded in the simultaneous tripartite construction of the stage in Scene 1. On one portion, Benjamin and Gurland arrive in Portbou and are told they must return to France. On another portion of the stage, there is a dialogue told in flashbacks between young Benjamin and his wife, Dora, and then a third portion of the stage is dedicated to a philosophical/political/theologic dialogue between Benjamin and Scholem and Hölderlin (or more accurately Benjamin as Hölderlin posing as a pseudo Benjamin and Hölderlin as Scardanelli!). Histories, dialogues, texts intersect, circulate, converge, and recede. Spectrographematically, run down, on the run, out of order, off its hinges, off its course, *Shadowtime* becomes "a sign of the times" which *takes* its time. 'Cause when it's all in the timing, it's *about* time. Flickering between "failed time" and flawed time, "reflective time" and "redemptive time," the text tears *into* time ("on the other side of time") and bides time (buys time), beating this time as contaminated time, beyond and beside time.

What time is it *now?* What time is it *now?*
What time is it *now?* What time is it *now?*
What time is it *now?* What time is it *now?*
What time is it *now?* What time is it *now?*[8]

Abandoning notions of chronology, causality, and historical contextualism, *Shadowtime* operates as an Einsteinian "function of energy" in perpetual recurrence, where the end is contained in an ever-receding beginning (or in the words of Jabès), in "the vertigo of a hypothetical beginning";[9] an irrepresentable resonant present that is always *just* out of reach.

Without static place, meaning, or tropos, this libretto foregrounds itself as linguistically diasporic. Operating through a more homiletic rather than rhetorical modality, through its seven scenes,[10] meaning wanders through a complex of codes, texts, borders; wanders like Benjamin's avatar through imagined levels of reality—not so much, nomadically, but *monadically.* Through Heinrich Heine (born Henry) and Hölderlin, through Groucho Marx and Karl Marx, Liberace and the Ba'al Shem Tov (disguised as a vampire), through Furies and angels and Einstein, revered Kabbalist and friend, Gershom Scholem, headless ghouls and Golems, Joan of Arc and Hitler, *Shadowtime* piles wreckage upon wreckage, trope upon trope. Each voice, like a letter, a sign, floating through a textual cosmos, erupts out of itself, out of its history, its "particular time / particular space."[11] Through brilliant intervention and re-inscription, Bernstein reverses, displaces, and seizes the apparatus of value coding and produces a perverted context "which is radiantly porous" and "where journey never ends."

But, what's interesting is that it never fetishizes the border or the blurring of borders, but the crossing, the voyage. It asks us to think about *how* the border is crossed. *Who* is crossing? In *what* ways? In *Shadowtime,* the border is not a separation but a step, a departure, a trespassing, an inclusive nonconclusive inclusion which is always already overdetermined and contaminated by the events of language. *Portbou* is reinvented as a portal, a door, a passage between countries, eras, genres, politics, and stands in for the "impracticable, the impossible passage, the refused, denied or prohibited passage, the non-passage."[12] (And, like Benjamin, we as readers are never *fully* assured "a safe passage.") What cannot pass comes to pass, not as a *non-pas* but *a-pas,* a passion, a *pas-de-pas* as parameters endlessly shift and the border *debords, abords,* and become spiralling centers in an endless process of promise ("on the shores of the promised"[13]), parasitism, grafting and divisibility. And if, according to Hélène Cixous, "when I cross a border it's my border I'm crossing, though I don't know which one I'm crossing or which side I end up on,"[14] *Portbou* simultaneously prohibits and gives passage. So, like working through so many languages, philosophers, poets, terrorists, thinkers, temporal and geographic codes, *Shadowtime* becomes a heterodidactics of the between—which questions ends, modes of ending. And, as such, does not embrace a transcendental concept of space but a topography of edges, a configuration of contours, sequences that wrench security out of a poetic labyrinth of vertiginous exigencies, a vortext of possibilities and substitutions.

Like how Kabbalah is rooted in *Torah, Shadowtime* is grounded in Benjamin's philosophies—"his ideas of intertwined natures of history, time, transcendence, timelessness, language and melancholy; the possibility for a transformational leftist politics; the interconnecting of language, things and cosmos; and the role of dialectical materiality, aura, interpretation and translation in art" (*Shadowtime synopsis*). Each are translations of the other.

Through a process of expansion and contraction both discourses become always already framed *within* an ever-spiralling discourse. Though both are *based on* the language of the "source text," they question any notion of a metalanguage or the transcendentalism of traditional criticism. But, as both Bernstein and Kabbalah engage in a process of "writing through" or "with" the other, it breaks down any hierarchical dichotomy of the "originary" texts. Enmeshed inside the sultry body of the other, meaning and truth are constituted contingently, indeterminately, in ongoing radical translation.

In the *Zohar,* this is particularly foregrounded in that rabbis (icons of legitimacy and authoritative discourse) are *in dialogue,* conflict, engaged in a nonhistorical, non-time-bound, never-ending always-circulating dialectics of discovery; fetishizing a notion that there *is no* single Truth, Authenticity, Legitimacy in a *unified* discourse. Similarly, *Shadowtime* sings,

Rings of desire, floods of wisps
Who's to say what, what's to say which
Whether what is is so because
Or whether what is is not.[15]

There are always already a superfluity of perspectives, positions, laws, which are always shifting. What is "true" is re-viewed as a network of possibility, re-told in a telling, a detailing, a taling of how the tell tolls, trials.[16] Or in the words of Bernstein,

The best picture
Of a picture
Is not the picture
But its reverse
Rehearing tales
Until they
Unfold
In the tolling[17]

As such, *Shadowtime* foregrounds how history is constructed, that truth is continually created ("tear's friction cobbles fact" [*indeed is*] "a hocus-pocus display"[18]) that memory is always slipping away (into capacious forgetting)—

. . . the facts I saw
what I had known

always disappearing
and the places
you saw
unable to trace
what's known
then gone . . ."[19]

Everything is inscribed in an "oily shadow a cozy vapour" that wafts through impressions, a "folded haze." What can possibly be fully apprehended? And to make matters more complex, the score is comprised of layers upon layers of sound. So even if one was "fully listening," it is impossible to fully "hear." The questions to be asked are: from *where* am i listening? With *whom* am i listening? For *what* purpose? The wholes ARE smashed and we are left to piece together the sparks, the fragments. In the shadows of desire.

Further, deferring easy consumption, Bernstein's libretto is inscribed with questions, interrogations ("are you ready to be the new Rashi?"—as he elevates art criticism to a sacred and mystical art), "What animates the letters? Do you mean to put divinity on trial?" (Scene 5: Pools of Darkness: 11, Interrogations). But, though these questions are not answered, in Scene 4 we are told, "the answer comes in the form of a question, an echo inside a shadow wrapped in cellophane." Additionally, the text is riddled with *answers* to questions that have never been asked (i.e., in *Aphorisms*), or if a question *is* asked, often the answers answer different unvoiced questions, positing itself almost as a pataphysical performance of the "elision of the elision without quotation."

In fact, *Shadowtime* questions all sense of conventional linear narrative structures. Through strategies of irritation and annoyance, hybridity, deformation, masking, and inversion, it presents itself as that which is not rational or irrational but relational, elational, or in Bernstein's terms, "arational." And if indeed, "just around the corner is another corner,"[20] *Shadowtime* celebrates a form of reason that is infinitely trajectoral. And, though "a trajectory is necessarily without heading and without assurance, [it is] a precipitation toward which trembles, vibrates at once orients and disorients,"[21] Bernstein presents not an unreasonable reason, a higher reason, a privileged reason, or a reason outside of reason, but in a hyperbolic surplus of spectrality, sacrality, alterity, a *raison d'être* ("knock knock, who's there?") where we *enter* in vertiginous dissymmetry (and like Benjamin, himself), in displacement, rupture, and disorientation.

So, just as "when every syllable a reason" (Jabès) or "every logic a semiotic" (Peirce), both Kabbalistic and Bernsteinian discourses posit an *anagogic logic* (a "flux logic"), and foreground how one cannot cling to an insurrectionary knowledge which assumes syntactic unity, topological reductionism; a finitist ambition of a nonreciprocal totalitarianism, evaluative centrality, and instead layers itself with "palimpsestic forms, cracked spines, archives of anteriority [and] vampiric codes" (77).

In Bernstein's text, Golems are speaking in constructed language. Each scene is inscribed with homophonic slippage, letter transposition, permutations, combinations, aphorisms. And all of these procedures are uncannily mirrored in Kabbalistic poetics. For example, in Scene 6, Part 6's "Cant's" is uncannily similar to the modulating techniques in Abraham Abulafia's model of meditation of the four-letter name of G-d used to reach transcendent heights—purely through the repetition and recombination of letters. In Bernstein's text there is insistent repetition/reproduction which evokes a mounting pleasure, an ecstatic (ex-stais) state of *verfremdungst.* Similarly, in "Tensions," each of the ten line's letters can be reassembled to make "each ear's sly fiction toy tutu unlit!"

According to Abulafia, if one writes a word, permuting and cycling the letters in every possible manner, he will progress to higher and higher states of consciousness. For, divine essence is sealed in these permutations, and every key of wisdom is given over to the individual who "gazes," "sees," and "understands." For, "when an individual looks into these permutations, he can see all of creation."[22]

Shadowtime III, The Doctrine of Similarity is dominated by number symbolism. Throughout this section it suggests the mystical practice of *Gematria* (the mathematics of Torah). *Gematria* is the calculation of the numerical equivalence of letters, words, or phrases, and thereby, gaining, insight into the interrelationship between words and ideas. The basic assumption behind this technique is that numerical equivalence is not coincidental, and there are different systems for identifying the numerical equivalence of individual letters.[23] But though Bernstein states that this section is an investigation into how "numeric patterns create reverberations within and between the text and music"[24] (in true Kabbalistic fashion), through its repetitions and permutations, the text *also* recognizes that each letter represents a different creative force.

According to the laws of *Gematria,* the numerical equivalence of two words reveals an internal connection between the creative potentials of each one. In Bernstein's homophonic translation of Ernst Jandl's *Der und Die,* we are forced to see the connection between each of the 338, three-lettered syntagms. Through its twenty-six lines (of thirteen words per line), through a somewhat perverted Abulafian process of *Hokhmah ha-Tseruf* (The Science of the Combination of Letters) or *Darkhei Tseruf ha-Otiyyot* (The Ways of the Permutation of the Letters), Bernstein performs a sacred ritual of combination which calls into the "dew" and "die" one experiences when one is able to "receive" the intellectual influx through the process of letter combination. For, according to the thirteenth-century mystic Abraham Abulafia, through the recombination of the sacred letters "He shall appear to him as if his entire body, from his head to his feet, had been anointed with anointing oil . . . and he will feel as if he will die."[25]

Further, in Hebrew, letters are also numbers. Thus each line of *Shadowtime* inevitably becomes a mathematical equation, a series of algebraic codes. Scene 1's Level 3's "1,2,3,4,5,6,7,8,9,10 / 1,3,2,4,8,5,10,6,7,9 / 9,6,4,5,8,3,2,7,1,10" can be read as a series of numbers, or as one step forward, two steps back *or* read Kabbalistically, each numeric cluster adds up to 55 which breaks down to 10 (5 + 5) and thereby references the 10 *sefirot* (vessels of light or utterances from which the world was created). Thus, this innocuous numeric sequence is coded with / loaded with all sorts of hidden treasures, and indeed does "mimic the primordial structures of the cosmos."[26]

Also, in this continuous recounting, Benjamin is literally (as well as figuratively) keeping time. His days are numbered. And of course, though playing out different sequences, but using 10 as the base, Bernstein shows how Benjamin is reimagined between one and zero, between something and nothing. In the shadows of time.

It's pretty obvious for a "close listener" to "hear" how this piece is not only Jewish in content, but certainly borrows or inherits a kind of Kabbalistic poesis—a heteroglossic/palimpsestic enunciative process where potential meanings are never fixed, never exhausted; a celebration of language as a productive economy of intersequential subterfuge, supplementarity and exchange; a religio-linguistic practice that remains *faithful* to a secret which secretes, a *s'ecrit* (a diasporic discourse inscribed in iteration and renegotiation).

Now, I'm not saying that Bernstein is familiar with and overtly imported Kabbalistic hermeneutics, but the uncanny similarities in *Shadowtime,* in particular, are worth noting. Albeit unconsciously or intuitively importing these cultural strategies, through the linking of modalized presents, Bernstein restages cultural temporalities into the invention of tradition and thereby questions inheritance as that which is not natural, transparent, or universal, but an irreducible legacy inscribed through cultural memory, *culturalingual* iterability and palimpsestic processes of prosthetic supplementarity. Through an ongoing process of bordering, re-bording marking and tracing, both discourses write themselves through a political economy of parasitism, grafting, and divisibility, and produce a paratactic sacrifice apostrophized in a liminal toponymy of accumulation.

In exile between France and America, between the past and his present, between different social and aesthetic contexts, between the imagined and the lived, between the text and the music, between the breath and the silences and discordance, the solo and the choral, between Marxism and mysticism. Between *die wahr* and *die wahrwelt,* the lived and the true, the real and the constructed. Between wartime and wartime, between "Beniamin" and "Benjamin," *Shadowtime* resists reification. It exists for us in pieces, fragments. But, as Bernstein also points out, it's not merely fragmented or disjunctive for its own sociopolitical sake (like perhaps the mythology of the free flow of random association), but rather as Bernstein himself says about Benjamin, he is "a good example of multipolar, rather than linear thinking. Benjamin's form of reflective writing suggests a poetics of multiple layers of figures. A line of thought may seem to go off into one direction then drops back to follow another trajectory only this new direction is not a non sequitur but rather echoes or refracts both the antecedent motifs and—this is the uncanny part—the eventual ones."[27]

Through "overlays, pleats, folds," *Shadowtime* foregrounds how like the world itself, "everything is intricately connected" and must be seen as inherently polyphonous, a transferential nexus or contextatic excess, a reproductive process, a sapirous reciprocity of quotation, restoryation, appendices, and resemblance.

Shadowtime becomes not merely a "Katabasis" (shadoworld), but a *Kabbalapoesis*—"[a] language lined with flesh, a text where we can hear the grain of the throat . . . a whole carnal stereophony: the articulation of the tongue, not the meaning of language."[28] A language not marked by "kataplexy" but a *Kabbalah-lexy* (which can never be "fully" accessed (or in the words of the text, can not merely be grasped but must be continually grappled with). But, somewhere between the layers of music, contemporary aesthetics, and historical myth, between palimpsested languages, politics, cultures, codes and between the unvoiced music and un-songed worlds Benjamin lives. Lives between layers of history where all that's accessible are moments, shards, fragments. But these fragments are not an arbitrary free play—but as Bernstein points out in his 2005 interview with Eric Denut, in the actual staging of the opera it is virtually impossible to hear unique words, voices but instead "verbal matter [becomes] part of the acoustic layering of the sound composition . . . not the singular threads but their composite . . . a chordal poetics in which synchronic notes meld into diachronic tones."[29]

Through a series of veilings and unveilings (as in the truth shall make you veiled or the veil of unknowing [*veil smear*]), *Shadowtime* avails, volleys in volé valleys, values, and calls into a vast repository of "involuntary memory." And if language itself can only fulfill itself through mourning, loss (as it all "[falls] into my capacious insomniac forgetting"[30]) marked by traces, absences, specters, echoes between "voluntary and involuntary memory" (a kind of cultural inheritance), between meaning and history, time and memory, we, as close listeners, "[unravel] / the threads / that hold / the leaves scattering,"[31] bear witness and remain in the shadow of the profound beauty of translation.

Notes

1. Charles Bernstein, *Shadowtime.* Scene 7: Stelae For Failed Time: Green Integer No. 122, Los Angeles, 2005, 118.

2. *Aggada,* which comes from the verb "le-haggid," meaning "to say" or "to tell," elaborates on biblical narrative, includes wise sayings, expressions of faith, expositions and expansions of Scripture, stories, anecdotes, or folktales, which allows the Torah to remain dynamic and open to varying interpretation. See Joseph Heinemann, "The Nature of Aggadah," in *Midrash and Literature,* ed. Geoffrey Hartman and Sanford Budick (New Haven, CT: Yale University Press, 1986), 41–55.

3. This is particularly evident in the *Zohar* (regarded as the premier "book" of medieval Jewish mysticism). But, it is not a single unified work but rather an anthology of texts from the Amoraic period up to the second half of the thirteenth century drawn from Babylonian and Palestinian Talmud as well as Jewish Apocalyptic literature. Comprised of three books and divided into five parts, it is more appropriately seen as a series of folds, a congeries of treatises, texts, extracts, or fragments drawn from many strata of mystical discourse. Not only are there numerous authors, but the *Zohar* is written in multiple fonts in several languages: sometimes Aramaic, sometimes Hebrew, sometimes both in the same sentence.

4. *Shadowtime,* 71.

5. Like in Kabbalistic hermeneutics, cosmic worlds, levels of reality, time exists simultaneously. There is no separation between this world and the future world. This sentiment is again present in the interview with Eric Denut, where Bernstein says, "That other world is always, anyway *this* world." See Charles Bernstein Interview, Eric Denut. The Argotist Online, 2005.

6. *Shadowtime,* 50.

7. Ibid., 118–119.

8. Ibid., 95.

9. Edmond Jabès, *From the Book to the Book,* trans. Rosmarie Waldrop, intro. Richard Samelman (Hanover: Wesleyan University Press, 1991).

10. The fact that *Shadowtime* is organized into seven scenes (and Scene 6 has 7 *Tableaux Vivants*) can be read as a Kabbalistic reference to the "Seven Double Letters":

Bet [ב], Gimmel [ג], Dalet [ד] Kaf [כ], Peh [פ], Resh [ר], Tav [ת]. According to the *Sefer Yetzirah* (*The Book of Creation*), these seven letters (which are called "Double" because they embody both a "hard" and "soft" sound and thereby question the whole nature of dualistic binaric thinking) were responsible for creating the

- 7 openings in the head (eyes, ears, nostrils, mouth)
- 7 planets (Saturn, Jupiter, Mars, Sun, Venus, Mercury, and Moon)
- 7 heavens (or firmaments: Vilon, Rakia, Shachakim, Zevul, Ma'on, Makhon, Aravot)
- 7 universes (for the Kabbalist, many universes can run concurrently; for once we transcend the universe as we know it, time shifts in meaning)
- 7 days of the week
- 7 lower sefirot (Chesed, Gevurah, Tiferet, Netzach, Hod, Yesod, Malkhut)
- 7 angels (Michael, Barakiel, Gabriel, Raphael, Chasdiel, Tzidkiel, Ariel)
- 7 rivers associated with the Holy Land (The Jordan, Yarmoch, Kirmyon, Poga, Pishon, Gichon, Chidekel)
- 7 deserts through which the Israelis passed during the Exodus from Egypt (Eitan, Shur, Sin, Sinai, Paran, Tzin, Kadmut)
- 7 cycles of 7,000 divine years (approx. 2,556,750,000 earthly years that the universe will go through)

11. *Shadowtime*, 70.

12. Jacques Derrida, *Aporias*, trans. Thomas Dutoit, ed. Werner Hamacher and David E. Wellbery (Stanford, CA: Stanford University Press, 1993), 73.

13. *Shadowtime*, 116.

14. Hélène Cixous, *Three Steps on the Ladder of Writing*, trans. Sarah Cornell and Susan Sellers (New York: Columbia University Press, 1993), 130.

15. *Shadowtime*, 109.

16. This is not to say that history does not exist or events did not happen, but rather explores how they are remembered, who is remembering them, and in what context.

17. *Shadowtime*, 121.

18. Ibid., 103.

19. Ibid., 114–115.

20. Ibid., 106.

21. Jacques Derrida, *Specters of Marx: the State of the Debt, the Work of Mourning, and the New International*, trans. Peggy Kamuf (New York: Routledge, 1994), 23. This type of trajectoral writing is evident throughout the *Bahir*. Not only does it often break off in the middle of one sentence and continue with the middle of another, but the answers to questions are sometimes missing (section 30); important enumerations are not brought to a conclusion (sections 88, 115). Sections 107–115 present a lengthy anonymous exposition, while 116 begins: "His pupils said to him" without any previous reference having been made to the teacher and his words. (See Gershom

Scholem, *The Origins of Kabbalah,* trans. Allan Arkusch, ed. R. J. Zwi Werblowsky (Princeton, NJ: Princeton University Press, 1987), 54.

22. As discussed in *Sefer ha-Ot* (Book of the Sign) and *Sefer haTseruf* (The Book of Blendings).

23. Four of the most common methods for calculation would be to determine the "Absolute Value," the "Ordinal Value," "the "Reduced Value," and the "Integral Reduced Value." The method that was calculated would determine which association. On some level, this system is akin to a Jakobsonian notion of working on both the syntagmatic and diametric axes of influence at the same time or the Saussurean notion of how choice is both simultaneously determined and free. Bernstein seems to be using a looser version of *gematria*—acknowledging language as a system of signs that can be repeated (reproduced) and continually redistributed, which opens the text for possible readings.

24. *Shadowtime,* 20.

25. Abraham Abulafia, in *Hayye ha-Olam ha-Ba* (Life of the Future World). See Moshe Idel, *The Mystical Experience in Abraham Abulafia,* trans. Jonathan Chipman (New York: State University of New York Press, 1988).

26. *Shadowtime,* 20.

27. Charles Bernstein Interview, Eric Denut. The Argotist Online, 2005.

28. Roland Barthes, *Pleasure of the Text,* trans. R. Miller (New York: Hill, 1975), 49.

29. Charles Bernstein Interview, Eric Denut. The Argotist Online, 2005.

30. *Shadowtime,* 122.

31. Ibid., 121.

Hijacking Language
Kabbalistic Trajectories

Adeena Karasick

> . . . gaze at a word, graft it, hew and carve it, combine its letters over and over again until your thought processes are turned over and your entire perception is altered. You will be showered with an influx of light. For, it is said, when an individual engages in these permutations, [s/he] can see all of creation.
>
> —Abraham Abulafia

Perhaps since the panel on Jewish Radical Poetics last year in New York, there has been a lot of talk about Jewish writing. Is Jewish writing something that foregrounds Jewish themes? Is it a stylistic methodology that defines itself through (as maybe Maria Damon might say) nomadicism, vagrancy, exile, or does it take on a more Bernsteinian flavor—and embody all "that which is formal, rhythmic, dialectical, dialogical and colloquial?" Or perhaps it's as Stephen Paul Miller says of Robert Alter, "a sort of mounting semantic pressure, a structure of intensity?"[1] How does *Jewishness* look, act, sound? I would have to contend that it's not necessarily about *what* is being said, but *how* language is being manipulated; how "meaning" is determined through an *experience* of *letters;* through a direct connection with them, their physical makeup and their interconnections, substitutions, combinations, and all the while questioning how this affects the foundations of thinking.

And in good company, i may add, these obsessions are also that of many Jewish secular thinkers: the Russian Formalists, Structuralists, post structuralists and key proponents of French feminist deconstructionist theory (Levi-Strauss, Jakobson, Derrida, Hélène Cixous, to name a few). With this said, I'd like to show how some of these formal concerns are uncannily akin to what might be termed a "Kabbalistic hermeneutics."

So, first what *IS* Kabbalah? As the ex-author for *Kabbalah for Dummies,* i can tell you, contrary to popular belief, & the mishugaas of Hollywood A-listers, with their misguided obsessions about red strings and bottled water, Kabbalah *IS NOT* a quick fix, cult fetish, self-help guide to modern angst, but rather is an "umbrella term" for a complex assemblage of mystical teachings, techniques for decoding the arcana, believed to be concealed within canonical Jewish texts.

Like in much deconstructionist theory and contemporary American poetics, in Kabbalistic practice, language is at the base of all thinking. So, even though this ancient hermeneutic methodology (which dates back to the second century) is grounded in an onto-theological discourse, notions of metaphysics, epistemology, and transcendency, its main focus is *on the way language functions.* Not only does it look at the meanings of terms and words, but also the sound and shape of letters, the vocalization points, the decorative additions, the frequency with which words and letters appear, their changes or absence or numerical value. All these procedures urge the reader to experience language in "non-traditional ways"—extract it from its *use* value and encourage one to somehow get inside these cosmic and erotic fields of discourse, harness language's inherent power, and experience the sensation of ever-expanding "meaning."

But, it is necessary to note *why* language is so crucial for the Kabbalists, is that because, for them, *THE WORLD WAS LITERALLY CREATED THROUGH LANGUAGE.*[2] According to the *Zohar,* the world was engraved and established with letters. And these twenty-two letters went out and created the "world above" and the "world below" (no hierarchy intended). And they believe, it is OUR DUTY, to *continue this process of creation.* And this is done by contemplating the Hebrew alphabet (the letters that make up the written language) *and by combining them!* For, it is through the substitutions and alterations of words (the intricate layering and juxtaposing of letters) that meanings and relationships in the *outside* world are continuously affected/re-created.

My G-d, this language IS Holy!

But this notion of "creation" (or the inherent creative POWERS of language) does not necessarily have to be understood on *A METAPHYSICAL LEVEL*—because if we remember from Foucault, our word-word connections can lead to social and political transformation and change; or just like for deconstructionists, our world IS always being re-created through language; its structures, systems, intra-semiotic operations. Like their semiaphiliac, secular political, post-structuralist antecessors, for the Kabbalists, each letter, each processual hermeneutic moment, every exegetical entry is a simulacric re-enactment of a continual creative process!

Throughout all my work this psycho-obsessive focus of the meticulous and detailed inner workings of language is always at play —sometimes invested intentionally, and sometimes it just filters through (cultural memory, inheritance). Certainly so in my reading of "The Western Wall" (*haKotel*) in *Dyssemia Sleaze*—each brick metonymically became like a letter, a syntagmatic trope, an instance of history, identity, blocks of meaning. The remains of the Wall, a fragment of history, like a shard of text, ruptured from its source though still resonates with its/his/her storic import that keeps changing as its socio/political and geographic matrices its continual social reformation {do walls make good neighbors?}, i was so consumed with how the *kotel* questioned whole notions of nature and culture / as new growth sprouted up between the bricks / blocks of meaning, how Kabbalistically it could be likened to the *Shekehinah* (the female indwelling presence of G-d, lips, word, mouth, how it continually speaks the unspoken). The wall then is filled with the secrets of her (quite literally as she is stuffed with paper, text, letters, inserted with desire). So, this structure, always a sign, at play, resonates massively and signifies all that is revealed and concealed, secret and resonant, a series of veilings and unveilings, invaginated surfaces, pockets, folds, ruptures, fragments of meaning.

Kabbalists use a series of formal linguistic procedures to achieve new or heightened perception; literally "to unseal the soul [*which, in the Kabbalistic imagination is partially physical*], to untie the knots which bind it"—(a kinda anti-deSadean system). This type of syntagmatic liberation is not totally unlike how the Dadaists used to break apart language in order to see G-d but MORE akin to a deconstructionist methodology whereby the text is re-examined, problematized, questioned, in order to expose the foundations of thinking practices, and expand it exponentially, while examining it contextually, multiperspectively.

And like how contemporary L=A=N=G=U=A=G=E poets employ such radical strategies to destabilize the text, *Kabbalists* use rhetorical techniques such as: *Gematria* (geometry, numerology), ellipsis, metaphrasis, ekphrasis, acrostics (or cross shtick), *Temurah* (which are anagrams)—as *Temurah* and *Temurah* and *Temurah* creeps into our petty place, *Temurah Temurah,* i love you *Temurah*—and a whole slew of slippery ellipses and multiple possibilities for layering and palimpsesting and diverting techniques to move text AWAY from a literal, linear narrative structure and into a lingua-erotic arena where the letters themselves are seen as balls of fiery potential. Black fire on white fire radiant and sparkling energies of desire embedded with infinite creative possibilities.

Gematria (Numerology)

What's interesting about *Gematria* is that in Hebrew, numbers are written as letters, so, one can, with equal legitimacy, read any page of the Torah (or any document, for that matter) as a series of words or a sequence of numbers, equations, arithmetic, or mathematical axioms. (Now *that's* a narrative destabilizer!)

Basically, *Gematria* consists of explaining a word or group of words according to the numerical value of the letters of substituting other letters of the alphabet for them within a set system. Over time, the system of *Gematria* became very complicated. Variations occur as certain letters are shaped differently when they are final letters. There are at least seventy-two different forms of *Gematria* used to decipher codes.

Gematria is not some hoo-hoo cosmic fantasy of codification, but a simple method of "calling into" the inherent heterogeneity or heteroglossia already in language. For the Kabbalists, these intricate combinatory procedures simply highlight how each word has multiple and perhaps infinite references; how language is an ever-expansive realm of multiplicity, divergence, and inconclusivity, and that *every word IS essentially a code for something else.*

Neqqudot (Vowels)

For Kabbalists, vowels play a significant role in expanding the literal meaning of text. Not only is the Torah scroll written without vowels and therefore pregnant with (in)finite vocalizable potential, but according to the Catalan Kabbalist Rabbi Jacob Ben Sheshet, the scroll of the Torah actually *should not be vocalized* because *no word should be limited.* To pronounce a word **one** way would be to limit and restrict all other possible pronunciations! Each word holds within it all possible articulations, references, associations. This is something i like to play around with a lot—this sense of embedding the text with many possible trajectories stemming from a single word, sound, nuance, reference all radiant, emanating with illuminative possibility. Also, for these Kabbalah dudes, the alphabet is gendered and the vowels are female—seen as *the form* and *soul to* the consonants, the energizing force, which causes the movement of the combinations of letters. As the vowels are not always (physically) present, they remain as a spectral presence, a present-non-present or resonant present, a series of illocatable traces forever haunting the consonants.

The five vowels

Cholam	Kametz	Tzereh	Chirik	Shuruk
◌ֹ	◌ָ	◌ֵ	◌ִ	◌ֻ

are very important (particularly in the *Sefer Yetzirah: The Book of Creation / or the Book of Letters*), as it is through specific vowel combinations / pronouncing them in specific ways that you can create a golem! (or in the words of Rocky Horror or Mary Shelley "... can make you a man!"). So, both on a theoretic AND practical level, on a mystical his/herstorical linguistic-semiotic or pop-cultural level, it seems both radical secular poetic thinkers *and* Kabbalists agree, *creation occurs through letters.*

Hokhmah ha-Tseruf (The Science of Combinations of Letters)

But one of the most crucial and interesting procedures for me, is *Hokhmah ha-Tseruf* (a process of linguistic "*Play,*" which consists of *Dillug* (jumping: which has to do with substitutions and combinations of letters) and *Kefitsah* (skipping from one concept to another). Both of these linguistic procedures are performed according to a set of flexible code words and identifiable structures.

According to Abulafia (the major proponent of *Hokhmah ha-Tseruf*), consonants are combined into a swift motion, which heats up your thinking and increases your joy and desire so much so that apparently you do not crave food or sleep and all other desires are annihilated. During this heightened state of contemplation, there is no desire other than the merging with these letters. i don't know about you, but when the writing is going well . . .

Abulafia was like the rebel Kabbalist of the thirteenth century (1240–1291). He was a Maimonides scholar, but instead of teaching the *Guide for the Perplexed* in a kind of "normal" way, he taught it based on the combinations of letters—that in order to fully understand it, you need to read it in conjunction with the pronunciation of the Divine Name with certain breathing techniques and singing and movements of the head. He believed that it was not enough to meditate on abstract truths as these were always too closely bound to *specific meanings,* but it was necessary to focus on the letters and their configurations, permutations. And it is only through doing this that you can reach *true mystical ecstasy* (check it out: Avraham Abulafia: the first language poet!). Each letter is seen as a body; which bodies forth between the body (corps), body (text) & bodies embodies bodes well swells (out of the page into yr body . . . and this body comprised of 613 organs and sinews, like 613 commandments, 613 *letters* of the Torah—Bodies. Letters, it's all the same[3]). In this context, divine connectivity is *an experience of language. Language that is visceral, somatic, and erotic.*

And THIS is something that is very close to my heart and my writing (and performance) practice. So, whatever it is i'm writing about: politics, fashion, pop culture, it's not that i'm writing about something overtly "jewey," but it's this awareness of language, of the intricacy of letters, sounds, movement that energizes the work.

Abulafia speaks about how to permute the letters back and forth and as a result of the activity and your concentration on the letters, your mind will become bound to them. The hairs on your head will stand on end and tremble. The blood within you will begin to vibrate because of the living permutations that loosen it. Your entire body will then begin to tremble, and all your limbs will be seized with shuddering. You will experience the terror of G-d and will be enveloped with fear of Him. You will then feel as if an additional spirit is within you, arousing you and strengthening you, passing through your entire body and giving you pleasure. It will seem as if you have been anointed with perfumed oil from head to foot. You will rejoice and experience a kind of (JEWY-sance). You will experience ecstasy and trembling—as if you are swallowed up by the letters and could die of rapture.

Also, according to the Kabbalists, all the letters make up the Name of G-d. So, no matter what you are writing you are in essence reciting the Sacred name. When you get up to read you are engaging in an act that is even MORE elevated, MORE complete than the Priests of the Temple times. Traditionally the masses sacrificed only rams, but in knowing and reciting the Sacred Name, you are sacrificing YOUR ENTIRE BEING!—Presenting before G-d, your bootylicious fat and your blood, your eyes which see the combinations of the names and your ears which pay heed to their sound. So, in reciting your work, you are reciting the Sacred Name and you are basically sacrificing YOURSELF on the altar of mystical union.

And it is written that you should constantly keep the letters of the Unique Name in your mind as if they were in front of you, written in a book of Torah. Each letter should appear as if it is always in front of you. Each letter should appear infinitely large. And you should keep this sensation with you, wherever you are . . .

(letters letters everywhere and not a trope to ink)

All of these techniques are often at play whenever i sit down to write, but certainly in doing the translation of the *Sefer Yetzirah,* in *The House That Hijack Built* (The *Sefer Yetzirah* or *The Book of Creation, Formation or The Book of Letters* IS the oldest text of Kabbalah. It's really a short treatise on cosmology and cosmogyny and tracks through how the world was created out of language.) In my McCaffereyesque "homolinguistic" or what Bernstein might call a "homophonic" translation, not only is there phonetic affinity but its focus is on the creation of meaning through the intersection of letters. My vision for the text was to have it ideally function simultaneously along (what Jakobson might call) its paradigmatic and syntagmatic axes.

Original: (*from Chapter 6:7*)

And when Abraham our father, may he rest in peace
looked, say, understood, probed,
engraved and carved,
He was successful in creation,
as it is written
"And the souls that they made in Haran"[4]

Translation:

Anon, über hombre, fathomed mostly in pieces, en process
A locus of cinders, stewed problematics, parables
Hungry and anchored
Housed in a sexy nexus of curated
Hazards wrought with
"Morsels of maiden whores"

Following Abulafia's techniques of the *Science of Combination of Letters* (of both free AND guided associations), the text becomes a practice of layering and infolding of meaning, full of puns, ellipses, and allusion.

Of course, this type of language play and questioning of the foundations of meaning also find parallels with Derridean deconstruction and post-structural methodologies used for "reading" texts—(though, it's important to note, as i have argued elsewhere, Derrida was *not* a Kabbalist, was *not* familiar with ancient Kabbalistic texts and methodologies, but these intersecting traces, uncanny linkages, are perhaps credible instances of cultural inheritance).

For example, like in Kabbalistic hermeneutics, a deconstructive practice invites the reader to see how language and meaning fold in on itself, are inscribed through discontinuous jumps which establish quasi-instantaneous links between sentences words or marks separated by hundreds of pages, and often incorporate nonlinguistic inscription; sublexical, graphic, and phonic units which force the reader to actively participate in the production of meaning and re-view language through an ever-widening lense. For both discourses, language is posited as a polyvocal process, a negotiation of passages, links, bonds, where form and content elide and become an intertextual web of possibility.

Also, just as it is customary to tear ones' clothes in mourning, a "de(con)-structive" or "combinatory" strategy which explodes words/concepts/contexts into constitutive/monadic elements tears them apart, or rips them from their locus (into shards, remnants, intertextilic fragments)[5] may also be seen as a sign of mourning. Abulafia's use of language carries the trace of death in its very inscription. For, just as death marks being, tearing words apart and endlessly recombining them signifies an ever-generative process.

For the Kabbalists, language manipulation is looked upon as the highest domain of study; it "is the knowledge of the force of the letters and their existence and their combination with each other, which enables the Kabbalist 'to create worlds.'" Every single word that is uttered through the mouth, every word that is written ascends aloft, splits firmaments. Every letter is seen as a web of mathematical and linguistic associations. Every letter a visceral moment of fiery potential. So, as for my poetics, a Kabbalistic poetics (if you will), is it a "Radical Jewish Poetics"?—i don't know, but what it asks, is to accept a meaning that is not fixed, but in flux, fluid; a logic that is often illogical; a rationality that is not irrational, but relational and affirms that like text itself, we must embrace contradiction, conflict, discordance. And, always remember that what's ecstatic is that which is outside of stasis, normalcy, complacency. What's mystical—is full of mystery. So, there's no need to understand this on a metaphysical, transcendentally hierarchic system of religiosity, but instead muck around in a sultry linguistic morass between otherness and familiarity, between what's veiled, unveiled, revealed, concealed, sealed, and salient; inside a semerotic lingua-static nexus of rupture (rapture), fractures, and fragments of light.

And this is Jewish Writing.

Notes

1. See "Pleasure," in *Skinny Eighth Avenue* (New York: Marsh-Halk Press, 2005).

2. According to the *Zohar*, "The world was engraved and established with 42 letters, all of them a crown of the holy name. When they had become joined, they ascended to its letters to the realm above and then descended to the realm below. They were adorned with crowns in the four corners of the world and [the world] was then able to survive. After this *the letters went out and created the world above and below;* the world of unification and the world of separation. And if, according to Abulafia, ". . . by contradicting the revealed structure of the Torah by means of letter combination, we [are able] to construct the hidden Torah, and by this construction, *the human*

intellect is also constructed," then each letter, each processual hermeneutical moment, every exegetical entry is a simulacric re-enactment of a continual creative process.

Also, according to the *Wisdom of the Zohar,* ". . . once [a wo/man] has produced a word from [H$^{e}_{i}{}^{r}_{s}$] mouth, that word becomes a sound and it cleaves atmospheres and firmaments and it goes up and another matter is aroused" (Vol. III, 952). Elsewhere, it is stated that "every single word of prayer that a [wo/man] utters through [H$^{e}_{i}{}^{r}_{s}$] mouth ascends aloft, splits firmaments, and enters the place that it enters" (Vol. III, 956).

3. There are said to be 613 limbs and sinews in the body, 613 positive and negative mitzvoth (commandments), 613 dark recesses in the soul.

4. From "The Book of Creation," in *The House That Hijack Built,* Adeena Karasick (Vancouver: Talonbooks, 2004).

5. A Kabbalistic hermeneutic can be said to operate or function in the way Matthew Barney describes the way the body develops under resistance—the way one tears down muscle cells in order to grow more of them (a kind of bodily deconstruction).

Letter to the Romans

Benjamin Friedlander

Let me be a Jewish poet after the fashion of Paul, who spoke new meanings with old words, and brought new conclusions to old meanings, saving the old conclusions for a new people, preparing a new future for the old people.

> Each pure life, each variety, fossilizes in public and accentuates the number of firmaments.
>
> —Kim Rosenfeld

> It is a strange language of trust, where individuals know each other intimately at the moment of betrayal.
>
> —Benjamin Hollander

To all God's beloved in Rome, who are called to be saints

The broad outline of Paul's life comes from his own letters, and from Luke's account in the book of *Acts.* A diaspora Jew of the tribe of Benjamin, Paul (born Saul) was a Pharisee, trained in scripture by Gamaliel the elder. Early on, he fiercely opposed the adherents of Jesus, condemning Stephen to death and overseeing the destruction of churches. Then, a visionary encounter on the road to Damascus shifted his loyalties. Traveling from Jerusalem with the high priest's authority, intending to make further arrests, he saw a blinding light, and heard a voice saying, "Saul, Saul, why do you persecute me?" Asking who spoke, he was told: "I am Jesus, whom you are persecuting; but rise and enter the city, and you will be told what you are to do." Three days later, when his sight had returned, Paul accepted baptism and became an apostle, founding congregations throughout the Greek-speaking world. His particular mission became preaching to the Gentiles, perhaps because, born outside Palestine (in Tarsus, in present-day Turkey), he had the requisite language skills and cosmopolitan experience. Arrested many times, he was a controversial figure, even among the followers of Jesus. According to legend, his last arrest ended in execution after several years in prison, but Luke is silent on this all-important point, and Clement, who knew Paul in Philippi, assumes a long, illustrious career.

Strange strange strange
the ways of the Word
in its illustrious
career, imprisoned as spirit
or set free as flesh.

I am not ashamed of the gospel: it is the power of God for salvation to every one who has faith, to the Jew first and also to the Greek

Some have described Paul's baptism as a conversion, but this missionary language implies that he abandoned one religion for another, an anachronistic, obscuring way of framing what is most radical in his theology: anachronistic, because Christianity as such did not exist in Paul's lifetime; obscuring, because the interdependence of Gentile and Jew is precisely what his letters advocate.

Did he remain a Jew until the end of his life? And what do we mean by "Jew" when we ask this question?

Paul himself conceived of his teaching as the answer to a call, wording that casts him in the tradition of the prophets. Echoing Jeremiah, he writes in Galatians: "For you have heard of my former life in Judaism, how I persecuted the church of God violently and tried to destroy it; and I advanced in Judaism beyond many of my own age among my people, so extremely zealous was I for the traditions of my fathers. But . . . he who had set me apart before I was born, and had called me through his grace, was pleased to reveal his Son to me, in order that I might preach him among the Gentiles" (1:13–15). The passage is equivocal. When Paul speaks of his "former life in Judaism," he may well mean that he has left Judaism behind, but his phraseology also permits us to conceive of a present life that is still Jewish, although antagonistic to tradition. And perhaps the passage is less equivocal than paradoxical: identifying with the prophets to articulate a dis-identification with his fathers, to whom the prophets preached, Paul sets forth to preach among the Gentiles.

A "calling," then, and not a "conversion."

But a calling within Judaism? Or a calling away?

Sad thoughts have fled,
Trouble and doubt, and now strange reveries
And odd caprices fill us in their stead.

—Emma Lazarus

Therefore you have no excuse, O man, whoever you are, when you judge another; for in passing judgment upon him you condemn yourself, because you, the judge, are doing the very same things

Paul's letters are the oldest books in the New Testament and take up about one quarter of the total pages. This has led many commentators to speak of Christianity as his creation—a view that two thousand years of Jewish hostility would seem to confirm. Certainly, the content of Paul's teaching is more extreme than that of Jesus. Zealous even as a Pharisee, he is at once more typical than Jesus of the Jews of his time, and more radical in his appraisal of Jewish tradition. Unlike Jesus, who exerts a certain fascination (and whose teachings are occasionally accepted as compatible with Jewish thought), Paul repels, a figure more alien than the God of the Gnostics.

Verily, kiddo, I walk
among monkeys as among
the foreskins and limbs
of monkeys—monkeys
in ruins

—Norma Cole

Complicating our understanding of Paul's message is the historical divide from across which we receive it. The religious upheavals of the first and second centuries C.E., when Judaism and Christianity first began to take shape in their present forms, constitute a kind of veil through which readers now, of necessity, must puzzle out Paul's writing—writing that came to function (irony of ironies) as a kind of law. This veil, the world we know, has a Christian warp and a Jewish weft. The warp is the appearance of Jesus and the subsequent transformation of his crucifixion and teaching into a new doctrine first within and then in opposition to Judaism. The weft is the destruction of the second temple in 70 C.E., less than a decade after Paul's death, a cataclysmic event that solidified the rabbinical role in the continuation and evolution of Pharisaic Judaism. (The rabbinic era proper began with the compilation of the Talmud, around 500 C.E.) Reading Paul through this veil makes it extremely difficult to identify the precise nature of his disaffiliation from tradition after accepting the call of Jesus. That he took issue with "the circumcision party" we know from his own letters; that he became a spiritual father to Marcionism, the most extreme form of anti-Judaism within Christianity, is historical fact. But Paul's place within Judaism? This remains a matter of dispute.

There will be tribulation and distress for every human being who does evil, the Jew first and also the Greek, but glory and honor and peace to every one who does good, the Jew first and also the Greek

> Whether the "poet" I struggle to bring to mind is a Jew or not a Jew makes no difference. . . . But it is a beginning of the work toward which the Jew, if the Jew takes thought, is particularly called.
>
> —Allen Grossman

In looking for echoes of Paul in writings by American Jews, I am not looking for echoes of Christianity; nor am I looking for poems that take up the life or death or cultural afterlife of Jesus, to whom Paul pays continual tribute. Writing of this sort is fairly common, as one might expect given the totality of Jewish immersion in Christian society. Engagements with Paul or Pauline ideas are much more difficult to find. A poem like Laura Riding's "The Last Covenant," which speaks directly to the problem ("And each new covenant made the other old; / And old was each new covenant"), is anomalous. Stray lines, oblique in their reference, are more typical. Scattered across the communal enterprise of Jewish writing, such lines constitute Paul's truest memorial—truest because most hidden.

The paucity of poetic response is not surprising when one considers the hostility with which Paul has long been held.[2] But another reason, surely, is the intimacy of his critique, an attack on tradition from within even more threatening than the external critiques ranged against Judaism by Paul's later followers. Looking beyond poetry, the Jewish response to Paul has generally taken two approaches. One response has been to regard Paul's challenge as a Christian challenge pure and simple, an approach that necessarily ignores or sets aside all that remains provocatively Jewish in Paul's thought. Another response has been to ignore Paul altogether, engaging Christianity solely through the figure of Jesus. For in Jesus, unlike Paul, the Jewish aspect remains traditional: a religious Jew can celebrate the teachings of Jesus and then rue their conscription into a new religion. The teachings of Paul permit no such celebration. Although his conscription into Christianity is no less retrospective than that of Jesus, there can be no doubt that Paul's reading of scripture would have been rejected by rabbinic authority even if the gospel of Christ had played no part in it at all.

Paul without Christ: this, indeed, is the formulation that most interests me, especially with regard to "secular Jewish culture." For Paul's setting aside of the law I see as an intrinsic possibility for Jewish life, a possibility that Paul neither discovered nor exhausted. Moreover, by linking Paul in this way to the cultural practices of so-called secular Jews, I mean, on the one hand, to take up Paul's theology as a practice of community, and, on the other hand, to suggest that those communities created by nonobservant Jews retain a theological significance.

They show that what the law requires is written on their hearts

> I was convicted of the allegory
> —Hannah Weiner

Stumbling over the word
of the prophet
on the way to a deferred
meaning, futures tumble
into an old conviction

But now the righteousness of God has been manifested apart from law

> a secret
> groundmass
> obliterating the old message
> —Abigail Child

Paul wrote his *Letter to the Romans* shortly before his arrest in Jerusalem, about 57 C.E. It is his longest theological testament and his most ingenious reformulation of three principles central to Jewish self-definition: law, circumcision, and covenant. His Christology is presupposed in this letter, but not emphasized. The question with which he is most concerned is the Gentile's place in a community of believers Jewish in orientation. This question was especially important for a congregation that had lived through the recent banishment of the Jews, a decree signed by Claudius in 49 C.E., probably in response to agitations over Christ. Before the ban was reversed by Nero (upon accession to the throne in 54), the Gentiles were necessarily in control of the church's local direction. Presumably, when Jewish believers returned to the capital, they opened or widened a rift over the status of traditional ritual practice.

Quite apart from the question's particular relevance for Rome, the status of the law was an issue for Paul and would have been a point of contestation even if the banishment had never occurred. In Galatians, Paul had argued vehemently that the Gentile followers of Jesus need not observe the laws of Moses. Citing Abraham allegorically, he even seemed to suggest that the Jewish followers need not observe—indeed, that those who did should be cast out like Ishmael, ceding to Gentiles the future owed them as children of Isaac:

> Tell me, you who desire to be under law, do you not hear the law? For it is written that Abraham had two sons, one by a slave and one by a free woman. But the son of the slave was born according to the flesh, the son of the free woman through promise. Now this is an allegory: these women are two covenants. One is from Mount Sinai, bearing children for slavery; she is Hagar. Now Hagar is Mount Sinai in Arabia; she corresponds to the present Jerusalem, for she is in slavery with her children. But the Jerusalem above is free, and she is our mother. For it is written, "Rejoice, O barren one who does not bear; break forth and shout, you who are not in travail; for the children of the desolate one are many more than the children of her that is married." Now we, brethren, like Isaac, are children of promise. But as at that time he who was born according to the flesh persecuted him who was born according to the Spirit, so it is now. But what does the scripture say? "Cast out the slave and her son; for the son of the slave shall not inherit with the son of the free woman." So, brethren, we are not children of the slave but of the free woman. (4:21–31)

In his book on Paul, *A Radical Jew,* Daniel Boyarin reads this passage with understandable distress. Operating under the assumption that Jewish identity is inconceivable apart from the law, he declares succinctly, "By understanding that the Law according to the flesh was the signifier of an allegorical Law of love according to the spirit, and that those, *including ethnic Jews,* who received the spirit were absolved of the requirements of the Law according to the flesh, Paul was . . . *annulling* Jewish difference." For Boyarin, in other words, Jewish antinomianism is a contradiction in terms.[3] A debatable point, of course, but what interests me here is not the truth or falsity of Boyarin's reading, but the way the law creeps back in to his commentary. For "annulment" is a legal term, and if Paul's allegory has any force at all, it is the force of law. This is the point Jacob Taubes makes in *The Political Theology of Paul,* that the *nomos* (law) of Paul's letters is not only Torah, but Roman law as well. The issue is authority. "It isn't *nomos* but rather the one who was nailed to the cross by *nomos* who is the imperator!" declares Taubes. What Paul would annul, in other words, is not "Jewish difference," but the power to adjudicate its definition.

Then what becomes of our boasting?

The body
is a spirit
on its own
life-support
system. Breaths
taken
to extremes
dissolve
the law
in garbled sounds

Do you not know, brethren—for I am speaking to those who know the law—that the law is binding on a person only during his life?

> But by whichever
> religious route
> to brute
> reality
> our forebears speed us
> —Mina Loy

Romans is a more judicious text than Galatians. Here too faith and spirit take precedence over law and flesh, but the latter two are no longer cast aside as slavery. Speaking as a Jew—that is, as a Jew loyal to a Jewish-Gentile congregation—Paul asks after the status of what Boyarin calls Jewish difference: "Then what becomes of our boasting? It is excluded. . . . For we hold that a man is justified by faith apart from works of law. Or is God the God of Jews only? Is he not the God of Gentiles also? Yes, of Gentiles also, since God is one; and he will justify the circumcised on the ground of their faith and the uncircumcised through their faith. Do we then overthrow the law by this faith? By no means! On the contrary, we uphold the law" (3:27–31). The argument is exquisite: although the law has lost its privilege, it remains in effect as a responsibility—which is a privilege in its own, more diminished way, "something to boast about, but not before God" (4:2).

Never once does Paul renounce his Judaism. But this begs the question: what does his Judaism become? That he preserves a place for Mosaic law in his community's religious life is not in itself proof that he himself obeyed the law. We must balance what he says in Romans with his earlier, more strident claim in Galatians. Nor is Romans without equivocation. His provocative comments on the "real Jew" and "true circumcision" remind us that Jewish difference is also a matter of internal difference, a disputation within Judaism, a choice, for Paul, between Abrahamic and Mosaic forms of covenant.

> the first thought
> snarls at the next thought,
>
> and the cuckoo in the nest . . .
> swallows everything.
>
> —Nada Gordon

But now we are discharged from the law, dead to that which held us captive

Certainly, whatever its place in Paul's daily life, the law has ceased to be the *basis* for his religion. Modeling himself on Abraham, who received God's promise before the law had even been handed down, Paul calls himself a Jew by virtue of his faith. Never mind that the end result is again obedience. Abraham too was obedient: leaving his father's house forever, lifting a knife to sacrifice his son, Abraham outdid even the Pharisees for zealousness. The problem with the law, then, is not the behavior that it compels, but the fact that it *compels* what should be given freely, and that it is focused on *behavior,* which is outward, external, physical, literal.

> As long as the outside does not put a value on you it remains outside but when it does put a value on you then it gets inside or rather if the outside puts a value on you then all your inside gets to be outside.
>
> —Gertrude Stein

The law, argues Paul, discovers transgression, and measures obedience from outward signs. Faith, by contrast, discovers obedience, and measures transgression from inward signs. From this it follows that circumcision, the external mark of an internal difference, must give way to righteousness, the internal mark of an external difference. "For he is not a real Jew who is one outwardly, nor is true circumcision something external and physical. He is a Jew who is one inwardly, and real circumcision is a matter of the heart, spiritual and not literal" (Romans 2:28–29). Covenant, likewise, is no longer a matter of blood relations, but conscious affiliation. The chosen people are now those who choose God, by answering his call. "For not all who are descended from Israel belong to Israel" (Romans 9:6), although "the gifts and the call of God are irrevocable" (11:29). Are the two verses in contradiction? One might say that Christianity begins in the setting aside of the second.[4]

The very commandment which promised life proved to be death to me

gift amnesia of fictitious
relatives renting above the carcass
—Rob Fitterman

The language of Paul's faith comes from Hebrew scripture (or its Greek translation, the Septuagint); when he speaks, he speaks in scriptural terms, giving scriptural precedent. When his speech overturns precedent, he is adept at revising the meaning of what puts him in conflict.

Paul's arguments, then, as distinct from his professions of belief, are precisely the points where he engages Jewish tradition: that faith achieves what the law merely aims to achieve, that true circumcision is inward, that the Jew and Gentile are one in their covenant with God—these are principles rooted for Paul in his reading of scripture, and they remain valid as principles independent of their Christological dimension.

Possible
To use
Words provided one treat them
As enemies.
Not enemies—Ghosts
Which have run mad
—George Oppen

In setting the Christ of Paul's letters outside Jewish tradition—the tradition as Paul would have known it—I mean to set aside the problem of his messianism as well, for it is not clear if Paul used the word "Christ" (Greek for "messiah," Hebrew for "anointed") in its original sense, to say that Jesus was God's anointed prophet (like the priests and Israelite kings, and even foreign rulers such as Cyrus, all of whom are called "christ" in the Septuagint), or in its later sense, to say that Jesus was Israel's predicted redeemer. As George MacRae notes in his essay "Messiah and Gospel," "the Pauline letters are distinctive in the New Testament as a major body of writings in which the Messiahship of Jesus is simply not an issue." Certainly Paul saw Jesus as Israel's redeemer, and certainly he saw him as the completion of a promise. But whether these two tenets had taken shape as a single, accepted office (the Messiah), recognizable as such to other Jews, who might then accept or reject the specific identification of Jesus as fulfillment, is in doubt; is, in fact, unlikely. Not only was there no coherent doctrine of the Messiah in the Second Temple era, even among eschatological sects, but the very term appears only rarely in significant documents of the time (including the Dead Sea Scrolls and Pseudepigrapha).

Messianism as we now understand it appears to be an innovation that did not gain currency until after Paul's death. Central to Christianity's self-understanding, it became a means of binding Hebrew scripture and Greek New Testament together. Its embrace by rabbinical Judaism is, then, a noteworthy instance of the post-Pauline character of modern Jewry, which developed out of the same traditional and creative influences that produced Christianity. Paul's Judaism is more ancient, is, in many ways, more distant from us than the Christianity to which he is given credit. It bears emphasis, then, that Paul's most profound challenge to the Judaism he knew was not his invocation of Christ, but his revocation of the law. Even among the followers of Jesus, Paul's antinomianism was controversial. His dispute with James (leader of the Jerusalem church, the strictest in its adherence to Jewish custom) indicates this:

> But when Cephas [Peter] came to Antioch I opposed him to his face.... For before certain men came from James, he ate with the Gentiles; but when they came he drew back and separated himself, fearing the circumcision party. And with him the rest of the Jews acted insincerely.... But when I saw that they were not straightforward about the truth of the gospel, I said to Cephas before them all, "We ourselves, who are Jews by birth and not Gentile sinners, yet who know that a man is not justified by works of the law but through faith ..., even we have believed ... in order to be justified by faith ... and not by works of the law, because by works of the law shall no one be justified." (Galatians 2:11–16)

The examples of Jewish law at issue here—circumcision and kashrut—are markers of ethnicity and so posed the greatest challenges for Paul in creating pluralistic communities. Yet Paul's critique is not limited to these examples, nor even to the larger but still limited portions of the law specific to ritual practice (such as keeping the Sabbath). His critique is aimed at law as such, which, in Paul's view, has ceased to provide an adequate basis for achieving the ends toward which it was appointed.

So the law is holy, and the commandment is holy and just and good

The totality of Paul's critique is especially surprising given the unequivocal character of his moral pronouncements: it is not for the sake of lax behavior or cultural relativism that he takes his extreme stand against James or Pharisaic Judaism. As Jacob Taubes puts it, "Paul is a zealot, a Jewish zealot, and for him this step is a tremendous one. The spiritual costs that he must bear he doesn't take upon himself for the sake of some blather in the spirit of this great nomos liberalism. He is totally illiberal; of that I am certain." Paul's struggle with the law is entirely in keeping with his effort to create a community that is holy, just, and good. In this sense, the *nomos* of his letter stretches to include even more than the law of Torah or Roman law. Natural law and the principles of reason are also implicated, as a key passage in Romans, perhaps the most moving in all of Paul's letters, makes clear: "I do not understand my own actions. For I do not do what I want, but I do the very thing I hate. . . . So I find it to be a law that when I want to do right, evil lies close at hand. For I delight in the law of God, in my inmost self, but I see in my members another law at war with the law of my mind and making me captive to the law of sin which dwells in my members. Wretched man that I am! Who will deliver me from this body of death?" (Romans 7:15–24). At issue here is not a freedom from the "yoke" of law, but something more fundamental—a reorientation of religious life. For Paul, this reorientation involves a turn to Jesus as savior. For present-day secular Jews—who, like Paul, turn aside from the law, but also, in some cases, from the very idea of a god who punishes or redeems—this reorientation is instead historical.

God, Law, and History: three orientations within Jewish tradition.

Potentially but not essentially overlapping, they establish the parameters of Judaism as such.

For we do not know how to pray as we ought, but the Spirit himself intercedes for us with sighs too deep for words

The law is a soap bubble, ever expanding, never separating from the ring, never becoming self-enclosed. Its film stretches thinner and thinner, impossibly containing the new possibilities of living that ever press against it, that sustain the bubble and give it shape.

An exhalation fills it—History or God—but what do we hear when we listen to this breathing?

What do we hear
when the spirit becomes word,
before word becomes flesh (if it ever does)?
What are the meanings
that the law obeys,
and, obeying, encloses?

Neither death, nor life, nor angels, nor principalities, nor things present, nor things to come, nor powers, nor height, nor depth, nor anything else in all creation

> The crowd roared and turned the page
> but was alone.
> The idea dawned, and it was day, colors displaying
> the imaginary conditions needed to produce
> languages not based on threats
>
> —Bob Perelman

Critiques of the law within Judaism have no continuous history, but present themselves episodically—or fail to present themselves, but persist as traces, as in Philo's censuring of those who, by reading allegorically, came to neglect the Torah's literal sense. A similar trace can be found in Maimonides, who was concerned that those who examine the law for philosophical content will cease to obey what they cannot understand. But Philo's testimony is especially pertinent: an Alexandrian Jew whose life overlapped with that of Paul, he confirms the currency of Paul's hermeneutic practice in the Hellenized world of first-century Judaism.

The correlation of reading and antinomianism is also evident in Kabbalah, where the notion of a "spiritual" law written in letters "visible only to mystics" leads to the radical conclusion that "things which are forbidden . . . according to the present manner of reading . . . may [in later days] be permitted or even ordained" (Gershom Scholem, *On the Kabbalah and Its Symbolism*); yet even our present manner of reading will lead, on occasion, to a rewriting of the law. The question is when or how this rewriting becomes out-and-out overthrow: at one end of the spectrum we find those creative readings that accommodate law to practical necessity (as in the "eruv," which extends the boundaries of the home symbolically so as to permit prohibited activities); at the other end, Spinoza's claim that "ceremonial observances" are not binding on "the Hebrews . . . since the destruction of their state" (*Tractatus Theologico-Politicus*).

Antinomianism then is a varied phenomenon, one that includes both libertine tendencies (as in the messianic movement of Sabbatei Sevi, which made use of the "blasphemous" formula "who permittest things forbidden") and those that tend toward a heightened piety (as in Izbicer Hasidism, which theorized a loosening of the law for those who achieve perfection within it). Nor is antinomianism purely marginal in its manifestations. The *Encyclopedia Judaica* cites Reform Judaism as an example, and one might extend this view to say that *any* movement away from observance, whatever its motivation, constitutes critique—that so-called secular Jewish culture, if that phrase means anything at all, constitutes a kind of radical sect within Judaism, one that owes much to the precedent of Paul.

Is there injustice on God's part? By no means!

> Che sara, have faith, trust the future or maybe it could be trust existence or your luck. . . . Anyhow, maybe "the greatest . . . is charity," caring for and taking care of things in the present.
>
> —Larry Eigner

If "secular Jewish culture" is a form of antinomianism, then it follows that this culture is also a part of the religious history of Judaism, and not, as is ordinarily conceived, the nonreligious extract of that history. A further corollary is that problems faced by this culture will often be translatable into Pauline terms. Ethics without adherence to the law? "Love does no wrong to a neighbor; therefore love is the fulfilling of the law" (Romans 13:10). Compatibility of traditions within mixed groups or families? "Practice hospitality. . . . Let not him who eats despise him who abstains, and let not him who abstains pass judgment on him who eats. . . . None of us lives to himself, and none of us dies to himself" (12:13, 14:3, 14:7). Hostility among Jews of divergent beliefs? "Do not boast over the branches. If you do boast, remember it is not you that support the root, but the root that supports you" (11:18). Paul's entire discourse concerns the continuation of Judaism in a new form.

But who are you, a man, to answer back to God?

And then there is the status of reason, so central to "secular" life: "I would rather speak five words with my mind, in order to instruct others, than ten thousand words in a tongue. Brethren, do not be children in your thinking; be babes in evil, but in thinking be mature" (1 Corinthians 14:19–20).

Has the potter no right over the clay?

> Pot rose, Dios sicken if alone.
> —David Melnick

Who stitched these clothes
we wear out without compunction?

Their colors fade
like old laws from books we never finished

but intend some day
to close

What shall we say, then?

> Transgression belongs to the law.
> —Jena Osman

To speak of a Pauline bent to "secular Jewish culture" is not so strange if one sees this culture as a transposition of Jewish habits, attitudes, and frames of reference into contexts that devout Jews will not necessarily accept or even recognize as Jewish. Is the nonobservant Jew Jewish? Is Paul? These are questions that belong to rhetoric as much as they do to theology: Who asks? Why? To what end? In which context?

Here I would pause to note that the word "secular" is not especially felicitous. Derived from the Latin *seculum,* "a generation, an age," it developed the meaning "temporal" or "worldly," serving within the church as a means of distinguishing between cloistered members of the clergy and those living in the world. Its subsequent usage shifted this distinction, perhaps in recognition of the church's diminishing authority: *secular* now refers to civil society, as distinct from the clergy as a whole. The church, in other words, setting itself in opposition to the secular, defines itself as eternal and sacred, not bound to time or place, not mortal—a distinction that parallels if it does not actually derive from Paul's opposition of spirit to flesh.

Yet however apt this distinction may be for Christianity, it makes little sense for Judaism, since Torah is precisely a regulation of human time and human behavior. In Judaism, the operative distinction is not between religious (ecclesiastical) and worldly (secular) spheres of action or influence, but between observant and nonobservant members of a community. Even so, the importation of this Christian concept is illuminating, for its very infelicity helps to indicate Paul's pertinence, that is, helps to indicate both the pathos and confusion that obtain when we conceive of Jewish culture in Christian terms. There are two reasons for this:

First, because Paul was not, historically speaking, a Christian when he made his critique, but a radical Jew, there is both pathos and confusion in importing a Christian concept to describe what is, in effect (if not intention), an antinomian form of Judaism: pathos, because it reiterates the erasure of Judaism that occurs when we define Paul anachronistically as Christian; confusion, because a Jewish antinomianism without Christ could never be conflated with Christianity.

Second, however, because Christianity distinguished itself from Judaism on the very basis of Paul's critique of the law, there is both pathos and confusion in defining "nonobservant Jewish culture" (a more exact description, I think, than *secular* Jewish culture) with a Christian term: pathos, because nonobservance inevitably arouses fear of absorption into Christianity; confusion, because, if ecclesiastical equates to spirit in Paul's critique, then "secular" is "flesh," and yet it is the Jew who falls away from flesh who becomes secular in this particular formulation.

Sophistry was never woven
from so many threads
unraveled from so many texts.
When the color schemes,
the shapes get swindled.
Keys that open different doors
look the same
when side by side. Unsparing logic,
it argues neither for nor against . . .

For there is no distinction between Jew and Greek

> This ran aground, cannot go on.
> Is it possible to begin twice?
> —Rachel Blau DuPlessis

Paul wrote his letters to entire communities, to men and women swayed by different voices within a movement that had not yet become committed to an orthodoxy, and this means that the coherence of his thought lies not in the totality of what he says (which is not, in any case, consistent), but in the totality of his address, in the particular diversities of people his letters were meant to reconcile. In writing to Rome, for example, Paul was addressing a group of believers who were not simply Jewish and Gentile. There were, presumably, varying degrees of observance of Mosaic law even among those born Jewish. This diversity was in part a reflection of the state of the new sect (a function of the assimilation of Gentiles with varying degrees of sympathy or acquaintance with traditional Jewish life; a function also of the differences between Judean Jews and the Hellenized diaspora). Partly, however, this diversity was due to Rome's particular history. I have already mentioned the banishment of Jews between 49 and 54 C.E. But Rome was also, as the empire's political and commercial center, a multiethnic city, and one would expect the local congregation to share in this character, especially since worship most likely occurred in small groups meeting in private homes spread throughout the city—a form of association that would have encouraged, or at least done nothing to impede, the introduction of new practices or the abandonment of old ones. Problems arose most clearly when meals were shared, since on those occasions adherence or nonadherence to kashrut became impossible to ignore. In Galatians, when Paul uses a food metaphor to describe the acrimony dividing his church, he is not straying far from the source of dispute: "But if you bite and devour one another take heed that you are not consumed by one another" (5:15). His primary concern, then, in writing his letters, is not *consistency,* but *constituency.* For the variations of Jewish and Gentile culture within the church were not reconcilable to a coherent set of beliefs or practices, but cohered, if at all, in the articulation of community, a sharing of blessings that was not, finally, theological, but rhetorical: "To the Jews I became as a Jew, in order to win Jews; to those under the law I became as one under the law . . . that I might win those under the law. To those outside the law I became as one outside the law . . . that I might win those outside the law. To the weak I became weak, that I might win the weak. I have become all things to all men. . . . I do it all for the sake of the gospel, that I may share in its blessings" (1 Corinthians 9:20–23).

If the root is holy, so are the branches

> *Windflower* overworld selvageflame sun coddle
>
> —Louis Zukofsky

If
I
were
a

tree
I
would
put
forth
my
leaves
to
be
eaten
by
time

—how could I not?

(Terrain slowly
pulled out
from under my feet

and every ounce
of me clinging
to hope of home)

Lest you be wise in your own conceits

> In hearts and houses silence and old fear
> Wall us apart, though in the flowing streets
> Our language boasts the universal bond.
> —Laura Riding

The common claim made on Paul's behalf, that he replaced Jewish particularity with Christian universalism, is not impressive to me: acceptance of Jesus as savior particularizes the covenant as surely as does circumcision. If the law is particular, then so is faith. Righteousness alone is universal, if anything can be, but righteousness—justice—is hardly the exclusive property of a Christian or Jewish covenant.

Experience teaches: the righteousness of the faithful is never guaranteed.

History shows: the purpose of the law is never simply justice.

Do not be conformed to this world but be transformed by the renewal of your mind

> truth is the ground of reality's
> appearance but reality intervenes
> against all odds
>
> —Charles Bernstein

Does time
require a dial
to be understood
in human terms? All we know
and are becomes
a decayed object
swept from sight
with a sweep of the hands.

The night is far gone, the day is at hand

> Faithful to your commandments, o consciousness
>
> —Delmore Schwartz

Those who give up ritual observance, yet name themselves Jews, are children of Paul, though they give up faith as well.

Those who name themselves Jews, yet welcome Gentiles in all their projects, are children of Paul, though they turn away from Christian gospel.

Those who mix with Gentiles, yet uphold a Jewish tradition of justice, are children of Paul, though they serve humanity instead of God.

Those who uphold justice as Jews, yet sacrifice tradition for the promise of a future, are children of Paul, though they dream of earth instead of heaven.

According to the revelation of the mystery which was kept secret for long ages

a flashing light on the road to Damascus
struck Paul blind and he heard a voice

> Luckily light is more than particle and wave, beyond syntax and grammar. It is the crunch of maw and mandible as you announce who you insist you are.
>
> —Tim Davis

Notes

1. The boldface verses come from Paul's "Letter to the Romans." These and other quotations from the New Testament are given in the Revised Standard Version.

2. As recently as 1906 *The Jewish Encyclopedia* could declare, "There is throughout [his] writings an irrational or pathological element which could not but repel the disciples of the Rabbis."

3. A subsequent book, *Dying for God,* develops a more nuanced understanding of Judaism's persistence within Christianity. Citing a sixth-century text in which a Christian disciple declares himself "a Jew secretly," an allusion to Romans 2:29 ("He is a Jew who is one inwardly"), Boyarin comments, "[He] knows that he can be both a Christian and a Jew, for the apostle to the Gentiles has already declared that one who is a Jew ἐν τῷ κρυπτῷ [*en to krupto,* "inwardly," but also "secretly"] is the true Jew. Indeed, it is the very essence of his claim to be a true Christian and not a fraudulent one that he be both a Jew and a Christian."

4. Thus Theodoret of Cyr, commenting on Romans 11:29: "In fact, of course, God did revoke the good gifts which he gave . . . King Saul, who received spiritual grace which later deserted him. Likewise Solomon, who received peace through the kindness of God, but after his transgression was deprived of grace. And then there are the Jews themselves, who always had their prophets to take care of them but who at the present time have been deprived of them."

A Note on Sources

My essay incorporates lines of verse or prose statements by twenty-one Jewish American poets. These come from the following books: Charles Bernstein, *Dark City* (Sun & Moon Press, 1994); Abigail Child, *Scatter Matrix* (Roof Books, 1996); Norma Cole, *Do the Monkey* (Zasterle, 2006); Tim Davis, *My Life in Politics* (Aperture, 2006); Rachel Blau DuPlessis, *Torques: Drafts 58–76* (Salt Press, 2007); Larry Eigner, *Areas Lights Heights: Writings 1954–1989,* ed. Benjamin Friedlander (Roof Books, 1989); Rob Fitterman, *Metropolis 1–15* (Sun & Moon Press, 2000); Nada Gordon, *Are Not Our Lowing Heifers Sleeker Than Night-Swollen Mushrooms?* (Spuyten Duyvil, 2001); Allen Grossman, *The Long Schoolroom: Lessons in the Bitter Logic of the Poetic Principle* (University of Michigan Press, 1997); Benjamin Hollander, *Rituals of Truce and the Other Israeli* (Parrhesia Press, 2004); Laura (Riding) Jackson, *The Poems of Laura Riding* (Persea Books, 1980); Emma Lazarus, *Selected Poems and Other Writings,* ed. Gregory Eiselein (Broadview Literary Texts, 2002); Mina Loy, *The Last Lunar Baedeker* (The Jargon Society, 1982); David Melnick, *Men in Aida, Book II* (Eclipse Editions, 2002); George Oppen, *This in Which* (New Directions Press, 1965); Jena Osman, *The Character* (Beacon Press, 1999); Bob Perelman, *Face Value* (Roof Books, 1988); Kim Rosenfeld, *Tràma* (Kruspskaya Press, 2004); Delmore Schwartz, *Last and Lost Poems* (New Directions, 1989); Gertrude Stein, *Everybody's Autobiography* (Exact Change, 1993); Hannah Weiner, *Spoke* (Sun & Moon Press, 1984); and Louis Zukofsky, *"A"* (University of California Press, 1978).

My understanding of Paul and his *Letter to the Romans* is based on a very small portion of the vast Pauline literature. I am indebted in particular to two recent texts that regard Paul from a Jewish perspective: Daniel Boyarin, *A Radical Jew: Paul and the Politics of Identity* (University of California Press, 1994), and Jacob Taubes, *The Political Theology of Paul,* trans. Dana Hollander (Stanford University Press, 2004). In sampling the small but provocative literature on Paul's Jewish background, I have also found useful the work of W. D. Davies, Mark D. Nanos, E. P. Sanders, and Alan Segal. My consultation of traditional Pauline scholarship has been more sparing. The following were especially useful: Gerald Bray, ed., *Ancient Christian Commentary on Scripture: Romans* (Fitzroy Dearborn Publishers, 1998); James D. G. Dunn, *The Cambridge Companion to St. Paul* (Cambridge University Press, 2003); Wayne A. Meeks, ed., *The Writings of St. Paul* (W. W. Norton & Company, 1972); Krister Stendahl, *Paul among Jews and Gentiles and Other Essays* (Fortress Press, 1976); and James C. Walters, *Ethnic Issues in Paul's Letter to the Romans: Changing Self-Definitions in Earliest Roman Christianity* (Trinity Press, 1993). Of the many recent attempts to read Paul philosophically I have found Theodore W. Jennings Jr., *Reading Derrida / Thinking Paul* (Stanford University Press, 2006), the most engaging. My essay also cites Kaufmann Kohler, "Saul of Tarsus," *The Jewish Encyclopedia* (Funk and Wagnall's Company, 1901–06), 11:79–87; and "The Letter of St. Clement to the Corinthians," *The Apostolic Fathers,* trans. Francis X. Glimm, Joseph M.-F. Marique, and Gerald G. Walsh (Catholic University of America Press, 1962), 9–58.

Coming to terms with Paul has taught me a great deal about Christianity's individuation within and separation from Judaism—a Judaism that was itself evolving in relation to Christianity. The following books (in addition to those cited above) have been most helpful on this topic: Daniel Boyarin, *Dying for God: Martyrdom and the Making of Christianity and Judaism* (Stanford University Press, 1999); Wayne A. Meeks and Robert L. Wilken, *Jews and Christians in Antioch in the First Four Centuries of the Common Era* (SBL Sources for Biblical Study 13, 1978); Jacob Neusner, William Scott Green, and Ernest Frerichs, eds., *Judaisms and Their Messiahs at the Turn of the Christian Era* (Cambridge University Press, 1987) (in particular George MacRae's essay "Messiah and Gospel"); and Jaroslav Pelikan, *The Christian Tradition, A History of the Development of Doctrine, 1: The Emergence of the Catholic Tradition (100–600)* (University of Chicago Press, 1971). Useful as well was William Scott Green and Jed Silverstein, "The Doctrine of the Messiah," in *The Blackwell Companion to Judaism,* ed. Jacob Neusner and Alan J. Avery-Peck (Blackwell Publishers, 2000). My remarks on Jewish antinomianism make use of insights and information drawn from Shaul Magid, *Hasidism on the Margin: Reconciliation, Antinomianism, and Messianism in Izbica/Radzin Hasidism*

(University of Wisconsin Press, 2003); Gershom Scholem, *On the Kabbalah and Its Symbolism*, trans. Ralph Manheim (Schocken Books, 1969); Gershom S. Scholem, *Sabbatai Sevi: The Mystical Messiah*, trans. R. J. Zvi Werblowsky (Princeton University Press, 1973); Alan Segal, *Paul the Convert: The Apostolate and Apostasy of Saul the Pharisee* (Yale University Press, 1990); Spinoza, *Complete Works*, ed. Michael L. Morgan, trans. Samuel Shirley (Hackett Publishing, 2002); and the entry on antinomianism (written in part by Gershom Scholem) in *Encyclopedia Judaica* (The Macmillan Company, 1971), 3:67–71.

I am also indebted to David I. Sheidlower, who long ago inspired me to think about Abrahamic Judaism, and to several friends and colleagues who offered hints, advice, and encouragement along the way: Carla Billitteri, Norma Cole, Kevin Davies, Rabbi Barry Krieger, Liam Riordan, Eric Selinger, Marwin Spiller, and Nathan Stormer.

White

Paul Auster

For one who drowned:
this page, as if
thrown out to sea
in a bottle.

So that
even as the sky embarks
into the seeing of earth, an echo
of the earth
might sail toward him,
filled with a memory of rain,
and the sound of the rain
falling on the water.

So that
he will have learned,
in spite of the wave
now sinking from the crest
of mountains, that forty days
and forty nights
have brought no dove
back to us.

Contributors

Paul Auster is the author of many books, including *Man in the Dark: A Novel, The New York Trilogy, The Brooklyn Follies: A Novel, Moon Palace, The Invention of Solitude,* and other works.

Merle L. Bachman is a poet and director of the BFA in Creative Writing at Spalding University in Louisville, Kentucky. She has published a literary criticism and creative nonfiction book, *Recovering Yiddishland: Threshold Moments in American Literature,* and a book of poems, *Diorama with Fleeing Figures.*

Charles Bernstein is Regan Professor of English and Comparative Literature at the University of Pennsylvania and a fellow of the American Academy of Arts & Sciences. In September 2004 he organized a forum on "Secular Jewish Culture / Radical Jewish Poetry" for the Center for Jewish History (video available on PennSound). Books include *Shadowtime* (libretto on Walter Benjamin), *Girly Man,* and *My Way: Speeches and Poems.* For more information, see epc.buffalo.edu.

Charlie Bertsch is the music editor at *Zeek* magazine and formerly held the same post at *Tikkun.* He has taught literature, film, and critical theory at the University of California, Berkeley, the University of Arizona, and Arizona State University. Presently, he is at work on two book projects, one about the cultural significance of punk and one on the "documentary impulse" in various media.

Maria Damon teaches at the University of Minnesota. She is author of *The Dark End of the Street: Margins in American Vanguard Poetry.*

Rachel Blau DuPlessis is an American poet-critic. Her critical writing includes *Blue Studios: Poetry and Its Cultural Work, The Pink Guitar: Writing as Feminist Practice,* and *Genders, Races, and Religious Cultures in Modern American Poetry, 1908–1934.* Earlier work includes *Writing beyond the End-*

ing: Narrative Strategies of Twentieth-Century Women Writers and *H.D.: The Career of That Struggle,* as well as an edition of *The Selected Letters of George Oppen.* DuPlessis's long poem project, begun in 1986, is collected in *Torques: Drafts 58–76* as well as in *Drafts 1–38, Toll* and *Drafts 39–57, Pledge, with Draft unnnumbered: Précis.* She has received Pew Fellowship for Artists, a residency at the Rockefeller Study Center at Bellagio, Italy, and a fellowship at the National Humanities Center, North Carolina. Her website is http://wings.buffalo.edu/epc/authors/duplessis.

Amy Feinstein is an assistant professor of English at Colgate University where she is completing a book on Gertrude Stein and the making of Jewish Modernism. Her work has appeared in *James Joyce Quarterly, Modern Fiction Studies, PMLA,* and *Shofar: An Interdisciplinary Journal of Jewish Studies.*

Thomas Fink, professor of English at City University of New York-LaGuardia, is the author of *"A Different Sense of Power": Problems of Community in Late-Twentieth-Century U.S. Poetry* and, with Joseph Lease, coedited a collection of essays on David Shapiro's poetry. His criticism has appeared in *American Poetry Review, Chicago Review, Contemporary Literature, Denver Quarterly, Jacket, Talisman, Verse,* and numerous other publications. He is the author of five books of poetry, most recently *Clarity and Other Poems.* His paintings hang in various collections.

Norman Finkelstein is a poet and literary critic. His books of poetry include *Restless Messengers* and the three-volume serial poem *Track: Track, Columns, and Powers.* His most recent book is *Passing Over,* a volume of poems containing work from the late 1980s through the mid-1990s. He has written extensively about modern and postmodern poetry, and about Jewish American literature. His books of criticism are *The Utopian Moment in Contemporary American Literature, The Ritual of New Creation: Jewish Tradition and Contemporary Literature, Not One of Them in Place: Modern Poetry and Jewish American Identity* and *Lyrical Interference: Essays on Poetics.* Recent poems, essays, and reviews have appeared in *American Letters & Commentary, Cincinnati Review, Contemporary Literature, American Literary History,* and *Twentieth Century Literature* and on the website of the Cultural Society. He recently completed a book on religious revisionism in contemporary long poems. Finkelstein was born in New York City in 1954. He received his B.A. from Binghamton University and his Ph.D. from Emory University. He is a professor of English at Xavier University in Cincinnati, Ohio, where he has taught since 1980.

Norman Fischer, a former abbot of the San Francisco Zen Center, is the author of *Taking Our Places: The Buddhist Path to Truly Growing Up.*

Benjamin Friedlander's collections of poetry include *A Knot Is Not a Tangle, The Missing Occasion of Saying Yes,* and the forthcoming *Citizen Cain.* He is also the author of *Simulcast: Four Experiments in Criticism,* and editor, most recently, of *Robert Creeley's Selected Poems, 1945–2005*. He is an associate professor of English at the University of Maine.

Michael Heller is a poet, essayist, and critic. Among his most recent volumes of poetry are *Eschaton* and *Exigent Futures: New and Selected Poems. Earth and Cave,* his mixed-genre journals of the 1960s when he lived in Spain, was published in 2007. A memoir, *Living Root,* appeared in the SUNY Press series on Modern Jewish Literature and Culture. A selection of his essays, *Uncertain Poetries,* was published in 2005. His most recent critical work is *Speaking the Estranged: Essays on the Work of George Oppen.*

Dr. Kathryn Hellerstein is an associate professor of Yiddish at the University of Pennsylvania. Her books include a translation and study of Moyshe-Leyb Halpern's poems, *In New York: A Selection, Paper Bridges: Selected Poems of Kadya Molodowsky,* and *Jewish American Literature: A Norton Anthology,* of which she is coeditor. She is also a major contributor to *American Yiddish Poetry: A Bilingual Anthology.* Her poems and many scholarly articles on Yiddish literature, and most recently, on women poets in Yiddish, have appeared in journals and anthologies. She has received grants from the National Endowment of the Arts, the National Endowment of the Humanities, and the Guggenheim Foundation and is currently working on a book and an anthology on women Yiddish poets (to be published by Stanford University Press).

Bob Holman is a poetry activist and coeditor of *Aloud: Voices from the Nuyorican Poets Café* and the author of *The Collect Call of the Wild.*

Adeena Karasick is a poet. She is author of *The Arugula Fugues, The House That Hijack Built, Genrecide, Memewars, Amuse Bouche, The Empress Has No Closure,* and *Dyssemia Sleaze.*

Hank Lazer is a noted critic and the author of fourteen books of poetry, including *The New Spirit, Elegies & Vacations, Days,* and *Lyric & Spirit: Selected Essays, 1996–2008*. Lazer is the associate provost for Academic Affairs at the University of Alabama.

Stephen Paul Miller is professor of English at St. John's University, Staten Island Campus. He is the author of several volumes of criticism and poetry, including *The Seventies Now: Culture as Surveillance, The Bee Flies in May, Skinny Eighth Avenue,* and *Being with a Bullet.*

Daniel Morris is professor of English at Purdue University. He is the author of several volumes of criticism and poetry, including *The Writings of*

William Carlos Williams: Publicity for the Self, Remarkable Modernisms: Contemporary American Authors on Modern Art, The Poetry of Louise Glück: A Thematic Introduction, and *Bryce Passage.* He is coeditor of *Shofar: An Interdisciplinary Journal of Jewish Studies.*

Ranen Omer-Sherman teaches English & Jewish Studies at the University of Miami. His essays on Jewish poets including Yehuda Amichai, Emma Lazarus, Dan Pagis, and Charles Reznikoff have appeared in journals such as *MELUS, Modern Jewish Studies, Prooftexts, Modernism/Modernity, Religion & Literature,* and *Shofar.* He is the author of *Diaspora and Zionism in Jewish American Literature* and *Israel in Exile: Jewish Writing and the Desert,* as well as coeditor of *The Jewish Graphic Novel: Critical Approaches.*

Alicia Ostriker is a poet and critic, the author of *Feminist Revision and the Bible,* and *The Nakedness of the Fathers; Biblical Visions and Revisions,* a combination of midrashic and autobiographical writing. Her most recent volume of essays is *For the Love of God: The Bible as an Open Book.* As a poet she has twice been a finalist for the National Book Award, has appeared in numerous anthologies of Jewish writing, and has been translated into many languages including Hebrew and Arabic. Her most recent volumes of poetry are the *Volcano Sequence* and *No Heaven.* Ostriker is professor emerita of English at Rutgers University, and she was poetry editor of *Lilith* for many years. She leads a monthly midrash writing workshop in New York City.

Bob Perelman is the author of numerous books of poetry, including *Iflife, Ten to One,* and, in collaboration with painter Francie Shaw, *Playing Bodies;* and two critical books, *The Trouble with Genius* and *The Marginalization of Poetry.* He teaches at the University of Pennsylvania.

Marjorie Perloff's most recent books are *The Vienna Paradox, Differentials: Poetry, Poetics, Pedagogy,* and, edited with Craig Dworkin, *The Sound of Poetry, The Poetry of Sound.* She is professor emerita of English at Stanford University and currently Scholar-in-Residence at the University of Southern California.

Jerome Rothenberg is an internationally known American poet, translator, and anthologist who is noted for his work in ethnopoetics and poetry performance. His many works include *Technicians of the Sacred* (1968), *Poems for the Millennium* in three volumes (1995, 1998, 2009), *A Big Jewish Book: Poems & Other Visions of the Jews from Tribal Times to the Present* (revised and republished as *Exiled in the Word,* 1977 and 1989), and *Poland/1931* (1974), reprinted in a single volume with *Khurbn* and *The Burning Babe* in *Triptych* (2007).

Meg Schoerke is a professor of English at San Francisco State University. She is a coeditor of the anthology *Twentieth-Century American Poetry* and coeditor of *Twentieth-Century American Poetics: Poets on the Art of Poetry* and author of *Anatomical Venus* (2004), a book of poems.

Joshua Schuster is an assistant professor of English at the University of Western Ontario. He has essays published in the *Journal of Modern Literature, Open Letter,* and *Other Voices,* and he is at work on a book titled *Organic Radicals: Poetry, the Life Sciences, and American Modernity.* A book of poetry, *Theatre of Public Safety,* was published in 2008.

Eric Murphy Selinger teaches American poetry and Jewish American literature at DePaul University, as well as at a variety of synagogues and libraries in the Chicago area. His books include *Jewish American Poetry: Poems, Commentary, and Reflections* (edited with Jonathan Barron) and most recently *Ronald Johnson: Life and Works* (edited with Joel Bettridge).

Index